DEC 22 1993	DATE DUE	
JUL 0 3 2006		

BLACKS IN THE NEW WORLD: *August Meier, Series Editor*

A list of books in the series appears at the end of this volume.

JOHN MERCER LANGSTON
and the Fight for Black Freedom
1829–65

John Mercer Langston

=== *and the Fight for* ===

Black Freedom

1829–65

William Cheek

AND

Aimee Lee Cheek

University of Illinois Press
Urbana and Chicago

Publication of this work was supported in part by a grant from
the San Diego State University Foundation.

This book is printed on acid-free paper.

Library of Congress Cataloging-in-Publication Data

Cheek, William F., 1933–
    John Mercer Langston and the fight for Black freedom, 1829–65 /
William and Aimee Lee Cheek.
        p.   cm.
    Includes index.
    ISBN 0-252-01550-9 (alk. paper)
    1. Langston, John Mercer, 1829–1897. 2. Afro-Americans—
Biography. 3. Afro-Americans—History—To 1865. 4. Slavery—
United States—Anti-slavery movements. 5. United States—Race
relations. I. Cheek, Aimee Lee, 1936–   . II. Title.
E185.97.L27C48   1989
973′.0496073′092—dc19
    [B]   88-14291
                                                                    CIP

To our beloved Pammy
and to the memory of
Wendy the adventurer

Contents

Preface

IN 1852, just twenty-two but already engaged in politics as well as black protest, John Mercer Langston stood on a crude platform facing an unfriendly white audience at a rural backwater on Ohio's Western Reserve. As he tried to speak for a white antislavery candidate for the state legislature, a heckler yelled out that the black man was promoting "nigger social equality" and that he associated with white women at Oberlin, the abolitionist college where he had taken his undergraduate degree and was currently studying theology. That was true, Langston replied. Advancing to the edge of the stand and looking straight at his tormentor, he added, "If you have in your family any good-looking, intelligent, refined sisters, you would do your family a special service by introducing me to them at once." Startled, the audience broke into such laughter and applause that the heckler had no other choice than to heed a friend's advice: "That darkey is too smart for you. Sit down."

Recounted by Langston in his autobiography, this incident seems suggestive of the personality of the man who, as orator, intellectual, and organizer, would take a commanding role in the nineteenth-century black American struggle for freedom and citizenship. But it is also perplexing. Is it grounded in fact? If so, what was the personal history that could endow so young a man, a black man in a repressive society, with the wit and audacity, to say nothing of the control and skill, that it implied? What were the social and political forces that had brought him to this juncture? And where would he be going from here?

Because scholarly work on Langston's life was scant, only the last of these questions has had a ready answer, and that the most obvious.

During a multifaceted career in black protest, politics, education, and the law lasting half a century, John Mercer Langston became the first black lawyer in the West, the first Afro-American elected to public office, a recruiter of black troops for the Union army, an inspector for the Freedmen's Bureau, the first law dean of Howard University, the U. S. minister to Haiti and Santo Domingo, the president of the Virginia state college for Negroes at Petersburg, and the first and only black representative of Virginia in Congress.

Such a career obviously merits study. Yet—even after limiting the scope of this volume to the period from Langston's birth on a Virginia plantation in 1829 to his emergence as a national leader with the close of the Civil War—the attempt to go beyond a bare-bones recital of major accomplishments to full-scale biography has entailed major difficulties. The most serious obstacle involves sources. Despite being cast in the heroic mold of the period, Langston's autobiography is useful, as is a published collection of his speeches. But he left only a skeleton set of personal papers. Not surprisingly, given his race, other private collections of manuscripts have failed to yield the volume and kind of material necessary for an in-depth study. More general sources largely reflect a white perspective, or, particularly in the case of newspapers of the time, are riddled with the omissions and distortions wrought by white supremacy.

It became apparent that if a three-dimensional Langston was to be located, it would be through his associations. Yet here, too, lay difficulties. Studies of Oberlin and the western antislavery movement— important to him personally and politically—have paid little attention to black participation. Moreover, the historical factors that blocked access to Langston's own life applied with at least equal force to the free black people of the North among whom he also lived and worked. In spite of pioneering and important exploration by scholars of the Afro-American experience, the community created by free blacks in the North—in contrast to the world made by the slaves—is only beginning to be mapped.

In addition, Langston's story was complex. His own parents, a wealthy white slaveholder and a part-Indian, part-black emancipated bondswoman, died when he was only four. Five years later, a court hearing abruptly severed his close relationship with white foster parents in Ohio and simultaneously awakened him to his identity as a Negro. Thereafter, he experienced the intricacies of urban black life and was caught up in a violent large-scale mob attack on blacks and white abolitionists. When he was fourteen, he began preparatory studies at Oberlin College, which was unique in admitting women as well as men and blacks as well as whites, and where he gained an exceptional education. Langston later became a lawyer and leading citizen in the town of Oberlin. In addition, he was active not only in the black civil rights movement in Ohio and the North, but also in anti-slavery politics.

The book that has emerged from these dilemmas is awkward to categorize. It is the result of combing the voluminous public record, which has proved fruitful despite its limitations, and the other available evidence, using the methods of social and political history as well as historical biography, and connecting Langston to his white antislavery and northern black communities. It is a work in black history that, within a black and white context, reveals the interaction of individual, social, and political history.

For want of a better term, it might be called a life-and-times biography. But, in contrast to older samples in this genre which often dealt with a well-known life and a times based primarily on standard information and interpretation, this study offers original research and new insights on a number of issues concerning both the culture and activism of the northern black community and the western antislavery movement. With the focus always on Langston, it examines, among other matters, black life in Cincinnati in the early 1840s, relations between blacks and whites in the college and biracial town of Oberlin, black participation in the celebrated Oberlin-Wellington Rescue of a fugitive slave, the black convention movement and the black nationalist-emigration movement in Ohio and the North, antislavery politics in Ohio, the John Brown affair, the recruitment of black soldiers during the Civil War, and the early black effort to shape a reconstruction founded on equality before the law.

Against such a landscape, this biography traces the path of an exceptional man, disadvantaged by a harrowing personal past as well as by slavery and prejudice but advantaged in ways that both separated him from and tied him to other black people. It shows how Langston's being exceptional helped to dictate his choice of strategies in his effort to reconcile his personal conflicts and combat the restrictions pressing upon him and his people and how that choice influenced the direction of the black struggle for freedom and citizenship.

Although the innermost Langston necessarily remains elusive, the public man, at least, is clear. To return briefly to his confrontation at the age of twenty-two, evidence exists to verify that the heckler lived in the locality, that Langston took part in the campaign, and that he already had developed advanced social views and uncommon ability as a public speaker. Although no independent account exists, the story does appear to be true—true in its critical facts and true to Langston's character.

Further, this study reveals the determined efforts of some leaders of the northern black community to confront the overweening forces arrayed against them. By centering a political movement for freedom and equality within the Afro-American culture, Langston and other resourceful and resilient men and women succeeded in affecting both their own destiny and the events of a critical era.

A second volume will deal with Langston's life in the interval between 1865 and his death in 1897.

Acknowledgments

Iₙ addition to the generosity of San Diego State University, which provided funds for typing the manuscript and a subvention to the University of Illinois Press, and the American Philosophical Society, which furnished two grants in aid, several individuals contributed significantly to this study, and we are in their debt: W. E. Bigglestone, archivist, Oberlin College; Marie I. Clark, local historian, Chillicothe, Ohio; Ann R. Wright, microfilm librarian, San Diego State University; Cheryl Harley and Cynthia Mather, research assistants; and Mary Giles, assistant editor, University of Illinois Press. We are grateful for the encouragement of our friends and family, especially Ethel B. Raveling. Our daughters Wendy and Pamela gave abundantly of their affection and faith; Pam read the entire manuscript and made valuable suggestions for its final revision.

Finally, we wish to thank our editor August Meier for his confidence in our vision, his patience where ours has sometimes failed during a very long endeavor, and his rigor, acuity, and understanding.

CHAPTER 1

Inheritor

1829–34

ON June 12, 1867, the white Virginians, much the same crowd that gathered every month on court day in Louisa County, seemed oblivious to expectations beyond the usual horse trading, laced with gossip and whiskey. But the newly freed men, women, and children who early thronged the hamlet, riding two or three to a mule or crowded into wooden carts, or walking in, some barefooted, before the sun burned through the dew-soaked morning, gave evidence by numbers alone that they sensed an occasion.[1] "A great deal of the old absolutism" still held them. Still, there were fewer instances of petty meanness lately and more promises of better wages come fall. The ancient fear and despair giving way to hope, they were cheerful as they passed the time in conversation, delving incident and character from the memories of the oldest among them, calling out the ghosts, to lay a foundation for the structure of the day. One of their own, the nationally prominent leader and orator John Mercer Langston, was to speak to them that afternoon.[2]

Langston, who had recently been appointed an inspector for the Freedmen's Bureau, arrived on the midday train. As he stepped out, the waiting crowd saw a well-dressed man in his late thirties, light in skin color, slender, and of medium height. His curly dark hair and beard framed regular features and full, intelligent, penetrating eyes; his movements and gestures were graceful. More arresting than any single physical characteristic was his presence. Courteous, self-possessed, proud to the verge of conceit (some said beyond), serious but with a flashing wit, he projected assurance and "personal magnetism."[3]

He did not apologize for his race. Just days ago at Leesburg, he and several white Republican traveling companions had been turned away from the hotel dining room kept by a Union man. Langston's friends had next appealed to the proprietor of another restaurant who, despite being a Democrat and an ex-Rebel, had responded: "I keep a hotel to make money, and yours is as good as anyone's. If you want to eat with a nigger I don't care a bang. Bring on your nigger." In bold strokes Langston had signed the register: "John Mercer Langston, Negro, Oberlin, Ohio."[4]

Journeying throughout the South for the Freedmen's Bureau and organizing councils of the Union League for the Republican party all along the way, going into areas like Louisa where whites and blacks drank copiously and most carried concealed weapons,[5] Langston would rely on his manner, far more than on federal troops or white politicians, to get him through.

Langston received a ceremonious welcome to Louisa Courthouse. The white president of the local Union League greeted him at the train while the five hundred black men composing nearly the entire membership of the league stood at attention and then divided ranks to form an aisle through which the guest was ushered to the village hotel. Although its public dining room also was off limits, young Major Marcus S. Hopkins, the Freedmen's Bureau officer for the region, dutifully if nervously preparing for the visit, had arranged for luncheon in private chambers. Having grown up on the Western Reserve not far from Langston's own home in Oberlin, Major Hopkins was acquainted with the black lawyer and abolitionist's prowess as an orator and had made diligent attempts to interest county notables in Langston's visit— only to evoke scorn at the idea "that any 'nigger' could talk law, politics, reconstruction or anything else with a degree of ability and intelligence to merit their attention." Nonetheless, as time for the speech-making drew near, the numerous whites on the outskirts of the crowd of some fifteen hundred appeared not wholly indifferent.[6]

Since passage of the Reconstruction Acts in March, white conservatives in Louisa County were exhibiting what Major Hopkins saw as a "real or pretended" interest in their black neighbors, some even speaking favorably of protection and education and a "fairer return" for labor. Registration for the coming election of delegates to the state constitutional convention was about to occur, with some two thousand black adult males in Louisa and Orange counties eligible to vote for the first time in their lives.[7] Although the Cincinnati *Gazette*'s man in the field predicted the Republican party would win the entire black vote in both counties, the recent blandishments by white Democrats seemed to confirm what Langston had long contended, namely, that the franchise was "a source of very great power."[8]

Politics aside, Louisa whites and blacks alike had particular reason to be curious about the speaker. As Langston assumed the platform with several white hosts, "objects of intense detestation to the mass of the white people," he could hear a dissonant yet harmonic chorus. "Ralph Quarles's boy," whites declared; blacks responded, "Lucy Jane Langston's son." Although dead for more than thirty years, the uncommon pair was not forgotten.[9]

Today Langston—the son of the white plantation owner and the black ex-slave—hewed to his practice of presenting himself as representative of both, a unifying element in a divided land. Although he had been recognized as a militant antislavery orator, his tone on this Virginia tour had been conciliatory: "so manly and generous and broad-spirited," it was reported of his speech at nearby Gordonsville the day before, "as to conquer all prejudice and take a deep hold upon the judgments of all classes."[10] Skillfully, Langston cast his lines, tendering a touching description of the Old Dominion's past greatness and "its present temporary depression and distress," projecting seductive images of its future as a free state in which black and white worked coequally toward an "unexampled prosperity and a superior civilization." To the roll of honored Virginians he attached the names of his father and other local men who had acted decisively in Langston's own behalf. Then, for more than two hours, he discussed Republican policy and the rebuilding of the South. Uncompromising on black citizenship and voting rights, he urged "nothing for the Negro because he was black, but because he was a man, he would ask everything for him that other men had."[11] Addressing blacks directly, in the morally earnest tone for which he was noted, Langston expounded his own hard-earned definition of liberty and the responsibilities his guardians and teachers on both sides of the color line had taught him to associate with it. It was a brief he had argued before black audiences for years, for self-reliance and well-directed energy, asking only a "fair opportunity" from whites, for the black acquisition of education, property, and moral character to the end of a "well ordered and dignified life."[12]

The strong musical tones of the finished orator, whose enunciation never hinted of plantation origin unless by premeditation, rang out across the grounds. A push began. Looking around, Major Hopkins noticed the blacks, "accustomed to yielding precedence," one by one surrendering the best places to whites. Ex-Confederate General William Fitzhugh Gordon, Jr., Louisa's commonwealth attorney, took over a seat on the platform, as Langston observed with surprise when he turned from his opening remarks to address the chair, for the man earlier had been identified to him as "the meanest rebel in the county." At the close of Langston's "admirable peroration," "there was one general rush to the platform, all trying to grasp him by the hand." Among the first was the visibly moved General Gordon, who murmured: "Langston, you are one of us." White and black, they congratulated him. "God bless you! God bless you!" blacks cried. "We knew your mother. We never expected to see this day!"[3]

When the exhausted orator retired, both a white Republican and the Rebel general helped him to his room. According to Langston, General Gordon insisted on plumping his pillow and begged his pardon for the "blasphemous, vulgar expressions" he had used against him. In the early evening Langston and other guests, Yankee and home-grown Unionists, at dinner in a private home, were startled by heavy raps on the door. The intruder turned out to be Gordon, with an invitation to address the white ladies at the Baptist church. That very night the native son spoke extemporaneously to a full house on "the duty of the American woman in this hour of our reconstruction." Afterward, the women, too, placed their gloved hands in his. The next morning Langston breakfasted at the first table in the hotel dining room as the general's guest, sitting at Gordon's right hand and facing his wife.[4]

How much of this peculiar drama was passion, how much policy? If these Virginians intended a contrived performance, part of the ancient deceit the white southerner had been practicing on the colored man for more than two hundred years, it went extravagantly far and, ultimately, failed in its probable purpose. Langston, who instructed blacks throughout the South in the next two years on how to vote and for whom, apparently was not persuaded. No more were black men and women. Within four days of his speech, the local Union League added some four hundred members; in the fall a black voting majority in Louisa County sent radicals to the Virginia constitutional convention. Still, for the moment, all of the actors seem to have departed from the political script, thrust beyond their reckoning by the intoxicating performance and emotions intensely felt if scarcely understood. Young Major Hopkins, for one, pronounced the white men sincere, observing: "A more perfect and delightful victory over prejudice than Langston gained was never won by an orator, and a more spontaneous ovation, honorable alike to its recipient and to those who gave it, was never more freely bestowed as a tribute to manhood, to intelligence, and to talent."[5]

The most poignant moment occurred after the breakfast. Escorted by Gordon and a dashing company, including white kinsmen of his own, Langston rode out to his father's old plantation. Only cataclysmic national events, in which he had taken a significant role, had enabled him to return to his birthplace after thirty-three years. In a remote corner of the grounds, he saw evidence of another triumph, that of his progenitors. The peculiar respect sometimes paid the scandalous dead, a kind of reparation for or transmutation of the enmity they arouse when alive, marked the stories the white Virginians told him of his parents. But the mute testimony of the place where they were buried was the most forcible indication of the effect of their unusual personalities. Through all the years no one had violated the graves. To their son it seemed a wonder. Unmarked and untended, overgrown by weeds and vines, the crumbling weathered mounds lay side by side, defiant.[16]

By 1800, Ralph Quarles, in middle age, was lodged securely among the up-country Virginia gentry. First born in a large, well-connected, and prosperous Spotsylvania County family,[17] he had early acquired a better than average education, a familiarity with plantation routine, and a head for business. During the War for Independence, according to his sons, the adolescent Quarles had joined the continental forces, served under Lafayette, perhaps in the nearby Yorktown campaign of 1781, and fought until victory came.[18] In the next years he had established his own plantation in economically undistinguished Louisa County, at the outset purchasing 370 acres between Hickory and Gold Mine Creeks, about three miles from the county seat, at a cost of one pound an acre.[19] He had come into his full inheritance upon his father's death in 1794, serving as coexecutor of the will alongside the aristocratic Colonel Garrett Minor, a kinsman of Dabney Carr, into whose family two of the Quarles brothers had married. Ralph's sister Frances had made a similarly good match in the estimable William Thomson II, who held successively most of the public offices in Louisa County.[20] Apparently a contented bachelor, Quarles concentrated on the management of his estate, the size of which, within a relatively short time, he more than doubled.[21]

The Gabriel slave revolt in the late summer of 1800, some forty miles to the south in Henrico County, jolted the even tenor of life for Quarles and his neighbors. They felt their vulnerability in a land that was thickly forested, hilly, and sparsely settled, with a total population in Louisa County of about twelve thousand divided fairly evenly between white, mostly poor, farming families and slaves, quite a number of the latter having trades.[22] Governor James Monroe's own assertion that the huge conspiracy extended into Louisa made defensive measures seem imperative.[23] Alarmed landowners strengthened the local militia, as William Thomson became first captain and then commander of the first battalion of the Fortieth Regiment. On Thomson's promotion, five county "Gentlemen," a Quarles brother among them, recommended Ralph Quarles to the governor and council "as a fit and proper person to act as Captain" in his stead.[24] Given his status and personal attributes, the appointment was assured.

Yet at about the same time, a new, unsettling factor had entered the tidy ledger of Captain Quarles's affairs, introduced in part by his sound financial management. While most local farmers struggled on small holdings to eke out a living from sandy soil impoverished by overcropping, ignorance of the necessity for contour plowing, inadequate manuring, and the growing of tobacco,[25] Quarles raised wheat, corn, other grains, and livestock, as well as the profitable tobacco, on his large acreage of fertile bottom land. With cash on hand he frequently extended loans, a practice encouraged by absence of banking facilities. As lender, he was entitled to hold as collateral any form of convertible property—grist mill, livestock, or slave.[26] On November 1, 1803, Quarles made a substantial loan to a hapless neighbor who had already been forced to place much of his property with an executor, and who died shortly thereafter. Perhaps moved by more than pecuniary considerations, Quarles sued for payment of the debt; the court ordered restitution from the dead man's "goods and chattels," or from those of the executor himself. In this transaction or one like it, "in pledge for money borrowed," Ralph Quarles acquired Lucy Jane Langston.[27]

She was a rare possession. Her "uncommon beauty and good qualities" made a lasting impression.[28] Quite young, still in her teens or early twenties,[29] she was of small stature but substantial build, with an easy and natural bearing. Partly black, partly Native American, probably by statute she should not have been a slave at all. While one Virginia law specified that the free or bond condition of the child followed that of the mother, another, enacted in 1691 and but little observed, prohibited the enslavement of Indians. Lucy, or Jane as she was often called, took the Langston name from her mother who, it was claimed, was a full-blooded Indian. Although Lucy Jane could not herself write her name, she may well have been the descendant of an educated man. Two Langstons, John and Gideon, were among the eight Indians who attended the College of William and Mary between 1753 and 1755—a coincidence of names with those of Lucy Langston's sons that suggests that one of these men was her grandfather.[30] Who her father was, beyond his having been, to some degree, of black African descent, there is no clue. Slave or free, it made no difference to his child's legal status. With "a slight proportion of Negro blood," Lucy would be a slave because her mother was a slave, legally or no; by Virginia statute she and her children would be mulattoes, to be treated in all respects as Negroes because her father had Negro blood.[31]

By 1806, Captain Quarles and his beautiful slave were the parents of a daughter named Maria. Although prudence dictated that such affairs be confined to the separate world of the plantation, out of view of the larger society, in that year he was impelled to take an extraordinary step. Shocked into empathetic recognition of their bondsmen's longing for freedom by the Gabriel uprising and rumors of other slave plots, Virginia's former revolutionaries had become increasingly suspicious of the free Negro, an "obnoxious" and dangerous lot whose numbers had multiplied since passage of the liberal emancipation law of 1782. After spirited debate during the 1804–5 legislative session on the practical and moral consequences of abolishing private manumissions, the General Assembly in 1806 passed an act declaring that all slaves freed after May 1 of that year must leave the state within twelve months, under penalty of being resold into slavery.[32]

Faced with this ultimatum, Quarles took action. On April 1, 1806, he drafted a careful document: "Be it known to all whom it may concern that I, Ralph Quarles of Louisa County, do hereby manumit and set free my negroe slaves Lucy, a woman, and Maria, a girl daughter of said Lucy. . . . And I do hereby declare the said slaves to be henceforward free persons at liberty to go where they please and to exercise and enjoy all the rights of free persons so far as I can authorize or the laws of Virginia will permit. . . ." Two weeks later, just before the deadline, the county court approved the manumission.[33] Lucy Jane Langston had the right to remain in Virginia, a free woman.

The next turning of this romance is unexpected and unexplained. The possibility exists that in freeing his bondwoman the Louisa County slaveholder hoped to disentangle himself, and her, from the emotional cords that bound them in their hopelessly unsanctioned and unsanctified union. In any case, Lucy Langston soon showed that she was not only legally but sexually independent of her former master. Ralph Quarles was not the father (the identity of the man or men is not known), but Lucy Langston was the mother of three children: William, Harriet, and Mary Langston. All were born after her manumission, likely during the first five years. According to an 1831 county registry of free Negroes, William Langston was then twenty-one, which would make his birthdate 1810. The "son of Lucy who was emancipated by Ralph Quarles," William was described as "a dark mulatto," "hair inclined to curl," "good countenance." As for Harriet and Mary, the 1830 federal census noted only that two free colored females between the ages of ten and twenty-four lived on the Quarles plantation.[34] It was to these children that their mother would will her property, including 290 acres of land.[35]

Despite this interval, the liaison between Ralph Quarles and Lucy Langston resumed, ultimately to become permanent and open. Between 1809 and 1815 the couple gave birth to their first son. A robust handsome boy, features "all of Anglo-Saxon stamp," who so greatly resembled his father that, at the age of twenty-one, "Quarles" was added to his name, he was called Gideon. In 1817, a second son was born. Charles Henry was like his mother "in blood, mind, and disposition."[36] The boys were cared for by Lucy, who also oversaw the keeping of the Great House. She lived in a modest abode at the other end of the garden, where she herself owned the feather beds and bedding, as well as the wheel and loom on which she spun and wove cloth.[37]

Quarles proved accountable and considerate to his mistress. He brought her mother onto the estate to spend her last years. When his and Lucy's young daughter Maria fell in love with the slave Joseph Powell, Quarles bought the man for her and set the married couple up in housekeeping on a nearby farm. Taught reading, writing, and something of business by her father, Maria and Joseph, whom she cautiously maintained in slavery until her death in 1846, managed the property profitably with the use of slave labor. The Powells had twenty-one children, one of whom would become an administrator in a Virginia black college.[38]

When Lucy Jane Langston once again became pregnant, she and Captain Quarles had been lovers for some twenty-five years. She was surely in her forties, he in his late sixties. "The child of my father's extreme old age," John Mercer Langston would call himself, and in another place, "the child of the advanced years of his parents."[39] Since one of his half-sisters later would tell him the birthdate, Langston, unlike so many of his black contemporaries, would be able to fix his beginnings in place and time.[40] To open his autobiography, *From the Virginia Plantation to the National Capitol*, published when he was sixty-four, Langston would commence with an affirmative sense of self: "JOHN MERCER LANGSTON was born upon a plantation located three miles from Louisa Court House, in Louisa County, Virginia, on the 14th day of December, 1829."[41]

John Mercer came into a self-contained world, regulated by the timeless rhythms of agricultural life. By the time of his birth, Captain Quarles, despite having disposed of a large portion of the more than

4,500 acres he had owned in 1815, remained one of the largest land-owners in the county, with a holding of more than 2,600 acres.[42] Cultivating the fields with grubbing hoes, broad hoes, harrows and shovel plows pulled by oxen or horses, baking the bread and pastries in three ovens, making the whiskey in a still, taking the honey from five bee-hives, manufacturing the liquid soap and candles from tallow, seeing to the work animals, cows, hogs, and sheep: such was daily life. Like other farmers in the Piedmont section, Quarles and his laborers readied the tobacco beds in the late winter months, sowed corn toward April's end, and planted the tobacco in the latter sunshine days of May or the beginning of June. The wheat was cut in late June and early July, tobacco suckered and topped all summer, the wheat trod out in sweltering August. The sowing of the wheat began at the end of August or early September along with the cutting of tobacco and the pulling of fodder. In the bracing autumn months the black men and women cured, stemmed, and prized tobacco and cut and harvested the corn. Often by late cold November the tobacco ripened and was hauled by wagon to the Richmond warehouse for sale. Sometime before Christmas, the whole plantation was swept up in hog-killing, when the fascinating horror of the slaughter, the arduous labor of the killing and the curing of the meat, the irresistible taste of cooked fresh pork, and the tantalizing smell of frying chitterlings mingled in a strange festival. When the Christmas season was over, Quarles and his men again took up their plows and cleared the fields.[43]

All of this required a sizable work force. In 1830, Quarles could employ six males and six females among his twenty-one slaves (nine of whom were less than ten years of age), as well as his two growing sons and probably Lucy's son William. Quarles was himself the only white person on the place. Rather than utilize a white overseer as large land-owners in Louisa County normally did, Quarles directed his laborers himself. His practice was to divide the slaves into work gangs, designating one as foreman on a rotating basis, to accomplish specific tasks. By so doing and by avoiding physical punishment of the slaves, during the last twenty years of his life Quarles was conducting an experiment with a twofold purpose. According to Langston, his father aimed to provide other planters with an object lesson in the increased efficiency produced by fair treatment and to prepare his slaves for self-government and eventual freedom.[44]

Quarles believed that slavery ought to be abolished, not by government but by the voluntary action of the individual slaveowner. So Langston claimed, and there is little reason to doubt it. On the other hand, how the troubled aristocrat reached this conviction is open to question. Doubts over the possible application of the natural rights philosophy to black slaves may well have assailed Quarles, along with Jefferson and other planters of the Revolutionary generation, while the intellectual hand-wringing over ridding the region of its burden of slavery persisted in the Upper South throughout Quarles's lifetime. Even within his own neighborhood, an influence for manumission and amelioration obtained. The Louisa County clerk for twenty-eight years was prosperous John Poindexter, a Separatist Baptist who often preached near Goldmine Creek, freed seventeen of his own bond servants, and led an active Benevolent Society pledged to humane treatment and eventual manumission of slaves. Langston's own account, however, simply states that his father held these "peculiar" beliefs about slavery, which in turn produced social ostracism, forcing him to lead "an exclusive life among his slaves" and, only then, to turn to a slavewoman for love. Almost certainly, the actual chain of circumstances is being reversed: Quarles's love for Lucy Langston, once their affair became open and lasting, led to his ostracism; both his affection and his exile contributed to the growth and expression of his radical ideas on the abolition of slavery and slave management.[45]

Given the century's racial attitudes, however, Langston's portrayal of his parents served important private and public needs. In justifying them, he was, to a degree, justifying himself, for he was the fruit of their illicit and racially mixed union, the mulatto bastard, the "mongrel." Even as he consistently denied that there was any wrong in interracial sexual pairing, he had repeatedly to answer the cruel charge: "I am not ashamed of my colored blood. I only wish I were as black as midnight darkness, but in my veins courses the blood of one of the best and most aristocratic families of Virginia, as well as the blood that makes me colored. My father was a white man, and a slaveholder; my mother, his wife, was colored and a slave. But I honor and love the memory of my father and my mother." In casting his father as a lonely man of conscience, rather than as an immoral slaveholder taking lustful advantage of his human property; his mother as intelligent and loving, accepting her lot "with becoming resignation" (even as he omitted explicit reference to her outside sexual involvement), Langston cloaked his parents with respectability, aristocracy, and affection. Heaven approved their union, because church and state would not.[46] As Langston struggled to reconcile his difficult racial legacy, on one level, at least, he would be able to transform the more common resentment or shame passed to black children by white fathers into gratitude and pride, even protectiveness. Although others of mixed blood, faced with the basic developmental problem of accepting or rejecting parental authority, might find themselves powerless to deal with the white father, a frustrating irresolution that could well plague their relations with other white authority figures, Langston consciously insisted upon a positive view of his father and mother that went toward shaping a positive view of himself. The family portraits he fashioned could be proudly displayed in a Victorian mansion, the darker shadings reflecting not character, but a society permeated by the evil of slavery.

Major purveyors of family legend to John would be his brothers Gideon and Charles, who grew into young manhood on the plantation. The general favorite, Gideon seemed the inheritor of "all the dash and the eloquence of his white and his colored-Indian progenitors." The 1831 county registry of free Negroes described Gideon as "a very bright mulatto, five feet 4 and 1/2 inches high, about 16 years of age, has a small scar just in brow of the right eye, black hair & rather inclined to be straight, good countenance." Less handsome, Charles seemed more complex: shy and sensitive yet impetuous, restive under discipline yet capable of firm self-control. "When aroused and his latent powers were called into requisition, he displayed masterful ability, logical power and commanding eloquence." In 1830, Charles was described as "a very bright mulatto, four feet 11 and 1/2 inches, 14 years old, small scar on forehead from cut, hair inclined to be light and straight."[47]

From the age of seven both boys reported to their father's private chambers for tutoring and recitations at five o'clock each morning year round before they went out to work the plantation. Drawing on his library of some forty volumes—a fair holding for a planter's household—a large map of America, and whatever other resources the place offered, Quarles instructed his sons in English studies (as opposed to classical), besides "general information and mental and moral improvement." It was an education for usefulness, a conjoining of head and hands that Langston came to consider man's "best earthly estate." Like most things, learning came more easily for even-tempered Gideon than for stubborn, delicate Charles, but both proved so bright and quick that their father was encouraged in the experiment—for so it could only be considered in a culture that held education of Negroes to be either futile or dangerous. Indeed, the 1831 Virginia assembly would prohibit the education of free Negroes, thus stifling efforts at schooling previously initiated around the state by black beneficial societies.[48]

John Mercer was born too late for paternal tutelage. But he remembered, or affected to remember, "my father, a perfect white man, . . .

dandying me on his lap." Because of his mother's precarious health, the baby was tended by a young slave, and it was under Lucky's watchful eye that he first toddled, then ran about the protective world his parents had made. He could taste honey fresh from the comb, feel the prickling of pine needles underfoot, watch the rhythmic shuttling of his mother's loom, play with slave children, dream in the warmth of a fire reflected on polished tables of cherrywood. Fascination alternated with fear as he daily renewed acquaintance with the livestock. His father's fine mount may have incited the initial awe that would make him a lifelong lover of horses. In the bright Virginia sunshine on a playground strewn with buttercups in spring and acorns and hickory nuts in fall, nature bid for his infant affections. The late child comes sometimes like a special gift, and wins a special love. From his parents and brothers, as well as other adults and children on the plantation, this child may have received such attention as to convince him his world was a beautiful, safe, and loving place.[49]

Yet Quarles's plantation did not go untouched by the increasing southern restrictiveness toward free Negroes during these years. Against the countervailing forces of newly militant white and black abolitionist agitation in the North, and in immediate response to the 1831 insurrection of Nat Turner and his band of fellow slaves in Southampton County, the Virginia assembly during notable debates of 1831–32, rejecting the argument that slavery was ruinous to whites while elaborating the view that slavery was a "positive good," passed a series of bills designed to make life intolerable for free blacks. A supplementary measure to put teeth in the 1806 banishment act included a requirement that commissioners of the revenue register all free Negroes so that a list of those remaining contrary to law could be presented to a grand jury annually. It was in response to the new law that in March 1831, Gideon and Charles, as well as their half-brother William Langston, were entered in the small leather-bound book, *Bonds Recorded*, at the county courthouse. Around this time, William Langston and his two sisters joined the outward migration of Virginia free Negroes that reached its height between 1830 and 1835, continuing until the war. Like many of the exiles, the Langstons went to southeastern Ohio, one sister settling in Jackson County, William and the other sister in Chillicothe in Ross County. A tall, good-looking young man, William soon found employment in the service of former Ohio governor Duncan McArthur.[50]

Even as outside events were increasingly infringing upon the special order of Ralph Quarles's fiefdom, he had to recognize the inevitability of coming defeat by an even more implacable foe. So long as he lived his wealth and position could protect his boys, but he was old. On October 18, 1833, appealing "In the name of God, Amen!" and "reflecting on the uncertainty of human life," Ralph Quarles made a final bid to justify his philosophy and satisfy his conscience. Cautiously estimating societal limits and shrewdly judging character, he wrote a will settling the major portions of his estate on his sons. Directing equal division among them, with each son to come into his inheritance at the age of twenty-one, he left to Gideon, Charles, and John Langston, "the three youngest children of Lucy, a woman whom I have emancipated," all of his lands lying on Hickory Creek—some 2,030 acres— and all of his personal property, all of his cash—death hard by, he deposited $3,930 in the federal bank in January 1834—and the proceeds of debts owed him, plus all of his federal and state bank stock. In the event "they should wish to remove to some other place during the time between my death and the youngest of them coming of age," he directed the lands be sold and proceeds reinvested for them. Quarles took pains to mollify three nephews, his next kin, by leaving them valuable chunks of land; in addition, to one he willed two male slaves, to another a family of ten. It was fear of possible attempts to invalidate the will, John Mercer Langston believed, that constrained Quarles from dividing his entire estate between his sons and freeing all of his slaves. He did liberate four valuable men, adding a general clause of manumission to "all other slaves that I may have any right or title to." To serve in the vital role of executors, Quarles secured the pledges of four influential men, all county slaveholders, two of them nephews named in the will. Within months one of those designated, William D. Gooch, moved his family to Ohio, thus becoming disqualified. The remaining three were to prove trustworthy and able. Since Quarles directed the estate not be appraised, no record of its value exists, but the bonds required of the executors aggregated $180,000.[51]

By April 1834, within six months of the formulation of his will, Captain Ralph Quarles was dead. During his final illness, only Lucy and their children, with his slaves, attended him; during the two days his body lay on its bier in the Great House, only they mourned. They interred him according to his directions in an obscure corner of his plantation. The little boy met grief and bereavement for the first time. Lucy Langston died shortly afterward. Still under orders, the slaves buried her beside their master. John would remember his nursemaid Lucky's embrace.[52]

Gideon had reached his majority, Charles was sixteen, but the baby John Mercer was only four years old. Concern over the boy's welfare had troubled Quarles's last months. Fortunately, a solution had been offered by William Gooch. Gooch had won the confidence of both Ralph Quarles and Lucy Langston. A man with a reputation for probity who often acted as a factor in business transactions, Gooch was the only white neighbor who called on them regularly. In her own will written February 15, 1834, Lucy Langston entrusted Gooch with property for one of her daughters and called him "my friend." On the verge of departure for Chillicothe, Gooch had promised to take the toddler into his household and see to his education. This agreement, doubtless joined with reports from William Langston about the possibilities for work and education for free black men in Ohio, determined Gideon and Charles on their course.[53] Uncle Billy, oldest and most experienced of the slaves freed by Quarles, and the three younger men, Burrel, twenty-five, James, Jr., twenty-four, and Arthur, twenty, all obligated by law to leave the state, decided to accompany them.[54]

While the emigrants readied for departure, there occurred two emotion-charged events, perhaps half-remembered by the boy or told him by his brothers. The first was separation from the slaves destined for the plantations of Quarles's two nephews. Jacob and Winney, an old couple, with their daughter and her seven children including John's nurse Lucky, were to go to the namesake Ralph Quarles, Abram and Lawrence to John Quarles. "They spent an hour or such matter gathering together the remnant of their little effects scattered here and there." Losing the last vestige of maternal care, the boy stood with his brothers and the four freed men at the door of "the great deserted mansion," into which they had moved, while each played his role in "this heartrending scene of parting."[55]

The second incident read from a different page of the annals of slavery. One dark night, when Uncle Billy's nervousness over their unprotected condition had been heightened by James's insistence on visiting a neighboring plantation, repeated pounding on the door of the Great House and a stentorian demand for entrance badly frightened John Mercer and his companions. As Burrel managed to throw the door wide, a huge black figure with wildly unkempt beard and long hair strode into the room. "Boys," he said, "I have come for something to eat!" If this "wonderful, mysterious person, coming from the wilderness," was a stranger to the child, the others knew him to be a fugitive slave, one of several such denizens of the forests and nearby Dirty Swamp, who periodically emerged to seek necessities in the slave quarters. The superstitious Uncle Billy interpreted the visit of this awesome figure to his young charges as auguring well for their own search for freedom.

Coincidence peppered Langston's life. For this occurrence he would claim a touching and meaningful sequel. In January 1865 after addressing battered black troops near Nashville, Tennessee, he was rather offended to be addressed as "John" by a white-haired, but still physically powerful, black corporal. "When you did not weigh ten pounds," the elderly soldier explained, "I held you in the hollow of this hand." Identifying himself as the Louisa fugitive, Robert J. declared he had entered the service "to fight until there is no more slavery in the land." "You were never a slave!" Langston blurted. "Always a slave, John," returned Robert J., "but always a fugitive slave, always a fugitive slave."

Describing the encounter for a reporter, Langston said, "I cannot give you the quiet powerful emphasis that he put upon repetition of these words, but it greatly strengthened my conviction that the perfectly black man *can* learn the lesson of freedom."[56]

Quarles's unusual concern and the unexceptionable constancy of the executors were among the factors that allowed Langston to hope that the white man might learn the same lesson. To teach it to these disparate peoples was his mission, a task for which he believed himself uniquely qualified by birth. He was a Virginian, with all that implied in nineteenth-century America, who represented the Great House and the slave quarters.

At dawn one morning in late September or early October of 1834, the little boy climbed into a carry-all, a wagon with canopied top and sides capable of lowering in inclement weather. Gideon had purchased the vehicle, along with a light wagon, harness and teams, clothing and camping equipment. All was ready. The four freed men had been registered by the county clerk; on September 8 the court compared the descriptions with their persons and ordered them certified. Gideon had secured authenticated copies of free papers for himself and his brothers. They guarded these precious scraps closely, perhaps tucking them in the oblong tin boxes often used by free Negroes. Without these documents they could neither travel in Virginia nor settle in Ohio.[57]

Rugged country lay between them and their destination. Though many Americans seeking changed and somehow freer lives in the new lands beyond the Alleghenies had taken the route, usage had hardly softened the natural perils of swollen streams, deep rivers, and narrow mountain paths. Avoiding the inns and taverns that offered solace to others, these black travelers had to depend on their own resources: camping in tents at night, eating food from their packs, dipping water from streams for tea and coffee heated over the campfire. Of the seven, Uncle Billy alone had ventured much beyond the perimeter of the plantation, accompanying his master on occasion to the Richmond markets. At the end of the first week, setting up camp for the night at the foot of the Alleghenies, the wayfarers were approached by a lone man on horseback. Traveling from Chillicothe, William Langston had undertaken to meet and guide them on. To John, it seemed the days passed more quickly then, as this new adult gave him the petting and playing he had missed. At one joyous moment, William lifted the small boy high and set him down on the saddle of his big horse, fitting his tiny boots in the shortened stirrups and jokingly assuring him that now the horse was his.

Finally through the mountains, they crossed the Kanawa River by ferry and, again by ferry, the Ohio River. They landed at Gallipolis in the free state of Ohio. Curiosity greeted them. With William setting the tone, they responded to questions with as much assurance as they could muster, but spent only one night before pushing on.[58]

Toward noon on the third day thereafter they came to Berlin Cross-roads, a small black settlement in Jackson County, and for Uncle Billy, Burrel, James, Jr., and the affable Arthur, the journey had reached its end. Each had been left money by Quarles, Billy having received $220 and the others $120 each,[59] and land was cheap there. Though freed men and women often headed for the larger towns of Ohio where jobs were more attainable, these men had enough of a stake to get started in a familiar environment, rural and black. No doubt, they were excited by the prospect of living in a community like the one in Milton Township where hope and endeavor were on the increase, one whose people, ex-Virginia slaves in the main, were bent on demonstrating that Negroes could be self-sufficient in a state of freedom.[60] (Three decades later John Langston would correctly single out Jackson County as one of the several farming districts in Ohio where blacks were "owners of large farms, which, in many instances, are well stocked and cultivated according to the most approved methods of agriculture.")[61] Not long after their arrival, the four Louisa County ex-slaves had their certificates of manumission recorded, in obedience to an 1804 law requiring the registration of all free blacks or mulattoes before they could reside in the state.[62]

The Langston brothers pushed on alone. They had been on the road three weeks; the horses had grown gaunt, the carry-all battered and worn, the travelers thin, tired, and dirty. With William pointing the way, the wagon rolled into the beautiful old town of Chillicothe.

NOTES

1. Washington *Chronicle*, June 14, 20, 1867; Marcus S. Hopkins, Freedmen's Bureau officer stationed in Gordonsville, Va., 1867–68, recalled incident at length in Washington *Star*, Nov. 23, 1882.

2. Marcus S. Hopkins to Gen. O. Brown, Feb. 28, 1867, Box 678, Mar. 31, Apr. 30, June 30, 1867, Box 679, Record Group 105, Records of the Bureau of Refugees, Freedmen and Abandoned Lands, National Archives (hereafter cited as Freedmen's Bureau ms., NA); Washington *Star*, Nov. 23, 1882; John Mercer Langston, *From the Virginia Plantation to the National Capitol; or, The First and Only Negro Representative in Congress from the Old Dominion* (Hartford, 1894; repr. New York: Johnson Reprint, 1968), p. 267.

3. Washington *Chronicle*, June 14, 1867; J. E. Rankin, introductory sketch, John Mercer Langston, *Freedom and Citizenship* (Washington, 1883; repr. Miami: Mnemosyne Reprint, 1969), pp. 38, 36.

4. New York *Mail and Express*, Oct. 25, 1890, in John Mercer Langston Scrapbooks, 4 vols., III, Moorland-Spingarn Research Center, Howard University (hereafter cited as JML Scrapbook).

5. William Frederick Mugleston, "The Diary of Marcus S. Hopkins, Virginia Freedmen's Bureau Officer," master's thesis, University of Virginia, 1965, pp. 33, 91.

6. Langston, *Virginia Plantation*, p. 267; Washington *Chronicle*, June 20, 1867; Washington *Star*, Nov. 23, 1882.

7. Hopkins to Brown, Mar. 31, Apr. 30, 1867, Box 679, RG 105, Freedmen's Bureau ms., NA.

8. Cincinnati *Gazette*, May 8, 1867; Langston, *Freedom and Citizenship*, p. 63.

9. Interview with John M. Langston, Chicago *Times*, Sept. 28, 1890, JML Scrapbook, III; Washington *Star*, Nov. 23, 1882; Langston, *Virginia Plantation*, pp. 17, 267.

10. Washington *Chronicle*, June 3, 10, 14, 1867.

11. Washington *Star*, Nov. 23, 1882; Washington *Chronicle*, June 10, 14, 1867.

12. Langston's message to the freedmen can be found in the New York *Herald*, June 3, 1867; Washington *Chronicle*, June 3, 4, 1867; several of the untitled, undated, 1867 newsclippings in John Mercer Langston Scrapbook, Fisk University Library; in more extended form in Baltimore *American*, n.d., included in J. M. Brown to Dear Recorder, Aug. 27, 1867, *Christian Recorder*, Sept. 14, 1867; and in full in Montgomery (Ala.) *State Sentinel*, Feb. 3, 1868, and Louisville *Courier-Journal*, July 16, 1869.

13. Washington *Star*, Nov. 23, 1882; Armistead C. Gordon, *Gordons in Virginia* (Hackensack, N.J., 1918), pp. 67–70; Langston, *Virginia Plantation*, pp. 269–70; Washington *Chronicle*, June 20, 1867.

14. Langston, *Virginia Plantation*, pp. 270–71; Washington *Star*, Nov. 23, 1882; San Francisco *Elevator*, Jan. 24, 1868; Washington *Chronicle*, June 20, 1867.

15. John M. Langston, "What I Saw in the South," Washington *Chronicle*, Aug. 13, 1867; Ibid, June 20, 1867; Hopkins to Brown, Oct. 31, 1867, Box 679, RG 105, Freedmen's Bureau ms., NA; Mugleston, "The Diary of Marcus S. Hopkins," passim; Washington *Star*, Nov. 23, 1882.

16. South Orange (N.J.) *Journal*, Oct. 26, 1876; Hoboken (N.J.) *Journal*, Oct. 25, 1876, both in JML Scrapbook, I; Chicago *Times*, Sept. 28, 1890, JML Scrapbook, III; Langston, *Virginia Plantation*, pp. 272–73.

17. Ralph Quarles was named first of ten children of William and Frances Quarles in William Quarles's will, probated Nov. 2, 1794, Will Book E, 1772–98, Spotsylvania County Courthouse. See account of the sales of William Quarles's estate, May 18, 1796, signed by Ralph Quarles, executor, in Will Book 4, Louisa County Courthouse (hereafter cited as LCC). Information about the Quarles family was made available by W. F. Baker of Newport News, Virginia, author of an unpublished genealogical study of the Baker family. He found 1751 guardianship papers for William Quarles, along with his brother Roger and sister Jane, putting them in the care of John Quarles of Caroline County.

18. *Speech of C. H. Langston before the U.S. District Court for Northern District of Ohio, Should Colored Men Be Subject to the Pains and Penalties of the Fugitive Slave Law? May 12, 1859, Delivered when about to be sentenced for Rescuing a Man from Slavery* (Cleveland, 1859); Cleveland *Leader*, May 7, 1859; Langston, *Virginia Plantation*, p. 13.

19. Deed Book F, p. 400, LCC.

20. William Quarles's will, probated Nov. 2, 1794, Will Book E, 1772–98, Spotsylvania County Courthouse; account of the sales of William Quarles's estate, Will Book 4; Order Book 1803–6, pp. 366, 397, 495, 15, 250, both in LCC.

21. The 1800 federal census listed Ralph Quarles in the 26–44 age category, and as the owner of 15 slaves. No other whites are listed on his plantation. Ransom B. True, "The Manuscript Returns of the Census of 1800," *Louisa County Historical Magazine* 4 (June 1972):43; Deed Book I, p. 612, LCC.

22. Joseph Martin, *A New Comprehensive Gazetteer of Virginia and the District of Columbia* (n.p., 1835), pp. 216, 219.

On the seven hundred to a thousand farms and plantations, with landholdings ranging from ten to six thousand acres and with nearly three-fourths of property owners holding between one hundred and six hundred acres, slavery predominated in 1800. The heads of more than two-thirds of all households (934) owned slaves. More than one-half of the owners had six or more slaves, while at least one-third held ten or more. Slavetrader Christopher Smith owned 150 people in 1800, and another sixty whites held twenty or more.

Slave artisans included blacksmiths, bootmakers, brickmakers, cabinet makers, carpenters, cartwrights, coopers, hatters, house joiners, housewrights, joiners, masons, saddlers, shoemakers, sulky makers, tailors, tanners, watch repairers, weavers and wheelwrights.

There were 132 free blacks in 1800. Eighty-one (36 black, 45 mulattoes) of these resided in the western part of the county, according to a list compiled in 1801 by that district's commissioner of revenue. Although roughly one-fifth resided with whites, predominantly these free blacks lived *on* a white plantation, meaning they either rented land and lived on it with their own people or else had their own place. Twelve of the thirty-seven free adults were skilled artisans: three carpenters, three spinners, two shoemakers, a weaver, a blacksmith, a farmer, and a tailoress. The others were predominantly farm laborers of one kind or another; see Ransom Badger True, "Land Transactions in Louisa

County, Virginia, 1765–1812: A Quantitative Analysis," Ph.D. diss., University of Virginia, 1976, pp. 28–32, 43, fn 4 on 43; True, "The Manuscript Returns of the Census of 1800," p. 22; and "A List of the Free Negroes and Mulattoes in the District of Peter Crawford 1801," ms. in Office of Clerk of the Circuit Court, LCC.

23. Herbert Aptheker, *American Negro Slave Revolts* (New York, 1943; repr. New York: International Publishers, 1963), pp. 225–26. According to the state's principal black witness, one of the black leaders, in an important organizational meeting, had spoken of having recruited several hundred Negroes from Louisa, Petersburg, and "adjacent counties"; see Gerald W. Mullin, *Flight and Rebellion: Slave Resistance in Eighteenth-Century Virginia* (New York, 1974), p. 144.

24. Order Book, 1803–6, p. 495, LCC.

25. Martin, *Gazetteer of Virginia*, pp. 216, 219.

26. See Ralph Quarles's will and inventory of his estate, Will Book 9, pp. 110, 143, LCC; Langston, *Virginia Plantation*, pp. 31, 13; Deed Book S, pp. 373–74; Deed Book T, pp. 385–86, both in LCC.

27. See Ralph Quarles versus William G. Poindexter, Order Book, p. 361; Indenture of Warner H. Broaddus, Aug. 19, 1803, Deed Book J, p. 705; and Broaddus will, Will Book 5, p. 154, all in LCC; Langston, *Virginia Plantation*, p. 13.

28. Washington *Star*, Nov. 23, 1882.

29. In 1830 the federal census listed one free Negro female, unquestionably Lucy Jane Langston, on the Quarles plantation, in the 36 to 55 age range. Population Census of 1830, Louisa County, Va., Reel 6, NA.

30. Langston, *Virginia Plantation*, p. 13; James Curtis Ballagh, *A History of Slavery in Virginia* (Baltimore, 1902; repr. New York: Johnson Reprint, 1968), pp. 49–50. Lucy Jane Langston's will is signed with an *X*; see Will Book 9, p. 133, LCC; College of William and Mary, Bursar's Book, 1754–69, p. 1.

31. Winthrop D. Jordan, *White Over Black: American Attitudes Toward the Negro, 1550–1812* (Chapel Hill, 1968), pp. 163, 167–69; Langston, *Virginia Plantation*, p. 13.

32. John H. Russell, *The Free Negro in Virginia, 1619–1865* (Baltimore, 1913; repr. New York: Negro Universities Press, 1969), pp. 65–71.

33. Deed Book K, p. 226, LCC. Between 1783 and 1807 twenty-seven Louisa County slaveowners manumitted 116 slaves; see True, "Land Transactions in Louisa County," p.31.

34. Langston characterizes these children as "born to Lucy Langston, before she was taken from the plantation into the Great House," giving no dates. Langston, *Virginia Plantation*, pp. 33–34; Bonds Recorded, No. 91, LCC; Population Census of 1830, Louisa County, Va., Reel 6, NA. When William Langston died in September 1886, his obituary stated his age was 74 years, 11 months; see Scioto *Gazette*, Sept. 23, 1886.

35. Will Book 9, pp. 220, 389, LCC.

36. Langston wrote that Gideon was born June 15, 1809, but his bond in 1831 described him as "about 16." Bonds Recorded, No. 90, No. 92, LCC;

Langston, *Virginia Plantation*, pp. 19–21, 13, 18. Writing in 1892 on the occasion of Charles's death, Langston noted only that Gideon was "much the senior" of his brother; see Cleveland *Gazette*, Dec. 24, 1892.

37. Langston, *Virginia Plantation*, pp. 18, 13; Will Book 9, p. 220, LCC.

38. Langston, *Virginia Plantation*, pp. 13, 18–19. Maria Powell's will, signed by her, appraisal of property, and estate settlement are recorded in Will Book 11, pp. 124–26, 148, 270, 273, 381, 537, LCC. She left a sizable estate. Her will directed that her six slaves, valued at $2,328, be sold, but that her husband, should he wish to leave the state, be freed. Langston wrote that a number of her children went to Ohio. Charles J. Powell, their son born in 1845, became in 1888 secretary and accountant of Virginia State College, where he lived with his family on campus until his death in 1916. A study of the family, compiled by Luther P. Jackson, *The Negro History Bulletin* 11 (Dec. 1947):51, with material also from Horace Mann Bond, is in Andrew Billingsley, *Black Families in White America* (Englewood Cliffs, N.J., 1968), pp. 106–9.

39. San Francisco *Post*, Apr. 5, 1877, JML Scrapbook, I; Langston, *Virginia Plantation*, p. 22.

40. Interview with Arthur D. Langston, St. Louis *Star-Sayings*, n.d., JML Scrapbook, II. During Langston's boyhood, public records referring to him reflect the century's casual attitudes toward age. Guardianship papers dated July 14, 1837, put his age at nine years. In the affidavit of William Langston, dated April 9, 1839, he is said to be "between eleven and twelve years." Both in Court of Common Pleas for Ross County versus William D. Gooch, Apr. 9, 1839, Court of Common Pleas, Box Case, No. 101, Ross County Courthouse, Chillicothe, Ohio (hereafter cited as RCC).

41. Langston, *Virginia Plantation*, p. 11.

42. His holdings in 1815 totaled 4,508 acres, plus 418 owned jointly with his brother-in-law William Thomson, and he paid taxes of $51.52. In 1830 the total was 2,609 acres, the tax $7.60; see "List of Land Tax Within Louisa County for the Year 1815"; "List of Land Tax Within Louisa County for the Year 1830," both in State Archives, Virginia State Library. See various land transactions in Deed Book M, p. 343; Deed Book Q, pp. 299, 301, 601; Deed Book R, pp. 73, 169, 246; Deed Book T, p. 463, all in LCC. In 1815 Quarles may well have been the largest landowner in the county. In 1810 only fifty or so property owners (5 percent) owned 1,000 acres or more, with the largest plantation not exceeding 3,000 acres; see True, "Land Transactions in Louisa County," pp. 51–52.

43. Will Book 9, p. 143, LCC; True, "Land Transactions in Louisa County," p. 53.

44. Population Census of 1830, Louisa County, Va., Reel 6, NA; Langston, *Virginia Plantation*, pp. 12, 16–17.

45. True, "Land Transactions in Louisa County," pp. 31–32, 34; Langston, *Virginia Plantation*, pp. 11–13. The repeated statement in newspaper interviews that Quarles manumitted all his slaves was probably part of Langston's protective handling of his father's memory, but an accurate account was given in the autobiography.

46. *Minutes . . . of the State Convention of the Colored Citizens of Ohio . . . Columbus . . . Jan., 1849 (Oberlin, 1849)*; Hoboken (N.J.) *Journal*, Oct. 25, 1876, JML Scrapbook, I; Langston, *Virginia Plantation*, pp. 12–13.

47. Cleveland *Gazette*, Dec. 24, 1892; Bonds Recorded, No. 90, No. 92, LCC.

48. Langston, *Virginia Plantation*, pp. 19–22; Will Book 9, p. 143, LCC; Langston, *Freedom and Citizenship*, p. 278; Luther P. Jackson, *Free Negro Labor and Property Holding in Virginia, 1830–1860* (New York, 1942; repr. Boston: Atheneum, 1968), pp. 19–20.

49. Louisville *Courier-Journal*, July 16, 1869; Langston, *Virginia Plantation*, p. 22; Will Book 9, pp. 143, 220, LCC.

50. Jackson, *Free Negro Labor*, pp. 12–13, 19–25; Bonds Recorded, No. 90, No. 91, No. 92, LCC; residences of sisters mentioned in William Langston's affidavit, Box Case, No. 101, RCC; William Langston obituary, untitled newsclipping, n.d., Henry Williams Scrapbook, Virginia State College Library.

51. Will Book 9, pp. 110–11, 143, 213, 384–85, LCC; Langston, *Virginia Plantation*, p. 25. The 1830 federal census listed the four executors: Nathaniel Mills held twenty-six slaves, Gooch, twelve slaves, and the two nephews, David Thompson, twenty-six slaves, and John T. Quarles, four slaves; Population Census of 1830, Louisa County, Va., Reel 6, NA.

52. Inventory of Quarles's estate was made April 26, 1834; Lucy Langston's will was partly proved June 10, 1834; see Will Book 9, pp. 143, 133, LCC; Langston, *Virginia Plantation*, pp. 17–18, 22; Hoboken (N.J.) *Journal*, Oct. 25, 1876; South Orange (N.J.) *Journal*, Oct. 26, 1876, both in JML Scrapbook, I.

53. Deed Book Q, pp. 102, 105; Deed Book S, pp. 373–74; Deed Book T, pp. 385–86, Will Book 9, p. 133, all in LCC. References to Gooch's promise to Quarles are numerous in Langston interviews, for example, San Francisco *Post*, April 5, 1877; Alliance (Ohio) *Monitor*, Oct. 13, 1876, both in JML Scrapbook, I.

54. Record of Negroes, 1804–55, Ross County Courthouse, Chillicothe, Ohio (microfilm edition of the Ohio Historical Society, Frame 98, Archives and Manuscripts Division, Columbus, Ohio).

55. Langston, *Virginia Plantation*, p. 27.

56. Ibid, pp. 29–30, 227–28; San Francisco *Post*, Apr. 5, 1877, JML Scrapbook, I.

57. Langston, *Virginia Plantation*, p. 31; Minute Book, 1831–35, LCC; Record of Negroes, 1804–55, RCC; Jackson, *Free Negro Labor*, pp. 4–5.

58. Langston, *Virginia Plantation*, pp. 31–35.

59. Will Book 9, pp. 110–111, LCC; Langston, *Virginia Plantation*, pp. 35, 157.

60. The first of a number of successful all-black farming settlements in Ohio, the Milton Township settlement in Jackson County was founded by the self-purchased Virginians, Thomas and Jemima Woodson, at a time (1830) when, as black friends subsequently noted, "that whole country was comparatively a new area, and that age a dark age." More than personal need lay behind their move. Despite their advanced years, the Woodsons, along with their fellow frontiersmen, the bulk of them ex-slaves (many, like the Woodsons, the

offspring of slave masters) were desirous of living in a place where "we should be all on perfect equality . . . free from the looks of scorn and contempt . . . free from all the evils attendant on partial and unequal laws." Inside of a decade, combating harassment almost every step of the way, the Woodsons converted a small farm into 372 well-tilled acres; accumulated several thousand dollars in earnings; and were directing forces in the establishment of a church, day and Sunday schools. Admired for their "piety, intelligence, and family government," the couple had seen to the education—not neglecting politics—of four sons, all of whom would become schoolteachers, with two of them, Lewis and Thomas, maintaining reputations as protest leaders. Daughter Sarah Jane, an 1856 graduate of Oberlin College, taught for a decade at Wilberforce University and later in black schools in the South. Like other commanding black figures before the war, the Woodson family was known for its sheltering of fugitives. By the early forties, the community comprised some fifty families, who were raising cash crops and educating their children. "Report of Committee Upon Agriculture," in *Minutes of the National Convention of Colored Citizens . . . Buffalo . . . Aug., 1843* (New York, 1843), p. 34, reprinted in *Minutes of the Proceedings of the National Negro Conventions, 1830–1864*, ed. Howard Holman Bell (New York, 1969); Lewis Woodson to Editor, Dec. 22, 1828, *Freedom's Journal*, Jan. 31, 1829; Carter G. Woodson, *Free Negro Heads of Families in the United States in 1830* (Washington, 1925), p. 129; Floyd Miller, *The Search for a Black Nationality: Black Emigration and Colonization, 1787–1863* (Urbana, 1975), pp. 94–105; A. D. Barber, *Report of the Colored People of Ohio* (Cincinnati, 1840), p. 5; C. B. Ray to Dear (Philip) Bell, Oct. 3, 1839, *Colored American*, Nov. 2, 1839; *Colored American*, Oct. 31, 1840; Daniel A. Payne, *History of the African Methodist Episcopal Church* (Nashville, 1891), pp. 213–14, 310; *Philanthropist*, June 29, 1842 (Woodson here is incorrectly identified, possibly a typographical error, as Thomas Hoodron); *Palladium of Liberty*, Sept. 25, Oct. 2, 1844; Martin Robison Delany, *The Condition, Elevation, Emigration, and Destiny of the Colored People of the United States, Politically Considered* (Philadelphia, 1852; repr. New York: Arno Press, 1968), p. 145; Rev. B. W. Arnett, ed., *Proceedings of the Semi-Centenary Celebration of the African Methodist Episcopal Church of Cincinnati Held in Allen Temple, Feb. 8th, 9th, and 10th, 1874* (Cincinnati, 1874), pp. 13, 21; *Philanthropist*, Dec. 8, 1845, Mar. 18, Oct. 14, 1846; Ellen NicKenzie Lawson with Marlene D. Merrill, *The Three Sarahs: Documents of Antebellum Black College Women* (New York, 1984), pp. 148–85; Wilbur H. Siebert, *The Underground Railroad from Slavery to Freedom* (New York, 1899), p. 424; *Colored American*, July 28, 1838.

61. Langston, *Freedom and Citizenship*, p. 112. The Langstons had a close identification with the colony. Besides the half-sister who lived there, Charles Langston owned property in Jackson County; see Delany, *Condition of the Colored People*, p. 145. Dr. Luther P. Jackson found in the 1860 census forty Virginia-born black heads of families living in Jackson County. Their property holdings varied from $300 to $6,800. All but four of them were farmers, and half were worth $1,000 or more. The "majority" of the black heads of families in Jackson County were property holders; see Jackson, *Free Negro Labor*, p. 113.

The richest black man in the settlement was the Rev. Noah Nooks, a delegate to the 1849 and 1850 Negro state conventions, and a resident of the settlement since its beginning. *Ibid*, p. 113, fn. 20; *Minutes . . . of the State Convention of the Colored Citizens of Ohio . . . Columbus . . . Jan., 1849* (Oberlin, 1849); *Minutes of the State Convention of the Colored Citizens of Ohio . . . Columbus . . . Jan., 1850* (Columbus, 1850); Woodson, *Free Negro Heads*, p. 129. Two other pioneers in the Jackson County settlement, who were to assume leadership positions in the state protest movement were schoolteacher and newspaper editor, W. H. Yancy (see chapter 3), and Methodist minister and political activist, W. Claiborne Yancy (see chapter 2).

62. Record of Negroes, 1804–55, RCC. Continued well after the 1849 repeal of the 1804 act requiring registration of Negroes, the Ross County record unfortunately is incomplete today. Arthur's registration is number 159, Burrel or "Burwell" is number 160, James Jr., number 162. Billy's doubtless was the missing number 161. Neither is there a record of the Langston brothers. The reason for their registration in Ross County, rather than in adjoining Jackson County, is unclear, although it was probably tied to their need for assistance from William Langston, who lived in Chillicothe, the Ross County seat.

CHAPTER 2

Love and Self-Reliance

1834–40

ALTHOUGH some of the prestige attached to Chillicothe as territorial and first state capital lingered, by 1834 commercial affairs had supplanted political in the lives of its citizens. Situated at the confluence of the Scioto River and Paint Creek, the town proved a natural marketing and milling center for the highly cultivated farms of the rich Scioto Valley. With the completion in 1832 of the Ohio and Erie Canal, the state's major economic lifeline running from Cleveland on Lake Erie to Portsmouth on the Ohio River, Chillicothe had become a bustling port, conducting trade with East and South. In a population of more than three thousand, southerners, migrants themselves or descendants of pioneers who settled the Virginia Military District of southwestern Ohio after the Revolution, predominated both in numbers and influence, perpetuating the customs and attitudes of their Virginia and Kentucky forebears. Although the "Old School" Presbyterian church, part of the Presbytery of Chillicothe that in 1827 had condemned slavery as a "heinous sin and scandal," promoted antislavery principles, white abolitionists constituted such a small minority that visiting black editor Charles B. Ray in 1839 reckoned them "too scarce to be found."[1]

During frontier days, blacks who accompanied their former masters, like the sixty freed slaves from Berkeley County, Virginia, brought to the area in 1793, had helped build the town as well as the river mansions nearby. Partly because of their conspicuous service, the first Ohio constitutional convention, held in Chillicothe in 1802, had come within a single vote of awarding the franchise to blacks, who numbered only 337 in the whole territory in 1800, fewer than 1 percent of the total population. In subsequent decades, hardening white supremacist attitudes found expression in a web of discriminatory legislation known as the Black Laws. Despite statutory and extralegal efforts to discourage black immigration, however, even harsher conditions in the South insured a continuing growth in Ohio's black population. The majority of Negroes settled in the geographically and climatically inviting south central and southwestern counties, especially along the Ohio, Scioto, and Little and Great Miami rivers. The great preponderance lived in rural areas, with fewer than 30 percent of Ohio's black population found in cities and towns before 1860.[2]

Heavily Virginian in their roots, by 1830 the black population of Chillicothe numbered about 300, one-tenth of the total; by 1840 it had grown to 410, the proportion of the total (3,977) remaining nearly constant. In 1830, 60 of the 71 black households, with an average size of 5.5 persons, were headed by males. Most worked as farm hands, town laborers, on the river and canals, or as domestics. Found in these categories were persons who later became artisans, like William Langston, who initially entered service before establishing himself as a carpenter. Five such "mechanics" were counted in Chillicothe by 1837. Black women found employment as washerwomen, day workers, seamstresses, and cooks. In the nearby countryside a small group of black farm owners prospered, modestly for the most part; in the town, Morris O'Free was the leading caterer, setting up late supper parties of fried tripe, pig's feet, and hot whiskey punch at the town house for the enjoyment of white gentlemen and ladies. During the general economic depression of the late 1830s, white abolitionists found Chillicothe blacks as a group "poorer than in most settlements," although "some" owned houses and lots and were in "good circumstances."[3]

Despite economic hardships and legal and social proscription, Negroes in Chillicothe early recognized that their situation demanded their "combination."[4] The first manifestation of racial solidarity and self-improvement in Chillicothe, as in other Ohio black communities, was the formation of churches separate from white congregations. In 1823, the first African Methodist Episcopal church west of the Alleghenies was established in Chillicothe as the result of the itinerant evangelizing of the Reverend Moses Freeman, who preached the "gospel of freedom to soul, mind, and body." A little later "Father" Freeman also received blacks "into the African connection" in Cincinnati and Columbus.[5] An African Baptist church was organized in Chillicothe in the early twenties, possibly by the Reverend David Nickens, likeliest candidate for the honor of first ordained black Baptist minister in Ohio. By the late thirties, both churches boasted a hundred or more members among whom women were notably active; moreover, black Chillicothe sustained an active adult temperance society and a youth temperance group comprised of the Sabbath school children.[6]

The religious impulse stimulated an early interest in education. In February 1827, a Chillicothe black meeting chaired by Lewis Woodson, twenty-one years old and only two years free of Virginia bondage— later an A.M.E. minister and a teacher in Pittsburgh as well as a pio- neering advocate of black nationalism[7]—organized the African Education and Benevolent Society. Its purpose was to dispel "moral gloom" through a "religious education" that would "prepare our chil- dren with dignity and propriety to pass through the vicissitudes of life." In initial cooperation with white Presbyterians, the society, termed by Nickens in retrospect "one general compact" formed by the "whole mass of respectable blacks," supported a school until at least mid-1832.[8] Later in the decade, the local chapter of the state black School Fund Society, formed in 1837, operated a school and by 1839, had purchased land on which to build an academy. In addition to educating its own children and some adults,[9] the Chillicothe black community prided itself on being "the mother and guardian of literature to the colored west of the Alleghenies." "With us," Nickens declared in 1832, "the spark kindled and burnt till brethren in neighboring towns caught the flame." The intellectual sparks, as well as the seeds of black cooperation and reform, were transmitted by such traveling preachers as the Meth- odists Freeman and Woodson and the Baptist Nickens, whose "pro- tracted meetings" and camp revivals in Chillicothe as well as Columbus, Cincinnati, and the rural areas spread current ideas, gospel and sec- ular. It was from its Ohio Conference in 1833 that the original en- dorsement of education by the African Methodist church came. Secretary Lewis Woodson recorded as the sense of the delegates that "Common schools, Sunday schools, and temperance societies are of the highest importance to all people, and more especially to us as a people."[10]

Doubtless, the African Education and Benevolent Society organized the "large meeting" of Chillicothe Negroes in the fall of 1827 that adopted resolutions pertaining to their rights and grievances, to be "laid before the legislature at its next session, signed by the people of color, petitioning that body to grant them full privileges of citizenship." This early political protest was expanded upon in a speech expressive of a developing black nationalism that Nickens gave in 1832. On July 5, to a gathering pointedly distinguished from "a mock pretense of cel- ebrating the Fourth, for that would betray in us a want of sound un- derstanding," Nickens called for solidarity and self-help in the face of a white culture that deprived "an oppressed people both of the means of a comfortable life and the means of grace, . . . to prepare us for the kingdom of glory." Once granted an equal opportunity by "our neighbors and lawgivers," he was confident "we could stand forth with the enlightened men of the earth." Stressing the achievements of ancient African civilizations and the progress made by the Chillicothe black community, the Reverend Mr. Nickens declared the significant question to be, "What can we do to ameliorate our condition? not, what can be done by others?"[11]

One response, indicative of the growth of black self-confidence and the efficiency of the lines of communication, was the organization on June 30, 1834, of the Chillicothe Colored Anti-Slavery Society. It was one of the first Negro auxiliaries in the nation of the American Anti-Slavery Society, formed in Philadelphia only six months earlier.[12] Under the steady and informed leadership of W. Claiborne Yancy, a one-time resident of the all-black settlement in Jackson County, later to be an A.M.E. traveling minister and an influential figure in the state black reform movement,[13] the members vowed to combat those "prejudices which prevent all from dwelling peacefully together as the children of one parent." Their "weapons of warfare," they declared, echoing the parent group's Declaration of Sentiments, would "not be carnal but mighty through God to the pulling down of strongholds."[14]

In the fall of 1834, passing courteously through the welter of Chillicothe blacks anxious for news of families and friends still in Virginia, Gideon and Charles Langston, having found temporary rooms, brought John to his guardian. From his first moments in the home of William and Matilda Gooch, the child felt protected and cared for like a son; or so, at least, it seemed in memory: warm, with smells of soap and supper, and comfortingly feminine, after the weeks of roughing it in wholly male companionship. The small, bustling lady of the house, truer to the reality of the hard-working plantation wife than the legend of the pampered southern female, and with an openheartedness peculiar to herself, immediately took him in hand. She stripped the filthy clothing from the begrimed four-year-old and gave him a thorough washing. Resplendent in a clean suit, the boy sat at her side at the evening table, while the handsome colonel and the three young ladies of the family coaxingly plied him with questions and sweetmeats, to which he shyly responded.

In retrospect, Langston could fully appreciate the rare naturalness of that welcome. The bath, refuting the racial stereotypes of untouchable, foul black skin and unsullied white southern femininity, was like

a baptism into the family, the most sustained and satisfying relationship of his childhood. A particular poignancy infused his memories,
for in the end, however inadvertently, his trust in the Gooches was
betrayed. These years assumed the contours of what has been called
the true paradise, the lost paradise. "All the years spent in that pleasant
home," he would confide to a reporter in 1877, "have made in my mind
a sunny picture to which I turn with unfailing delight as the years
pass on."[15]

The family, in his sentimental description, represented southern aristocracy uncorrupted.[16] Only a few years removed from serving as an
agent to purchase slaves and from holding a dozen slaves himself,
Colonel Gooch seemed to his Negro ward a model gentleman, "who
could, indeed, be trusted as husband, father and friend."[17] Matilda
Chiles Gooch, her own daughters all but grown, gave the appealing
orphan easy access to her affections. The little boy's days centered
around her; at night, according to one account, he slept in the same
bed with her and her husband. The youngest Gooch daughter, Virginia, an enthusiastic student at the fashionable Chillicothe Female
Seminary, drew the task of teaching the child speech and manners.
Finding him quick and eager, Virginia soon expanded her lessons to
include memorization of the alphabet and Bible verses, then reading
and writing. Gently, this girl whom he loved "as a sister," communicated
her own "great and unusual" fondness for books. After two or three
years of her tutoring, Johnnie, ever anxious for the respect and confidence of all the Gooches, was "well on in the easy primary lessons of
spelling, reading, geography and arithmetic, with simple instruction in
printing and writing," and could recite portions of the Sermon on the
Mount and other Biblical selections.[18]

Not long after the child's arrival, the Gooches, while retaining possession of their stone house situated on 188 acres along Paint Creek,
had moved to a 147-acre farm in a choice location, about a mile below
town along the Ohio Canal. Here the boy could experience the pleasures of gentrified country life. The chain of hills afforded "from a
thousand points, as many panoramas." Canal traffic was a kaleido-
scope, as barges carried colorful vegetables, fruits, and barrels of flour
destined for New York, and in the opposite direction, boatloads of
families with possessions heaped about them headed for new lands in
the West. It seemed to the little boy, or to the remembering man, that
his life flowed as easily as the canal, sparkling in the sunlight.[19]

Colonel Gooch did not get around to formalizing the guardianship
of the boy until July 14, 1837, and then only as a footnote to the more
important business of his brother Charles. Both Gideon and Charles,

soon after arrival, had enrolled in the preparatory department of abolitionist Oberlin Institute. When Charles was nineteen, approaching the age at which he would receive his legacy, he appeared before the Ross County Court of Common Pleas and chose Gooch as his guardian. Simultaneously, the court appointed Gooch guardian of John Langston. With two associates as securities, Gooch put up a $20,000 bond. The brief, perfunctory document recording the action, ultimately of vital importance to Johnnie and the man he considered his father, made no mention of race.[20]

During these formative years, the boy lived without a conscious recognition of his mixed blood. He was called Johnnie Gooch. "He did not know," wrote Langston's friend the Rev. J. E. Rankin, "he had a drop of colored blood in his veins." Inevitably, townspeople gossiped. Rumor charged Gooch with appropriating his ward's inheritance, as well as his brothers' portions, to his own use; but Gooch's social status discouraged open challenge. Moreover, the boy's hair was dark and wavy; his skin lighter than that of many southern Europeans; his lips no more generous than most. Common racial tests proved unrevealing. Johnnie Gooch, riding to town barefooted one day, was overtaken by a white countryman who scrutinized him closely, especially his exposed heels and soles, and finally remarked that "his [Johnnie's] foot was as white as his own." If such incidents shocked the boy into a suspicion that something set him apart, he was equipped neither intellectually nor emotionally to unravel the mystery. Rather, he trusted in his parents' protection; he imagined his "fortress, and ever-present help in time of trouble" was Mrs. Gooch's apron.[21]

When he was seven or eight years old, Johnnie was enrolled in the public school of Chillicothe. He remembered setting out eagerly on a Monday morning, wearing a neat, close-fitting jacket and pants of Kentucky blue jean, with "stylish fashionable cap and shoes," carrying a brand-new dinner bucket, and holding Colonel Gooch's hand, to walk the mile and a half up the canal towpath to school. Gooch made quick arrangements with the principal, and the boy was entered in an advanced level of the primary department, a class taught by the "kind-hearted" Miss Annie Colburn. Gooch, backed by wealth and position, may well have resorted to the legal precedent set in 1834, when the Supreme Court of Ohio had ruled that anyone less than one-half black was legally white and thus entitled to the privileges of the common schools.[22]

Johnnie's class met in the gallery of the Methodist church. Seated on rude slab benches with neither backs nor desks to lean upon, the pupils were expected to work for six hours daily. Johnnie's legs dangled far short of the floor, compounding his discomfort. Driven to desperate measures, he informed his teacher that his father wanted him home early every day to help get up the cows. To his own surprise, his unpracticed duplicity succeeded until Gooch discovered the scheme and put an end to it. When Miss Colburn sweetly inquired if he was sorry, the boy, already squirming on his uneasy perch, replied honestly, "No, madam!" Adjustments made, the boy attended school regularly, becoming "earnest" in his work.[23]

The Gooches continued to treat him as a "scion of their affection and family." Virginia's persistent tutelage in deportment erased any trace of the plantation Negro child. John learned to fish and was given his own tackle; he learned to hunt and was given his own gun and dogs. "He acted as if he had in prospect a future, apparently as propitious and happy as the son of any home could have sought or desired."[24]

In 1839, William Gooch, although well past middle age, was swept once more into the westward movement. The Star of Empire currently was taking its flight to Missouri, ballyhooed as a state "combining advantages that no other state does": St. Louis would become "the greatest island city in the world." Over his wife's protests but with the hearty concurrence of his two young sons-in-law, Gooch determined to move his whole family to Missouri. He found and purchased land in Cooper County and sold his Chillicothe properties, realizing a tidy profit.[25]

Almost as an afterthought, the problem of nine-year-old Johnnie came up. The scene was one Langston would replay often in later years. "I was called into the room where Mr. and Mrs. Gooch seemed to have been in very earnest consultation. 'John,' he said in his grave, kind manner, 'John, we are going away from here; very far away—out West. Do you wish to go with us or shall we find you another home here?' What a question. I wondered if he had asked his daughters the same one, but I answered unhesitatingly, 'Why sir, I want to go with you.' His reply was as brief as it was satisfactory. 'You shall,' and I was dismissed."[26]

The departure was set for early April. From the day of this unsettling interview until the time of embarkation, the boy saw "many colored people" about the farm and sensed "that they had an evident desire to see and speak with me. I avoided them," he recalled. "I had never been associated with them at any period within my recollection and had no desire to be now." Johnnie left school at the end of March to join his family in the last week of preparation. It took three days to load the household goods, farm equipment, and animals onto the canal boat chartered by Gooch to carry them down to Portsmouth, where they would take the steamboat on to St. Louis.[27] The family boarded at night, expecting to wake nearly at Portsmouth. But the morning of April 9 dawned with their barge scarcely fifteen miles from home, still in Ross County, mired by a break in the canal. After breakfast the boy went ashore and began skipping pebbles in the muddy water. At about 8 o'clock, glancing idly toward Chillicothe, he noticed indistinct movement far up the towpath. Gradually he discerned two men on horseback, riding hard toward him.

The horses glistened with sweat when the men pulled up. One was William Langston. The other, a stranger to Johnnie, was the town marshal, James Robinson, who motioned to Gooch to come ashore. The boy had run to Matilda Gooch's side. "The anxious look on all the faces around me caused me to watch . . . very closely. I saw a paper taken from an inside pocket, and saw Mr. Gooch motion it away as if he comprehended its import without hearing." Sobbing wildly, overcome with dread, the boy clung to the distraught woman.[28]

The men left in haste, the boy sitting behind Colonel Gooch's saddle and hugging him tightly. It was after noon when they reached the old stone statehouse converted to courthouse. "I remember seeing on our way an unaccountable number of colored people. I remember hearing repeatedly the word 'kidnapping.' " A hearing was hurriedly arranged, interjected into the schedule by Judge John H. Keith as a favor to his "personal friend" Gooch. Gooch secured the services of attorney John L. Taylor, U.S. congressman, "then as ever, the pink of gracious courtesy and gentility."[29]

William Langston had instigated habeas corpus. In a state that forbade a black to testify against a white in court, it was an extraordinary action. A possible explanation offered by a local journalist long afterward was that "a horrible hullabaloo" had been raised, and "legal proceedings were resolved upon." But if supported by the agitated black community and possibly advised by white abolitionists, William Langston's access to legal remedy probably came by way of his post in the servant's quarters of the venerable ex-governor and town founder Duncan McArthur. William Langston's lawyer was Allen G. Thurman, an ex-Virginian who had brought his own slaves to freedom in Chillicothe in 1819, practiced law since 1835, and, subsequently, would gain a national reputation, in part for his legal acumen but, in larger measure, for his role as one of the Democratic party's most consistent defenders of southern interests and white supremacy.[30]

Racial tensions and anti-abolitionist feeling, partially a reaction to the hard, economically depressed times, were high in the area at the moment. Night riders reportedly had driven a number of black families from their houses in the surrounding countryside and had threatened "with lynch law and destruction of their property" white farmers who employed or housed blacks. Some of the victims had gone so far as to bring their complaints to the grand jury, then in session.[31] In the circumstances, the news of a young mulatto heir to a large fortune being "kidnapped" to slave state Missouri electrified the townsfolk. To the eyes of the badly frightened child, it seemed that an angry, menacing, mainly black throng filled the courtyard. Whites elbowed and pushed into the crowded courtroom. Attracted by the commotion, strangers in town on business came to watch the show. Two of the travelers, the pro-status quo "Observer" and the abolitionist "Justice," would report on the "novelty," as "Observer" put it, to out-of-town newspapers.[32]

The case against William Gooch, directed to "shew cause why he shall not be removed from the guardianship of John Langston, a coloured boy and a minor," was called. William Langston sturdily declared his doubts about Gooch's stewardship: one of the original sureties during John's guardianship proceedings in 1837 had since failed in business; should Gooch take John to Missouri, none of his relatives would be near enough to guard his interests; the portion of Quarles's estate destined for John would probably amount to some eight to ten thousand dollars. Although the colored man was not charging Gooch either with kidnapping, as the crowd had it, or malfeasance, his statement strongly implied that in a slave state, both John's freedom and inheritance would be jeopardized.[33]

The harried Gooch, family and possessions stranded down the canal, replied stoutly. While it was true that one of his sureties had failed, it was also true that one of his wards, Charles Langston, since that time had become twenty-one, thus in full receipt of his inheritance and out of his care. Therefore, he deemed his official bond "amply sufficient." Moreover, the terms of Quarles's will made it impossible for John to receive any money until he reached his majority, and except for the $100 yearly paid by the executors, Gooch had "not received any portion of the legacy devised to the said John."

Carefully, inadequately, the affidavit explained: "The said William D. Gooch prompted by the best motives and feelings toward said John Langston . . . has treated him in the kindest manner, [an effaced clause] and that he desires to act towards him precisely and exactly as the laws of this State and this Honorable Court may direct." In taking the boy to Missouri, Gooch averred that first, he "was advised that he was fully authorized" to do so; and second, "that it was as much in compliance with the anxious wishes of the said minor himself, as from a belief in the necessity of a faithful discharge of duty . . . that he was taking him with his family to his new residence."[34]

Thurman eloquently pressed his case. Should Gooch prove unable or unwilling to protect the colored boy, he might be enslaved, his legacy stolen, Thurman contended. His heated argument brought him perilously near a critical view of slavery. "Alarmed at himself," the abolitionist "Justice" noted, "and seeming to dread, lest peradventure, some of the by-standers might mistake his benevolent feelings for abolitionism, he took occasion to wash his hands of it, by declaring his abhorrence of the fanaticism." Judge Keith, rebuking Thurman for indiscretion and admonishing that the case had "nothing to do" with abolitionism, pronounced his own opinion "that the principles of abolitionism carried out, would *dis-member* the union!"[35]

Abolitionism, what was it, that so upset dignified adults? In spite of his misery, the boy wondered. "Habeas corpus," "ward of the court," "slavery," "mulatto," "Negro." The unfamiliar words buffeted the bewildered child, who sat "weeping as if his heart was breaking in the deep bereavement which he experienced." Only once was he permitted to speak. When the judge asked what he wanted, Johnnie burst out with a passionate plea to go with Gooch.[36]

His attempt proved futile. Doubtless swayed by the imperatives of property—the inheritor, more than the mulatto orphan vulnerable to enslavement, engaged the court's interest—as much as by Thurman's pleading, Judge Keith rendered his decision. In attempting to take John beyond the court's purview, Gooch had violated the terms of guardianship. The conservative "Observer," pleased by Keith's pronouncement and his scathing indictment of antislavery agitation, reported that he "stated the facts, the reasons, and the law, sustained the rule, and decided that, under all the circumstances, the boy ought not to be taken out of the jurisdiction of the court."[37]

In his petition William Langston had requested that Richard Long, the New Englander who had bought Gooch's farm, be appointed guardian of John in his stead. Long was an avowed abolitionist, perhaps consulted by William in advance of the suit. Judge Keith, freshly delivered of his censure of the diabolical doctrine of abolitionism, committed John Langston to the abolitionist's care. Beaten, Colonel Gooch told the boy goodbye, "tarrying only to leave with him his fatherly caress and benediction."[38]

John Langston, nine years and four months of age, was alone. With the gently reared child's faith in a just and rational universe, he searched desperately for meaning in the catastrophe. No one seemed to explain. Was it because the canal boat had stuck in the mud? Review of events yielded only confusion: the excited exhaustion of leave-taking melding into sleep on the swaying barge, the disappointment of the morning, the shock of seeing William Langston's brown face, the tears, the rough texture of Gooch's coat against his cheek, the jouncing on the horse's hard back, . . . half-remembering, perhaps, another horse-back ride and himself laughing and adoring this now alien black man. And the angry colored people thronged in the courtyard, muttering of "kidnapping"; the white lawyers and white judge arguing over him; "Why boy, y'r foot is as white as mine!" His father, somehow guilty, powerless, leaving him behind.

It was a second orphaning, a retroversion to the heartbreak of his infancy. Nearly forty years later, speaking of this rent with "the only friends I knew in the wide world," Langston said, "No late sorrow has obliterated or lessened one pang of the anguish I suffered then."[39] As he grew older, he came to an understanding of the nature of the immense injustice done him, not in that Chillicothe courtroom, that had acted, he would conclude, to safeguard his interests, but in the whole society. When he was a child, he could only mourn the Gooches and hope desperately to see them again. When he became a man, he retained the dream of being reunited, but he understood the inter-vening forces: his personal injury was merged into the flux of incident and ideology in the struggle against slavery in the South and racial injustice in the North.

Langston would assert that no one was at fault in the affair, but that was the judgment of the adult, not the child. A child's strong but prim-itive sense of justice demands that blame be laid: on William Langston, the instigator; on Gooch, who failed him; on himself, with the child's egocentric notion that he is the causal agent for adult misadventure. Or he might have fixed on the alien fact of his race, before ignored, but abruptly an important, even treacherous part of himself. But con-sciously, he blamed Allen Thurman. He hated him "because he felt that he had heartlessly taken him from his best and truest friends." "For two years I hated him with all of a child's impotent, unreasoning wrath"—until his fear and confusion had subsided, and he did not need to hate him any longer. When as a grown man he met U.S. Senator Thurman, he felt compelled to identify himself as the child in the case and confess his old anger. The senator floridly rejoined, "Langston, I saved, I made you; and so far from hating, you should love me."[40]

After the hearing, the boy was sent back to the Gooch farm to stay with the affluent Puritan Richard Long. A crusty New Englander in his late forties, with a wife of about his own age and five children, Long had sufficiently established credentials in the southern-dominated community to be named a trustee of the prestigious Chillicothe Female Seminary.[41] A prominent figure in the Ohio Anti-Slavery Society, he had been elected one of its managers in 1838 and, the year after, a vice-president. When the young abolitionist tornado Theodore Dwight Weld had whirled across southern Ohio in 1834 and 1835, it was Long who had served as his Chillicothe contact.[42] Told his new living arrangements would be beneficial because Long was an "abolitionist"— that word again—John asked at the first opportunity what an "abolitionist" was. A gentleman who "loves colored people, and would have them all treated very kindly," he was informed. With this advice, the nine-year-old, expectant of balm for his wounds, was staggered by his first encounter with Richard Long. In the clipped accents of his region, Long demanded: "What, sir, can you do?" John confessed he could do nothing. In a "terrible" tone, Long inquired: "How do you expect to live?"

Under this precise and disciplined Yankee, the child soon realized life could be a "solemn and earnest thing." Long's disposition and philosophy, combining "all the severer elements of Puritan purpose and life," refused to honor the boy's private miseries. Children were not to be pampered. Where the Gooches had expected Johnnie to be a small gentleman, occupied with books and dogs and boyish pleasures, young enough to luxuriate without shame in the starched circle of his mother's apron, Long expected him to be a little man. His premise was that the "highest style of boyhood was realized, when it could be said of one that he was a good worker."[43]

John began at once, driving a horse and cart to haul brick from the kiln to the farmyard for a new building. He remembered working diligently, in hope of praise, excited despite his troubles to be able to manage the horse. On the third day Long deigned to comment that he might someday make a good driver. In time, the boy developed such skill that Long made him driver of his pair of sorrels, pulling the wagon weekdays and the carriage on Sunday. By then too, feeling anything but the poor little drudge, he had branched out into other farm endeavors, hoeing in the fields, or steering a light plow down the furrows.

A time of worship preceded and succeeded each workday. While Long "read and expounded . . . the Word," the entire household, including the Negro cook and hired man, were expected to attend, the children and John following along in their Bibles, sometimes each reading a verse aloud, singing and praying. From time to time, Long entertained visiting clergymen, who contributed their talents. Long was a deacon of the "Old School" (predestinarian, non-evangelical) Presbyterian church, whose minister, Hugh Stewart Fullerton, was noted for his assistance to both free blacks and fugitives. In line with the Ohio Anti-Slavery Society's call for the support of colored schools, the church (in 1837) had paid $20 a month to Miss Clarissa Wright to teach

Chillicothe blacks; the minister and the farmer were doubtless among the "but four or five individuals" Schoolmarm Wright could count on "to lend a helping hand." On Sundays John was expected to do his chores promptly so that he might drive the family to church, where he attended both Sabbath school and services, "seated always with the family."[44]

During "The Great Change," as Langston titled it, the boy must have tried anxiously to understand the requirements of his new role, that of a colored boy. "Thinking every day of the Gooches, and wondering whether Mrs. Gooch had forgotten him," he surely was wondering whether she had rejected him, whether as a colored boy he somehow forfeited not only her presence but also his right to her affection. Moreover, along with other lost privileges, he no longer attended school. Being Negro seemed to mean that one worked, like the colored laborers he had always seen. One learned, if at all, haphazardly, as a secondary result of religious instruction. As for human relationships, if the stern Presbyterian Long was an example of someone who "loved colored people" and wanted them "treated very kindly," the colored boy might have to redefine the terms. But glimmerings of the black world, perhaps, as well as some solace, were provided by the "quite frequent" visits of his half-brother William, who "always brought him some beautiful, or interesting, or pleasant thing."[45]

The boy's greatest comfort, however, as the days went on in their "grave, solemn tread," was the final response to Long's demand: he could "do" something. Accustomed to thinking himself frail and young, he felt his body growing stronger, his hands more skilled. A child's routine of "leisure" and dependency had given way to a boy's regimen of "labor" and "self-care." He was proud to be able to handle the good horses and work the farm. Years later he would boast at a New York county fair that he could plant, sow, and reap at the age of ten, and "turn as straight a furrow and husk as many ears of corn as any man in the state."[46] Hard work, self-reliance, achievement could help to compensate for, and in part, to overcome, the disadvantages of being classed as a Negro. In an embryonic form, the idea may have taken hold. He was alone; he missed the Gooches terribly and believed he always would; but he was not helpless.

He lived with the Longs about a year and a half. The contrast of their "strict and severe discipline of life" with the "loving and indulgent" Gooches gave him an intimate acquaintance with the dominant American family types, the Cavalier and the Puritan. For the "trying and taxing duties" that would be his, Langston concluded, Long's practical approach was beneficial. Yet despite his acknowledgment of the advantages of the work ethic, reinforced and expanded by his years among the New Englanders of Oberlin and his political and personal affinities for them, he retained his admiration for the conception of aristocracy personified by the chivalrous William Gooch and the hospitable, cultured Gooch family; and in some ways he modeled himself and his family life after them. His contemporaries would often be moved to comment on his poise and manners: his "air of a gentleman."[47] He bore himself with ease and grace of the sort best learned in childhood, gained in a good measure in the Gooch household.

More basic, perhaps, was his lack of early training in servility. He would call it the "touch of slavery," and ask: "How long will it take the American Negro, how long will it take the intellectual Negro, how long will it take any man who has been 245 years in slavery to rid his soul of the slave spirit?" For nine years he had no sense of inferiority. His experience with the Longs was more ambiguous; still, it may be significant that the 1840 census taker apparently listed him in the household with no notation of race.[48] Nonetheless, whatever the mitigating factors, his sense of being abandoned by and being labeled as racially distinct from the only family he knew could only have incurred large psychological costs.

When his older brother Gideon sent for him in the late months of 1840, he left his home on the canal without much reluctance. Having lived there for nearly as long as he could remember, with white families, wrestling with half-formed ideas and impressions of what it meant to be not-white, John Langston, Negro, set out for Cincinnati, the most race-conscious city in the state.

NOTES

1. Caleb Atwater, *A History of the State of Ohio* (Cincinnati, 1838), p. 339; Eugene Holloway Roseboom and Francis Phelps Weisenburger, *A History of Ohio* (New York, 1934), p. 174; Federal Writers' Project of Ohio, *Chillicothe and Ross County* (Washington, 1938), pp. 18–19, 27; Francis P. Weisenburger, *The Passing of the Frontier, 1825–1850* (Columbus, 1941), pp. 17, 20, 364–65; C. B. Ray to Dear (Philip) Bell, Sept. 16, 1839, *Colored American*, Oct. 5, 1839.

2. Richard Albert Folk, "Black Man's Burden in Ohio, 1849–1863," Ph.D. diss., University of Toledo, 1972, p. 6; Federal Writers' Project, *Chillicothe and Ross County*, p. 27; Frank U. Quillin, *The Color Line in Ohio* (Ann Arbor, 1913; repr. New York: Negro Universities Press, 1969), pp. 13–20; David A. Gerber, *Black Ohio and the Color Line, 1860–1915* (Urbana, 1976), pp. 10, 14–15.

3. Carter Woodson, *Free Negro Heads of Households in the United States in 1830* (Washington, 1925), p. 129; Population Census of 1840, Ross County, Ohio,

Reel 21, National Archives; A. D. Barber, *Report of the Colored People of Ohio* (Cincinnati, 1840), pp. 5, 11–12, 7; Augustus Wattles, *Memorial of the Ohio Anti-Slavery Society to the General Assembly . . . Ohio* (Cincinnati, 1838), pp. 18–19; Federal Writers' Project, *Chillicothe and Ross County*, p. 27; *Philanthropist*, Nov. 26, 1839. William Langston's connection with ex-Governor Duncan McArthur is reported in his obituary by John Mercer Langston; see untitled news-clipping, n.d., Henry Williams Scrapbook, Virginia State College Library.

   4. David Nickens, "Address to the People of Color in Chillicothe," July 20, 1832, *Liberator*, Aug. 11, 1832.

   5. Gerber, *Black Ohio and the Color Line*, p. 20; Daniel A. Payne, *History of the African Methodist Episcopal Church* (Nashville, 1891), pp. 21, 61–62; William T. Martin, *History of Franklin County* (Columbus, 1858), pp. 191–92; Daniel Alexander Payne, *Recollections of Seventy Years* (Nashville, 1888), pp. 104, 106, 123; Rev. B. W. Arnett, ed., *Proceedings of the Semi-Centenary Celebration of the African Methodist Episcopal Church of Cincinnati Held in Allen Temple, Feb. 8th, 9th, and 10th, 1874* (Cincinnati, 1874), pp. 12–13, 18; Allen Temple, Centennial Commission, *Centennial Guide Allen Temple A.M.E. Church . . . 1924* (Cincinnati, 1924), p. 11.

   6. After serving as pastor of the African Baptist Church in Chillicothe, Nickens by 1835 was in Cincinnati as pastor of the black Union Baptist church on Baker Street, a post he retained until his death in 1838 at the age of forty-four. He worked with the Weld-Wattles group of white abolitionists on education and reform within the Cincinnati black community; see Nickens, "Address," *Liberator*, Aug. 11, 1832; William J. Simmons, *Men of Mark: Eminent, Progressive and Rising* (Cleveland, 1887; repr. Chicago: Johnson Publishing, 1970), pp. 375–76; Gilbert H. Barnes and Dwight L. Dumond, eds., *Letters of Theodore Dwight Weld, Angelina Grimke Weld, and Sarah Grimke, 1822–1844*, 2 vols. (New York, 1934), I, p. 192; Wendell P. Dabney, *Cincinnati's Colored Citizens: Historical, Sociological, and Biographical* (Cincinnati, 1926; New York: Johnson Reprint, 1970), pp. 371–72; Wattles, *Memorial . . . 1838*, pp. 18–19.

   7. Woodson promoted morality and religion among black children and adults in Chillicothe and elsewhere in Ohio in the late twenties and early thirties; see Floyd J. Miller, *The Search for a Black Nationality: Black Emigration and Colonization, 1787–1863* (Urbana, 1975), pp. 94–104; *Freedom's Journal*, Apr. 6, 1827, Jan. 31, 1829.

   8. *Freedom's Journal*, Apr. 6, 1827; Nickens, "Address," *Liberator*, Aug. 11, 1832.

   9. Wattles, *Memorial . . . 1838*, p. 19; Columbus *Ohio State Journal*, Sept. 10, 1839.

   10. Nickens, "Address," *Liberator*, Aug. 11, 1832; Payne, *History of the A.M.E. Church*, pp. 44, 51, 56, 59, 61–63, 97–98, 309–11; Allen Temple, Centennial Commission, *Centennial Guide*, pp. 8–18; John B. Shotwell, *A History of the Schools of Cincinnati* (Cincinnati, 1902), p. 441; Richard Clyde Minor, "James Preston Poindexter, Elder Statesman of Columbus," *Ohio State Archaeological and Historical Quarterly* 56 (1947):268.

11. *Freedom's Journal*, Dec. 14, 1827; Nickens, "Address," *Liberator*, Aug. 11, 1832.

12. Scioto *Gazette*, Aug. 6, 1834; Benjamin Quarles, *Black Abolitionists* (New York, 1969), pp. 28–39.

13. An "eyewitness" to slavery, possibly in Virginia, Walter Claiborne Yancy was living in Jackson County in 1830. Then between twenty-four and thirty-five years of age, he headed a household of five. A resident and community leader in Chillicothe for much of the thirties, Yancy was "admitted on trial" as a preacher in the A.M.E. church in 1837, subsequently becoming an elder and then a traveling preacher. In the fall of 1837, he was elected president of the first black convention held in the state and was selected to head the School Fund Society, which the delegates created for the "moral and religious elevation of the colored people of Ohio." As the society's agent, Yancy raised funds, visited, and set up black schools. In 1843, he lectured for the Garrisonian Ohio American Anti-Slavery Society and the following year for the state's Liberty party. Also in 1844, in the employ of the white abolitionist Ladies Education Society, Yancy visited various black settlements around the state, giving lectures and superintending moral and educational matters. More than half a century later, when asked about the black protest movement in Ohio before the war, the black Cincinnati educator Peter Clark recalled Walter Yancy as one of its most active leaders; see A. Brodie to Editor, Aug. 2, 1842, *Philanthropist*, Aug. 27, 1842; Woodson, *Free Negro Heads*, p. 127; Payne, *History of the A.M.E. Church*, pp. 118, 130–31, 146; *Ohio State Journal*, Sept. 10, 1839, Sept. 15, 1840; *Philanthropist*, Sept. 8, 1837, Sept. 11, Oct. 2, 1843, Feb. 14, June 12, Aug. 28, 1844; Peter H. Clark to John W. Cromwell, Dec. 21, 1901, quoted in John W. Cromwell, *The Negro in American History* (Washington, 1914), p. 37.

14. Scioto *Gazette*, Aug. 6, 1834.

15. John Mercer Langston, *From the Virginia Plantation to the National Capital; or, The First and Only Negro Representative in Congress from the Old Dominion* (Hartford, 1894; repr. New York: Johnson Reprint, 1968), p. 38; San Francisco *Post*, Apr. 5, 1877, in John Mercer Langston Scrapbooks, 4 vols., I, Moorland-Spingarn Research Center, Howard University (hereafter cited as JML Scrapbook).

16. Langston, *Virginia Plantation*, pp. 37–40.

17. Deed Book Q, pp. 102, 105; Deed Book S, pp. 373–74; Deed Book T, pp. 385–86, all in Louisa County, Va., Courthouse; Population Census of 1830, Louisa County, Va., Reel 6, NA; Langston, *Virginia Plantation*, pp. 37–38.

18. Chillicothe *Leader*, Nov. 2, 1889; Langston, *Virginia Plantation*, pp. 39, 40, 43; interview with Arthur D. Langston, St. Louis *Star-Sayings*, n.d., JML Scrapbook, II; San Francisco *Post*, Apr. 5, 1877, JML Scrapbook, I; J. E. Rankin, introductory sketch, John Mercer Langston, *Freedom and Citizenship* (Washington, 1883; repr. Miami: Mnemosyne Reprint, 1969) p. 9.

19. Deed Record 38, 39, 40, pp. 425, 569, 311, Ross County Courthouse, Chillicothe, Ohio (hereafter cited as RCC); Scioto *Gazette*, Mar. 21, 1844.

20. Guardianship for Charles Langston and John Langston, July 14, 1837, Ross County Probate Court, case 4311, RCC.

21. Interview with Arthur D. Langston, St. Louis *Star-Sayings*, n.d., JML Scrapbook, II; Langston, *Virginia Plantation*, pp. 39, 42, 44; Rankin, introductory sketch, Langston, *Freedom and Citizenship*, p. 33; Chillicothe *Leader*, Nov. 2, 1889.

22. Langston, *Virginia Plantation*, p. 43; Lorain County *News*, Aug. 4, 1870; *Williams* versus *School Directors*, 6 *Ohio State Reports* 570 (1834).

23. Langston, *Virginia Plantation*, pp. 43–45, 48.

24. Ibid., pp. 42, 47, 41.

25. Scioto *Gazette*, July 30, 1840; Deed Record 38, 39, 40, pp. 425, 569, 311, RCC.

26. San Francisco *Post*, Apr. 5, 1877, JML Scrapbook, I.

27. Ibid.; Langston, *Virginia Plantation*, p. 48.

28. Chillicothe *Leader*, Nov. 2, 1889; Langston, *Virginia Plantation*, p. 48; San Francisco *Post*, Apr. 5, 1877, JML Scrapbook, I.

29. San Francisco *Post*, Apr. 5, 1877, JML Scrapbook, I; Langston, *Virginia Plantation*, p. 50; Chillicothe *Leader*, Nov. 2, 1889.

30. Chillicothe *Leader*, Nov. 2, 1889; H. Wayne Morgan, *From Hayes to McKinley, National Party Politics, 1877–1896* (Syracuse, 1969), pp. 190–91, 294, 302.

31. "Justice" to Editor, *Philanthropist*, July 2, 1839; Barber, *Report . . . 1840*, pp. 11–12.

32. "Observer" wrote his account for an administration organ, the Chillicothe *Advertiser*, Apr. 20, 1839. "Justice" attempted to respond to "Observer" and, when the *Advertiser* returned his letter because of its "incendiary" nature, sent both letters with his further observations to the *Philanthropist*, which printed the entire text on July 2, 1839.

33. *The Court of Common Pleas for Ross County* versus *William D. Gooch,* Apr. 9, 1839, Court of Common Pleas, Box Case No. 101, RCC; "Justice" to Editor, *Philanthropist*, July 2, 1839.

34. Box Case No. 101, RCC.

35. "Justice" to Editor, *Philanthropist*, July 2, 1839.

36. Langston, *Virginia Plantation*, pp. 49–52; San Francisco *Post*, Apr. 5, 1877, JML Scrapbook, I; St. Louis *Star-Sayings*, n.d., JML Scrapbook, II.

37. "Observer" to Editor, Chillicothe *Advertiser*, Apr. 20, 1839, reprinted in *Philanthropist*, July 2, 1839.

38. Box Case No. 101, RCC; Langston, *Virginia Plantation*, pp. 51–52.

39. Chillicothe *Leader*, Nov. 2, 1889; San Francisco *Post*, Apr. 5, 1877, JML Scrapbook, I.

40. Ibid.; Langston, *Virginia Plantation*, p. 53.

41. Population Census of 1840, Ross County, Ohio, Reel 21, NA; Scioto *Gazette*, Aug. 6, 1840.

42. *Report of the Third Anniversary of the Ohio Anti-Slavery Society . . . Granville . . . May, 1838* (Cincinnati, 1838), p. 11; *Report of the Fourth Anniversary of the Ohio Anti-Slavery Society . . . Putnam . . . May, 1839* (Cincinnati, 1839), p. 19; *Weld-Grimke Letters*, I, p. 194.

43. Langston, *Virginia Plantation*, pp. 54–56.

44. Ibid., pp. 56–57; *Report of the First Anniversary of the Ohio Anti-Slavery Society Held near Granville . . . Apr., 1836* (Cincinnati, 1836), p. 8; Barber, *Report . . . 1840*, p. 5; Wilbur Henry Siebert, *The Mysteries of Ohio's Underground Railroads* (Columbus, 1951), p. 61.

45. Langston, *Virginia Plantation*, pp. 54–55, 73, 88.

46. Ibid., p. 59, 54–56; Potsdam, N.Y., *Courier and Freeman* n.d., 1889, JML Scrapbook, II.

47. Langston, *Virginia Plantation*, p. 58; William Wells Brown, *The Black Man: His Antecedents, His Genius, and His Achievements* (New York, 1863; repr. New York: Johnson Reprint, 1968), p. 237.

48. New York *Freeman*, May 14, 1887, JML Scrapbook, II; Population Census of 1840, Ross County, Ohio, Reel 21, NA.

CHAPTER 3
―――――
Culture and Kinship

―――――

1840–43

P LACED in an amphitheater of hills giving onto the Ohio River,
where boats and barges teemed against the backdrop of the slave
shores of Kentucky, the Queen City of the West—Porkopolis to the
unromantic—provided a spectacle of Jacksonian aspirations. Animated, striving, growing in four decades from frontier settlement to
sixth largest city in the nation, it was a town of red and white houses on
clean well-paved streets with tiled walkways, attractive shops, and neat
and elegant private residences, and a town of swampy bottoms, rickety
tenements, and mean malodorous alleys; protean and joltingly democratic, where yesterday's raisin cake vendor was today's state congressman; progressive and reform-minded, boasting a system of public
schools in which even the poorest Irish child might receive a free education but no black child could; violence prone, with "gentlemen of
property and standing" not loathe to form a mob against abolitionists
and blacks; above all, exuberantly committed to exemplifying the potential of free men working in a free society and shamelessly dedicated
to placating its good customers of the South. With an economy that
revolved around commerce and trade—hogs, cattle, whiskey, flour, lumber, and a variety of manufactured products—leading businessmen
took pains to nourish the commercial match with southern cotton that
had been struck early on. Even in the midst of the nationwide depression set off by the Panic of 1837 and despite losses to business, the city
grew at record rates, its population swelled by immigrants from the
hard-hit eastern urban centers. Mechanics and builders were busy. Carriages bearing generously petticoated ladies rattled over the cobble-
stones; rich southern planters in tall beaver hats pushed through the

throngs of horny-handed Ohio and Kentucky farmers; burly German butchers festooned stalls in the famous market with garlands of sausages; newly arrived Irish families stood in bewilderment on the docks; rough rivermen, black and white, sought out satisfaction in brothels and bars. Steamboats anchored while others lined up for berths, travelers above deck, cargo and slave coffle below. On the waterfront muscular black roustabouts hoisted bales of cotton, tierces of tobacco and salt pork, barrels of flour, sugar, coffee, molasses, fish, and whiskey. Black porters hustled for baggage to carry to the elegant hotels where Kentuckians liked to pass summer months; black draymen clattered from wharf to warehouse; black stewards looked to the buying of fresh produce; well-dressed black waiters pocketed their tips.[1] The alert farmboy who simply walked the broad streets of Cincinnati acquired an education.

Yet beneath the bustle, for a boy who was black, harder lessons lay. Although Negroes wore the shirt of Nessus throughout Ohio, discrimination was nowhere more entrenched than in Cincinnati. All black Ohioans had to contend with the state's infamous Black Laws. Following the denial of the franchise to blacks in the Ohio constitution of 1802, the state had acted to discourage black immigration through such requirements as registration and the posting of surety; to exclude Negroes from jury service and from testifying in legal cases involving white persons; to bar them from the militia; to deny them the benefits of the Poor Law and of institutions for the physically or mentally infirm; and, despite equal taxation of black-owned property, to exclude black children from the public school system.[2] In Cincinnati, moreover, Negroes met with all but universal segregation, proscription, and the threat of violence. News that a slave had disappeared from a ship, or that white southerners were in town to search for their missing bondservant, usually set off a hue and cry in which city authorities joined to look for signs of stolen property in the homes and shops of black residents and white abolitionists. On two occasions, in 1829 and in 1836, large-scale riots directed against blacks had engulfed the city, the first resulting in the exodus of a large number of black residents, the second, costly to white abolitionists as well as to blacks, in the destruction of the presses of the *Philanthropist*, an antislavery newspaper then edited by James G. Birney.[3]

In this volatile setting, John Mercer Langston first experienced the life of a black community. As luck would have it, he came to Cincinnati just at the moment when a white backlash, triggered by the rising black socioeconomic status in combination with other factors, was about to erupt into yet another of Cincinnati's periodic manifestations of mob violence. Nonetheless, it was here that the impressionable boy first was exposed to enterprising black men and women who had established themselves as skilled workers and property owners, to vigorous black institutions, and to black community leaders. The evidence supports the mature Langston's own judgment: "If there has ever existed in any colored community of the United States, anything like an aristocratic class of such persons, it was found in Cincinnati. . . . In fact the entire negro community of the city gave striking evidences, in every way at this time, of its intelligence, industry, thrift and progress; and in matters of education and moral and religious culture, furnished an example worthy of the imitation of their whole people."[4] During his two years in Cincinnati, John Langston, barely eleven when he arrived, began to learn about the black kinship and culture that would sharpen his perceptions and help to give purpose and direction to his own life.

Drawn by the ever-expanding economic opportunity to Cincinnati—which some Negroes called "the emporium of the West"—the black population was the largest in the state, having grown from an estimated 690 in 1826 to an official 2,240 by 1840 (5.1 percent of the city's 44,000 population). The black residents tended to be young and of southern origin; indeed, self-bought, manumitted, or free-born southerners fueled much of the dynamism and egalitarian idealism observed in the youthful black Cincinnati society of 1840, where 80 percent of its people were less than thirty-six years of age.[5] The 1840 residential and occupational directory listed 313 "Colored" persons, who doubtless constituted the most successful group, 74 percent of whom had come from slave states or the slaveholding District of Columbia, principally from Virginia and Kentucky. Augustus Wattles, a dedicated white abolitionist who as a young man immersed himself in black community life in 1834, calculated that 1,129 Negroes in Cincinnati had known slavery. Four hundred seventy-six of these ex-slaves had purchased themselves at a total cost of $215,522, or an average of about $450 per person, while many were currently involved in purchasing family members or friends. When a concerned Wattles visited a family to learn the reason for irregular school attendance, he found the youngsters in the care of the eldest child, a ten-year-old, who explained, "I'm staying at home to help buy father." An 1845 canvass by Wattles's brother John revealed 369 self-emancipated slaves, about one-fifth of the adult population, who had paid $166,050 for their freedom. Such men and women, the black editor Charles B. Ray of New York was disposed to declare after a protracted stay in 1839, had the "proper materials in their character to become industrious, economical, and reputable citizens."[6]

Combining skills learned in slavery[7] with the ingenuity suggested by their playful saying, "If you can't find it, make it,"[8] and benefiting from the assistance of committed white sympathizers, black Cincinnatians had registered economic gains. As migrants flowed into the city in the late thirties, the demand for essential services had increased: workers were necessary to hew and dig and haul, whitewash the walls, scrub the clothes and floors, mend and polish the shoes, cook the food, saw the wood. Although always indifferent in reporting the women who doubtless performed many of these tasks, the city directory in 1840 listed 146 Negroes so engaged, almost double the figure of four years earlier. Because Irish immigrants, who would compose 12 percent of the population by 1850, had just begun to arrive, blacks had as yet few competitors for such work.[9] Blacks also took advantage of the depression-induced lower cost of living and the institution of a near-barter economy. Moreover, river and canal commerce, which continued to thrive, provided major employment opportunities. In 1840, nearly one-fourth of the black work force had jobs on the steamboats, several hundred of which operated from Cincinnati's wharves, and in other connected services and trades. "Besides their ordinary wages, which are good," Ray observed, black rivermen availed themselves of plentiful "opportunities for trading at great profit" in "the lower country."[10] Among the 287 Negroes listed as employed in the 1840 directory, ninety-two (an increase of 250 percent in four years) can be classified as semiskilled, that is, workers at jobs demanding some talent and understanding of the marketplace: thus, whitewasher, drayman, steward, cook, huckster, butler, trader, gardener, fruit dealer, barkeeper. The traditional classification of such workers as unskilled is cast in doubt by the fact that thirty-eight of the eighty-eight Negroes worth $1,000 or more according to the 1850 census fall in this category. Furthermore, although laborers are always characterized as unskilled, six black Cincinnatians held this title and somehow managed to accumulate $1,000 or more by 1850. Indeed, three of the black community's most respected men were listed in unskilled occupations: the intellectual stevedore John I. Gaines ($3,000); huckster Richard Phillips ($13,000); huckster Joseph Fowler ($18,000).[11] Traditional classifications of work are patently inadequate to measure either the worth or worthfulness of mid-nineteenth-century black Cincinnatians.

In 1840, ninety blacks were recorded in twenty-one skilled occupations: 46 barbers, 10 carpenters, 6 shoemakers, 4 coopers, 3 bricklayers, 3 plasterers, a schoolteacher, a livery stable owner, and assorted other artisans. "Colored mechanics were . . . getting as much skilled labor as they can do," an observer remarked. Like the port cities of St. Louis and Boston, but in substantially more occupations, Cincinnati was beginning to employ black men in a variety of jobs that required a certain amount of expertness and responsibility.[12] From 1836 to 1840, the number of blacks in the higher occupational tier increased from 83 to 182.[13]

The river city's rise in population particularly benefitted black barbers. It was no accident that a black parade in Columbus in the mid-1850s featured a giant razor and a plow, for throughout Ohio, barbering, a trade relegated exclusively to Negroes, along with farming, offered the most economic security to black men. An exemplar of the economic potential of barbering in Cincinnati was William W. Watson, an able community leader and young John Langston's future protector. Purchased from slavery by a family member only eight years before, by 1840 Watson owned two brick houses and lots in town and another 560 acres in the Mercer County black farming settlement, as well as his own barbershop expanded to include a bathhouse advantageously situated in the heart of the business district of Cincinnati. By 1850, when the number of black barbers had risen to 134 from the 46 a decade earlier, Watson would rank as one of the community's outstanding financial successes, with declared property holdings of $5,500.[14] His actual worth may have been greater: white abolitionist James Freeman Clarke put it at some $30,000, while black abolitionist Frederick Douglass put the barber on the same rung as Henry Boyd, the carpenter and bedstead manufacturer who was widely advertised as the richest black man in Cincinnati. Besides the possibility of abolitionist exaggeration, the discrepancy in the reports of the wealth of such prospering and publicly protesting blacks as Watson may have arisen from several related factors: a copy of the census was deposited in the courthouse; blacks were excluded from public facilities maintained by property taxes; black success might invite white retaliation. On the last point, the case of Henry Boyd would seem pertinent. Boyd's renowned furniture factory was burned again and again until finally, in 1859, no longer able to obtain fire insurance, he closed his business.[15]

Despite the special strains of purchasing family members from slavery and of coping with white harassment, by 1840 an impressive number of black Cincinnatians, persuaded that to possess a homestead was to be "independent and wealthy,"[16] had become property owners. Noting that their property "consists in that which is permanent and valuable, in household lots, and country land, two thousand or more acres of which they own in one plot," the Reverend Charles Ray in 1839 assessed their holdings as proportionately higher than in other black communities in the North. Moreover, "they are still accumulating faster than our people elsewhere."[17] White abolitionist Amzi D. Barber reported in 1840 that nine-tenths of black-owned houses and lots in the city had been purchased within the last four years. Besides individual holdings, a joint stock enterprise titled the Iron Chest Company, whose vice-president was Gideon Langston, had been organized in September 1838. From the dollar weekly investments of its members, the company had erected three large brick buildings that it rented to whites. Including the $19,000 valuation on three black churches, the total property worth of Cincinnati Negroes in 1840 was estimated at $228,600.[18]

Negroes lived in some ten clusters located around the city's outer perimeter and in the center of town. Although many blacks lived close together for purposes of self-defense, society, and access to their own community institutions, the residential segregation practiced in Cincinnati during the pre-war era—given the constant stream of low-income immigrants—was more economic than racial. The bulk of the unskilled, black and white, tended to concentrate in the most densely settled areas. In the east central section, where both "Germany," named for its large number of Germans, and "Bucktown," named for its large number of blacks, were situated, some 950 blacks and 8,000 whites found shelter.[19] Within the section, housing conditions varied considerably, from the relative comfort of Germany, where the black schoolteacher and whitewasher Owen T. B. Nickens and other respected black leaders lived, to the misery of Bucktown, called the "Bottoms" by the compassionate. In this wretched basin of tenements and shanties drained by an odiferous stream that carried the bloody run-off from pork processing houses, black and white "herded together," with as many as six family members living in an eight-by-twelve room; poverty, disease, violence, and criminality were good neighbors.[20]

Abolitionist commitment, in combination with a large, growing, and youthful black population and the improving economic conditions, had helped to account for an invigoration of black institutional life in Cincinnati in the mid-thirties. Building on a foundation of black community-directed efforts extending back at least a decade,[21] a group of young white abolitionists—the famous "Rebels" of Lane Seminary led by the Connecticut Yankees Theodore Dwight Weld and Augustus Wattles—had rendered valuable assistance.[22] Working closely with black leaders[23] —including former Chillicothe Baptist minister David Nickens,[24] A.M.E. minister William Paul Quinn,[25] painter William M. Johnson,[26] and schoolteacher Owen Nickens[27] —the "Rebels" in 1834 had instituted an extensive program of instruction and uplift in an effort, as Weld put it, to create a "spectacle of free black cultivation."

Three young white women teachers brought in from the East, called the "Sisters," had worked zealously in the project.[28] Besides a lyceum and a library, the activities had included day and night schools for both sexes and all ages, with instruction on topics ranging from the ABCs, sewing, and housekeeping to mathematics, abolitionism, and salvation.[29] Morally and materially, the abolitionists had contributed to the upsurge in black property holdings during the late thirties. "Before you commenced schools," a black Cincinnatian confided in 1840, "I did not feel any interest in laying up property. I did not feel that I had a home here. If I earned property, I knew not but my house would be pulled down over my head by a mob. All I cared for was to have enough to eat and wear." Outside the city, black Cincinnatians' large landholdings in Mercer County resulted from Augustus Wattles's investment of their funds in the all-black farming community he instigated; at home, whites, on occasion following an example set in Mercer County, may have recorded property in their names while making out second titles to the actual black owners.[30]

The schooling and moral reform efforts had likewise borne fruit. By 1839, the Colored Education Society, founded in 1836, was overseeing three private schools for Negro children in the city, two of them entirely supported by the black community, and one by the white Ladies' Anti-Slavery Society of Cincinnati, while black financial contributions had risen from $150 in 1835 to $900. Such a performance, backed by petitioning by blacks and white abolitionists, doubtless had inspired the city council's unprecedented allocation of black tax money to support a short-lived school in 1839–40 for the "children of the colored people."[31] Under a constitution drafted by schoolteacher Owen Nickens, the Moral Reform Society—organized shortly after its educational counterpart and with many of the same officers—had pledged its members of both sexes to uphold the "true principles of morality and integrity" and specifically to work for "suppression of intemperance, licentiousness, gambling, sabbath-breaking, blasphemy, and all other vices." At the end of the decade one-quarter of the adult black population of the free-swinging port city belonged to temperance societies, with the result that black whiskey peddlers had to operate surreptitiously, and black drunks seldom appeared on the streets.[32]

Respectable black life in Cincinnati had long centered on the churches, particularly the abolitionist Bethel A.M.E. and Union Baptist. Rebelling against the requirement that Negroes come last to the communion table, several black Methodists in 1824 had withdrawn from the predominantly white church and, inspired by the itinerant missionary Moses Freeman, had formed an A.M.E. congregation. Both

Freeman and convert Owen Nickens, who was appointed a "local preacher," later recalled meetings in a cellar dubbed "Jerico," while other gatherings occurred in homes, a blacksmith shop and a house for processing lime. In 1834, the congregation had purchased a lot on Sixth Street east of Broadway, where, using the combined labors of the fellowship, it had erected a church designed by one of the members.[33]

One of the oldest black Baptist churches in the West and probably the largest, the Union congregation had separated from the white Baptists in 1831, although continuing an uneasy coalition with them.[34] In 1839, the black Baptists had moved from a small brick church they had constructed to the imposing structure on Baker Street formerly occupied by their white counterparts. Within five years, by using proceeds from fairs conducted by women of the church, converting donated goods into cash, and relying on contributions from members, the barber Watson in particular, the church had paid all but $2,000 of the $9,000 purchase price; by 1848, it had cleared the entire debt.[35] During the 1840s, when young John Langston attended, the ministers were two ex-Virginians, Charles Satchell, also a self-employed dyer,[36] and the Oberlin-educated fugitive, William P. Newman.[37] Both, Langston recalled, "were possessed of large ability, piety, and eloquence." Under their leadership, coupled with Watson's faithful service, the Union Baptist functioned as a missionary church to the black destitute and a "mother church to nearly all the colored churches of its order in the great valley and in Canada."[38] Fervent in condemning slavery and in opposing the church's pro-slavery apologists (as was the Zion Baptist, founded in 1843 by the pioneer minister-missionary Wallace Shelton)[39] the Union Baptist congregation infused its other major interests—the Sabbath school and the "secular education of youth"—with Christian abolitionist principles.[40]

Worship in these churches combined emotional release with reform values. Newman in later years confirmed a white woman's account of her visit to an undisclosed black church that, in all probability, resembled the Union Baptist: "No surly pew occupant placed a forbidding hand on the pew door. Seats, hymn-books, crickets, and fans were at my disposal. The hymn was found for me. Everybody sang. It was infectious. I was among people to whom Sunday was neither a bugbear nor a bore. And such *hearty* singing!—sometimes too fast, sometimes too slow, but to my ear music, because it was soul, not cold science. . . . I went home happy, for I had not fed on husks." Similarly, on a Sunday afternoon in late 1850, Swedish traveler Fredrika Bremer called at the Bethel A.M.E. church that John Langston had also attended during his sojourn in Cincinnati. The house was filled. The celebrants sang their

own hymns, which Bremer found crowded with "naiveté, imagery, life."
The singing "ascended and poured forth like a melodious torrent,
heads, feet and elbows moved all in unison amid evident enchantment
and delight." A "very black" young minister, in "flowing eloquence,"
alluded to the recently enacted Fugitive Slave Law and entreated the
congregation to pray for the runaway and for a nation that would pass
such oppressive legislation. The year before a British minister and his
wife came away from a tea invitation at the neat and clean dwelling of
the Zion Baptist minister Wallace Shelton assured that blacks "were
deeply and justly disaffected towards the American people and the
American laws."[41]

Arguably, the extensive religious conversions that occurred during
the late 1830s, stimulated by pious blacks as well as evangelizing white
radicals, had helped to move black Cincinnatians toward self-help and
protest. In 1840, Amzi D. Barber, an Oberlin theological student and
former teacher of black children in Cincinnati, reported about five
hundred conversions over the past four years, bringing the total membership in the Union Baptist, Bethel A.M.E., and M.E. churches to
some eight hundred. Religion for some was "excitement merely."[42]
Nevertheless, if evangelical Christianity, the Oberlin brand in particular
with its emphasis on moral excellence, stirred many whites to acts of
benevolence, the most potent manifestation being the abolitionist crusade, that same force mixed with Afro-American religion brought
from the South, with its stress on emotional and sensory fulfillment—
the two faiths having in common a respect for freedom, education, and
individual responsibility and dignity—was seemingly not less effective
in energizing a black self-helping movement in the city and around the
state. If the revolution in race relations was to occur, if "the cause of
truth and justice, . . . one God will sanction," as the devout Gideon
Langston put it, was to prevail, it had to begin, Cincinnati's black
leadership generally agreed, in the churches. The poet Madison Bell,
who worshipped in the Bethel congregation during this period, later
reflected: "These Negro churches have done more to educate the heart
and mind for freedom's blessings held in store than every other means
combined."[43]

By the time John Langston arrived in the city, twenty-two men, including his brother Gideon, had emerged as leaders in church and
society as well as educational, moral, and abolitionist enterprises.
Nearly three-fourths of the group were native Virginians. All were
employed: six as barbers, four carpenters, three hucksters, two white-
washers; one each as schoolteacher, painter, plasterer, tanner, dyer,
steward, and livery stable operator.[44] Newspaper readers[45] and keen

observers, these leaders profited from occupations that positioned them to receive and transmit political intelligence. This was particularly true of the barbers: Andrew J. Gordon, one of the state's premier black orators; the literate W. H. Yancy, co-editor of *The Colored Citizen*, one of two black newspapers published briefly in the city during the 1840s; John Liverpool, a pioneer leader in Cincinnati and corresponding secretary in Ohio for the early national black convention movement; John Hatfield and William O'Hara, key conductors for the underground railroad;[46] and William W. Watson.

Certain traits distinguished them, individually and as a group. Augustus Wattles, who enjoyed more intimate terms with the black community than any other white man, singled out the leaders' honesty, uprightness, and industry. Baptist minister Newman, working among them in the late thirties and forties, was struck by the pride and strength the leaders seemed to derive from their community's advancing "number, intelligence, and wealth." The well-traveled New Yorker Charles Ray believed that—to a greater extent than in any other black community he had visited—"important principles" prevailed among the leaders, primarily union and "confidence in each other's integrity." Taking in leadership and community, Ray pronounced black Cincinnatians "the best population of our people I have ever seen or heard of."[47] Moreover, these black men of property and standing embodied a sense of racial obligation, the essence of which several had articulated in 1837: " 'Ethiopia shall soon stretch forth her hand to God,' is the declaration of infinite goodness and wisdom. It must take place, and will doubtless be effected by human agency; and who so proper as educated colored people to be the heralds of the gospel, and teachers of science and civilization to their benighted brethren in all lands."[48] Speaking in 1845, Salmon P. Chase of Cincinnati, the future senator, Ohio governor, and chief justice of the U.S. Supreme Court, who had already made a name for his legal defense of fugitive slaves and in antislavery politics, would sum up the achievements of the black community. Contrasting the situation in his boyhood twenty years before, when "the colored inhabitants [were] hardly in a better condition than slaves," to their current "visibly improved condition," Chase declared: "Debarred from the public schools, you have established schools of your own; thrust by prejudice into the obscure corners of the edifices in which white men offer prayer, you have erected churches of your own. . . . Excluded from the witness box, you have sought that security which the law denies, in a favorable public opinion propitiated by your good conduct."[49] On the self-help foundation of the thirties, the leadership would build a broad array of political and protest activities in the two decades before the war, working aggressively in cooperation with other black communities in the state to further the objectives of full freedom and equality.

Although Gideon Langston and other leaders of the Cincinnati black community eased the way, eleven-year-old John, fresh from the Chillicothe farm and still harboring wistful memories of the Gooches, doubtless was more confused than impressed by his introduction to the black social and political culture of the city. Any hopes he had had of living with his brother Gideon had been dashed. Although Gideon, who had settled in Cincinnati after brief study in Oberlin Institute's preparatory department, had already established himself in business, opening a barbershop and, shortly thereafter, the only black-owned livery stable in the city, he had remained a bachelor and, as such, was unprepared to care for the boy.[50] Instead, he had found John a boarding place with John Woodson, a fellow community leader, whose home was situated on Sixth Street, east of Broadway and north of the canal, in the section known as Germany. Like Gideon, Woodson, a master carpenter, was an officer and stockholder in the Iron Chest Company. "Steady, industrious, and cherishing proper ideas of what is necessary for [Negro] elevation," as *Philanthropist* editor Gamaliel Bailey said of him and two other black builders, Woodson, a former Virginian, was compiling a solid record of involvement in local and state organizations for education, moral elevation, and self-help. As superintendent of the Sabbath school of the Bethel A.M.E. church, Woodson, whom Langston characterized as "fairly educated" and efficient, entered John into its membership. John doubtless also joined the children's temperance group, which had existed for more than five years and was of special interest to Woodson, himself an officer of the Moral Reform Society and a promoter of its charge to impress on adults and children alike "the importance of temperance, morality, virtue and industry."[51]

On weekdays John went to the basement of the black Baptist church on Baker Street, some distance away, to the school taught by the Reverends Mr. Denham and Goodwin. Langston would remember the white teachers, who had been at the work for several years, as even-tempered, enthusiastic men of considerable learning, able to win the respect and confidence of their pupils. Charging $3 per quarter in advance and affording the rare opportunity of a full year term, the school enjoyed a healthy enrollment, drawing not only on local children but also on those who, like John, had been sent from other more deprived areas for the educational advantages. An average of sixty-five boys and girls attended. According to Langston's recollection, the pupils displayed a high order of morality and of scholarship; Cincinnati schoolchildren had been praised for eagerness since the opening of the first Lane Rebel project school in 1834, when children had "begged to be taken in."[52]

Nevertheless, on initial acquaintance, Johnnie's new school, like his new surroundings as a whole, must have seemed strange and restricted. Although his schooling had been neglected of late, it was soon apparent that he was one of the better scholars. Years of enforced ignorance and poverty had left deep imprints on young minds. Some of John's classmates, several years further on, may have been among those students at Hiram Gilmore's High School in 1848 who struck visiting black abolitionist Martin Delany as having learned "comparatively nothing, except perhaps a little business education and some music for show purposes," but no science and no English composition—"They don't capitalize i." The effects of limited opportunity were also apparent at John's Sabbath school, where white abolitionists, while praising the "neat dress, good order, and appearance of intelligence" of the pupils, noted with regret that this was the solitary instruction some received.[53] For John, moreover, the Bethel church's demonstrative services may well have seemed strange after the proper Presbyterians of Chillicothe. And what was he to make of men and women of the black upper class, like Woodson and his associates, whose constant striving to maintain home and institutions contrasted sharply with the easy circumstances of the white families he had known. Even while the boy responded to the culture—learning new words and phrases: "you creature, you!," "a squash of fat," and "*studies* about it";[54] stopping off at a confectioner's shop for a sugarplum or a stick of candy from the big barrel; playing at marbles or splashing in the canal on hot summer days; sniffing the strong odors of frying pork or fatback in narrow alleys; listening to the music of the black boatmen, one man singing the stanzas, others coming in on the chorus[55] —he had few clues to the puzzle of his own place in it. The grammatical questions of "I" were simple for Johnnie Langston, the psychological more than ordinarily complex and painful.

The city's turbulent racial and anti-abolitionist climate that spring and summer of 1841 could only heighten his anxieties. An important ruling by the Ohio supreme court, the activities of blacks and some white abolitionists to help slaves escape set against the often violent attempts to reclaim them, the building white resentment of the rising black prosperity and confidence, and economic unrest all contributed to the impending conflict. In late May, the state's highest court, conforming to arguments earlier advanced by Cincinnati attorney Chase in the Matilda case, decided that any slave voluntarily brought by an owner or permitted by him to travel into Ohio became a free person. In response, playing on fears of damage to the southern trade, the influential Cincinnati *Enquirer*, a Jacksonian newspaper, renewed its periodic alert concerning the malign influences of abolitionism. Condemning the practice of assisting fugitive slaves as particularly disruptive of relations with the South, the *Enquirer* began a sultry summer of demanding action against those responsible.[56]

New to the city and young as he was, John nonetheless doubtless already knew something of the operations of the underground railroad, in which his brother Gideon, as well as his landlord John Woodson and such notables as William W. Watson were involved. Helping slaves off the steamboats or from over the river and concealing them once they were in the city, blacks, assisted by white sympathizers, over the years had made Cincinnati a major portal from slavery to freedom. While members of the Bethel church regularly helped runaways, the enterprises of the Iron Chest Company also included the care and protection of fugitives. "Such matters are almost uniformly managed by the colored people," abolitionist James G. Birney had confided to Lewis Tappan in 1837, an assertion echoed by Levi Coffin, who was called the superintendent of the underground railway, when he took up residence a decade later. Although necessarily clandestine—one black man referred to "under-railway" agents as being "initiated into the mysteries of Syble"—and dangerous, the work engendered the kind of personal satisfaction expressed by the trusted agent John Hatfield: "I never felt better pleased with anything I ever did in my life, than in getting a slave woman clear, when her master was taking her from Virginia."[57]

If John's imagination could enter into not only the adventure, but also the morality of violating the law to aid a fellow human being to freedom, the boy was all the more alarmed by the recurrent mob action against those who succored fugitives. "When . . . their hiding places were discovered it mattered little what the color of the protector was," as Langston remembered, "popular feeling was quickly aroused and in not a few cases manifested itself in violence against those concerned in such transaction." Thus, the entire black community had reason for concern in early August when a letter purportedly from a fugitive to his still-enslaved wife came to light. Naming two black residents of Cincinnati, William O'Hara, a barber, and "George" Casey (probably William Casey, a riverman), from whom help could be expected, the escapee advised his wife to tell her trusted friends "that if they can once get to Cincinnati, they can get liberty; and that the colored men in the boats will whisper in their ears where to find abolitionists." Enraged by this evidence of a "nefarious conspiracy," the *Enquirer* declared the city overrun by free blacks, "laboring, when they do labor, in competition with white citizens, and when they do not, subsisting by plunder." It called on township trustees to enforce the seldom observed law of 1807 requiring blacks to post $500 bond within twenty days of their arrival in the state. If they had not posted bond, and could not, it demanded that they leave the city.[58]

In the company of landlord or brother, Johnnie Langston no doubt attended the ceremonies held on August 1, 1841—despite the growing hostility—to commemorate the abolition of slavery in the British West Indies. Since 1838, when black Cincinnatians had held a watch-night service to mark the official termination of the apprenticeship system in the British possessions, celebration of the First of August had become an annual event, as it was in a growing number of black northern communities. With many of the black leaders taking part, William M. Johnson presided over the 1841 observance, an elaborate family-oriented affair that opened at Bethel A.M.E., continued at Baker Street Baptist, and concluded with "an elegant temperance dinner" prepared by a black caterer and served outdoors. Young Joseph Henry Perkins—who on a like occasion in 1849 would proudly describe black contributions and excoriate "the fiery famished brood of Anglo Saxons, that continue to suck at the vitals of Afric's bleeding, but unoffending children"—acted as orator of the day. Woodson's foreman, J. L. Tinsley, led the toast to "The day we celebrate—Honored for an event which must ultimately result in the abolition of slavery throughout the world"; A. M. Sumner declared that the West Indies independence "admonished all oppressors in every nation that the day is at hand when the hand of Almighty God will sunder the chains of the oppressed in every land."[59] As much as the forthright rhetoric, the success of the well-organized celebration evinced the considerable socioeconomic progress and political awareness that the Cincinnati black community had attained.

Nonetheless, these very factors were stimulating rancor among whites. On a psychological level, the Englishman Edward Abdy's observation, made during a visit to Cincinnati in 1834, was still apt: whites spoke of self-improving blacks "with a degree of bitterness that dictated a disposition to be more angry with their virtues than with their vices." Whether or not blacks actually "assume [d] the air of fellows in authority" or "took the inside of the pavement upon all occasions," as critics charged, more than one Cincinnatian was angered simply by respectable and responsible black behavior. "White men . . . are naturally indignant," a white working man explained, "when they see a set of idle blacks dressed up like ladies and gentlemen, strutting about our streets and flinging the 'rights of petition' and 'discussion' in our faces."[60]

The economy and the weather exacerbated the festering discontent. In early August, drought and heat dropped the Ohio River to an unprecedented low water mark, throwing many white laborers, as well as black, out of work. Meanwhile, overall economic conditions remained unstable, with new bank closings eminent. As the *Enquirer* continued to charge blacks and abolitionists with the major responsibility for business difficulties and job losses, the *Philanthropist* indulged in provocative statements of its own. No doubt inspired by the First of August proceedings, the *Philanthropist* shortly afterward rebuked those southern editors who were threatening to sever business relations over the ruling in the Matilda case. "Madmen! a pretty thing for you to be talking of non-intercourse, while nothing but respect for the power of the free states protects you from the desolating vengeance of the united black race of the Western Hemisphere."[61]

Little was needed to trigger a riot. As August turned to September, the incidents began. Not far from the Woodson home where Johnnie lived, a youthful white gang pelted several well-dressed black men with gravel. As other blacks joined in, a fight ensued that wounded several persons on both sides; rumor had it that a white youth was "so badly cut, that his bowels fell out." Sometime after midnight of the following day an armed white party burst into a black hotel, the Dumas House on McAllister Street, demanding a black man's surrender to them, only to be repulsed. Yet another scuffle between whites and blacks, reportedly with some injuries to the former, broke out in the Lower Market soon after.[62]

By Friday, September 3, even a black child could recognize that a full-scale white attack seemed inevitable. As numbers of Kentuckians swelled the crowds and city officials made no move to intervene, Johnnie Langston heard "high and open threats, conveyed in vulgar base expressions which indicated the possibility and probability of an early attack." It was Langston's recollection—which subsequent events seem to confirm—that stiffening for the onslaught, black elders armed themselves with guns, planned their defense, and—in an all but unique action in the history of pre-war race riots—chose a leader to direct it. The man was Major J. Wilkerson. A twenty-eight-year-old self-purchased mulatto who acted as an A.M.E. missionary to establish churches and schools in the West, Wilkerson would offer this family history in his memoirs: "A Virginian by birth, born not far from Little York, a town of no little renown, and as to his blood, he is of the Bengal of Africa, Anglo-Saxon of Europe, Powhatton of America; but strictly the grandson of Col. Wilkerson, who fought with one of the bravest of the brave, namely General Gates, at the battle of Saratoga, N.Y." Langston recalled that the Cincinnati black community had full confidence in the man.[63]

By 8 o'clock that night a white mob, having assembled openly in Fifth Street Market, moved purposefully toward the black homes and businesses clustered around Sixth and Broadway, the section where Johnnie Langston boarded. In the "outrageous, barbarous and deadly attack upon the entire class of the colored people" that followed, as Langston put it, the mob assaulted blacks "wherever found upon the streets, and with such weapons and violence as to cause death in many cases, no respect being had to the character, position, or innocence of those attacked." Behind windows and doors and on rooftops of houses at Sixth and Broadway and along the alley leading from New to Sixth, armed blacks waited. After razing a Negro confectioner's shop and shouting down the mayor, who had attempted to remonstrate with them, the mob—brandishing bludgeons and demanding of white residents where the Negroes lived—advanced into New Street.[64] Suddenly the black defenders, doubtless under orders from Major Wilkerson, launched their counterattack, opening fire from the alley with rifles and muskets and wounding several whites. "The crowd gave back towards Broadway," a white witness reported. "The negroes rallied, and came into the street firing their guns, and throwing missiles at the crowd as it was retreating . . ., and pursued the crowd to Broadway." To cover the black charge, shots were fired into the retreating mob from a frame house in Broadway occupied by black steamboat steward Asbury Young.[65] Reportedly yelling out "a wild shout of triumph and defiance," some fifty armed black men succeeded in pushing the mob "full one hundred yards from their houses." Despite a heavy rain shower and further firing from the black defenders, by 1 a.m. the attackers collected themselves sufficiently to drag an iron six-pounder from the river to the corner of Sixth and Broadway, stuff the cannon with boiler punchings, and discharge it at least three times down Sixth. Far into the night the fighting continued, until a military contingent summoned by the mayor moved in to keep the mob at bay.[66]

Although the black defense had succeeded, the struggle was not over. An early morning meeting at the court house, presided over by the mayor, hastily agreed to the demands of white citizens: enforcement of

the Black Laws, including the requirement for bonding, return of all
fugitive slaves, repudiation of the doctrines and activities of abolitionists, and, most immediately, complete disarmament of blacks and arrest
of Negro law-breakers. With the riot area under martial law for blacks
and mob law for whites (none of whom were arrested), "swarms of
improvised police officers" spread across the city in search of Negroes,
dragging off servants or waiters or barbers, combing black residences
for men and arms, collecting what the *Enquirer* described as enough
weapons to supply "an Algerine pirate vessel." In a futile gesture toward conciliation, some Negroes met to promise compliance with the
laws and thank city officials for their efforts to protect them. Herded
into the square at Sixth and Broadway and penned in by a guard of
soldiers, blacks were not permitted to leave even when they gave bond;
late in the day, some three hundred black men, sound and maimed,
were marched off to jail while whites struck and kicked and jeered
at them.[67]

Early that morning John Langston was in Woodson's home when a
black neighbor dashed in to warn him of the impending arrests. Although allegedly the jailing was for their self-protection, Langston
would write, in actuality "the colored men were imprisoned because
it had been thoroughly shown by their conduct that they had become
so determined to protect themselves against whatever odds, that great
and serious damage might be expected were they again assaulted."[68]
After watching Woodson and his assistant Tinsley hide themselves in
the chimneys of the house, the boy took off through the back yard and
garden, jumped over the fence into the alley, and headed down Main
Street to the canal bridge. He was determined to warn Gideon, whose
barbershop was near Fourth and Main, more than a mile away. In the
middle of the bridge, John heard police officers behind him ordering
him to stop. Terrified, he raced onward until nearly to his goal, stumbled into a drugstore, and fainted. The white druggists, friends of his
brother, carried him to Gideon's rooms, where he was revived and told
his story. Well aware of the city order and already in hiding, fearful of
the danger of Johnnie's having been followed, Gideon settled in behind
barred doors and windows to listen and wait, his exhausted brother at
his side. Gideon's five employees hid with them. Finally, in the concealing dusk, the boy ventured out with the helpful white merchants to a
confectionary to buy food for the hungry men, who had eaten nothing
for some fifteen hours.

Listening in the darkness, Johnnie heard the "howls, and yells, and
screams, and oaths, and vulgarities" of the rioters as they dragged
the press of the *Philanthropist* down Main Street and threw it into the

river.[69] They destroyed the bakery of naturalized Englishman Cornelius Burnett, who often succored fugitives, and attacked an abolitionist book depository. Raiding parties searched out Negroes' homes where "windows were broken, doors smashed, children frightened, and poor women insulted." Late in the night they descended on Sixth and Main, battered the Bethel church, and again attacked the houses where only women and children remained. The *Chronicle* reported "scenes of greater real atrocity, though with less personal injury" than on the evening before; the *Gazette* acknowledged that the city had been "in a complete anarchy, controlled mostly by a lawless and violent mob." Although Governor Thomas Corwin had issued a proclamation calling for cessation of the violence, neither military companies, police, nor the large numbers of deputized citizens had offered effective resistance to the rioters. At length, after a few arrests were finally made, the mob dispersed from sheer exhaustion.[70]

Sunday, John came out of hiding to a dazzlingly sunshiny day. The "solemn, awful tread and tramp" of the mounted constabulary intruded on an almost religious silence. Like Ismael, the boy was struck by the cruel dissonance of natural serenity and human violence: "It would have been a day fit for the calm and peaceful worship of our Heavenly Father in a civilized and Christian community. As it was, however, the horrid sight of the vast company of such policemen, . . . with the recollection of the sad, dire events of the preceding nights and days, drove every feeling of love and veneration out of the hearts of those who had thus been outraged and terrified."[71]

It had been the most destructive and violent rioting in the city's history; indeed, it may well have been the most severe urban outbreak against blacks in pre-Civil War America. Although Langston remembered a high death toll among white attackers and black defenders, no accurate count of the dead and wounded, or of the amount of property damage, was attempted.[72] In accordance with the rioters' demand that the law of 1807 be enforced, however, a city official did disclose the posting of bonds by more than a hundred blacks and mulattoes; Kentucky slaveholders, invited to inspect the black prisoners before their release, claimed one as a fugitive slave.[73] Not appeased, a group of anti-abolitionists formed a new society to forward their aims. On the other hand, while the *Philanthropist*, picking up a few new subscribers and renewed support from the old, continued publication, Langston believed that the riot had also served to embolden such antislavery adherents as Salmon P. Chase and Samuel Lewis, who subsequently joined with Gamaliel Bailey in giving force to the fledgling Liberty party.[74]

The effect on the black community was profound. An abolitionist's census of black Cincinnatians in 1845 showed that despite a population increase of about six hundred since 1840, the private property holdings had dropped nearly $50,000 during the five-year period—an indication, however imperfect, of the extent of the property loss and the difficulty of economic rebuilding in a time of increased financial retrenchment. In the months immediately following the riot, another white observer of black Cincinnatians noted "a manifest depression of their energy and zeal in behalf of the schools and even of their private interests"; blacks themselves began serious consideration of emigration to Canada. By the fall of 1842, a black Oberlin student reported that nine of the city's most respectable black families, in addition to several young men, already had left for Canada, explaining: "times are very dull, money very scarce, nothing doing, & prejudice very great." At the same time, black community leaders took pains to contradict a rumor that a number of Negroes desired or intended to move to Liberia. Within two months of the riot, before a large crowd assembled at the abolitionist Sixth Presbyterian church, such leaders as George Cary, William O'Hara, John Liverpool, Charles Satchell, A. M. Sumner, and W. W. Watson repudiated the American Colonization Society and its Liberian project.[75] Over the long term, the riot of 1841—as repeated references to it in public gatherings demonstrated—exercised a strong hold on the black consciousness. At the 1843 National Convention of Colored Citizens in Buffalo, New York, Sumner, speaking for Watson and Andrew J. Gordon as well as himself in opposition to the adoption of the Reverend Henry Highland Garnet's militant *Address to the Slaves,* argued that it could endanger not only those free Negroes living in the South, but also those who lived in the border areas of free states. "We of Cincinnati," he declared, "[are] ready to meet anything that may come upon us unprovoked, but we [are] not ready injudiciously to provoke difficulty." Alongside the legacy of prudence left by the riot, because of the black defense there was also a legacy of pride, as black abolitionist William C. Nell, visiting the city with Langston fifteen years later, would observe. From the perspective of his own years in the black movement, Langston would write that the riot and the restrictive measures failed to "hush the voices of the eloquent colored men themselves, who through such experiences, were learning what their rights were, and how to advocate and defend them."[76]

For young John Langston, the riot may well have served as an emotional watershed. The desperation that pushed the boy over Woodson's fence to seek out and warn the one person he could claim as his family in that dangerous city was a telling measure of his lonely insecurity in this new life. The pulse-pounding moment on the canal bridge when he was identified as a Negro, his race to his brother, his venture into the night to procure food for Gideon and his workers, may all have made him feel intensely a participant in the black experience. Repelled and frightened by the depravity of the white attackers, thrilled by the courage of the black defenders, he could have felt the sense of unity engendered in members of groups by sudden adversity, and, later, the survivor's sense of uniqueness, value, and kinship to one's fellows. The knowledge that white abolitionists, too, were suffering could take him toward an appreciation of the possibilities of black-white union for the cause. Moreover, it is possible that the very savagery of the riot served to vent the violent and inexpressible anger, fear, and grief that had seized him when he was torn from the Gooches, moving him toward a sense of closure and to an acceptance of his black identity.

Toward the beginning of John's second year in Cincinnati, he looked up from his school desk at the sound of a familiar voice and saw William Gooch. Together on a bench, Johnnie and Gooch passed an emotional afternoon reviewing their separate existences, the boy asking eagerly after Mrs. Gooch and Virginia, the colonel, who was back in Ohio to make final settlement of his property in Chillicothe, assuring him of their affectionate concern. John promised that when he reached his majority he would rejoin the Gooch family in Missouri. Gooch's departure left the boy deeply affected but not despairing; in school and out, he had duties to attend to and associations to explore.[77]

Shortly after the riot, John had changed his address from the eastern to the south central part of the city, a move that brought him close to school and to Gideon, and into the household of the redoubtable William W. Watson. The boy doubtless thrilled to Watson's classic story of bondage and freedom, a story already well known among abolitionists. In 1832 in Lexington, Kentucky, standing on an auction table, Watson, then twenty-four and a "sable son" of Virginia, pointing to his weeping wife and little daughter, had successfully pled with potential buyers to abstain from bidding and was purchased by his brother-in-law for $650. A Cincinnati barber, the latter had raised the purchase price by persuading two white merchants to endorse his note on which he had then borrowed at exorbitant interest. Working in his brother-in-law's shop and also as a waiter, Watson not only had paid off the note within the year, but also subsequently purchased four other family members for a total exceeding $3,000, while embarking on his own barbering business and making his substantial investments in real estate. In her published justification for *Uncle Tom's Cabin*, Harriet Beecher Stowe, a resident of Cincinnati during the time she was gathering material for the book, would name Watson, along with five other former slaves she had met there, as men who exemplified the capability of the race, "conquering for themselves comparative wealth and social position" by their "self-denial, energy, patience, and honesty."[78]

John Langston, who found Watson's brick house with its well-furnished and pleasant rooms and parlors attractive, rightly perceived the social position of Watson and his wife Ruthellen as "conspicuous and influential." Besides the large number of family members and inmates—seventeen recorded in the 1840 federal census—frequent visitors kept the household lively. Noting in 1850 that Watson, his "esteemed friend," was the first black Cincinnatian to offer him hospitality, Frederick Douglass would advise: "He who would know whether colored people know how to live in a state of freedom might soon receive the desired information by making Mr. W. W. Watson a visit."[79] Because the children of Cincinnati's enterprising black families, "the very best and most highly educated and cultured young persons," as Langston put it, congregated in the Watson's parlor, John made new friendships and deepened others initiated during his first tentative months in the city. The most notable was with Peter Clark, himself the son of the successful barber Michael Clark. A precocious youngster exactly John's own age, Peter Clark—so forward in his studies that he would be employed as a teaching assistant after only two years of study at Gilmore's High School where he "finished" his education—was destined to become an eminent educator and political leader. Riveted in young manhood by common reform concerns, the relationship between Langston and Clark would endure until Langston's death, when Clark would refer brokenly to the loss of the "only friend who remains to me from my boyhood days."[80]

Like others in the industrious Watson household, where the 1840 census recorded nine males employed, John, while continuing his schooling, began to work at his landlord's barbershop and bathhouse. On Saturdays from early morning to the midnight closing he blacked boots, ran errands, and carried towels for whatever tips came his way. Rendered inconspicuous by age and role, John could closely observe the black barbers and their patrons, the majority of whom were white, although—since Watson and his companions in black reform repeatedly reproved those Cincinnati barbers who operated racially segregated shops—black customers doubtless were accommodated. The propensity of men to talk over the small beer of the week in such a setting acquainted the boy with current issues and ideas. At the same time, he could appreciate the personal qualities of the black barber—diplomacy, a liking of good talk and companionship, and a need to be abreast of events both abroad and in his own provincial sphere—that often made him an able politician and community leader, not only in

Cincinnati but elsewhere. Watson and his staff "pleased and won" their customers, John concluded, by skill, efficiency, decorum, and honesty. As for the patrons, one at least provided John an object lesson in thrift and temperance: the well-heeled dandy, who often tossed 50 cents and sometimes a dollar to the boy for polishing his boots, "commenced drinking and gaming, and I have lived to see him willing to black my boots for 10 cents had I asked him." Under the masks of lather, moreover, men sometimes revealed their passions and prejudices. Peter Clark, Langston's friend, who as a young man worked in his father's barbershop, would relate that a white man whom he was shaving had asked to be introduced to colored women. When Clark refused, the customer sneeringly referred to his shop's serving "niggers," whereupon Clark hurled the shaving cup to the floor, avowing never to shave a white man again unless to "cut his throat." If Watson and his workers also resented being at the beck and call of offensive white men, the bootblack might note the mechanisms of self-defense under their own disguises of accommodation: unimpeachable politeness, but perhaps an accidental nick of an offensive customer's chin, a topcoat brushing so assiduous it scraped the shoulders beneath, a flattering appraisal of an unappealing cut of hair or beard. Past midnight in the sweepings of the day, when black masks descended, the young bootblack would count out his earnings before his encouraging elders, who offered counsel on customer-pleasing, hard work, and frugality. Delighted to have mounting savings as well as pocket money, John began to envision himself a "successful and thrifty man."[81]

Business, however, he observed, was to be balanced with larger obligations. A staunch Baptist, who agreed with white abolitionists that the Sabbath should be reserved for worship, Watson refused to open his shop from the Saturday closing until five o'clock Monday morning. Any financial loss he suffered was set against a psychological gain that could hardly have escaped John's notice—the transformation from Saturday night's barber, as liable to be called "boy" as John himself, to Sunday morning's "Reverend Watson" and "Mr. Watson" in a society whose religious and secular joys and sorrows existed outside of white reckoning. John again enjoyed the reflected glory of his landlord's prestigious position in the church for, like Woodson at the Bethel A.M.E., Watson served as superintendent of the Sabbath school for the Union Baptist on Baker Street, of which he was also a trustee. This man of "vigorous mental parts, with limited education," as Langston described him—whose command of religious discourse was such that black political gatherings frequently called upon him to offer prayer— taught the most advanced Bible class, in which he enrolled Johnnie. In this church where good oratory and, as a white visitor remarked, "hymns beautifully and exquisitely sung" were staples, the boy, who doubtless joined in the singing, added to his store of knowledge of the rhythms and variety of black oral expression and to his appreciation of the black American's religious music—music that depicted an enlarged universe, roaming between past history, present circumstance, and future promise, bestowing a sense of peace and inner freedom, calling up thoughtful reflection. Most importantly, John experienced in the Union Baptist church, as in the Bethel A.M.E., the power of black self-determination. The black church, a mature John Langston would maintain in describing the founding of the African Methodist Episcopal church, not only represented "the organized Christian protest of the colored American against unjust, inhuman, and cruel complexional discriminations," but also offered him the "opportunity to be himself, to think his own thought, express his own conviction, make his own utterance, test his own powers, cultivate self-reliance, and thus, in the exercise of the faculties of his own soul, trust and achieve."[82]

During his second year at Denham and Goodwin's school, John progressed rapidly to the point where he and one other boy, probably Peter Clark, composed the highest class. Despite the traditional nature of the curriculum—ancient history, advanced arithmetic and grammar, and elementary science—the preoccupations of students and teachers meant that John was acquiring the rudiments of an antislavery education as well. Assigned to write an essay on Alfred, king of the Saxons, a sixteen-year-old black pupil in a similar Cincinnati school had responded: "at one time [Alfred] did not know his a,b,c, but before his death he commanded . . . nations. . . . I think if the colored people study like King Alfred they will soon do away with the evil of slavery. I cant see how the Americans can call this a land of freedom where so much slavery is." Just as the white Ohio schoolboy William Dean Howells, wearing a paper hat and flourishing a wooden sword, dreamed of the martial glory of English and American heroes,[83] John and his classmates fastened for inspiration, not only on these classic figures, but also on modern black liberationists. Particularly with the events of the riot "impressed upon the memory of the lad who witnessed, as he was terrified by them," John was excited by the slave mutineers of the *Amistad* and the valiant Cinque, or, as Langston and other contemporaries spelled it, Chinque. In the summer of 1839, Cinque, said to be an African prince, had led an uprising of his fifty-two fellow captives aboard the Spanish schooner *Amistad*. Though the Africans had gained control of the ship, they were overtaken by a U.S. government brig off the coast of Long Island and arrested, but not before Cinque had dived overboard, swimming "like an otter, first upon his back, then upon his breast," and evading his captors for nearly an hour. With ex-President John Quincy Adams handling the case for the Africans—eventually decided in their favor by the U.S. Supreme Court —abolitionists extracted full publicity value from it, using such devices as the sale of Cinque's picture for a dollar. Like other black communities, Negroes in Cincinnati not only tacked the likeness to their walls and told their children Cinque's story, but they also contributed to the defense fund. After the Africans finally won their freedom, Gideon Langston, speaking for his fellow townsmen, would be able to thank Adams personally for his "able defense . . . by which means a number of our fellow men were raised from a level with the brute creation, and placed in the scale of human existence." So meaningful would the memory be that John Mercer Langston would name his first daughter Chinque.[84] At the same time, Haiti, much in the news because of the attempt of several congressmen—Adams's "untiring efforts" won Gideon Langston's praise—to extend official recognition to the black Caribbean republic, caught John's interest. Excited by the Haitian revolution and its heroes, whom black Cincinnatians frequently toasted at First of August celebrations—and after one of whom, Dessalines, Langston would name his first son—the boy familiarized himself with Haitian history.[85]

John's early rhetorical efforts doubtless drew on antislavery topics. Like the youthful white orators in the common schools—whose "vehement action" led Harriet Martineau to wonder in mock dismay which of them would "speak in Congress hereafter"—John and his classmates frequently participated in plays, special exercises, and public exhibitions, the boys decked out in starched collars, the girls in "kid slippers, neat pantalettes and tastefully-plaited and ribboned hair." With his extended family and adult friends present to hear and applaud, John, honored to be chosen for special parts, soon discovered how much he liked reciting and speaking.[86]

Having tasted the exhilaration of performing, the boy, accompanying his brother or Watson to public forums addressed by white abolitionists or black community leaders, witnessed the power of oratory to express ethical values and laudable goals, as well as to inspire protest and resistance. None ranked higher in the boy's pantheon of heroes during these months than four talented young black orators: Joseph Henry Perkins, whom Peter Clark would call the "great orator of the Ohio valley";[87] John I. Gaines, then barely in his twenties but already active in state as well as local black reform; Andrew J. Gordon; and Gideon Langston. In 1850, Frederick Douglass would single out both

Perkins and Gaines for their "great powers over the minds and feelings of our people."[88] A barber noted for his dignity, Gordon[89] would be the speaker at a notable ceremony in 1845 (after John had left the city) to honor Salmon Chase. Presenting the attorney with an engraved silver pitcher in recognition of his contribution toward establishing a slave's right to freedom if brought voluntarily by his owner into the state, Gordon praised not only Chase's service to the enslaved, but also his sensitivity to "the deprivation of rights endured, and the wrongs inflicted upon the free colored people"; in return, the normally restrained Chase made his most radical utterance to date: a firm declaration of support for the Negro's rights to civil and political equality, including suffrage.[90]

Although all of these "fearless and able defenders of the rights of their people" inspired John, his brother Gideon, who "manifested large ability and learning with commanding and surprising qualities of oratory," excited his warmest admiration. Probably John was present on the brisk March 1843 evening when the "gifted and eloquent" Gideon, as Gaines characterized him, severely denounced colonization as having "no other tendency than to sacrifice the free colored population for the purpose of rendering the system of slavery more secure." Abolition of slavery, Gideon declared, was the only means to achieve the "entire liberation" of the Negro. A leader in the state black reform movement as well as in Cincinnati, Gideon would be chosen in November 1843 to head the black delegation that welcomed John Quincy Adams to the city—privately because blacks were barred from participating in the official welcoming ceremony. In his remarks, Gideon—whom Adams described in his diary as a "young mulatto, son of wealthy Virginia planter, but bearing the name of negress mother"—expressed gratitude for the congressman's fight against the "gag rule" in the House of Representatives, as well as his other antislavery contributions. "Although we have no honors of state to confer," Gideon said, "yet we offer you a far higher reward in the approbation of a grateful people. Injuries we write upon sand, but favors on marble, not to be erased; and these acts of yours are as indelibly written on the tablets of our hearts, and can never be obliterated." The occasion provided John Langston with a proud family memory, the more poignant since Gideon, apparently the victim of tuberculosis contracted after the livery stable owner's exposure to severe winter weather, would soon be forced to drop from public life and would die at the age of forty-six.[91]

When the thirteen-year-old left the river city to return to Chillicothe in the spring of 1843, invitations from Woodson and Watson to stay with them whenever he might return helped soften his real regret at leave-taking. Of Watson, at least, John had early news, for the Baptist deacon offered "an impressive appeal to the throne of Grace" at the black state convention in Columbus in August, attended by both Charles and William Langston, delegates from Chillicothe. Indeed, in the fraternity of talent and need that developed between black Ohioans, such meetings were inevitable. Growing into manhood, John Mercer Langston would maintain his ties with these men and their families, who had become, in a real sense, his own. In his maturity, he would express his gratitude to the outspoken leaders of the black community, "all of whom, it was the privilege and advantage of the boy John to hear and to know, their eloquent efforts serving him in large measure as inspiration and purpose."[92] His experience in Cincinnati had left him little ground to doubt that black people, afforded half a chance, could earn their way and justify their claim to full citizenship rights in American society—and defend themselves by force of arms when appropriate to their struggle. The determination, sacrifice, and achievement exhibited daily by the reform-minded men and women with whom he had associated undergirded his future resolve to win them at least that half a chance.

NOTES

1. Charles Dickens, *American Notes and Pictures from Italy* (London, 1908), p. 162; George Wilson Pierson, *Tocqueville and Beaumont in America* (New York, 1938), pp. 554–565; Harriet Martineau, *Retrospect of Western Travel*, II (New York, 1838; repr. New York: Haskell House, 1969), pp. 37–52; Ohio Writers Project, *Cincinnati, a Guide to the Queen City and Its Neighbors* (Cincinnati, 1943), pp. 58–59, 35–36; Leonard L. Richards, *"Gentlemen of Property and Standing"; Anti-Abolition Mobs in Jacksonian American* (New York, 1970), pp. 136–50; Robert McColley, *Slavery and Jeffersonian Virginia* (Urbana, 1964), p. 176; David Carl Shilling, "The Relation of Southern Ohio to the South during the Decade Preceding the Civil War," *Quarterly Publication of the Historical and Philosophical Society of Ohio* 8 (Jan. 1913):6–15; *Colored American*, Oct. 17, 1840; Carter G. Woodson, "The Negroes of Cincinnati Prior to the Civil War," *Journal of Negro History* 1 (Jan. 1916):1–22.

2. Helen M. Thurston, "The 1802 Ohio Constitutional Convention and the Status of the Negro," *Ohio History* 81 (Winter 1972):21–37; Betty Culpepper, "The Negro and the Black Laws of Ohio, 1803–1860," master's thesis, Kent State University, 1965, 16–17; Leonard E. Erickson, "The Color Line in Ohio Public Schools, 1829–1890," Ph.D. diss., Ohio State University, 1959, passim.

3. Richard C. Wade, *The Urban Frontier* (Chicago, 1964), pp. 223–29; John Mercer Langston, speech, "Action of the Federal Government," ms., John Mercer Langston Papers, Fisk University Library; A. D. Barber, *Report of the Colored People of Ohio* (Cincinnati, 1840), passim; *Rights of All*, Aug. 7, 1829; Cincinnati

Sentinel, Aug. 20, 1829, quoted in *Rights of All*, Sept. 7, 1829; Marilyn Bailey, "From Cincinnati, Ohio to Wilberforce, Canada: A Note on Antebellum Colonization," *Journal of Negro History* 68 (Oct. 1973):427–40; Richards, *"Gentlemen of Property and Standing"*, pp. 92–100; Ohio Anti-Slavery Convention, *Report on the Condition of the People of Color in the State of Ohio . . . Putnam . . . Apr., 1835* (n.p., 1835), p. 2; *Philanthropist*, Feb. 27, 1838, Nov. 11, 1840, May 19, Mar. 24, 1841.

4. John Mercer Langston, *From the Virginia Plantation to the National Capitol; or, The First and Only Negro Representative in Congress from the Old Dominion* (Hartford, 1894; repr. New York: Johnson Reprint, 1968), pp. 61–62.

5. The Board of Managers of the Colored Education Society to Editor, *Emancipator*, Apr. 22, 1837; C. B. Ray to Dear (Philip) Bell, Sept. 13, 1839, *Colored American*, Oct. 12, 1839; C. B. Ray to My Dear Bell, Sept. 16, 1839, *Colored American*, Oct. 5, 1839; Population Census of 1840, Hamilton County, City of Cincinnati, Reel 398, National Archives.

6. David Henry Shaffer, *The Cincinnati, Covington, Newport and Fulton Directory for 1840* (Cincinnati, 1840), pp. 467–77; *Report on the Condition of the People of Color . . . 1835*, pp. 8–9, 12, 6; Augustus Wattles to Mr. Editor, Mar. 6, 1834, Utica *Western Recorder*, n.d., reprinted in *Emancipator*, Apr. 22, 1834; John O. Wattles, "Colored People in Cincinnati," Cincinnati *High School Messenger and Reformer*, n.d., quoted in *Philanthropist*, Apr. 30, 1845; *Colored American*, Oct. 5, 1839.

7. On Afro-American work patterns and culture developed in slavery and around it, see Ira Berlin, *Slaves without Masters: The Free Negro in the Antebellum South* (New York, 1974); John Blassingame, *The Slave Community: Plantation Life in the Antebellum South* (New York, 1979); Dena J. Epstein, *Sinful Tunes and Spirituals* (Urbana, 1977); Eugene D. Genovese, *Roll, Jordan, Roll: The World the Slaves Made* (New York, 1974); Herbert Gutman, *The Black Family in Slavery and Freedom 1750–1925* (New York, 1976); Lawrence W. Levine, *Black Culture and Black Consciousness* (New York, 1979); Gerald W. Mullin, *Flight and Rebellion: Slave Resistance in Eighteenth Century Virginia* (New York, 1972); Leslie Howard Owens, *This Species of Property* (New York, 1976); Albert J. Raboteau, *Slave Religion* (New York, 1978); Thomas L. Webber, *Deep Like the Rivers* (New York, 1978); Peter Wood, *Black Majority: Negroes in Colonial South Carolina* (New York, 1974).

8. Frances Trollope, *Domestic Manners of the Americans*, ed., Donald Smalley (New York, 1949), p. 427.

9. Edward Deering Mansfield, *Personal Memories, Social, Political, and Literary, with Sketches of Many Noted People, 1803–1843* (Cincinnati, 1879; repr. New York: Arno Press, 1970), pp. 305–7; Ohio Writers Project, *A Guide to the Queen City*, pp. 58–59; Shaffer, *Cincinnati Directory . . . 1840*, pp. 467–77; J. H. Woodruff, *Cincinnati Directory, 1836–1837* (Cincinnati, 1836); Cincinnati *Gazette*, Dec. 4, 1839.

10. Shaffer, *Cincinnati Directory . . . 1840*, p. 483; Mansfield, *Personal Memories*, p. 307; Population Census of 1840, Hamilton County, City of Cincinnati, Reel 398, NA, lists 229 boatmen out of 1,005 blacks recorded as employed. In 1840, thirty-three steamboats were built in Cincinnati; Charles Cist, *Cincinnati*

in 1841: Its Early Annals and Future Prospects (Cincinnati, 1841), pp. 252–55; *Colored American*, Oct. 12, 1839.

11. Shaffer, *Cincinnati Directory . . . 1840*, pp. 467–77; Francis J. Mastrogiovanni, "Cincinnati's Black Community, 1840–1850," master's thesis, University of Cincinnati, 1967, pp. 97–100.

12. Shaffer, *Cincinnati Directory . . . 1840*, pp. 467–77; *Philanthropist*, July 21, 1840. According to the 1840 city directory, blacks were engaged in 46 different occupations. By 1850 it had increased to 66. In St. Louis in 1850, blacks worked in 33 different categories of employment; in Boston, 44. Shaffer, *Cincinnati Directory . . . 1840*, pp. 467–77; Patricia Mae Riley, "The Negro in Cincinnati, 1835–1850," master's thesis, University of Cincinnati, 1971, pp. 59, 66.

13. Woodruff, *Cincinnati Directory, 1836–1837*; Shaffer, *Cincinnati Directory . . . 1840*, pp. 467–77.

14. *Frederick Douglass' Paper*, Aug. 11, 1854; *Philanthropist*, July 14, 1840; Shaffer, *Cincinnati Directory . . . 1840*, p. 476; Harriet Beecher Stowe, *Uncle Tom's Cabin* (Boston, 1852; repr. Columbus: Charles E. Merrill, 1969), p. 320; Mastrogiovanni, "Cincinnati's Black Community, 1840–1850," p. 40.

15. William Loren Katz, ed., *The Free People of Color* (New York, 1969), p. 251; *Anti-Slavery Bugle*, Aug. 10, 1850; George Washington Williams, *A History of the Negro Race in America*, 2 vols. (New York, 1883), II, pp. 138–40.

16. "Report of Committee Upon Agriculture," *Minutes of the National Convention of Colored Citizens . . . Buffalo . . . Aug., 1843* (New York, 1843), p. 31, reprinted in *Minutes of the Proceedings of the National Negro Conventions 1830–1864*, ed. Howard Holman Bell (New York, 1969).

17. *Colored American*, Oct. 5, 1839. Amzi Barber, who taught school in black Cincinnati in the mid-thirties, reported in the spring of 1837 that "above 20" blacks in Cincinnati had purchased land in Mercer County; see Amzi D. Barber, "Of the Present Condition of the Colored People in Cincinnati, Apr. 1837," *Report of the Second Anniversary of the Ohio Anti-Slavery Society . . . Mt. Pleasant . . . Apr., 1837* (Cincinnati, 1837), p. 62. See also *Philanthropist*, Apr. 30, 1845, and *North Star*, June 9, 1848, for reports of "many" black Cincinnatians owning farms and tracts of land in the country.

18. Barber, *Report of the Colored People of Ohio*, pp. 12–13.

19. Useful in drawing these conclusions were three masters' theses: Riley, "The Negro in Cincinnati, 1835–1850," pp. 92–95, 101–4; and the maps, pp. 86–91; Mastrogiovanni, "Cincinnati's Black Community, 1840–1850," pp. 14–19, 28–38; Leonard Harding, "The Negro in Cincinnati, 1860–1870: A Demographic Study of a Transitional Decade," master's thesis, University of Cincinnati, 1967, pp. 20–28. See also Ray to Dear Bell, Oct. 3, 1839, *Colored American*, Nov. 2, 1839. On black residential clusters in Cincinnati in 1850, see Henry L. Taylor, "On Slavery's Fringe: City-Building and Black Community Development in Cincinnati, 1800–1850," *Ohio History* 95 (Winter-Spring 1986):5–33.

20. Shaffer, *Cincinnati Directory . . . 1840*, p. 474; Population Census of 1840, Hamilton County, City of Cincinnati, Reel 398, NA; Trollope, *Domestic Manners*, ed. Smalley, p. 52; Cincinnati *Gazette*, n.d., quoted in *Philanthropist*, Mar. 24, 1840.

21. Rev. B. W. Arnett, ed., *Proceedings of the Semi-Centenary Celebration of the African Methodist Episcopal Church of Cincinnati Held in Allen Temple, Feb. 8th, 9th, and 10th, 1874* (Cincinnati, 1874), pp. 13–20, 62; John B. Shotwell, *A History of the Schools of Cincinnati* (Cincinnati, 1902), p. 447.

22. Gilbert H. Barnes and Dwight L. Dumond, eds., *Letters of Theodore Dwight Weld, Angelina Grimke Weld, and Sarah Grimke, 1822–1844*, 2 vols. (New York, 1934), I, pp. 132–35, 211–21, 250–54; Augustus Wattles to Henry Howe, n.d., printed in Henry Howe, *Historical Collections of Ohio* (Cincinnati, 1847), p. 356.

23. *Weld-Grimke Letters*, I, pp. 192, 218, 179; Augustus Wattles to Susan Lowe, Apr. 28, 1835, Augustus Wattles Papers, Kansas State Historical Society; Shotwell, *A History of the Schools of Cincinnati*, p. 447.

24. See chapter 2 for biographical sketch of David Nickens.

25. Quinn's ministry soon took him elsewhere. Daniel A. Payne, *History of the African Methodist Episcopal Church* (Nashville, 1891), pp. 131, 137, 146, 170.

26. Virginian William M. Johnson and his wife are in the 10–24 age category in the 1840 census; a female child and an elderly man reside in the household. An agent for the *Colored American* and the *Liberator* in Cincinnati, Johnson was prominent in local protest meetings and presided at the 1841 First of August ceremonies. He was the president of the 1843 black state convention in Columbus. Population Census of 1840, Hamilton County, City of Cincinnati, Reel 398, NA; *Colored American*, Sept. 2, 1837; *Philanthropist,* Feb. 20, 1838, Mar. 5, 1839, Aug. 18, 1841, Oct. 2, 1843.

27. After joining the A.M.E. church in December of 1824 in Cincinnati, native Virginian Owen Nickens was appointed a "local" preacher. In March, 1834, independent of the Lane Rebels, he started the "first successful colored school" in the city; three months later he was in New York, representing the state at the national black convention. The 1840 census puts Nickens in the 36–55 age category, head of a family of four. In 1844, with ex-Tennessean A. M. Sumner, whose own experience as a schoolteacher added up to a "score of years," he edited Cincinnati's initial black newspaper, *The Disfranchised American*. When public education finally came to black Cincinnati in 1852, Owen Nickens was awarded one of the three black teaching positions. As late as 1874, Nickens was teaching in a rural Ohio community. Owen T. B. Nickens to Rev. B. W. Arnett, Feb. 4, 1874, printed in *Proceedings of the Semi-Centenary*, ed. Arnett, p. 31; Payne, *History of the A.M.E. Church*, pp. 61–63; Shotwell, *A History of the Schools of Cincinnati*, p. 447; *Minutes of the Fourth Annual Convention, for the Improvement of the Free People of Colour in the United States . . . New York . . . 1834* (New York, 1834), p. 9, reprinted in *Proceedings of the National Negro Conventions*, ed. Bell; Population Census of 1840, Hamilton County, City of Cincinnati, Reel 398, NA; *Palladium of Liberty*, May 1, 1844; *Philanthropist*, Apr. 24, 1844; *Eighth Annual Report . . . Colored Public Schools, Cincinnati, June 30, 1857* (Cincinnati, 1857), p. 13.

28. Theodore Weld to Louis Tappan, Mar. 18, 1834, *Weld-Grimke Letters*, I, p. 135; on the "Sisters," Emeline Bishop, Phoebe Matthews, and Susan Lowe, see Ibid., pp. 211–21, 250–54.

29. Edward Abdy, *Journal of a Residence and Tour in the United States of North America from April 1833 to October, 1834*, 3 vols. (London, 1834), II, pp. 400–4; *Report on the Condition of the People of Color . . . 1835*, passim; A. Wattles to Editor, July 3, 1834, *Emancipator*, Aug. 26, 1834.

30. *Colored American*, Oct. 17, 1840; *Free Labor Advocate*, n.d., quoted in *Anti-Slavery Bugle*, Nov. 6, 1846; *Report of the Second Anniversary of the Ohio Anti-Slavery Society*, p. 62; Emma Wattles Morse, "Sketch of the Life and Work of Augustus Wattles," Wattles Papers.

31. *Philanthropist*, Dec. 9, 1836, July 21, 1840; Barber, *Report of the Colored People of Ohio*, p. 13; Cincinnati Board of Education, *Annual Report*, June 30, 1840. From April 1830, a year after initiation of the public school system, until at least the end of 1843, blacks regularly petitioned the city council for a share of the public school funds; see Shotwell, *A History of the Schools of Cincinnati*, p. 447; Abdy, *Journal*, II, pp. 393–94, 400–1; *Philanthropist*, Dec. 24, 1842; Cincinnati *Herald*, Dec. 22, 1843.

32. *Report of the Second Anniversary of the Ohio Anti-Slavery Society*, pp. 59–64; Barber, *Report of the Colored People of Ohio*, p. 13; *Philanthropist*, Mar. 26, 1839. John Wattles's census listed 509 members in 1845. *Philanthropist*, Apr. 30, 1845.

33. Arnett, ed., *Proceedings of the Semi-Centenary*, pp. 13–21; Daniel Alexander Payne, *Recollections of Seventy Years* (Nashville, 1888), p. 104; Nickens to Arnett, Feb. 4, 1874, *Proceedings of the Semi-Centenary*, ed. Arnett, p. 31.

34. Oberlin *Evangelist*, Aug. 28, 1844; William J. Simmons, *Men of Mark: Eminent, Progressive, and Rising* (Cleveland, 1887; repr. Chicago: Johnson Publishing, 1971), pp. 375–77; Wendell P. Dabney, *Cincinnati's Colored Citizens: Historical, Sociological, and Biographical* (Cincinnati, 1926; repr. New York: Johnson Reprint, 1970), pp. 370–71.

35. Simmons, *Men of Mark*, p. 377; Barber, *Report of the Colored People of Ohio*, pp. 12–13; Katz, ed., *The Free People of Color*, p. 253; Cincinnati *Enquirer*, June 2, 1841; *Philanthropist*, July 14, 1841; Cincinnati *Gazette*, July 23, 1844; Oberlin *Evangelist*, Aug. 28, 1844; *North Star*, June 9, 1848. The oldest church in black Cincinnati was the Union Chapel M.E. church on Seventh Street, organized in 1815; see Arnett, ed., *Proceedings of the Semi-Centenary*, p. 59. A city directory for 1846 lists five black churches: African Union Baptist; Zion Baptist; Bethel African Methodist; Episcopal Methodist; and New Wesleyan African. Charles Cist, *The Cincinnati Miscellany . . .* (Cincinnati, 1846), p.81.

36. The first pastor of the church was David Nickens, "probably the first ordained colored minister in Ohio," who served from 1835 until his death in August 1838. Simmons, *Men of Mark*, pp. 375–76. Charles Satchell, his successor, held the position for the next seven years. In the 1840 census Satchell and his wife are in the 24–36 age category; two children and an elderly woman were also in the house. Satchell was elected president of the Moral Reform Society of the Colored of Ohio in 1838. He attended the 1844 black state convention in Columbus. Simmons, *Men of Mark*, pp. 371, 376; Shaffer, *Cincinnati Directory . . . 1840*, p. 475; Population Census of 1840, Hamilton County, City of Cincinnati, Reel 398, NA; *Philanthropist*, Feb. 20, 1838; *Palladium of Liberty*, Sept. 25, 1844.

37. On Newman, see chapter 4.

38. Langston, *Virginia Plantation*, p. 62; Oberlin *Evangelist*, Aug. 28, 1844; Dabney, *Cincinnati's Colored Citizens*, p. 371.

39. In the 1820s and 1830s Wallace Shelton organized Baptist churches in various parts of Ohio. An ex-slave, he was the chaplain of the first Ohio black state convention in 1837. The same year, he was one of nearly two hundred black Cincinnatians who petitioned the state legislature to abolish the "Black Laws." In the late thirties and early forties, Shelton occupied pulpits in Dayton and Columbus. In early 1843, he and thirty-nine other members of the Baker Street Baptist church in Cincinnati decided to form the Zion Baptist church, of which he was the minister for thirty years. An underground railroad agent, Shelton was active in local and state protest causes throughout the forties and fifties. In 1873, he became the acting pastor of the newly organized Mt. Zion Baptist church. Lewis G. Jordan, *Negro Baptist History* (Nashville, 1930), p. 61; *Frederick Douglass' Paper*, Aug. 11, 18, Sept. 1, 1854; *Philanthropist*, Sept. 8, 1837, Feb. 20, 1838, Aug. 13, 1839, May 31, July 12, 1843, June 10, Nov. 11, 1846; Columbus, Ohio, Chapter of the Frontiers of America, Inc., ed., *Negroes' Contribution in Franklin County 1803–1953* (Columbus, 1954), p. 7; Arnett, ed., *Proceedings of the Semi-Centenary*, p. 62; Wilbur Henry Siebert, *The Mysteries Of Ohio's Underground Railroads* (Columbus, 1951), p. 31; *State Convention of the Colored Citizens of Ohio . . . Columbus . . . Jan., 1849* (Oberlin, 1849); Cleveland *Leader*, Oct. 25, 1858. A picture of the "Father of the Zion Baptist Church" is in Dabney, *Cincinnati's Colored Citizens*, p. 94.

40. Simmons, *Men of Mark*, p. 376.

41. *Provincial Freeman*, Jan. 19, 1856, Dec. 8, 1855; Fredrika Bremer, *The Homes of the New World*, 2 vols. (New York, 1853), II, pp. 157–59; Ebenezer Davies, *American Scenes and Christian Slavery* (London, 1849), pp. 156, 152–53.

42. *Weld-Grimke Letters*, I, pp. 179, 192, 218; Barber, *Report of the Colored People of Ohio*, p. 13; Augustus Wattles, *Memorial of the Ohio Anti-Slavery Society to the General Assembly of the State of Ohio* (Cincinnati, 1838), p. 17; *State Convention of the Colored Citizens of Ohio . . . 1849*; Payne, *History of the A.M.E. Church*, pp. 193–94.

43. *Philanthropist*, Nov. 22, 1843; J. Madison Bell, "Poem—Now and Then," in *Proceedings of the Semi-Centenary*, ed. Arnett, p. 91.

44. The twenty-two leaders were Thomas Bascoe, Va., plasterer; Henry Boyd, Ky., carpenter and bedstead manufacturer; George Cary, Va., huckster; Thomas Crissup, Va., carpenter; Joshua B. Delany, Ohio, steward; Thomas Dorum, Ky., whitewasher; Joseph Fowler, Va., huckster; A. J. Gordon, Va., barber; John Hatfield, Pa., barber; Dennis Hill, Md., tanner; William M. Johnson, Va., painter; Gideon Quarles Langston, Va., barber and owner of a livery stable; John Liverpool, Va., barber; Owen T. B. Nickens, Va., whitewasher; William O'Hara, Va., barber; Richard Phillips, Md., huckster; Charles Satchell, Va., dyer; A. M. Sumner, Tenn., schoolteacher; John Tinsley, Va., carpenter; William W. Watson, Va., barber; John Woodson, Va., carpenter; W. H. Yancy, Va., barber. A partial list of sources for the twenty-two leaders include the newspapers, directories, censuses, antislavery convention reports,

published church records, and masters' theses cited throughout this chapter. Also beginning to be active in the early forties in black protest were two very young men, John I. Gaines, stevedore, and Joseph Henry Perkins, who worked in navigation, and by the late forties, Langston's contemporary, Peter H. Clark. All three were to become major local and state leaders. Gaines and Clark are profiled in chapter 5; for Perkins, see note 87 of this chapter. The Reverend Wallace Shelton became an important leader in the city when he finally settled there permanently in the early forties (note 39).

45. John Wattles found 700 newspaper subscriptions in an adult black population of 1,903, of whom 343 could read and write; see *Philanthropist*, Apr. 30, 1845; list of subscribers in *Philanthropist*, June 30, Nov. 17, 1841; George Cary to Editor, Aug. 18, 1837, *Colored American*, Sept. 2, 1837; Ray to Bell, Sept. 16, 1839, *Colored American*, Oct. 5, 1839.

46. On Gordon, see note 89 of this chapter. The two black newspapers were *The Disfranchised American* (1844) edited by O. T. B. Nickens and A. M. Sumner, and *The Colored Citizen* (1845–46) edited by W. H. Yancy and the Reverend Thomas Woodson. On Liverpool's association with the national convention movement, see *Minutes and Proceedings of the First Annual Convention of the People of Colour, . . . June, 1831* (Philadelphia, 1831), p. 9; *Minutes and Proceedings Of The Second Annual Convention, . . . June, 1832* (Philadelphia, 1832), p. 15; both reprinted in *Proceedings of the National Negro Conventions*, ed. Bell. For the underground railroad activities of O'Hara, see *Philanthropist*, Oct. 23, 1840, and Cincinnati *Enquirer*, Aug. 9, 1841; for Hatfield, see Laura Haviland, *A Woman's Life-Work* (Chicago, 1889; repr. New York: Arno Press, 1969), p. 166, and Wilbur Henry Siebert, *The Underground Railroad from Slavery to Freedom* (New York, 1899), p. 422.

47. *Emancipator*, Apr. 22, 1834; *Provincial Freeman*, Nov. 3, 1855; *Colored American*, Oct. 12, 1839.

48. Statement of the Board of Managers of the Colored Education Society, *Emancipator*, Apr. 13, 1837.

49. *The Address and Reply on the Presentation of a Testimonial to S. P. Chase, by the Colored People of Cincinnati* (Cincinnati, 1845), pp. 19, 33–34.

50. Henry Cowles, "Oberlin College Catalogue and Records of Colored Students, 1835–62," ms., Henry Cowles Papers, Oberlin College Library; Cleveland *Gazette*, Dec. 24, 1892; Charles Cist, *Cincinnati Directory for the Year 1842* (Cincinnati, 1842), p. 395.

51. Langston, *Virginia Plantation*, pp. 60–61; *Philanthropist*, Feb. 20, 1838, July 14, 21, Nov. 4, 1840, Dec. 21, 1842; Katz, ed., *The Free People of Color*, p. 252; Dabney, *Cincinnati's Colored Citizens*, pp. 357, 106–7. The 1840 census lists Woodson and his wife in the 24–36 age category. Population Census of 1840, Hamilton County, City of Cincinnati, Reel 398, NA; *Report of the Second Anniversary of the Ohio Anti-Slavery Society*, p. 64.

52. Langston, *Virginia Plantation*, p. 60; Barber, *Report of the Colored People of Ohio*, p. 13; Shotwell, *A History of the Schools of Cincinnati*, pp. 452–53; Abdy, *Journal*, II, p. 401.

53. *Philanthropist*, Nov. 26, 1839, July 14, 1840; *Report of the Second Anniver-*

sary of the Ohio Anti-Slavery Society, pp. 59, 65; *North Star*, June 9, 1848. On Hiram Gilmore's High School, see sketch written by Peter H. Clark and L. D. Easton in Shotwell, *A History of the Schools of Cincinnati*, pp. iii, 453–54.

54. Trollope, *Domestic Manners*, ed. Smalley, pp. 427–28; *Weld-Grimke Letters*, I, p. 216. "Studying" meant prayerful reflection.

55. *Emancipator*, Dec. 21, 1843; Epstein, *Sinful Tunes and Spirituals*, pp. 165–66.

56. J. W. Schuckers, *The Life and Public Services of Salmon Portland Chase* (New York, 1874), pp. 41–44; *Philanthropist*, June 30, Aug. 18, 1841; Cincinnati *Enquirer*, June 26, 1841.

57. Katz, ed., *The Free People of Color*, p. 253; *Anti-Slavery Bugle*, Aug. 24, 1850; *Philanthropist*, Nov. 4, 1840; Arnett, ed., *Proceedings of the Semi-Centenary*, p. 19; Siebert, *The Mysteries of Ohio's Underground Railroads*, p. 31; Abdy, *Journal*, III, p. 23; Dwight L. Dumond, *Letters of James Gillespie Birney*, 2 vols. (New York, 1938), I, p. 376; Levi Coffin, *Reminiscences of Levi Coffin* (Cincinnati, 1892; repr. New York: Arno Press, 1968), p. 297; "Cincinnatus" to Frederick Douglass, July 3, 1848, *North Star*, Aug. 11, 1848; interview with John Hatfield, Benjamin Drew, *The Refugee: A North-Side View of Slavery* (Boston, 1856; repr. Reading, Mass.: Addison Wesley Publishing, 1969), p. 256.

58. Langston, *Virginia Plantation*, p. 62; *Philanthropist*, June 30, 1841; Cincinnati *Enquirer*, Aug. 9, 10, 1841. Although George Cary, president of the Iron Chest Company (of which O'Hara was treasurer), did aid fugitives, William Casey, whose occupation and residence in Post Office Alley abetted his underground railroad work, was even better known in this capacity; see *Philanthropist*, Nov. 4, 1840; Shaffer, *Cincinnati Directory . . . 1840*, p. 468; Haviland, *A Woman's Life-Work*, pp. 112, 129, 135, 161, 166; Coffin, *Reminiscences*, pp. 308, 330–32, 339, 347–48; Cincinnati *Herald*, n.d., quoted in *Anti-Slavery Bugle*, July 7, 1848.

59. *Philanthropist*, Aug. 18, 1841; *Colored American*, Aug. 25, 1838; J. H. Perkins, *Oration, Delivered on the First of August, 1849, Before the Colored Citizens of Cincinnati* (Cincinnati, 1849), p. 25.

60. Abdy, *Journal*, I, p. 117; Cincinnati *Enquirer*, Sept. 9, 10, 25, 1841; "A Workey" to Editor, Cincinnati *Enquirer*, Sept. 10, 1841.

61. Cincinnati *Enquirer*, Aug. 10, 1841; *Emancipator*, Sept. 23, 1841; *Philanthropist*, Aug. 4, 1841.

62. All of the city's newspapers covered the riot. See reprints in *Philanthropist*, Sept. 8, 1841. See summaries of precipitating events in Cincinnati *Gazette*, Sept. 6, 1841; Cincinnati *Chronicle*, Sept. 4, 1841; Cincinnati *Enquirer*, Sept. 3, 4, 9, 1841; see also Richards, *"Gentlemen of Property and Standing"*, pp. 124–29; and Woodson, "The Negroes of Cincinnati," pp. 12–16.

63. Langston, *Virginia Plantation*, p. 63–64. An elder of the A.M.E. church, Wilkerson acted as the principal fundraiser for the church's Union Seminary, a manual labor school set up some twelve miles west of Columbus in 1845. During the Civil War, Wilkerson reportedly became a Quaker. Major James Wilkerson, *Wilkerson's History of His Travels and Labors in the United States, as a*

Missionary, in Particular that of the Union Seminary (Columbus, 1861), pp. 25, 4, 33–34, and passim; Payne, *History of the A.M.E. Church*, pp. 161, 185–86; A. G. B. to Editor, *Anglo-African*, Feb. 28, 1863.

64. Langston, *Virginia Plantation*, p. 63; Cincinnati *Gazette*, Sept. 6, 1841; Cincinnati *Chronicle*, Sept. 4, 1841, Cincinnati *Republican*, Sept. 6, 1841, both quoted in *Philanthropist*, Sept. 8, 1841; Cincinnati *Enquirer*, Sept. 9, 1841.

65. James Hall et al. to Editor, Cincinnati *Enquirer*, Sept. 18, 1841. Young, a steamboat steward and later cook, by 1850 would be one of the wealthiest blacks in the city, with property valued at $3,900. The ex-Virginian also served as a trustee of the Colored Orphan Asylum. Shaffer, *Cincinnati Directory . . . 1840*, p. 477; Riley, "The Negro in Cincinnati, 1835–1850," p. 74; Cleveland *True-Democrat*, Feb. 22, 1848.

66. *Liberator*, Sept. 17, 24, 1841; Cincinnati *Enquirer*, Sept. 9, 1841; *Philanthropist*, Sept. 8, 1841.

67. Cincinnati *Gazette*, Sept. 6, 1841; Langston, *Virginia Plantation*, p. 64; Cincinnati *Chronicle*, Sept. 6, 1841, quoted in *Philanthropist*, Sept. 8, 1841; *Philanthropist*, Sept. 8, 1841; Cincinnati *Enquirer*, Sept. 9, 1841.

68. Langston, *Virginia Plantation*, pp. 64–65; see similar argument in *Philanthropist*, Sept. 8, 1841.

69. Langston, *Virginia Plantation*, pp. 65–66.

70. Cincinnati *Chronicle*, Sept. 6, 1841, quoted in *Philanthropist*, Sept. 8, 1841; *Philanthropist*, Sept. 8, 22, 1841; Cincinnati *Gazette*, Sept. 6, 1841.

71. Langston, *Virginia Plantation*, p. 67.

72. Leonard P. Curry, *The Free Black in Urban America, 1800–1850* (Chicago, 1981), p. 107; Langston, *Virginia Plantation*, p. 64. Casualty reports varied: 30 whites seriously wounded, Cincinnati *Gazette*, Sept. 6, 1841; 15–20, primarily whites, injured, 4 dead (2 white, 2 black), *Niles' National Register*, Sept. 11, 1841; J. Nicholson, a white man from Newport, Ky., dead, 2 unnamed black men dead or dying, Cincinnati *Enquirer*, Sept. 6, 1841.

73. Cincinnati *Enquirer*, Sept. 8, 10, 1841; Cincinnati *Gazette*, Sept. 7, 1841; *Philanthropist*, Sept. 22, 1841.

74. Cincinnati *Enquirer*, Sept. 10, 11, 14, 18, 21, 25, 1841, Jan. 24, 1842; Richards, *"Gentlemen of Property and Standing"*, p. 129; Joel Goldfarb, "The Life of Gamaliel Bailey, Prior to the Founding of the National Era . . ." Ph.D. diss., UCLA, 1958, chapter 16, cited in Richards, *"Gentlemen of Property and Standing"*, p. 128; Langston, *Virginia Plantation*, p. 66.

75. *Philanthropist*, Apr. 30, 1845; "Annual Report of the Ladies Education Society," *Philanthropist*, June 29, 1842; "A Colored Man" to Editor, *Philanthropist*, Dec. 28, 1842; William E. Walker to Hamilton Hill, Oct. 7, 1842, Oberlin College Library; Cincinnati *Chronicle*, n.d., quoted in *Philanthropist*, Nov. 10, 1841.

76. *Minutes of the National Convention of Colored Citizens . . . Buffalo, N.Y. . . . Aug., 1843* (New York, 1843), p. 18, reprinted in *Proceedings of the National Negro Conventions*, ed. Bell; William C. Nell to Editor, *Liberator*, Nov. 21, 1856; Langston, *Virginia Plantation*, pp. 66–67.

77. Langston, *Virginia Plantation*, pp. 69–71; Deed Record 40, Ross County Courthouse, Chillicothe, Ohio; San Francisco *Post*, Apr. 5, 1877, JML Scrapbook, I.

78. Langston, *Virginia Plantation*, p. 61; *Colored American*, Oct. 17, 1840; *Philanthropist*, July 14, 1840; *Anti-Slavery Bugle*, Aug. 10, 1850; Stowe, *Uncle Tom's Cabin*, pp. 319–21.

79. Langston, *Virginia Plantation*, p. 61; Population Census of 1840, Hamilton County, City of Cincinnati, Reel 398, NA; Frederick Douglass, "Character and Condition of Colored of Cincinnati," *North Star*, n.d., quoted in *Anti-Slavery Bugle*, Aug. 10, 1850.

80. Langston, *Virginia Plantation*, p. 61; Peter Clark to Caroline Langston, Dec. 11, 1897, Caroline W. Langston Papers, Fisk University Library. See "Reminiscences—Professor Peter H. Clark," at John Mercer Langston Memorial Meeting, St. Paul's Church, St. Louis, Feb. 6, 1898, newsclipping, n.d., John Mercer Langston Papers, Fisk University Library; Dovie King Clark, "Peter Humphries Clark," *The Negro History Bulletin* 5 (May 1942):176; Simmons, *Men of Mark*, p. 245.

81. Langston, *Virginia Plantation*, p. 72; *Report of the Proceedings of the Colored National Convention . . . Cleveland . . . Sept., 1848* (Rochester, 1848), p. 17, reprinted in *Proceedings of the National Negro Conventions*, ed. Bell; Cleveland *Leader*, Aug. 2, 1866; Simmons, *Men of Mark*, pp. 244–45.

82. Langston, *Virginia Plantation*, pp. 72, 61; *Report of the Second Anniversary of the Ohio Anti-Slavery Society*, p. 65; Barber, *Report of the Colored People of Ohio*, p. 13; Bremer, *Homes of the New World*, II, p. 157; Langston, *Freedom and Citizenship*, pp. 135–36.

83. Langston, *Virginia Plantation*, p. 60; Ohio Anti-Slavery Convention, *Report on the Condition of the People of Color of Ohio*, p. 5; W. D. Howells, *A Boy's Town* (New York, 1890), pp. 124–25.

84. Langston, *Virginia Plantation*, pp. 66, 181; Howard Jones, *Mutiny on the Amistad* (New York, 1987), passim; Brown, *The Rising Son*, pp. 325–28; Joseph Sturge, *A Visit to the United States in 1841* (London, 1842; repr. New York, A. M. Kelley Reprint, 1969), p. 50, appendix E, xxxi–li; *Weld-Grimke Letters*, II, p. 811; *Philanthropist*, Nov. 18, Dec. 9, 1840, Nov. 22, 1843. One of the Amistad captives, Mar-gru [Sarah Kinson] attended Oberlin while Langston was a student there.

85. *Philanthropist*, Nov. 22, 1843; Langston, *Virginia Plantation*, pp. 355, 157.

86. Martineau, *Retrospect of Western Travel*, II, pp. 52–53; *Philanthropist*, Dec. 9, 1836, Jan. 26, 1844; Langston, *Virginia Plantation*, p. 60.

87. Of the major Cincinnati black leaders of the period, least is known of Perkins. The 1840 census lists him and his wife in the 10–24 category. A student at Hiram Gilmore's High School in the mid-forties, he attended the 1844 state convention and delivered the 1849 First of August oration in Cincinnati. Shotwell, *A History of the Schools of Cincinnati*, pp. 454–55; Population Census of 1840, Hamilton County, City of Cincinnati, Reel 398, NA; *Palladium of Liberty*, Sept. 25, 1844; Perkins, *Oration*.

88. *Anti-Slavery Bugle*, Aug. 24, 1850.

89. Andrew J. Gordon, a native Virginian listed, along with his wife, in the 10–24 age column in the 1840 census, took a leading role in black affairs on a local, state and national level for more than two decades. In 1843, having served as secretary of a meeting in New York to determine whether to have a national convention, he served as a delegate from Cincinnati to the convention held in Buffalo, N.Y., in August. President of the 1853 Ohio state convention at Columbus, Gordon was a barber in Cleveland during the fifties, where he served as a member of the "Committee of 9," the city's black underground railroad directors. Back in Cincinnati by the fall of 1859, he advised a black meeting against adopting a strong resolution in favor of John Brown, reminding those present of the damage done the community by the 1841 riot. In June 1860 he was elected a trustee of the Colored Public Schools for the Western District of Cincinnati. Shaffer, *Cincinnati Directory . . . 1840*, p. 471; Population Census of 1840, Hamilton County, City of Cincinnati, Reel 398, NA; *National Convention . . . 1843*, p. 3, reprinted in *Proceedings of the National Negro Conventions*, ed. Bell; *Frederick Douglass' Paper*, July 6, 1854; *Official Proceedings of the Ohio State Convention of Colored Freemen . . . Columbus . . . Jan., 1853* (Cleveland, 1853); Cincinnati *Enquirer*, Nov. 16, 1859; Cincinnati *Gazette*, June 26, 1860.

90. *Address and Reply on the Presentation of a Testimonial to S. P. Chase*, p. 17 and passim. On Chase's serious Commitment to black America, see Frederick J. Blue, *Salmon P. Chase: A Life in Politics* (Kent, Ohio, 1987).

91. Langston, *Virginia Plantation*, p. 67; Gaines's comment, *Eighth Annual Report . . . Colored Public Schools, Cincinnati*, p. 12; John Quincy Adams, *Memoirs of John Quincy Adams* (Philadelphia, 1886), pp. 428–29; *Philanthropist*, Mar. 15, Nov. 22, 1843, Oct. 14, 1846; John Mercer Langston, "The Langstons," Cleveland *Gazette*, Dec. 24, 1892.

92. *Philanthropist*, Oct. 2, 1843; Langston, *Virginia Plantation*, pp. 73, 67.

CHAPTER 4

Morality and Politics

1843–49

O N the first Sunday of March 1844, the fourteen-year-old boy, in a state of high excitement edged with fatigue, stared curiously through the window of Oberlin's "good temperance hotel." He had come to enter the preparatory department of Oberlin Collegiate Institute. The final leg of his three-day journey from Chillicothe, forty-eight miles of northern Ohio's notorious muck and mire, had been passable only by rented wagon and team and had taken from five o'clock in the morning until well after midnight. Thus it was in the cool morning light of the Sabbath, when the evangelical village, which professed not to hold with display of any sort, virtually paraded both principles and personalities, that John Mercer Langston got his first look at the center that, for him, would hold. For the next quarter of a century, with brief exceptions, he would be connected with Oberlin as a student and professional man; his whole life he would think of himself as one "educated . . . at Oberlin College, Ohio, soundly in politics, as well as morality."[1]

The Langston family had already made its mark at the school that figured so importantly in nineteenth-century black education, both through the contributions of the relatively few Negroes trained there and the larger inspiration it offered to blacks across the North. Founded in 1833 to save and transform the Godless West primarily through the training of teachers and ministers, the tiny colony and institute started with two unorthodox educational schemes: the innovative manual labor plan designed to allow impecunious students to pay their way while strengthening their bodies through physical labor, and the hitherto untried coeducation of the sexes. When economic necessity quickly forced Oberlin's founders to seek assistance, the rebellious seminarians from Lane in Cincinnati struck a bargain. They agreed to study theology at Oberlin, thus bringing in funds from their eastern abolitionist supporters as well as attracting several prestigious faculty members, on the condition of equal admittance of black students. Although an occasional Negro had won acceptance to colleges previously, only Oneida Institute had practiced open admission. The presence of female students made the experiment even more controversial. Nevertheless, over predictions of Oberlin's destruction in the "shipwreck of Amalgamation," the trustees by a single vote approved an equal admissions policy on February 10, 1835. The consequent enrollment of many of the "Rebels," the appointment of abolitionist faculty members, and a notable three-week antislavery lecture series by Theodore Dwight Weld in November,[2] set Oberlin firmly in an abolitionist mold.[3] By January 1836, trustee John Keep, who had cast the deciding vote, would assure New York philanthropist Gerrit Smith that Oberlin was the "only institution where the subject of Slavery is allowed an untrammeled treatment & where *prejudice* is so far conquered that colored people are admitted, to the full enjoyment of all & the same privileges with others."

Among the students were "two, from Virginia of color," Keep further noted, "& they are as well received & treated as others."[4] Gideon and Charles Langston, in registering for the 1835 fall semester in the preparatory school, had become the first Negroes enrolled at Oberlin. The brothers boarded with the college, probably dining at the public boarding house like other students, doling out pennies for washing and handkerchief mending. Each purchased a "Polyglott Bible." With newly acquired axes, they chopped wood for warmth and hacked at stumps still jutting thickly on the village green. Gideon earned a few cents by working for a carpenter, probably on the hall financed by Arthur Tappan's donation or the two other college buildings under construction. On March 6, 1836 both were baptized and received into membership of the Oberlin church.[5] During the 1836 summer session, the brothers were enrolled in the Oberlin branch school that, because the onslaught of students had overstrained meager facilities, was set up at Sheffield. The forty pupils included the third Negro to enroll, James Bradley, who had studied at Lane. While Gideon settled in Cincinnati, Charles, according to sketchy records, reenrolled in the preparatory department in 1841 and studied until the spring of 1843.[6]

The Langston brothers did not prove to be harbingers of "hundreds of negroes . . . flooding the school," as some colonists had feared. Of the approximately 8,800 students at Oberlin before the Civil War, scarcely 3 percent were Negroes. The majority of black students, like the majority of white, were enrolled in the preparatory and female departments. One (incomplete) listing indicates that during the entire pre-war period about two of every three black students at Oberlin studied only one year, and that in the preparatory department. Of the one hundred blacks enrolled in the college from 1840 through 1865, thirty-two (seventeen men, fifteen women) earned degrees.[7]

By 1844, when John Mercer took up his studies, only an estimated twenty-eight black male and thirteen black female students had been enrolled, but in that year—reflecting a somewhat more inviting anti-slavery atmosphere—the figure shot up dramatically, with some twenty-one young men and one young woman listed.[8] By that date only four black students had been admitted to the college: George Boyer Vashon of Pittsburgh, scheduled to become Oberlin's first black graduate in August 1844; William Cuthbert Whitehorne of Jamaica, a missionary convert in the class of 1845;[9] Virginia fugitive slave William P. Newman, the Baptist minister who had left the college after completing the sophomore year in 1843;[10] and William Howard Day, a native of New York City and member of the class of 1847.

While white Oberlin students generally came from farms, primarily in Ohio, New York, and New England, and possessed slender purses, slight preparation, and "pious intentions," black students' backgrounds were multifarious, ranging from Africa to southern slavery to northern cities; their circumstances likely to be even more straitened; their training less; their motivations, although equally pious, transmuted to service for the race.[11]

"I am a poor boy and would like to go to school,"[12] as one Negro wrote, was perhaps the most common personal revelation, black or white, in the letter of application. Probably it was the rare black student who did not work while in residence. "I propose to sell goods in Oberlin and pursue my studies," announced Edward J. Roye, the future president of Liberia, a student in 1846–47.[13] Asking for the position of "sweeping" Oberlin Hall, Joseph T. Cook, enrolled in 1855, confessed he could "boast no friends with bloated purses ready to support me in my arduous undertaking but depend upon my own exertions for carrying me through the labyrinths which usually hedge up a students pathway."[14] For responsible abolitionist fathers like John B. Vashon, a barber and pioneer racial activist, and John C. Peck, a clothing dealer, both of Pittsburgh, determined their sons and daughters have opportunities denied themselves, an Oberlin education was purchased at "considerable sacrifice." As the devout Christian Peck explained, "Money is so very hard to get that it will require the strictest Economy to enable me to give [his son David] an Education." David J. Peck would be the first black American to earn a medical degree from a reputable institution.[15]

Regarding educational background, few entering black students were as advanced as eighteen-year-old William Howard Day. Writing from Northampton, Massachusetts, where he had become an accomplished printer, Day could also boast of a reasonably good training in Latin, Greek, and the English studies "such as are generally taught in schools." Day's mother and later his white guardian had seen to his education in both private and public schools.[16] "His attainments are very limited," the Rev. Theodore S. Wright's summation of one of his youthful flock at black First Presbyterian church in New York City, and applicant Martin R. Delany's "I can't be expected to equal those who have been under the strict criticism of good Teachers,"[17] were the more common laments. (Pittsburgh activist Delany, who later studied medicine briefly at Harvard, did not attend Oberlin.) St. Louis cooper John B. Meachum wrote of his two sons, whose "moral and spiritual" care he was about to surrender to Oberlin, "It is only 5 years since I bought them from slavery, at which time they did not know their Alphabet. Besides, the means of Instruction in St. Louis have always been very circumscribed and interrupted for colored people. Sometimes a teacher would continue a few months, and then away again for years, mostly on account of the opposition of wicked and unfeeling men. . . ."[18]

Sabram Cox, an assistant to Elijah P. Lovejoy at the time of the white abolitionist editor's death at the hands of a mob, was recommended to Oberlin as a "steady, industrious seriously inclined young man," a characterization that aptly identified the salient traits of most Oberlin students, whatever their color.[19] "Of hopeful piety and respectable talents" was the way Daniel A. Payne, minister of the A.M.E. Israel Bethel in Washington and future bishop, portrayed the young blacks he desired to send to the school.[20]

Like most white students, black applicants sought higher education as the means to "future usefulness," principally as preachers and teachers. Most blacks had already adopted the idea, which Oberlin attempted to reinforce, that their favored position entailed an obligation to devote their talents to bringing up the race. In recommending a young friend, Austin Steward, the author of a celebrated ex-slave autobiography, argued the case for the responsibility of the intellectually advantaged Negro: "We want him and other Black men to be well edicated with speashall rafferent to labouring amounge our destitute people." An early desire to teach other Negroes provided the educational motivation for Fanny M. Jackson, who took an A.B. degree in 1865 and afterward was teacher and principal for many years at the Institute for Colored Youth in Philadelphia. Black student Davis Day speculated that more "colored youths" did not attend Oberlin because they were "not aware of the privileges" or thought "they could do no good if they should obtain an education." On the contrary, Day urged male and female to "come one and all," embrace Christianity, "and then commence the work of preparing our minds for usefulness, that we may soon be able to go out into the world, spreading light and truth all around us."[21]

Despite their paucity of prior education and finances, black students as a whole apparently performed in the classroom nearly as well as white. In 1862, E. H. Fairchild, principal of the preparatory department and a one-time teacher of black students in Cincinnati, noted that some Negroes had been "among our most successful students, and some have evinced their manhood by a dullness hardly surpassed by any of our white students." Pointing out that blacks had graduated with honor from all departments, he stated, "their reports will show that their average is not materially below that of whites."[22]

Like white students, Negroes gained early experience in "usefulness" by winter teaching jobs. Oberlin's vacation was purposely extended from November to March, to allow students to earn expense money and disseminate knowledge and a few radical notions.[23] Black-supported schools, as well as the white common schools, were beneficiaries.

In 1843–44 John Mercer, returned from Cincinnati, was a pupil at the Chillicothe black school, where Oberlin student Charles Langston had taught during the 1841–42 session.[24] The school during John's enrollment had the uncommon luck of securing the services of two of the Oberlin College students described above, Vashon and Whitehorne. With only four or perhaps five black Americans having received bachelor's degrees to that point,[25] the two students were, in Langston's words, "forerunners . . . for a whole race in the ways of highest scholarship." Highly regarded in Oberlin as orators as well as scholars, each would be elected valedictory speaker by his respective graduating class. With "their peculiarly handsome endowments of manner and address," the young men made a strong impression in the Chillicothe black community and on young Langston.[26]

John saw in Vashon, in particular, much to emulate. As a boy, George, like John Mercer, had associated with a reform-minded black aristocracy. His father, John Vashon, a member of the First Board of Managers of the American Anti-Slavery Society and financial supporter of abolitionist editor William Lloyd Garrison, had helped organize a Pittsburgh education society designed to prove "that the intellectual capacity of the black man is equal to that of the white." In its school, taught by black nationalist Lewis Woodson, formerly of Chillicothe, George developed an interest in poetry. His hero-worship of Lord Byron, manifested in insistence on pronouncing every syllable of the poet's full name, brought him teasing from his older schoolmate Delany. Entering Oberlin College in 1841 as a sixteen-year-old freshman, George impressed Professor James A. Thome as "one of the best minds in the class." He pursued his interest in poetry with a rendition of an original poem that a female student deemed *"exquisitely grand"* for his literary society and, later, with publication of "Vincent Ogé," an epic on the 1790–91 Haitian uprising. " 'Freedom!' is the rally-cry," went a couplet, "That calls to deeds of daring."[27]

Involved in abolitionism since boyhood, Vashon's "burning eloquence" at the 1843 First of August celebration in Oberlin would be recalled years later. The ardent nature of his oratory was apparent in an address he would deliver just after John Mercer's arrival in Oberlin. At his turn in the college's monthly rhetorical exercises, Vashon defended the "true reformer" against ridicule as "fanatic and enthusiast": "He feels that he advocates the cause of truth—he knows that truth must eventually triumph, and so far as he is concerned, it matters little whether his efforts bring about the consummation, or his life-blood flows as the prelude of that triumph."[28] For John Mercer Langston, Vashon would be successively academic and career model and national reform colleague.

It was the need to name a guardian that had brought John back to Chillicothe. At the boy's request, the Ross County Probate Court had appointed William Langston on April 20, 1843. Still unmarried, William boarded John with the well-fixed barber Harvey Hawes, a property owner who had secured the $1,200 guardianship bond. A state black convention delegate in 1839, Hawes had served as treasurer of the statewide black School Fund Society and as one of the directors of the local chapter. Ex-Virginians and admirers of aristocratic bloodlines, the elderly Hawes and his wife coddled John as a "little Virginia gentleman."[29]

Enrolled in November 1843 at the "large and substantial" schoolhouse erected two years earlier with the help of both Hawes and Charles Langston, John Mercer quickly discovered two ambitions. He wished to excel among classmates who, reflecting black Chillicothe's long and continuing emphasis on education and tutelage by white and black Oberlin teachers, were, as Charles had reported, "generally interested in their studies." That achieved, and with the example of

Vashon, Whitehorne, and his brothers before him, he aspired to attend Oberlin. But William Langston, himself illiterate—his challenge to Gooch had been signed with an "X"—and prospering modestly as a carpenter, intended to set John to learning a trade. It required the concerted efforts of Vashon, Charles, and Gideon Langston, but at length William agreed to a single year of preparatory school. The boy accompanied Vashon on his return to Oberlin.[30]

John Mercer's first sight of the radical village was both typical and unforgettable. Raw and unprepossessing, still girt round with thick forest, Oberlin was a secluded settlement of fewer than two thousand persons. About one hundred fifty two-story frame houses, most painted white, three dry goods stores, and a book store were clustered around the green, a twelve-acre plot boasting seven commodious college buildings. To one side stood the newly constructed brick meeting house, the largest church in Ohio. On that Sunday morning, the muddy streets and boardwalk appeared to John to contain the entire populace. "By nine o'clock everyone seemed to be upon the streets, pressing on, with earnest purpose depicted in his face, looking neither to the right nor left, in the effort which he was making to get either to the early prayer-meeting or the Sabbath school." But when the chapel bells tolled at half-past ten, the earlier crowd "seemed small now, as compared with the vast swelling company of students and people pressing to the great church, the only one in the place." In a community and college whose "prominent characteristic . . . was piety," according to Oberlin's historian,[31] John Mercer had awakened to a sort of walking race toward a goal that most, unhesitatingly, would have identified with the Millennium.

Seated beside Vashon in the church's circular gallery where students were placed, John eyed the vast auditorium, the raised pulpit, and behind it the large organ and choir of more than a hundred singers. Black men and women sat, not in "negro pews" or special gallery, but intermingled with whites, often in the choir itself—a sight, a visitor remarked, that "strikes a stranger forcibly." Former Lane professor John Morgan, who would become John's adviser and friend, feelingly read the Sermon on the Mount. The boy, whose mind went chasing back to his own recitations of the scripture for Virginia Gooch, observed that cheeks were moist with tears. To him the congregation appeared transfixed when Charles Grandison Finney began to speak.[32]

The most renowned revivalist of the age, Finney had converted thousands in "burned over" western New York state before agreeing to resign from the Broadway Tabernacle in New York City to become professor of theology at Oberlin in 1835. Although conservative churchmen abhorred both his perfectionist doctrine and unconventional revival methods, it was a measure of Finney's success that such influential reformers as Weld were his converts, "Finney men." What Langston would call the "Oberlin movement,"[33] recognizing a distinctive outer-directed reform philosophy, rested on the perfectionism propounded by Finney, which held out as a practical possibility to everyone the achievement of salvation through the exercise of one's own free will. The convert must concentrate, not on the after-life, but *"at being useful in the highest degree possible."* [34] Further, because Oberlin defined racial prejudice and slavery as evils and predicated personal holiness on active participation in reform, perfectionism made for a powerful antislavery impulse. "To establish universal liberty by the abolition of every form of sin" was a stated goal of the institution. Finney urged students to be "anti-devil all over!"[35]

"A more eloquent pulpit orator never lived," in Langston's judgment. Typically, the six-foot-two inch evangelist with penetrating blue eyes under beetling brows might groan for the soul's salvation at one moment and pray for a Liberty party victory the next, while piling up evidence like the lawyer he had been before receiving his "retainer from the Lord Jesus Christ." On that first Sunday, although Finney preached for ninety minutes in the morning, broke for forty-five, and took up his text again until he could speak no longer, it appeared to John that the congregation hung on his words "as if for life itself." The boy, who would study Finney's platform techniques as well as his doctrines, found him a "vanquishing son of eloquence." Physically and emotionally exhausted at sermon's end, like the rest of the congregation, the novice "moved away in silence." "Everything which President Finney says seems so very clear and so well adapted to each one," black student Caroline V. Still would confide in 1864. Young Langston "had never had his soul moved" by such preaching.[36]

On Monday, in search of lodging, Vashon took the boy to the home of Professor George Whipple. Like some of his penurious colleagues and townsmen, Whipple accepted student boarders. "Even the children in our families are neglected," a mother complained ruefully, "so we may pray and care for the children of others who are sent here to be educated." The going rate was modest: "Board one dollar a week payable monthly in advance, room rent 6 ct. a week, fuel about 50 cents a month." Explained the landlord of African student Sarah Kinson (Mar-gru), one of the *Amistad* captives, the terms were "as low as can be and live." Twenty-nine blacks, more than half of them students, were living in eighteen white households at the time of the 1850 census; the landlords included Asa Mahan, college president, Professor Henry Cowles, editor of the Oberlin *Evangelist*, and instructor James H. Fairchild, future Oberlin president.[37]

Whipple and his wife received John cordially. A Lane Rebel who had taught black Cincinnatians and been among the most adamant in insisting that Oberlin admit blacks, Whipple had been professor of mathematics and natural philosophy since 1838, during which time he had helped to rescue a fugitive slave from would-be captors. Mrs. Whipple, too, took an interest in black students, seeking out boarding places for them.[38] John Mercer was granted an upstairs room in the Whipple home, introduced to their daughter who, he learned, would be his classmate, and ushered into the dining room.

At table with the family and various boarders, including a young black woman, John found himself seated between his handsome, well-born hostess and Miss Jane Trew, a young teacher. In the racially and sexually integrated room, trying to adjust to the New England table and parry the fervent questions of the ladies, the boy watched one course after another disappear with dismaying promptness. He was left "greatly embarrassed" and hungry,[39] free to reflect that although he could hardly complain about Oberlin hospitality, it might well starve him.

"Here I discovered at once that I breathed a new atmosphere," he would marvel thirty years later. "Though poor, and a colored boy, I found no distinction made against me in your hotel, in your institution of learning, in your family circle." Still, it is unreasonable to expect that the return passage from a black environment to an at once alien and disturbingly familiar world could be made without emotional strain. Admonished by Vashon to be "obedient, docile and agreeable," the boy, surely struggling to restrain his anxieties, exerted himself to be inoffensive. At least once he fled into the traditional black role of servant. One of Oberlin's "many pleasant stories" about him involved a party given by the Whipples and attended by several distinguished guests. Despite repeated urgings to sit with the company, John Mercer insisted upon waiting on tables. Langston, who in manhood would be criticized for "vanity" and called "as proud as Lucifer," in his Oberlin boyhood created an impression of "youthful modesty and timidity."[40]

Gradually, Langston would claim, he came to feel "at ease" among these cultured Christian reformers. Professor Whipple, who left Oberlin in 1847 to become the first secretary of the American Missionary Association, the Oberlin-influenced interdenominational humanitarian agency headquartered in New York City, a post he would hold for thirty years, would prove a "fatherly and judicious counsellor and friend." Although they would differ on religious doctrine, Langston grew to "love and respect" him. In 1867, when Whipple and his one-time boarder shared the platform at a meeting of teachers of colored schools in Washington, D.C., Langston would take advantage of the occasion to express "the liveliest gratitude to his old teacher."[41]

On that first Monday Vashon also saw to his young friend's registration. Entrance to the "People's College," as friendly newspapers called it, or "the celebrated Abolition School," the Cincinnati *Enquirer*'s term of opprobrium, was uncomplicated and cheap. The preparatory department required a familiarity with the three Rs, testimonials of good character, and a $15 a year tuition fee. Excluding clothing and books, total expenses for a year came to about $70, a bargain of such proportions that, despite Oberlin's cranky practices, the enrollment had averaged a healthy 528 annually since 1840. There were two possible courses of study: the less demanding English branch terminating with the preparatory years, or the classical, college preparatory branch. Disregarding William Langston's strictures, Vashon, probably with his friend Charles's concurrence, entered John in the classical branch.[42]

The boy took up his studies in a class of nearly two hundred, one-fourth of whom were female. In dingy classrooms, where students sat at backless benches and wrote at tables, he was initiated to classical studies through Greek and Latin grammars and readers and Cicero's orations. English grammar and oral and written expression, geography, a comprehensive arithmetic running from simple numeration to cube roots and progressions, and a study of the Four Gospels composed basic course work, rounded out by weekly compositions, discussions, and declamations. Counting the hours that John Mercer, like other students, was expected to devote to manual labor, it made for a full schedule, the whole calculated to produce "a strong mind in a sound body, connected with a permanent, vigorous piety."[43]

Political instruction grounded in abolitionist and republican values began early for the preparatory students. John Mercer and the other "preps" celebrated the Fourth of July with an address from tutor Nelson Hodge, his normally witty mien exchanged for sobriety on this occasion. Delineating the North—"domain of liberty," prosperity, enterprise, intelligence, and virtue—from the South—the "realm of slavery," poverty, decay, ignorance, and vice—Hodge bade his pupils consider their own destiny in deciding the slavery question, charging them to be true to themselves, the interests of man, the principles of the Declaration of Independence, and their God.[44] Abolitionist discourse, whether by faculty, students, or visiting speakers, would be an integral part of John Mercer's Oberlin curriculum.

John, like other black students, found his instructors empathetic
and encouraging. Officially, Oberlin's "practical abolitionism" was pre-
mised on equal, not compensatory treatment. Noting that applicants with insufficient preparation—necessarily more black than
white—could not be admitted to Oberlin, J. H. Fairchild asserted that
"no adaptation of the course of study to the special needs of colored
pupils was ever made." Even though the faculty doubtless attempted
to maintain impartiality, the emotional investment of the teachers
was evident in President Mahan's 1842 declaration that the black
students' general conduct and "considerable improvement" in scholarship were "a source of pleasure to the officers." In similar vein, Professor Thome delightedly informed Weld in 1841 about "some fine
young colored men and girls (young ladies) here now; some who with
a thorough education will become noble minds."[45] Sympathy toward
black students was combined with an unusually democratic approach
to the student-teacher relationship. Not "distant coolness," but
"kindness and friendship . . . and in many instances the most familiar
sociability," was observed by black abolitionist Delany on an 1848 visit—
"*the students love the Professors*." The often-critical Delany noted a commensurate boost in student self-confidence: "instead of confused
awkwardness, as is usually the case among students," the recitations were "ready and cheerful, full of life, with kind and smiling
professors and tutors." Consequently, black students generally remarked, as did student John M. Brown, the future A.M.E. bishop, in
1844, that nowhere else could a Negro get an education "as cheap
as he can at Oberlin, and at the same time be respected as a man."
John Mercer would join with Fanny Jackson in asserting that the faculty
and instructors, without exception, "regard a colored man as a *man*,
and do not consider that they are conferring a favor upon him by so
doing."[46]

Yet, among the ambiguities in Oberlin's social contract that John
Mercer, even as a preparatory student, consciously or unconsciously,
may have found troubling was the lack of black teachers, either on the
regular faculty or among the college students acting as instructors in
the preparatory department. The faculty and trustees were aware of
the problem. As early as 1841, Professor Thome was inspired by young
George Vashon's scholarly bent to speculate favorably on the possibility
of a Negro faculty member. In 1852, a "portion of the community,"
which may well have included Langston, petitioned the trustees asking
appointment of "a colored Professor." A "smaller number of the community" presented a counter-petition. "Why should Oberlin not set
such an example?" demanded the *Voice of the Fugitive*, the black Canadian newspaper. Because Oberlin's financial support derived primarily

from sympathizers with the black educational experiment, the question was the more pertinent. But the trustees first postponed a decision and then, in August 1853, resolved that "intrinsic merit irrespective of color" governed the choice of faculty. Despite the availability of its own black graduates to a faculty whose new appointments went all but exclusively to alumni, apparent fear of critical reaction in the rapidly shifting circumstances of the prewar period, perhaps combined with the faculty's own unresolved anxieties on race, tended to produce paralysis. Not until 1864, "against the old custom of giving classes only to white students," did the faculty appoint a Negro college student, Fanny Jackson, to teach preparatory pupils. She considered this relatively modest step morally courageous. Despite her apparent success, Langston's plea in 1870 to "not let the fact of color be a reason for not employing . . . a black man . . . in every way fitted for a teacher in any department" would go unheeded. No Negro would be appointed to the Oberlin faculty until 1948.[47]

In class and out, in white-dominated abolitionist Oberlin John Mercer's feeling of racial responsibility was accentuated. His own emotions surely approximated the tension vividly described by Fanny Jackson: "I never rose to recite in my classes at Oberlin but I felt that I had the honor of the whole African race upon my shoulders. I felt that, should I fail, it would be ascribed to the fact that I was colored." Nor was the imperative of being "representative of the race," which for Langston would be a life-long preoccupation, wholly self-imposed. It stemmed as well from white Oberlin's tendency to view its "intelligent, handsome" black students, improving themselves intellectually, culturally, and morally, as, in Langston's words, "another and additional evidence of the sure amelioration and progress of the race whose blood and features marked their nationality."[48] Moreover, like the fugitive slave on the abolitionist platform, the black student was perceived as an agent for the antislavery conversion of white students.

For teachers seeking the superior black student as evidence for racial equality, John was certain to stand out. Marked as the youngest Langston brother and Vashon's protege, the light-skinned, slightly freckled boy with large, earnest eyes was further set apart by his comparative youth, emphasized by a slight, wiry frame, among white and black classmates likely to be far more mature. Mannerly and shy, his deportment doubtless hinted at his contrasting cultural backgrounds. His fine diction, remarked upon by a white student of the following decade, probably was in evidence even then. His earlier schooling was uneven but not inferior.[49] In a system emphasizing recitation, the boy possessed the advantage of an exceptionally fine memory; moreover, he had a propensity for clear and logical thought.

Despite his intellectual advantages, however, John would speak of having floundered "in great despair, thinking he never could learn." Although a part of him responded positively to his instructors' high expectations, perhaps, at the same time the exigencies of representing the race may have exacerbated the gifted adolescent's common fear of failure. It was Finney, he said, who offered him a lifeline, with the Emersonian advice: "John, the secret of success is self-reliance."[50] However undefined, to the boy, who was at least half-realizing it for himself, the counsel offered by the famous man was meaningful.

The name he affixed to his compositions was J. Mercer Langston. Not an unusual practice at Oberlin, where a black classmate was (James) "Monroe" Jones and a future general and Ohio governor, wearing a white paper hat while scraping plates in the dining hall, was (Jacob) "Dolson" Cox, the name inversion nevertheless may have signaled a psychological changing of the guard. The question of name was interconnected with the self he was told to rely upon, particularly the twice-orphaned black child. Comparing himself to the *Uncle Tom's Cabin* character, Langston would say: "Like Topsy I growed. God was my father and my mother. I was called John Gooch, or John, anything else, according to where I was living."[51] By emphasizing "Mercer," with its connotations of respectability and standing, over the common "John," the very designation of the average man, the boy may have been attempting to halt the arbitrary handling of his identity and mask painful past roles. Like former slaves who renamed themselves in freedom, he may have perceived the change as an assertion of his autonomy. The adolescent's search for individuality and preoccupation with his future found expression in the dignified polysyllables. In adult life, he would be referred to by various combinations of surname and initial, but to school friends he was and remained Mercer.

"With every influence upon him calculated to develop and sustain his scholarly qualities and character," the boy pursued his studies with "assiduity and vigor." His growing resolution to continue beyond the preparatory year was reinforced at the August 1844 commencement, when he saw George Boyer Vashon become Oberlin's first black graduate. Vashon's valedictory oration, "Liberty of Mind," contended that "genius, talent, and learning are not withheld by our Common Father, from those whom the prejudice against color would doom to unthinking degradation." John Mercer went home to Chillicothe in November, his ambition encouraged by Professor Whipple, who entrusted him with a letter to his guardian recommending his return for a full collegiate course.[52] His hopes were fixed on attaining his place in the forming procession of black Oberlin graduates.

John Mercer Langston

Asa Mahan

Charles Grandison Finney

John Morgan

"The old worthy matchless men" Langston called his professors. Mahan, Finney, and Fairchild served successively as presidents of Oberlin. For Langston, Mahan, Finney, and Morgan were valued advisers as well as inspirational teachers; Fairchild (following page) was a fellow town leader; Monroe, as a member of the Ohio legislature, and Peck, as editor of the Oberlin newspaper, were collaborators in antislavery politics. (Oberlin College Archives)

James H. Fairchild

Henry E. Peck

James Monroe

Norton S. Townshend

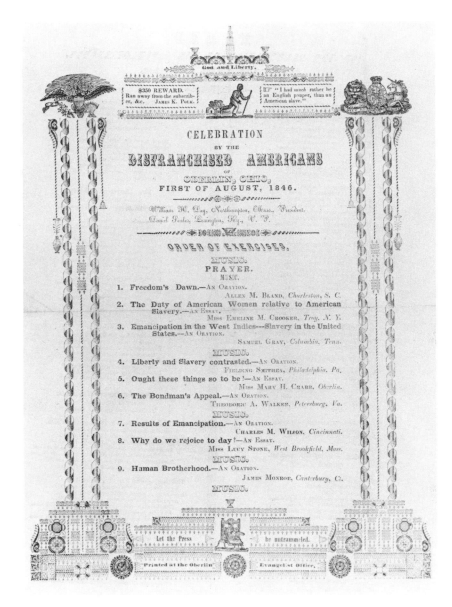

Program of the 1846 Oberlin celebration of the First of August, commemorating the emancipation of slaves in the British West Indies, illustrates the cooperative relationship developed between black activists, white feminists, and white abolitionists. Two black students, William Howard Day and Daniel Seales, were in charge. In addition to other black male students, the program included several white female students, among them Lucy Stone making her first public address. The only white male speaker was the future antislavery politician James Monroe. (Oberlin College Archives)

LUCY STONE
(From a photograph in the
Oberlin College Library)

ANTOINETTE BROWN
(From *Autographs for Freedom*
[Auburn—1854])

Lucy Stone, abolitionist and feminist leader, was eleven years older than Langston but only two classes ahead and helped him with his studies. Antoinette
Brown, ordained minister and women's rights advocate, took theology classes
with Langston as an auditor because women were barred from regular admission. (Oberlin College Archives)

John had been with his brother Charles only a short time when several black farmers from Hicks Settlement, eight miles from Chillicothe, came to call. Designated to act as the school committee by black families in the rural area, the delegation requested the elder Langston's assistance in finding a teacher, but Charles could recommend no one. As the last resort, the farmers asked Charles to let his brother take the job. Because the boy was obviously too small to apply the rod, the committee guaranteed the good behavior of the scholars. Besides this not inconsiderable inducement in a period when a country schoolteacher might be brained by a poker and an abolitionist white teacher complained of a "rude company" of black pupils,[53] the farmers offered meager pay and uncertain accommodations.

Only a few weeks before his fifteenth birthday, the smallest boy in the schoolroom but one, John Mercer became a teacher. After ringing his morning bell, he daily supervised recitations and taught the rudiments of geography and the three Rs. Once he had exchanged the initial boarding round with his pupils' families for permanent lodging with a black farmer who desired private tutoring in reading and Bible lessons for himself and his small son, John rode five miles on horseback to and from the school each day. After two months, virtually the entire settlement converged on the church building that had sheltered the school for the closing ceremonies that John, himself but a year removed from eager participation in such occasions, directed with a flourish. The shyness he experienced in Oberlin apparently did not hinder the teacher. He felt he had done well. Years later Samuel Cox, young Langston's only pupil at the Hicks school smaller than he, by then principal of Chillicothe's black schools, would offer confirmation in fond recollections of his "first and most beloved teacher."[54]

John's salary had been paid monthly in the coins collected from his pupils' families. It was indicative of the settlement's poverty that no coin was larger than a quarter. Carefully wrapping the entire sum in newspaper and his best pocket handkerchief, the boy balanced the weighty bundle in front of him as he rode the horse back to Chillicothe.

At home, John Mercer showed off in "pride with a little sense of self-sufficiency." When black Oberlin student Samuel B. Devore, Vashon's successor at the Chillicothe school, asked Charles to substitute teach for two weeks, the latter took the occasion to apply a brotherly squelch. John was the teacher of the family, he teased, "quite bold enough and self-reliant to attempt almost anything." Devore offered the job, and, despite misgivings about his reception by his former classmates, John took it. He managed to get by with only one thrashing, which he administered to a mischievous and, not entirely coincidentally, very small boy. According to one biographical sketch, young Langston also delivered his first public address at this time, putting forth black claims to the common schools.[55]

Teaching, Langston would reflect, was calculated to promote the Oberlin students' "desire and determination to make the most of themselves as scholars and useful members of society." For John and other black students, this periodic descent from the ivory tower tended to counter potential disaffection from the race. The young black intellectual learned to contend with, if not fully resolve, the complexities of class and cultural barriers between himself and his people. As a young black woman from Oberlin confided, her pupils at first "expected we should feel very important, above them," until she convinced them that a superior education "did not make us proud." Richer in experience and self-confidence, John was also gratified by his earnings. The recompense, material and moral, was sufficient to persuade him to devote subsequent vacations to similar work.[56]

Charles compensated John for his earlier teasing when the argument with William Langston revived over the boy's return to Oberlin. Still determined to apprentice John, the carpenter demanded indignantly what Vashon and Whitehorne would be able to do with their college degrees. Certainly, his skepticism was not misplaced. In later years, John Mercer Langston would tell of a white Chillicothe mob that chased a black man to the ground and killed him. Like Mark Twain's fictional "white-shirted nigger," the mere sight of whom enraged Pap Finn, the victim wore a white shirt; this badge of respectability had been his death warrant. Whether this incident had occurred or lay in wait, William's common sense informed him that white society would willingly surrender neither profession nor place to the educated Negro. "Time will take care of the boy's interests!" Charles responded. "Let us do our duty." Finally, it was agreed the youth could return for the full college course, undertaking to complete preparatory work in time to enter the freshman class in the fall of 1845.[57]

Nevertheless, an incident on John's return journey wounded him so deeply that he may well have been tempted to share William's cynicism. The first evening stopover of his stagecoach was at Columbus. Naively, the boy followed the other passengers toward the Neil House, a three-hundred-room stage hostelry famed for comfort and courtesy. Abruptly, a white man blocked John's way. "We don't accommodate niggers," he said. "Just step down the alley and you will find a nigger boarding house."[58]

Furiously embarrassed, his new self-esteem in tatters, the boy stood hesitantly beside his trunk in the darkening rain. A passing black man elicited the tale, shouldered his trunk, and led him to shelter. His hosts on that bitter night were "a man and his family, colored persons, whom he learned subsequently to respect and honor." In all likelihood, the man was the multifaceted David Jenkins, whose advertisement in the newspaper he edited, the lately defunct *Palladium of Liberty*, had offered lodging for young men "by the week, day, or month on reasonable terms," and who would put Langston up frequently during subsequent years of co-involvement in reform. A major figure in the black civil rights drive in Ohio over three decades, the steady Jenkins was well qualified to comfort the "heart-broken" boy in his "surprise and sore indignation." The next morning John started to climb into the stage. The same agent who had accosted him before loudly demanded he ride outside with the driver. Indignation had mounted overnight. Besides, it was still raining. John refused. At this juncture, an agitated white passenger, witness to the previous indignity, insisted that everyone dismount, the passenger list be read, and the seating be made according to order of the reservations. The first name on the way-bill was John M. Langston. With his white benefactor at his side, he was transported and lodged on equal terms for the remainder of the journey. But his encounter with discrimination, "absolutely more deadly" to his feelings "than the quickest poison" to his body, had made an indelible impression.[59]

Once back in Oberlin, he registered for the spring semester and, a mark of his new maturity, signed up for a room in Tappan Hall, the men's dormitory. He set about furnishing room 69. All singles, the rooms in Tappan were spare, closetless, eight by sixteen feet, equipped solely with a stove and the advice: "Wood costs only the labor of getting it." He would be expected to fetch his own water and do his own housekeeping. He would eat in the commons, where the diet, although no longer strictly Grahamite vegetarian, still conformed closely to the "plain and holesome" kind intended by the founders. Meals were, a student grumbled, "rather down hill."[60]

In dormitory and dining hall, for the first time on his own, John Mercer would grapple, more intimately than during his stay in the Whipple household, with the intricacies of interracial student relationships. In that regard, his preparatory year had been less than happy. He had failed to develop a close affinity with any white student. If his shyness was partially to blame, factors outside himself also inhibited the development of natural relationships between white and black Oberlin students.

The faculty attempted to regulate black-white student relations on the basis of equal treatment and freedom of association. Professor Henry Cowles explained in 1851: "colored and white students of the same sex, walk together when both are agreed to do so. . . . eat together if both prefer it. . . . meet in the same classes for recitations if they happen to be studying the same branches. . . . worship together before the same common Father. . . ." Black and white students also shared places of abode, both dormitories and private houses, but evidently did not room together. In Tappan Hall, single rooms made that impossible; in Ladies' Hall, black and white apparently did not avail themselves of the opportunity. Further, to combat prejudice, the faculty let it be known that abuse of black students would not be tolerated, early on expelling a white student from a prominent family who called a fellow student a "black nigger." More fundamentally, as a modern institution might attempt to use psychological counseling, Oberlin trained its formidable religious resources on the problem. "Prejudice in Oberlin is preached against, prayed against, sung against, and lived against," asserted Langston and his young friend Fanny Jackson in 1864. The comprehensiveness of the efforts against racism Cowles expressed thus: "Our great business here is to educate mind and heart, and we should deem ourselves to have small cause to be proud of our success if we should fail to eradicate, in no long time, the notion that 'nature' has made any such difference between the colored and the white 'classes' that it would be wrong for either to associate with the other."[61]

Yet, in aspiring to be an island of racial equality, Oberlin was washed by the ebb and flow of surrounding white supremacist attitudes. Langston endorsed as "fair and truthful" Fanny Jackson's 1864 evaluation of Oberlin. Although it came nearer to being free of discrimination "than any other place in the United States," she observed, "human nature in Oberlin is about the same as human nature in New York, until it has taken a collegiate course, and not infrequently it requires a theological to purify it entirely." Not until "America washes her robes of her national sin, and stands before the world with clean hands and spotless garments, . . . may we expect to find Oberlin entirely free from prejudice."[62]

Incoming students, whether attending despite Oberlin's racial policies or, in the words of a prominent white alumnus, "drawn hither by half-formed sympathy on his or his parents' part with the spirit of the place," were likely to transport prejudice among their personal effects. Although committed to "immediate emancipation," a white applicant submitted, "I have ever lived among whites exclusively, and to be now associated with blacks would be disagreeable, admitting it to be right." Stern parental admonitions against associating with black students followed many sons and daughters to Oberlin, as John Mercer would have personal reason to know. A Massachusetts girl reassured the home folks: "You can tell any body that asks that we dont have to kiss the Niggars nor to speak to them without we are a mind to. I dont think that thare six pure Niggars here that go to school. . . . I have not kissed a Niggar yet nor ant a going to nor hant seen any one else." Moreover, the preconceptions of some white students tended to block their recognition of black individuality. Lawrence W. Minor, a black college graduate in 1850 who was active in the Ohio civil rights drive and would become president of Alta Vista College in Texas, was seen by a white classmate as "lazy, incurably lazy" and unlikely to rise. Some white students categorized black academic abilities: "good in languages, but stumbled when they came to mathematics." Some, even after classroom experience with excellent black students, perhaps would have given a mildly befuddled nod to an alumnus' assignment to the Negro of "a certain adamantine limitation in the region of the skull." John Mercer surely had encountered most of these attitudes among preparatory students, the "less cultivated" and newest to Oberlin ideas, and thus the most likely to express prevalent American sentiments.[63]

John Mercer was no more immune than other black students to the slight or the "sly thrust." Potentially if not actually, he was the "darky" in the dining hall who extended the customary Oberlin "brother" to a white boy who retorted: "that want my name, my name was Ben, he never called me brother again." He knew the core of prejudice beneath the forced veneer of politeness, and that many who paid lip service to "the oppressed race" were thinking "nigger." From time to time, in the interaction of young persons outside the sphere of official restraint, the underlying hostility surfaced. Although authoritative plain talk was in understandably short supply on this topic, in 1866 Female Department principal Marianne Dascomb reported an occasional "manifestation of prejudice against color"; James H. Fairchild, connected with Oberlin from the beginning of his studies in 1834 to the end of his presidency in 1889, conceded that "in a few rare instances a colored and a white boy have had a quarrel. . . ." Doubtless, there were other incidents like the shoving match between five crinolined young women for space on the village's narrow wooden boardwalk; the white girl who tumbled onto the unpaved street below applied "several vile epithets to the colored ladies." More serious was the two-vote defeat, during the war years, of a black candidate for preparatory class valedictorian, reportedly by "hard lying and prejudice."[64]

The tipping of the social equation toward lionization or patronage was equally difficult for the black student. Like others, John Mercer had to deal with insincere compliments, the "milk and water article, such as it degrades one to receive." In the dining hall, an Oberlin critic alleged, "a contest ensues to see who shall enjoy the pleasure of their [black students] company, and mingle in their conversation."[65] Moreover, white students genuinely interested in the "oppressed race" subjected the racial representative to flattering, but emotionally wearing, probing, akin to that John Mercer had experienced at the Whipple dining table.

Black-white student relationships also had to overcome the black students' own societally engendered anxieties and hostilities. More than one Negro student "imagined," in President Fairchild's diplomatically couched phrase, "that some disrespect was shown him by a fellow [white] student." John Mercer's own first reaction to a white student's friendly overture would be astonishment.[66]

Interracial relations between the sexes presented special problems. Young men sat on one side of the dining room tables; young women on the other. "Colored gentlemen and ladies" intermingled with white, and to feminist Lucy Stone, two classes ahead of John Mercer, there appeared "no difference." In classrooms they worked side by side. So long as relationships remained platonic, Oberlin rested comfortably on the principle of "freedom of association." But the need to defend the institution against the salacious rumors that dogged it during at least its first three decades dictated in part, one must surmise, the regulation and guidance of student behavior. Authorities probably attempted to discourage interracial romances by such means as denying the special permission required before a student couple could go for a walk. Noting the absence of racially mixed couples from the streets, a visitor declared, "Practical equality has not promoted miscegenation, nor any other evil."[67] In actuality, however, a student's gossip in 1861 that "a fellow here . . . Married a Darky Lady worth about $25000.00 For her money" may have had some substance. E. H. Fairchild in 1862 disclosed that only one interracial student marriage had occurred during nearly thirty years, between a young white man and "a lady quite his superior in talent, education, and energy, in whom there was an 'invisible admixture of African blood.'" When her race was discovered after six months of their teaching in an Ohio River village, both were fired. "This is the beginning and end of amalgamation in this Institution," Fairchild concluded ironically, "and such has been its punishment."[68]

In attempting to deal with their opposites in sex and race, John Mercer and his classmates were groping in uncharted emotional regions. The observations of even reluctant white participants in the social experiment make it clear that they felt the physical attractions of some black students. Lawrence Minor's classmate deprecated his character but appreciated his good looks and charm. "The best appearing chap I have seen here is black," admitted the boy who would not be called "brother"; the girl who would not kiss a "niggar" thought Negro students dressed "a great deal better" than white students. Probably there was more than one episode like the one early in John Mercer's college life, when a black student fell in love with a white girl classmate who refused to marry him. The distraught youth threatened to drown himself in the village well, despite the sympathetic remonstrances of Lucy Stone. At length, in desperation, she advised him that if he were determined on suicide, he should cut his throat rather than ruin the school water supply; outraged, the young man snapped out of his depression. A tragicomic incident of young love, but—in manner that Langston resented—it tended to define the limits of social equality. Yet, at some level of consciousness, more than one Oberlin student, black and white, surely entertained the proposition that a men's literary society debated publicly just before the war: "Res, That the amalgamation of the white and black races in this country is feasible, proper, and should be encouraged."[69]

Sarah Candace Pearse, a white student who would be graduated from the Ladies' Department in 1851, apparently accepted Oberlin's special dispensations so wholeheartedly that she somehow forgot societal restrictions on the social intercourse of white females and black males. Her 1848 winter teaching job was in Cincinnati. "John M. Langston, a classmate and a superior gentleman and scholar, . . . ," Sarah's husband would later recall, "delivered a package at her boarding place for her but did not ask to see her." It betokened a gallantry the girl did not grasp. Naively, she inquired at their next meeting, " 'Why did you not call for me?' " " 'Do you not know,' " John Mercer rejoined, " 'that it would have cost you your position?' "[70]

The frustrations of never being more than Brother to the Oberlin Sister, of always being barred, outside Oberlin, from calling at the white girl's parlor, grated on Langston. The nineteen-year-old college senior would startle the 1849 state black convention with his angry denunciation of the sexual limitations placed upon him and other Negroes by American society. "If you ask a white man whether you may associate with his daughter, or whether you may marry her," he railed, "he will tell you, no! I want to separate myself from such a government."[71] It would be easy to read this outburst as a sign that John Mercer's hopes for close relations with a young white woman had been stymied. More significant even than a possibly thwarted romance, however, was the fact that he had achieved sufficient intimacy with at least a few white students, female and male, on grounds so nearly approximate to equality that he dared to demand the full extension of the doctrine of freedom of association.

On the first Sunday he spent in Tappan Hall, a "beautiful" morning just before classes began, the white boy from Akron who had the adjacent room knocked at his door. His name was Henry Howe. He invited John Mercer to his room, where the boys read Latin and played checkers. "Colored boy as I was, and one too who had never before had a young white friend who was willing to treat me as his friend," Langston would confess to Howe nine years later, "I was somewhat astonished at your conduct. I felt as Topsy felt when Eva spoke a word of kindness and love to her."

Despite Langston's uneasiness, the morning proved a prelude to an enduring friendship. Perhaps it was based partly on the Negro boy's need for reassurance after his bitter rejection in Columbus. Perhaps it grew from the boys' joint pleasure in flouting school rules, for Oberlin forbade checkers, along with "any similar game of chance or skill," and gaming was particularly unseemly on the Sabbath. For three of their four undergraduate years, John Mercer and Henry, who in old age would declare he had tried to "live for the good that I could do," would occupy adjoining rooms. With a third boy, "Teddy," they shared the escapades of college life, "whether memorable," Mercer reminded Henry, "laughable, or ridiculous."[72]

"Teddy" most likely was Edward Daniels of Boston. Notable as land reformer, newspaper editor, and Radical Republican in Reconstruction Virginia, Daniels at Oberlin offered Langston substantial proof of his affectionate loyalty. John Mercer and Edward "read the same books, played the same games, ate at the same table" until discovered by the latter's guardians in Massachusetts. They first remonstrated with Edward and then "ordered him either to give up his negro associate or relinquish all claim to their kindness." As Langston would recount proudly in an 1872 stump speech for his old comrade, then waging an ultimately unsuccessful congressional campaign in northern Virginia, Edward's decision was "but the work of a moment. Rather than sacrifice a principle," he determined to "forego all the pleasures of home and kin, and he did so." Henceforth, Daniels had been "as true to the Negro generally," as to Langston "individually."[73] In that "pure atmosphere," as students often called it, black and white did sometimes find it possible to make friends, not merely for the season of youthful idealism but for the years.

Oberlin's singular institutionalized egalitarianism, despite its ambiguities and shortcomings, allowed John Mercer a broad experience with white peers upon which he would test and expand his evolving commitment to full social equality, up to and including the interracial union that had been his parents' own. Oberlin's rare experiment in biracial education persuaded him that its advantages far outweighed its imperfections. The interest and respect extended by his white friends compensated in part for the wounds to self-esteem inflicted by a rejecting larger society. "You nor I can not begin to tell how much your conduct at that time did towards making me what I am," Mercer confided to Henry. "It led me to feel that after all there might be something in me. This is the feeling that brings success to effort."[74]

By dint of a heavy schedule, John Mercer finished his preparatory course in time to be admitted to the college for the fall 1845 semester. In keeping with the Oberlin plan, plain living and hard thinking ordered his days. The school bell rang daily at 5 a.m., allowing time for fetching wood and water, housekeeping, and perhaps a few minutes of study before breakfast, followed by attendance at chapel. Classes began at 7 o'clock. Dinner was at noon, a simple supper at half-past six. Like other male students, Langston may have chopped in the school garden or on the farm that supplied the foodstuffs; female students attended to washing and ironing. John Mercer took up the habit of "early rising, with late retirement" that would be a life-long pattern.[75]

In the college nine professors, seven of them clergymen, imparted a classical education strongly laced with the evangelism of Charles G. Finney and the ethics of President Asa Mahan, emphasizing morality and freedom of inquiry. The course of study conformed closely to that of leading eastern colleges. Fanny Jackson recalled "plenty of Latin, Greek and mathematics." Broadly speaking, the first year concentrated on the classics, the second on mathematics, the third on science, the fourth on philosophy.[76]

John Mercer apparently thrived on the heavy doses of Latin and Greek that so dismayed a black classmate, James Monroe Jones, that he threatened to drop out. The twenty-four-year-old Jones had advanced from preparatory department into freshman class with Langston. The story went that Monroe's doughty father Allen, a Herculean blacksmith who had bought freedom in Raleigh, North Carolina, and transported his considerable family in a two-horse wagon to Oberlin specifically for the children's education, grabbed an ax. "Now, James, you take your choice," he said. "You go back to college, or you lay your head on this chopping block and I will chop it off." The reluctant scholar would be graduated in 1849, as, subsequently, would three of his brothers.[77] Monroe may well have envied young Langston, who found it amusing to read Latin with Henry Howe. If John Mercer's enthusiasm or aptitude anywhere waned in mathematics, physiology, chemistry, physics, philosophy, or political economy, he characteristically compensated by hard work. Furnished with wide-ranging curiosity, he explored knowledge in the nonspecialized manner of the times and came out a lover of learning.

The closest linking of course work to contemporary concerns was mental and moral philosophy, an inclusive senior course distinguished at Oberlin for two qualities: the moral point given each discussion and the dynamic teaching of Asa Mahan. Langston affectionately regarded Mahan as "a man of great learning and profound ability, in the departments of metaphysics and theological science,—a teacher of rare skill and efficiency, and a lecturer and preacher of unusual power." Charismatic and contentious, an eclectic who drew on German Idealism, particularly Kant, combined sometimes incongruously with Coleridge and Cousin, as well as Finney's New Theology, Jefferson's enlightenment rationalism, and Scottish common-sense, Mahan developed an ethical basis for reform. The object of moral philosophy as he defined it was "to ascertain our duties, and the reason or ground of our obligation to perform them." The duty of the true Christian, he contended, was to labor for "the correction of existing abuses, and the conformity of all institutions . . . to the fundamental of universal reason and the pattern on the mount." Since the "modern church" had "so flagrantly failed as a universal reform society which it is bound to be," Mahan was convinced that "reformatory movements which constitute the glory of the present age" were essential to society's moral health. A full decade before passage of the Fugitive Slave Law, he, like Finney, delineated the citizen's obligation "to regard the law of right or the will of God as of supreme authority above all human enactments." Just as he and Finney were among the five moral philosophers in the American academic world who preached abolition, his textbook on moral philosophy was the only one in the country that directly assaulted the institution of slavery. In 1859, following Langston to the podium after a celebrated fugitive rescue, Mahan would rejoice that the rescuers, some of whom he had taught the "principles of liberty," remained "still true to their duty."[78]

The young Langston profited from the teachings of Mahan and Finney on free will: that people, as moral agents, responsible for personal salvation, could and should exercise control over their own lives. Moreover, he gained an understanding of the reformer's need for tolerance. As Mahan expressed it, "I had much rather err with an honest inquirer, than be right with the bigot. . . ."[79] Langston's own reform philosophy would be a reworking of the pattern laid down by

Mahan. Through such instruction, he absorbed an ethical and evangelical optimism that encouraged him to hold to the prospect of a better day and a better humankind.

Rhetoric, emphasized as a key vocational skill, was required all four years. Under the instruction of Professor Thome, aided by James Monroe, an American Anti-Slavery Society lecturer prior to his theological studies at Oberlin, John Mercer worked at the mechanics of elocution, studied the lives and speeches of the great orators, notably Demosthenes and Cicero, and read English literature. Like all male students, he met a weekly requirement of compositions, speeches, and extempore discussion. Monthly, each young man delivered an original public declamation.

Early in his freshman year, both men's literary societies invited John Mercer to membership. Typically, the literary society offered collegians a bracing departure from the regimen of recitation and weekly lecture; in a school where "the Club, the Saloon, public games, social attractions were wholly unknown," it was the more stimulating.[80] Black students in the college regularly received bids to the Oberlin societies.[81] Sallie Holley, the white abolitionist who was Langston's classmate, doubtless expressed the Oberlin consensus when she declared that black graduates excelled in oratory and public reading, exhibiting "an exuberance of nature, a tropical fervor that gives a charm to their performances."[82] Like Vashon, Langston chose the Union Society.

His initial debate assignment dealt with a controversial topic: "Do the teachings of phrenology interfere with man's moral agency?" When his turn came, he faltered, "Mr. President," and stopped. So paralyzed was the boy that he could gauge neither when nor how he regained his chair. On return to consciousness, John Mercer broke into tears of "grief and humiliation," shrugged off the proffered sympathy of which he felt "wholly unworthy," and fled to his room. Behind a locked door, he cried silently throughout the night. At the morning bell he roused, "as if moved by some power above and outside of himself."

Confronting the red-eyed, puffy face in his small wall mirror, the boy made "the solemn vow of his life." Never again would he fail in any attempt to deliver a speech, nor would he allow "any opportunity to make one pass unimproved." That very morning, in his telling, he agreed to substitute for a fellow member in an upcoming debate. Within the week the fledgling orator mounted the podium and redeemed the second half of his pledge, in an address of "ease and spirit." The "joy and satisfaction" he took from the applause was commensurate to his earlier "deep mortification and dejection."[83]

Able to joke about it in later years, Langston himself recognized that he had bridged an important maturational crisis. The emotional extremity of his reactions suggests how deeply embedded already, at the age of fifteen, was this timid boy's desire to be a public speaker. In this youthful dark night of the soul Finney might have recognized similarities to the conversion experience. In that near cataleptic moment, like the dumbness visited on many Biblical prophets, the accumulating pressures of John Mercer's anomalous position had come due. Faced with proving himself a worthy member of a mainly white group, as well as with demonstrating ability at the task at which he most desired to excel, the controls he had learned to exercise over his anxieties perhaps had not so much failed as over-functioned, preventing all communication. The silent, locked away agony of his struggle with guilt and failure, like Finney's own tears when "It seemed as if my heart was all liquid . . . ," brought him to his own transcendent moment. He pledged himself not to religion, however, but to self-reliance and oratory. The idea, awakened by early admiration of black orators and intensified in evangelical Oberlin where words, the Word, possessed transforming powers, would become for him a faith that eloquence could win acceptance for the racial representative and promote social change.

His enthusiasm for rhetoric was affirmed, both in style and content, in his first recorded address. Delivered May 23, 1848, it was a plea to Union Society members to participate actively in the newly reconstituted society. Apt to venture far out on burgeoning verbal and philosophical branches, the young orator displayed the "recent touches of the oratorical professor"[84] noticeable in Oberlin's students: references to Milton, Burke, and Sheridan, a quote from Scott's "Lay of the Last Minstrel," tries at parallelism achieved mainly at heavy cost in redundancy, the clear organization, the flourishing finish. Through oratory and debate, he argued, "Mind is brought in contact with mind and our latent and dormant powers are aroused to animation and lively activity—the hidden scintillations of our minds are made to display themselves in unwonted and unbeclouded splendor—, . . . and in short, we are most especially forwarded in our intellectual advancement. . . ." Moreover, the times demanded the "greatest minds." In Europe, he pointed out, "Revolution now follows revolution. Kings flee and queens desert their thrones, royal authority sinks into insignificancy." Flushed with democratic-republican optimism, John Mercer voiced faith in the "age of progress and advance. . . . Men must act and first they must be prepared." Whatever the merit of an idea, or zeal behind it, "if the power of expression be wanting, all is naught." His own inarticulate episode edged the truism. In an unembarrassed entreaty for "manly conduct," eighteen-year-old J. Mercer Langston beseeched the members to attend to duty "in the name of our future literature—in the name of humanity—in the name of the Society and for the sake of a merited and permanent reputation." Girding on oratory like scabbard and blade, he dared to reveal a broad range of personal ambitions. He urged the necessity to be "accurate in discrimination, fluent in thought, original in plan, and apt in suggestion whether we would be writers or influential orators, whether we would be a philosopher or a sagacious statesman, whether we would be successful advocates at the bar or wise legislators in the halls of Congress."[85] In retrospect, his words seem a remarkably accurate foretelling.

Langston's thoughts about his future were being shaped, not merely by his encounters with white reformers, but also by his continuing associations with black activists, both in Oberlin and out. Separate black meetings and racially integrated meetings led by blacks were a part of college and village life. During the month John Mercer had first arrived, in March 1844, the current black student leaders, John M. Brown, later bishop in the A.M.E. church,[86] Edward P. Davis, future school principal and A.M.E. minister,[87] and state protest leader and future emigrationist William P. Newman figured prominently in a black meeting to agitate for repeal of the Black Laws and welcome the Columbus newspaper, the *Palladium of Liberty*. In May 1846, Sabram Cox, William Howard Day, and Lawrence W. Minor led a memorial service for Charles T. Torrey, a white underground railroad worker who had died in prison. In addition, black students and townspeople, fugitives in the main, often met at the Liberty School building, which the adult Langston called their "Faneuil Hall, in which the Negro made his most eloquent and effective speeches against his enslavement."[88] The need of Negroes in white-dominated Oberlin to make an independent statement, to demonstrate black manhood, and to play an unfettered black role found expression in such sessions. Further, the black students gained the opportunity to assert their identity with and commitment to their people's cause, "the thousands who with us are disfranchised" and "three millions of our brethren in bonds." As the March 1844 meeting resolved, the black students felt their obligation to support black enterprises generally "as lovers of liberty and of our country" and to turn their personal advantages to account for the benefit of the "oppressed colored citizens of the United States" of which they were "a portion."[89]

Blacks originated and directed the single most important antislavery demonstration of the Oberlin calendar. By black request, the initial First of August celebration was held in 1842 and thereafter was observed by most Oberliners in preference to the "cruel mockery" of the Fourth of July. "How can we enjoy our freedom while our fellow men are in bondage?" was the "ruling idea" of supplications at the morning prayer meeting in 1842. Besides President Mahan, Vashon and Newman spoke during the day-long festivities that concluded with a "plain" banquet, provided free by blacks, for eighty Negroes and one hundred seventy whites. In 1844, Whitehorne called for "Revolutions Effected by Reason, Not by Force," while Day condemned his "guilty" nation and exhorted, "Colored friends, then struggle on—struggle on!"[90]

Utilizing their control of the First of August program, blacks demonstrated the reciprocal supportive relationships they had developed with a small band of white feminists, who bolted that "place" that Oberlin, despite its heterodox practices, assigned women, and who played their own role in John Mercer's political education. Students like Lucy Stone, Antoinette Brown, Sallie Holley, Maria Goodall, Emeline Crooker, and Mary Crabb, who had come to cherish ideas of their own liberation through appreciation of black bondage, were able to advance from sympathetic interest to some cooperative endeavors with black students and residents. Lucy Stone's entree was teaching at the Liberty School, established in 1844 as a separate entity to replace the "common school department" of Oberlin Institute for the elementary education of black adults. (Black children attended the village elementary school.) An experienced teacher in her late twenties, the girlish-appearing Stone was confronted in her first class by a towering black man, who protested for the group that it was improper for men to be taught by a woman. She convinced them to give her a try and proved so successful that when the Ladies' Boarding Hall took fire, "a whole string of colored men . . . arrived on the scene one after another, to save her property, each demanding breathlessly, 'Where is Miss Stone's trunk?' " When the faculty, who allowed essay reading but prohibited public speaking by women, rejected Stone's plea to allow female students to hold debates, the aged mother of one of her black scholars opened her parlor to the determined young women. Thus prepared, the Misses Stone, Crooker, and Crabb accepted the invitation of Day and the other "young colored men" in charge to address the 1846 First of August celebration, along with five black men and a sole white male, the pronounced egalitarian James Monroe. "Why do we rejoice today?" was the first of thousands of public addresses Lucy Stone was to deliver over the next nearly half century. Similarly, in 1847, Antoinette Brown, who would become the first ordained woman minister, was featured on the program.[91]

Notably, it was through the combined pressure of black students and townspeople and white female activists, both groups more favorably disposed toward William Lloyd Garrison and his followers than was Oberlin generally, that a hostile faculty finally allowed Stephen and Abby Kelley Foster to argue disunionism in church and state at the college chapel in September 1846. Disappointed by the treatment of the Garrisonian "come-outerism twins," as one white Oberlinite derisively dubbed them, a black meeting approved a resolution drawn by Lawrence Minor that "in no way can the cause of Anti-Slavery reform be so effectively retarded as by distrusting the fidelity of the advocates of freedom." President Asa Mahan, who had debated Foster, had stated that the couple "are not sincere and safe advocates of equal rights." But, without disputing Mahan's loyalty to their cause, the black meeting praised the Fosters as "true and honest friends of the oppressed" and Garrison himself as the "Leonidas of the Anti-Slavery Movement."[92] This independent, pragmatic stance toward abolitionism that tried to cooperate with the political wing, strongly Oberlin-influenced in Ohio, while recognizing the contributions of the moral suasionist Garrisonians, reflected the attitude of the state black leadership generally. Young Langston would adopt a similarly politically oriented, but non-doctrinaire, outlook.

Although discretion demanded the connections of white female activists and black students go unacknowledged, two post-college incidents of discriminatory treatment, one involving Day and the second Langston, would provoke Stone and Brown to public affirmations of friendship for their schoolmates.[93] On a more personal note, in old age Lucy Stone would recall having assisted the "clever colored boy" John Mercer Langston at his studies. He requited the sympathy and inspiring example of young feminists by embracing, well before graduation, belief in equal rights for women. In future he would gracefully chide his alma mater for unwillingness to elevate its "great experiment . . . this co-education of sexes" to the point of full equality. John Mercer's endorsement of women's rights would be one of his contributions to the first national black convention he would attend.[94]

In the months preceding his formal introduction to the black movement in early September 1848, the young Negro intellectual was forced to renewed reflections on American prejudice. Only a week after Langston's idealistic address to the Union Society, as if to emphasize the profound gap between college dreams and cultural realities, Charles Langston was very nearly lynched. In late May 1848, Charles, soon to be appointed western representative of the Sons of Temperance and empowered to charter organizations west of the Alleghenies,[95] had joined forces on a lecture tour with Martin Delany. The latter was promoting subscriptions to the *North Star*, the black newspaper recently commenced in Rochester, New York, under the editorship of Frederick Douglass. Anticipating trouble, Delany observed that rumors of the approaching repeal of some of Ohio's Black Laws had angered the white populace. Even small children in Lisbon, in eastern Ohio, "flip[ped] out disparagement against the colored stranger." On May 23 at Columbus, with the assistance of his "worthy and talented friend" Charles Langston, Delany was relieved to be able to hold a meeting.[96]

Reaching the village of Marseilles in northern Ohio after sunset a week later, the black abolitionists decided on the advice of local sympathizers to hold a meeting at the schoolhouse. But as they walked toward it, young rowdies dogged their steps. Once inside, the hecklers proved so raucous that Charles Langston, initially taken for white by many, refused to gratify the "disrespectful spirit." To a local wit's motion to "adjourn by considering this a darky burlesque," he and Delany, who boasted of himself "there lives none blacker," pushed their way back to the hotel. From their upper-story room the two men saw the mob ignite a roaring bonfire and place a fortunately well depleted tar-barrel in the center. To a cacophony of drum, tambourine, clarinet, and violin, the whites shouted: "Burn them alive—kill the niggers—they shall never leave this place—bring them out—rush in and take them—which is their room—Niggers!" Well after midnight, still deliberating on the benefits of lynching as opposed to selling the two men in the South, the citizens dispersed, leaving six guards and an ostler boy who slept in the hotel barroom to sound the alarum on a bass drum. While the watchmen slumbered in the early dawn, Charles and Delany stole out to the barn where their village allies had concealed their horse and carriage. Not until buggy squeaks and thudding hooves sounded did the guards awake. The frustrated captors got off a few stones, "howled and yelped," and "threatened us not to come back again."[97] While Charles Langston continued to the East, to confer with Douglass in Rochester on plans for an upcoming black national convention, Delany made an Oberlin stop, where he doubtless gave John Mercer full details.[98]

Black leaders from across the North, with John Mercer Langston a member of an enthusiastic Oberlin delegation, crowded into Cleveland's hotels, tabernacle, and courthouse September 6–8, 1848, for the black national convention, the ninth such gathering since 1830. The presiding officer was Frederick Douglass. In his early thirties, but with seven years of antislavery lecturing, his enormously successful slave narrative, and a triumphal tour of the British Isles behind him, he was a "phenomenon" becoming an institution.[99] Prominent among the Ohio delegates was Charles H. Langston, who would be Ohio's representative on the national central committee appointed to carry on the convention's work (although apparently soon disbanded). William Howard Day, elected secretary, and the Langstons constituted part of an Oberlin-educated vanguard that also numbered Sabram Cox, now an Oberlin farmer, and the talented musician Justin Holland.[100] An optimistic tone prevailed, the delegates voicing, in much the same terms the college boy had used in the spring, a belief in "the great law of progress, written out by the hand of God." Virtually all of the current themes of the black struggle against slavery and for civil rights were aired. Delegates ended by endorsing the results of the Buffalo convention that scarcely a month before had launched the Free Soil movement. But they added the proviso that "such persons and parties alone as have a tendency to enhance the liberty of the colored people of the United States" deserved support. "It will be a long time before we gain all our rights," they conceded, nevertheless, gradual improvement in the black condition was "evident."[101]

J. Mercer Langston's participation was modest. Besides remarks "commending those who helped runaways," he joined Day in a strong advocacy of admitting women to full delegate privileges because the rules covered "all colored persons present," and they "considered *women persons*"; the convention acquiesced with "three cheers for women's rights." Douglass, who gave the neophyte reformer a brief encouraging mention in the *North Star*, would recall more than a quarter of a century afterwards having heard Langston's "eloquent voice" for the first time and predicting then "that voice would some time be heard in the nation."[102]

At the state black convention in Columbus in January 1849, with Charles Langston the president, John Mercer was more assertive. As a member of the business committee, he helped formulate an aggressive series of resolutions, many suggested by two recent Oberlin black meetings,[103] ranging from endorsement of the Higher Law to resistance to all racial oppression or proscription. John Mercer, still rankled by his boyhood exclusion from the Columbus hotel, probably inserted the demand that white abolitionists boycott all discriminatory stage houses and hotels in Ohio.[104]

But young Langston's most prominent contribution was an ardent advocacy of black emigration, a topic destined for extensive debate during the next decade. Speaking spontaneously to a resolution repudiating the American Colonization Society's agitation for black Ohioans to go to Liberia, John Mercer advanced the argument that white racism undermined black manhood. So long as strong prejudice endured, and he saw "little hope for its removal," Negroes were barred from an American nationality; yet a nationality was essential "before we can become anybody." "We have already drunk too long the cup of bitterness and woe," he protested, "and do gentlemen want to drink it any longer?" Declaring his own willingness to go wherever he could be free, he advised blacks to leave the country. To remain would be "humiliating, virtually acknowledging our inferiority to the white man."

The actual resolution drawn up by John Mercer and the youthful Zanesville barber W. Hurst Burnham, however, predicated black emigration on prior universal emancipation: "taking our freed brother as our coadjutor . . . , we are willing, it being optional, to draw out from the American government, and form a separate and independent one. . . ."[105] In contrast to some abolitionists, John Mercer obviously did not believe that elimination of slavery would eliminate prejudice. Moreover, since abolition of slavery, even to the optimistic, seemed a long way off, it is apparent that, despite the student's passionate personal avowals, his proposal was essentially theoretical, an attempt to formulate a future course for black Americans. "An actual black nationality," Langston would call "the dream of my youth."[106] Because the dream reveals much about Oberlin's influence on him and because he would retain that dream, returning to it in one form or another for several years, it is important to pause to scrutinize his incipient nationalism.

The germ of the young black intellectual's enthusiasm, shared at the convention by the highly respected David Jenkins and several other delegates, almost surely was the nationalistic zeitgeist that seemed to grip all Europe and strongly touched America. "Revolution now follows revolution," John Mercer had exclaimed jubilantly in the heady spring of 1848, as the fire of popular uprisings, having ignited in France, spread rapidly to Germany, Italy with the dream of the *risorgimento*, and the Hapsburg Empire. In England, too, workers united in the short-lived Chartist movement. Although the aims of the more than fifty separate revolts were not all the same, indeed sometimes worked at the cross-purposes that contributed to their gradual crushing out, culminating in Hungary with the rout of forces under Louis Kossuth, the charismatic Magyar leader, in the late summer of 1849, the animating spirit was democratic and nationalistic. In the United States the revolutions reinforced the widely held belief in a God-directed movement toward universal liberty. Young Americans, led by Senator Lewis Cass of Michigan, the 1848 Democratic presidential nominee, trumpeted the message that the United States had a mission to forward that progress, even through active intervention in Europe. Blacks and abolitionists, on the other hand, while quick to point out the contradiction of a slaveholding nation's attempting to export democracy and freedom, showed equal zeal in interpreting the revolutions as signs, as John Mercer had put it, of "an age of progress and advance." A Cleveland black meeting in April 1848 greeted the French upheavals as "bright omens of the future rapid progress of that nation, and of the race." Shortly afterward John I. Gaines welcomed Delany to Cincinnati with the declaration, "the spirit of the age, in which you and I live, is progressive. . . . God designed in his infinite wisdom and providence that men should be free—as free as the air we breathe, and enjoy and possess the higher degree of civilization. . . ." Obviously drawing the parallel between black Americans and other oppressed peoples, Gaines expressed confidence that, if "stayed for the time being, [freedom] must come and will come."[107] Moreover, while earlier in the decade black intellectuals had been prone to speak, like William Cuthbert Whitehorne, of obtaining liberty "not by force of arms, but by the peaceable efforts of reason," the rhetoric of revolution increasingly entered black oratory. With the majority of the 1849 delegates, John Mercer voted to purchase and distribute five hundred copies of a pamphlet containing two rallying cries for black uprisings, David Walker's 1829 *Appeal . . . .*, and Henry Highland Garnet's 1843 *Address to the Slaves*. Citing the participation of individual Negroes in the French revolutions and the Chartist struggle, in 1850 Langston would proudly proclaim, "Colored men have acted in all the mighty movements of the world for Freedom."[108]

If shaped by the nationalistic climate, John Mercer's dream of a black nationality certainly contained the stuff of personal experience and his perceptions, as a young black intellectual, of the racial situation. His friendship with George Vashon, an admirer of the Haitian revolutionists and short-term emigrant to the Island Republic, as well as his boyish hero-worship of the black liberationists of Haiti and the *Amistad*, were conducive to his receptivity to nationalist ideas. Moreover, his uncommon range of experience in white society allowed him to gauge acutely the depth and pervasiveness of white supremacist attitudes, which, in turn, led to his doubt that black Americans would ever be allowed to exercise their full humanity.

Not simply civil rights, but full social acceptance seemed to be comprehended in his vision of nationality. In impetuous defense of his resolution, the student boldly brought up both white bars on interracial marriage and racial discrimination at Oberlin. John Mercer's scornful repudiation of a country that prohibited racial intermarriage was based on an insight similar to that recorded earlier by Alexis de Tocqueville, who observed that the test of true equality in a society was its willingness to accept marriages that disregarded traditional class divisions. In his statement on Oberlin, apparently referring to the Liberty School for black adults, Langston averred that "you will find a colored school, brought into existence on account of prejudice even there. Will any gentleman deny this?" Two Oberlin men, Day and farmer Thomas Brown, a school trustee, immediately rose with refutations before President Charles Langston declared the discussion out of order. While the validity of John Mercer's specific charge cannot be determined, the more interesting point is that he dared to attack a hitherto sacrosanct institution. Reluctant to jeopardize the unusual degree of opportunity that Oberlin extended, few blacks ever criticized it publicly. That John Mercer, by every indication a successful and popular scholar, should have felt the need and freedom to do so suggests both an abiding sensitivity to racial slights and a maturing conception, nurtured by his political education, of the full dimensions of equality. Indeed, by his senior year, several vital traditions embraced by Oberlin—the evangelical, republican, democratic, abolitionist, self-reliant, and Afro-American—had been so inculcated in the student as to cause him here to openly affirm his black declaration of independence.

Importantly, in striking a claim to a black nationality, young Langston was seeking another country that was not so much geographical as moral and psychological. He was expressing his own militant consciousness of manhood and hoping to inspire more aggressive attitudes in his people. "Trusting as we do in the omnipotence of truth, we are willing and ready to 'battle on and battle ever,' " he had prefaced his advocacy of emigration. "Dearly as I love my native land, I am willing to go wherever I can be free." J. Mercer Langston, nineteenth birthday celebrated just days before, did not intend to suffer injustice grinningly. Liberation, in the fullest sense, was central in his thought. "The spirit of our people must be aroused," he urged passionately, "and they must feel and act as men."

Despite John Mercer's heated arguments, the delegates resolved overwhelmingly to "remain in the United States, and contend for our rights at all hazards."[109] The idealistic losing debater probably did not feel overly disappointed. His embrace of emigration was as yet abstract and ambiguous, while he held to the hope that America might fulfill the liberal promise of its own revolution by recognizing the black claim to freedom and equality, thus allowing blacks their nationality in their native land.

Within the month that hope was strengthened by striking victories for blacks in the Ohio assembly. Dr. Norton S. Townshend of Lorain County and John F. Morse of Painesville, both Liberty and Free Soil politicians with strong Oberlin connections, took advantage of a deadlock in the lower house between Whigs and Democrats to bargain for amendments to the Black Laws. The agreement eventually struck with Democratic legislators, ironically even more anti-black than the Whigs, resulted in abrogation of the laws requiring the posting of bonds and barring the testimony of black witnesses in court; moreover, the 1848 legislation providing for the establishment of common schools for Negroes was rewritten and liberalized. Further, Salmon P. Chase, the antislavery lawyer from Cincinnati, was elected to the U.S. Senate.

In the *North Star*, Frederick Douglass gave credit for the repeal to "our colored brethren in Ohio [who] combatting every opposition, resisting every obstacle, . . . forced the dominant class in their own state to notice and respect their efforts." In Oberlin, Negro students and townspeople organized a day-long celebration of joy. By black invitation President Mahan preached; in the afternoon six "young gentlemen of color," John Mercer surely among them, argued that education, more than Christian gospel, offered the chief means of black elevation.[110]

As the August 1849 commencement approached, John Mercer worked at perfecting his graduation address. Instead of an antislavery theme, his topic was "The Sacrifices and Recompenses of Literary Life." Besides a genuine taste for scholarship, the subject was expressive of his protest against the white presumptions that circumscribed black manhood. In his nineteenth year—six years younger than the average Oberlin graduate—he was preoccupied with questions of manhood: what pertained to him as himself, a human being, a black man, an American.

But a cholera epidemic that had ravaged southern Ohio and spread north forced cancellation of the commencement ceremonies. In contrast to the usual elaborate proceedings that attracted spectators from miles around, Professor Morgan and President Mahan officiated at modest exercises. Eleven graduates of the college course received diplomas. James Monroe Jones and John Mercer Langston thus became the fourth and fifth Negroes to earn the A.B. degree from Oberlin College. Always Langston would regret the lost opportunity to speak the words with which he would have crowned his college career.[111]

At other times he would try to sum up the college years. Formally, in his autobiography: "Education, which meant the development of the whole human being in intellectual, moral and spiritual powers, with due consecration of all learning, genius, talent and influence to God and humanity, without distinction of sex or color, was recognized as the duty and privilege of every child of man. And upon all subjects of freedom—the unconstitutionality of slavery, its utter violation of the maxims of the Bible, and its outrage of all the fundamental doctrines of genuine democracy—its position was clear, comprehensive, and decisive." Sentimentally, at the age of sixty-five, to his professor and friend James H. Fairchild, he celebrated "the old worthy matchless men, who figured so conspicuously and effectively in the early history of Oberlin College. I recall with sentiments of profound gratitude the names of Mahan, Finney, Morgan, yourself and others. . . ." At twenty-four, to Henry Howe, he proclaimed college "the most interesting and pleasant portion of my life," and remembered "the beautiful ways that so much delighted and charmed our boyhood."[112]

"Homo sum; atque nihil humani a me alienum puto." Already, at the state black convention in January, John Mercer Langston had enunciated "that nervous masculine sentiment in favor of his own humanity" declaimed first by the Roman slave Terence. The phrase would serve as leitmotif of his oratory and guiding principle of his actions. The literary life or any other, the college graduate was ready to assert, should be his to consider; no longer the shy colored boy, he claimed the rights belonging to all men. Perhaps that phrase, pronounced in Latin, best symbolized the meaning of his Oberlin education. "Though man be wrapped in chains his *humanity is deathless*," John Mercer had come to believe. "I am a *man*, and there is nothing of humanity, as I think, estranged to me."[113]

NOTES

1. John Mercer Langston, *From the Virginia Plantation to the National Capitol; or, The First and Only Negro Representative in Congress from the Old Dominion* (Hartford, 1894; repr. New York: Johnson Reprint, 1968), p. 77; Cleveland *Herald*, n.d., 1845, quoted in Oberlin *Evangelist*, Sept. 10, 1845; Cleveland *Gazette*, Dec. 2, 1893.

2. John J. Shipherd to Br. [N. P.] Fletcher, Dec. 15, 1834, Oberlin College Archives; Robert S. Fletcher, *A History of Oberlin College*, 2 vols. (Oberlin, 1943), I, pp. 85–170, 177–78.

3. Gilbert H. Barnes and Dwight L. Dumond, eds., *Letters of Theodore Dwight Weld, Angelina Grimke Weld, and Sarah Grimke, 1822–1844*, 2 vols. (New York, 1934), I, pp. 242–45; James H. Fairchild, *Oberlin: Its Origins, Progress and Results* (Oberlin, 1860), pp. 18, 26.

4. John Keep to Gerrit Smith, Jan. 16, 1836, Oberlin College Archives.

5. *Catalogue of the Trustees, Officers and Students of the Oberlin Collegiate Institute, Together with the Second Annual Report*, Oberlin, 1835 (Cleveland, 1835); William E. Bigglestone, "Straightening a Fold in the Record," Oberlin *Alumni Magazine* 68 (May-June 1972):11; "Day Book" (or "Cash Journal"), Apr. 1, 1835-May 24, 1836; "Untitled Document," Nov. 28, 1835, Box I, both in Oberlin College Treasurer's Vault; "Oberlin First Congregational Church Records, 1834–1856," Oberlin College Archives.

6. "1836 Folder," "Misc. Archives," Oberlin College Archives; Fletcher, *Oberlin College*, I, p. 189; Henry Cowles, "Oberlin College Catalogue and Records of Colored Students, 1835–1862," ms., Henry Cowles Papers, Oberlin College Library (hereafter cited as Cowles List).

7. N. P. Fletcher, "Critical Letters," 1837, No. 3, Oberlin College Archives; Fletcher, *Oberlin College*, II, p. 710; Cowles List; Ellen N. Lawson and Marlene Merrill, "The Antebellum 'Talented Thousandth': Black College Students at Oberlin Before the Civil War," *Journal of Negro Education* 52 (1983):142, 151–52. James H. Fairchild, third president of Oberlin, estimated that between 1835 and 1883, collegiate degrees were awarded to sixty of some 1,000 Negro students. See James H. Fairchild, *Oberlin: The Colony and the College 1833–1883* (Oberlin, 1883), p. 112.

8. Cowles List.

9. Upon graduation Whitehorne went to Belize, British Honduras, where he was a merchant for five years. From 1850 on he lived in Panama City, Panama, first editing the *Mercantile Chronicle* and then the *Star and Herald*. On June 4, 1879, at the age of 57, he died in Chame, Panama. William Cuthbert Whitehorne, Alumni Records, Oberlin College Archives; San Francisco *Elevator*, June 22, 1872.

10. Newman was noticeably active during his five years in school at Oberlin. In 1839, he was one of twenty-nine Oberlin residents who agreed to "devote the 4th of July, in the future, to labor in our respective occupations, the avails of which, we pledge to the cause of emancipation." When blacks at Oberlin determined to celebrate the First of August in 1842, they selected Newman and George B. Vashon to speak for them; he also delivered an oration the following year. According to fellow student, William Howard Day, Newman was the "first colored man [to] cast a ballot in the county of Lorain." In August of 1843, he was among the six Lorain County delegates elected to the state convention in Columbus and was elected chairman of its nine-man business committee. Newman co-authored the 1843 "Address to the Citizens of Ohio," a spirited essay on the "unjust and impolitic course which is pursued toward us," which the convention had published in black Ohio's premier newspaper, the *Palladium of Liberty*. In the fall of 1843, in "poor health" and with "scarcely a dollar in my purse," Newman left school in order to "make arrangements for a common school" for blacks in Canada West. Maintaining a mailing address at Oberlin, he would move back and forth from Canada to Ohio over the next several years, devoting his services to various projects directed toward black elevation. In 1844, as the agent of the Ladies Education Society of Ohio,

Newman visited and lectured in "a large number of colored settlements, several of which no agent of the Society has ever before seen." During his agency, Newman was responsible for obtaining teachers for the black communities in addition to raising funds for the society and for the Union Baptist church of Cincinnati. In late 1848, he returned to Cincinnati, where he had lived in the middle thirties, to become pastor of the Union Baptist church. Following passage of the Fugitive Slave Law, Newman went back to his work in Canada. Operating the sawmill at Dawn, in Chatham, when not teaching and preaching, he did not get on well with two of the community's leaders, white Oberlinite Hiram Wilson and the black minister, Josiah Henson. He left Canada in the late fifties, first trying Haiti, where he clashed with the Catholic church, and later Jamaica. In 1863, hearing through a friend that Secretary of the Treasury Salmon Chase "thought it to be my duty to aid the Union Cause," Newman, with his wife and six children, returned to his "native country" to "aid in putting down the Soul-Monger's rebellion." "I am a war Parson!" he explained in his letter to Chase. In 1864, Newman was a delegate from Cincinnati to the national black convention in Syracuse. Later that year he resumed his pastorate in the Union Baptist church. He died in Cincinnati on August 31, 1866, the first victim of a cholera epidemic. His church erected a monument to him in its new cemetery and paid $1,000 for a homestead in Appleton, Wisconsin, for his widow and family; see Cowles List; *Philanthropist*, July 2, 1839, Oct. 14, 1843, Aug. 28, Apr. 24, 1844; Oberlin *Evangelist*, Aug. 17, 1842, Aug. 16, Dec. 20, 1843, Jan. 3, Aug. 28, 1844, Jan. 3, 1849; *The Aliened American*, Apr. 9, 1853; *Palladium of Liberty*, Dec. 27, 1843; Wendell P. Dabney, *Cincinnati's Colored Citizens: Historical, Sociological, and Biographical* (Cincinnati, 1926; repr. New York: Johnson Reprint, 1970), p. 371; W. P. Newman to Editor, Oct. 1, 1850, *North Star*, Oct. 24, 1850; *Voice of the Fugitive*, Jan. 15, 1851; Robin Winks, *The Blacks in Canada* (New Haven, 1971), pp. 164–65, 196, 199–201, 203, 231, 395; W. P. Newman to Editor, *American Baptist*, n.d., quoted in Anti-Slavery *Bugle*, Mar. 16, 1861; William P. Newman to My Dear Sir, Nov. 30, 1863, Salmon P. Chase Papers, Library of Congress; *Proceedings of the National Convention of Colored Men . . . Syracuse . . . Oct., 1864* (Boston, 1864).

11. Fletcher, *Oberlin College*, II, pp. 507–36.

12. Nathaniel D. Morris to Kind Sir, Jan. 1845, Oberlin College Archives.

13. A native Ohioan who described himself in his letter of application as "a colored man about 30 years old," Roye had taught briefly in Chillicothe before giving it up to try sheepherding in Iowa. He would become president of Liberia in 1871; see Edward J. Roye to Rev. Sir, Sept. 22, 1845, Oberlin College Archives; Cowles List; Allen Johnson and Dumas Malone, eds., *Dictionary of American Biography*, 22 vols. (New York, 1928–44), XVI, p. 212.

14. J.T.Cook to Hamilton Hill, Dec. 25, n.d., Oberlin College Archives; Cowles List.

15. J.B.Vashon to R. E. Gillett, Nov. 19, 1840; J. B. Vashon to H. Hill, Jan. 13, 1847; John Peck to Hamilton Hill, Feb. 1, 1842, all in Oberlin College Archives. On John Peck and his son, David J. Peck, see Victor Ullman, *Martin R. Delany: The Beginnings of Black Nationalism* (Boston, 1971), pp. 18, 24, 31, 41,

44–45, 47–48, 70, 79, 87, 113, 138–39, 152. Cowles lists David J. Peck as a student at Oberlin 1841–43, Cowles List. Peck's daughter Louisa attended Oberlin in 1851, Vashon's daughter a private school in Philadelphia. See Cowles List; Lawson and Merrill, "The Antebellum 'Talented Thousandth,' " 145, fn. 17.

16. William H. Day to R. E. Gillett, June 29, 1843, Oberlin College Archives. See profile, chapter 5.

17. Theodore L. Wright to Levi Burnell, Mar. 2, 1837; M. R.Delany to Rev. Mr. Mahan, Feb. 19, 1841, both in Oberlin College Archives.

18. J. B. Meachum to Dear Brother, May 29, 1839, Oberlin College Archives. Climpson and Nathaniel Meachum attended Oberlin in 1839, Cowles List.

19. A.L.Shumway, *Oberliniana, 1833–1883* (Cleveland, 1883), p. 22; Meachum to Dear Brother, May 29, 1839, Oberlin College Archives.

20. Daniel A. Payne to Rev. Asa Mahan, Feb. 14, 1844, Oberlin College Archives.

21. Wright to Burnell, Mar. 2, 1837; Austin Steward to Prest. Asa Mahan, Feb. 25, 1847, both in Oberlin College Archives; Fanny M. Jackson Coppin, *Reminiscences of School Life and Hints on Teaching* (Philadelphia, 1913), p. 17; Davis Day, "Instruction of Colored People," *Philanthropist*, Oct. 13, 1841. Davis Day was a student at Oberlin in 1839, Cowles List.

22. E.H. Fairchild, "Are Negroes Susceptible to High Cultivation?," Oberlin *Evangelist*, June 4, 1862.

23. For Oberlin as supplier of teachers for black schools during the winter, see Augustus Wattles to Henry Cowles, Jan. 20, 1836, Sept. 14, 1837, both in Cowles Papers; *Philanthropist*, June 11, Oct. 22, 1839; *Palladium of Liberty*, Oct. 16, 1844; John M. Brown to H. Hill, Dec. 29, 1848, Oberlin College Archives.

24. *Philanthropist*, June 29, 1842.

25. Amherst graduated Edward Jones in August 1826; two weeks later Bowdoin graduated John B. Russwurm. In 1828, Edward Mitchell was graduated from Dartmouth; in 1836, John Sykes Fayette from Western Reserve College, and possibly William G. Allen from Oneida Institute. Walter George Robinson, Jr., "Blacks in Higher Education in the United States Before 1865," Ph.D. diss., Southern Illinois University, 1976, pp. 11–13, 51–52, 102.

26. Langston, *Virginia Plantation*, pp. 74–75.

27. Ullman, *Martin R. Delany*, pp. 11–19; Benjamin Quarles, *Black Abolitionists* (New York, 1969), pp. 24, 20; Floyd J. Miller, *The Search for a Black Nationality* (Urbana, 1975), pp. 94–105; Martin Delany, *The Condition, Elevation, Emigration, and Destiny of the Colored People of the United States, Politically Considered* (Philadelphia, 1952; repr. New York: Arno Press, 1968), pp. 119–20; Cowles List; James A. Thome to Theodore Dwight Weld, Apr. 13, 1841, *Weld-Grimke Letters*, II, p. 864; Harry N. Frost, ed., *Register of the Members Both Graduate and Non-Graduate of Phi Delta Literary Society, Oberlin College* (Oberlin, 1891), p. 18; Fletcher, *Oberlin College*, I, p. 250; George B. Vashon, "Vincent Oge," in *Autographs for Freedom*, ed. Julia Griffiths (Rochester, 1854), pp. 44–60.

28. Cleveland *True-Democrat*, Mar. 10, 1847; Oberlin *Evangelist*, Aug. 16,

1843; George Boyer Vashon, "Conservatism and Change," Oberlin *Evangelist*, Apr. 10, 1844. Immediately upon graduation from Oberlin, Vashon studied law under Pittsburgh jurist Walter Forward. A struggle for admission to the Pennsylvania bar, including two appeals through the courts, proved fruitless, but he passed an open court examination in New York and was admitted in January 1848. Soon after he went to Haiti, where he taught two years at the College Faustin before returning to New York in an attempt to establish a practice in Syracuse. In 1854 he became professor of *belles lettres* at Central College at McGrawville, New York, a short-lived (1849–58) coeducational, racially integrated Baptist institution, the first to employ black men on the faculty. In 1855, he was the Liberty party candidate for attorney general of New York, the first Negro to run for public office in the state. Subsequently, Vashon became principal of the colored schools of Pittsburgh (1857–63); principal of Avery Institute at Allegheny, Pennsylvania (1863–67); solicitor for the Freedmen's Bureau; and from 1872 to his death in 1878, professor in Greek and modern languages at Alcorn University in Mississippi; see Cleveland *True-Democrat*, Mar. 10, 1847, Jan. 21, Feb. 8, 1848; *North Star*, Jan. 28, 1848; *Frederick Douglass' Paper*, Sept. 8, 1854; William Wells Brown, *The Rising Son; or, The Antecedents and Advancement of the Colored Race* (Boston, 1874; repr. Miami: Mnemosyne Reprint, 1969), pp. 476–78; Albert A. Wright, "Biography of George Boyer Vashon," Oberlin College Alumni Meeting, June 1879; Jackson (Mississippi) *Daily Times*, Aug. n.d., 1878, both in Oberlin College Archives; *People's Advocate*, n.d., quoted in Oberlin *Review*, Nov. 20, 1878, in George Boyer Vashon, Alumni Records, Oberlin College Archives.

29. Guardianship for John Langston, Apr. 20, 1843, Ross County Probate Court, Apr. 20, 1843, Case 4311, Ross County Courthouse, Chillicothe, Ohio; *Ohio State Journal*, Sept. 10, 1839; *Philanthropist*, Mar. 26, 1839; Langston, *Virginia Plantation*, pp. 73–74. Several pieces of property bought and sold by Harvey Hawes between 1826 and 1848 are listed in Ross County, General Index of Deeds, Ross County Courthouse. In the 1840 census he and his wife are in the "36 to 54" age category; Population Census of 1840, Ross County, Ohio, Reel 21, NA.

30. *Philanthropist*, June 29, 1842. Joseph Carter Corbin, who became an educator in postwar Arkansas, serving first as the state superintendent of education and later as principal of Branch Normal College in Pine Bluff, was a younger classmate of Langston's at this time; see William J. Simmons, *Men of Mark: Eminent, Progressive and Rising* (Cleveland, 1887; repr. Chicago: Johnson Publishing, 1970), pp. 583–86; Langston, *Virginia Plantation*, pp. 74–76; the *Court of Common Pleas for Ross County* versus *William D. Gooch*, Apr. 9, 1839, Court of Common Pleas, Box Case, No. 101, Ross County, Chillicothe, Ohio. In 1860, carpenter William Langston had property valued at $3,000. Luther P. Jackson, *Free Negro Labor and Property Holding in Virginia 1830–1860* (New York, 1942; repr. Boston: Atheneum, 1969), p. 113, fn. 20.

31. Cleveland *Herald*, n.d., 1845, quoted in Oberlin *Evangelist*, Sept. 10, 1845; Henry Howe, *Historical Collections of Ohio* (Cincinnati, 1847), p. 315; New York *Independent*, Mar. 24, 1853; Langston, *Virginia Plantation*, pp. 77–78; Fletcher, *Oberlin College*, II, p. 574.

32. New York *Independent*, Dec. 12, 1861; Langston, *Virginia Plantation*, p. 79.

33. Langston, *Virginia Plantation*, p. 99.

34. C.G. Finney, *Lectures on Revivals* (New York, 1835), pp. 374–75. On Oberlin perfectionism, see Charles Grandison Finney, *Memoirs of Rev. Charles G. Finney* (New York, 1876), pp. 350–51; Jonathan Blanchard to Editor, *Philanthropist*, Oct. 8, 1839; H. E. Johnson, "Charles G. Finney and Oberlin Perfectionism," *Journal of Presbyterian History* 46 (Mar. 1968):43, 45, 47, 51.

35. Fletcher, *Oberlin College* I, pp. 251–53; Cleveland *Herald*, n.d., 1845, quoted in Oberlin *Evangelist*, Sept. 10, 1845; W. L. Garrison to My Dear Wife, Aug. 28, 1847, William Lloyd Garrison Papers, Boston Public Library.

36. *Courier and Freeman* (Potsdam, N.Y.), n.d., 1889, John Mercer Langston Scrapbooks, 4 vols., II, Moorland-Spingarn Research Center, Howard University; Langston, *Virginia Plantation*, p. 79; John Mercer Langston, *Freedom and Citizenship* (Washington, 1883; repr. Miami: Mnemosyne Reprint, 1969), p. 12; Carrie V. Still to Jacob White, Nov. 25, 1864, Jacob White Papers, Moorland-Spingarn Research Center, Howard University; Langston, *Virginia Plantation*, p. 79.

37. Langston, *Virginia Plantation*, p. 80; Zeruiah Porter Weed to S. S. Jocelyn, July 5, 1859; W. W. Wright to Lewis Tappan, Nov. 11, 1846, both in American Missionary Association Archives, Amistad Research Center, Tulaue University (hereafter cited as AMA Papers); Population Census of 1850, Lorain County, Ohio, Reel 705, NA. On Sarah Kinson, see Ellen NicKenzie Lawson with Marlene D. Merrill, *The Three Sarahs: Documents of Antebellum Black College Women* (New York, 1984), pp. 2–40.

38. George Whipple to Theodore Dwight Weld, Jan. 8, 1835, *Weld-Grimke Letters*, I, pp. 193–94; Fletcher, *Oberlin College*, II, p. 689; Samuel D. Cochran et al. to Editor, *Philanthropist*, Mar. 24, 1841; Wright to Tappan, Nov. 11, 1846, AMA Papers.

39. Langston, *Virginia Plantation*, pp. 80–81.

40. Langston, *Freedom and Citizenship*, pp. 141–42; Langston, *Virginia Plantation*, p. 80; Shumway, *Oberliniana, 1833–1883*, p. 104; William H. Ferris, *The African Abroad, or His Evolution in Western Civilization, Tracing His Development Under Caucasian Milieu*, 2 vols. (New Haven, 1913), II, p. 745.

41. Langston, *Virginia Plantation*, p. 81; August Field Beard, *A Crusade of Brotherhood: A History of the American Missionary Association* (Boston, 1909; repr. New York: AMS Press, 1972), pp. 207–10; Langston, *Freedom and Citizenship*, p. 10; O. O. Howard to George Whipple, Dec. 2, 1873, Oliver O. Howard Papers, Bowdoin College Library; *National Intelligencer*, June 8, 1867.

42. Cleveland *Herald*, n.d., 1845, quoted in Oberlin *Evangelist*, Sept. 10, 1845; Albany *Patriot*, n.d., quoted in Oberlin *Evangelist*, Nov. 19, 1845; Cincinnati *Enquirer*, June 2, 1841; *Catalogue of the Officers and Students of the Oberlin Collegiate Institute, 1844–5* (Oberlin, 1844), pp. 30–31; J. A. Thome to Theodore Dwight Weld, Sept. 12, 1843, *Weld-Grimke Letters*, II, pp. 982–83; New York *Independent*, Mar. 24, 1853; Cincinnati *Gazette*, Aug. 6, 1845; Langston, *Virginia Plantation*, p. 80.

43. *Catalogue of the Oberlin Collegiate Institute, 1844–5*, pp. 14, 29; "Reminis-

cences of the Class of Eighteen Hundred & Fifty," ms., Oberlin College Library; James H. Fairchild, "Address on Oberlin: Its Origin, Progress, and Results," Oberlin *Evangelist*, Oct. 10, 1860.

44. Shumway, *Oberliniana, 1833–1883*, p. 149; Oberlin *Evangelist*, July 31, 1844.

45. Fairchild, *Oberlin: The Colony and the College*, p. 112; *National Anti-Slavery Standard*, Oct. 13, 1842; Thome to Weld, Apr. 13, 1841, *Weld-Grimke Letters*, II, p. 864.

46. M. R. D.[elany] to Frederick Douglass, July 24, 1848, *North Star*, Aug. 4, 1848; Daniel A. Payne, *The Semi-Centenary and the Retrospection of the African Methodist Church in the United States of America* (Baltimore, 1866), p. 65; J. M. Langston and Fanny M. Jackson to Editor, June 28, 1864, *National Anti-Slavery Standard*, July 9, 1864.

47. Thome to Weld, Apr. 13, 1841, *Weld-Grimke Letters*, II, p. 864; Oberlin College, Board of Trustees Minutes, Feb. 18, Aug. 25, 1852, Aug. 22, 1853, Box 16, R. S. Fletcher Papers, Oberlin College Archives; *Voice of the Fugitive*, May 20, 1852; Coppin, *Reminiscences*, pp. 12, 18–19; Lorain County *News*, Aug. 4, 1870; Juanita D. Fletcher, "Against the Consensus: Oberlin College and the Education of American Negroes, 1835–1865," Ph.D. diss., The American University, 1974, p. 216.

48. Coppin, *Reminiscences*, p. 15; John Mercer Langston, "A Representative Woman—Mrs. Sara K. Fidler," *A.M.E. Church Review* 4 (July 1887):474.

49. Fairchild, *Oberlin: The Colony and the College*, pp. 112–13; Denton J. Snider, *A Writer of Books* (St. Louis, 1910), p. 100; "Reminiscences of the Class of Eighteen Hundred & Fifty."

50. Lorain County *News*, Aug 4. 1870.

51. On Langston's name change, see J. Mercer Langston, "Speech Before the Union Society, May 23, 1848," ms., John Mercer Langston Papers, Fisk University Library; Lucy Stone, "Oberlin and Women," Cleveland *Leader*, July 5, 1883; Lorain County *News*, Aug 4, 1870.

52. Langston, *Virginia Plantation*, pp. 81–82, 89; Oberlin *Evangelist*, Sept. 11, 1844.

53. Langston, *Virginia Plantation*, p. 82; A. D. Barber, *Report of the Colored People of Ohio* (Cincinnati, 1840), p. 1.

54. Langston, *Virginia Plantation*, pp. 82–85; Harriet A. Little, "John Mercer Langston, A.B., A.M., LL.D.," *A.M.E. Church Review* 4 (October 1887):187.

55. Langston, *Virginia Plantation*, pp. 85–87. Devore attended Oberlin in 1844 and 1850, and had been a teacher and engaged in business in Mercer County, see Cowles List; Little, "John Mercer Langston," 187.

56. Langston, *Virginia Plantation*, p. 88; Camilla Stevens to Lucy Stone, July 26, 1846, Box I, Fletcher Papers; Langston, *Virginia Plantation*, p. 87; Little, "John Mercer Langston," 187.

57. Langston, *Virginia Plantation*, pp. 89–90; untitled, undated news-clipping, 1876, John Mercer Langston Scrapbook, Fisk University Library.

58. A Traveller to Editors, *Ohio State Journal*, Nov. 25, 1845; untitled, undated news-clipping, 1876, Langston Scrapbook (Fisk); Scioto *Gazette*, Aug. 26, 1885; Langston, *Virginia Plantation*, pp. 90–91.

59. *Palladium of Liberty*, Feb. 28–Nov. 12, 1844; "Miscellaneous Bills," Langston Papers; Langston, *Virginia Plantation*, pp. 91–92.

60. *Catalogue of . . . Oberlin Collegiate Institute, 1845–6* (Oberlin, 1845), p. 10; Fletcher, *Oberlin College*, II, pp. 596, 600, 610–11; *Catalogue of . . . Oberlin Collegiate Institute, 1845–6*, p. 35; Snider, *A Writer of Books*, p. 104.

61. S.B. to Prof. H. Cowles, Aug. 25, 1851, and Henry Cowles to S. B., Sept. 2, 1851, both in Oberlin *Evangelist*, Sept. 10, 1851; Fletcher, *Oberlin College*, II, p. 596, fn. 7; Fairchild, *Oberlin: The Colony and the College*, p. 113; *Proceedings of the General Anti-Slavery Convention Called by the Committee of the British and Foreign Anti-Slavery Society, and Held in London from Tuesday, June 13, to Tuesday, June 20, 1843* (London, 1843), p. 206; *National Anti-Slavery Standard*, July 9, 1864; Oberlin *Evangelist*, Sept. 10, 1851.

62. *National Anti-Slavery Standard*, July 9, 1864.

63. Address of Jacob Dolson Cox (Class of '45), W. G. Ballantine, ed., *The Oberlin Jubilee 1833–1883* (Oberlin, 1883), p. 285; E. W. Gray to Asa Mahan, Dec. 23, 1843, quoted in Fletcher, *Oberlin College*, II, p. 521; F. A. Collester to Dear Mother, Apr. 19, 1852, Box 3, Fletcher Papers; "Reminiscences of the Class of Eighteen Hundred & Fifty"; Coppin, *Reminiscences*, p. 15; Snider, *A Writer of Books*, p. 105; *National Anti-Slavery Standard*, July 9, 1864.

64. *National Anti-Slavery Standard*, July 9, 1864; B. D. Wright to My Dear Sisters, May 1, 1846, Box 16, Fletcher Papers; M. P. Dascomb, "Report of Female Department for 1865–1866," R. S. Fletcher Files, Oberlin College Archives; Fairchild, *Oberlin: The Colony and the College*, p. 113; "Record of the Proceedings of the Ladies Board," Box 6, Fletcher Papers; Boston *Commonwealth*, n.d., quoted in *National Anti-Slavery Standard*, June 11, 1864.

65. *National Anti-Slavery Standard*, July 9, 1864; Delazon Smith, *A History of Oberlin, or New Lights of the West* (Cleveland, 1837), p. 57.

66. Fairchild, *Oberlin: The Colony and the College*, p. 113; J. Mercer Langston to Henry [Howe], Apr. 10, 1854, Langston Papers.

67. Alice Stone Blackwell, *Lucy Stone, Pioneer of Women's Rights* (Boston, 1930), p. 47; "The Social Problem Solved," *The Congregationalist*, n.d., quoted in New York *Independent*, Nov. 16, 1865.

68. John Carey Leith to Dear Father, May 6, 1861, Oberlin College Archives; Oberlin *Evangelist*, June 4, 1862; Lawson, *The Three Sarahs*, pp. 248–53.

69. "Reminiscences of the Class of Eighteen Hundred & Fifty"; Wright to My Dear Sisters, May 1, 1848; Collester to Dear Mother, Apr. 19, 1852, both in Fletcher Papers; Blackwell, *Lucy Stone*, p. 56; Fletcher, *Oberlin College*, II, p. 772.

70. L. F. Parker, "Sarah Candace Pearse Parker," (Lit. 1851), ms., dated 1900, copy in Sarah Candace Pearse, Alumni Records, Oberlin College Archives. She is mentioned as a Cincinnati teacher in Helen M. Cowles, *Grace Victorious; or, The Memoirs of Helen M. Cowles* (Oberlin, 1856), p. 51.

71. *Minutes . . . of the State Convention of the Colored Citizens of Ohio . . . Columbus . . . Jan. 1, 1849* (Oberlin, 1849).

72. Langston to Henry, Apr. 10, 1854, Langston Papers; *Laws and Regulations* (Oberlin, 1840); *Catalogue of . . . Oberlin Collegiate Institute, 1845–6*, p. 10;

Catalogue of . . . Oberlin Collegiate Institute, 1846–7 (Oberlin, 1846), p. 11; *Catalogue of . . . Oberlin Collegiate Institute, 1847–8* (Oberlin, 1847), p. 10; Henry Willett Howe, Alumni Records, Oberlin College Archives.

73. Washington *National Republican*, Oct. 24, 1872. On Daniels, see James McPherson, *The Abolitionist Legacy: From Reconstruction to the NAACP* (Princeton, 1975), pp. 76–77.

74. Langston to Dear Henry, Apr. 10, 1854, Langston Papers.

75. Blackwell, *Lucy Stone*, pp. 53–54, 46; Antoinette Brown Blackwell, "Reminiscences of Early Oberlin," ms., Blackwell Family Collection, the Arthur and Elizabeth Schlesinger Library on the History of Women in America, Radcliffe College; "Reminiscences of the Class of Eighteen Hundred & Fifty"; Langston, *Virginia Plantation*, pp. 92–95.

76. Fletcher, *Oberlin College*, II, pp. 694–702; Coppin, *Reminiscences*, p. 12.

77. James Monroe Jones, Alumni Records, Oberlin College Archives; "Oberliniana," Oberlin *Alumni Magazine* 57 (Apr. 1961):12; John Craven Jones, Alumni Records; William Allen Jones, Alumni Records; Elias Toussaint Jones, Alumni Records, all in Oberlin College Archives.

78. On the teaching of mental and moral philosophy in American colleges in this period, see Wilson Smith, *Professors and Public Ethics* (Ithaca, 1956). J. M. Langston to Maj. Gen. O. O. Howard, Aug. 15, 1871, Howard Papers; Fletcher, *Oberlin College*, I, pp. 472–88; Asa Mahan, articles on "Reform," Oberlin *Evangelist*, May 8, June 19, Aug. 14, 1844; Cleveland *Leader*, May 25, 1859.

79. Fletcher, *Oberlin College*, I, p. 234.

80. Ibid., II, pp. 738–39; "Reminiscences of the Class of Eighteen Hundred & Fifty."

81. Among the black members of the literary societies were George B. Vashon; William Cuthbert Whitehorne; William Allen Jones (teacher, dentist, and gold miner in British Columbia, Canada); B. F. Randolph, who was murdered in South Carolina in 1868 while actively campaigning for the Radical Republicans; Fanny Jackson; and Oberlin's first black female graduate, Lucy Stanton. Harry N. Frost, ed., *Register of the Members Both Graduate and Non-Graduate of Phi Delta Literary Society, Oberlin College* (Oberlin, 1891), pp. 18, 31, 34; Cleveland *Leader*, Oct. 21, 1868.

82. *National Anti-Slavery Standard*, Sept. 9, 1865.

83. Langston, *Virginia Plantation*, pp. 93–95; Shumway, *Oberliniana, 1833–1883*, p. 104.

84. New York *Independent*, Sept. 12, 1867.

85. J. Mercer Langston, "Speech Before the Union Society," Langston Papers.

86. Born in Delaware and educated in the East, where he was trained as a barber, John M. Brown attended Oberlin from 1841–44. As a result of the efforts of Brown and others, the 1845 Annual Conference of the A.M.E. church founded Union Seminary some twelve miles outside Columbus to educate future ministers and all others interested in "the cultivation of their minds." Land was purchased, but no buildings erected for several years. In

the meantime the seminary's quarters was the basement of the Bethel A.M.E. church in Columbus, and Brown was its first principal. In late 1848, he reported that he had a "large and flourishing school of 53 scholars. . . . I both serve a Church and teach a school. . . . The Students of Oberlin (Colored) are all around me. . . . All are doing good." Of gentlemanly demeanor and a fluent speaker, Brown was active and influential in the black protest movement in Ohio until 1853, when his church called him elsewhere. A long and useful life, including a number of years spent in postwar Washington where he and Langston worked together, awaited the future bishop (ordained 1868) of the A.M.E. church; see Simmons, *Men of Mark*, pp. 805–8; Brown, *The Rising Son*, pp. 449–50; Cowles List; J. M. Brown to Hamilton Hill, July 21, 1845; J. M. Brown to Hamilton Hill, Dec. 29, 1848, both in Oberlin College Archives; Daniel A. Payne, *History of the African Methodist Episcopal Church* (Nashville, 1891), pp. 149–50, 186–87, and passim.

87. Brown's position as principal of Union Seminary was taken over by Edward P. Davis, who attended Oberlin from 1840–44 and was a minister in Columbus at the time of his appointment. It was under Davis that the seminary was moved to its originally proposed site in Franklin County. In 1852, editor Henry Bibb noted that Union Seminary under the Rev. Davis's charge had "a farm of 172 acres paid for, partly cleared and under cultivation. The number of pupils have varied each term, during the past year from 30 to 65." Davis continued as the head of the always struggling seminary until 1863, at which time it was merged with Wilberforce University at Xenia, Ohio. In the fifties, Davis was involved in black policymaking, delivering one of the principal speeches at the 1850 state convention at Cleveland and acting as the secretary of the 1853 state convention. Following the demise of Union Seminary, Davis served his church as a minister and conference leader until his death in September 1866; see Cowles List; S. J. Woodson to Editor, *Christian Recorder*, Nov. 10, 1866; *Voice of the Fugitive*, Sept. 23, 1852; Edward P. Davis, "Origin and Progress of Union Seminary Institute," *Christian Recorder*, Apr. 18, 1863; Anti-Slavery *Bugle*, Aug. 17, 1850; *Official Proceedings of the Ohio State Convention of Colored Freemen . . . Columbus . . . Jan., 1853* (Cleveland, 1853); Payne, *History of the A.M.E. Church*, pp. 399, 402–14, 423–38; PET. to Editor, Oct. 1, 1866, *Christian Recorder*, Oct. 13, 1866.

88. Edward Davis and John M. Brown to Editor, *Palladium of Liberty*, July 10, 1844; *Anti-Slavery Bugle*, July 24, 1846; Langston, *Virginia Plantation*, p. 101.

89. *Anti-Slavery Bugle*, July 24, 1846; *Palladium of Liberty*, July 10, 1844.

90. Oberlin *Evangelist*, Aug. 17, 1842, Sept. 11, Nov. 6, 1844.

91. Antoinette Brown Blackwell, "Autobiography," chapter 5, ms.; Blackwell, "Reminiscences of Early Oberlin," both in Blackwell Family Collection; Oberlin *Evangelist*, July 17, 1844, Aug. 19, 1846; Blackwell, *Lucy Stone*, pp.51–52; Program of First of August Celebration, 1846, Fletcher, *Oberlin College*, I, opposite page 250; Antoinette Brown to Lucy Stone, n.d., 1847, Blackwell Family Collection.

92. Betsey Cowles, "Mr. and Mrs. Foster at Oberlin," *Anti-Slavery Bugle*, Oct. 9, 1846.

93. *Anti-Slavery Bugle*, Jan. 14, 28, Feb. 4, Apr. 22, 1854; J. Mercer Langston to Julia Griffiths, Oct. 29, 1854, *Frederick Douglass' Paper*, Nov. 10, 1854; Antoinette L. Brown to Julia Griffiths, Nov. 8, 1854, *Frederick Douglass' Paper*, Nov. 24, 1854; J. M. Langston to Julia Griffiths, n.d., *Frederick Douglass' Paper*, Dec. 1, 1854.

94. Mrs. Orna Langhorne quoted in *Southern Workman*, n.d., quoted in Cleveland *Gazette*, May 28, 1892; Lorain County *News*, Aug. 4, 1870; *North Star*, Sept. 29, 1848.

95. *North Star*, June 2, Sept. 15, 1848.

96. *North Star*, Apr. 7, May 5, July 14, 1848.

97. *North Star*, July 14, 1848; Delany, *Condition of the Colored People*, pp. 36, 45–48, 192–97.

98. *North Star*, July 28, Sept. 8, Aug. 4, 1848.

99. Cleveland *True-Democrat*, Sept. 7, 1848; *Report of the Proceedings of the Colored National Convention . . . Cleveland . . . Sept., 1848* (Rochester, 1848); John Morgan to Mark Hopkins, Dec. 15, 1847, quoted in Fletcher, *Oberlin College*, I, p. 270. Morgan, and doubtless Langston, encountered Douglass and his moral suasionist friends, William Lloyd Garrison and Stephen Foster, when they stopped off in Oberlin during commencement week of 1847; see W. L. Garrison to My Dear Wife, Aug. 28, 1847, Garrison Papers; D. McB. to Editor, Aug. 25, 1847, Cleveland *True-Democrat*, Sept. 3, 1847. On Douglass, see Waldo E. Martin, Jr., *The Mind of Frederick Douglass* (Chapel Hill, 1984), and Waldo E. Martin, Jr., "Frederick Douglass: Humanist as Race Leader," in *Black Leaders of the Nineteenth Century*, ed. Leon Litwack and August Meier (Urbana, 1988), pp. 59–84.

100. *National Convention . . . 1848*; Cleveland *True-Democrat*, Aug. 7, Sept. 11, 1848; *North Star*, Oct. 20, 1848.

101. *National Convention . . . 1848*.

102. Ibid.; *Anti-Slavery Bugle*, Oct. 13, 1848; *North Star*, Sept. 29, 1848; Washington *National Republican*, July 7, 1875.

103. Cleveland *True-Democrat*, Sept. 11, 1848; *North Star*, Jan. 12, 1849.

104. *State Convention . . . 1849*.

105. Ibid.

106. Langston, *Virginia Plantation*, p. 356.

107. Langston, "Speech Before the Union Society"; Cleveland *True-Democrat*, Apr. 27, 1848; John I. Gaines, "Address," May 12, 1848, *North Star*, June 2, 1848.

108. Oberlin *Evangelist*, Sept. 11, 1844; *State Convention . . . 1849*; "Actions of the Federal Government in behalf of Slavery," ms., Feb. 27, 1850, Columbus, Langston Papers.

109. *State Convention . . . 1849*.

110. Stephen E. Maizlish, *The Triumph of Sectionalism: The Transformation of Ohio Politics, 1844–1856* (Kent, Ohio, 1983), pp. 121–46; Frederick J. Blue, *Salmon P. Chase: A Life in Politics* (Kent, Ohio, 1987), pp. 68–72; Leonard Erickson, "Politics and Repeal of Ohio's Black Laws, 1837–1849," *Ohio History* 82 (Summer-Autumn 1973):154–75; *North Star*, June 29, 1849; Oberlin *Evangelist*, Feb. 28, 1849.

111. Langston, *Virginia Plantation*, p. 96; George N. Allen to George Whipple, Aug. 1, 1849, AMA Papers.

112. Langston, *Virginia Plantation*, p. 101; John Mercer Langston to My Dear Friend, Jan. 5, 1895, James H. Fairchild Papers, Oberlin College Library; Langston to Dear Henry, Apr. 10, 1854, Langston Papers.

113. *State Convention . . . 1849*. Examples of his use of the quotation in two major addresses are in *Annual Report Presented to the American Anti-Slavery Society* (New York, 1855); Montgomery (Alabama) *State Sentinel*, Feb. 3, 1868.

CHAPTER 5

Career, Reform, and Thwarted Hopes

1849–50

B Y the end of Langston's collegiate days, if not before, "thinking of beginning to do something," as he later phrased it to a gathering of young men, he determined on becoming a lawyer.[1] It was a career to which his speaking talent and background, a life tied to courtrooms with almost Dickensian knots, disposed him, as its prestige attracted him. To a great extent, incontestably, lawyers led the age: Clay, Calhoun, and Webster among the seniors, Seward, Chase, and Sumner among the risers. Tocqueville had called the law in America the aristocracy of professions.

For Langston, who already thought of himself as a representative of his race, the challenge of achieving a racial breakthrough was a major inducement. To date, only three Negroes had gained entry to the American legal profession, all in the East. In 1844 in Portland, Maine, Macon B. Allen, later accredited in Massachusetts as well, had become the first Negro admitted to the bar. In 1847, after an open court examination in Boston, Robert Morris also had won the right to practice law in Massachusetts.[2] But both Maine and Massachusetts enfranchised Negroes and accorded them greater legal protection than in most other states; in fact, Massachusetts would become, just before the Civil War, the only northern state to permit Negroes to serve as jurors. Unfortunately, John Mercer could look to the frustrating experiences of his friend George Vashon in Pennsylvania, which had disfranchised Negroes in 1838, as the nearest potential parallel for his hopes. After finally succeeding in breaking the color line in New York, which allowed a restricted black suffrage, by passing an open court examination in January 1848, Vashon accepted a teaching position in Haiti and said, "My native State may claim the honor of casting me off; I am perfectly willing to accord it to her. And with pleasure [I] set down to the credit of New York whatever merit there may be in receiving me unto her bosum. . . . and now panoplied in the privileges of my profession, I am ready to bid farewell to the land of my birth in order to work out my destiny in the glorious field which the Island Republic offers to my labors."[3]

Young Langston realized the odds were against him. In Ohio the entire legal status of blacks and mulattoes remained a tiresomely ambiguous proposition. Suffrage depended on the local election judges who determined by sight whether a prospective voter was nearer white than black and thus entitled to cast his ballot. Nor did the pattern of racial discrimination exclude the courtroom. The state still barred Negroes from serving as jurors, and only that year, 1849, had the legislature abrogated the ban on Negro testimony in cases involving whites. Even so, observers acknowledged that the repeals would not be observed in the southern counties where the Negro population was greatest; in actuality, Ross County, for only one example, would continue to record Negro immigrants until 1855, six years after repeal of the state law authorizing the practice.[4]

But, Langston knew, the stakes were high. The case had been well put by a Cleveland journalist, criticizing the Pennsylvania bar's refusal of Vashon: "If God had painted him white, he would have been admitted. The colored people have rights; why not have learned men of their own kindred to vindicate them?" Like John Mercer's protest-minded colleagues in the black movement, who had pledged at an Oberlin meeting and again at the state black convention in January 1849 not only to support one another in claiming their consitutional rights, but also "in having the laws oppressing us tested," the young man was persuaded of the immense need to know the law both to protect and to extend black legal privileges.[5]

Oberlin diploma and pride in hand, young Langston queried antislavery lawyers and law schools. In response, a prominent attorney, whom he regarded as a special friend of the Negro, declared his inability to take the colored man into his office as a student, and "kindly" advised him to try his luck in the British West Indies. (The counsel was nearly identical in import, and perhaps source, to that offered him under different circumstances by Senator Salmon P. Chase in the autumn of 1850.) Forgiven by an older Langston as "natural enough under the circumstances," the letter of rejection arrived when he was already discouraged by equally negative advice from an elderly, highly respected Negro, who ridiculed his hopes because legal studies "would doubtless prove too intricate for the comprehensions of a colored man."[6]

By Christmas of 1849, however, Langston had attached himself to an abolitionist lawyer from Cleveland. Sherlock J. Andrews, a Weld convert, friend of Oberlin, and onetime Whig congressman, was willing to associate with Langston's scheme to integrate the white man's club, but only as his crowded schedule permitted. Judge of the superior court of Ohio and presently chairman of a committee studying the possibilities for a law school on the Western Reserve, Andrews consented to furnish Langston the essential texts and provide occasional explication. In his middle-aged benefactor, reputedly a "fiery and eloquent advocate . . . and withal a perfect gentleman," John Mercer discovered a man sympathetic to the idea of full citizenship rights for blacks.[7] Yet, for reasons not explained, the arrangement soon terminated. Quite probably, Andrews's election as a delegate to the 1850–51 convention to devise a new Ohio constitution made further lessons impractical.

Informed by a college friend, himself now a law student, of a possible opening at his own school at Ballston Spa in Saratoga County, New York, John Mercer applied in a letter reciting his qualifications and promising advance payment of all fees. The owner, J. W. Fowler, replied that although the faculty and trustees unanimously opposed his admission, a personal interview might reverse their stance. Langston's arrival at Ballston Spa coincided with the school commencement, featuring an address by the distinguished Philadelphia lawyer, orator, and abolitionist David Paul Brown. Loftily entitled "The Aristocracy of Eloquence," a phrase the impressed Langston would appropriate for a speech of his own eight years later, Brown's oration confirmed and strengthened his ambition.[8] Expectantly, he underwent interrogation by Fowler. But, after renewed discussion with his trustees and faculty, Fowler reported their conclusion that prospective white students, particularly those they hoped to attract from the South, would refuse to attend classes with a Negro. Nonetheless, the law principal himself, studying John Mercer's physical characteristics, proposed two devious alternatives. He could "edge" into the school by sitting silently in the recitation room off from the classroom and, if no one objected, moving closer by degrees until, eventually, he was incorporated into the class. Or he might "pass," masquerading as a Spaniard or Frenchman from some part of the Americas. Disappointed, hurt, and indignant, Langston rose from his chair and, if his recollection may be trusted, vowed in ringing tones: "Before I would consent to the humiliation and degradation implied in either of your propositions, I would open my veins and die of my own act! I am a colored American; and I shall not prove false to myself, nor neglect the obligation I owe to the Negro race!" Shrugging aside Fowler's apologies, he added: "I do not need sympathy! I need the privileges and advantages of your law school." The law principal proffered the aggrieved candidate the chance to speak in his lecture hall, to which Langston agreed, with the tart proviso, or so he agreeably remembered, that his topic would be Fowler's "treatment of a young educated colored man, the first of his class to ask admission as a student to any American law school." Fowler hastily withdrew the offer. Langston's journey came to an improbable conclusion with the inexperienced westerner's inclusion in a wealthy white abolitionist's glittering dinner party, the guests including his student friend as well as a discomfited Fowler, an experience of social acceptance counterpoised with rejection that salved, although it could not cure, the hurt.[9]

It appeared for some time, however, as refusal piled on top of refusal, that these memories would be the only fruit of his efforts. Application to Timothy Walker's noted Cincinnati Law School brought the perhaps anticipated disappointment. In words growing monotonous by repetition, Walker, who had admitted that slavery "brutalizes the black population and debilitates the white," explained that his "students would not feel at home" with a Negro, and Langston "would not feel at home with them."[10]

"Shall black talent be buried?" John Mercer's rhetorical appeal in January 1850 surely was also a cry of the heart. Young, gifted, and balked, he could be tempted to view his personal dilemma as a test of the white abolitionist and Negro faith in education as the means for racial progress, an enlarged vision that entailed only larger discouragement. More than four decades later, when he recalled this chapter of his life, pain and outrage flowed onto the pages. "Nearing his majority," at the outset of his effort to make himself "a useful man," feeling that he could do great things but afraid he would be prevented, he had been "denied."[11] Yet, even while he continued to pound futilely at the locked doors of the legal profession, he found a constructive channel for his energies and idealism. Barely twenty years of age, he began to work intensively in black protest and reform.

The center for Langston's efforts, as it would be throughout the pre-war decade, was the Ohio black convention movement. To understand Langston's involvement, it will be necessary to examine the structure and leadership of the movement, the most aggressive and sustained of the various black movements in the northern states. On at least twenty-one occasions—eleven since 1837 and ten times from 1850 until the outbreak of war—a record of frequency and longevity unmatched in any other state, the "combined wisdom and talent" of black Ohio concentrated in state conventions.[12] In the late thirties and into the forties, when the priority was to stimulate organization of privately funded black schools, delegates gathered in late summer or early fall; later, with focus on such legislative reform as acquisition of common school privileges, repeal of the Black Laws, and full enfranchisement, the conventions generally coincided with opening sessions of the state assembly in January. In accord with the latter purpose, Columbus, the state capital, was most often the site, but the conventions also had resort to Cincinnati, the urban black population center; Cleveland, hub of the abolitionist Western Reserve; Dayton, located in the southwest region where the predominant number of blacks resided; and, on the eve of war, Xenia, in Greene County, by then, with the establishment of Wilberforce University, a black intellectual center and home of a large black population.

More than three hundred different men and women participated in the eleven conventions for which figures exist, the number of delegates varying from a low of sixteen to a high of seventy-one, with a median of forty-five. The activist backbone of the movement was in the well-organized, vocal black communities of Cleveland, Columbus, Cincinnati, Oberlin, and Chillicothe, never without delegates. But, although the four urban areas and Oberlin supplied the dominant leadership, the rural areas, where the bulk of the black population lived, were broadly and consistently represented, with the exception of Brown and Gallia Counties in the south. The black "literati," as an 1851 delegate called them, the convention-goers ordinarily were elected by meetings called in their own localities. The 1849 convention, which may be taken as typical, included "pastors of churches, school teachers, students, farmers, plasterers, house painters, sign and ornamental painters, glaziers, paper hangers, wheelwrights, joiners, printers, barbers, independent barbers (shave anybody, white or colored), and blacksmiths."[13]

Operating on several levels, the conventions offered those who attended certain political, psychological, and social benefits. First, they were training sessions in democracy and leadership. Facilitated by parliamentary procedure, free speech reigned. Delegates elected officers, served on committees, drafted resolutions and petitions, and took part in floor debate to hammer out policy and arrive at consensus. Subsequently, they presented the convention's work at local meetings where democratic procedure and debate likewise governed. Published minutes of the convention, copies of which were sent to prominent white abolitionists and politicians, circulated throughout the black community. Second, the conventions were sources of vital information and insight. Delegates shared knowledge of available land, markets, employment, or teachers; volunteered their own experience in organizing benevolent, economic, and political associations; discussed tactics and strategy for handling a local problem or a statewide issue; and, at the meetings held in Columbus, conferred with friendly white politicians. Informally, delegates had the chance to talk of crops and cattle, of business prospects, family, and community, or of the latest atrocity tale or rescue story. Finally, the conventions were exercises in confidence-building as well as healthy outlets for tension. In particular, oratory, the quality of which was often remarked upon by outsiders, provided the release of language and evoked a rededication to the struggle. On hearing their own speakers, the emotions of the black Ohioans may have been akin to those described by Ralph Ellison, the Negro novelist and essayist. He observes that the eloquence of the orator, like other artists, creates "moments of exultation wherein man's vision is quickened, . . . moments of high consciousness; moments wherein we grasp, in the instant, a knowledge of how transcendent and how abysmal and yet how affirmative it can be to be human beings."[14]

Continuity in the Ohio black movement was insured by the State Central Committee. From the early forties onward, a group of seven to ten stalwarts, sometimes appointed by the convention and sometimes, it would appear, self-perpetuating, the Central Committee, in consultation with other acknowledged leaders around the state, issued calls for conventions, carried out, where possible, their dictates, and when it was deemed essential or expedient, implemented policies of its own devising.[15]

The charge sometimes was leveled at black leaders in other northern states that they represented no one but themselves.[16] Whatever the validity of that criticism elsewhere, it did not pertain in Ohio. The representative nature of the conventions, in combination with the lecture and organizational tours frequently undertaken by convention-appointed agents—most often David Jenkins and John Mercer Langston during the fifties—and the crowd-attracting First of August celebrations at which the convention movement leaders served as orators, helped to build a constituency and assure an ongoing dialogue. In addition, several of the men who achieved reputations extending beyond their home territory took commanding roles in black-organized educational (School Fund Society), temperance (Sons of Temperance), and religious (Methodist and Baptist) institutions that had statewide networks. A few held white-sponsored antislavery agencies that required extensive travel and visitation.

Langston and his colleagues in the movement appealed with most effect to men who were restless and willing to risk themselves to obtain relief: the artisans, semiskilled enterprisers, and self-employed businessmen, the small group of educated ministers and teachers, the independent farmers residing in the countryside. Their constituency also included the wives and daughters of black male leaders as well as women with some formal education and those in skilled trades.

By the time of young Langston's involvement, a solid leadership core of some twenty men, three-quarters of whom would continue into the fifties, had emerged. (Table 1).[17] Of major importance during the early years were the Reverend Walter Claiborne Yancy of Chillicothe, who was later a resident of Butler County; schoolteacher A. M. Sumner, barbers Andrew J. Gordon, William H. Yancy, and William W. Watson, riverman Joseph Henry Perkins, minister Wallace Shelton, and barber and livery stable proprietor Gideon Q. Langston, all important figures in the Cincinnati of John Mercer's boyhood; the carpenter and boatman John Malvin and barber John L. Watson of Cleveland; barbers L. D. Taylor and James P. Poindexter, and painter and plasterer David Jenkins, all of Columbus. Also active from the mid-forties onward were John M. Brown, barber, teacher, and minister in Columbus; the Reverend William P. Newman, who lived occasionally in Cincinnati and Oberlin; Charles H. Langston, teacher in Chillicothe and then dentist and teacher in Columbus; along with Cincinnati steamboat provisioner John I. Gaines and barber Alfred J. Anderson of Hamilton in Butler County. Newspaperman William Howard Day of Oberlin became prominent at decade's end; teacher Peter H. Clark of Cincinnati was not widely known until the state convention in January 1852.

With but four exceptions (two of whom had southern parentage), their origins were in the South, with a preponderant number coming out of Virginia. Several had enjoyed comparatively privileged beginnings: the three Langston brothers had benefited from the concern of a wealthy white father, while stable black parentage had nurtured the aptitudes of Gaines, his nephew Clark, and Jenkins. Of those whose status can be determined, eleven were born free and five had been slaves. The early life of Lorenzo Dow Taylor, who attended every state convention until his death in 1857, was concealed, lamented Charles Langston in his memorial, "in that black and impenetrable obscurity in which slavery always seeks to envelop itself and its victims." Two were fugitives, Newman and John L. Watson. The latter, a long-time antislavery lecturer, joked that in heaven his old master would greet him, "Ha, ha John—you here? I have been looking for you; you have been gone thirty years."[18] From their predominantly southern roots the leaders derived commonalities of language, experience, and cultural style, especially humor and a chivalrous manner; from their western environment, a tendency to disregard caste and class. Together, these qualities helped to minimize the potential for regional and class disharmony within the leadership, while contributing to the generally democratic outlook of the leadership's appeal to its people.

Among the leadership, color was not the measure of the man. Nine at least of the men under consideration were mulattoes. How many others had white ancestry is difficult to determine, in part because they themselves appear to have placed so little importance upon it. In contrast to the East, where black reformers at loggerheads occasionally did resort to censure on the basis of skin color, those in the forefront in Ohio mentioned lightness or darkness nearly always in the positive sense. Gaines, for example, would point out his own blackness or that of a particularly successful schoolchild, but only to underscore his conviction that a black man was as fully capable as a mulatto. Day did once quell a black nationalist during debate by announcing that the latter's two wives had both been "white," but such an exchange was rare.[19]

Although none lived in easy circumstances, most, if not all, were property owners; several possessed considerable means. Moreover, the leaders utilized occupation, position, or work location to promote their cause. Barbers like John L. Watson, proprietor of the "largest bathhouse west of the Alleghenies," and Poindexter, whose shop was near the Neil House, "headquarters of public men," and across from the State House, sharpened wits with customers of influence and power; Jenkins's contracts to paint and plaster public buildings allowed access, which he tactfully exploited, to white officeholders; Brown and Shelton used their respective Methodist and Baptist pulpits to preach a gospel of liberty and equality for all; Sumner, Jenkins, and Charles Langston capitalized on their successive national appointment as "Patriarch" of the Sons of Temperance to promote education and political rights as well as moderate habits; Malvin, Perkins,[20] and Gaines, by virtue of their situations on the waterways, assisted fugitives to the North; Newman and W. C. Yancy combined itinerant ministries with establishing black schools and raising funds for abolitionist enterprises.

Although studies of New York state and Detroit have found that the majority of black abolitionists were ministers,[21] only three of the twenty Ohioans were occupied in the ministry full-time, and another minister made his living as a teacher. Noting that nineteenth-century black leadership "generally came from ministerial ranks, for most other professions were virtually closed to blacks," one scholar has speculated that the factor separating the great majority of black ministers who did not

Table 1. Biographical Data for Black Leaders in Ohio, 1837–60

Name	Status	Color	Origin	Residence	Dates	Occupation	Education	Wealth	Sources
Anderson, Alfred J.	Born free	M	Va.	Butler Co., Hamilton, Ohio	Feb. 24, 1824–95	Barber	Diligent self-study; 3 months' formal education; highly literate	Property holder	Parham, *Official History*, 297–99; *North Star*, May 5, June 2, 1848; *Philanthropist*, Oct. 2, 1843; *Anti-Slavery Bugle*, Dec. 27, 1856
Brown, John M.	Born free	M	Del.	Columbus	1822(?)–87+	Barber, teacher, minister	Oberlin College 1841–44	?	Simmons, *Men of Mark*, 805–8; Brown, *The Rising Son*, 449–50
Clark, Peter H.	Born free (father freed)	M	Ohio—father, Ky.	Cincinnati	March 1829–1925	Barber, teacher, editor, clerk	Graduate, Gilmore high school; highly literate	Property holder	Gerber, "Peter Humphries Clark," pp. 173–90; Cleveland *Gazette*, March 6, 1886; Simmons, *Men of Mark*, 244–49; Brown, *The Rising Son*, 522–24; Clark, "Peter Humphries Clark," 176
Day, William Howard	Born free	M	N.Y.	Oberlin, Cleveland	Oct. 19, 1825–Dec 2, 1900	Printer, editor, teacher	Graduate, Oberlin College	Property holder	Blackett, *Beating Against the Barriers*, 287–386; Simmons, *Men of Mark*, 701–4; Brown, *The Rising Son*, 449–50; "William Howard Day," Alumni Records, Oberlin College; Harrisburg (Pa.) *Telegraph*, Dec. 3, 1900

Table 1. Continued

Name	Status	Color	Origin	Residence	Dates	Occupation	Education	Wealth	Sources
Gaines, John I.	Born free	B	Ohio	Cincinnati	Nov. 6, 1821–Nov. 27, 1859	Stevedore, proprietor of boat store	Limited formal education; diligent self-study; highly literate	$3,000 in 1850	Brown, *The Rising Son*, 450–52; *Matthews*, "John Isom Gaines," 41–48; *Liberator*, April 27, 1860; Shotwell, *A History of the Schools*, 457–58; Riley, "The Negro in Cincinnati," 73; Cleveland *Leader*, June 9, Aug. 4, 1860
Gordon, Andrew J.	?	?	Va.	Cincinnati, Cleveland	?–1859+	Barber	Highly literate	?	Shaffer, *Cincinnati Directory*, 1840; *Population Census*, 1840; *Address and Reply to Presentation of Testimonial of S. P. Chase*
Jenkins, David	Born free	B	Va.	Columbus	1811–Sept. 5, 1877	Barber, printer, plasterer	Private tutor; highly literate	Considerable property	Parham, *Official History*, 267–68; *National Convention*, 1848; Mahoning (Ohio) *Free Democrat*, Jan. 14, 1853; Ohio *State Journal*, Feb. 25, 1870
Langston, Charles H.	Born free	M	Va.	Chillicothe, Columbus	1815(?)–Nov. 1892	Teacher, dentist	Oberlin College, 1836, 1839, 1842—43	Inheritance; real estate owner	Cleveland *Gazette*, Dec. 24, 1892; A. D. Langston to George M. Jones. Nov. 1906, postcard in Charles Langston File, Oberlin College Archives

Table 1. Continued

Name	Status	Color	Origin	Residence	Dates	Occupation	Education	Wealth	Sources
Langston, Gideon Q.	Born free	M	Va.	Cincinnati	1809(?)–48(?)	Proprietor of livery stable	Oberlin College, 1836, 1839	Inheritance; owner of well-appointed livery stable	Cleveland *Gazette*, Dec. 24, 1892; A. D. Langston to George M. Jones, Nov. 1906, postcard in Charles Langston File, Oberlin College Archives
Malvin, John	Born free (slave father)	M	Va.	Cleveland	1795–1880	Carpenter, steamboat cook, sawmill engineer, canal boat captain	Paid slave to teach him to read and write; wrote autobiography	$1,000 in 1860, $3,000 in 1870	Peskin, ed., *North into Freedom*, passim; Goliber, "Cuyahoga Blacks," 101
Newman, William P.	Runaway slave	?	Va.	Oberlin, Cincinnati	?–Aug. 5, 1866	Minister	Completed sophomore year at Oberlin College	?	Simmons, *Men of Mark*, 376; Oberlin *Evangelist*, Aug. 17, 1842; *North Star*, Oct. 24, 1850; Newman to Chase, Nov. 30, 1863, Salmon P. Chase Papers, Library of Congress
Perkins, Joseph Henry	?	?	?	Cincinnati	10–24 age category 1840; last evidence 1867	Businessman	Gilmore high school; highly literate	?	*Population Census*, 1840; Cleveland *True-Democrat*, Jan. 26, 1850; *Anti-Slavery Bugle*, Aug. 24, 1850; Perkins, "Oration," 1849, *op. cit.*; Cincinnati *Gazette*, Feb. 23, 1867; Shotwell, *A History of the Schools*, 457–58

Table 1. Continued

Name	Status	Color	Origin	Residence	Dates	Occupation	Education	Wealth	Sources
Poindexter, James P.	Born free	M Father white; mother Cherokee & black	Va.	Columbus	Sept. 25, 1819–1907	Barber, also minister after 1862	Private lessons from Englishman; highly literate	Property holder	Minor, "James Preston Poindexter," passim; Simmons, *Men of Mark*, 258–65
Shelton, Wallace	Slave, probably emancipated	?	?	Cincinnati	?–Last evidence 1874	Minister	Highly literate	Property holder	*Frederick Douglass' Paper*, Aug. 18, 1854; *State Convention*, 1849, *Philanthropist*, Feb. 20, 1838; Arnett, ed., *Proceedings*, 60, 62
Sumner, A. N.	?	?	Tenn.	Cincinnati	24–36 age category in 1840; last evidence 1858	Teacher	A "score of years" teaching experience by 1844; co-editor of newspaper	Property holder	*Population Census*, 1840; Shaffer, *Cincinnati Directory*, 1840, 475; *Philanthropist*, Feb. 20, 1838; *Palladium of Liberty*, May 1, 1844; *Philanthropist*, April 22, 1844; *State Convention*, 1858
Taylor, L. D.	Freed slave	B	Va.	Columbus	1815–April 24, 1856	Barber	"Did not much excel in knowledge of letters"	?	*State Convention*, 1857; *Palladium of Liberty*, Sept. 25, 1844

Table 1. Continued

Name	Status	Color	Origin	Residence	Dates	Occupation	Education	Wealth	Sources
Watson, John L.	Runaway slave	?	Va.	Cleveland	?–last evidence Jan. 1850	Barber	Highly literate	Prosperous barbering business	*State Convention*, 1849, 1850; Cleveland *True Democrat*, Aug. 16, 1850; *Palladium of Liberty*, Oct. 9, 1844
Watson, William W.	Freed slave	M, 3/4 B	Va.	Cincinnati	24–36 age category in 1840;last evidence 1855	Barber, waiter	"Vigorous mental parts"; literate	$5,500– $30,000 in 1850	*Colored American*, Oct. 11, 1840; *Population Census*, 1840; Shaffer, *Cincinnati Directory*, 1840, 476; Riley, "The Negro in Cincinnati," 73; *Anti-Slavery Bugle*, Aug. 10, 1805; Langston, *Virginia Plantation*, 61
Yancy, W. Claiborne	Born free	?	Va.?	Chillicothe Butler Co., Hamilton, Ohio	24–36 age category in 1830–last evidence 1844	Minister	Highly literate	?	*Philanthropist*, Aug. 27, 1842; Woodson, *Free Negro Heads*, 127; *Philanthropist*, Sept. 8, 1837; Feb. 14, Aug. 28, 1844; Cromwell, *The Negro in American History*, 37
Yancy, William H.	Probably Slave, probably emancipated	?	Va.?	Cincinnati	55–100 age category in 1830–46	Barber	Co-editor of newspaper	?	Woodson, *Free Negro Heads*, 27; Cist, *Cincinnati Directory*, 1842, 447; *Philanthropist*, Dec. 8, 1845; *Palladium of Liberty*, March 20, April 2, May 1, 1844; *Philanthropist*, June 10, 1846

Table 1.   Continued

Sources: *The Address and Reply on the Presentation of a Testimonial to S. P. Chase, by the Colored People of Cincinnati* (Cincinnati, 1845); Rev. B. W. Arnett, ed., *Proceedings of the Semi-Centenary Celebration of the African Methodist Episcopal Church of Cincinnati Held in Allen Temple, Feb. 8th, 9th, and 10th, 1874* (Cincinnati, 1847); R. J. M. Blackett, *Beating Against the Barriers* (Baton Rouge, 1986); William Wells Brown, *The Rising Son* (Boston, 1874; repr. Miami; Mnemosyne Reprint, 1970); Charles Cist, *Cincinnati Directory for the Year 1842* (Cincinnati, 1842); Dovie King Clark, "Peter Humphries Clark," *Negro History Bulletin*, 5 (May 1942); John W. Cromwell, *The Negro in American History* (Washington, 1914); David A. Gerber, "Peter Humphries Clark: The Dialogue of Hope and Despair," in Leon Litwack and August Meier, eds., *Black Leaders of the Nineteenth Century* (Urbana, 1988); Thomas J. Goliber, "Cuyahoga Blacks: A Social and Demographic Study, 1850–1880," (master's thesis, Kent State University, 1972); John Mercer Langston, *From the Virginia Plantation to the National Capitol; or, The First and Only Negro Representative in Congress from the Old Dominion* (Hartford, 1894; repr. New York: Johnson Reprint, 1968); Richard Clyde Minor, "James Preston Poindexter, Elder Statesman of Columbus," *Ohio State Archaeological and Historical Quarterly* 56 (Oct. 1947); Samuel Matthews, "John Isom Gaines: The Architect of Black Public Education," *Queen City Heritage* 45 (Spring 1987); *Minutes . . . of the State Con-*
vention of the Colored Citizens of Ohio . . . Columbus . . . Jan., 1849 (Oberlin, 1849); *Minutes of the State Convention of the Colored Citizens of Ohio . . . Columbus . . . Jan., 1850* (Columbus, 1850); William Hartwell Parham, comp. *An Official History of the Most Worshipful Grand Lodge of Free and Accepted Masons for the State of Ohio* (n.p., 1906); J. H. Perkins, *Oration, Delivered on the First of August, 1849, Before the Colored Citizens of Cincinnati* (Cincinnati, 1849); Allan Peskin, ed., *North into Freedom: The Autobiography of John Malvin, Free Negro, 1795–1880* (Cleveland, 1966); Population Census of 1840, Hamilton County, City of Cincinnati, Reel 398, National Archives; *Proceedings of a Convention of the Colored Men of Ohio . . . Cincinnati . . . Nov., 1858* (Cincinnati, 1858); *Proceedings of the State Convention of the Colored Men of the State of Ohio . . . Columbus . . . Jan., 1857* (Columbus, 1857); *Report of the Proceedings of the Colored National Convention . . . Cleveland . . . Sept., 1848* (Rochester, 1848); Patricia Mae Riley, "The Negro in Cincinnati, 1835–1850," (master's thesis, University of Cincinnati, 1971); David Henry Shaffer, *The Cincinnati, Covington, Newport and Fulton Directory for 1840* (Cincinnati, 1840); John B. Shotwell, *A History of the Schools of Cincinnati* (Cincinnati, 1902); William J. Simmons, *Men of Mark: Eminent, Progressive and Rising* (Cleveland, 1887; repr. Chicago, Johnson Publishing, 1970); Carter G. Woodson, *Free Negro Heads of Families in the United States in 1830* (Washington, 1925).

advocate abolitionism publicly from those who did was the latter group's theological training.[22] In pre-war Ohio, however, on the local as well as the statewide level, ministers composed a minority of the leadership, and abolitionist ministers with theological training were scarcely in evidence, unless the Oberlin educations of Newman and John M. Brown can be considered equivalent. The activist centers looked less to the ministers than to the artisans (especially the barbers) and the men of business and letters; essentially rural areas often found leadership in blacksmiths or farmers.

Nevertheless, Ohio's black reform notables were influenced by evangelical perfectionist Christianity, with Oberlin as a major source. The closest they ever came to defining a common faith was a brief statement adopted by the 1849 convention: "to respect and love that as the religion of Jesus Christ, and that alone, which, in its practical bearings, is not excitement merely, but that which loves God, loves humanity, and thereby preaches deliverance to the captive, the opening of the prison-doors to them that are bound, and teaches us to do unto others as we would have them do to us." Agreement on a religion that emphasized personal, practical, and political reforms rather than heavenly salvation constituted one of the leadership's strongest bonds. It allowed the ministers and church elders, the latter the more numerous representatives of organized religion, to work in general harmony with those who for various reasons, including scorn at what they deemed cowardice in the churches' failure to oppose slavery, were not church members. Such concord did not prevent A.M.E. minister Brown and other delegates from hotly resisting various attempts, some instigated by John Mercer Langston, to censure churches and ministers who did not espouse antislavery positions. But on the whole, while careful to award those ministers in attendance special attention, commensurate to the power of the black church, the black leadership, including Brown, appeared to value denominational ties far less than firm moral rectitude and zeal in the furtherance of black liberation.[23]

The Ohio principals were, nearly to the man, uncommonly literate. Thanks to Oberlin and Gilmore's High School in Cincinnati, more than a third boasted formal educations; others had combined diligent independent study with snatches of scholarship from haphazard sources—a literate slave, intelligent customers in the barbershop, or a private tutor. The lucidity of convention documents and other records testifies to the general success of their efforts. But even so, the considerable differences in educational levels were a potential source of friction that seems largely to have been avoided because of the leaders' shared belief in education as the means of mental, moral, and material advancement.

Ex-slave Taylor "did not so much excel in the knowledge of letters," confessed C. H. Langston, but his scholarship, directed by the Proverbial injunction to "'get wisdom, and with all thy wisdom get understanding,'" surpassed others of superior opportunities.[24] Riverman Joseph Henry Perkins, in his 1849 First of August oration, subsequently circulated in pamphlet form, articulated the collective wisdom: "To prepare our posterity to assume a higher position in society we must educate them, morally, practically, and intellectually, make them mechanics and tillers of the soil, . . . make their lives proverbial for virtue, industry, economy, and temperance." Exclusion of Negroes from the means of education, the leadership maintained, was detrimental to society's "purity, prosperity, and stability." In the 1844 "Address of the State Convention to the Citizens of Ohio," Sumner, Jenkins, and J. L. Watson, in arguing for common school privileges, demanded, "What advantage . . . is it to our white fellow-citizens, that we grow up in their midst an ignorant, degraded, immoral, vicious and indolent people? . . . . What injury is it . . . if colored people become educated, honest, intelligent, high-minded, useful, wealthy . . .?"[25]

The Ohio black leadership's vision of how life should be lived embraced a combination of Christian, republican, abolitionist, and Afro-American values. As early as 1837, W. C. Yancy, Malvin, Sumner, Shelton and others in attendance at the first black Ohio Convention were speaking of themselves, in the same breath, as "Christians and republicans." By 1843, Yancy, as an agent of the Liberty party of Ohio, was arguing against the "unconstitutional encroachments of the slave-power upon the rights and interests of the people of the free states." In 1849, Gaines, in his First of August oration in Columbus, published together with the one given by Perkins in Cincinnati, denounced that "bastard, Anglo Saxon Republicanism" of "our own country" that "has intrigued at home and abroad for the ostensible purpose of reducing and keeping in most abject servitude, a loyal portion of her citizens." The Afro-American experience had given the leadership a recognition of the key role blacks had in freeing themselves, leading to a respect for the principle of civil disobedience and a faith in the power of resistance, an awareness of the need to be prepared to exploit opportunity, an acknowledgment of the importance of cultivating patience, persistence, self-control, and personal and racial dignity, a conviction of the undeniable rightness of the black cause, and an appreciation of the moral victory.

The Ohio black leaders' commitment to these values, reaffirmed at every convention, would be nowhere more boldly stated than by Charles Langston in his 1859 "card" justifying John Brown's action at Harper's

Ferry. The "renowned fathers of our celebrated revolution taught the world that 'resistance to tyrants is obedience to God,' " Langston asserted, and that "all men are created equal, and have the inalienable right to life and liberty." These men "proclaimed *death*, but *not slavery*, or rather 'give me liberty or give me death.' " In establishing a government to promote "liberty, justice, and happiness," the great revolutionaries had affirmed the right of the people "to abolish it, and to institute a new government" if it ever became destructive of such ends. John Brown's actions, Charles Langston summed up, "were in perfect harmony with and resulted from the teaching of the Bible and of the revolutionary fathers, and of every tried and faithful" abolitionist here and abroad.[26]

The personal backgrounds of these largely self-made men tended to lead to the self-reliant reform philosophy they espoused. In the face of the "adamantine wall of prejudice and Negro hate propped and supported" by law, as Charles Langston observed in eulogy of Taylor, "an almost superhuman energy and perseverance" were required to rise above the barrier "to moral and intellectual eminence." John Langston remembered Gaines's "determination not to exist merely, but to live, and to act a manly part in life."[27] The leadership shared a belief in the value of hard work, thrift, education, morality, religion, and family—those qualities ascribed by John Mercer Langston to Cincinnati's "aristocratic" black community, those qualities extolled in white abolitionist hamlets and small towns across the North. Moreover, the leaders were conscious that individual failure to adhere to high standards exposed the race to condemnation: "Our slightest faults are engraven on stone," warned Perkins, "and our brightest virtues are written on water."[28] In public life as in private, their disciplined performances, at the state conventions, in regional gatherings like the First of August celebrations, at community meetings, gave even hostile white observers scant opportunity to resort to standard racial deprecation. Rather, black and white alike remarked on the "unaffected dignity" with which Cincinnati barber Gordon presided over a state convention; the "courteous," "genial manner" of Columbus barber Poindexter; the "impressive and dignified . . . manners and bearing" of Butler County barber Anderson.[29] Furthermore, because the leaders did not live in racial isolation, confidence based on their own individual accomplishments and a perceived progress of their people in the critical areas of education, morality, and property holding was heightened by their daily observations of whites of every class.

For all the black handicaps, the vital measurements of worth of a mid-nineteenth-century American, at least in Ohio, where the white masses were generally poor and without education or skill, did not too much separate the races. In 1854, after reviewing figures on the wealth and property of black Ohioans (a value he assessed at more than $5 million), John Mercer Langston would declare it evident that "we are not more ignorant and degraded than other men." Quoting an 1849 comment by Secretary of State Samuel Galloway praising black Ohioans' advancement during the past decade, in which the official singled out the "order and intelligence" of black conventions and associations, Langston would demand: "What more could he have said, gentlemen, of the masses among the white people of this state?" By 1849, the leadership's self-confidence had reached the point that self-reliance became the recommended course of action, not just for the black individual, but for the collective struggle for political rights. "We ought to show to the world that we [are] capable of doing our own business," 1849 convention president Charles Langston remarked in successfully urging that a white man be excluded from the committee seeking use of the state legislators' hall for a public session. The delegates went on to recommend "to our brethren throughout the Union, that they, thanking their white friends for all action put forth in our behalf, pursue an independent course."[30]

Besides an increasingly audacious and straight-speaking Charles Langston, by then prominent in Columbus's black community, the preeminent leaders with whom John Mercer Langston would work most closely during the fifties were Malvin and Day of Cleveland; Jenkins and Poindexter of Columbus; and Gaines and Clark of Cincinnati. Like the Langstons, each of these men demonstrated a longevity, remarkable among reformers, in the cause of racial elevation.

A man of dignified yet forceful persistence, John Malvin was notable for his steadying hand, consistency, and reasonableness. In 1832, the free-born Virginian established residence in Cleveland where, through his principal trade as carpenter and joiner as well as such supplementary work as piloting his own lake vessel, he attained a modest prosperity.[31] Like other state leaders, Malvin was an instigator of both civil rights initiatives and black community-building. In 1833, he succeeded in integrating the First Baptist church and worshipped there with his wife Harriet for the next forty-seven years. With some aid from the local American Anti-Slavery Society, of which he was a member, Malvin began organizational work that culminated in what was possibly the town's first black meeting in January 1837. As chairman, Malvin proposed commissioning a black agent to traverse the state, assessing conditions in black settlements and gaining signatures on a petition for repeal of the Black Laws, work that led to the first black state convention that fall and establishment of the School Fund Society. Elected an officer in the parent organization, the self-educated Malvin helped form a local branch that operated a subscription school for several years.[32] During this period he was a founder of the Young Men's Union Society, which aspired to promote moral, mental, and political awareness through reading, debating, and exchange of ideas.[33] A dominant figure in black agitation in Cleveland for a generation and more,[34] the reliable and uncontentious Malvin served periodically on the State Central Committee, acted as vice-president of the state conventions of 1837 and 1857, and held the same office in the black Ohio State Anti-Slavery Society from 1858 until the outbreak of war.[35] Plain-spoken and not a powerful or especially skilled orator, Malvin was notable for his sense of perspective and seemingly indestructible faith. In his *Autobiography*, published in 1879, a year before his death at the age of eighty-five, he wrote: "Distinctions which are founded on human policy, without reference to the divine or natural law, and which tend to the degradation of a set of human beings, cannot be lasting, and must sooner or later succumb to the dictates of reason and humanity."[36]

William Howard Day served black Ohio as lecturer, editor, teacher, and political activist from 1844 until late 1855 when, for reasons of health and finances, he moved to Canada.[37] The light-skinned son of a Negro sailmaker who was a naval veteran of the War of 1812 and the campaigns against the Barbary pirates and an active abolitionist mother who was a founding member of the first A.M.E. Zion church, Day was adopted after his father's death by a prosperous white abolitionist in Northampton, Massachusetts. His new father insisted that Day receive an excellent formal education and training as a printer. While an Oberlin undergraduate (1843–47), Day worked as a typesetter for the Oberlin *Evangelist* and attracted attention as a "bold, eloquent" orator.[38] A cultivated speaking style, described by one auditor as a "mournful cadence of a deep and beautifully-toned voice," a positive attitude—the "Good Time Coming" was a favorite theme—and a striking appearance,[39] helped to make him an effective spokesman for the black movement and a useful campaigner for the Free Democratic (Free Soil) party on the Western Reserve.[40] In 1851, he joined the Cleveland *True-Democrat* as a compositor and reporter.[41] From April 1853 to May 1854, he was editor of *The Aliened American*, a black-supported weekly published in Cleveland.[42] Married in 1852 to the accomplished Lucy Stanton, first Negro graduate (1850) of the Oberlin Ladies Department (the couple would later divorce), Day supplemented his income by teaching subjects ranging from the classics to vocal music and shorthand.[43]

During Day's Canadian years (1855–59), he operated a farm and a print shop, lectured, and worked for the education of fugitive slaves in

Canada West (now Ontario).[44] From 1859 through late 1863, he toured England, Ireland, and Scotland, raising funds for the all-black Buxton Settlement at Chatham. Subsequently, although Day never achieved the national stature that had been predicted for him—in part, perhaps, because of a combative personality and, on occasion, less than responsible behavior—his career was substantial. In keeping with his lifelong beliefs in education and political agitation as the principal means of black advancement, he would be superintendent of schools for the Freedmen's Bureau operations in Maryland and Delaware, edit a newspaper, *Our National Progress* (1871–75), promote and supervise various educational projects for the A.M.E. Zion church, and campaign for the Pennsylvania State Equal Rights League and the Republican party. A resident of Harrisburg, Pennsylvania, from 1872 until his death in 1900, Day, recognized by blacks and whites as the city's pre-eminent black leader, would serve for eighteen years as a member of the school board, including a full term as its elected president.[45]

If it were possible to identify a mainspring for the state movement, David Jenkins, continuously active from its beginning until after the Civil War, would be the likeliest candidate. A free-born, privately tutored Virginian, Jenkins came to Columbus in 1837. Besides working as a barber and farmer, he set up his own house-finishing business and by the mid-forties held plastering and painting contracts with city and state, having accumulated "considerable real estate" along the way.[46] Disquieted by the absence of black self-help and abolitionist initiative in Columbus, in 1837 Jenkins organized in his own parlor what a co-agitator remembered as the "first public meeting" of the city's Negroes. Subsequently, he started a long-lived debating society, participated in the state and local School Fund Society, and served a term as "patriarch" of the Sons of Temperance.[47] He edited black Ohio's first newspaper, the weekly *Palladium of Liberty* (1843–44). As a devotee of "constant agitation," the shrewd, personable Jenkins traveled widely to speak on political, moral, and intellectual elevation, carrying along a reserve of handbills, the blanks of which he filled in to announce his meetings. "Too long have we permitted our common enemy to trample on our rights—too long have we remained silent," he exhorted the 1844 convention.[48]

Once he had acquainted himself with Ohio's constitution and laws, Jenkins assumed the self-appointed (and eventually formalized) duties of lobbyist for Negro rights. Over two and a half decades, the dark-skinned, neatly attired activist attended so many sessions of the state assembly, and engaged in so "many a sharp colloquy" with legislators, that a Democratic newspaper would charge him with responsibility for all the "abolition" measures introduced. In the mid-sixties, a Cincinnati *Gazette* reporter, noting that Jenkins had become known as the Ohio assembly's member at large, acknowledged that amendments suggested by the "intelligent and witty colored man" had been adopted. In 1873, Jenkins ventured to Canton, Mississippi, to teach school, and later served a full term in the state legislature before his death in 1877.[49]

As a leader, fellow Columbian James Preston Poindexter combined diplomatic skill and a powerful religious conviction. Son of a part-Negro, part-Cherokee free woman and a white journalist for the Richmond *Enquirer* and orphaned at an early age, at ten Poindexter began to work as a barber, the profession he would follow for more than fifty years. At eighteen, he and his bride came to Ohio, where they lived briefly in a farming community before settling in 1838 in Columbus. In old age Poindexter told historian Wilbur Siebert that the "first impressive thing he heard of in the town" was the underground railroad, in which he, like the other state black leaders, took an active part.[50] He joined the Second Baptist church and occasionally preached there; from 1858 until near the end of the century, he was its regular minister. Of "temperate habits," Poindexter was a moving force in the local temperance society that had 220 on its membership rolls by 1843.[51] The next year the Sons of Protection, a black insurance society that paid sick and burial benefits, was formed; Poindexter served as its president for thirty of its forty-three years of existence. Through the local debating society, he expanded upon the private lessons he had received from a scholarly Englishman, in time becoming a "convincing speaker," debater, and owner of a "fine library."[52] Admired for a "gentle and obliging" nature and for his ability to stick to his principles in spite of "personal, partisan, and political friendships," Poindexter attended nearly every state convention and was frequently elected to the state central committee. In post-war Columbus, he would serve four elected terms on the school board and two on the city council. Having helped to shape strategy and policy for black Ohioans for more than four decades, Poindexter, eighty-eight, died in 1907.[53]

Native Cincinnatian John Isom Gaines, whom John Langston had admired in post-riot Cincinnati, was as proud of his pure African ancestry as he was of his community service. He was the eldest son of Isom and Elizabeth Gaines (the grandmother of Peter Clark), who were known, according to Langston, for their "practical common sense" and Christian deportment. "Forced into active life at an early age" by his father's death, Gaines worked up to ownership of a successful riverfront grocery.[54] He steadily improved upon a meager formal education by "diligent application," as well as an early and sustained participation in black protest activities, beginning with the 1837 state convention when he was only sixteen.[55] Along with his nephew Clark, Day while he remained in Ohio, and both Langstons, Gaines functioned as an intellectual in the Ohio reform movement, filling his speeches, written addresses, and published letters with learning, from an informed interpretation of the latest events to his own distillation of the timeless "truths" of the Greeks, the Bible, and European scholarship.[56] On a practical level, he made two major contributions to the Ohio black movement during the fifties, both to be discussed later at more length: first, as the chief foe of black emigration; second, as the single person most responsible for securing a common school education for the Negroes of Cincinnati. An "animated and powerful" speaker, Gaines, notwithstanding the demands of his business, mounted many white abolitionist and black platforms around the state during the forties and fifties.[57] Sometimes directly challenging prejudice by seeking to integrate public facilities, Gaines saw the resolution of American racism in "the power of Christianity, amalgamation . . ., the progress of letters," while the Negro's particular charge was "self-exertion" and "mutual dependence."[58] Langston, who would deliver Gaines's convention eulogy, recalled that once the eccentric white Kentuckian Cassius Marcellus Clay, dining with Gaines at the home of Cincinnati black merchant Samuel Wilcox, had insisted that the teetotaler Gaines drink a glass of "sparkling Catawba" wine with him. Thereupon, the latter drew back and declared, " 'I abstain from principle.' " Even though "greatly disabled" by disease for several years before his death in 1859, Langston would note, Gaines "seemed determined to spend his last energies in behalf of his greatly outraged race" and, although unable to walk, a few days before he died, had insisted on being carried to a school board meeting to defend a measure he deemed significant.[59]

A fierce individualist, Langston's boyhood friend Peter Humphries Clark was one of the foremost educators of nineteenth-century Ohio. Born in Cincinnati, he was the son of barber Michael Clark, and the grandson of the famous explorer William Clark and his one-time slave Elizabeth (who had later married Isom Gaines). Educated at Gilmore's High School and briefly apprenticed to a white stereotyper, Clark worked with John I. Gaines and others to shape the Negro public school system in Cincinnati.[60] For nearly three decades as schoolmaster and, part of that time, high school principal, he helped turn out many of the black teachers for city and state.[61] Small and thin, with "sharp features" and arresting eyes, Clark also served the reform movement as editor and agitator. In 1855, he and his wife Frances Williams, an 1853 graduate of Oberlin, began publication of the *Herald of Freedom,* a

short-lived weekly devoted to "free discussion of the Anti-Slavery question and to an uncompromising advocacy of the rights of man."[62] He
later did editorial work for Frederick Douglass's newspaper and, regularly crossing the river to slave state Kentucky, edited the Free Soil
Newport *News*, published by the often-mobbed W. S. Bailey. Clark lectured widely, at one point writing an antislavery drama that he read to
audiences "with the understanding that there would be a slight charge
at the door."[63]

Resentful of the white prejudice that he felt repeatedly blocked his
personal ambitions and his people's advancement and given to public
pessimism, in an apparent effort to resolve his frustration Clark embraced various and often contradictory enthusiasms, including Unitar-
ianism, African Methodism, and socialism.[64] After the war, for a
combination of political and personal reasons, he shifted allegiances
between factions of the Republican party before becoming Ohio's most
prominent black Democrat. Alongside other factors, the competition
for black votes that he helped to instigate resulted in a state civil rights
law and school integration. In 1886, the Republican-controlled school
board of Cincinnati, seizing upon convincing evidence that Clark had
attempted to bribe a witness in a political corruption case to aid his new
Democratic allies, removed him from the city schools. Thereafter, em-
bittered and disillusioned, he would teach for many years at the Charles
Sumner High School in St. Louis before his death in 1925 at the age of
ninety-six.[65]

For John Mercer Langston, the state black meeting in Columbus in
the second week of January 1850 marked his own assumption of a
leadership role. From Jenkins's call to order of the fifty-nine delegates
from twenty-five counties, an unusually large representation, to rousing choruses, over and again, of "Old Johnny Bowdown, or the History
of the Black Laws of Ohio," through to the final, hearty cheers for
"Liberty, Equality, and Fraternity" three days later, the twenty-year-old
was so ubiquitous and vociferous that a colleague teasingly referred to
"Senator Langston."[66]

The major issue facing John Mercer and fellow delegates was the
proposed revision of the Ohio constitution, unchanged since 1802.
Fully aware that earlier constitutional revisions in Pennsylvania and
New York had resulted, respectively, in total disfranchisement and restricted suffrage, and that the constitution newly adopted in Illinois
went so far as to bar black immigration, black Ohioans recognized, as
Poindexter put it, "An important crisis has come upon us."[67] The gains
registered in the preceding year—enactment of a school law and repeal
of several Black Laws—had aroused considerable white resentment that

could result in new provisions inimical to black interests. Moreover, the congressional debate over admission of California and New Mexico, involving the question of slavery's extension, had increased public volatility on racial matters, shifting the Negro from the woodpiles to the parlors of the northern consciousness. Even as resentment of the "Slave Power" grew, so did perturbation over the "nigger question." United in the conviction that upon their own actions depended "probably, the weal of the disfranchised in this state of our birth and adoption," the black leaders viewed the Ohio Constitutional Convention's possible effects in polar extremes: their rights were in "imminent danger," but, on the other hand, their full enfranchisement might be won.[68]

Even before the convention, young Langston had been busy collecting statistics on the number of Negroes in each county, the amount of property they held, and the taxes they paid, their self-improvement efforts and their "intellectual attainments." His purpose here was ably stated by his black Oberlin classmate, the Cleveland musician and music teacher Justin Holland: "Let us by an overwhelming show of facts, deprive the trading politicians of even a decent excuse for further opposing our enfranchisement."[69] Doubtless, John Mercer had participated in the Oberlin black meeting in November that, looking toward the state convention, had organized a local Colored American League and employed Day to conduct a fund-raising drive aimed at supporting "efficient men to advocate *the right of the colored man to a vote.*"[70] Convention president J. L. Watson, boosted for office as "the anti-slavery wheelhorse of the Reserve" by John Mercer against a movement for some younger man, returned the favor by appointing Langston chairman of the business committee, charged with devising a "plan to attain our rights here." Rallying the delegates, Watson averred, "If they do take our rights from us, they shall take our rights from us in our presence. . . . Let us press on—, let the hand of the colored man be seen moulding public opinion in this State from centre to circumference."[71] With Watson and Day, young Langston occupied the platform at an evening public session in the hall of the House of Representatives, which drew an overflow crowd of both whites and blacks. Because the legislators' decision in 1849 to grant the black convention use of the hall for the first time had sparked adverse criticism, repetition of the concession was taken as an encouraging sign. Mixing song and speechmaking in approved abolitionist style, the program, opening and closing on rousing pleas for enfranchisement by Watson and Day, featured John Mercer in a quartet's rendition of "Feebly the Bondsman Toiled," and other plaintive melodies, as well as a "neat, chaste speech" on the lately reinvigorated abolitionist theme, the American people's inconsistency in upholding liberty and slavery. The evening's aftermath was heartening, for the chief Whig publication in the capital complimented the program, white spectators demonstrated a rare willingness to acknowledge the merit of the black orators, and several state legislators invited Negro delegates to call at their rooms.[72]

On the convention floor, in youthful anxiety to state his position on virtually every question, John Mercer neither avoided touchy issues nor, although mannerly and respectful, seemed very solicitous of the opinions of more experienced men. Although his eloquent defense of Watson's qualifications for the presidency was a diplomatic way of making amends to the veteran, whom he had taxed at the 1849 session with lacking the courage to express openly his convictions on emigration, John Mercer incautiously provoked stormy debate by advocating another delegate's resolution condemning the inaction of black Methodists on slavery. "If we ask white men to be anti-slavery, we ought to ask the same of colored men," he reasoned. He scornfully chastised the A.M.E. church and its *Christian Herald*, edited by A. R. Green, as well as black preachers who "sacrifice the principles of virtue, humanity, and universal brotherhood, to sordid and mercenary objects." Predictably, black Methodists of both denominations took umbrage. Only strong appeals from classmate James Monroe Jones, Watson, and others, plus an overwhelming vote to table the resolution, finally persuaded the hostile camps to drop the "vexed issue." To avoid such a tussle, Langston's business committee earlier had voted to reject the resolution; in charging ahead anyhow, John Mercer gained his stated desire to be "correctly reported before the people of the State of Ohio," but at the cost of offending such influential Methodists as J. M. Brown. Impatient and independent, the youth had not embraced what one convention correspondent termed "the doctrine of the wise man—'A time for all things.' "[73]

Moreover, Langston was equally critical of, as he put it, "great men," specifically Frederick Douglass. In appealing for establishment of a newspaper, a cause he would advocate until its realization in 1853, Langston upbraided Douglass for having "proved recreant" to his promise to the 1848 national convention to allow access to his columns. Although easterners' overnight trips or merest spats were reported, "Men at the West cannot be noticed. . . . the *North Star*, edited by Frederick Douglass, is not the organ of the colored people." Douglass's failure to report Day's canvass for the Oberlin Colored American League apparently sparked Langston's criticism; other delegates also took aim at the editor for self-aggrandizement in his report of the 1848 conclave.[74] Still, it could have been objected that John Mercer's remarks were inappropriate for one so little seasoned in the cause.

Despite his willingness to engage in controversy, however, Langston's approach was essentially positive, marked by spontaneity and optimism. In off-the-cuff advocacy of the proposed newspaper, he began, "It may be objected that there is no reading among the colored people.—Why, sir, even colored boys are learning their country's history, and there is hardly one of them who cannot tell you of the great things now transpiring. Old men, in the winter of their age—on the back declivity of their lives—are learning their letters." Beyond simple literacy, some Negroes had considerable intellectual attainments. In oratory, "Colored men can boast of a Douglass and a Remond. In our own state we can boast of J. I. Gaines, J. H. Perkins, and in our own convention of William H. Day, John L. Watson, and a host of others." "The colored man has the germ of a literature peculiar to himself." Used properly, the talents of black Ohioans would "make a paper such as shall be to us an honor."[75] John Mercer's rash outspokenness, if sometimes exasperating, when coupled to his appreciation for other movement leaders and their goals was transformed into a winning enthusiasm. Moreover, to black activists singing contemptuously of "Old Johnny Bowdown," his very lack of deference, even directed at perceived shortcomings within the black movement, could seem exhilarating. The youngster, who in addition to his other functions even chaired one session of the convention, so impressed six delegates that they supported him against Day, the obviously better qualified and successful candidate, to present the address on Negro enfranchisement to the Ohio Constitutional Convention.[76]

The plan for the enfranchisement campaign that Langston put before the delegates, enlarging upon the machinery already set in motion by Oberlin blacks, centered on establishment of the Ohio Colored American League, with an executive committee responsible for finances and organization. Six lecturer-agents were to canvass the state, helping to circulate petitions for equal rights that should be presented to the constitutional convention. In approving the league, the black Ohioans elected Langston recording secretary and agent for the southern portion of the state.[77]

During that crucial year of 1850, while events in Washington were reshaping the course of the whole antislavery conflict and vitally altering the conditions of black lives, the young reform apprentice, like a knight errant commencing a quest, was thoroughly initiated. Scraps of old bills are suggestive: board for the month of February, 24 cents a day, plus 23 cents postage for letters and pamphlets, to Jenkins in Columbus; $3 to a printer for bills to advertise his lectures; $35.50 in March for appropriate garments—frock coat, doeskin pants, fancy silk pants, fancy silk vest.[78] In early February, John Mercer and Watson addressed a Cleveland gathering and reaped a generous $15 collection for the campaign. From then on, first from Jenkins's home and later from Cincinnati and Chillicothe, Langston mainly worked the populous, racially conscious southern rural and urban areas. The kind of hearing he, Watson, and fellow agents received, even from well-disposed whites, is indicated by a laconic entry in the diary of a pious student at Geauga Seminary in the northeastern corner of the state. "I attended a lecture on slavery this evening," noted James A. Garfield on April 2, 1850. "The darky had some funny remarks and witty too. Looks like rain."[79]

Probably Garfield heard not Langston but one of his co-laborers. Langston's own argument for enfranchisement, outlined in conscientious student style to be adaptable for different audiences and adjustable with the current of events and preserved by him perhaps less for reasons of sentiment than practicality, for he would have to plead for Negro suffrage for another twenty years, sounded a more sober note. With Ohioans manifesting increasing concern over the threat of the slave states to northern interests in economic advancement, social mobility, and the spread of democratic institutions, he settled on the gambit of presenting the equal rights argument in the context of "Actions of the Federal Government in Behalf of Slavery." Charging northern politicians with "servility" to slavery forces, the young black abolitionist, predicting "a change coming about," urged a dual approach: "First, convert our friends and relatives in the South"; "Second, elect to Congress men who will stick to Northern interests." In Ohio, "although most [Black Laws] have been wiped from the Book still we have but commenced the work." Oppressive legislation, joined to segregation and exclusion from civil and social institutions, "answer the question why are the Colored People not more elevated, intelligent and refined." His defense of the black claim for the elective franchise, based on natural rights and American nativity, encompassed a radical definition of black labor as "equivalent to capital, and far more desirable," a delineation of black contributions to the national defense in American wars, evidence of black Ohioans' capacity to exercise the franchise "in an intelligent and manly manner," an ironic discussion of taxation and representation: "as the Slaves in the South enjoy this right, as an offset, we of the Free States should be entitled to it." Even in outline form, some of the young orator's lines conveyed the black struggle in heroic terms: "A Mountain of Prejudice is to be surmounted. A Herculean task is before us." And, in rueful reference to the Revolution, "Our orators and toastdrinkers have studiously avoided allusion to the participation of colored men in the great struggle for freedom." African Americans "have had no impartial Historian to sound their deeds of valor."[80]

In July, John Mercer joined his voice to that of the master orator whom the young man, even while denouncing his supposed neglect of Ohioans, had termed reverentially "the *immortal* Douglass." Mending western fences, Frederick Douglass had published in mid-June an approving notice of the "very spirited and commendable efforts" of black Ohioans for the past two years "to secure the Right of Franchise," along with the observation that progress in the civil rights campaign was apparent, particularly in the "marked change in the tone of the press of Ohio, which may be traced in part to their [blacks'] own efforts at self-elevation."[81] When Douglass accepted an invitation to address the Fourth of July dedication of a temperance hall in Cincinnati, Negro leaders in that city and Columbus decided to exploit his talents.[82] In the Queen City, a black welcoming delegation marched with him from the railroad station to the Dumas House, the black hotel, where he spoke from the balcony, beginning a crowded eight days of speeches and such fundraising events as the Colored Orphan Asylum's reception and the Bethel A.M.E. church's well-patronized fair. Besides entertaining Douglass at his home, Langston's friend W. W. Watson arranged to open the Baker Street Baptist church for his lectures, with a "promptitude and alacrity" that the black abolitionist, often barred by timid black churchmen from use of their facilities, found refreshing. In addition, white abolitionists Andrew Ernst and his wife Sarah Otis Ernst, president of the Cincinnati Ladies Anti-Slavery Sewing Society, honored the visitor at a racially mixed gathering whose guest list was nearly a personnel roster of the city's underground railroad.[83]

Not to be outdone in hospitality, David Jenkins and other movement leaders, who had invited Douglass to boost the civil rights campaign in Columbus, staged an equally varied program. John Mercer doubtless was among the greeters at Jenkins's home, where Douglass boarded during his stay. Talk at the reception centered on "the subject of our common freedom and elevation." In a lighter mood, much of the company subsequently embarked with the distinguished visitor on a country ride to a spa, Hart Springs, where a black farmer converted his "quiet domicile," encircled by horses and carriages, into a sort of hotel for the occasion.[84]

After this respite, Douglass made afternoon and evening addresses in the senate chamber of the State House on July 15, with Langston also speaking at the night session. Despite oppressive heat, a good crowd heard the afternoon lecture, and such a large number appeared early that night that an estimated five hundred spectators remained massed at the door. Well into the program, a rumor began that in Douglass's earlier speech he had called the framers of the constitution "cowards," and—even as he was insisting that "prejudice against color would gradually disappear"—the scraping and stamping of feet rumbled in the balcony, fistfuls of gravel rattled on the stairs, and "vulgar exclamations" sounded. State auditor John Woods, who was sitting in the balcony, made citizen's arrests of several ringleaders, but the disturbance spread outside the hall. A bogus fire alarm was set off. Ringing the bell, the crowd paraded the fire engine around the State House, deterred only by police from going for the pumps. When the speakers left the platform, the crowd swept Douglass toward the door where the mob began throwing stones, but friendly whites diverted their attention, allowing Douglass and Langston to escape. Still, far into the night searching gangs harassed the section of Columbus where most blacks lived.[85]

The following morning, in front of the Neil House, scene of Langston's humiliation five years earlier, the Ohio Stage Company forcibly ejected Douglass from his seat. It seems likely that Douglass, an old hand at calculating such incidents, was not quite so surprised as he let on, for, should he have been unacquainted with the company's notorious segregation policy, his challenge-minded hosts, who had publicized a similar incident as recently as January, would surely have alerted him. Lending to the air of premeditation was the thoroughness of the groundwork: Douglass had paid for a first-class ticket, reserved early, and even boarded the stage before other passengers, one stop before the Neil House. When Douglass indignantly refused the stage line's demand that he sit on top, only to be turned out by two burly employees and denied a refund, he entrusted his case to a lawyer. While the attorney later secured an out of court settlement, Douglass got full propaganda value from the incident in the press.[86]

Protest made, Douglass and Langston shared a hired horse and buggy on the journey east. The black abolitionists, professional and tyro, brought their news to communities through east central Ohio along the National Road all the way to Pittsburgh. In New Concord by July 18, their lectures left a local editor "as much surprised as pleased, at the ease and fluency" they displayed; he testified "to the reasonable, moderate and persuasive nature of their remarks." He regretted to learn they had been mobbed in Columbus.

"Those missionaries of human elevation," as a Pittsburgh journalist dubbed Douglass, thirty-three, and his twenty-year-old traveling companion,[87] offered their audiences a study in contrasts. Douglass, copper-colored, was "cut out for a hero," a strongly built man with a leonine head and a height of more than six feet. Although often called handsome, "his carriage is not graceful," an Ohio reporter observed, "his form being heavy and somewhat bent." Nor were his features regular: his mouth was a cupid's bow, his chin too short for the breadth of jaw and cheekbones, his nose large and sharp, his face too suffused with strong emotion to be entirely pleasant. Rather, the imposing fore-head under the thick curly mane, the brooding eyes, the sensitive mouth together made "one of the most expressive countenances that one may see in the largest bodies of men";[88] the frame, the massive head, the voice, even the color, seemed to exude natural power.

Inches shorter and pounds lighter, John Mercer's frame was still wiry and slender, and his manly height did not much exceed the average, about five feet eight or nine. His movements were sure and natural. His hair and sideburns were neatly trimmed and curly; forehead high and gently rounded; nose, mouth, and chin evenly proportioned. His countenance would be characterized by a contemporary as mild and amiable. But while nothing of the rake was in it, certainly, the face of the young Langston, captured in a photograph from this period, with its direct gaze and uncompromising jaw, rather seems to hint at an ardent nature, a fierce pride that he normally concealed with a modest deportment, a flashing temper that he must struggle to control. Around the luminous eyes is a peculiar expression, a pucker already etched between the brows, both wince and frown, partaking of pain and determination. Douglass, too, bore a fierce furrow where the bridge of spectacles might have rested. That look, half-vulnerable, half-aggressive, might have seemed to the discerning observer the mark of kinship between the novice and his illustrious companion.[89]

Among abolitionist orators, Douglass had few peers. At his side, Langston had an invaluable opportunity to study the broad range of his rhetorical battery. Beginning in a low conversational tone and mak-ing few gestures, using language on the platform as skillfully as on paper, calling on a ready wit, gift for satire and pathos, and talent at mimicry, Douglass, at appropriate moments, would roll forth his me-lodious, rich voice in tones as full and deep as an organ.[90]

On this tour, the younger lecturer politely deferred to the elder, tailoring his remarks to fill out the program when he was in good form, or spell him when he was tired. Not that this betokened a slack-ening of effort, for Langston's anxiety to impress audiences with the importance of his cause probably was rivaled only by his desire to cut a figure for his distinguished companion. More than the thought of suiting himself for the hot weather, one imagines, led him to purchase another new black satin vest and pair of trousers just before the trip.

Young Langston won a glowing report in Pittsburgh. After an arduous day of morning and afternoon meetings in two separate churches, he was allotted the opening of the evening program before a large audience of "all creeds, colors, sexes, parties." John Mercer ably discussed black enfranchisement. When, at a rather late hour, his exhausted co-laborer appeared, "the young man modestly gave way to his senior," but Douglass's voice was gone. Still, the audience did not feel cheated. "This young man is a strong reasoner, and possessed of a goodly portion of intellectual acquirements," the Pittsburgh *Tribune* noted. "He studied in the Oberlin College, we are told, and the evidence of oratorical ability he exhibits, while addressing his audience, are alike creditable to his instructors and to himself in their application."[91]

While Douglass returned to Rochester after a four-week tour of some 1,400 miles and twenty-six meetings, better informed as to the character of the Ohio leadership and through his own scrapes with "very rough treatment"[92] the obstacles they faced, the black Ohioans and white antislavery allies continued to wage the civil rights campaign against ever-hardening opposition. Indeed, from the opening day of the Ohio Constitutional Convention in May, it had been clear that Negroes had not exaggerated the dimensions of the threat to their legal status. A petition urging banishment of black residents was presented nearly with the initial banging of the gavel; in subsequent sessions, a stream of anti-Negro petitions demanded revival of the rescinded Black Laws and adoption of such measures as prohibition of Negro immigration and provision of state aid for colonization. Moreover, some delegates attempted, unsuccessfully, to bar the reception of counter-petitions for Negro enfranchisement.[93] When Dr. Norton S. Townshend of Lorain County presented one such petition signed by Day, whom he described as a "nearer white than black" constituent, an opponent suggested heatedly that the new constitution specifically exclude persons of mixed blood from citizenship rights.

Still, in the petition battle at least, Langston and fellow agents, along with white abolitionists, managed to outnumber their opponents. In the final count, some twenty-nine petitions from ten different counties, bearing a total of more than 1,500 names, asked equal political and legal rights for the Negro; three additional petitions from three counties, with two hundred names, asked specifically that the Negro be permitted to vote.[94]

Despite the success of their petition drive, and against his own youthful will for optimism, by the end of summer John Mercer Langston, with other movement leaders, had to recognize that the prospects for enfranchisement were dim. Discouragement was manifest on several levels. Charles Langston, agreeing with John Mercer on the need for an outlet for black westerners' literary talents, had laid plans to publish a volume of selections by Negro authors, but in late September informed contributors of a postponement "in consequence of circumstances which could not be foreseen or avoided by men." Probably the postponement became permanent. Another sign, reflecting not only political developments but also fear of a local cholera outbreak, was the poor turnout for the state mass convention in Cleveland on the First of August. Attempting to rally blacks from "alarming apathy," the delegates endorsed the principle that the price of liberty is eternal vigilance and vowed to "keep as nearly as possible to the enemy, and struggle boldly and manfully for our rights upon this soil."[95] But brave words could not disguise dwindling hopes.

On September 12, 1850, in a letter to Senator Salmon Chase, John Mercer and Charles Langston confessed their "doubt as to the best course to pursue" to achieve black enfranchisement and wondered, "Is the public sentiment of the country such as to preclude the idea of the successful attainment of our Political rights and equality in this state at present?"[96] The Ohio Constitutional Convention offered one response on February 8, 1851, when the enfranchisement proposal was defeated, 75–15. Moreover, Townshend, Langston's short-term mentor Andrews, and other antislavery delegates, mainly from the Western Reserve, failed down the line in attempts to include blacks in the state militia, provide for equal and nonsegregated public schools, and, in other ways, put Negroes on an equal footing. On the other hand, state financial aid to the American Colonization Society, a proposition warmly supported in southern Ohio, was defeated. The attempt to limit public schooling to whites was forestalled. Further, in contrast to three other western states that during the decade followed the example of Indiana in barring black immigration, the much discussed exclusionary provisions never came to a floor vote. Except for a new constitutional (rather than legislative) debarment from the state militia, blacks emerged legally unscathed. As a means of defending their Thermopylae, as Day had expressed it, the black campaign offensive had been a qualified success.[97]

"Shall we be robbed of our Elective Franchise?" Langston had pleaded with audience after audience. "Your answer will be no. All things forbid any other."[98] The logic of his own argument, the praise it had won, the time spent, would combine in his disappointment at the outcome of his initial venture into reform. Even on that day in early fall when he and his brother formulated their letter to Chase, John Mercer, a few months short of his twenty-first birthday, confronted the probable failure of two of his goals for black manhood—personal professional choice and full citizenship. Coincidentally, on that same day the U.S. House of Representatives, following earlier action by the Senate, as if in reply to the Langstons' query about the national sentiment toward Negroes, gave final approval to the Fugitive Slave Act.

NOTES

1. New York *Globe*, Oct. 15, 1882, John Mercer Langston Scrapbooks, 4 vols., II, Moorland-Spingarn Research Center, Howard University.

2. *Niles' National Register*, July 27, 1844, quoted in *National Intelligencer*, July 20, 1867; *North Star*, Jan. 28, 1848; James Oliver Horton and Lois E. Horton, *Black Bostonians* (New York, 1979), p. 56.

3. *North Star*, Jan. 28, 1848; New York *American*, n.d., quoted in Cleveland *True-Democrat*, Feb. 9, 1848. See note 28, chapter 4.

4. *Ohio State Journal*, Feb. 24, 1849; Record of Negroes, 1804–55, Ross County Courthouse, Chillicothe, Ohio. (Microfilm edition of the Ohio Historical Society, Frame 98, Archives and Manuscripts Division, Columbus, Ohio.)

5. Cleveland *True-Democrat*, Mar. 10, 1847; *North Star*, Jan. 12, 1849; *Minutes . . . of the State Convention of the Colored Citizens of Ohio . . . Columbus . . . Jan., 1849* (Oberlin, 1849).

6. John Mercer Langston, *From the Virginia Plantation to the National Capitol; or, The First and Only Negro Representative in Congress from the Old Dominion* (Hartford, 1894; repr. New York: Johnson Reprint, 1968), p. 106; Salmon P. Chase to C. H. and J. M. Langston, Nov. 11, 1850, Salmon P. Chase Papers, Library of Congress; Mary J. Safford to Editor, Apr. 5, 1869, *National Anti-Slavery Standard*, Apr. 17, 1869.

7. Harriet A. Little, "John Mercer Langston, A.B., A.M., LL.D.," *A.M.E. Church Review* 4 (Oct. 1887):180; Golbert H. Barnes and Dwight L. Dumond, eds., *Letters of Theodore Dwight Weld, Angelina Grimke Weld, and Sarah Grimke*, 2 vols. (New York, 1934), II, p. 795; New York *Independent*, Mar. 27, 1850; Williams Brothers, *History of Lorain County* (Philadelphia, 1879), p. 46.

8. Langston, *Virginia Plantation*, pp. 109, 106; *Anti-Slavery Bugle*, June 25, 1853; John Mercer Langston, *Freedom and Citizenship* (Washington, 1883; repr. Miami: Mnemosyne Reprint, 1969), p. 62.

9. Langston, *Virginia Plantation*, pp. 106–10; Washington *National Republican*, Mar. 1, 1888. The law student friend was Timothy W. Higgins. T. W. Higgins signed an I.O.U. to Langston of $20 "on order for value received," possibly in May 1850. See "I.O.U.," John Mercer Langston Papers, Fisk University Library.

10. George Wilson Pierson, *Tocqueville and Beaumont in America* (New York, 1938), p. 569; Langston, *Virginia Plantation*, p. 110; Elyria *Independent-Democrat*, Oct. 25, 1853.

11. *Minutes of the State Convention of the Colored Citizens of Ohio . . . Columbus . . . Jan., 1850* (Columbus, 1850); Langston, *Virginia Plantation*, pp. 104–10.

12. Frederick Douglass, "Colored Citizens of Ohio," *North Star*, June 29, 1849. Peter Clark, in old age, claimed that "The people of Ohio held conventions annually for more than thirty years. Usually they printed their proceedings in pamphlets." Peter H. Clark to John W. Cromwell, Dec. 21, 1901, quoted in John W. Cromwell, *The Negro in American History* (Washington, 1914), p. 37. Douglass in 1849 wrote that "for the last six years annual conventions of colored freemen have assembled at Columbus . . . to devise ways and means for bettering their condition. These annual conventions, we dare say, have been more faithfully and regularly held than those of the colored freemen of any other state in the Union," *North Star*, June 29, 1849. Records or calls for Ohio state conventions are as follows: *Philanthropist*, Sept. 8, Oct. 13, 1837; *Ohio State Journal*, Jan. 15, 1839, and *Philanthropist*, Feb. 26, 1839 refer to a convention in Columbus the previous October; *Ohio State Journal*, Sept. 10, 1839; *Liberator*, Oct. 18, 1839; *Philanthropist*, Oct. 22, 1839; *Ohio State Journal*, Sept. 15, 1840; call for state convention, in *Philanthropist*, May 26, 1841; *Philanthropist*, Oct. 4, 1843; *Palladium of Liberty*, Dec. 27, 1843; *Philanthropist*, Sept. 16, 1844; *Palladium of Liberty*, Sept. 25, Oct. 2, 16, Nov. 13, 1844; call for state convention in *Philanthropist*, June 11, 1845 and Cincinnati *Gazette*, June 18, 1845; call for state convention in *Anti-Slavery Bugle*, Dec. 10, 1847; Cleveland *True-Democrat*, Sept. 19, 1848; *State Convention . . . 1849*; *State Convention . . . 1850*; *Minutes of the State Convention of the Colored Citizens of Ohio . . . Columbus . . . Jan., 1851* (Columbus, 1851); *Proceedings of the Convention of the Colored Freemen of Ohio . . . Cincinnati . . . Jan., 1852* (Cincinnati, 1852); Cleveland *True-Democrat*, Sept. 9, 1852; *Frederick Douglass' Paper*, Oct. 1, 1852; *Official Proceedings of the Ohio State Convention of Colored Freemen . . . Columbus . . . Jan., 1853* (Cleveland, 1853); *Frederick Douglass' Paper*, June 16, 1854, refers to a convention in Dayton the previous October; *Proceedings of the State Convention of Colored Men . . . Columbus . . . Jan., 1856* (Columbus, 1856); *Proceedings of the State Convention of the Colored Men of the State of Ohio . . . Columbus . . . Jan., 1857* (Columbus, 1857); *Proceedings of a Convention of the Colored Men of Ohio . . . Cincinnati . . . Nov., 1858* (Cincinnati, 1858); *Proceedings of the First Annual Meeting of the Ohio State Anti-Slavery Society . . . Xenia . . . Jan., 1860* (Xenia, 1860).

13. *State Convention . . . 1851*; *State Convention . . . 1849*.

14. Ralph Ellison, *Going to the Territory* (New York, 1986), pp. 211–12.

15. *State Convention* reports, passim; *Anti-Slavery Bugle*, Dec. 18, 1852, Oct. 1, 1853; W. H. Burnham to J. M. Langston, Feb. 6, 1854, and Peter H. Clark to J. M. Langston, Jan. 22, 1854, both in John Mercer Langston Papers, Fisk University Library; *Liberator*, Feb. 15, 1856.

16. Jane H. Pease and William H. Pease, *They Who Would Be Free: Blacks' Search for Freedom, 1830–1861* (New York, 1974), pp. 288–97.

17. The leaders were determined by their prominence in various local, state, and national meetings; by their involvement in various civic, church, and protest activities; and by their recognition among their peers. Unless otherwise cited, the source for the leadership profile drawn in the following pages is found in Table 1.

18. *State Convention . . . 1857*; Cleveland *True-Democrat*, Jan. 30, 1850.

19. *Anti-Slavery Bugle*, May 21, 1853; *State Convention . . . 1858.*

20. We have been unable to identify the specific occupation of Joseph Henry Perkins. The 1840 census lists him in the occupational category of "navigation." Population Census of 1840, Hamilton County, City of Cincinnati, Reel 398, NA.

21. Gerald Sorin, *Abolitionism: A New Perspective* (New York, 1972), p. 101; David M. Katzman, *Before the Ghetto: Black Detroit in the Nineteenth Century* (Urbana, 1973), p.19.

22. Sorin, *Abolitionism: A New Perspective*, p. 19.

23. *State Convention . . . 1849*; *State Convention . . . 1850*; *State Convention . . . 1851.*

24. *State Convention . . . 1857.*

25. Joseph Henry Perkins, *Oration, Delivered on the First of August, 1849, Before the Colored Citizens of Cincinnati* (Cincinnati, 1849); *Palladium of Liberty*, Nov. 13, 1844.

26. *Philanthropist*, Oct. 13, 1837; Walter Yancy to Editor, *Philanthropist*, Jan. 4, 1843; J. I. Gaines, *Oration, Delivered on the First of August, 1849, Before the Colored Citizens of Columbus, Ohio* (Columbus, 1849); Charles H. Langston, "Card," Cleveland *Plain Dealer*, Nov. 18, 1859.

27. *State Convention . . . 1857*; John M. Langston, "Eulogy on the Life and Character of John I. Gaines, Delivered at the First Annual Meeting of the Ohio State Anti-Slavery Society, Xenia, Ohio, Jan. 3d, 1860," *Liberator*, Apr. 27, 1860.

28. Perkins, *Oration . . . 1849.*

29. Oberlin *Evangelist*, Feb. 2, 1853; Richard Clyde Minor, "James Preston Poindexter, Elder Statesman of Columbus," *Ohio State Archaeological and Historical Quarterly* 56 (1947):285–86; William Hartwell Parham, comp., *An Official History of the Most Worshipful Grand Lodge of Free and Accepted Masons for the State of Ohio* (n.p., 1906), p. 267; *Anti-Slavery Bugle*, Dec. 27, 1856.

30. "Memorial of J. Mercer Langston, to the General Assembly of the State of Ohio," quoted in *Frederick Douglass' Paper*, June 16, 1854; *State Convention . . . 1849.*

31. Allan Peskin, ed., *North into Freedom: The Autobiography of John Malvin, Free Negro, 1795–1880* (Cleveland, 1966), pp. 29, 38, 50, 55–56, 59. In 1860 Malvin put his material wealth at $1,000; a decade later it had increased to $3,000; see Thomas J. Goliber, "Cuyahoga Blacks: A Social and Demographic Study, 1850–1880," master's thesis, Kent State University, 1972, p. 101.

32. Peskin, *North into Freedom*, pp. 54, 56–57; *Emancipator*, Nov. 14, 1839; *Philanthropist*, Jan. 20, Sept. 8, 1837; *Ohio State Journal*, Sept. 10, 1839; Russell H. Davis, *Black Americans in Cleveland* (Washington, 1972), pp. 45–47; *Philanthropist*, June 29, 1842.

33. Cleveland *Herald*, Mar. 29, 1839.

34. Peskin, ed., *North into Freedom,* passim; *Philanthropist,* May 26, 1841; Cleveland *True-Democrat,* Sept. 19, 1848, Feb. 19, 1849, Sept. 30, 1850, Feb. 25, 1851; *Anti-Slavery Bugle,* July 20, Aug. 17, 1850; Cleveland *Forest City Democrat,* Feb. 17, 1854; Cleveland *Leader,* July 23, 1855, Feb. 8, 1858; W. W. Brown, "Colored People of Cleveland," *Anti-Slavery Bugle,* Dec. 5, 1857.

35. *Philanthropist,* Sept. 8, 1837; *State Convention . . . 1857; State Convention . . . 1858.*

36. Peskin, ed., *North into Freedom,* p. 86.

37. See, in particular the biography of Day in R. J. M. Blackett, *Beating Against the Barriers* (Baton Rouge, 1986), pp. 287–386; William Howard Day, Alumni Records, Oberlin College Archives; William H. Day to Editor, May 18, 1857, *Provincial Freeman,* May 30, 1857; William J. Simmons, *Men of Mark: Eminent, Progressive and Rising* (Cleveland, 1887; repr. Chicago: Johnson Publishing, 1970), p. 702; W. H. Day to Gerrit Smith, Mar. 27, 1856, Gerrit Smith Papers, George Arents Research Library, Syracuse University; *Provincial Freeman,* Sept. 29, 1855.

38. Blackett, *Beating Against the Barriers,* pp. 287–89; Simmons, *Men of Mark,* p. 701; Cleveland *True-Democrat,* Sept. 7, 1847; Oberlin *Evangelist,* Nov. 6, 1844, Sept. 1, 1847.

39. William Wells Brown, *The Rising Son* (Boston, 1874; repr. New York: Johnson Reprint, 1970), p. 449; *Frederick Douglass' Paper,* Aug. 5, Sept. 2, Dec. 16, 1853; Cleveland *True-Democrat,* Jan. 26, 1850; *Liberator,* July 28, 1853.

40. *Anti-Slavery Bugle,* June 29, Aug. 24, 1850; *Frederick Douglass' Paper,* Oct. 15, 1852.

41. Cleveland *True-Democrat,* Dec. 24, 1849; *Frederick Douglass' Paper,* May 13, 1852; Simmons, *Men of Mark,* p. 702; William Howard Day, Alumni Records.

42. *The Aliened American,* Apr. 9, 1853; *Frederick Douglass' Paper,* May 19, 1854.

43. Simmons, *Men of Mark,* p. 702.

44. Ibid.; Chatham Tri-Weekly *Planet,* Aug. 23, 1858; William H. Day to Gerrit Smith, June 21, 1858, Smith Papers.

45. Blackett, *Beating Against the Barriers,*pp. 315–86; Harrisburg *Telegraph,* Dec. 3, 1900; William Howard Day, Alumni Records.

46. Parham, comp., *Official History,* p. 267; Martin Robison Delany, *The Condition, Elevation, Emigration, and Destiny of the Colored People of the United States, Politically Considered* (Philadelphia, 1852; repr. New York: Arno Press, 1968), p. 99; Mahoning *Free Democrat,* Jan. 14, 1853; *Report of the Proceedings of the Colored National Convention . . . Cleveland . . . Sept., 1848* (Rochester, 1848).

47. J.P. Ward, "David Jenkins and His Work," *Ohio State Journal,* Feb. 25, 1870; *Ohio State Journal,* Sept. 10, 1839; *North Star,* Sept. 15, 1848.

48. Parham, comp., *Official History,* p. 267; *Palladium of Liberty,* Dec. 27, 1843–Nov. 13, 1844, passim, Oct. 16, 1844.

49. Parham, comp., *Official History,* pp. 267–68.

50. Minor, "James Preston Poindexter," 267–68; Simmons, *Men of Mark,* p. 259; Wilbur Henry Siebert, *The Mysteries of Ohio's Underground Railroads* (Columbus, 1951), p. 60.

51. Minor, "James Preston Poindexter," 268–69, 283; *Minutes of the National Convention of Colored Citizens . . . Aug., 1843*, p. 38, reprinted in *Minutes of the Proceedings of the National Negro Conventions, 1830–1864*, ed. Howard Holman Bell (New York, 1969).

52. Simmons, *Men of Mark*, p. 261; *Ohio State Journal*, Feb. 25, 1870; Minor, "James Preston Poindexter," pp. 274, 269.

53. *Palladium of Liberty*, Sept. 25, 1844; *State Convention . . . 1849, 1850, 1851, 1856*; Minor, "James Preston Poindexter," 274, 281–86; Simmons, *Men of Mark*, p. 265. For Poindexter's post-Civil War role in Ohio politics and society, see David A. Gerber, *Black Ohio and the Color Line 1860–1915* (Urbana, 1976), pp. 188–89, 204, 214, 223–24, 228–29.

54. John M. Langston, "Eulogy on the Life and Character of John I. Gaines," Brown, *The Rising Son*, p. 450; *Liberator*, Nov. 21, 1856; Cleveland *Leader*, Dec. 2, 1859. See also Samuel Matthews, "John Isom Gaines: The Architect of Black Public Education," *Queen City Heritage* 45 (Spring 1987): 41–48.

55. *Liberator*, Apr. 27, 1860; J. C. C. to Editor, *National Anti-Slavery Standard*, Apr. 6, 1867; Brown, *The Rising Son*, p. 450.

56. On his speeches, see, in particular, John I. Gaines, *Oration Delivered on the First Of August, 1849* (Cincinnati, 1849); John I. Gaines, "Response to speech by Martin Delany," *North Star*, June 2, 1848; John I. Gaines, "A Plea for Colored Americans," *Anti-Slavery Bugle*, May 21, 1853; on letters, see, in particular, John I. Gaines to Editor, Jan. 16, 1854, *Frederick Douglass' Paper*, Jan. 27, 1854; Gaines to Editor, Jan. 8, Mar. 3, 1855, *Provincial Freeman*, Jan. 20, Mar. 24, 1855.

57. *Liberator*, Apr. 27, 1860; *Anti-Slavery Bugle*, Aug. 17, 1850, May 21, 1853.

58. Cincinnati *Atlas*, n.d., quoted in *Voice of the Fugitive*, Apr. 8, 1852; Gaines to Editor, Jan. 8, 1855, *Provincial Freeman*, Jan. 20, 1855.

59. *Liberator*, Apr. 27, 1860; Cleveland *Leader*, Dec. 2, 1859.

60. "Peter Humphries Clark," Cleveland *Gazette*, Mar. 6, 1886; John B. Shotwell, *A History of the Schools of Cincinnati* (Cincinnati, 1902), p. 454; Simmons, *Men of Mark*, p.244.

61. Shotwell, *A History of the Schools of Cincinnati*, pp. 455–59.

62. Brown, *The Rising Son*, p. 523; Henry Cowles, "Oberlin College Catalogue and Record of Colored Students, 1835–1862," ms., Oberlin College Library; *Herald of Freedom*, quoted in *Frederick Douglass' Paper*, June 15, 1855.

63. Simmons, *Men of Mark*, pp. 245–46; Cleveland *Gazette*, Mar. 6, 1886.

64. Peter H. Clark to Mr. McLain, Sept. 17, 1850, quoted in Carter G. Woodson, *The Mind of the Negro as Reflected in Letters During the Crisis, 1800–1860* (New York, 1926), pp. 132–33; Cincinnati *Enquirer*, Nov. 22, 1850; *African Repository* 27 (Jan. 1851):20–21; *State Convention . . . 1852*; Simmons, *Men of Mark*, p. 245; Cincinnati *Commercial*, Mar. 27, 1877; Herbert G. Gutman, "Peter H. Clark: Pioneer Negro Socialist, 1877," *Journal of Negro Education* 34 (Fall 1965):413–18.

65. David A. Gerber, "Peter Humphries Clark: The Dialogue of Hope and Despair," in *Black Leaders of the Nineteenth Century*, ed., Leon Litwack and Au-

gust Meier (Urbana, 1988), pp. 173–90; Gerber, *Black Ohio and the Color Line*, pp. 219, 225, 227, 229–43. See also Lawrence Grosman, "In His Veins Coursed No Bootlicking Blood: The Career of Peter H. Clark, *Ohio History* 86 (Spring 1977):85–93; and Dovie King Clark, "Peter Humphries Clark," *Negro History Bulletin* 5 (May 1942):176.

    66. *State Convention . . . 1850*; Cleveland *True-Democrat*, Feb. 14, 1850.

    67. Cleveland *True-Democrat*, Jan. 21, 1850; *State Convention . . . 1850*.

    68. Ibid.

    69. Cleveland *True-Democrat*, Feb. 14, 1850; *State Convention . . . 1850*. For a biographical sketch of Justin Holland, see Simmons, *Men of Mark*, pp. 250–54.

    70. Cleveland *True-Democrat*, Dec. 24, 1849.

    71. *State Convention . . . 1850*; Cleveland *True-Democrat*, Jan. 21, 1850.

    72. *Ohio State Journal*, Jan. 13, 1849; Cleveland *True-Democrat*, Feb. 14, 1850; *Anti-Slavery Bugle*, Jan. 19, 1850.

    73. *State Convention . . . 1850*; *State Convention . . . 1849*; Cleveland *True-Democrat*, Jan. 26, Feb. 2, 6, 1850; *State Convention . . . 1850*.

    74. Cleveland *True-Democrat*, Jan. 26, 1850; *State Convention . . . 1850*; *State Convention . . . 1849*.

    75. Cleveland *True-Democrat*, Jan. 26, 1850.

    76. Cleveland *True-Democrat*, Feb. 6, 1850.

    77. *State Convention . . . 1850*; Cleveland *True-Democrat*, Feb. 2, 1850.

    78. "Langston Paid to David Jenkins," Feb. 9, 1850; "Received Oct. 14, 1850 of J. M. Langston"; "Mar. 15, 1850," all in Langston Papers.

    79. Cleveland *True-Democrat*, Feb. 14, 2, 1850; Harry James Brown and Frederick D. Williams, eds., *The Diary of James A. Garfield* (East Lansing, 1967), I, 1848–71, p. 38.

    80. "Actions of the Federal Government in Behalf of Slavery," ms., dated Feb. 27, 1850, Columbus, in Langston Papers. Compare for similarities to "Address to the Constitutional Convention of the State of Ohio, Now Assembled," *State Convention . . . 1851*.

    81. *State Convention . . . 1850*; *North Star*, June 13, 1850.

    82. Frederick Douglass to Samuel May, June 13, 1850, William Lloyd Garrison Papers, Boston Public Library; *North Star*, June 27, 1850.

    83. *North Star*, July 18, 1850; *North Star*, n.d., quoted in *Anti-Slavery Bugle*, Aug. 24, 1850; *Anti-Slavery Bugle*, Aug. 10, 1850.

    84. *Anti-Slavery Bugle*, Aug. 10, 1850.

    85. *Ohio State Journal*, July 16, 1850; *North Star*, n.d., quoted in *Anti-Slavery Bugle*, Aug. 24, 1850; Akron *Beacon*, n.d., quoted in Cleveland *True-Democrat*, July 27, 1850; Columbus *Standard*, n.d.; Akron *Beacon*, n.d.; and New Concord *Free Press*, n.d., all quoted in *Anti-Slavery Bugle*, Aug. 17, 1850.

    86. *Anti-Slavery Bugle*, Jan. 19, 1850; Cleveland *Plain Dealer*, July 26, 1850; *North Star*, n.d., reprinted in *Anti-Slavery Bugle*, Aug. 24, 1850.

    87. New Concord *Free Press*, n.d.; Pittsburgh *Tribune*, n.d., both quoted in *Anti-Slavery Bugle*, Aug. 17, 1850.

    88. Concord, R. I., *Herald of Freedom*, Dec. 10, 1841, quoted in Philip S. Foner, *Frederick Douglass* (New York, 1964), pp. 47–48; Akron *Beacon*, n.d.,

quoted in *Anti-Slavery Bugle*, Aug. 17, 1850; Cincinnati *Gazette*, Apr. 28, 1852.

89. Photograph of John Mercer Langston, Oberlin College Archives; Brown, *The Rising Son*, p. 448.

90. Akron *Beacon*, n.d., quoted in *Anti-Slavery Bugle*, Aug. 17, 1850; Concord, R. I., *Herald of Freedom*, Dec. 10, 1841, quoted in Foner, *Frederick Douglass*, p. 48.

91. "Receipt of Adams, Stewart & Co. July 9, 1850," Langston Papers; New Concord *Free Press*, n.d., and Pittsburgh *Tribune*, n.d., both quoted in *Anti-Slavery Bugle*, Aug. 17, 1850.

92. *North Star*, n.d., quoted in *Anti-Slavery Bugle*, Aug. 24, 1850.

93. Thomas C. Nelson, "The Aliened American: The Free Negro in Ohio, 1840–1851," master's thesis, University of Toledo, 1969, pp. 88–89; Charles Thomas Hickok, *The Negro in Ohio, 1802–1870* (Cleveland, 1896; repr. New York: AMS Press, 1975), pp. 53–54; Frank U. Quillin, *The Color Line in Ohio* (Ann Arbor, 1913; repr. New York: Negro Universities Press, 1969), pp. 61–62.

94. *Ohio Standard*, n.d., quoted in *Anti-Slavery Bugle*, June 29, 1850; Quillin, *The Color Line In Ohio*, pp. 63, 61.

95. C. H. Langston to Frederick Douglass, Sept. 22, 1850, *North Star*, Oct. 3, 1850; *Anti-Slavery Bugle*, Aug. 17, 1850; Cleveland *True-Democrat*, Aug. 10, 1850.

96. C.H. and J. M. Langston to Chase, Sept. 12, 1850, Chase Papers.

97. Nelson, "The Aliened American," pp. 91–100; Quillin, *The Color Line in Ohio*, pp. 70–87; Hickok, *The Negro in Ohio*, pp. 55–66; *Anti-Slavery Bugle*, Dec. 14, 1850; Leon Litwack, *North of Slavery* (Chicago, 1961), p. 263; Cleveland *True-Democrat*, Jan. 26, 1850.

98. "Actions of the Federal Government in Behalf of Slavery," Langston Papers.

CHAPTER 6

"A Nationality, Before We Can Become Anybody,"[1]

1850–52

THE shadow of the Fugitive Slave Law loomed over Langston's thought and actions in the early 1850s. "This abomination of all abominations," he cried in outrage, struck down "all the shields of liberty."[2] Part of the compromise package designed to avert sectional crisis and remove slavery from politics, it plummeted northern blacks to the depths of anger and despair, setting the tone for a decade that would seem an endless voyage on the roily moral and emotional waters of a dangerous sea. Each new development—from act of the federal government to local election to sometimes bloody resistance to slave catchers—tossed them from troughs of disillusion to crests of optimism. Between came brief periods of apparent stasis, an ebb in the flow of racism, or, conversely, a tide so strong it seemed foolhardy to challenge it, a pulling back from sectional confrontation, a surface acceptance of compromise. But the sick feeling remained. Langston would have echoed the sentiment of Ralph Waldo Emerson: "We wake up with a painful auguring, and after exploring a little to know the cause find it is the odious news in each day's paper, the infamy [of the Fugitive Slave Law]."[3] Some, like Emerson, hoped the law would prove unenforceable; but the federal government was to be consistent in enforcement efforts, while each instance of resistance by whites and blacks would exacerbate the tension in North and South.[4] In such a changeable, heightened emotional climate, where men took each action or reaction to be an omen of the eventual outcome of the struggle for freedom, it was not unnatural that John Mercer should have been gripped by ambivalence over his own and his race's destiny. Even as the young man engaged in a number of activities aimed at eventual black liberation and nationality within the American republic, he was increasingly attracted to the vision he had articulated nearly two years earlier. A black nationality achieved by emigration, he painfully, hopefully, defiantly began to believe, might be the only way for American blacks to develop their fullest human potential.[5] Even while John Mercer became in late 1850 the first Negro admitted to theological studies at Oberlin College, undertaking the work as a stepping stone to a legal career, he was considering rejecting the nation whose prejudice seemed unalterable. By January 1852, in a move whose repercussions would be felt across the black North, these ideas and emotions would come to the surface.

Designed to strengthen the largely unenforced law of 1793 requiring the return of fugitive slaves to their owners, and placate secession-threatening southerners, the Fugitive Slave Law, which Langston was not alone in thinking of dubious constitutionality, put at hazard the freedom of all blacks, subjecting them to kidnap and false claims. At the same time, it forbade ordinary citizens, white or black to assist the fugitive, but required them to aid in his or her arrest. Indignantly, speaking on demand of his 1851 state black convention colleagues, John Mercer outlined its provisions: "It strips man of his manhood and liberty upon an *ex-parte* trial; sets aside the constitutional guarantee of the writ of Habeas Corpus, which, under the constitution, can never be suspended, except in cases of rebellion or invasion, declares that the decision of the commissioner, the lowest judicial officer known to the law, upon the matter of personal liberty—the gravest subject that can be submitted to any tribunal, shall be final and conclusive; holds out a bribe in the shape of double fees, for a decree contrary to liberty and in favor of Human Slavery [$10 if the alleged fugitive were remanded to his or her claimant, $5 if he or she were deemed to be free]; forbids any enquiry into the facts of the case by confining it to the question of personal identity." The law shattered "all the great bulwarks of Liberty. . . . It kills alike, the true spirit of the American Declaration of Independence, the Constitution, and the palladium of our liberties." It was "unworthy the name of law." "By *prohibiting* what is *right*, and commanding what is *wrong*," he explained, furnishing the appropriate passage from Blackstone, the act reversed the definition of real law. It was, rather, "a hideous deformity in the *garb* of law."[6]

John Mercer's own immediate reaction, with his brother Charles, was to write Salmon Chase, Ohio's Free Soil senator, asking advice on the black American future. Clearly divided in their own minds, the brothers posed two alternative visions: continuation of the black and, to a by now somewhat lessened degree, abolitionist struggle for equal rights and, thus, perhaps, an eventual unrestricted black American nationality; or emigration. What was the likelihood, they wondered, if Negroes themselves requested it, of a congressional land grant in the territories acquired from Mexico, where blacks might "peaceably settle and enjoy our own Political rights as do the inhabitants of other territories?" Failing this, "should we . . . quit the land of our birth and seek an asylum in a foreign clime, or remain here—until assisted by our Friends 'until success shall crown efforts,' and the great principles on which our Government was founded shall exist in practice as well as in theory?"[7]

Future considerations aside, the present need was to protest the new enactment. The Langstons joined with other blacks in Ohio, and across the North, in public articulation of profound disgust. The 1851 state black convention, with both men prominent, associated congressmen who had voted for "this fiendish enactment" with the despotism of Nero and Caligula, the tyranny of Charles I, the capricious cruelty under the reign of terror in France. On the community level, black vigilance committees were established or revitalized, and plans refined for helping fugitives to Canada. Incitements to civil disobedience were open and repeated. Blacks, rural and urban, endorsed the motto of a Muskingum County meeting: "Watch, fight, and pray." Declaring their preference that the nation be "shattered into a thousand fragments" rather than "quietly submit" to any law that would "compel us to deliver our oppressed brethren into the hands of their heartless pursuers," John Malvin, Lawrence W. Minor, and other Cleveland blacks vowed to "exert our influence to induce slaves to escape and protect them from recapture." A Columbus meeting, led by Charles Langston and stalwarts Jenkins and Taylor, while urging fugitives to leave for a "land of liberty," appointed a five-man committee to protect against seizures by slaveholders or their agents and advised all Negroes to be constantly prepared for self-defense.[8] The significant escalation of black rhetoric, with overtones of violence, would continue throughout the crisis-ridden decade.

White reaction, too, was forceful. Like "a bomb-shell suddenly thrown into a peaceable crowd," the enactment detonated waves of indignation across the North. Denunciation was particularly vigorous on the Western Reserve. Oberlin, expressing "mortification and shame," pledged that while "our fugitive brother remains in our midst, we will stand by him to the last." A mass gathering twelve miles away at Elyria openly planned an underground resistance network for Lorain County to be conducted by "good men and true." In a foreshadowing of the major political realignments of the decade, prominent

Democrats and Whigs rubbed shoulders with Free Soilers in two massive demonstrations in Cleveland. "No enactment ever given birth to by the American Congress," John Mercer noted in grim gratification, "has ever created so much dissatisfaction and excitement as the Fugitive Slave Law of 1850. This is not to be wondered at when we remember that mankind are not entirely divested of their humanity."9 Surely, while one part of his mind fastened on emigration, another, interpreting white indignation as a good omen for blacks, assured him that such moral fervor might be harnessed to bring about black liberation and nationality within the American republic.

But even as the first protests sounded, Negroes from throughout the North, some free persons as well as fugitives, individually and in groups, began the exodus to Canada that, by some estimates, would involve some twenty thousand persons during the pre-war decade. Moreover, it was quickly apparent that the Langstons were not alone in the black intellectual circle in their consideration of the imperatives for abandoning the country. Within a week of the bill's passage, Oberlin-educated William P. Newman, one-time (and possibly still) fugitive slave, resigned the pastorate of Cincinnati's noted Union Baptist church. He accepted a call to Chatham in modern-day Ontario, even though, only six years before, after repeated tours as a teacher and minister in Canada West, he had warned would-be immigrants of adverse conditions and racial prejudice all but matching that in Ohio. But, as was plain from a lengthy, bitter letter written in Cleveland while he and his large family awaited passage, the minister had lost faith in his country. "A mission of bonds and death," not freedom, was the now-apparent goal of the government, he exhorted his "brethren, the objects of hate and the victims of oppression. . . . Would not the Devil do well to *rent out hell* and move to the United States, and rival, if possible, President Fillmore and his political followers!" Counseling resistance "even to death," Newman pledged to "kill any so-called man who attempts to enslave me or mine."10

If emigration or flight to neighboring Canada was acceptable as a means of self-liberation, John Mercer and his black movement colleagues had long viewed Liberian colonization of free blacks, under the aegis of the all-white American Colonization Society, in a wholly negative light. Over the years most articulate blacks in Ohio and across the North, rankled also by the society's southern support and repeated failures to assist black colonists adequately, agreed with Gideon Langston's 1843 denunciation: "Colonization has no other tendency than to sacrifice the free colored population for the purpose of rendering the system of slavery more secure." Even the 1849 pro-emigration resolution drawn up by John Langston and his friend W. Hurst Burnham had expressed determination "never to submit to any scheme of colonization, in any part of the world, in or out of the United States, while a vestige of slavery lasts." Ohio black conventions consistently adopted resolutions stating opposition to the society "because [as the 1851 convention report put it] its object is the expatriation of 600,000 defenceless free colored persons, which is cruel and unjust, and our opposition is deepened, when we consider that the greater part of the Churches and professed Christians of the country, are with that society. . . ." When the American Colonization Society requested an appropriation from the Ohio legislature in early 1851, Day, Malvin, and young barber H. Ford Douglass, "as taxpayers and citizens," would rail "against an appropriation of one cent" to send Ohio blacks to Africa. Despite such opposition, "taking advantage," as Frederick Douglass claimed, "of the depressed, disheartened and anguish-smitten state of our people," in the Fugitive Law's aftermath the A.C.S. began to make more headway with Negroes in the North.[11]

Only five days after the Fugitive Slave Law's adoption, "disgusted as he was by the bitter prejudice of the times," Peter Clark announced his willingness to go to Liberia. Together with two of Langston's Oberlin contemporaries—William R. Casey, son of riverman William Casey, Cincinnati's prominent underground railroad conductor, and Lawrence Minor, just graduated and active with Cleveland blacks in castigating "this guilty nation"—Clark organized the Liberia League. Two months later, the young men told their hopes of being teachers or bookkeepers in Liberia to the A.C.S.'s vigorous Cincinnati chapter, which extended its warmest endorsement and promises of financial aid.[12] Their destination was "Ohio in Africa," a just-purchased ten-thousand-acre tract donated by a wealthy white Cincinnatian and promoted by David Christy, the society's energetic local agent. But they would never arrive. How far Minor and Casey, who both remained in Ohio to be active in the black movement, actually pursued their intention is uncertain, but Clark, at least, traveled to the docks in New Orleans, where he found a "dirty little lumber schooner" chartered for the transportation of 120 emigrants. Appalled at the vessel, the frail young man refused to embark. Within six months, most of those who sailed were either dead or imprisoned, victims of smallpox or long incarceration at Charleston, South Carolina, where the captain had put in for medical assistance.[13] Such experiences scarcely were calculated to increase the black intelligentsia's confidence in the Colonization Society.

By the time of the state black convention in January 1851, John Mercer and Charles, whose design in soliciting Senator Chase's advice had been to submit it to the delegates, had changed plans. This was true despite Chase's encouragement, in a gloomy assessment of black American possibilities, of emigration. A proponent of equal civil and political rights for blacks, Chase nonetheless candidly admitted his "long held" opinion. "Natural law" having ordained the races for different geographical latitudes, he argued, once the artificial constraint of slavery should be removed, the "natural" separation of white from black would recur. This widely held thesis Chase tempered, however, by declaring that "no *violence*—no *compulsory* emigration,—no legalized injustice of any description" should be countenanced. "If the Declaration of Independence is not a fable and a cheat, the colored people, *in virtue of their manhood* have the same natural rights as other men." To the Langstons' specific inquiries, the first-term senator had replied that he saw no chance for black Ohioans to attain political rights "at present." The grant of a portion of the western territories for black settlement seemed out of the question. "Those among the colored people, whose circumstances permit," he advised, should emigrate to the West Indies or Liberia or wherever they could find a welcome. From similar pronouncements over the next months, it would appear that Chase's sentiments were representative of a small group of antislavery radicals, most of whom, as radical Republicans late in the decade, ironically would oppose a move from within the party aimed at black colonization.[14]

But the fact that the Ohio Constitutional Convention by January 1851 had rendered no decisions on issues vital to Negroes made publicizing Chase's advice seem inopportune. The Langstons were aware that black emigration discussion could be perverted by advocates of financial assistance to the Colonization Society, both in Constitutional Convention and state legislature, into evidence of Negro support. Moreover, even though chances for a successful resolution of the black enfranchisement campaign were dim—wryly, Jenkins, in accepting the black convention presidency, remarked, "I have been battling for the last ten years in this State for the attainment of the elective franchise, with what success I leave you to judge"[15] —promotion of emigration would detract from and, to a large extent, undercut their own efforts and those of their few faithful allies, most notably Dr. Norton Townshend of Lorain County, in the Constitutional Convention.

Furthermore, young Langston, a believer in thorough preparation, may have judged their emigration scheme still too immature for exposure. Based on their query to Chase, it seems likely that the brothers had hoped that the thorniest problem connected with a mass emigration—where blacks should settle—might be solved by a federal grant of a portion of the territory acquired through the war with Mexico. Indeed, the idea had gained some currency among Ohio anti-slavery politicians. In 1849, the remarkable Free Soil-influenced lower house of the state assembly had instructed Ohio congressmen to procure passage of federal law authorizing apportionment of a section of the new territories for the benefit of all free blacks, giving each settler title to eighty acres free of charge and establishing schools and government for their protection.

A similar proposal would be endorsed by the Cleveland *True-Democrat*, Day's Free Soil employer. Although the *Anti-Slavery Bugle*, the western Garrisonian organ published at Salem, Ohio, scorned the scheme as "colorphobia wearing the garb of philanthropy," the black leadership, usually quick to disown any white-sponsored plan for black colonization, had remained silent. Still, Chase's negative assessment of the chances for congressional approval, and perhaps like results from other soundings, may have discouraged the Langstons from any attempt to put the black convention on record in favor of settlement in the western territories. Interestingly, in a meeting with a delegation from the black convention, including both Langstons, it was the Ohio Governor Reuben Wood, an anti-slavery Democrat, who suggested that, "with the prejudice of the whites, if Congress would approve to the use of the colored some portion of our domain and the colored could feel willing to emigrate, it might be the best thing both for them and the whites."[16] But with most Free Soilers, along with other white northerners, determined to keep free Negroes as well as slaves out of the territories, Congress ultimately would show no interest in allowing blacks a share in the national domain, even blocking them from homestead rights. Their exclusion from the West would heighten black interest in emigration.

Although the Langston brothers thus did not bring up nationalist-emigration at the 1851 convention, their remarks on other topics did reveal much of the militance and consciousness of group solidarity that are elements of nationalist thought. Charles espoused a pragmatism edged with violence in response to a motion by H. Ford Douglass that no colored man could "consistently" vote because of the pro-slavery nature of the Constitution, an old issue presumably revived by Frederick Douglass's recent disavowal of the Garrisonian position. Charles called on blacks to vote "or do anything else under the constitution, that will aid in effecting our liberties, and in securing our political, religious, and intellectual elevation." Granted the pro-slavery nature of the Constitution, "made to foster and uphold that abominable, vampirish and bloody system of American slavery," that was no reason to abstain from politics. He himself would vote "on the same principles, (circumstances being favorable) that I would call on every slave, from Maryland to Texas, to arise and assert their *liberties*, and cut their masters' throats if they attempt again to reduce them to slavery." Citing the American Revolution's slogan, "Resistance to Tyranny is obedience to God," Charles confessed, "I have long since adopted as my God the freedom of the colored people of the United States, and my religion, to do anything that will effect that object." The Langstons joined in the defeat of the anti-voting measure, 28–2. In a no less resolute statement urging establishment of a state black newspaper, John Mercer, a convention vice-president, avowed that Ohio blacks had "interests peculiar to ourselves" and must "talk to each other, and to the world." Both Langstons supported, and Charles served on the three-man committee of correspondence for, the calling of a black national convention to be held in Buffalo the following September. With such eastern leaders as Martin Delany responding that the groundwork was insufficient, the call would go unheeded until 1853.[17] But the attempt to achieve black northern unity within the country, like the emigration movement, would be a major manifestation of black nationalism in the decade.

Within Ohio at the moment, however, black organizational resources were low. A reduced attendance—only thirty-seven delegates from nineteen counties—was one reflection of the heavy toll on black morale exacted by the Fugitive Law. With the past year's statewide league apparently aborted, the 1851 convention postponed action on John Mercer's proposals for a newspaper and confined formal organization to the usual appointment of a State Central Committee. Nonetheless, although it was not a time for new initiatives, the delegates showed determination to carry through on the old, protesting efforts within the Constitutional Convention to again restrict the common schools to white children and reiterating the demands for enfranchisement.

Their most notable success was the interview secured with Governor Wood. The reasons for this unprecedented favor were related to the anti-Fugitive Law agitation, Wood's eagerness to reinstate his party's alliance with the Free Soilers, and the fact that the governor, elected several months earlier with some anti-slavery support, already faced a fall reelection campaign under a new constitutional provision. The nine-man black delegation, headed by Ford Douglass, included both Langstons and Day who, in a forceful address, asked the governor to put in writing an endorsement of black enfranchisement. "Is not this due the colored men who under the restrictive clause of the present Constitution have cast their ballots for you as standard bearer of their principles, is it not due to your own heart, throbbing in favor of the great interests of Humanity . . .?" Day demanded. Professing interest "in the welfare of the colored," Governor Wood admitted indecision on black political rights, but thought it "wonderful they were interested." Through Day's Cleveland newspaper employer, the interview was widely publicized. Possibly the governor did exercise quiet influence, not certainly for black enfranchisement but against the proposed harsh restrictions, on the Constitutional Convention's Democratic majority, for his winning reelection campaign did receive the support of such antislavery radicals as Chase and Townshend. In future, as the Democratic party settled firmly into a conservative, anti-black mold, the interview with the Democratic governor would seem even more remarkable. For the moment, the governor's "shuffling, evasive, cowardly answer," as the *Anti-Slavery Bugle* called it, together with the Constitutional Convention's subsequent rejection of black claims, may have pushed a wavering young Langston closer toward a black nationalist-emigration.[18]

"When many years ago I looked around me," Langston would volunteer in 1882, "all was dark as night. When I spoke of studying law I was laughed at; when I spoke of studying theology the idea was pronounced chimerical." In the fall of 1850, frustrated by his failure to gain entrance to a law school or lawyer's office, John Mercer sought out Professor John Morgan in Oberlin. The "melting-hearted, but alligator-hided" Irishman, whom Langston compared to Daniel O'Connell in his concern for the Negro, advised Mercer to undertake a full course of study in the department of theology. The department had never had a black graduate, and Morgan discerned the opportunity for Oberlin and the black intellectual to achieve a racial breakthrough.[19] The weight of popular opinion, backed by widely accepted scientific theories of the Negro's inferior intellectual abilities, held, as Langston put it, "that theological and metaphysical study treated as matter of science was too profound and intricate for the Negro brain and intellect." Only that year Dr. Josiah C. Nott, most prominent exponent of the "new American ethnology," had edified the Southern Rights Association in Mobile with his well-publicized "proofs" of the Negro's innate unfitness for anything but servitude. Even educator Horace Mann accepted such findings to the extent that he believed the "Caucasian excels the other [race] in intellect; the African excels the others, even Caucasian, in the affectional or emotional part of their nature."[20]

Not averse to thinking himself an intellectual standard bearer for the Negro in the assault on white supremacist ramparts, Langston found

Morgan's suggestion appealing. "We struggle against opinions," he exhorted black compatriots about this time. "Our warfare lies in the field of thought. Glorious struggle! Godlike warfare!" In forced retreat from his major career objective, he relished this proposed secondary attack. Moreover, his undergraduate exposure to theological subjects had been positive. Without surrendering his legal ambition, Langston entered the theological department, too late, however, for inclusion in the 1850 school catalogue.[21]

A stiff, three-year course, the theological curriculum centered on didactic and polemic theology, sacred and ecclesiastical history, and exegesis of Old and New Testaments, utilizing Greek, Latin, and Hebrew. Along with Morgan, the Reverends Finney, Cowles, and, after the spring of 1852, Henry E. Peck, a young abolitionist firebrand from Rochester, New York, who would become Langston's friend, carried the teaching load. Old lawyer Finney maintained that the theological students were taught "to reason consecutively,—*to think on their legs*—to draw illustrations living from nature around them—and understand the law of God,"[22] all useful training for a would-be attorney. Finding the subject matter absorbing and demanding, young Langston particularly appreciated as well the emphasis on logic and analysis.

As word of the Negro theological student spread, curiosity-seekers took to dropping in on his classes. When he was called upon to recite, Langston would recall sardonically, the visitors, invariably by their facial expressions and often verbally, would betray surprise at his ability to handle such abstruse materials. Sometimes they tactlessly conveyed their astonishment directly to him; sometimes they quizzed his professors: " 'Does he really seem to understand and comprehend the truths, the profound principles of theology?' "[23] The seminary walls were not so thick as to permit the incipient black nationalist to forget about prejudice.

On the other hand, such doubts scarcely seemed to perturb fellow "theologs." Proud as a group of their intellectual independence and their status at the top of the student hierarchy, the seminarians shared John Mercer's delight in confounding critics. Having overridden Morgan's stern objections in admitting Oberlin graduate Antoinette Brown to membership, although as a woman she was permitted to pursue theology only as an auditor, the Theological Literary Society lost no time in acquiring its first Negro member. Langston straightway was elected "scribe" of the society, and reelected in March 1851. Faculty engaged alongside students in the society's oratorical exercises, essays, and informal argumentation, whose frequently radical tenor was typified by the debate in the angry aftermath of Senator Daniel Webster's support of the Compromise of 1850: "Ought Webster to Be Hung?" In one of his own debates in June 1851, Langston doubtless voiced a trenchant negative on the "propriety of supporting the American Bible and tract societies, considering their relation to Slavery and slaveholders."[24]

He took another whack at religious supporters of the Peculiar Institution in an address on "Qualifications of the Pulpit Orator," delivered at the August 1851 commencement. The theologs had given him additional proof of their regard by electing him to represent the first-year class. In "clear and forcible" style,[25] he transformed his dull-sounding topic into a striking exposition of Christian, democratic-republican, and abolitionist reform—"the all-embracing doctrine of universal liberty." The minister must develop the "moral courage" to protest "every unjust discrimination growing out of caste and accidental difference," to "stand forth in vindication of all reforms in Church and State, which are the legitimate demand of truth and love," and to champion in "trumpet tones" the cause of "the dumb, the disfranchised, and the enslaved." Sparing neither the "soulless and obsequious" doctors of divinity, "heartless" statesmen, "a time-serving Congress," nor "the huge, the colossal, the mercenary dimensions of slavery itself," the black seminarian charged churchmen with the obligation of combating "every species of oppression and wrong."

The commencement audience, particularly those who knew that John Mercer aspired not to the pulpit but to the law, may have suspected that his prescription for the "successful pulpit orator" might apply equally well to the lawyer-reformer: "Cultivated rhetoric, vigorous imagination, fine discriminating logical powers, accurate and extensive knowledge, sincere respect for his fellow-men, a soul absorbing philanthropy, and a warm and benign earnestness." His auditors were impressed. An Ohio congressman was overheard to joke, "It is said in my neighborhood that in Oberlin they think as much of a white man as a colored man, if he behaves himself." But if the college were to produce a few more specimens such as Langston and three other recent black commencement orators, "we cannot say so."[26]

In contrast to many poverty-stricken Oberlin theologs, who stuffed mail-bags with entreaties for loans and jobs,[27] John Mercer was fortunate to be able to afford both study and a host of reform activities. Twenty-one years of age in December 1850, he had come into his legacy. It is impossible to determine its size, but by the fall of 1851, he owned properties in Lorain County, where Oberlin was situated, valued for tax purposes at a robust $4,590. Moreover, the potential emigrationist had begun to acquire real estate in other localities. By 1854, he had rentproducing property in Columbus, where his agent was Charles Langston, who practiced dentistry and taught and was himself owner of an 1,100 acre farm leased to a white tenant in Jackson County.[28] Nevertheless, uncertain when he could expect to earn a living, the student landowner adhered to the careful money habits of his boyhood. He lived frugally, rooming at low cost "at Mr. Ells'," scrupulously recording such minor purchases as rubber leggings and umbrella and extending small loans, with interest, to friends and relatives. Not until the final year of his theological course, apparently tempted while buying textbooks, did he succumb to the luxury of possessing Webster's dictionary at a cost of $15.[29]

In the fall of 1851, John Mercer saw a way to turn his financial independence, which freed him from the necessity of the vacation teaching jobs he had held frequently since he was fourteen, and his popularity with other students to the advantage of the currently troubled Negro public schools. With few exceptions, such as the racially integrated public schools in Oberlin, Cleveland, and several other localities, schooling of black children had been dependent on private financing until the school law of 1848 provided that tax money could be used for their benefit. That law was repealed in 1849, when new legislation provided that those Negro children excluded from white common schools should share proportionately with white children in each district's state-furnished school funds, while receiving the local tax revenues derived from Negro-owned property. Moreover, Negro taxpayers would elect the black school directors—the first voting privilege most Ohio blacks had ever enjoyed.[30]

But the law, as Langston and black colleagues alleged, was "generally misunderstood, and in many cases, notoriously perverted; to the great injury of the cause of education among us, thus defeating the object of the framers of the act." Recalcitrant local officials frequently blocked black efforts to establish schools under the law. In 1850 and again in 1851, the Ohio secretary of state reported some local authorities were evading the requirement to enumerate Negro school-age children, on which turned the distribution of state funds. In Toledo, white abolitionist Laura Haviland kept school in a Negro church for some six months before officials, who had predicted her departure would mean "the end of that Negro school . . . and that wouldn't be long, for the Negroes were too poor to pay her," finally agreed to turn over public funds for its support.[31] In Cincinnati, organization of schools was well underway by the early fall of 1849, but the city council refused to appropriate funds to the Negro school directors, claiming the black franchise provision of the school law violated the state constitution. A black mass meeting, led by John Langston's friend John Gaines and his old landlord John Woodson, determined on suing the city, whereupon fundraising began and the services of Flamen Ball, Senator Chase's law partner, were secured. In 1851, specifying the "equal footing" granted "colored youth . . . in respect to Common schools," the Ohio Supreme Court ruled in favor of the black trustees. Peter Clark, teacher in one of the schools, whose closing had stimulated his interest in colonization, would donate his back salary to help defray costs of the suit. Later he paid tribute to Gaines, his short, ebony-skinned uncle, as a metaphor for the black community: "At last the little black man triumphed over the city of Cincinnati."[32]

Nevertheless, with Negro education still subject to local racial attitudes, the interpretation of cloudily worded statutes by judges and elected officials, and the vagaries of state politics, triumph was tenuous and incomplete. In 1853, a Democratic legislature would award black schools a share in all school funds. But simultaneously the lawmakers would make it easier to deny school privileges by requiring a minimum of thirty Negro children be available before a school had to be provided, and would rescind the right of blacks to elect school trustees, making them subject instead to white school boards. In 1856, a Republican assembly, lobbied by Gaines and Clark, would restore the election privilege, but only to Cincinnati Negroes.[33] Yet by the fall of 1851, the one thing certain was that ostensibly public education was still largely dependent on private efforts: if Negro children were to be educated, Negro taxpayers would have to organize their own schools and demand that local officials fulfill their legal obligations.

On the evening of September 14, 1851, young Langston and several other students called a meeting in the Oberlin chapel. Summoned to the chair, John Mercer explained the black school predicament, argued for a new student organization to provide assistance, and suggested appointment of a representative to work with black communities throughout the state. He could have reminded them of similar earlier activities by Oberlin-connected white and black abolitionists, including the Reverend Dennis Day, a black student who helped direct student teachers to black schools from 1840 until his departure in 1849. The result of the initial session, and two others shortly after, was the formation of a Young Men's Anti-Slavery Society, eighty-five strong. The society's objective was "the social and moral elevation of the colored race." Langston was elected the school agent. Inviting the Young Women's Anti-Slavery Society to share expenses, the members pledged to provide him a horse and carriage, plus $20 a month. Although, as

Langston remembered it, he voluntarily footed his own bills, he was furnished a more vital resource, an association holding itself responsible for the supply of teachers.[34]

In the next months, and during succeeding vacation periods, young Langston guided horse and buggy across the state from the lake country to the Ohio River, "arousing, directing, and utilizing public feeling among the colored people for their educational welfare." As among the tens of thousands in the South after the war, so among Ohio's twenty-five thousand he tried to strike the sparks of informed hope. Education was essential, he argued, if black Ohioans were to lend their "aid in promoting the abolition of American slavery, and in devising some judicious plan for the elevation of the half-free of the Northern states." It was "the glory of any people . . . the sure palladium of their Liberty—the positive evidence of their permanent and growing elevation." In the black communities, "in public address or private effort," he explained the steps necessary to attain funding and organize school districts, promising, as further encouragement, an Oberlin-trained teacher.[35]

The need for such impetus and direction had been recognized by the two preceding state black conventions in their calls for a state superintendent of colored schools. In January 1852, after Langston's initial tour as school agent, he would chair the black convention's committee on education, composed of Day, Gaines, Clark, and Charles Langston, which again called for black election of a school superintendent. From his committee's recommendations, some problems John Mercer had encountered may be inferred. Besides the lack of state direction and encouragement, and insufficient funding reflected in the paucity and poverty of school facilities, other hampering factors were an uneducated Negro clergy possessed of less than "just and enlarged views of *truth*"; teachers academically unqualified and lacking the requisite "deep interest in the welfare of the communities"; and, on the part of the black citizenry, not only ignorance of privileges but also confusion of sympathies in changing from existing private classes to public schools. Some blacks in Columbus, for instance, reportedly had been reluctant to make the switch from private classes. To inform blacks of recent legal developments, the Ohio supreme court's decision in the Cincinnati case was inserted in the convention's published minutes. Langston's education committee strongly recommended, meanwhile, that rather than church-supported or other private schools, "the free schools in the State be supported and encouraged in preference to all others, for upon them depend the education of the colored youth of Ohio."[36]

Apathy reigned in some black communities. In February 1854, John Mercer received a plea for assistance, eloquent of black indifference and official neglect, from William Hurst Burnham. A popular barber, who by 1855 would resume his trade in Cleveland, and a frequent convention delegate who had championed Langston's emigration proposals in 1849, Burnham complained of life in Zanesville, "this dark spot" where he felt "almost blotted out of existence." Situated in Muskingum County, Zanesville in 1850 had 224 black residents, nearly 3 percent of a total population of 7,705. His wife (Josephine Minor, who knew Langston through her studies at Oberlin), Burnham noted wryly, "says tell John that in our blessed city can be found an awful set of darkies and in the same breath wants to know, if you can, send a teacher (*a white one*). . . ." Since the couple was "boarding" and thus lacked the facilities for overnight guests, Burnham could not, as he wished, invite Langston to lecture, but promised to send "some material aid." He closed on a statement of need: "In this county we have but one school (in Putnam) and in that there is forty scholars or about 36 in regular attendance. . . . In our own city we have over a hundred children and no school. Help us can't you."[37]

Clearly, the Oberlin student teachers that Langston helped direct to black communities were vital to the early black common school movement. When Laura Haviland left Toledo's grudgingly recognized Negro school in 1852, for example, it was with the assurance of replacement by John G. Mitchell, a black Oberlin student who would be graduated in 1858 and later become theological dean at Wilberforce University. In the fall of 1854, white abolitionist John Wattles, Augustus Wattles's younger brother and agent to black communities for the Cincinnati Ladies' Anti-Slavery Society, asserted, perhaps over-optimistically, that "nearly all the colored schools in the state" had profited from "competent colored teachers" during the previous winter. In 1859, Anson Smyth, Ohio commissioner of common schools, in a general condemnation of educational conditions for Negro children, declared "their teachers, whether white or colored . . . poorly qualified, and are employed because they can be had at small salaries," but admitted to some qualified exceptions.[38] It took the dedication of the Oberlin students to endure the lower pay than teachers in white schools enjoyed, and the "mere sheds and basements" in which many had to teach—"wretched apologies for educational advantages," sputtered black abolitionist William C. Nell of Boston after an 1856 lecture tour with Langston. By 1862, E. H. Fairchild, principal of the Oberlin preparatory department, would assert: "The entire colored school system in Ohio and Indiana, and to some good extent in the Canadas, rests on the pupils taught in Oberlin College." Moreover, a survey of blacks educated at Oberlin showed that "a very large majority" were then engaged in teaching black schools.[39]

Unfortunately, incomplete and unreliable state records make it impossible to gauge statistically the black community response to Langston's efforts. No figures were kept in 1851–52, the first winter of his school agency; the following year only 22 black schools with 939 pupils (of a possible 6,862) were reported in the common school system. But by 1853–54, official records showed 48 schools with 2,439 pupils (of a possible 9,756). If the figures seem dubious, the trend of ever-growing black support of public education, at least, was clear. By 1860–61, a reported 159 black schools showed an enrollment of nearly 7,000 (of 14,247), almost a tenfold increase over the previous eight years.[40]

These increases occurred in the face of radically varying local conditions. In the single year of 1858, there were reports of a fully integrated school in Deer Creek in northeastern Stark County; good but all-black schools in a rural settlement in Shelby County; and, in the Quaker community of Harveysburg in southern Warren County, visited by school agent Langston early in the decade, a flourishing colored school taught by one black teacher and one white; but in Springfield township near Cincinnati, white school directors obstructed Negroes' educational efforts at every turn. The Springfield Negro children would "have to go without schooling," the Cincinnati *Gazette* puckishly noted, "and then be reproached when they grow up for not knowing as much as white folks."[41]

Despite grave problems, the black educational state in Ohio may not have been too much inferior to the white. In most rural sections and among poor whites in the cities of Ohio, as across the North, public education was still rudimentary. In a study of Newburyport, Massachusetts, for example, a modern scholar, who found that 40 percent of working-class parents in 1850 admitted their children had not been enrolled in school during the past year, concluded: "The opportunities for formal education past the age of ten or eleven" in Newburyport "were effectively nil for working class children." In Cincinnati, enrollment figures for the years 1854–63 were about proportionately equal for blacks and whites. Daily attendance, moreover, was extremely low for both. For the school year 1856–57, Cincinnati whites of school age were estimated at 40,986, but only 16,673 (40 percent) were registered for school, and daily attendance averaged 10,439 (just above 25 percent). For the same year, Cincinnati blacks of school age were an estimated 1,345, of whom 618 (45 percent) were registered, and daily attendance averaged 280 (just above 20 percent).[42]

The relative improvement in educational advantages was striking. In 1853 David Jenkins observed that public funding for Columbus's Negro schoolchildren had increased within a few years from $300 to $1,500 per year and jubilantly reported "great progress . . . and in nothing more than our school privileges." On the black slate, multiplication by five meant a significant advance had been chalked in. Ohio State Representative James Monroe of Oberlin, speaking before the assembly on January 22, 1857, would appraise the situation favorably: "At the present time not only are the mass of the colored acquiring a common education, but a considerable number among them are graduates of colleges, thoroughly educated, and are doing what they can to improve and elevate their people." Langston himself, in the same month, noting the "influence of our common schools and our religious organizations" in improving black capabilities, would assert, "In our literary qualifications, we compare favorably with other inhabitants of this commonwealth."[43]

Although the Young Men's Anti-Slavery Society apparently disbanded in late 1853, and Langston's formal stint as school agent presumably came to a close, his involvement in supplying teachers and stimulating black schools, if less intense than in those first crucial years, would continue. In his 1857 address, Monroe would fit a title to the role, explaining that an Oberlin Negro had for years "acted as a sort of superintendent of the colored schools" of Ohio. In later years, an admirer would assert that Langston "did more, perhaps, than any other man to reform the public school system of the State."[44]

It was somewhat paradoxical that at the very commencement of his travels for school reform in the fall of 1851, the agent of the Oberlin Young Men's Anti-Slavery Society was also Ohio's leading advocate, with his brother Charles, of a radical solution for black America's problems. Worsening conditions on nearly every level had hardened their emigrationist resolve. Prejudice—"most cruel and bitter, . . .—unjust, unnatural and opposed to the civilization of the age," the 1852 Ohio black convention complained—seemed to be intensifying. Each passing month saw another entry in the ledger of maltreatment, ranging from such meanness as the newly segregated seating in Cleveland's major theater, discriminatory treatment in Ohio's prisons, and the expulsion of indigent, elderly, and ill blacks from Cincinnati's tax-supported poor house,[45] to the vast injustice of the Fugitive Slave Law. Besides the depressing effects of each reported fugitive recaptured or free person kidnapped, blacks had witnessed ample evidence of federal determination to enforce the law. In February 1851, after some fifty Negroes, moving "like a black squall," forcibly rescued the fugitive Shadrach from a Boston courtroom, President Fillmore himself issued a special proclamation ordering the prosecution of the rescuers. And in early April, as both black and white Bostonians watched helplessly, hundreds of police oversaw the sad march of Thomas Sims, a fugitive from Georgia, to the docks for shipment south. Economically, too, while the nation reveled in unprecedented prosperity, poor blacks faced competition with steadily increasing numbers of immigrants, particularly Irish, for jobs in Cincinnati and other northern cities.[46]

In politics, while the "Young America" movement, arguing the Manifest Destiny of Central American expansion, free trade, and interventionist aid to republican elements in European nations, reached new heights, the vast majority of Americans, with the original northern outcry over the Fugitive Law fading to a murmur, seemed determined to regard the Compromise of 1850 as the final settlement of the slavery question. Both the confident Democratic and faltering Whig parties would write that position into their platforms in the spring of 1852, while badly divided Free Soilers seemed on the verge of disappearance. To further depress black spirits, a drop in the projected rate of increase of the free black population, noted in the 1850 census, had revived predictions of eventual extinction of the race in America. Ohio Congressman Lewis D. Campbell, an antislavery Whig whose opinion on the black condition was solicited by the Ohio black Central Committee in late 1851, was blunt: "I regard the 'present position' of your race in this country, as infinitely worse than it was ten years ago. . . . I see nothing to justify a promise of much to your 'future prospects.' "[47]

Coinciding with falling black hopes was resurgent black, and white, excitement over the European liberation movements that had inspired John Mercer's youthful admiration. Louis Kossuth, the charismatic Hungarian patriot who symbolized the very spirit of rebellious nationalism, made a much-heralded landing in New York in December 1851, the commencement of a six-month national tour that seemed to throw the whole North and West into an evangelistic, expansionistic, militaristic frenzy. In early February he swept through Ohio. As it turned out, when pressed by a New York City black delegation led by caterer George Downing, who paid homage to the "great principle" enunciated by Kossuth "that a man has a right to the full exercise of his faculties in the land which gave him birth," Kossuth would disappoint black and white abolitionists, who had hoped for an open condemnation of slavery, by a statement of neutrality on American "domestic issues." Nonetheless, the public's mania for the Hungarian exile presented opportunities for abolitionists like John Mercer Langston, who argued: "You can talk about liberty abroad, but if you would be consistent, you must labor for the emancipation and elevation of the slaves at home." Nor did Kossuth's silence on slavery immediately diminish the appeal of his idealistic rhetoric: "To fight for liberty," he told a New York audience, "is to fight for nationality." Black Ohioans responded. Expressing their sympathy for Kossuth and other European revolutionists, blacks in Cleveland declared, "Constitutional liberty by means of universal suffrage, trial by jury, etc., and the improvement of the social condition of the people, are ideas for which, like the people of Europe, we are striving here." A Columbus gathering, with Charles Langston as secretary, similarly proclaimed, "So long as we can sympathize with the wronged and outraged Hungarians struggling for liberty at home or fleeing to other lands to escape Russian tyranny and oppression, our hearts cannot but yearn over the bleeding and panting fugitive fleeing from slavery and despotism in this Free Republic."[48]

As these statements indicated, nationalistic impulses undergirded by republican ideology merged with militant intentions. Since passage of the Fugitive Slave Law, black civil disobedience in Ohio and across the North had become more overt. Despite the risks, blacks throughout the decade publicized assistance rendered to fugitives; in 1854, the Cleveland Committee of Nine began to issue quarterly balance sheets of "passengers" and expenditures; the January 1855 report claimed 275 travelers over the previous eight months at a cost of nearly $500. These public avowals were clearly a tactic to enlist support, but they were also expressions of outrage and pride. With white reporters present at the January 1852 state convention, Peter Clark would boast that at one point on the Ohio River, presumably near Cincinnati, the "forwarding agents" had counted 138 fugitives "put through" to Canada during a single year. As convention president, Langston would appoint members of the Central Committee "agents *ex-officio* of the underground railway"; delegates would discuss a system of cipher to be used in telegraphing. "Is there no force competent to break up this extensive system of negro stealing?" fumed the Cincinnati *Gazette*. "It is nothing less." But the 1852 convention delegates resolved to obey the Higher Law, to defy the Fugitive Law, and to guard their liberty by the "mildest means in our judgment, adequate to the end."[49]

The means that African Americans, spurred by dramatic slave rescues of the preceding months, were willing to endorse had moved far by now from the mildness of moral suasion. In addition to the forcible rescues of Shadrach in Boston and Jerry in Syracuse, a bloody encounter had occurred near Christiana, Pennsylvania, where more than a score of gun-firing, pitchfork-wielding black farmers and several whites engaged in battle with southern slave catchers. Two fugitives escaped, two white southerners and three black defenders died, and other defenders faced federal charges. Messages of solidarity and support went out from black Ohio. Praising the "noble, honorable, and manly example of the Christiana Patriots" as "worthy the imitation of every colored man in the country, whether bond or free, when his liberty is assailed," blacks in Columbus approved Charles Langston's recommendation that black Ohioans employ an able lawyer to assist in their defense. A Cleveland gathering, making explicit the comparison with the European revolutionaries, expressed sympathy "with the men at Christiana and Syracuse, who like the Fathers of the Revolution, preferred to risk life, rather than to sacrifice liberty." Citing all three rescues, the 1852 convention would claim to "have learned from their example that liberty is dearer than life, and eternal vigilance its only guarantee." The "brave and beautiful bearing of the free blacks," lauded by abolitionist Gerrit Smith,[50] in resisting the Fugitive Law, violently and nonviolently, increased racial solidarity and pride; the tragic need to put up such resistance increased the desperation of the search for a remedy.

In urging emigration, Langston had the backing of some radical white antislavery opinion. Besides Chase, several other long-time advocates of black civil and political equality made known their feelings that blacks should leave the country. Their advice, if partially formed by their ambivalence on race, also reflected the disillusionment of partisans after too many losing battles—with the Compromise of 1850, they may have felt, the decisive one. Under the circumstances, as millions of Europeans voluntarily sought to better their condition through emigration to the United States, and thousands of Americans moved westward, there was a certain logic in thinking blacks might do the same. In April 1851, the *National Era*, edited by Gamaliel Bailey (formerly of the Cincinnati *Philanthropist*), the Washington antislavery organ that, young Langston observed, many black Ohioans read regularly, volunteered that Negroes "must become possessed with the same spirit of self-relying enterprise" as the whites. "Were we a colored man, we would never rest from our wanderings till we had found a place where our children might grow up into the dignity of a noble manhood." Printed in serial chapters in the *National Era* in 1851, Harriet Beecher Stowe's *Uncle Tom's Cabin* concluded on the same note. In December, in response to a request for advice from the Ohio black Central Committee composed of Gaines, Day, Jenkins, and John Jackson of Cincinnati, the humanitarian Horace Mann formulated an elaborate proposal for black emigration and establishment of separate black communities "in

the West Indies, on the coast of Africa, or elsewhere. . . . It is *your* duty,"
Mann charged, "to project some broad and comprehensive plan" to
redeem and elevate enslaved blacks everywhere. More tentatively,
Norton Townshend, close to Ohio black leaders and Mann's colleague
in Congress, in his own letter to the Central Committee also posited
emigration as a possible solution. Even abolitionist James G. Birney, the
Liberty party presidential candidate in 1840, old, weary, and partially
paralyzed, finally had come to believe American prejudice all but in-
vincible. Long affectionately regarded by Cincinnati blacks, Birney
would prepare a message to read to the Ohio black convention, but
would be so overcome by the ovation he received on entering the hall
that he had to turn it over to another. Emigrate, he advised, pointing to
Liberia. "By remaining, you only destroy yourselves."[51]

Beyond external factors, Langston had private reasons for taking up
the nationalist cause that were connected to his internal pursuit of
liberation. To a young man wrestling with definitions of manhood,
black nationalism held out the promise of achieving eventual social
acceptance and full citizenship in some other land; to one apprehensive about being allowed to undertake his chosen career, it might promote the idea that he could control his own destiny. As an orphan,
as a Negro rejected in his native land, as an intelligent and highly
educated man not entirely at home in either the black or white worlds,
Langston could draw a heightened sense of belonging from occupying an assertive position in a black-initiated movement for self-
determination.

Young Langston's 1849 black nationalist summons—"Our people
must be aroused. They must feel and act as men."—echoed urgently in
the Central Committee's convention call, issued in October 1851. The
time had come when blacks "must act or perish, . . . when silence is a
crime." Both John Mercer and Charles responded by preparing to lead
a full debate aimed at adoption of a nationalist-emigration policy.
Charles, in particular, "studied the subject with great care." Doubtless,
the brothers probed the opinions of black friends interested in various
emigration possibilities. During 1851, emigration discussion had occurred in Indiana; Trenton, New Jersey, where Canadian settlements
had been considered; and New York, where a movement led by Lewis
H. Putnam for African emigration had gained the governor's approval.
Closer to the Langston brothers were Henry Bibb, with a Canada-based
movement, and Martin Delany of Pittsburgh. In September, a black
convention in Toronto, including a dozen American delegates, had not
only urged slaves and free blacks to spurn the United States for Canadian residence, but had also proposed a union of blacks in Canada, the

United States, and the West Indies. A major purpose of the league would be to facilitate the establishment of black agricultural communities in Canada and the British West Indies. Bibb, a Kentucky fugitive and author of a slave narrative, had lectured frequently in Ohio before moving to Canada in 1850 and had spearheaded the convention through his newspaper, the *Voice of the Fugitive*. Doubtless consulted by Charles Langston, the *Voice's* agent in Columbus, Bibb contributed an encouraging assessment of black possibilities in Canada; after the Ohio conclave, the editor would deem Charles for his championing of emigration a "noble specimen of manhood." Besides Africa, Canada, and the West Indies, a few blacks were beginning to consider Central America because of its proximity and racially mixed populations. Apparently inspired by Delany, Dr. David J. Peck, John Mercer's Oberlin contemporary, undertook a Central American mission in the winter of 1851–52 that—after Delany's election in absentia as mayor of Greytown (San Juan del Norte)—was aborted by a landing of U.S. Marines. Delany himself, smarting from his racially inspired ejection from the Harvard Medical School, in the next several months would collect his thoughts for the influential pro-emigration work that would be published in April, *The Condition, Elevation, Emigration and Destiny of the Colored People of the United States, Politically Considered*. Probably from such sources, the brothers wrote a two-hour justification for a nationalist-emigration, arriving at the convention with manuscript in hand.[52]

When the five-day meeting convened in mid-January in Cincinnati, forty-five delegates from eighteen counties were in attendance at the Union Baptist church, which John, as a boy, had attended with Watson. Despite record cold, the convention attracted full-house crowds day and night, and unusually broad press coverage. In contrast to its ridicule of "proverbial" "misapprehension and misapplication of words" at a Negro church conference, the Cincinnati *Gazette* found the convention a "very respectable concourse."[53]

Twenty-two-year-old John Mercer Langston was elected president, a tribute to his abilities and the statewide following he had built through his enfranchisement and educational endeavors. In his acceptance, he expressed surprise. "My inexperience and youth wholly precluded any such hope on my part. I thank you for the honor—indeed it is an honor in my humble opinion, greater than the honor done Millard Fillmore by the American people, in calling him to the Presidency of this country. For in his position he is trammelled by an unjust public sentiment, a sentiment adverse to him or freedom. While the object of this Convention is, to oppose this public sentiment and further the cause of Liberty and Equality."[54]

President Langston served immediate notice of his intentions, outlining as the convention's major concerns: "the education of our children—the agricultural interests of our people—the temperance movement among us—the course which we are to pursue during our stay in this country and the plan of emigration which we shall adopt if we see fit to go out of this country." With a plea for "calm and deliberate consideration," Langston, whom the *Gazette* judged "an impressive speaker, and, withal, an energetic and prompt presiding officer," "took strong ground in favor of *some* form of emigration that should secure the nationality of his race." Repudiating the leaders and goals of the American Colonization Society, he made an "animated and eloquent" appeal "in favor of the colored people occupying some territory" where, in words reminiscent of Kossuth's seductive phraseology, "they could be respected among the nations of the earth."[55]

The Langstons' formal address, which John Mercer delivered while Charles dominated discussion in committee and on the floor, expanded upon the theme, combining a bitter attack on the American Colonization Society with an exploration of the nature of prejudice. The thesis, reported Peter Clark in two letters written in 1852 and 1901—bookends of a tragic half century—was the "Mutual repellency" between black and white, "growing out of the relation of master on the one hand, and slave upon the other"—or, as he put it in 1901, "growing out of a consciousness, on the part of the whites, that they were the oppressors, and among the blacks, that they were the oppressed." Thus, "in consequence of this repellency they could never live together on terms of equality." In 1901, Clark would conclude, "Time has vindicated the position taken by Mr. Langston" and deem it "the best speech of his life." The *Gazette's* summary, although too brief to yield a clear interpretation, did indicate a black nationalism crackling in its militance. After pointing "to the significant fact that nearly every one of the distinguished gentlemen who had written letters to the Convention had heartily approved of the policy of general emigration—and the devotion of these men to the best interests of the black race was unquestioned—. . . , he warned his race that when they decided to remain in this country they tamely and meanly assented to the absorption and EXTINCTION of their race. He would never consent to this. Mr. Langston's scathing denunciation of all who would assent to the policy of amalgamation," concluded the *Gazette*, "will be remembered by all who heard it."[56]

Submitting the majority report of the committee on emigration, Charles Langston, H. Ford Douglass, and Peter Clark called for a national black convention to investigate the possibilities of a nationalist-emigration and to appoint an agent to visit "various portions of the western continent, with a view to determining the most suitable point for the settlement of our people, and the establishment of an independent nationality." The proponents, who also included George J. Reynolds, a Sandusky coppersmith, argued, first, "that a participation in the government was essential to the development of a manly and independent character in the people" (John Mercer's 1849 argument); second, that blacks should "establish a nationality on the American continent to influence the institution of slavery, by the spectacle of a commonwealth of colored persons." In contrast to the position espoused by John Mercer in 1849 when emigration was foreseen only after complete emancipation, these black intellectuals now argued that "the concentration of the colored race" in continental proximity offered "the only relief from the oppressions of the American people" and would, besides, "react favorably upon the institution of slavery." Encompassed in these points were several ideas: refutation of proslavery claims of racial inferiority, provision of a safe haven for fugitives, and formation of a liberating army. Charles Langston specifically proposed that in emigrating en masse to Central or South America, the emigrants might "unite with some Government there, and then make the demand upon the United States to liberate their brethren from their bonds." Moreover, the nationalists argued, "if the time should ever come, when the tardy justice of the whites should compel the slave to appeal to arms, there would be near at hand a nation to whom a black Kossuth might appeal for 'material aid.' "[57]

The minority report on emigration, written by barbers L. D. Taylor of Columbus and L. C. Flewellen of Cincinnati, ex-Georgia veteran of the Florida Indian wars, contended that blacks possessed neither the desire nor the means for a mass emigration, "and had we them no nation has signified as yet a disposition to receive us as a body." The opponents of emigration, mainly businessmen and churchmen with long experience in the black movement, were led by John I. Gaines, David Jenkins, and William Howard Day, strongly seconded by W. W. Watson, Wallace Shelton, and John M. Brown. Gaines, who was fiercely committed to "survive or perish" on home grounds, scorned the emigration proposal as "nothing more nor less than the 'old coon' colonization," and argued there was "no disposition on the part of the great majority to emigrate and there never will be." Gaines would explain later that same year that he based his own hopes "in the power of Christianity, and in the strong nerves of the blacks themselves," even while conceding the "gloomy" prospect. Along with Jenkins, who had moved away from his tentative emigrationism of 1849, Gaines would be an outspoken and effective opponent of all emigration and colonization movements throughout the decade.[58] Day opposed a general emigration because he believed perseverance might obtain for the colored people their full American citizenship, but did not object to individuals' emigrating, though he would not emigrate himself. In actuality, Day was one of only two major participants in the 1852 debate who did leave the country by mid-decade.[59] H. Ford Douglas also moved briefly to Canada in 1856, but by 1858 he was leading a civil rights drive in Illinois.[60]

Militant notes—talk of physical force, violent resistance, a black Kossuth, and slave uprisings—sounded throughout the emigration debate and spilled over into other convention business. President pro tem Charles Langston, speaking extemporaneously, had opened the convention on a combative note, declaring the blacks must fight for their rights if they could obtain them in no other way. In this he was seconded by David Jenkins. Proponents and opponents of emigration outdid one another in defending their positions on the basis of their willingness, as Charles put it, "to die for freedom." Charles, a white abolitionist observed, evidently depended "upon the grace of gunpowder more than the grace of God. . . . upon fight or flight rather than upon intellectual or moral force." Advocates of caution and moderation met with jeers. Even the highly respected Gaines, attempting to reply to John Mercer's pro-emigration address, found himself frequently interrupted. The convention shouted down a wary Ross County delegate's objections to the militant language of the resolution on Kossuth, then clamored for another speech from young Langston, who responded "in an impassioned and eloquent manner," and the resolution passed unanimously. Whatever the truth in Charles Langston's charge that blacks were too passive: "We do not appreciate our rights as the Hungarians do. We seem determined to remain slaves. We want the spirit of men. . . .," the majority of the delegates, angry and aggrieved, seemed bent on asserting their manly readiness for forceful resistance and even rebellion. Moreover, they sought to infuse a like spirit in their people. Speaking to the resolution on the European revolutionaries, Ford Douglass urged "the idea of preparing the mind for the employment of physical force to obtain liberty in the regular Anglo-Saxon style."[61]

Like Cleveland and Columbus blacks earlier, delegates proclaimed their kinship with Kossuth and German socialist Gottfried Kinkle, to both of whom they offered pecuniary and military aid. Several other resolutions also indicated a significantly broadening social consciousness. Besides planning to gather information on the history of antislavery movements throughout the world, the germ of an idea that young Langston would develop into one of his finest pre-war speeches, the convention advocated that "the Russian Serf, the Hungarian Peasant, the American Slave and all other oppressed people, should unite against tyrants and despotism." Nearer to home, in a move toward solidarity with Ohio's large number of German immigrants, the delegates recommended (and eventually would see realized) the teaching of the German language in black common schools as "a great auxiliary to our cause." Urged by Clark, in a foreshadowing of his later espousal of socialist ideas, the delegates discussed forming labor associations composed of blacks, immigrants, and other working-class groups.[62] Clearly, Langston and others of the black leadership had been stimulated by the European revolutionaries not only to nationalism, but also to an accompanying conception of the unity of the oppressed, and at least a rudimentary socialism, that, in turn, tended to mitigate the racism often attached to nationalistic movements. Indeed, in contrast to the strain of racial chauvinism that would be criticized in Delany's later leadership, John Mercer Langston and his allies in the Ohio nationalist-emigration drive were not recorded in any claim of white inferiority or black superiority.

The militant nationalistic mood of the whole convention found expression in the resolution encouraging the formation of black military companies. A defiant gesture toward the new Ohio constitutional ban on black membership in the militia, the recommendation specified that blacks should obtain military training to assist state or nation in case of foreign invasion; but in the context of discussions of fighting for rights and lending aid to future slave uprisings, the direct action implications were clear. Indeed, a similar proposition at the 1847 black national convention in Troy had met with cautious rejection; however, a New York convention in early 1851 had revived the topic, and in 1852, several months after the Ohio convention, Robert Morris and C. L. Remond would advocate before a Massachusetts legislative committee the organization of a black militia in Boston.[63] Two years later, in the fall of 1854, Cincinnati blacks would form a company called the Attucks Blues, in honor of the Revolutionary martyr Crispus Attucks, practice drills under visiting militia captains, secure uniforms and equipment with funds partially raised by fairs and other benefits conducted by black women, and, by 1855, be ready for a public parade. Despite threatened mob violence "if we dared to 'insult the people,' " an officer of the company recalled, white-trousered legs stepped out briskly to the rhythm of a Negro brass band, the men bearing guns and cartridge boxes marked "U.S." Judged "well drilled, well uniformed, and well officered," the company subsequently would be congratulated personally by Salmon Chase "on its great triumph over the prejudices which sought to deter you from making your appearance on the streets of Cincinnati."[64] Recognizing its value for black morale, the 1857 Ohio black convention would recommend the Cincinnati company, which, like white militias, had both ceremonial and social functions, for emulation by other black communities. On July 25, 1855, presenting a company flag donated by black women, public schoolteacher Mary Ann Darnes, who with her sister Josephine had attended the Oberlin literary department, urged the Attucks Blues, if ever called to service, to fight for the principles of liberty and justice: "The time is not far distant when the slave must be free, if not by moral and intellectual means it must be done by the sword."[65]

In agreement upon these issues, both sides in the emigrationist debate also joined in fierce denunciation of the American Colonization Society. The Langstons and their allies recognized that fear of encouraging the "wicked system" of Liberian colonization, as the convention minutes put it, had long stifled serious consideration of other emigrationist alternatives. Since the 1829 Cincinnati black exodus to Canada that had inspired national discussion of emigration, black Ohioans had given it only fitful attention. In the winter of 1838–39, a group of young black men in Cleveland, after nightly sessions extending over weeks, did settle on talented sixteen-year-old J. M. Whitfield's recommendation of emigration aimed at concentrating blacks near the national borders, particularly in California; after the 1841 riot, as has been noted, some families and individuals had left Cincinnati in search of less troublous places; and by 1848 the respected Cincinnati schoolteacher A. M. Sumner was contemplating an African inspection tour, convinced that a number of blacks North and South were willing to emigrate under the proper conditions. Moreover, although the major thrust of Ohio's self-help movement was toward citizenship, separatism was discernible in the all-black agricultural settlements, importantly represented at the 1852 convention by Henry Hurd of Mercer County. Still, while a large number of blacks had emigrated after passage of the Fugitive Slave Law, no one had sufficiently disentangled "emigration" from "colonization" to permit development of black emigration policy. By staging the emigration debate in Cincinnati, the heart of the Colonization Society strength, John Mercer, who strongly condemned colonization at every opportunity, and his equally vociferous colleagues engineered a confrontation of sorts. With several prominent white colonizationists looking on, the black delegates chastised the society and African colonization, resolving, with only two dissenting votes, to oppose it "body and soul."[66]

The emigration debate extended over two days, enlisting most of the delegates. "No little talent and eloquence was exhibited by the learned young orators," noted an observer, "and sound sense and sparkling wit by the older and less learned members." Put to a vote, the proposal was defeated, 36 to 9. "This terminated the question which is at this hour," the convention secretary noted, "absorbing the interest of the leading colored minds of this State."[67]

But the issues raised in Cincinnati would continue to agitate black northerners in the months and years ahead.[68] Indeed, the Langstons and fellow advocates had laid the groundwork for a major black movement of the decade. By insisting on the distinction between the emigrationist and colonizationist positions, they had opened the door for serious discussion of emigration. By advocating emigration on the basis of self-determination and nationalism, emphasizing black self-respect, they had isolated the most effective arguments for the movement, arguments, moreover, that promoted a more positive black self-image whether or not the projected black nation could be realized. Besides thus defining the terms, they had even put forward practical considerations: the calling of a national convention, the appointment of an agent, the designation of Central America as destination, that anticipated events in 1854. It was with reason that Clark, looking backward after half a century, would term John Langston's "memorable address" and the 1852 Ohio convention "the beginning of the Emigration Movement in which Dr. Martin R. Delany afterwards became prominent."[69]

Just as significant was the Langstons' contribution to the development of a black nationalist consciousness. Self-respect, self-help, solidarity, insistence on the rights of human beings and citizens, including self-defense, were basic to their concept of a black nationality. The convention's endorsement of the black common schools and calls for establishment of a black newspaper and black agricultural communities, along with its more strikingly militant resolutions, indicated that beleaguered blacks were marshalling their spirits for resistance. "To promote union, and render our action beneficial," President Langston appointed a central committee for each county represented, to organize the state "after the manner of the great political parties." Further, delegates laid plans for an unusual second state convention to be held in Cleveland that fall. Soon Ohioans would renew agitation for a national convention. Black nationalism, in the forms both of union within the country and emigration from it, would grow in coming months.[70]

For the moment, however, John Mercer incurred the wrath of Frederick Douglass, his touring companion of some eighteen months before. Alarmed by emigration's potential drain on black leadership, the editor ridiculed Langston's "talk about preserving races, proceeding from our side, . . . [as] ridiculous. If with us resided the wealth, intelligence, literature, arts, science, and with the whites, slavery, ignorance, poverty and degradation, the reasoning might be saved by a shadow of plausibility." Stating an idea to which he would return in the last years of his life, Douglass positioned the world's "hope . . . [in] the fusion of races." Without attempting to refute Langston's thesis of the intractability of racial prejudice, he observed ad hominem that "our friend," in calling for a strong black identity, should remember he had more white than black blood.[71]

More criticism came from the *Anti-Slavery Bugle*'s correspondent who, while praising Langston's "decided ability" as presiding officer, called mass emigration "visionary and undesirable." In like vein, a Cincinnati abolitionist newspaper regretted the emigrationist interest and noted of Charles Langston, "And yet he has that high order of talent which ought to keep him here for the advocacy of the rights of his less able brethren." But from Canada, Bibb lamented that the convention majority "concluded to stay in the States to be spit upon, as well as disfranchised and oppressed."[72]

Probably little chastened by Douglass's chiding, John Mercer had to take more seriously the three latter observations, for they reflected his own fluctuating feelings of the past three years. What were the dictates of racial responsibility? Unlike Day, the theological student did not consider emigration merely a personal decision. Because his concern was with racial policy, he had to confront doubts as to its practicality and desirability for a whole people. The young black nationalist, who neither posed emigration again at a state convention nor agitated it in the press, would continue to wrestle with problems of the black destiny in private conversation. Not until the fall of 1854 would his ambivalence over black nationhood be publicly resolved.[73]

NOTES

1. John Mercer Langston, quoted in *Minutes . . . of the State Convention of the Colored Citizens of Ohio . . . Columbus . . . Jan., 1849* (Oberlin, 1849).

2. *Minutes of the State Convention of the Colored Citizens of Ohio . . . Columbus . . . Jan., 1851* (Columbus, 1851).

3. Gay Wilson Allen, *Waldo Emerson: A Biography* (New York, 1981), p. 552.

4. Stanley W. Campbell, *The Slave Catchers: Enforcement of the Fugitive Slave Law, 1850–1860* (New York, 1972), pp. 96–147.

5. *State Convention . . . 1849.*

6. *State Convention . . . 1851.*

7. C.H. and J. M. Langston to Salmon P. Chase, Sept. 12, 1850, Salmon P. Chase Papers, Library of Congress.

8. *State Convention . . . 1851*; *North Star*, Dec. 5, 1850; Cleveland *True-Democrat*, Sept. 30, 1850; Ohio *State Journal*, Oct. 16, 1850.

9. *Anti-Slavery Bugle*, Oct. 19, 1850; Oberlin *Evangelist*, Oct. 9, 1850; Cleveland *True-Democrat*, Nov. 2, 1850; Cincinnati *Gazette*, Oct. 16, 17, 20, 31, 1850; William C. Cochran, *The Western Reserve and the Fugitive Slave Law* (Cleveland, 1920; repr. New York: Da Capo Press, 1972), pp. 96–99; *State Convention . . . 1851*.

10. William P. Newman to Frederick Douglass, Oct. 1, 1850, *North Star*, Oct. 24, 1850.

11. *Philanthropist*, Mar. 15, 1843; *State Convention . . . 1849*; *State Convention . . . 1851*; Cleveland *True-Democrat*, Feb. 25, 1851; *Frederick Douglass' Paper*, July 31, 1851. For biographical material on H. Ford Douglass, see Vincent Harding, *There Is a River: The Black Struggle for Freedom in America* (New York, 1981), p. 167.

12. William J. Simmons, *Men of Mark: Eminent, Progressive, and Rising* (Cleveland, 1887; repr. Chicago: Johnson Publishing, 1971), pp. 244–45; Peter H. Clark to Mr. McLain, Sept. 17, 1850, quoted in Carter G. Woodson, *The Mind of the Negro as Reflected in Letters During the Crisis, 1800–1860* (New York, 1926), pp. 132–33; Cleveland *True-Democrat*, Sept. 30, 1850; Cincinnati *Enquirer*, Nov. 22, 1850; *African Repository* 27 (Jan. 1851): 20–21.

13. Cleveland *Gazette*, Mar. 6, 1886; Ohio *State Journal*, Jan. 11, 1850; Cincinnati *Gazette*, Nov. 5, Oct. 31, 1850; *African Repository* 26 (July 1850): 216; Cincinnati *Enquirer*, Mar. 8, Nov. 22, 1850; John B. Shotwell, *A History of the Schools of Cincinnati* (Cincinnati, 1902), pp. 448–49.

14. C. H. and J. M. Langston to Salmon P. Chase, Sept. 12, 1850; Chase to C. H. and J. M. Langston, Nov. 11, 1850, both in Chase Papers; George M. Fredrickson, *The Black Image in the White Mind: The Debate on Afro-American Character and Destiny, 1817–1914* (New York, 1972), pp. 100–17; Eric Foner, *Free Soil, Free Labor, Free Men: The Ideology of the Republican Party Before the Civil War* (New York, 1971), pp. 276–80.

15. *State Convention . . . 1851*.

16. Concord *Free Press*, n.d., quoted in *North Star*, June 29, 1849; *House Miscellaneous Document*, 31 Cong., 1 sess., no. 19 (1850), cited by Leon F. Litwack, *North of Slavery: The Negro in the Free States, 1790–1860* (Chicago, 1970), p. 253; Ohio Laws 47, 395–96, quoted by Cochran, *Western Reserve and the Fugitive Slave Law*, p. 66; Cleveland *True-Democrat*, Feb. 27, 5, 1851.

17. *State Convention . . . 1851*; M. R. Delany to C. H. Langston, William H. Day, and J. M. C. Simpson, *North Star*, Apr. 3, 1851.

18. Cleveland *True-Democrat*, Feb. 5, 1851; *Anti-Slavery Bugle*, Feb. 22, 1851; Richard H. Sewell, *Ballots for Freedom: Antislavery Politics in the United States, 1837–1860* (New York, 1976), pp. 209–11; Stephen E. Maizlish, *The Triumph of Sectionalism: The Transformation of Ohio Politics, 1844–1856* (Kent, Ohio, 1983), pp. 157–58, 170–71.

19. New York *Globe*, Oct. 15, 1882, John Mercer Langston Scrapbooks, 4 vols., II, Moorland-Spingarn Research Center, Howard University; Robert S. Fletcher, *A History of Oberlin College*, 2 vols. (Oberlin, 1943), I, pp. 159, 192; II,

pp. 688–89; John Mercer Langston, *From the Virginia Plantation to the National Capitol; or, The First and Only Negro Representative in Congress from the Old Dominion* (Hartford, 1894; repr. New York: Johnson Reprint, 1968), p. 112.

20. Langston, *Virginia Plantation*, p. 114; Fredrickson, *The Black Image in the White Mind*, pp. 71–82; Horace Mann to E. R. Johnson, Oct. 5, 1852, New Bedford *Standard*, quoted in *Frederick Douglass' Paper*, Oct. 22, 1852.

21. *State Convention . . . 1851*; Langston, *Virginia Plantation*, pp. 112–13, 115; *Triennial Catalogue of the Officers and Students of Oberlin College for the College Year 1850–51, 1851–52, 1852–53* (Oberlin, n.d.).

22. Fletcher, *Oberlin College*, II, pp. 727, 733.

23. Langston, *Virginia Plantation*, p. 114.

24. Oberlin College Theological (Literary) Society Records, 1844–53, Oberlin College Archives; Antoinette Brown to Lucy Stone, 1848, Blackwell Family Collection, the Arthur and Elizabeth Schlesinger Library on the History of Women in America, Radcliffe College.

25. Oberlin *Evangelist*, Sept. 10, 1851; J. E. Rankin, introductory sketch, John Mercer Langston, *Freedom and Citizenship* (Washington, 1883; repr. Miami: Mnemosyne Reprint, 1969), p. 11.

26. Langston, *Freedom and Citizenship*, pp. 11–12; Cleveland *True-Democrat*, Sept. 3, 1851.

27. L. T. Parker to My Dear Bro Whipple, June 6, 1853, "Gentlemen of the Association," Sept. 23, 1853, John A. Reed to Dear Sir, June 6, 1854, all in American Missionary Association Archives, Amistad Research Center, Tulane University (hereafter cited as AMA Papers).

28. Oberlin tax receipt, Nov. 11, 1851, Lorain County tax receipt, Nov. 14, 1853, Columbus tax receipt, Nov. 8, 1853, Langston to F. B. Boney, Jan. 19, 1854, C. H. Langston to J. M. Langston, telegram, Mar. 31, 1854, Langston to Boston, Kelly & ?, Jan. 25, 1854, all in John Mercer Langston Papers, Fisk University Library; Martin R. Delany, *The Condition, Elevation, Emigration, and Destiny of the Colored People of the United States, Politically Considered* (Philadelphia, 1852; repr. New York: Arno Press, 1968), p.145.

29. *Triennial Catalogue . . . of Oberlin College, 1851–52, 1852–53*; receipt of J. M. Fitch and G. W. Eells, receipt from J. M. Fitch, Oct. 10, 1852, misc. I.O.U.s and bills, receipt, March 11, 1853, all in Langston Papers.

30. Leonard E. Erickson, "The Color Line in Ohio Public Schools, 1829–1890," Ph.D. diss., Ohio State University, 1959, pp. 54–116, 177–86.

31. *Proceedings of the State Convention of the Colored Citizens of Ohio . . . Cincinnati . . . Jan., 1852* (Cincinnati, 1852); Ohio Secretary of State, *Annual Report . . . on Common Schools . . . , 1850*, p. 26, *1851*, p. 14; Laura S. Haviland, *A Woman's Life-Work: Labors and Experiences* (Chicago, 1889; repr. New York: Arno Press, 1969), pp. 180–83; Toledo Board of Education, Minutes, 1848–58, pp. 192, 205, cited in Erickson, "Color Line," p. 210.

32. Gaines's own account in *Eighth Annual Report of the Board of Trustees for the Colored Public Schools of Cincinnati* (Cincinnati, 1857), pp. 12–13; *History of Schools for the Colored Population from the Special Report of the Commissioner of Education on the Improvement of Public Schools in the District of Columbia, 1871* (repr.

New York: Arno Press, 1969), II, pp. 371–72; Shotwell, *A History of the Schools of Cincinnati*, pp. 455–56; *The State on Relation of Eastern and Western School Districts of Cincinnati vs. City of Cincinnati, et al.*, *Ohio Reports* 19:178 sq.; Cleveland *Gazette*, Mar. 6, 1886; Cincinnati *Commercial*, n.d., quoted in Cleveland *Leader*, Dec. 2, 1859.

33. Charles T. Hickok, *The Negro in Ohio, 1802–1870* (Cleveland, 1896; repr. New York: AMS Press, 1975), pp. 98–102; Erickson, "Color Line," pp. 198–200; Cincinnati *Commercial*, n.d., quoted in *Anti-Slavery Bugle*, Sept. 3, 1853; *Anti-Slavery Bugle*, May 21, 1853, June 30, 1855; *National Anti-Slavery Standard*, Feb. 16, 1856; *History of Schools for the Colored Population*, II, p. 372.

34. Oberlin Young Men's Anti-Slavery Society—Records, ms., Oberlin College Archives; *Philanthropist*, July 7, Oct. 13, 1841; Buckeye *Sentinel* (Elyria, Ohio), June 25, 1844; D. Day to the Colored Settlements, Oct. 7, 1844, *Palladium of Liberty*, Oct. 16, 1844; D. Day to Lucy Stone, Feb. 20, 1846, R. S. Fletcher Papers, Oberlin College Archives; Henry Cowles, "Oberlin College Catalogue and Records of Colored Students, 1835–1862," ms., Henry Cowles Papers, Oberlin College Library (hereafter cited as "Cowles List"); Langston, *Virginia Plantation*, p. 141.

35. Langston, *Virginia Plantation*, p. 141; J. M. Langston et al., Report of the Committee on Education, *State Convention . . . 1852*.

36. *Minutes of the State Convention of the Colored Citizens of Ohio . . . Columbus . . . Jan., 1850*; *State Convention 1851*; *State Convention 1852*; Frederick A. McGinnis, *A History and an Interpretation of Wilberforce University* (Blanchester, Ohio, 1941), p. 26.

37. *State Convention . . . 1849*; *State Convention . . . 1850*; *State Convention . . . 1851*; Cleveland *Leader*, June 14, 1855; *Tenth Annual Report of the Colored Schools of Cincinnati* (Cincinnati, 1859), pp. 3, 6; W. H. Burnham to Langston, Feb. 6, 1854, Langston Papers. Josephine Minor studied in the Oberlin preparatory department in 1846. She was one of five children, born in slavery in New Orleans, who were sent to Oberlin for an education. One brother was Lawrence Minor, B.A. 1850; another, Patrick Henry Minor, became a lieutenant in the 1st U.S. Colored Battery in Kansas. See obituary, Patrick Henry Minor, Leavenworth *Bulletin*, quoted in New Orleans *Tribune*, Apr. 19, 1865; Ellen N. Lawson and Marlene Merrill, "The Antebellum 'Talented Thousandth': Black College Students at Oberlin Before the Civil War," *Journal of Negro History* 52 (1983):144, 151, 153.

38. Haviland, *A Woman's Life-Work*, pp. 180–83; *Liberator*, Nov. 3, 1854; Ohio Commissioner of Common Schools, *Annual Report*, 1858–59, pp. 54–55.

39. W.C. Nell to William Lloyd Garrison, *Liberator*, Nov. 14, 1856; E. H. Fairchild, "Are Negroes Susceptible to High Cultivation?," Lorain County *News*, n.d., quoted in Oberlin *Evangelist*, June 4, 1862.

40. Erickson, "Color Line," pp. 213, 216.

41. *Liberator*, n.d., quoted in *Anti-Slavery Bugle*, Apr. 17, 1858; *Anti-Slavery Bugle*, May 1, 1858; *The Free South*, n.d., quoted in *National Anti-Slavery Standard*, Oct. 9, 1858; Langston, *Virginia Plantation*, p. 141; Cincinnati *Gazette*, n.d., quoted in *Anti-Slavery Bugle*, Aug. 7, 1858.

42. Stephan Thernstrom, *Poverty and Progress* (Cambridge, 1964), p. 23; Richard A. Folk, "Black Man's Burden in Ohio, 1849–1863," Ph.D. diss., University of Toledo, 1972, pp. 249–50, in particular, pp. 233–59, in general. Compare Stanley K. Schultz, *The Culture Factory: Boston Public Schools, 1789–1860* (New York, 1973), and Carl F. Kaestle, *The Evolution of an Urban School System: New York City, 1750–1850* (Cambridge, 1973).

43. David Jenkins to Frederick Douglass, May 23, 1853, *Frederick Douglass' Paper*, June 3, 1853; *Anti-Slavery Bugle*, Feb. 21, 1857; John Mercer Langston, "Address to the Legislature of Ohio," *Proceedings of the State Convention of the Colored Men of the State of Ohio . . . Columbus . . . Jan., 1857* (Columbus, 1857).

44. Oberlin Young Men's Anti-Slavery Society—Records, Oberlin College Archives; *Anti-Slavery Bugle*, Feb. 21, 1857; Langston, "Address to the Legislature"; C. W. Mosell, "Lord, Deliver Us from Our Friends," *Christian Recorder*, Sept. 13, 1883.

45. *State Convention . . . 1852*; William H. Day to Editor, Cleveland *True-Democrat*, Sept. 4, 1851; *Anti-Slavery Bugle*, Feb. 15, 1851; "P" to *Anti-Slavery Bugle*, Sept. 3, 1852; Cincinnati *Nonpareil*, n.d., quoted in *Anti-Slavery Bugle*, July 3, 1852. A poor law passed during the legislature's 1851–52 winter session specifically prohibited Cincinnati authorities from extending relief to black paupers.

46. Benjamin Quarles, *Black Abolitionists* (New York, 1969), pp. 205–07; Campbell, *Slave Catchers*, pp. 98–100. By 1850, Irish immigrants comprised 12 percent of Cincinnati's population.

47. Donald S. Spencer, *Louis Kossuth and Young America: A Study of Sectionalism and Foreign Policy, 1848–1852* (Columbia, Mo., 1977), pp. 11–14, 43–64; Campbell, *Slave Catchers*, pp. 75–79; Cincinnati *Gazette*, Mar. 11, 1851; Fredrickson, *Black Image in the White Mind*, pp. 154–59; Horace Mann to John I. Gaines et al., Dec. 31, 1851, L. D. Campbell to John I. Gaines et al., Jan. 5, 1852, both in *State Convention . . . 1852*.

48. Spencer, *Louis Kossuth and Young America*, pp. 49–58, 122–25, 76–81; *Anti-Slavery Bugle*, Nov. 29, 1851, May 7, 1853; *Frederick Douglass' Paper*, Jan. 8, 1852; Cleveland *True-Democrat*, Nov. 22, 1851.

49. *Frederick Douglass' Paper*, July 6, Sept. 8, 1854, Jan. 26, 1855; *State Convention . . . 1852*; Cincinnati *Gazette*, Jan. 19, 1852.

50. Campbell, *Slave Catchers*, 100–1; *Anti-Slavery Bugle*, Nov. 29, 1851; Cleveland *True-Democrat*, Nov. 22, 1851; *State Convention . . . 1852*; Gerrit Smith to Governor Hunt, Feb. 20, 1852, *Liberator*, Mar. 5, 1852.

51. Foner, *Free Soil, Free Labor, Free Men*, pp. 280; *National Era*, Apr. 24, 1851; Cleveland *True-Democrat*, Jan. 26, 1850; Mann to Gaines et al., Norton S. Townshend to John I. Gaines et al., Jan. 8, 1852, both in *State Convention . . . 1852*; *Anti-Slavery Bugle*, Jan. 31, 1852; Cincinnati *Gazette*, Jan. 19, 1852; Ohio *Times*, Jan. 15, 1852, quoted in *Voice of the Fugitive*, Aug. 12, 1852; James G. Birney, *Examination of the Decision of the Supreme Court of the United States, in the Case of Strader, Gorman and Armstrong vs. Christopher Graham, Delivered at Its December Term, 1850: Concluding with an Address to the Free Colored People* (Cincinnati, 1852), p. 43; *Liberator*, Feb. 13, 1852; Gerrit Smith to Governor Hunt,

Feb. 20, 1852, *Liberator*, Mar. 5, 1852; A. J. Knox to Garrison, Mar. 12, 1852, *Liberator*, Mar. 26, 1852.

52. *State Convention . . . 1849*; *Anti-Slavery Bugle*, Nov. 8, 1851; Ohio *Times*, n.d., quoted in *Voice of the Fugitive*, Feb. 12, 1852; Howard Holman Bell, *A Survey of the Negro Convention Movement, 1830–1861* (New York, 1969), pp. 141–51; Floyd J. Miller, *The Search for a Black Nationality: Black Emigration and Colonization, 1787–1863* (Urbana, 1975), pp. 107–8, 111–33; *Voice of the Fugitive*, Jan. 1, Feb. 12, 1852; Victor Ullman, *Martin R. Delany: The Beginnings of Black Nationalism* (Boston, 1971), pp. 138–40; Peter H. Clark to John W. Cromwell, Dec. 21, 1901, quoted in John W. Cromwell, *The Negro in American History, Men and Women Eminent in the Evolution of the American of African Descent* (Washington, 1914; repr. New York: Johnson Reprint, 1968), pp. 37–38. On Delany, see Nell Irvin Painter, "Martin R. Delany: Elitism and Black Nationalism," in *Black Leaders of the Nineteenth Century*, ed., Leon Litwack and August Meier (Urbana, 1988), pp. 149–71.

53. *State Convention . . . 1852*; *Ohio Times*, quoted in *Voice of the Fugitive*, Feb. 12, 1852; Peter Clark to Henry Bibb, Jan. 31, 1852, *Voice of the Fugitive*, Feb. 12, 1852; *Anti-Slavery Bugle*, Jan. 31, 1852; Cincinnati *Nonpareil*, n.d., quoted in *Anti-Slavery Bugle*, Feb. 7, 1852; Cleveland *True-Democrat*, Jan. 24, 1852; *National Anti-Slavery Standard*, Feb. 5, 1852; Cincinnati *Gazette*, Aug. 17, Jan. 15, 16, 19, 1852.

54. *State Convention . . . 1852*.

55. *State Convention . . . 1852*; Cincinnati *Gazette*, Jan. 15, 1852; *Ohio Times*, n.d., quoted in *Voice of the Fugitive*, Feb. 12, 1852. William Lloyd Garrison, in reviewing Delany's *Condition, Emigration . . .*, would note the similarity of Delany's theory with Kossuth's, that by emigration a people "may ultimately become 'a power in the earth.' " *Liberator*, May 7, 1852.

56. Clark to Bibb, Jan. 31, 1852, *Voice of the Fugitive*, Feb. 12, 1852; Clark to Cromwell, Dec. 21, 1901, Cromwell, *Negro in American History*, pp. 37–38; Cincinnati *Gazette*, Jan. 19, 1852. The *Gazette* called it "an able effort," while the *Times* termed it "splendid." *Ohio Times*, n.d., quoted in *Voice of the Fugitive*, Apr. 8, 1852.

57. *State Convention . . . 1852*; Cleveland *True-Democrat*, Jan. 24, 1852; Clark to Bibb, Jan. 31, 1852, *Voice of the Fugitive*, Feb. 12, 1852; *Ohio Times*, n.d., quoted in *Voice of the Fugitive*, Feb. 12, 1852.

58. *State Convention . . . 1852*; Cleveland *True-Democrat*, Jan. 24, 1852; *Ohio Times*, n.d., quoted in *Voice of the Fugitive*, Feb. 12, 1852; Cleveland *True-Democrat*, n.d., quoted in *Frederick Douglass' Paper*, Feb. 5, 1852; *Anti-Slavery Bugle*, Aug. 14, 1852; Gaines to Douglass, Jan. 16, 1854, *Frederick Douglass' Paper*, Jan. 27, 1854; *Liberator*, Apr. 27, 1860.

59. *Anti-Slavery Bugle*, Jan. 31, 1852; Cincinnati *Gazette*, Jan. 19, 1852; *State Convention . . . 1852*. Although prominent at the Chatham emigration convention in August 1858, Day journeyed south to Cincinnati in November specifically to attend the black state convention and declare that on the same spot where he had opposed emigration six years before, after becoming an emigrationist himself he had returned to resist emigration. On Day's emigration

activities, see R. J. M. Blackett, *Beating Against the Barriers: Biographical Essays in Nineteenth Century Afro-American History* (Baton Rouge, 1986), pp. 310– 23.

60. *Provincial Freeman*, July 12, 1856; *Frederick Douglass' Paper*, Mar. 25, 1859.

61. *Ohio Times*, n.d., quoted in *Voice of the Fugitive*, Feb. 12, 1852; Clark to Bibb, Jan. 31, 1852, *Voice of the Fugitive*, Feb. 12, 1852.

62. *State Convention . . . 1852*; Langston, "The World's Anti-Slavery Movement," *Freedom and Citizenship*, pp. 41–67; *Ohio Times*, n.d., quoted in *Voice of the Fugitive*, Feb. 12, 1852; Herbert G. Gutman, "Peter H. Clark: Pioneer Negro Socialist, 1877," *Journal of Negro Education* 34 (Fall 1965):413–18. By 1869, Cincinnati's black public schools would employ seventeen teachers, fifteen of whom were black and one-time pupils of the city system. The other two teachers were German, one taught music and the other taught the German language. Shotwell, *A History of the Schools*, p. 372.

63. *State Convention . . . 1852*; *Ohio Times*, Jan. 17, 1852, quoted in *Voice of the Fugitive*, Feb. 12, 1852; Cincinnati *Gazette*, Jan. 19, 1852; *Proceedings of the National Convention of Colored People . . . Troy, New York, Oct., 1847* (Troy, 1847), p. 17, in *Minutes of the Proceedings of the National Negro Conventions, 1830–1864*, ed. Howard Holman Bell (New York, 1969); *Liberator*, Apr. 4, 1851; *Anti-Slavery Bugle*, May 22, 1852.

64. *Ohio Times*, n.d., quoted in Cleveland *Leader*, Sept. 7, 1854; Cleveland *Leader*, Oct. 3, 1854; *Anti-Slavery Bugle*, Oct. 7, 1854; *Liberator*, Nov. 21, 1854, July 20, 1855; *National Anti-Slavery Standard*, July 28, 1855; W. W. Tate to Editor, Sept. 4, 1855, *Provincial Freeman*, Sept. 8, 1855; San Francisco *Elevator*, May 10, 1873. Julius Hawkins, arrested and required to post bond during the 1841 Cincinnati riot, reportedly was the first company captain; see Cincinnati *Enquirer*, Sept. 8, 1841, and Wendell P. Dabney, *Cincinnati's Colored Citizens, Historical, Sociological and Biographical* (Cincinnati, 1926; repr. New York: Johnson Reprint, 1970), p. 200.

65. *Proceedings of the State Convention of the Colored Men of the State of Ohio . . . Columbus . . . Jan., 1857* (Columbus, 1857); Cleveland *Leader*, June 25, July 12, 21, 28, Aug. 3, 1858; Cincinnati Board of Education *Annual Report*, June 30, 1855, 159; George W. Williams, *History of the Negro Race in America, 1619–1880* (New York, 1883; repr. New York: Arno Press, 1968), II, pp. 145–56. Mary Ann and Josephine Darnes, Oberlin literary department students in 1852 and 1853, were daughters of William Darnes, a barber, with property holdings of $2,500, who attended the January 1852 convention. Patricia Mae Riley, "The Negro in Cincinnati, 1835–1850," master's thesis, University of Cincinnati, 1971, pp. 97–100; Cowles List.

66. *State Convention . . . 1852*; *Colored American*, Mar. 2, May 18, 1839; Whitfield to Douglass, *Frederick Douglass' Paper*, Nov. 25, 1853; *African Repository*, 24 (Aug. 1848):243–44; Cincinnati *Gazette*, Jan. 10, 1852.

67. *State Convention . . . 1852*; *Ohio Times*, n.d., quoted in *Voice of the Fugitive*, Feb. 12, 1852.

68. *Frederick Douglass' Paper*, Mar. 11, 25, Apr. 29, Oct. 22, 1852; Bell, *Negro Convention Movement*, pp. 141–48; William H. and Jane H. Pease, *They Who*

Would Be Free: Blacks Search for Freedom, 1830–1861 (New York, 1974), pp. 258–60. By October 1853, David Jenkins, heading a committee formed to oppose the upcoming national emigration convention in Cleveland, estimated that about one-fourth of Ohio's black population favored some form of emigration. David Jenkins et al. to the Colored Citizens of Cleveland, Oct. 6, 1853, *Frederick Douglass' Paper*, Oct. 28, 1853.

69. *Ohio Times*, n.d., quoted in *Voice of the Fugitive*, Feb. 12, 1852; *State Convention . . . 1852*; Clark to Cromwell, Dec. 21, 1901, Cromwell, *Negro in American History*, pp. 37–38.

70. *State Convention . . . 1852*; *Ohio Times*, quoted in *Voice of the Fugitive*, Feb. 12, 1852.

71. *Frederick Douglass' Paper*, Feb. 5, 1852.

72. *Anti-Slavery Bugle*, Jan. 31, 1852; *Ohio Times*, n.d., quoted in *Voice of the Fugitive*, Feb. 12, 1852; *Voice of the Fugitive*, Feb. 12, 1852.

73. W. H. Burnham to Langston, Feb. 6, 1854, Langston Papers; Cleveland *Herald*, Aug. 26, 1854; *Speech of H. Ford Douglass, in Reply to Mr. J. M. Langston Before the Emigration Convention, at Cleveland, Ohio. . . .* (Chicago, 1854), pp. 7, 16.

CHAPTER 7

"To Work Out My Destiny,"[1]

1852–54

DURING the two and a half years that followed his call for a black nationality, John Mercer Langston's horizon, and his hope, expanded markedly. Even as he widened his involvement in the abolitionist and black civil rights movements, he began to engage in radical politics—an engagement that would provide his long-sought avenue to the legal profession, just as political developments would seem the evidence of potential for national reform that would cause him to relinquish his emigrationist dreams.

Ironically, given the weighty role that politics would play in shaping Langston's future, and that he would assign to it—politics, the seasoned black campaigner would affirm late in life, was the "natural and vital atmosphere of the intelligent American"—the young man's first political foray smacked less of seriousness than of student prank. In Oberlin—"the greatest sinque of Free Soil iniquities this side of Uncle Tom's Cabin, New Hampshire, and Hell," according to one critic—Democrats constituted an embattled minority. Nevertheless, emboldened by the presidential nomination of Franklin Pierce on a platform accepting the finality of the Compromise of 1850 and warning against renewal of antislavery agitation, local Democratic diehards called a ratification gathering in mid-June 1852. In the crowd of nearly a hundred were "Democrats, Whigs, Free-Soilers, and 'boys,'" including John Mercer and his henchmen. Hardly had the opening speaker concluded his talk when loud shouts, "Langston, Langston," erupted. "A colored gentleman of *very* Democratic principles," as the correspondent of a Cleveland Free Soil paper chortled, the twenty-two-year-old theological student launched into a fifty-minute assault on the venality of

Democrats—and Whigs, to boot, for the latter had just nominated General Winfield Scott for president while echoing the Democratic endorsement of the Compromise. Langston's remarks met with "unbounded enthusiasm." The meeting shortly adjourned with three groans for the Democratic national ticket.[2]

Although inconsistent with the separatist ideology Langston had expressed at the Ohio black convention in Cincinnati only six months before, his political activities, which quickly became regular and extensive, were in keeping with the young black intellectual's sense of racial obligation. Even as he had put his passionate case for black mass emigration, he had renewed his vows to "oppose unjust public sentiment and to further the cause of Liberty and Equality."[3] Moreover, both emigration advocacy and political activism issued from a common conviction: to be fully a man, the black man must participate fully, freely, and equally in public life. Whatever Langston's eventual decision on emigration, so long as he remained in the United States his duties were to assert himself as a man, to promote a black consciousness even while affirming a common humanity, to exacerbate the mounting tension between the North and the Slave Power. While occupied by his theological studies and educational labors among black Ohioans, John Mercer was cognizant of the advantages of his Oberlin connections and determined to take every opportunity to enhance the antislavery cause.

Reinvigorated by the publication of *Uncle Tom's Cabin*, the white abolitionist movement early presented Langston with one such opportunity. In April 1852, an important anti-slavery convention was staged in Cincinnati by the Ladies Anti-Slavery Sewing Society. Active since 1841 in assisting black Cincinnatians—as well as such fugitives as Henry Bibb, editor of the *Voice of the Fugitive* and a convention speaker, who publicly thanked one woman present for having tried to hide him during his unsuccessful first escape from Kentucky a dozen years before[4]—the Ladies Society was organized around evangelical abolitionism. Nonetheless, the group and their president, Sarah Otis Ernst, welcomed to the convention representatives of broadly divergent anti-slavery views. Besides such Cincinnatians as the Reverend Levi Coffin, "president" of the underground railroad, businessman Henry W. Blackwell, and Dr. William H. Brisbane, ex-South Carolina slaveholder, the notables included Frederick Douglass; Samuel Lewis, venerable Ohio abolitionist-politician; George W. Julian, ex-Free Soil congressman from Indiana; Charles Lenox Remond, Negro lecturer of the American Anti-Slavery Society; Charles C. Burleigh, also a long-time Garrisonian lecturer; and the Reverend John G. Fee of Kentucky, the convention president. In all, some two hundred male and female delegates were in attendance, composing the largest convention of "the friends of freedom" yet assembled west of the Alleghenies.

As major business, the delegates roundly castigated both the Whig and Democratic parties for attempting to stifle discussion of slavery. They condemned the conciliatory attitudes toward slaveholders exhibited by much of the church and clergy. And, in an indication of how far abolitionists had moved from the Weldian moral suasion and Garrisonian nonresistance dominant during the previous two decades, they warmly endorsed Douglass's advice to resist the Fugitive Slave Law, or any other unjust law, by force of arms.[5]

John Mercer attended the convention—his first important abolitionist affair—as delegate from the Oberlin Young Men's Anti-Slavery Society.[6] Considerately received, he acted as a secretary and was prominently mentioned in the city and abolitionist press. Besides making valuable new contacts and renewing old, Langston had the opportunity to smooth over differences with Douglass, his recent adversary on emigration. On the final and climactic evening of the three-day convention when "the Douglass" was the featured speaker—before a standing-room-only crush of two thousand persons, white and black—the theological student slipped easily into the familiar role of program opener for his erstwhile traveling companion. In his address Langston, doubtless a moving force in the abolitionists' resolution to "turn deaf ears to all colonization agents," chose to rework the major theme of his remarks to the January black convention. In "highly creditable" style, he excoriated the American Colonization Society and enlarged upon the features and strengths of racial prejudice.[7]

Langston's earnestness and animation impressed the New England veteran Charles Burleigh, who informed Garrison of the young speaker's ability. In turn, John Mercer invited the itinerant lecturer to accompany him to Oberlin, where he arranged two separate appearances, one under the aegis of the Young Men's Anti-Slavery Society and the other, the Young Men's Lyceum. Although sharp airings of ideological differences had marked some previous visits by "Come-outers," harmony followed the genial long-haired Garrisonian and his popular black student sponsor north from Cincinnati. His lectures well attended, Burleigh departed Oberlin bolstered in purse and in spirits.[8]

Although Langston, who supported all sincere abolitionist endeavor, was hospitable to Burleigh personally, the political abolitionists, not the Garrisonians, were voicing the ideas to which he was most receptive. Having thrilled to former Congressman Julian's call, voiced at the Cincinnati abolitionist convention, for a new political organization to overthrow the Whig and the Democratic parties, Langston welcomed the political developments of the late summer of 1852. Meeting in Pittsburgh in August, the Free Soil party, name now changed to Free Democratic, nominated Senator John P. Hale of New Hampshire for president and Julian for vice-president. The platform, a slightly more radical version of the 1848 manifesto, included a condemnation of the Fugitive Slave Law and an unprecedented call for diplomatic recognition of Haiti. Despite the defeat of New York abolitionist Gerrit Smith's attempt to insert an equal rights plank, radicals took additional encouragement from the convention's recognition of black delegates and election of Frederick Douglass as a secretary. Langston had the chance to hear firsthand accounts from several returning delegates—Gerrit Smith, abolitionist editor Sherman W. Booth of Wisconsin, John Mercer's old economics professor Amasa Walker, and Douglass, the last of whom drew a crowd of 2,500 on two hours' notice—who, one after another, stopped off in Oberlin to plump for the Free Democratic ticket.[9]

John Mercer attended the Lorain County Free Democratic ratification meeting at the county courthouse in Elyria on August 27. Abolitionist Congressman Joshua R. Giddings of Ashtabula, facing an arduous campaign for his eighth term, and ex-Congressman Joseph M. Root of Lorain County, noted for his resistance to the Compromise of 1850, addressed the gathering. Included on the speakers' roster, Langston won a not-inconsiderable tribute from the Whiggish Elyria *Courier*. Although he "committed an egregious blunder" in charging that the nomination of Winfield Scott had been dictated by the South, still the black theological student made the best speech of the day.[10]

Soon afterward Langston began to campaign for the Free Democratic county congressional committee. Besides boosting the national ticket, he campaigned for the reelection of Congressman Norton S. Townshend of Avon township. A champion of black rights, Dr. Townshend had been elected to the Ohio Assembly in 1848 where his pivotal role in amending the Black Laws and sending Salmon Chase to the Senate, although reviled by Whigs, had won him Oberlin's strong support for his successful 1850 congressional bid. In 1852, however, following a Democratically directed reapportionment of his district, Townshend, like Giddings and other Free Democratic candidates on the Western Reserve, faced an uphill fight.[11] John Mercer, who often went out with other student speakers, found the prevailing sentiment of the district "anti-negro and of positive pro-slavery character in its hatred of such a community and college as those of Oberlin." Nevertheless, the twenty-two-year-old black campaigner, as principal speaker, drew five hundred persons to a Friday afternoon meeting in early

September at Ripleyville in Huron County, and a respectable crowd to a second rally that same week in Pittsfield.[12]

The hamlet of French Creek proved the novice stump speaker's most severe test. Appearing with three white companions, Langston was to deliver the closing address. While the third white speaker was on the stand, a man in the crowd shouted out: "Are you in favor of nigger social equality?" The question set off a volley of cat-calls, foot-stomping, and hand-clapping. Hastily, the embarrassed young speaker surrendered the platform to Langston. Starting off by repeating the heckler's words, John Mercer caught the crowd's attention with a strong anti-black, anti-abolitionist argument that he then reversed, explaining that the abolitionist movement involved "freedom as the birthright of all." Social equality depended upon individual choice. "Only the enemy of human rights" would attempt to obtrude the spurious issue of black social equality into the discussion. By that time the crowd was listening quietly, and the heckler decided to try again. "You learned that at Oberlin!" he baited. Calmly, John Mercer agreed to the truth of the charge. "You learned another thing at Oberlin!" bawled the man. "You learned to walk with white women there!" Boldly, Langston again admitted the accusation was true. Advancing to the platform's edge to beard his harasser, he advised, "If you have in your family any good-looking, intelligent, refined sisters, you would do your family a special service by introducing me to them at once." Pleased by his audacity, the crowd laughed and applauded. "An old gray-headed Democrat" drawled to his discomfited friend, "Joe Ladd, you damn fool, sit down. That darkey is too smart for you! Sit down!"[13] Clearly, Langston's initial venture into the rough give and take of the hustings called on, and aided the development of, those personal traits and rhetorical skills that would be essential for the black politician in the future.

During the campaign, John Mercer also had the honor of presiding over an Oberlin appearance of the barnstorming team of the Free Democratic presidential nominee, Hale, and Senator Chase. As president of the Oberlin Young Men's Anti-Slavery Society, he extended its platform to them on October 1, 1852. Chase discussed the corruptness of old parties and compromise measures while Langston and his friends listened "during perfect stillness." The excited young black abolitionist doubtless agreed with the society's secretary that the visit would "long be remembered by the friends of the oppressed."[14]

Other leaders of the black Ohio movement shared Langston's interest in the Free Democratic campaign. Like him, they relished the prospects of punishing the Whigs for their part in the Fugitive Slave Law and of building a strong antislavery alternative to the Democrats. At the same time, the black leadership hoped to influence the Free Democrats—now largely shorn of the Democratic "barnburners" who had been the most antagonistic to black rights of the various elements in the 1848 Free Soil coalition—to endorse black enfranchisement in Ohio. Their hope that the state party might be persuaded to depart from the national platform on this issue was grounded in the knowledge that such prominent Ohio Free Democrats as Chase and Samuel Lewis earlier had helped to lead the Liberty party to support black suffrage. The size and enthusiasm of black gatherings in the late summer strongly indicated that the militance that had marked the January debate on emigration had been transferred to antislavery politics. Some one thousand blacks turned out for the First of August celebration in Cincinnati, where they applauded white abolitionist Brisbane's description of the Whig and Democratic parties as both being "sold to the slaveocracy." Watson, Clark, W. R. Casey, Gaines, and Ford Douglass added their own forceful comments. Later that same month, in preparation for a state black convention planned for early September, one of the largest meetings of blacks recorded in Cincinnati pounded approval of a string of resolutions aimed at political equality. John Hatfield presided over the meeting, with Gaines, Casey, and Clark prominent. So forthright were the demands that the white press complained about the "intemperate language." The black Cincinnatians went so far as to endorse disunion, should it prove impossible to abolish slavery, certain that one or the other was "necessary to our ever enjoying, in its fullness and power, the privileges of an American citizen." Moreover, they issued a blunt reminder to "Free Soil friends": "We demand . . . that while they are laboring for the overthrow of Slavery, they do not forget that a large portion of this State are deprived of their just rights as citizens."[15]

The state black convention held in Cleveland on September 8–10 provided the most dramatic demonstration for black rights during the campaign. The conclave, which had been approved at the state black convention the preceding January, was an unusual black mass gathering. It attracted some five hundred men and women from around the state and was billed as the largest Ohio black convention ever held, featuring what was probably the first public reunion of black military veterans. The eight former soldiers and sailors included John B. Vashon of Pittsburgh, veteran of the War of 1812, and Lovell C. Flewellen of Cincinnati, an ex-Georgian who had fought as a volunteer in some of the Indian wars in 1836. Flewellen spoke of the "ingratitude manifested towards us after all we had done, by the whites of the country." The veterans sat in striking array while William Howard Day—himself the son of a black veteran and the arranger of the ceremony—claimed for blacks "an equal participation in the exercise and enjoyment of those American rights which large numbers of that race . . . had fought, suffered, and died to establish." In addition to Vashon, other out of state leaders in attendance included Peyton Harris of Buffalo, David Lett of Michigan, and Dr. J. W. C. Pennington of New York City. The famed abolitionist and women's rights advocate Sojourner Truth, to whom Langston paid tribute in a special introduction, also addressed the gathering. John Mercer, who started the proceedings with an earnest speech on freedom, was elected a vice-president, while Oberlin black farmer Sabram Cox served as president.

Besides adopting nearly intact the aggressive resolutions for equal rights formulated in August by the Cincinnati black meeting, the convention added two important items. Despite Sojourner Truth's unlettered eloquence in her strongly religious plea for forbearance, the Ohioans reaffirmed their earlier stand in favor of violent resistance to enforcement of the Fugitive Slave Law, whenever necessary. This position was justified because "the government had forsaken us, and joined hands with the robber." In addition, presaging a major thrust of the national black movement, the Ohioans went on record in favor of instruction and training as a means of gaining access to the mechanical trades. The latter resolution, however, should not be interpreted as a sign that black Ohioans were in dire economic straits. Speaking on special invitation, James Freeman Clarke, a white abolitionist minister from Boston whose book on the black northern condition would be published later in the decade, declared the overall economic health of black Ohio to be generally favorable, a judgment that the large convention turnout would seem, to some degree, to substantiate.

The second day of the convention was designated as a jubilee to celebrate "some of the events which colored people had helped to make conspicuous." A white Cleveland militia heralded the black celebration with two salutes: "the first thunders of artillery that ever awaked the echoes of these hills in honor of the colored people," Day exulted, "but they shall not be the last." A large parade, complete with brass band, wound through the major thoroughfares. Noticeable in the line of march were uniformed members of various benevolent and fraternal organizations, women's associations, and vigilance committees. Black Oberlin female students had stitched a large standard that women of the Cleveland vigilance committee carried: "Education is our greatest Hope! Colonization equal to Pious Hatred! The *Bible* and *Uncle Tom's Cabin*! Buckeyes, are our Chains *All Forged*?" Rain forced afternoon ceremonies indoors. Langston read special communications, one from a leader of the local German community, and Day delivered the major address. On the final day, delegates chose a new Central Committee and expressed interest in holding a national black convention. All in all, the large attendance, the distinguished speakers from far and near, the militant resolutions, and the public response stirred John Mercer and his colleagues to optimism. "This meeting will be of vast benefit to our cause in this section," reported Lawrence W. Minor, the 1850 Oberlin graduate. "It is generally conceded that a few more such demonstrations will redeem our noble Buckeye State."[16]

The immediate political effect, however, was disappointing. The Free Democratic state convention, meeting in Cleveland a few days afterward, refused to endorse a resolution for black enfranchisement offered by Day. Thereupon, the black journalist bitterly criticized the Free Democrats for preferring expediency to principle in an article that the Cleveland *True-Democrat*, his Free Soil employer, declined to print, but which the rival Whiggish *Herald* displayed prominently. Only candidates who supported the black cause, Day warned, would receive black votes. Another black admonition came from southern Ohio. A Warren County black convention, repudiating openly racist candidates, also criticized the Free Democratic acceptance of state jurisdiction over slavery and declared that both the Declaration of Independence and the Constitution were aimed at securing "equal rights to all men."[17]

On election day, Langston cast his first ballot in a presidential campaign. The results were daunting. Not only Hale and Julian but, closer to his heart, congressional candidate Townshend fell victims to the national Democratic sweep that sent Franklin Pierce to the White House. Yet, at second glance, from the fledgling black campaigner's perspective, things might have seemed not so bad. Hale gained 31,682 votes in Ohio, more than in any other state, and only a small decline from the 1848 vote. The Western Reserve gave Hale and Julian healthy majorities and, despite the Democratic gerrymandering, elected two Free Democratic congressmen, incumbent Joshua Giddings and newcomer Edward Wade of Cleveland, brother of Ohio Senator Benjamin F. Wade. Most important, the Whig losses were staggering, making some sort of major party realignment appear inevitable in the near future.[18]

As for black enfranchisement, Langston may have discerned several possibilities for turning the Free Democratic losses to advantage. The Free Democrats now faced the task of organizing for the 1853 state races. The strength demonstrated by party members on the Western Reserve, generally the most radical in their antislavery beliefs, meant that precisely those Free Democrats most responsive to black persua-

siveness might take the upper hand in the state campaign. Since ignoring black rights obviously had not won votes, Langston and his allies
were in a better position to argue that a consistent and forthright
antislavery platform, including equal rights for blacks, might. Even
though such a position would cost the Free Democrats in the statewide
races, it might benefit them in election of representatives to the Ohio
assembly. Moreover, a reform campaign could be expected to enlist
energetic abolitionists to perform vital organizational work, thus
strengthening the party as an antislavery force in any future coalition.

At the same time, Langston may have been encouraged by a new
surge of interest in black humanity similar, although shorter in dura-
tion, to that which had occurred during the abolitionist awakening of
the thirties. Evangelical-inspired attempts earlier in the decade to restore moral fervor to the antislavery movement by emphasizing the
Negro as an individual, rather than sectionalism and the institution of
slavery, had made limited progress.[19] But the 1852 election had seemed
to indicate that sectionalism and antiextensionism were losing their
effectiveness as antislavery issues. Events would prove just how misleading this was, but, in the meantime, to fill the gap, the black man himself moved nearer to the moral center of antislavery agitation. Both
Uncle Tom's Cabin, popular on the stage as well as in print, and recur-
ring real-life dramas of fugitive recaptures or escapes contributed importantly to building new sympathy with the black plight.

His effectiveness on the hustings already demonstrated, Langston
was advantageously placed to translate awakening sympathies into political action. He went to work immediately with the New Year. A delegate to the Free Democratic Lorain County convention in Elyria in
early January 1853, he served on a three-man committee on resolutions
that drafted a series of radical proposals. In addition, he offered a
sharply worded condemnation of two repressive measures then before
the Democratic-dominated state legislature—one providing for the appropriation of state funds for Liberian colonization; the other, for the
barring of black immigration and the forced registration of black and
mulatto residents. Both bills would be defeated, but only after protracted black protest. These attempts "to revive the Black Law and
colonization spirit," Langston urged, must be regarded "as efforts of
tyranny and oppression not to be borne, but to be reprobated as Anti-
Democratic and utterly Anti Christian." In hearty accord, the Lorain
Free Democrats also adopted the resolution that Langston had helped
to formulate declaring it the "duty of the Free Democracy of Ohio
to do all in their power to insure the colored people of the state in
the possession and enjoyment of the elective franchise." Furthermore,

suiting action to words, the conclave elected the black theological student as one of its four delegates to the Ohio Free Democratic convention in Columbus on January 12.[20]

At Columbus, John Mercer saw the black leadership's long prodding of the Free Democrats for black enfranchisement bear fruit. Echoing the Lorain County resolution, the Free Democratic state convention approved a platform that endorsed black suffrage.[21] This turn-about from the party posture of only six months before doubtless reflected a larger decision to wage a reform campaign, designed to elect representatives to the Assembly, against the now blatantly anti-Negro Democrats. The black enfranchisement plank was part of a strong antislavery platform to which was joined a call for an Ohio temperance measure similar to the popular Maine Liquor Law. As further indication of their reform intentions, the Free Democrats chose as their gubernatorial candidate the old Liberty party leader Samuel Lewis.

Determined to capitalize on the Free Democrats' change of heart, Langston moved directly from these party deliberations to the Ohio black convention that met in Columbus one week later. The forty-nine free men of color, representing twenty-three counties, elected as president A. J. Gordon of Cleveland, a barber, the Cincinnati orator John Mercer had known in his childhood. As vice-president and a member of the business committee, Langston was an influential voice in shaping the convention's resolutions. In contrast to their stance a year earlier, the Langston brothers now eschewed any mention of emigration and devoted their energies to strengthening the struggle for equal rights. Even H. Ford Douglass, the only delegate quoted on emigration, now maintained that he advocated not a mass migration, but merely "that under some circumstances colored men may advance their interests by emigration." As for the long-despised Liberian colonization, the delegates denounced the proposed appropriation of public funds for that purpose as "not only unconstitutional, but self-degrading." The resolutions concerning the protection and advancement of the free Negroes of Ohio also condemned the bill then before the legislature to forbid blacks to enter Ohio and require registration of all black residents, with a vow that "like the 'Fugitive Bill,' being unconstitutional . . ., it should be discountenanced and resisted to the last." Moreover, in an effort to assess black voting potential, the convention requested the vigilance committees in every county to report the total number of possible mulatto voters. After Langston expounded on the "great evil of liquor-drinking," the black delegates roared unanimous approval of the Free Democracy-backed proposal for an Ohio temperance law.

Following up on their resolutions, Langston and his colleagues launched two major undertakings: a statewide black society and a newspaper. Aimed at achieving full political and civil rights, the newly created Ohio State Anti-Slavery Society incorporated such time-tested devices as the central committee, the agent-lecturer, and local auxiliaries. Charles Langston prepared sample constitution and bylaws for auxiliaries, specifically open to both sexes. John Mercer, who had pled for a newspaper ever since his first state convention in 1849, once again ably argued the duty of supporting a medium that would enable black Ohioans to "give utterance to their thoughts" and "speak as occasion might call, of their insults and wrongs."[22]

William Howard Day, who back in late December had gone East searching for financial support for such a venture, was chosen both as editor and as the state society's first agent. Within the year he would be succeeded in the latter post first by David Jenkins, and then by Langston himself.[23] On April 9, 1853, a sample number of *The Aliened American*, edited and published by Day, would appear. Its motto: "Educate your children—and Hope for Justice." By then, through the sale of stock primarily to black supporters who doubtless included such enthusiasts as the Langston brothers, and with himself and his wife major investors, Day had acquired the wherewithal to buy a press and set up a Cleveland printing office. In August, a second issue belatedly appeared. Thereafter, *The Aliened American* was "punctual" in its weekly visits until the late spring of 1854. At that time, Day's precarious health forced his resignation. Although the State Council purchased his interests, the announced suspension of publication became permanent. But during its short life, *The Aliened American*, much praised for its editing, the quality of articles from both male and female contributors, and "large and fair" appearance, would be an influential and useful tool for the Ohio black movement.[24]

The growing salience in antislavery agitation of the rights of the northern free men of color was evident at the April 1853 annual meeting of the Cincinnati antislavery convention. In contrast to the previous year, free black men's rights ranked high in the order of business—a fact that must have gratified John Mercer, a secretary of the convention and one of its major orators. Besides Langston, prominent black participants included the black Garrisonian Charles Lenox Remond of Salem, Massachusetts, and John I. Gaines, the three men sharing the platform at a special evening session devoted to the black cause. Day was a secretary and member of the business committee. As in 1852, the Ladies Society had attracted representatives from across the antislavery spectrum. At the one extreme, William Lloyd Garrison himself, on his first visit to Cincinnati, led a notable contingent from the American Anti-Slavery Society ranks; at the other, Samuel Lewis, convention president and Free Democratic gubernatorial candidate, and George Julian stood out among the antislavery politicians. Because the "nearest duty is the first duty," the delegates vowed unanimously, abolitionists, before condemning slaveholders, were bound to grapple with and try to suppress "whatever in legislation or public sentiment manifests a proscriptive and tyrannous spirit against the colored man in the State where they live." Ohio's political disenfranchisement of colored citizens, therefore, should be "vigorously denounced and held up to public condemnation until it ceases to exist."[25]

Vigorous denunciation Gaines and Langston were happy to supply. At their evening session, Gaines, in a stirring "Plea for Colored Americans," threatened black rebellion. He dreaded the idea of "this broad land of ours . . . drenched in a brother's blood—but if liberty, fraternity, equality—if the government of God can only be secured and preserved by it—thrice welcome it, Sir, as a messenger from on high to shatter the fetters of the bondsman, and to let the oppressed go free." That, in the one-time "riot city," only a river's width from slavery, the normally temperate Gaines should evoke Toussaint L'Ouverture and black revolution was one measure of the alteration in public sentiment.[26]

Preceding Garrison to the platform on the second morning, John Mercer made one of the major addresses of his early career. He developed a favorite theme: slavery was the "sum of all villainies," the oppressor of white and black and the corrupter of church, state, society, and literature, North and South. Slavery, he declared, "comes into the Northern States and makes slaves of the colored people." In scathing allusion to the Ohio bills to register and exclude black residents, and the state law barring black paupers from public assistance, he asked, "Why should I be driven out of the State? Have we not labored for the support of the government ever since its formation, and your benevolent institutions, and, withal, of your penitentiary?" "I stand here with invisible manacles upon me," he cried, "I have not the freedom you desire me to have."[27]

Although, in the main, his attack focused on the attitudes of white supremacists, Langston also took the occasion to reject two attitudes prevalent among abolitionists: racial romanticism, which centered on the idea that blacks, although less talented intellectually, were more gifted emotionally than whites; and color-blindness, a basic tenet of Garrisonian abolitionism, which refused to recognize differences between the races and, consequently, did not acknowledge the legitimacy of black societies and other "complexional institutions."[28] Racial romanticism recently had come to the fore with *Uncle Tom's Cabin*. Although not mere stereotypes, Harriet Beecher Stowe's characters tended to be aggressive or nonresistant according to their proportion of white blood: if black, they relied largely on faith and love; if mulatto, on manly courage and intellect. Despite Langston's praise for Mrs. Stowe's masterpiece as "written in defense of liberty and against slavery," he argued: "The black man, though he has a black skin, is intellectually and morally a man." He possessed "the same intellect as the white man, and the same sort of sensibility, which is, when cultivated, as tender as his.—He has the same executive will too." With equal firmness, he rejected suggestions of black superiority. "For we have all the virtues and vices of other men," he insisted, and repeated it for emphasis.[29]

Although Langston's insistence on the black share in the common humanity had been part of this prepared address, his rebuke of colorblindness was impromptu. It came in response to Remond, who had opened his speech by noting that he "would not speak as a colored man, but as *a man*." (To another forum, Frederick Douglass would retort that Remond's remark constituted a "cowardly" repudiation of connection with his race.)[30] Langston prefaced his own remarks with a measured declaration of his position. "I am anxious every word I utter, every gesture I make, shall be as a colored man. My only apology in appearing before you is the color of my skin." His complexion was not cause for sympathy. Rather, in the "great contest . . . . between liberty and slavery," his color was providential. "I am of necessity placed on the side of anti-slavery. Had I been a white man and inherited the condition and property of my father, I might have been a pro-slavery man today. But thanks to God, who created me, and the men who have educated me, I am in spite of myself an anti-slavery man." Because of his "blood connection," he could "speak with some freedom and boldness" as the "advocate of the American slave." This conception of the multiple levels of his identity—black, pleading for the slave and free black; human; American—reinforced the passion of his concluding plea: "My friends; if you would save your country and government and all its great interests, you must one and all labor for the overthrow of Slavery, or it will overthrow you and everything else. We must come to the rescue of our country from this great curse."

The speech received fuller coverage than any other Langston had made to date, fixing him more firmly as a black abolitionist to be reckoned with. The Wilmington, Ohio, *Herald of Freedom*, one of four newspapers that printed it in full, noted his superior talent for oratory and judged his native intellect "seldom surpassed by any of his own or any other race." Ignoring Langston's implied rebuke of Remond, the Garrisonian press praised him; the Ohio Anti-Slavery Society and other Garrisonian affiliates, before many months had elapsed, would begin issuing speaking invitations. Moreover, the Oberlin seminarian strengthened his reputation with evangelical and political abolitionists. His own political antislavery hopes were inspirited by George Julian's declaration of the Whig party's decease and prediction that the Democratic party, "having no principles but some negative and obsolete ones to bind it together, and having no outside pressure, must fall to pieces."[31]

By mid-1853, the prospect of black northern unity emerged as a further diversion from Langston's thoughts of black nationalist emigration. Although earlier efforts by Day to arrange a conference of black northerners had failed, Frederick Douglass's proposal for a national black convention to plan for a National Council and an industrial school quickly generated enthusiasm. Accordingly, a summons to a black national convention to be held in Rochester, New York, July 6–8, 1853, was issued in May and signed by forty-two prominent men from nine states. One of only four Ohio signatories, John Mercer was elected a delegate by an Oberlin black meeting. The large Ohio delegation to the convention included his brother Charles, Day, Jenkins, Clark, and Gaines, all of whom would occupy major offices or committee assignments. More than at any other pre-war black national convention, the 140 delegates who gathered in Rochester's stately Corinthian Hall numbered in their ranks the recognized leaders of the race. Presided over by J. W. C. Pennington, they included such Garrisonians as Remond and William C. Nell of Massachusetts and Robert Purvis of Pennsylvania; convention movement pioneers William Whipper, John Peck, John B. Vashon of Pennsylvania, and Jehiel C. and Amos G. Beman of Connecticut; leaders of civil rights struggles in their respective states like George T. Downing of Rhode Island, Leonard A. Grimes of Massachusetts, John Jones of Illinois, and James McCune Smith of New York; former newspaper editor Charles B. Ray of New York; a few, like J. M. Whitfield of New York, who would shortly become prominent in the emigrationist movement; and a liberal sprinkling of highly educated young men: Day, the Langstons, William J. Wilson of New York, and George Vashon.[32]

Both his committee and speaking assignments, more prominent that those usually granted so young a man, made it clear that John Mercer

Langston's reputation had preceded him. He was appointed to a three-man committee chaired by Downing, the thirty-four-year-old successful innkeeper and caterer in Newport, to report on black engagement in commerce. Affirming the need for blacks to lead and direct in their professional lives, the committee ascribed "much of the increased respect" shown blacks, to their "awakening, especially throughout the less densely settled portions of the country, to active business relations; that we are beginning to become producers as well as consumers."[33]

The report on social relations, drawn up by Wilson, Whipper, and Ray, however, concluded just the opposite. That report paternalistically scolded blacks for financial mismanagement, "lethargy, depression, discouragement, and seeming content"—a racial stereotype in direct opposition to the definition of black identity that Langston had been at pains to offer in Cincinnati. Moreover, it declared that free blacks constituted "a body of consumers and non-producers." The young Ohioan could not remain silent. "Fired up," like several of his western colleagues, John Mercer "sprang to the platform." Referring to a memorandum he had just jotted, based on his previously compiled statistics, Langston "told how many persons in Cincinnati were employed in various departments, at what wages, and with what property results, defending each branch of business with the clearest insight into its nature and relations, as productive. . . ." On grounds that labor was "equivalent" to capital and workers to "producers," he rattled off a list that began with Cincinnati's two hundred bootblacks, the job he had performed in Watson's barbershop, and ended with three bank tellers and a landscape painter, the latter a reference to the highly regarded artist Robert S. Duncanson who, as Langston noted, had just gone for a year's study in Rome. Putting black property holdings in Cincinnati at $800,000 and in Ohio at more than $5 million, he contended, "They proved that wherever there was wealth, there was health, virtue, and all manner of respectability; and that they demanded deference to a great extent." In what proved the major floor dispute of the convention, Langston aggressively insisted upon his definition of black labor as productive, moving that the social relations report be amended to "conform to the fact, which is, that we are, to a great extent, producers." Downing concurred and attempted to add Langston to the social relations committee to strike the "obnoxious passages" and rewrite the report. At length, with rejection of the whole report by a vote of 63 to 31, the Oberlin debater and his allies triumphed. This display of economic understanding, judgment, and wit struck one white observer as equal to "any debate among white men I ever heard."[34]

In a formal program on the second night that attracted many white spectators, Langston shared the platform with four other orators, Douglass, Pennington, Remond, and Gaines. Not only did these men heap scorn on the American Colonization Society, but subsequent resolutions also condemned it, declaring that blacks had "long since determined to plant our trees on American soil and repose beneath their shade." Despite the controversy over nationalist-emigration that flared soon after the convention, any discussion on that topic went unreported. Rather, delegates occupied themselves with ambitious organizational schemes that, if realized, would have resulted in a virtual black nation within a nation. Following Douglass's urging, they approved the establishment of an industrial school for black youths and of a National Council which, through an elaborate committee system, would control cooperative endeavors in business, consumer affairs, labor, and cultural matters. Although the location of the school, a bone of contention between East and West, was left to the discretion of the National Council,[35] a significant portion of the funding, Douglass indicated, would be supplied by Harriet Beecher Stowe from her solicitation of English philanthropists.[36]

Although meeting with initial enthusiasm in black communities across the North and in the abolitionist press, the National Council and the proposed industrial school—and with them the hope of black national unity—quickly became mired in ideological and sectional disputes and personal acrimony. Within several weeks of the Rochester convention—a timing surely calculated to undermine its work—the black nationalist Martin Delany, personally as well as ideologically alienated from Douglass, issued his own call for a national emigration convention to meet in Cleveland a year hence, thus entering a competing claim on black attention.[37] Meanwhile, Douglass, on hearing that several prominent black Garrisonians had been publicly critical of him and of the convention, exploded into print with bitter denunciations of his one-time coworkers in the American Anti-Slavery Society. At that, the antagonisms that had simmered since Douglass's open break with the Garrisonians two years before boiled over. During the extended and painful period of vituperative mutual recrimination that followed, Garrison and his followers opposed the industrial school idea as well as the council, branding them as mainly black, rather than color-blind, institutions.[38] By January 1854, confronted by the dissension between Douglass and the Garrisonians, Mrs. Stowe made it known that she would not allocate the funds raised in England to the school proposal, preferring other antislavery projects instead.[39] As if all this were not trouble enough, disputes rocked the National Council from its very first meeting, when a late-arriving Day, representing Ohio, found that his eastern cohorts, despite the absence of a quorum, had made a number of decisions that appeared to him to slight the interests of Negroes in the West. Subsequently, Day and Douglass, whose editorial rivalry only intensified their argumentativeness, used both their newspapers and the council to continue the battle.[40] Boycotted by Ohioans who charged the easterners with having excluded them from planning, the lackluster national black convention at Philadelphia in October 1855 abandoned the attempt to realize the program set in motion two years before. Simultaneously, the national black convention movement ground to a halt. Weighted too heavily with exciting but impractical organizational schemes, hobbled by ideological and sectional strife, and buffeted by personal ambitions and animosities, the National Council created by the most illustrious of the national black conclaves held during the three decades preceding the Civil War had carried the seeds, not only of its own destruction, but also of the entire pre-war movement.[41] Diplomatically remaining outside the controversy—a fact that doubtless ingratiated him with all factions—John Mercer Langston attended the National Council only once, the third and final meeting held in New York City in May 1855, and then only as an honorary nonvoting member.[42]

As much as business transacted by the 1853 National Convention at Rochester, the caliber of the black North's representative men impressed observers. Langston's participation—Douglass complimented him for having "borne a very distinguished part"—represented another significant broadening of the Ohioan's political and social perspectives. At twenty-three, John Mercer's background, experience, ability, and personal qualities—the modesty appealingly combined with confidence, the schooled logic with "fiery" emotion—that had helped to propel him to leadership in the Ohio black movement, already had won him not only access to the national black platform, but also the good opinion of black abolitionists of differing reform perspectives. Douglass, for example, saw to it that John Mercer was one of a handful of delegates summoned by perfumed notes to a sumptuous tea attended by wealthy white abolitionists and arranged by Julia Griffiths, the young Englishwoman who assisted in Douglass's newspaper office. Miss Griffiths found Mr. Langston "a gentleman of fortune, a shining scholar and a brilliant orator—He could easily gain admission to the first circles of any country, *but his own*."[43] Despite his argument with Langston at the convention, Charles Ray was among the New York City delegates, including James McCune Smith, Philip A. Bell, and A. N. Freeman, who, immediately upon adjournment, hosted John Mercer's initial visit to the city. There, along with Charles Langston, Day, William C. Nell, and John Jones, the well-off Chicago tailor, John Mercer spoke at a series of meetings. Reporting one of his speeches, made off the cuff, the New York *Tribune* declared it would have "honored the Halls of Congress." Nell invited John Mercer to accompany him home to Boston, mecca of eastern abolitionism, to speak at a morale-building session. With editor Garrison himself taking notes for the *Liberator*'s report, Langston shared speaking duties with Nell, Remond, Purvis, and W. J. Watkins, associate editor of Douglass's paper. The convention, all reportedly agreed, had constituted "an era in the cause of the colored population, whether bond or free." They urged blacks to push forward the "car of Liberty and Equal Rights."[44]

Although invited by Nell to stay through the First of August celebration at Framingham where luminaries of the American Anti-Slavery Society would perform, John Mercer felt obliged to return to Oberlin. He was scheduled to take over as agent of the Ohio State Council from the indefatigable Jenkins, who had spent March, April, and May on the road. More immediately, Langston expected to speak at a West Indies emancipation celebration in Lorain County, but, on arrival, he found it had been cancelled. He then accepted an invitation to address the celebration at Frankfort in Ross County, Johnnie Gooch's home territory.

However painful the past associations, the Ross County picnic grove became the setting for an emotional triumph. Although anti-abolitionist sentiment previously had dominated the area, the festivities attracted some twenty-five hundred rural people, mainly white. But just as Langston mounted the speaker's stand, "dark heavy clouds came up, and with their broad folds overspread the whole sky. Nor was it long before they discharged upon us their entire contents, drenching mother and babe, man and boy, the beau and the lass." While some of the picnicers found shelter in their wagons, Langston was completely exposed to the downpour. "I suppose it is a fact," he reported to William C. Nell, "that I was more thoroughly wet than any other person." His ardor undamped, however, the black abolitionist talked for an hour and a half. He described the crusade to "bring liberty and manhood to the American bondman, and life, peace, and joy to his drooping heart," and expounded "the rational hope of 'the good time coming.' " Apparently enthralled, the farm folk listened in the rain. "As I had the ability," John Mercer related, "I poured the truth upon their hearts so as to make them think, feel, and, if possible, act. That I did them some good, I fully believe." On this evidence that "the cause goes forward," he drew hope that "we shall, before many years, be able to make Ohio the anti-slavery state of the Union."[45]

The accolades of the eastern press, the attention of the rain-soaked Ohioans attested to the degree to which the theological student had been able to develop his rhetorical skills. During his third and final year of studies, he and other senior theologs, with years of rhetorical practice behind them and a youthful confidence in their range of knowledge, devoted special attention to extemporaneous speaking. At informal sessions, begun by announcement of a topic, students competed to deliver addresses without notes, "as finished as might be in thought, dictum, arrangement of matter and illustration." A description by a visitor to a Theological Society meeting in 1863 gives the flavor of John Mercer's experience: "After an animated discussion of the 'Wine' question, in wh. all took the right side, and gave their reasons, an extempore exercise took place, highly beneficial I shld. imagine. A topic and name were given by each member, and when the Pres. drew a name, the owner thereof had to come forward, take a topic from the mass, and speak on it *five* minutes immediately: 'Who was Melchisidec,' 'Was the Flood universal,' 'Nature or Art, which is ahead,' 'Unity of the Human Species,' 'Matrimony &c,' were well treated." In New York City or southern Ohio, on the political stump or antislavery platform, and, later, most particularly, before judges and juries, Langston's uncommon expertise at extemporaneous address gave him an edge. In the end, he believed, this training was the major factor in success before the bar.[46]

Notwithstanding his accomplishments, John Mercer almost certainly gave less than unalloyed satisfaction to his mentors. Reputedly, he was "the only student permitted to study theology here while not a Christian." His Christianity is an open question. Langston himself never discussed his personal religious views at any length. But it was true that, in a community in all but perpetual revival—proud of its freedom of thought and liberality of sentiment but convinced that those qualities led inevitably to a religious life in some, preferably evangelical, church[47]—since the age of fourteen, John Mercer stubbornly had resisted all entreaties to undergo conversion and embrace salvation. The most notable public occasion for such an entreaty was the Oberlin graduation ceremony in 1852, when he was awarded his master's degree. If a soul proved recreant to Charles Grandison Finney's judgment, the evangelist was not loathe to appeal directly to the Lord; in Langston's case, Finney first instructed: "My son, you ought to consecrate yourself to the Master's work and preach," and then, in the closing prayer, "implor[ed] the Lord to open the eyes and heart of the young man and teach him his duty as to the choice of his calling for life." The young man remained obdurate.

In his autobiography, Langston rather vaguely observed: "Such was the natural and inevitable effect" of the theological study that he "could not fail to be reached by its moral and religious results." On other occasions, he affirmed his belief in the necessity of leading a Christian life, and the belief that such a life might be attained by obedience to personal conscience, "the voice of God in his soul." Although at Oberlin and afterward he attended church regularly, it appears that he did not believe he needed formal affiliation with a particular religious denomination to instruct his conscience. Oberlin theological students enjoyed an uncommon freedom of remark and inquiry. The Oberlin teachings as Langston interpreted them—the reliance on reflection or intuition to make duty clear, the belief that reason was a sublime faculty "related to eternal and absolute truths," the notion that an inborn spiritual faculty, taught and cultivated, enabled man "to recognize God in his spiritual manifestations, to discern and appreciate spiritual truths, and to feel and relish the gentle distillations of the spirit of divine love as they fall upon his heart like dew upon the grateful earth"—reinforced his impulse toward self-reliance and his unorthodoxy.[48]

In the final weeks of his theological studies, John Mercer expressed his liberal religious leanings to two separate forums. The first was a public meeting to help his Cincinnati companion, Peter Clark; the second, a graceful small essay he wrote in late August 1853 for Julia Griffiths *Autographs for Freedom*, a fund-raising giftbook hawked at abolitionist conventions and bazaars. Clark, a Unitarian, recently had amazed white observers and scandalized some conservative blacks by his able exposition of Thomas Paine's "republican principles of freedom" and his condemnation of a religion that taught Negroes to "bear toil and stripes" in hope of "a mansion of bliss in the regions above." Subsequently, the schoolteacher had been accused of atheism by several Negro school trustees and fired by the then-controlling white school board. The Langston brothers and Gaines joined Clark in public denial of the charges while, at the same time, protesting against any religious tests to determine fitness for professional position. Although young Langston's words were not recorded, it is certain that he, like Clark, preferred a religious focus on this world, rather than other-worldly concerns.[49] Just as vehemently, as his essay in *Autographs for Freedom* made clear, Langston objected to organized religion's hypocrisy on the slavery issue. "The majority of our most distinguished divines find employment in constructing discourses, founded upon perverse expositions of sacred writ, calculated to establish and fix in the minds of the people the impression that slavery is a divine institution," he charged hotly. As enemies of the slave, he considered the "influence of the Church" matched only by the "power of the State." In his skepticism, Langston—like Clark and some other black intellectuals of his century—seemed to express hostility not to Christianity but to a church that justified slavery and, as a black minister expressed it, "asks us to wait patiently for the time when the colored people would wear a crown of gold in the 'Sweet bye and bye.' "[50]

But these views did not separate him from the Oberlin evangelicals. His refusal to rely on Christianity "as a grand relief for the wrongs of the oppressed" did. Not content with this final resort endorsed by most Oberlin clergymen, Langston depended most strongly on education of the intellect and sensibilities. "Educate him!"—not "Convert him!"—would be his life-long plea for the black man. Moreover, not Christian humility but "courage, moral and physical," was to his mind the "most brilliant and beautiful quality" a person could possess: "the highest type of moral courage, the purpose and power to do that which seemed to him, in spite of the prepossession and customs of society, right and proper."[51] Langston believed in a revolutionary God, his white clergyman-biographer would declare. Langston believed in a God who "would not stand idly by if the oppressed made an effort to secure what God had given and man had taken"; and, at the same time, he drew "courage and persistence" from the belief that every "earnest man's life is a plan of God." The key to God's plan for him, he seems to have concluded, was his mixed blood that put him perforce on the side of liberty in the overweening moral struggle of his generation. His doctrine seems to have been closer to that enunciated by his brother Charles than to that of any church: "I have long since adopted as my God the freedom of the colored people of the United States, and my religion, to do anything that will effect that object."[52] Shortly before he died, Langston still insisted he was a member "of no church."[53]

Accustomed to being called heretics themselves, Oberlin's pious professors naturally would have been disappointed when their gifted Negro student drew back from full acceptance of their doctrine. The question of Langston's "spirituality" would be posed in 1862, as a possible objection to his employment, by American Missionary Association secretary George Whipple, John Mercer's own early protector; the A.M.A.'s Oberlin agent would reply he could not vouch for it, but feared that Langston was "deficient in that respect."[54] In a God-preoccupied, church-controlled era, Langston's unorthodox religious views were bound to place him under suspicion. To maintain his individualistic, self-reliant stance would indeed demand the moral courage he described.

Like student activists of any generation, this "shining scholar" apparently had fallen behind in his requirements to the point that he could not sit with other class members at the commencement exercises on the fourth Wednesday in August 1853. Subsequently, work completed, he obtained official status as one of the ten Oberlin seminary graduates of 1853. Analytically, through emphasis on hermeneutics and exegesis of Biblical texts, psychologically, in attempts to explain "every phenomenon of the human understanding and every condition of the human heart concerning virtue or vice," and in terms of general knowledge, Langston felt the whole course "educated and sustained his highest conceptions of truth, with his best logical powers."[55] With such tools, he was confident, he could tackle virtually any intellectual endeavor, including the law.

In July 1853, Langston announced happily that he lately had adopted the law as his profession. Free Democratic party activities had brought the Oberlin student into the orbit of Philemon Bliss, a leading attorney and newspaper publisher at nearby Elyria. A Connecticut Yankee schooled at Fairfield Academy and Oneida, forced by poverty to drop out of Hamilton College before graduation, Philemon Bliss had come West in the late thirties and settled in Elyria. Early he had cooperated with his one-time Oneida friends, numerous among the Lane Rebels at Oberlin and in Weld's Band, to spread the antislavery message. Investigating political opportunities for furthering abolitionism as early as 1839, and quickly winning a reputation as a lawyer of "great mental ability," Bliss had won Lorain County's first probate judgeship in 1848, presiding over the Fourteenth judicial circuit until 1851.[56] In January 1853, Bliss and Langston, as two of the three-member business committee, had cooperated in drafting the radical resolutions passed at the Lorain County Free Democratic convention; both men had represented the county at the state party convention that month. Impressed by his young coworker, Bliss had agreed to tutor him in his office.[57]

Apprehensive that his Negro apprentice might be unable to secure suitable boarding in Elyria—the bustling county seat where attitudes, although predominantly antislavery, fell far short of Oberlin's racial tolerance—Bliss arranged a room for him in the county courthouse and invited him to take meals with the Bliss family. Langston had scarcely unpacked before he attended an American Colonization Society lecture and, when it appeared the colonizationist had won over his audience, impetuously rose and announced his own rebuttal would be offered at the courthouse, naming the day and the hour. That night, troubled by how his rash action might affect his unjelled relations with his new patrons, John Mercer slept badly; in the morning, skipping his habitual study, he hurried to the breakfast table to explain himself. To his relief, Bliss declared his determination to preside at Mercer's meeting and, not to be outdone, Martha, his wife, insisted on gracing the podium with her "large and beautiful chandelier." Thus bolstered, and with arguments by then well-honed, Langston's anti-colonizationist speech, according to his own accounting, not only discomfited the A.C.S.'s agent, but also brought lecture invitations from surrounding communities.[58]

Shortly thereafter, Bliss made further public acknowledgement of confidence in his "young friend." In an editorial note, he scornfully mentioned Timothy Walker's rejection of the colored man's application to his Cincinnati law school and offered his own opinion that Langston's "intellectual worth and liberal education would do honor to any one, white or black." John Mercer was determined "to pursue his studies," Bliss announced, and "demonstrate to the extent of his abilities that it is not necessary for a man to be white in order to be a lawyer."[59]

Despite these brave words, both student and mentor knew that, in actuality, whiteness was nearly the only inflexible requirement in the often slipshod process, particularly in the West, by which attorneys were produced in the pre-Civil War era. Generally involving law office apprenticeship rather than a formal program, when the aspirant knew "some law," mainly Blackstone, and had in hand recommendations attesting to his moral character, the procedure culminated in an often-indifferent examination before a frequently ill-informed judge or board of lawyers. Bliss assured Langston he would be prepared "to meet any question of color, in his case," apparently without going into details, but warned sternly that his legal knowledge must be letter-perfect, "for we must have no failure." Over the next twelve months, as much as political and black activism allowed, John Mercer heeded Blackstone's admonition: the law was his "jealous mistress, brooking no divided love." Bliss instructed him in theory, expounded legal principles, repeatedly subjected him to review. Student and preceptor worked on real and personal property, contracts and evidence, practice and pleading. To overcome the lack of moot court practice, Bliss sent Langston into the county courthouse to observe, afterward catechizing him strictly.[60]

Vital as this rigorous training was to Langston's future, momentous political developments from the fall of 1853 to the fall of 1854, the period of his law apprenticeship, also would significantly shape the outcome. In 1853, radical political realignment favoring the antislavery cause made considerable progress in Ohio, thanks to a well-organized, vigorous Free Democratic campaign throughout the state, to which John Mercer contributed. By late September, he had addressed mass meetings within a wide radius of Oberlin. Once again he campaigned for Norton Townshend, this time a candidate for the Ohio senate. On election day, although the Democrats retained control of the statehouse and the legislature, it was apparent that the Free Democratic gamble on antislavery, equal rights, and temperance had paid off handsomely. Attracting large numbers of orphaned Whigs, Free Democratic gubernatorial candidate Samuel Lewis, in defeat, won more than fifty thousand votes, outpolling Whig and Democratic opponents in Clinton County and throughout the Western Reserve—an increase of nearly 60 percent over Hale's total the previous year. Thirteen Free Democrats, including Senator Townshend, were sent to the assembly. Antislavery radicals had demonstrated impressive strength that would be wielded to good effect in the months ahead.[61]

Themselves hoisting the black enfranchisement banner to the Free Democratic standard, the black leadership, meeting in state convention at Dayton in late October, appointed Langston to present an appeal to the next state legislature. Assured of Senator Townshend's collaboration, at least, the law student scrupulously prepared his brief. Fleshing out his earlier arguments with historical and legal research, he also corresponded with movement colleagues—who, in turn, subjected themselves to the insults of county clerks—to gather current data[62] from which he concluded that black property subject to Ohio taxation was worth more than $5 million. He produced a closely reasoned plea that the general assembly "strike from the organic law of the State all those clauses which make discriminations on the ground of color," arguing that it was "unjust, anti-democratic, impolitic, and ungenerous to withhold from us the right of suffrage."[63]

On the last Tuesday in March, 1854, John Mercer Langston, styling himself "representative of the 25,000 half freemen of Ohio," accompanied by a small black delegation, arrived at the Ohio statehouse to read his memorial to the legislators. While the young orator stood expectantly in the vestibule, Senator Townshend, citing rules permitting private citizens personally to present memorials and petitions—female representatives of the temperance and women's rights movements included—moved that Langston be heard.[64] Earlier, at Townshend's request, Day had been admitted to senate galleries as reporter for the *Aliened American*, but then, on a straight Democratic vote, had had privileges revoked.[65] Now, true to form, with one senator snickering that Townshend was "the colored people's representative—that *he* could say well what they desired to present," the legislators refused to give Langston audience. Furiously disappointed, John Mercer stalked out of the hall. His labors, however, were not entirely lost.

Within weeks Townshend's committee stoutly reported a bill, promptly tabled, providing for a constitutional amendment to extend enfranchisement to black Ohioans. The report was based on Langston's plea, which was printed in full. "The various reasons for extending the right to colored persons are so ably set forth in the memorial of J. Mercer Langston. . . .," Townshend noted, that "nothing further in the way of argument seemed to be required."[66]

The senate's action seemed to John Mercer racism undisguised. Senators voted "with their eyes blinded by prejudice and negro hatred," he stormed in the *Aliened American*. If it were "fit and proper" that non-voting female representatives of various causes should be heard, and he thought it was, surely "it was equally fit and proper that I should be heard in behalf of the colored people of Ohio, and their rights." The sole reason for the senate's exclusion of him was "that I am a *colored* man, and appeared before them as the representative of colored men." Two years earlier black nationalist-emigration had seemed to him the only escape from such prejudice; now he vowed retribution. "Since we cannot have a hearing before the Legislature," he urged black Ohioans, "let us resolve to have a full and impartial one before the tribunal of the people, one whose effect shall fill our hearts with joy and gladness, while it fills the hearts of enemies with fear and trembling. And *now*, gentlemen, is the time to bestir ourselves—*now* is the time for us to make our voices heard—*now* is the time for us to enter upon a brave and manly defense of our cause, remembering that to the high endeavor, the undaunted effort, there is promised the glad and glorious success."[67]

More than youthful ardor, John Mercer's urgency sprang from his sense of propitious national upheaval. True to 1852 presidential campaign promises, for two years the Pierce administration and Congress had tried to clamp down slavery discussion. Noting their inefficacy, John Mercer, in a New York City speech in July 1853, had taunted: "Go . . . and padlock all the whites at the North—go padlock all the mouths of all the slaveholders at the South—go padlock all the mouths of the men and women North and South —still you cannot check agitation. No; the voices of babes would cry it out, and the winds of heaven would return it again. As long as there remained a vestige of slavery," he predicted, "so long there would be agitation."[68] Already events had proved him a sound prophet. The Kansas-Nebraska Act, an act that specifically repealed the Missouri Compromise prohibition of slavery north of the line 36°30', introduced by Senator Stephen A. Douglas of Illinois in January 1854 and finally passed in late May, outraged much of the North.

Taking advantage of the company he kept, Langston threw himself into efforts to channel anti-Nebraska protest into new political organization. In January, soon after the bill was submitted, Oberlin had manned the barricades against "this nefarious scheme," holding one of the first indignation gatherings in the north, and warning balefully through the *Evangelist* that unless the pro-slavery power could be arrested, "we shall have nothing to expect but universal slavery—its admission as a national institution." Philemon Bliss served on a committee of seven to direct agitation in Lorain County.[69] Langston prevailed upon his mentor and others on the committee, who included some of his former professors, to send him out on the stump. A black campaigner to attract Whigs and Democrats to a new coalition was, even in Lorain, a risky proposition, but it proved sound. "Mercer Langston has addressed large and enthusiastic audiences," an Oberlin correspondent exclaimed, "and the people turn out to hear, whenever liberty is the issue." Langston, Bliss, and theologian Henry Peck led a July 1 Oberlin mass gathering of county voters in endorsement of "the divorce of the Federal Government from slavery, and putting it actively on the side of Freedom." To cheers they announced "no more compromises—no yielding to the South." Whigs, Democrats, Free Democrats, old Liberty men attended. "To see the weather-beaten veterans of the old parties rise up, and throw off the yoke of bondage to party, and declare for the right and true" was evidence the antislavery backfires John Mercer had helped to ignite were at full blaze. "The whole county is rapidly taking anti-slavery ground," a partisan observed. "Free men will not stick to old organizations."[70]

Like agitation throughout Ohio resulted in a huge Anti-Nebraska state convention in Columbus on July 13 "to unite the sober judgment of the people of Ohio on the outrage perpetuated upon them by the repeal of the Missouri compromise."[71] More than a thousand delegates, along with thousands of alternates and onlookers, were on hand. The convention made several nominations for offices in the state's off-year elections and adopted an anti-extensionist platform. Unsatisfied, Langston's townsmen, "deeply moved by the recent triumphs of the slave power," issued the "Oberlin Anti-Slavery Platform": "The time has come when the people of the North should rally and combine their energies, not only to prevent the spread of slavery, but to crush the system itself." On August 8, the fusion party in the Fourteenth Congressional District nominated Philemon Bliss for the U.S. House of Representatives.[72]

With a crisis psychology dominant, John Mercer Langston addressed a meeting on August 21 during the Oberlin commencement week.

"Let Slavery triumph now," participants concluded, "and the fate of the nation will be sealed." The gathering, whose other leaders included Bliss, Townshend, and Joseph R. Swan of Columbus, the coalition nominee for the Ohio supreme court, determined on "two strings we can pull, and both shall be *well pulled*"—the election of "good men" to Congress, and "aid in pouring into Kansas an Anti-Slavery population which shall resist and prevent the ingress of Slavery." To forward the latter aim, the Kansas Emigrant Aid Association of Northern Ohio, powered by Oberlin, before long would be exporting men, money, and guns.[73] For the former, Langston and his allies intended to keep anti-Nebraska fires stoked for Philemon Bliss's candidacy.

In this atmosphere of building antislavery excitement, the long and heatedly discussed black national emigration convention, called a year before by Martin Delany, met in Cleveland August 24–26. For months, Ohio black leaders, most particularly Gaines, ruefully acknowledged by an opponent as "the most ultra anti-emigrationist in the West, and also the most talented one," as well as the redoubtable Jenkins, had worked in tandem with other northern blacks to foil Delany's plans. Besides combating the emigrationist argument in numerous letters and special meetings, Gaines and his allies argued for self-help, racial solidarity, and antislavery on such occasions as the particularly successful 1854 First of August celebration at Dayton, addressed by Day, Langston, and Gaines. Black Ohioans were urged to boycott the convention. When Delany gaveled the meeting to order, a total of only 101 "executive delegates," nearly half of whom were from Pittsburgh and its environs—and only fifteen Ohio men and women in their number— were on hand. Clearly, the competing antislavery claims on black attention in combination with the anti-emigrationist campaign had cut deeply into Delany's potential following, particularly in Ohio.[74]

Langston's own position was peculiar. He went to the convention but because avowed emigrationists alone were credentialed as delegates, he joined Gaines, Day, and John Malvin on the sidelines, "only in the attitude of idle spectators."[75] For compelling public and personal reasons, his attitude toward emigration had changed. Flushed both with the recent stirring antislavery developments and, more than he probably dared confess, with irrepressible hopes for a happy near conclusion of his legal studies and other personal projects, the twenty-four-year-old Langston must have listened uneasily to the arguments he himself had put with such conviction at the ages of nineteen and twenty-two. Black nationhood through mass emigration, so exciting in the context of European revolution, now seemed as impractical as the eventually somewhat tarnished movement of Louis Kossuth himself.

What was more, in a North seemingly, at least from a Lorain County viewpoint, at antislavery fever pitch, pessimistic speculation over immutable racial prejudice hardly seemed opportune. Even though the anti-Nebraska agitation contained a strong anti-black component, John Mercer could foresee, had seen already, a significant political transformation, and was working on a weekly, sometimes daily, basis to accomplish it. Now the Whig party was fatally wounded; a new major antislavery party was forming; a more antislavery North surely would be the result. The Declaration of Independence and the Constitution, the law student had come to believe, offered an unbreakable contract of freedom and citizenship to American blacks.

How much Martin Delany knew of John Mercer's current views is a mystery. Although Langston had corresponded with friends on the topic, he had said nothing publicly since January 1852. Certainly, the young man's failure to register as a delegate alone should have made evident his lack of enthusiasm. Just as unfathomable are Delany's motives, in a convention arranged to bar all dissent—for example, floor requests to hear Gaines were denied—in deliberately suspending the rules during informal session on the second evening and calling on Langston for a speech.[76] Perhaps the doctor believed the young nationalist whose arguments had helped clarify and mobilize the emigration movement would be too embarrassed, before an audience of emigrationists, to recant.

Langston's response was "a lengthy and rhetorical speech, replete with classical elegance . . . . To the surprise of many," he professed his change of heart. No longer did he consider white American prejudice overweening and unshakable. "A colored man of science, learning, and industry," John Mercer asserted, "could gain, and would be as much respected here as the white man." Consequently, he would remain in the United States—in the words of the 1853 National Convention declaration—to plant his " 'American tree.' " If the Constitution and the Declaration of Independence "were for freedom," then "success was certain for the colored man in common with the white man in the United States." Langston intended "to work out my destiny in Lorain County, Ohio."[77]

With the house "in a ferment of emotion," Langston's erstwhile comrade, H. Ford Douglass, brandishing John Mercer's discarded black nationalist-emigrationist theories, lashed his inconsistency with "withering sarcasm." Douglass rejected the role of "a young robin" expected to swallow obediently Langston's assertions, and those of Frederick Douglass and J. McCune Smith, that "the principles of emigration are destructive to the best interests of the colored people." And he assailed "the bombastic outpouring of the gentleman from Ohio, who in the abundance of his wisdom, has thought it proper to enlighten us on the many mistakes of his past life, all of which he very modestly attributes to his 'youthful enthusiasm.' "[78]

Although, as he had surely foreseen, John Mercer remained a light-ening rod for emigrationist wrath in coming weeks, renunciation of his young dreams won warm approval from George Vashon, his student protector who likely had shared them. Defending Langston, along with Gaines and Day, as having "always taken an earnest part in every move-ment for the colored man's welfare," the short-term Haitian emigrant attacked the emigration convention for its "tendency to see distinctions between the races—the very thing our enemies are racking Science and Revelation to discover," and for the encouragement it offered white colonizationists. At the same time, Langston had the virtually solid support of the Ohio black leadership. Clark and Gaines led black Cin-cinnatians in repudiation of emigration and colonization; Jenkins from Columbus published blacks' determination "to make *this* the battle-ground of their liberties." In the words of the black Cincinnatians, Langston himself finally was undivided in his commitment to remain on American soil, "to be that 'agitating element' in American politics."[79]

From Cleveland John Mercer had planned to journey to Salem, where he was to address the twelfth anniversary gathering of the West-ern Anti-Slavery Society, Garrisonianism's Ohio outbranch, but "im-perative circumstances" forced him to an uncharacteristic last-minute cancellation and a quick return to Elyria.[80] He did face urgent busi-ness. Within a fortnight the reformed emigrationist would take his examination before the Ohio bar.

On the morning of September 13, 1854, at Philemon Bliss's request, the five-member district court, convened in Elyria, appointed a com-mittee of three examiners. All local lawyers, two were Democrats, "men of age with fixed principles and feelings," Langston would recollect. The third was Gerry Boynton, younger and a Whig "of improving liberal sentiments," who later would become "an ardent Republican." Not one of these "elegant gentlemen" cottoned to the notion of a Ne-gro colleague. But, from the opening question: "What is law?" through real and personal property, John Mercer slid through "as if greased." Bliss's training had been "so rigid," he later boasted, that he passed every line of questioning and "staggered" the examiners by his profi-ciency. Boynton, in whose office the examination had taken place, afterward assured him privately that the committee report would give him his due.[81]

That afternoon the examiners submitted written certification to the judges that Langston was intellectually qualified to discharge the duties of an attorney, and that he was of appropriate moral character and age, and a citizen of Ohio and the United States. The two Democrats hastily interjected, however, that the applicant was colored. At that, the presiding officer, a supreme court justice from southern Ohio, remarked Pilate-like that a colored lawyer was unlikely ever to plead before him, therefore, his fellow jurists, all from northern Ohio, should decide. Boynton then played his trump. Quietly reminding the court that "Judge Bliss is taking care of [Langston's] case," and having to remind no one that Bliss was the coalition party's congressional candidate, he made two quick points: the examiners' report called Langston a "citizen"; by 1842 state supreme court decision, a "nearer white than black" mulatto was entitled to the rights of a white man.

Disgruntled, the chief justice, "with manifest warmth of feeling," ordered Langston to rise. "I stood before him," he recalled thirty-five years after, "and was informed that I was white enough." Through "a beautiful hocus pocus arrangement," he was "construed into a *white man*" and sworn in. After taking his oath and receiving his certificate, the new attorney nervily asked the judge why he had had to stand, and "I was told that it was material to know by actual sight what my color was."[82]

A month afterward, Philemon Bliss was elected to Congress. "Ohio All Anti-Nebraska!" trumpeted the Cleveland *Leader*. Coalition candidates captured all twenty-one congressional seats, while, in the leading state contest, Swan won seventy-eight of eighty-eight counties for election to the supreme court. Bliss barely squeaked by in heavily Democratic Ashland County, but, with Lorain contributing nearly half of his votes, succeeded in rolling up an impressive majority. In Ohio, the coalition that some northerners already were calling the Republican party was well joined.[83]

"I was present at the party's birth. I helped to dress it," Langston justifiably would assert in later years.[84] Before most northerners, white and black, John Mercer Langston had thrown in his lot with what he would earnestly contrive to make the party of freedom. His tireless campaigning had contributed to the coalition's formation and initial victory. In so doing, he had demonstrated that, if it unquestionably were true that Ohio blacks had only a few hundred votes to inject into a political system of coalition and compromise, it was not true that they "had nothing to bargain with."[85] As Stephen A. Douglass had demonstrated during his defense of the Nebraska bill in the Senate, when he branded Chase and Sumner "the pure, unadulterated representatives of Abolitionism, Free Soilism, Niggerism,"[86] racism would be a major Democratic defense tactic against the antislavery insurgents. While some Republicans would try to counter by denying any sympathy for

blacks, a few, both because of personal commitment and practical political necessities, would employ the tested abolitionist method of bely-
ing the "nigger" stereotype with the Negro reality. The presentable,
personable Negro from Oberlin, capable of coolly facing down a heckler with a laugh at the latter's expense, of stubbornly lecturing for
ninety minutes in the rain, from the start exemplified the usefulness to
the new party of the black campaigner.

Although Langston, as raconteur in middle age, understandably
stressed the importance of his dazzling examination performance in
winning his unprecedented admission to the Ohio bar, he could not
have failed to recognize that it also reflected the new political realities
that he himself had helped to create. Bliss the coalition congressional
candidate was simply a more persuasive figure than Bliss the Free
Soiler, as was Langston, the coalition campaigner, rather than Langston, "the representative of colored men." One of the most remarkable
fruits of the anti-Nebraska harvest was the creation of the first Negro
lawyer in the West.

In that part of the country it was customary for the newly authorized lawyer to treat his examiners to dinner; but if that celebration was
almost certainly prevented by the intrusion of an older custom of racial separation, it should not be assumed that a sense of the irony of
his situation precluded feelings of genuine elation. It had taken John
Mercer four years, since before the passage of the Fugitive Slave Law
until after the Kansas-Nebraska Act, but he had proved wrong the
white and black nay-sayers and demonstrated "to the extent of his
abilities that it is not necessary for a man to be white in order to be a
lawyer."[87]

The preceding spring, while catching up on correspondence, letters
to friends of his undergraduate and theological years, and notes to
young women of his acquaintance, he had given over a few spoilt sheets
to doodling. His handwriting normally was less the penman's than the
student's, rather small and meant to move quickly across the page. In
doodling, his strokes were more expansive, underscored with squiggles
and bold lines, expressive of large dreams. What he wrote, over and
over, was his name, *John Mercer Langston, John M. Langston, J. M. Langston, Langston, Langston,* with only slight variations in the *L* and *g*, then
a large and fancy *Langston, Elyria* with a much looped *E*, a big impressive *Langston* with the cross of the *t* and tail of the *n* looped into and
merging with an equally large *Ohio.* For that unguarded moment, the
brilliant young black man felt confident he could take on the world and
win the laurels of profession and society. *Langston Esqr.* Again. *Langston
Esqr.*[88]

NOTES

1. Cleveland *Herald*, Aug. 26, 1854.

2. *Colored American*, May 20, 1893; Knoxville *Whig*, Dec. 24, 1853, quoted in Clayton S. Ellsworth, "Oberlin and the Anti-Slavery Movement Up to the Civil War," Ph.D. diss., Cornell University, 1930, p. 115; Cleveland *True-Democrat*, June 19, 1852.

3. *Proceedings of the Convention of the Colored Freemen of Ohio . . . Cincinnati . . . Jan., 1852* (Cincinnati,1852).

4. *Philanthropist*, June 23, 1840, Aug. 9, 1853, Feb. 7, Aug. 28, 1844; "McD" to Editor, *Emancipator*, Dec. 21, 1853; Wilbur H. Siebert, *The Mysteries of Ohio's Underground Railroad* (Columbus, 1951), p. 34; Levi Coffin, *Reminiscences of Levi Coffin, the Reputed President of the Underground Railroad* (2d ed., Cincinnati, 1880), pp. 300–1; Cincinnati *Gazette*, Sept. 20, 1850; *Anti-Slavery Bugle*, Oct. 5, 1850.

5. Cincinnati *Gazette*, Apr. 28, 29, 30, 1852; *Herald of Freedom* (Wilmington, Ohio), Apr. 30, May 7, 1852; *Western Citizen*, n.d., quoted in *Frederick Douglass' Paper*, June 3, 1852; *Voice of the Fugitive*, May 6, 1852; Cincinnati *Times*, n.d., quoted in *Frederick Douglass' Paper*, May 13, 1852; *Anti-Slavery Bugle*, May 8, 15, 29, 1852; *Liberator*, May 7, 14, 28, 1852.

6. Oberlin Young Men's Anti-Slavery Society Records, ms., Oberlin College Archives.

7. Cincinnati *Gazette*, Apr. 28, 1852; *Frederick Douglass' Paper*, May 6, 1852; *Anti-Slavery Bugle*, May 8, 1852; *Voice of the Fugitive*, May 6, 1852.

8. *Frederick Douglass' Paper*, May 20, 1852; Charles C. Burleigh to Garrison, Apr. 30, 1852, *Liberator*, May 14, 1852; Cleveland *True-Democrat*, June 11, 1852; *Anti-Slavery Bugle*, July 3, 1852; Oberlin Young Men's Anti-Slavery Society Records.

9. *Liberator*, May 7, 1852; Richard H. Sewall, *Ballots for Freedom* (New York, 1976), p. 244; Cleveland *True-Democrat*, Aug. 13, 26, 1852; *Frederick Douglass' Paper*, Aug. 26, 1852.

10. Elyria *Independent Democrat*, Sept. 1, 1852; Frederick J. Blue, *The Free Soilers: Third Party Politics, 1848–1854* (Urbana, 1973), pp. 136, 189, 193–94, 198, 261; Elyria *Courier*, Sept. 1, 1852.

11. N.S. Townshend, "The Forty-Seventh General Assembly of Ohio—Comments upon Mr. Riddle's Paper," *Magazine of Western History* 6 (1887):623–28; Cincinnati *Gazette*, Sept. 12, 1850; Ellsworth, "Oberlin and the Anti-Slavery Movement," pp. 110, 115; Blue, *The Free Soilers*, p. 261.

12. John Mercer Langston, *From the Virginia Plantation to the National Capitol; or, The First and Only Negro Representative in Congress from the Old Dominion* (Hartford, 1894; repr. New York: Johnson Reprint, 1968), pp. 137–39; Cleveland *True-Democrat*, Sept. 8, 1852.

13. Langston, *Virginia Plantation*, pp. 137–39. The Population Census of 1850, Roll 705, Ohio, Lorain County, Ohio, Avon township, NA, lists Joseph P. Ladd, 28, profession: Swedenborgian minister.

14. Oberlin Young Men's Anti-Slavery Society Records.

15. Sewell, *Ballots for Freedom*, pp. 97–101; *Frederick Douglass' Paper*, Aug. 13, 1852; *Anti-Slavery Bugle*, Aug. 14, Sept. 11, 1852; untitled clipping, n.d., John Mercer Langston Scrapbooks, 4 vols., II, Moorland-Spingarn Research Center, Howard University.

16. *National Anti-Slavery Standard*, Aug. 19, 1852; Elyria *Courier*, Sept. 8, 1852; Cleveland *Plain Dealer*, Sept. 9, 1852; Cleveland *True-Democrat*, Sept. 9, 19, 1852; *Anti-Slavery Bugle*, Sept. 18, 1852; *Frederick Douglass' Paper*, Aug. 6, Sept. 17, Oct. 15, 1852; Lawrence W. Minor to Frederick Douglass, *Frederick Douglass' Paper*, Oct. 1, 1852.

17. W. H. Day to Democracy of Ohio, Sept. 15, 1852, Cleveland *Herald*, n.d., quoted in *Frederick Douglass' Paper*, Oct. 15, 1852; *Frederick Douglass' Paper*, Oct. 15, 1852.

18. Cleveland *True-Democrat*, n.d., quoted in *Frederick Douglass' Paper*, Oct. 29, 1852; Blue, *The Free Soilers*, pp. 261–62, 269–70.

19. Merton L. Dillon, *The Abolitionists: The Growth of a Dissenting Minority* (DeKalb, 1974), pp. 199–204.

20. Elyria *Independent-Democrat*, Jan. 12, 19, 1853; Cincinnati *Gazette*, Apr. 21, 1853.

21. Blue, *The Free Soilers*, p. 271; Salmon P. Chase to E. S. Hamlin, Feb. 4, 1853, *Diary and Correspondence of Salmon P. Chase* (Washington, 1903; repr. New York: DaCapo Press, 1971), pp. 249–50.

22. Blue, *The Free Soilers*, p. 271; *Official Proceedings of the Ohio State Convention of Colored Freemen . . . Columbus . . . 1853* (Cleveland, 1853); Oberlin *Evangelist*, Feb. 2, 1853.

23. *Frederick Douglass' Paper*, Jan. 7, 1853; *State Convention*, 1853; David Jenkins to Frederick Douglass, May 23, 1853, *Frederick Douglass' Paper*, June 3, 1853; *National Anti-Slavery Standard*, July 19, 1853.

24. *The Aliened American*, Apr. 9, 1853; New York *Tribune*, May 3, 1853; W. H. Day to Editor, May 9, 1853, New York *Tribune*, May 21, 1853; *Anti-Slavery Bugle*, Aug. 27, 1853; Cleveland *True-Democrat*, Aug. 24, 1853; *Frederick Douglass' Paper*, July 29, Sept. 2, May 19, 1854; John N. Still to Frederick Douglass, Apr. 18, 1854, *Frederick Douglass' Paper*, Apr. 28, 1854; Cleveland *Herald*, Aug. 26, 1854; Cleveland *Forest City Democrat*, Jan. 25, 1854; *National Anti-Slavery Standard*, July 19, 1853.

25. Cincinnati *Gazette*, Apr. 20, 21, 22, 1853; *Anti-Slavery Bugle*, Apr. 30, May 7, 21, 1853; *Liberator*, Apr. 22, May 6, 1853; *Herald of Freedom*, Apr. 29, 1853.

26. *Anti-Slavery Bugle*, May 21, 1853. Compare black Ohioans' opposition to adoption of Garnet's "Address . . ." in 1843 National Convention. *Minutes of the National Convention . . . Buffalo . . . 1843* in *Proceedings of the National Negro Conventions*, ed. Howard H. Bell (New York, 1969).

27. Cincinnati *Gazette*, Apr. 21, 1853; *Anti-Slavery Bugle*, May 7, 1853; *Frederick Douglass' Paper*, May 20, 1853; *Herald of Freedom*, Apr. 29, 1853.

28. George M. Fredrickson, *The Black Image in the White Mind* (New York, 1971), pp. 97–129.

29. *Herald of Freedom*, Apr. 29, 1853; Cincinnati *Gazette*, Apr. 21, 1853;

Anti-Slavery Bugle, May 7, 1853; *Frederick Douglass' Paper*, May 20, 1853; *Liberator*, May 6, 1853; Cincinnati *Gazette*, Apr. 22, 1853.

30. *Liberator*, May 6, 1853; Speech of Frederick Douglass at annual meeting of American and Foreign Anti-Slavery Society, New York City, May 1953, in *The Life and Writings of Frederick Douglass*, ed. Philip S. Foner, 5 vols. (New York, 1950, pb., 1975), II, p. 246.

31. *Herald of Freedom*, Apr. 29, 1853; *Anti-Slavery Bugle*, May 7, 1853; *Frederick Douglass' Paper*, May 20, 1853; *Liberator*, May 6, 1853; Cincinnati *Gazette*, Apr. 21, 22, 1853.

32. *Frederick Douglass' Paper*, May 6, 20, June 17, 1853; Cleveland *True-Democrat*, June 13, 1853; *Proceedings of the Colored National Convention, Held in Rochester, July 6th, 7th, and 8th, 1853* (Rochester, 1853); Howard Holman Bell, *A Survey of the Negro Convention Movement, 1830–1861* (New York, 1969), p. 166; *Frederick Douglass' Paper*, Sept. 8, 1854. Ohioans prominent at the convention included Day, a vice-president; Clark, secretary; C. H. Langston and Gaines, business committee; Jenkins, finance committee; A. J. Gordon, A. M. Sumner, and the Rev. Benjamin Templeton. No complete delegate list is available.

33. *Colored National Convention, 1853*, pp. 27–28.

34. Ibid., pp. 20–26; New York *Tribune*, July 15, 1853. Langston's appreciation of Duncanson (1821–72), one of the major artists of his day, as a black "producer" contrasts with recent criticism faulting the painter for not taking a more active role in the black struggle. Compare David C. Driskell, *Two Centuries of Black American Art* (New York, 1976), pp. 39–44.

35. New York *Tribune*, July 15, Sept. 27, 1853; *Frederick Douglass' Paper*, n.d. quoted in *Anti-Slavery Bugle*, July 23, 1853; Rochester *American*, n.d., and Rochester *Democrat*, n.d., both quoted in *Liberator*, July 28, 1853; *Colored National Convention, 1853*, passim.

36. Frederick Douglass to Harriet Beecher Stowe, Mar. 8, 1853, quoted in *Colored National Convention, 1853*, pp. 33–38; *Frederick Douglass' Paper*, Mar. 4, 18, Apr. 1, May 6, 1853.

37. *Frederick Douglass' Paper*, May 6, July 25, 1853; Delany to Douglass, Mar. 23, 1853, and "Remarks," *Frederick Douglass' Paper*, Apr. 1, 1853; William H. Pease and Jane H. Pease, *They Who Would Be Free: Blacks Search for Freedom, 1830–1861* (New York, 1974), pp. 260–63; Bell, *A Survey of the Negro Convention Movement, 1830–1861*, pp. 134–35, 152–56; Floyd J. Miller, *The Search for a Black Nationality, Black Emigration and Colonization, 1787–1863* (Urbana, 1975), pp. 134–44.

38. *Frederick Douglass' Paper*, extracts, quoted in *Liberator*, Aug. 26, 1853; W. C. Nell to W. L. Garrison, Aug. 19, 1853, *Liberator*, Sept. 2, 1853; Robert Purvis to Garrison, Aug. 22, 1853, *Liberator*, Sept. 16, 1853; *Liberator*, Aug. 12, 1853–Jan. 27, 1854, passim; *Frederick Douglass' Paper*, Mar. 31, July 28, 1854; William C. Nell to George T. Downing, Sept. 12, 1854, in William C. Nell Papers, Boston Public Library. Even after Douglass and Garrison, at the pleading of their friends, dropped the quarrel from their respective newspapers, it continued to surface at antislavery gatherings. For example, see Syracuse *Chronicle*, n.d., quoted in *Liberator*, Oct. 13, 1854. For discussions of Douglass's split with

the Garrisonians, see Waldo E. Martin, Jr., *The Mind of Frederick Douglass* (Chapel Hill, 1984), pp. 38–48; Philip S. Foner, *Frederick Douglass* (New York, 1964), pp. 137–54.

39. *Frederick Douglass' Paper*, Jan. 2, 1854; H. B. Stowe to Garrison, Dec. 19 (1853), anti-slavery letters to Garrison, Boston Public Library, quoted in Foner, *Frederick Douglass*, pp. 151–52; H. B. Stowe to Ladies Anti-Slavery Society in Glasgow, quoted in *Liberator*, Jan. 6, 1854; Benjamin Quarles, *Frederick Douglass* (Washington, D. C., 1948; repr. Boston: Atheneum, 1968), p. 131; *Frederick Douglass' Paper*, n.d., quoted in *Liberator*, Apr. 14, 1854; W. C. Nell to Garrison, *Liberator*, Jan. 27, 1854; *Liberator*, Feb. 24, 1854; *Aliened American*, Apr. 1, 1854, quoted in *Liberator*, Apr. 14, 1854.

40. *Frederick Douglass' Paper*, Oct. 23, Dec. 2, 1853, July 28, 1854; Day, O. S. B. Wall, John Booker, Justin Holland, William C. Nell to Douglass, Aug. 7, 1854, *Frederick Douglass' Paper*, Sept. 1, 1854; *Liberator*, Dec. 23, 1853, Feb. 24, 1854; *Aliened American*, Apr. 1, 1854, quoted in *Liberator*, Apr. 14, 1854; R. J. M. Blackett, *Beating Against the Barriers: Biographical Essays in Nineteenth-Century Afro-American History* (Baton Rouge, 1986), pp. 305–9; Bell, *A Survey of the Negro Convention Movement*, pp. 165–78.

41. David Jenkins to Douglass, Dec. 25, 1854, *Frederick Douglass' Paper*, Jan. 4, 1855; Jenkins to Douglass, June 16, 1855, *Frederick Douglass' Paper*, June 29, 1855; Bell, *A Survey of the Negro Convention Movement*, pp. 178–80; *Proceedings of the Colored National Convention, Held in Franklin Hall . . . Philadelphia, October 16th, 17th, and 18th, 1855* (Salem, N. J., 1856).

42. New York *Tribune*, May 10, 11, 1855; New York *Times*, May 11, 12, 1855; New York *Herald*, May 10, 1855.

43. New York *Tribune*, July 15, 1853; *Frederick Douglass' Paper*, Aug. 19, 26, 1853, June 16, Nov. 10, 1854.

44. New York *Tribune*, July 19, 1853; *Liberator*, July 22, 29, 1853; *Frederick Douglass' Paper*, July 22, Aug. 5, 1853.

45. Langston to William C. Nell, Aug. 19, 1853, *Liberator*, Sept. 2, 1853; *National Anti-Slavery Standard*, July 19, 1853.

46. Langston, *Virginia Plantation*, pp. 116–17; Mary Dascomb and Louisa Fitch to James Monroe, Nov. 12, 16, 1863, quoted in Robert S. Fletcher, *A History of Oberlin College*, 2 vols. (Oberlin, 1943), II, p. 778.

47. A.L. Shumway, *Oberliniana, 1833–1883* (Cleveland, 1883), p. 103; J. H. Fairchild, "Oberlin: Its Origin, Progress and Results," Oberlin *Evangelist*, Oct. 10, 1860.

48. Langston, *Virginia Plantation*, pp. 115–16, 113; John Mercer Langston, "The Intellectual, Moral, and Spiritual Condition of the Slave," in *Autographs for Freedom*, ed. Julia Griffiths (Rochester, 1854), pp. 147–49; First Congregational Church, Treasurer's Records, 1860–65, ms., Oberlin College Archives; New York *Independent*, Sept. 25, 1851.

49. Newport *News*, n.d., quoted in *Anti-Slavery Bugle*, Feb. 12, 1853; Cincinnati *Commercial*, n.d., and Cleveland *True-Democrat*, n.d., quoted in *Anti-Slavery Bugle*, Sept. 3, 1853; *Frederick Douglass' Paper*, Aug. 26, 1853; *Liberator*, Sept. 30, 1853.

50. Griffiths, ed., *Autographs for Freedom*, pp. 149–50; William Waring, "Skepticism Among Negroes," address to Literary Society of Bethel Church, Washington, D.C., Jan. 3, 1882, *People's Advocate*, Jan. 21, 1882.

51. Oberlin *Evangelist*, Feb. 28, 1849; John Mercer Langston, *Freedom and Citizenship* (Washington, 1883; repr. Miami: Mnemosyne Reprint, 1969), p. 76.

52. J. E. Rankin, introductory sketch, Langston, *Freedom and Citizenship*, p. 33; Cincinnati *Gazette*, Apr. 21, 1853; *Minutes of the State Convention of the Colored Citizens of Ohio . . . Columbus . . . Jan. 1, 1851* (Columbus, 1851).

53. Langston to Azariah Root, Dec. 14, 1894, John Mercer Langston, Alumni Records, Oberlin College Archives.

54. J. P. Bardwell to George Whipple, Oct. 31, Nov. 5, 1862, American Missionary Association Archives, Amistad Research Center, Tulane University (hereafter cited as AMA Papers).

55. *Frederick Douglass' Paper*, Nov. 10, 1854; *Catalogue of the Officers and Students of Oberlin College, for the College Year 1852–53* (Oberlin, 1853), pp. 9, 40, 48; Oberlin *Evangelist*, Aug. 31, 1853; *Quinquennial Catalogue of the Officers and Graduates of Oberlin College* (Oberlin, 1916), p. 488; Langston, Alumni Records; Langston, *Virginia Plantation*, pp. 112–13.

56. New York *Tribune*, July 19, 1853; *Philanthropist*, Aug. 28, 1838, Dec. 17, 1839; Williams Brothers, *History of Lorain County* (Philadelphia, 1879), pp. 49, 137; U.S. Government, *Biographical Directory of the American Congress* (Washington, D. C., 1971), p. 604. Admitted to the bar in Elyria in 1838, Bliss, after a brief western sojourn for health reasons, lived in Elyria from 1846 to the spring of 1861, when President Lincoln appointed him chief justice of Dakota territory. Subsequently, he moved to St. Joseph, Missouri, where he served as associate justice of the Missouri supreme court (1866–72), and dean of the law division of the University of Missouri at Columbia (1872–89). He died in 1889 at St. Paul, Minnesota, at the age of seventy-six. He served two terms in Congress, March 4, 1855–March 3, 1859, as a Republican.

57. Elyria *Independent-Democrat*, Jan. 12, 19, 1853.

58. Langston, *Virginia Plantation*, pp. 117–20. The Population Census of 1850, Roll 705, Ohio, Lorain County, Avon township, NA, lists Philemon Bliss, his wife Martha, two males, 5 and 3; three females, 50, 23, 13.

59. Elyria *Independent-Democrat*, Oct. 25, 1853.

60. Anton-Herman Chroust, *The Rise of the Legal Profession in America*, 2 vols. (Norman, 1965), I, pp. 105–6; John P. Frank, *Lincoln as a Lawyer* (Urbana, 1961), p. 11; Langston, *Virginia Plantation*, pp. 122–24.

61. Elyria *Independent-Democrat*, Sept. 28, 1853; Blue, *The Free Soilers*, pp. 272–73; Sewell, *Ballots for Freedom*, p. 252.

62. Cleveland *True-Democrat*, Sept. 28, 1853; Elyria *Independent-Democrat*, Oct. 25, 1853; Peter H. Clark to John Mercer Langston, Jan. 22, 1854; O. S. B. Wall to John Mercer Langston, Jan. 25, 1854; W. H. Burnham to John Mercer Langston, Feb. 6, 1854; John Mercer Langston to Auditor of Gallia County, Jan. 29, 1854; sample letter by Langston requesting information from county auditors, Jan. 19, 1854; all in John Mercer Langston Papers, Fisk University Library.

63. "Memorial of J. Mercer Langston to the General Assembly of the State of Ohio," *Frederick Douglass' Paper*, June 16, 1854; William C. Nell, *The Colored Patriots of the American Revolution* (Boston, 1855), pp. 336–41.

64. Nell, *The Colored Patriots*, pp. 336–41; *Anti-Slavery Bugle*, Apr. 1, 1854.

65. *Anti-Slavery Bugle*, Jan. 14, 28, Feb. 4, 11, Apr. 23, 1854; Cleveland *Forest City Democrat*, Jan. 24, Feb. 17, 1854; New York *Times*, Jan. 30, 1854; New York *Tribune*, Feb. 9, 1854.

66. *Aliened American*, n.d., quoted in *Anti-Slavery Bugle*, Apr. 1, 1854; "Report of the Select Committee on Petitions and Memorials from Colored Persons, in the Senate," Apr. 19, 1854, *Frederick Douglass' Paper*, June 16, 1854.

67. John Mercer Langston to the Colored Men of the State of Ohio, Mar. 25, 1854, Langston Papers; *Aliened American*, n.d. quoted in *Anti-Slavery Bugle*, Apr. 8, 1854.

68. New York *Tribune*, July 19, 1853.

69. Cleveland *Forest City Democrat*, Jan. 25, 1854; Oberlin *Evangelist*, Feb. 15, Mar. 15, 1854; Cleveland *Herald*, Feb. 8, 1854.

70. C.W.K. to Editor, July 3, 1854, Cleveland *Leader*, July 6, 1854; Oberlin *Evangelist*, July 6, 1854.

71. Rufus P. Spalding, Cleveland attorney, quoted in J. W. Schuckers, *Life and Public Services of Salmon Portland Chase* (New York, 1874; repr. Miami: Mnemosyne Reprint, 1969), p. 165, fn.

72. John A. Reed to Dear Sir, June 6, 1854, A.M.A. Papers; Oberlin *Evangelist*, Aug. 16, 1854; Cleveland *Leader*, Aug. 15, 1854.

73. Oberlin *Evangelist*, Aug. 30, 1854; Cleveland *Leader*, Aug. 26, Sept. 2, 1854; S. L. Adair to Jocelyn, Aug. 25, 1854, A.M.A. Papers; Ellsworth, "Oberlin and the Anti-Slavery Movement," pp. 136–64.

74. Samuel A. S. Lowery to Editor, Jan. 31, 1855, *Provincial Freeman*, Feb. 17, 1855; John I. Gaines to Editor, *Frederick Douglass' Paper*, Jan. 27, 1854; David Jenkins to Editor, *Frederick Douglass' Paper*, Oct. 23, 1853; J. M. Whitfield to Editor, *Frederick Douglass' Paper*, Nov. 25, 1853; *Frederick Douglass' Paper*, July 6, 1854; *Liberator*, Aug. 25, 1854; Cleveland *Leader*, Aug. 25, 1854; *Proceedings of the National Emigration Convention of Colored People . . . Cleveland, Ohio . . . August, 1854* (Pittsburgh, 1854), pp. 16–18. Women delegates, normally uncounted in black conventions, boosted attendance figures by one-third.

75. George B. Vashon, "The Late Cleveland Convention," *Frederick Douglass' Paper*, Nov. 17, 1854.

76. W. H. Burnham to Langston, Feb. 6, 1854, Langston Papers; *Emigration Convention . . . 1854*, p. 13; W. H. Day, "Proceedings of the Colored People's Convention," Cleveland *Herald*, Aug. 26, 1854.

77. Vashon, "Convention"; Lowery to Editor, Jan. 31, 1855, *Provincial Freeman*, Feb. 17, 1855; Day, "Convention."

78. Day, "Convention"; *Emigration Convention . . . 1854*, p. 13; *Speech of H. Ford Douglass, in Reply to Mr. J. M. Langston Before the Emigration Convention . . . August, 1854* (Chicago, 1854).

79. Vashon, "Convention"; David Jenkins to Editor, Oct. 17, 1854, *Frederick Douglass' Paper*, Oct. 27, 1854; *Frederick Douglass' Paper*, Oct. 20, 1854.

80. Minute Book of the Western Anti-Slavery Society, Proceedings of Twelfth Anniversary, Library of Congress; *Liberator*, Sept. 8, 1854.

81. Langston, *Virginia Plantation*, pp. 123–24; St. Louis *Globe-Democrat*, Oct. 5, 1890; Chicago *Times*, Sept. 28, 1890, both in Langston Scrapbook, III.

82. Langston, *Virginia Plantation*, pp. 124–25; *Ohio State Journal*, Sept. 28, 1889; Cincinnati *Gazette*, June 6, 1867 (quotes altered from third to first person).

83. Cleveland *Leader*, Oct. 12, 13, 1854; Sewell, *Ballots for Freedom*, p. 273. On the Republican party in its early years, see William E. Gienapp, *The Origins of the Republican Party, 1852–1856* (New York, 1987).

84. Boston *Globe*, Sept. 26, 1891; Boston *Herald*, Sept. 26, 1891, both in Langston Scrapbook, III.

85. Pease and Pease, *They Who Would Be Free*, pp. 204–5.

86. David Donald, *Charles Sumner and the Coming of the Civil War* (New York, 1960), p. 253.

87. Elyria *Independent-Democrat*, Oct. 25, 1853.

88. Blue note paper, dated Elyria, Apr. 25, 1854, and reverse side of Dear Henry, 1854, Langston Papers.

CHAPTER 8

Law, Marriage, and Public Place

1854–56

I N late March of 1854, six months before his bar examination, Langston had made final payment on the $3 thousand purchase price for
a lush fifty-acre farm near Lake Erie. In mid-September, the newly
accredited attorney moved to the farm. Situated about nine miles from
Oberlin and fourteen from Elyria, the homestead was part of Brownhelm township, settled in 1817 and 1818 by a colony from Stockbridge,
Massachusetts. "Puritan in thought, purpose, education and character," as Langston found them, the former New Englanders tended not
only one of the most fertile farming areas on the Western Reserve, but
also vigorous antislavery sentiments, and, to a "really and truthfully
exceptional degree," a humane social climate. In an important respect,
however, the 1,200-strong citizenry had not had its abolitionism tried.
No Negro had ever before lived in Brownhelm.[1] Langston's professional, domestic, and political ambitions—his public pronouncements
and private hopes for a fully realized black life in white America—
would be tested against the limits of racial equality in an all-white
abolitionist community.

By his telling, the move was precipitated by the "considerably dis-
turbed" state of his health. His physical indisposition had, in fact been
noticeable during his New York City appearances the preceding
summer,[2] and by January had forced him to consult a physician. Apparently the problem, common for students of the day, was overwork.
Although he was only twenty-four, even a robust, energetic constitution
like his might well rebel under the rigorous study discipline of years
climaxed by anxious engrossment in the law. Lecturing, campaigning,
and reform activities added to the strain. At the same time, the drives

that fueled these activities—the need to submerge private insecurities in the public cause of abolition and black advancement, as well as the continual pressures to be exemplary—surely exacted a toll. An additional factor may well have been worry over potential failure, first, to gain admission to the bar, and then, to win a practice. Certainly, as John Mercer tried for this racial breakthrough, he had been "warned a thousand times that the fate of the Negro was sealed, and in the decree which fixed the destiny of the blackhued son of the race, his own position was determined and settled!" As Frederick Douglass had observed, potential white clients would not employ black lawyers "to the obvious embarrassment of their causes, and the blacks taking their *cue* from whites, have not sufficient confidence in their abilities to employ them." The editor, overlooking Robert Morris's apparently comfortable practice in Boston, had deemed Langston's predecessors "great failures."[3] At any rate, whatever the causes for John Mercer's condition, the doctor's suggested cure, a typical remedy for the harassed scholar, was at least two years of fresh air and physical exercise, to begin as soon as he completed his legal studies. Langston's purchase of the Brownhelm farm not only provided the setting to fill the prescription, but also established him in the independent, self-reliant life of the yeoman farmer that was the predominant national ideal, one continually urged on their followers by the Ohio black leadership. And it permitted a prudent fallback from the risks of professional failure.

The farm, which included a two-story frame house, a barn, a cornhouse, and other buildings, as well as fields and orchard, John Mercer rented in late January 1854 to an English family, Thomas Slater, his wife, and their son John. Slater "was a servant in the old country," Langston would recount. Eventually, with his Negro landlord doing the legal work, Slater would collect enough money from an English estate to set himself up as the farmer of a substantial acreage. When the English immigrant retained a subservient manner even then, Langston remonstrated. But Slater explained that he had served his former master "so long and so faithfully with my hat in my hand or under my arm in their presence that when I went into the presence of this man I involuntarily took off my hat and put it under my arm and I could not help it." Fully aware of the irony, the black American, in pure mid-century democratic spirit, would admonish the Englishman: "Slater, put on your hat." By terms of the contract between Langston and Slater, the latter was obligated to furnish one-half the seed, tend the stock, and cultivate the farm "in good and husbandlike manner," while the two would split the profits. Moreover, the Slaters, installed in the farmhouse, agreed to accommodate Langston with room and board, and do his "washing and mending."[4]

While Langston's choice of white tenants may have been, in part, a propitiatory gesture toward his white neighbors, the decision to live under the same roof with them doubtless reflected his reform philosophy. Like white abolitionists Augustus Wattles and Theodore Dwight Weld, who had chosen to live with black families, John Mercer believed "reformers ought to live up to the principles which they seek to impress upon mankind." "If they are preachers of Liberty and Equality, without distinction of sex or color," he held, reformers were obligated, within reason, to manifest their beliefs in their daily lives. For most of his life, a white domestic would be included in the Langston household.[5]

One day quite soon after his move onto the farm, when he and the younger Slater were grubbing out the fall's turnip crop, a white stranger approached and asked for "Lawyer Langston." John Mercer's reaction was peculiar. Perhaps his caller's inability to distinguish him from his English farmhand struck him as ludicrous. Or perhaps he felt the need somehow to contain his suddenly soaring hopes. In any event, Langston, whose quick wits early had seized on humor as means of self-defense, decided to play a practical joke. Wiping away a little dirt and sweat, he informed the visitor he could find Mr. Langston at the house and escorted him there. Shortly thereafter, having washed and donned his "Sunday clothes," the attorney made a dramatic reappearance in his own parlor. "I am Mr. Langston," he announced. Undeterred, the stranger introduced himself as Hamilton Perry and explained his mission. Perry, "not a regular member of the bar but what was called a pettifogger," as Langston would put it, was about to face young Stevenson Burke of Elyria, a crack young lawyer then six years into what would become an eminent legal career.[6] Burke's client, the plaintiff, was suing for immediate possession of his house, which was occupied by Perry's client. Perry asked Langston's assistance. "I was so pleased I could hardly hold myself back," Langston would recall. Still, he uneasily queried Perry as to whether he really "wanted me, for the assistance of a Negro might prejudice his case." On being reassured, Langston "gladly consented, although I was fearful he would change his mind before the day of trial."

As Langston told the story, a week later, on a Saturday afternoon in early October, the case was tried. To handle the throng, augmented by some who had traveled "from miles around" to witness the novel spectacle, Brownhelm Justice of the Peace Samuel Curtis prudently moved the trial from his home office to a capacious barn. Perry began the defense but early yielded to his black colleague. Convinced "that his all was staked upon it," Langston conducted the cross-examination, presentation of defense witnesses, and summation. He "labored and spoke in it with the earnestness and power of one who would win victory against any and every opposition." The hearing, begun at 1 o'clock, had continued for more than eight hours before argumentation to the jury began, but the spectators did not budge. Finally, the jurymen, without stirring from their seats, unanimously declared for the defendant. On the midnight drive home where, for consolation or celebration, Mrs. Slater's best cup of tea and "most inviting country supper" awaited, John Mercer, health problems presumably forgotten in the excitement, announced triumphantly to his hired man: "I shall never do another day's work on the farm. I am going to practice law."[7]

The inadvertent assistance of temperance advocates enabled him to keep his word. A ban on sale of alcoholic beverages for consumption on store premises, sought by Langston's allies in the Free Democratic party for the past two years, had just been enacted by the Ohio legislature. With Carson Leagues and other temperance groups on the Reserve, particularly in the Oberlin vicinity, eager for enforcement, the prospects for retail liquor dealers looked grim. Temperance committees, armed with witnesses and lawyers, were descending upon dealers, and mass arrests were underway. As for opponents of the anti-liquor law, the Cleveland *Leader* noted complacently, only their lawyers stood "much chance of realizing much profit in the contest."[8]

The morning after his first trial, John Mercer was indulging in Sunday breakfast and a self-congratulatory review of his triumph when a knock came at the door. It was a white liquor dealer, seeking Langston to defend him against prosecution under the new law. A staunch temperance man himself, who had "descanted at length on the evils of intemperance" and supported legal curbs on whiskey sales, John Mercer accepted the dealer's retainer with alacrity. Any possible qualms he could rationalize, in the words of his clerical biographer: "A young lawyer is compelled to take the clients who first knock at his office door." All that Sunday, according to Langston's recollection, a steady stream of liquor vendors came knocking.[9]

From this beginning Langston speedily made his mark in the backwoods as a criminal lawyer. Even discounting his claim that he "cleared quite every one charged with crime whose defense he attempted," the balance of acquittals obviously was so markedly in his favor that clients of the type he first attracted continued to give him business. Often poorly educated English or Irish immigrants, they were mainly Democrats. Such men sought out the Negro attorney, more than probably, not simply for his growing reputation, but with the concomitant notion that, with some antislavery judges and juries, their own less than respectable status and minority politics might be enhanced by association with his ambiguous status and minority race. Moreover, they may have sensed that Langston's desperation to win approximated their own. Within the year after his first case, Langston would be engaged full-time in practice of the law.[10]

In the fall of 1854, in the flush of first success, John Mercer felt the time had come for a "most serious change"[11]—his marriage. Although his own needs and desires were paramount, the ideal of black womanhood described by Ohio black reformers and exampled, in part, by reform-minded black women unavoidably influenced his choice of a wife. The ideal black woman, as defined by Ohio black leaders, had much in common with her white sister. Essential attributes of the latter, it was insisted in protracted public discussion, were piety, chastity, submissiveness, and domesticity. Likewise expected to exhibit "native modesty, industry, . . . virtue, cleanliness of person," the black lady—to a greater extent than her Caucasian sister—was supposed to display "Christian intelligence" and education, or "at least a love for learning." "We want educated colored young men and young women; yes, educated young women," Oberlin black student Davis Day had counseled in 1841, "for although many of our people think there is no need of educating their daughters, yet rely upon it, the elevation of our race depends in a great degree upon the talents and education of our females." In actuality, black women educated at Oberlin made major contributions to black schooling in Ohio.[12] Moreover, through necessity, the black woman was expected to be more independent and somewhat more assertive than the white. She was encouraged to move toward "a new sense of character, to a new self-respect."[13]

Ohio's upstanding black females regularly extended woman's sphere in behalf of black elevation. Expected to manage the household and do the daily marketing, black "ladies" always seemed to be conducting fairs and festivals whose proceeds went to furnish instruments for the band and uniforms for the Cincinnati Attucks Blues, to hire the halls for black conventions and reform meetings, or to other community projects. As elsewhere, black women in Ohio played "an active and untrammeled" role in their churches. In old age, Sarah Jane Woodson Early, the daughter of the pioneer black Ohio communitarians Thomas and Jemima Woodson—who was graduated from Oberlin College in 1856 and taught first at Wilberforce University and at schools in the South from 1868 until her retirement in 1888—recalled that in her own A.M.E. church, women had raised funds to build the churches and support the ministers, assisted in prayer and class meetings as well as in Sabbath schools and, when necessary, opened their own homes for public worship. She also remembered the power of women preachers—some of whom were especially "talented in speech" and "eloquent in prayer." Reflecting on women's religious experience, Early, who was superintendent of the Negro division of the Women's Christian Temperance Union from 1888 until 1892, noted: "The freedom which they enjoyed in their worship and the satisfaction arising from equal rights in church privileges made the work more precious and secured to them greater hopes for future success." For women, the church was "an open door by which to enter the arena of public action."[14]

Not uncommonly, the black woman who was employed as a teacher, or as a milliner, dressmaker, shirtmaker, or tailoress (one observer estimated a hundred or so such skilled tradeswomen in Cincinnati in the mid-fifties) was likewise the one who solicited for the black newspapers and raised money to publish proceedings of the conventions.[15] As Ohio's black females strove to promote moral purity, taking an assertive role in a moral reform society that was pledged to "treat the licentiousness of both sexes alike," or in organizations such as the temperance-directed Daughters of Samaria, so they were attentive to the arranging of decorations that adorned the festivities for freedom, to the sewing of banners that flew in parades for equality, to the cooking of enormous quantities of food, whose excellence was universally acclaimed, for the First of August celebrations.[16] If these black women instructed their children, teaching the domestic arts and instilling patience, perseverance, and self-reliance, they also organized various benevolent societies, ranging from the Female American Association of Cincinnati, which cared for the sick and infirm, to the Cincinnati orphan asylum, whose active members included W. W. Watson's wife Ruthellen, and Peter Clark's mother Eliza, to the Colored Ladies Benevolent Sewing Society of Cleveland, which canvassed for clothing, sewed, and ordered goods for the benefit of runaway slaves.[17] While seeing to the needs of boarders and members of extended-kinship families, both common in middle-class black homes, the women in charge might also furnish food and lodging to runaways.[18] On occasion, their aid to fugitives went further. In 1848, a spontaneously assembled group of black women thwarted several white southerners in their attempt to locate a fugitive slave, stimulating a black man's feeling invocation: "God bless the ladies of Cincinnati, they are ahead in every work."[19]

Black women often attended protest gatherings and conventions, although not as official delegates, sometimes contributing a song or toast to the proceedings.[20] At the 1849 state convention in Columbus they did more. Irritated at not being allowed a say, they held a caucus and through Jane P. Merritt, the wife of one of the delegates, submitted a resolution that William Howard Day, chairman of the business committee, read to the convention: "Whereas, we the ladies have been invited to attend the Convention, and have been deprived of a voice, which we the ladies deem wrong and shameful. Therefore, RESOLVED, That we will attend no more after tonight, unless the privilege is granted." After some debate, the resolution won adoption.[21] Nonetheless, apart from the noted antislavery lecturer and poet Frances Ellen Watkins, the published reports of the conventions of the fifties noted only one woman's voice, that of the Oberlin-educated Sara G. Stanley. On behalf of the Delaware Ladies Anti-Slavery Society, Stanley—a freeborn North Carolinian (1838?–1916) who taught in black schools in Ohio during an eight-year period before going South with the American Missionary Association to teach the freed people, to whom she considered herself bound "by the ties of love and consanguinity; they are socially and politically 'my people' "—wrote a rousing letter to the 1856 convention: "To you we would say, be true, be courageous, be steadfast in the discharge of your duty."[22]

In addition to delivering an occasional abolitionist address and joining in strategically timed protests against segregation, black women in Ohio contributed essays, letters, and poems. Noteworthy in this regard were Lucy A. Stanton and Frances Williams, the first and second black women graduates of Oberlin (1850 and 1853): Stanton assisted her husband, William Howard Day, with the publication of his newspaper, *The Aliened American*, which boasted a number of women correspondents; Williams worked as an editor with her husband, Peter Clark, on his *Herald of Freedom*.[23] When the Langstons and their male cohorts in 1858 formed the Ohio State Anti-Slavery Society to work for freedom and the franchise, they appointed a large number of women to county committees charged with holding meetings of the local affiliates of the new society, making private solicitations for donations, and collecting general statistics on black life in their respective localities.[24]

In upcoming years of black reform, John Mercer Langston would count on black women, not only for bringing order and peace to their homes, and for their "business understanding and tact,"[25] not only for the encouragement and prodding of their husbands to speak out against black wrongs as well as to assert black rights, but also for energetic engagement in the campaigns for freedom, enfranchisement, and black political power. For Ohio's black leaders generally, and for Langston, the ideal black woman combined the accepted feminine virtues with intelligence, education, a degree of independence, and racial commitment.

John Mercer believed he had found such a woman in Caroline Matilda Wall. Born in Rockingham, Richmond County, North Carolina in 1833, Caroline was the daughter of Colonel Stephen Wall, a planter who served as a state senator, and his slave Jane. "A noted man," Langston would write in the 1880s, "remembered even to this day by those of his old neighbors who still live," "of superior intelligence and business enterprise,"[26] Wall took to bed at least three of his slave women, all of whom bore him children. Rody was the mother of Albert and John; Priscilla Ely the mother of Napoleon. Prissy's sister Jane Ely—whom Stephen Wall's brother Mial would describe to Caroline in the early 1850s as enjoying "fine health" and looking "as young as ever, or very nearly so"—was the mother of Orindatus Simon Bolivar, called O. S. B. or "Datus," born about 1826, Caroline, Sara, and Benjamin Franklin. All of the children bore the Wall name.[27]

Caroline escaped the scars of bondage, as Langston explained, by her removal "ere she could have understood what slavery was." Wall emancipated her and her sister Sara when they reached a suitable age and sent them to Harveysburg in southwestern Ohio's Warren County. "A good anti-slavery neighborhood," as Quaker Levi Coffin called it, the village of about 450 persons, noted for the proximity of medicinal springs, offered a soothing draught of tolerance in Ohio's racist hinterlands. Predominant among the settlers were Hicksite and Orthodox Friends, sects that supplied long-term activists to the abolitionist movement with the Hicksites especially prominent in the Garrisonian Western Anti-Slavery Society.[28] Moreover, a progressive black settlement flourished nearby. As early as 1842, Harveysburg was the site of a First of August celebration attended by a racially mixed company and staged by Warren County and Clinton County Negroes.[29] At Wall's direction, and with generous subsidies from him, Caroline and her younger sister Sara settled with a white guardian, Nathan Dix; gradually, Wall freed other offspring and entrusted their care and education to the village Friends. The Wall children probably attended the mainly white Harveysburg Academy, although by 1848 a separate, unusually well-conducted black school, taught by one white and one black teacher, would be in operation. Given their "affluent circumstances, under wise and suitable guardianship," as Langston observed, the Wall children were able to pursue "all those amenities and dignities of personal character, in addition to general education, which render life always, in any class of people, worthy and honorable." Any distinction made toward the Wall children, he added, "was in their favor."[30]

In a fulsome encomium, Langston would state that Wall freed Jane to accompany her children, but a letter from Mial Wall to Caroline

in 1853 indicates that both Jane and Prissy were then on the plantation. Langston also would fail to mention that Wall had three slave
mistresses. But if Wall's "sterling qualities" were not tarnish-free, his
conduct toward his children does seem to have been uncommonly responsible. In his will he left $1 thousand to each of his seven freed
offspring, property to Jane's four children, and entrusted his brother
with $15 thousand, the bulk of which was to go toward "aiding, de-
fending, and securing the just rights" of his mulatto children both in
North Carolina and Ohio.[31]

In 1850, Caroline came to Oberlin, studying for a year in the preparatory department before entering the women's collegiate level, the
"ladies literary course." When she and Sara, who would be graduated
from the women's college in 1856, joined the First Church soon after
their arrival, it seemed to Langston that the congregation was deeply
stirred by their appearance and behavior "especially as they would
make public profession of their conversion. They were then the representatives of the best type of the colored girl—intelligent, handsome,
graceful and attractive, winning the sympathy of everyone, as it became
known that they were orphans, who had neither as yet, reached her
eighteenth year."[32]

Sometime that year the "young, handsome North Carolina lady"
caught John Mercer's eye. They were introduced, but not until his
school tour of the state for the Young Men's Anti-Slavery Society in the
winter of 1851–52 did their friendship begin to take form. On his stop
in Harveysburg, Langston was a guest in Caroline's home. Here he
realized that Caroline was more than pretty, more than "talented, refined, and pleasant." He was struck by the dignified self-possession
with which the young girl, who was in charge of the household, ordered
affairs and exercised amiable authority over Sara and her brothers and
half-brothers. Moreover, then and in later meetings, he detected "in
her conversation and behavior, that she was fully informed as to the
condition of the colored people . . . and deeply and intelligently interested in their education and elevation." It was true that twice within the
past year Caroline had publicly manifested such an interest. At Oberlin
in July 1851 she had gotten into something of a scrape by forthrightly
demanding rectification of a grievance. It began when Penelope Lloyd
and Josephine Darnes, both black student friends of hers, had encountered three white girls, one a student, on the village boardwalk, a
treacherous passage far too narrow to accommodate simultaneously so
many crinolines. Because neither party would yield, the white student
had lost her footing and tumbled to the clay street below, upon which
she "retaliated by applying several vile epithets to the colored ladies."

Spunkily rising to the defense of the insulted black women, Caroline, with the collaboration of one of them, wrote and read aloud in their composition class "an article said to be quite personal and giving an account of the whole affair." A Quaker upbringing did not mean that Caroline's was an entirely pacific nature. In consequence of her action, the austere Oberlin Ladies' Board, composed of the principal of the female department and faculty wives, had ordered that all those involved in the shoving incident should be rebuked in front of their class, that the white student should apologize publicly, and Miss Wall and her friend must "acknowledge the impropriety of their conduct in writing a composition of the character they did."[33] Later, in November 1851 at Harveysburg, eighteen-year-old Caroline, along with Sara and O. S. B. Wall, had become one of the twenty-nine signatories of the constitution for a new antislavery society for Clinton and Warren counties. The society's avowed purposes were threefold: "The immediate and unconditional emancipation of the Slave, . . . aiding and assisting the fugitive," and the elevation of the "colored people among us."[34]

Although the two attractive young persons uncovered fertile common grounds for future cultivation during Langston's visit to the cozy Wall household, the friendship proceeded at a measured pace. Neither Mercer, as she called him, nor "Sister Carrie," as he fondly addressed her, were lacking in romantic opportunities. Mial Wall's avuncular letter to Caroline in March 1853 on the selection of a husband was prompted by the discovery that she had "several Beaux and it may be I am writing to a Married Lady." In the event it was not too late, and with a gentlemanly apology for possibly trespassing on her feelings, Wall counseled the independent, dark-skinned Caroline: "Use the best discretion in the Selection as it is the most critical time of a person's life." Friends "capable of discriminating between men" should be consulted, "and together with your own good judgment thare is little to fear." He hoped her husband might be "a man of good appearance, fine disposition, moral habits, possessing industrious and business talents. I care not what his occupation is, if respectable, men of any occupation succeed well if *he is the man*, if not a failure may be expected in any."[35]

To judge by fragments of correspondence and a teasing note from Carrie's brother O. S. B. Wall, the handsome law apprentice himself was the object of several young ladies' affections. In January 1853 elected a delegate to the Free Democratic state convention in Columbus from Harveysburg, O. S. B. had subsequently moved to Oberlin, where he had set himself up as a shoemaker and become further involved with Langston in black reform. In January 1854, he twitted Mercer on "your girls" at Oberlin. All seemed to have "high hopes for the future.

John Mercer Langston
(Brady Collection)

Caroline Langston in later years.
(From John Mercer Langston, *From the Virginia Plantation to the National Capitol* [1894])

Fanny M. Jackson, prominent educator. While studying for her bachelor's degree, which she received in 1865, Fanny Jackson helped Caroline Langston raise funds to buy regimental banners for the black soldiers Langston was recruiting. (Oberlin College Archives)

Edmonia Lewis. As her attorney, Langston successfully defended Edmonia Lewis against charges of poisoning two other women students, both white. She later achieved fame as a sculptor. (Schomburg Center for Research in Black Culture, The New York Public Library, Astor, Lenox and Tilden Foundations)

The Langstons' house at 207 East College St., Oberlin. Fanny Jackson recalled that Langston's "comfortable home was always open with a warm welcome to colored students, or to any who cared to share his hospitality." (Oberlin College Archives)

Of course, some of them must be disappointed." Every day, Datus teased, he saw "some one of them." Only that day he had seen little Mary W. (possibly a pun on Carrie W.) and "did wish I could tell her you sent particular compliments to her but could not without telling an untruth that you know I cannot do."[36]

During the preceding fall, Carrie and Mercer apparently had quarreled. An indignant Mercer had scribbled absurdly: "Of course I am not intending to write you a letter at this time. And for the good and satisfactory reason that I am under no obligation to do any such thing. . . ." But then he had broken off, perhaps for a more conciliatory, or, at any rate, more logical approach.[37]

By the spring of 1854, however, the courtship had progressed. Carrie accompanied Mercer on a "reading tour" to Toledo, apparently unchaperoned. Perhaps, too, she had not furnished herself with the proper authorization from the college. If so, Carrie, who had been hauled before the Ladies' Board once before for a lesser rule violation—"having been out on a pleasure ride and detained beyond the usual study hour at eve"—had knowingly risked dire consequences. On March 9, Carrie's anxious suitor wrote from Elyria. First formally begging her pardon for "daring to write you a short note without asking leave," Mercer explained that he was worried about her "prosperity. . . . I want to know," pleaded her "humble friend," "what the Ladies Board have seen fit, in the plenitudes of their wisdom and mercy, to do with you. . . . I remained in Oberlin all day yesterday in order to hear the upshot of this matter, but without success. Please do me the favor to let me hear from you soon."[38]

But the repercussions, if any, were minor. Within a week the Young Ladies' Literary Society, of which Carrie was an active member, elected her corresponding secretary. On the same evening, March 15, 1854, Carrie and Sara Wall, possibly having been coached by their well-informed friend, debated in the affirmative the question: "Resolved, that the system of colonization is calculated to rivet the chains of the oppressed." Like the undergraduate men's society to which Mercer had belonged, Carrie and sister members of the Ladies Society took as their province a broad range of current problems. In particular, they debated matrimony through such inquiries as to whether it were "proper for ladies to make proposals of marriage" and whether married life was "more conducive to a woman's happiness than single?" In the fall of 1854, at the beginning of what would have been her senior year, Carrie tendered her resignation from the society.[39] On the question of the conduciveness of marriage to a woman's happiness, she had come down on the side of the affirmative.

Mercer invited a good friend to stay at his farm for several days to help him argue out the matrimonial decision. But, in truth, his mind was already made up. Strongly influenced not merely by the black movement's notions of the model woman, but by Oberlin's radical females who had brought him along to a commitment to women's rights, and by those intelligent, refined women of his boyhood, Matilda and Virginia Gooch, Langston liked Carrie's educated intelligence and independent spirit, developed through years of relying on her own "good judgment." He liked the strength of this young woman, her lack of submissiveness, her humor and common sense, her willing identification with the race to which she was joined by her maternal blood. Perhaps he saw in her even then the wife of more than thirty years who would still address him as "My darling Mercer," write with witty uncomplaint of household and family problems, scold spiritedly because he failed to inform her of his next visit home: "Why don't you speak up and tell what you intend to do?" and urge him not toward the safe, conservative, profitable, and comfortable, but the radical, difficult, expensive, and dangerous. "Some one must take the lead in very advanced steps as to the capability of the Negro," she would advise her husband in the late 1880s, with neither in doubt as to whom she meant, "but who will dare to take the lead? it cannot be a coward."[40]

Formally, with a touch of the old diffidence, Mercer chose to propose by letter, entrusting it to his friend whom he sent off toward Oberlin at sunset. Carrie mercifully kept him in suspense no more than a day or so; Mercer penned into his contract with the Slaters, in the clause dealing with his room and board, "and wife." On the twenty-fifth of October, 1854, John Mercer Langston, twenty-four, was married to Caroline Matilda Wall, twenty-one, at the home in Oberlin where she boarded. Professor Morgan, a friend to both, performed the ceremony. The day after their wedding, Carrie and Mercer, as official witnesses, stood at the sides of her brother O. S. B. Wall and Amanda A. Thomas, her classmate in the women's literary department at Oberlin, when the pair took their own vows in Cleveland. The Langstons then continued their short "wedding tour," first to Cincinnati where they were entertained handsomely by the William W. Watson family and received by other prominent members of the developing black upper class, and then to Harveysburg, where they spent a few days with one of Carrie's closest friends. Afterward, the young couple returned to their country home where they could begin to forge the loving compatibility that, from all available evidence, was to undergird their long companionship.[41]

During the winter of 1854–55, the first of two they would spend on
the farm, John Mercer, besides attending to his law practice, settled
into the role of gentleman farmer. Although the Slaters performed
most of the chores until they moved farther west sometime in 1855,
when Langston presumably hired other help, some jobs fell within the
owner's purview. Years later at a New York county fair, Langston would
declare himself to have been "a neighbor to old John Brown's brother,
and many a time have I paid him fifty dollars in cash for a calf, and
watched that calf until it became a cow, and many a time have I placed
a big bucket under that cow and milked from it twenty quarts of milk in
five minutes, making from that milk seventeen pounds of butter a
week, which was sold to buy groceries for the family." Furthermore, he
boasted of sitting behind "the best Morgan horse in Lorain County"
and sweeping the races at the fairs. He was no stranger, he assured
fair-goers, to "occasions like this."[42]

Long, quiet country nights allowed John Mercer to indulge his taste
for reading, study, and reflection. Cultural concerns, he believed, were
a vital ballast to keep the reformer from becoming submerged in his
own reform; indeed, they were at the core of his definition of manhood. "Who dares to say," he demanded of a critic, "that the very
leaders of the Liberty movement shall not give a large share of their
time to the investigation and study of Theology, Medicine, and Law,
and thus gain an accurate appreciation of the bearings of these Sciences upon the happiness of man? Indeed, this is their duty." Literature and the arts, "the great Volume of Nature," and "the mysterious,
the subtle and the delicate movements of the human heart," all were
legitimate concerns of the reformer; abolitionists, even black abolitionists, he argued, had the "right to *study* and *reflect* upon all subjects
connected with the weal of mankind."[43]

Mercer and Carrie also delighted in their new roles of host and
hostess. Friends of the young couple from Oberlin, as well as "leading
reformers, white and colored," came to visit, some for days at a time.
Such visits gave Mercer occasion to show off his orchards and timothy-
covered meadows; his cattle, sheep, and horses; and his woods studded
with chestnut and hickory trees. He and his guests could engage in
animated discussions on a variety of topics in the parlor or, in clement
weather, outside under the towering pine that shaded the west corner
of the two-story frame house. Some Brownhelm neighbors also took to
stopping by. They did "not find the latch string drawn in," observed
white farmer James Frisbie, who lived nearby on the family homestead
on Middle Ridge. "He will ask you in very politely, and be ready to

converse with you on law, theology, politics, history, the arts and sciences, agriculture, the news of the day, etc., etc." Frisbie himself had "frequently visited, talked, and eaten with Mr. Langston."[44]

Yet even as Langston set about demonstrating, as he would put it, his "claim to humanity, and all those things that pertain to a dignified life,"[45] he repeatedly encountered racial discrimination. Even on his honeymoon, prejudice had intruded. When Mercer, but four days married, accompanied William W. Watson to Cincinnati's Melodeon Hall to hear his former Oberlin theological classmate Antoinette Brown address the Temperance Association, the two men, who would have been "most glad" to pay the 10 cent entrance fee, were stopped at the door and "informed that men of *our complexion* could not gain admission." Langston quickly sent a note to the Reverend Brown, expressing confidence that if "real reformatory material" were in her make-up she would show "the spirit of a true woman" and rebuke the association "for this miserable conduct." Actually, it turned out to be the proprietor of the hall, not the temperance association, that had set the exclusion policy. Miss Brown rose to the occasion with what Langston would deem a "scorching, but Christian rebuke." Protesting the "whole color-phobia spirit," she declared that "men of talent, refinement and education, who could have spoken as fervent and eloquent words as had been uttered there by any speaker that afternoon" had been excluded. Drawing on a bold if slightly pulpit-worn device, she substituted the name of Christ for Langston, "representing Him as virtually excluded from a temperance audience in Cincinnati; and on the Lord's day." Subsequently, the society endorsed her statement and vowed not to use the hall again until the color bar was dropped. But by that time, Langston and Watson had been driven from the hall.

"How uncalled for! how unkind and unchristian!" the indignant bridegroom fumed. Within ten minutes of his ejection from the hall, venting his anger, he dashed off a description of the incident for Julia Griffiths, who inserted it in *Frederick Douglass' Paper*. Noting Watson's high social and economic status, Langston demanded, "If wealthy, influential and respectable colored men are insulted and maltreated, what will be done to the poor and degraded among us?"[46]

The letter's publication brought replies from several sources. Antoinette Brown explained her actions and the temperance society's resolve, at which Langston expressed satisfaction and considered the matter closed. However, Samuel Lowery, a free Negro from Nashville and an advocate of emigration, pointedly contrasted Langston's expressed faith that blacks could overcome American prejudice with his having been barred from a public lecture "because he was *colored, and invited out*." Moreover, Francis Barry of Berlin Heights, Ohio, a white self-styled "universal reformer"—who shortly before had used the *Liberator* to ingenuously announce the nonexistence of God and invite responses from anyone who disagreed—embarked on a series of letters arraigning Antoinette Brown and Langston for insufficient reform purity. Specifically, he argued that Brown should have refused to address the temperance group, and Langston should not have excused her participation, because no principled abolitionist could act in an organization or meeting that excluded blacks.[47]

Although Langston usually avoided public argument of the sort that frequently embroiled abolitionists, white and black, the Garrisonians in particular, Barry's criticism goaded him into replying. Restricting abolitionists only to those groups that allowed black participation, Langston pointed out, was "equivalent to saying that they shall speak on no other subject than Slavery. . . . Because in our country, the Literary, the Historical, the Philosophical, the Theological, and the Temperance Associations are all *Pro-Slavery*. That is, *the large majority in these Associations make distinctions on the ground of color*." In the face of this numbing reality, he concluded, all that should be asked of any lecturer in circumstances like Miss Brown's was to administer "a severe, a Christian *rebuke*, in the name of right and insulted humanity, of all such miserable, and worse than heathenish conduct."[48]

Close to home, local temperance enthusiasts offered their own unwelcome support of Langston's thesis. An association called the "Ark," open to both sexes, had been gotten up in North Amherst, not far from Brownhelm. James Frisbie and several others proposed Langston for membership. He was voted in unanimously, but disgruntled members later raised such a fuss that the vote had to be reconsidered at a second meeting in early March 1855. (A similar group in Cleveland had recently split over the question of admitting Lucy Stanton Day resulting in formation of a new group opposed to "colorphobia.") Frisbie, noting sarcastically that in closely associating with Langston he had not been "aware of feeling a single 'nigger streak' about me," read an essay fervently arguing that he was "a *fit* person to sail in the Ark." After spirited debate, Langston was voted in, 36–17. An abolitionist from the hamlet of Fruit Grove expostulated, "Truly, a colored person might be a very Socrates, Demosthenes, Euripides, possessing all the excellencies of a thorough education, and a deep and comprehensive reading, with all the culture and refinement of the most finished and elegant modern society, and yet he cannot escape the foul effects of this fell power— . . . pervasive, influential, almost omnipotent prejudice." Langston's admission was "certainly an anti-slavery triumph. But it is a sad one."⁴⁹

Along with such painful incidents, John Mercer faced the quotidian challenge of Colonel Frank Peck. The original owner of Langston's property had warned him before purchase that the only man in the immediate vicinity likely to stir up trouble was Peck, who owned the adjoining farm and regularly used a lane cut through what would be Langston's land. Peck's own brother paid a call to deliver the same caution. One of the early Massachusetts pioneers, the colonel, title derived from service in the volunteer frontiersman "Cornstalk militia," was, as Langston put it, "distinguished for the inveteracy of his Hunker Democracy and his unconquerable hatred of abolitionism and the Negro." As Langston worked in a potato field shortly after his move to the farm, he spotted Peck striding stiffly through the lane on his way to the post office, and on his return, accosted him. Langston's first respectful "Good morning, Colonel Peck!" elicited only silence, so he repeated it "very emphatically." In a "gruff, savage" growl, Peck demanded, "Who are *you*!" After a brief exchange, Peck began damning "the abolition, negro-loving school of Oberlin" and swearing he wanted nothing to do with any Oberlin-educated colored man, to which Langston replied by defending the college and brazenly suggesting it would benefit Peck's family if he should send his children there to be educated "and to be advanced morally and enlightened politically."

From this unlikely commencement, an improbable amicability developed. Carrie Langston also established a friendship with Mrs. Peck⁵⁰ who, along with her children, it was reported, rejoiced "in the distinctive appellation of Abolitionists." Even after the Langstons in the spring of 1856 removed to Oberlin, they continued to visit the Pecks. In the autumn of that year John Mercer, who clearly delighted in teasing his unregenerate "Democratic friend," decided that Peck was one of the local curiosities to which a visiting black abolitionist, William C. Nell of Boston, should be exposed. In his report to the *Liberator*, Nell included an appreciative account of his welcome, adding of Peck that "The strangest of all strange facts is, that though an active administration man, and a supporter of Buchanan for the Presidency, he treats the colored man as a brother beloved."⁵¹

The story of Nell's visit was one that Langston would consider both funny and instructive enough to be included in speeches to the freedmen in 1869. At Peck's farmhouse, he and Nell had been met at the door by the colonel, who ushered them inside where Nell was "introduced to his beautifully-dressed wife and daughter." Suspecting that Peck, given such juicy provocation, would quickly revert to "his great hobby . . . that the negro was made for slavery, . . . the arrangement was made by Divine appointment as found in the Constitution," Langston was not disappointed. While he conversed with the women, "my friend talked politics with the Colonel, who very soon got out the [Democratic] *Journal of Commerce*, and, with his hand upon my friend's knee, began with earnest and violent gesticulation. 'I,' says the Colonel, 'see the color of his face.' He says, 'Hold on, Langston.' I did hold on. They talked for hours. The evening wore away, and the next morning my friend returned to Boston.

"In a week, along came a 'Garrison *Liberator*,' one for myself and one for the Colonel. In it was an article about the visit of my friend to the Colonel, relating what a nice man he was. I saw the colonel soon. He says, 'I have got something I want to read to you.' He took out the *Liberator*. Says I, 'What news? Anything about the Negroes rising in rebellion, fire, devastation, murder or such like?' Says he, 'Hold on, Langston.' I held on. The Colonel began to read—it was full a column and a half—it was all about his family; says he, 'Ain't that nice.' Says I, 'Don't you remember who wrote it; it came from the head, heart and hand of a negro.' 'Don't, don't, don't talk that way,' said the Colonel."

Driving home his point, Langston would conclude: "The character, you understand, the moral life, the ability of that black man, refuted forever the arguments. Forever after the Colonel said, in spite of himself, 'I tell you, he is my equal, and superior, too.' "[52]

Unquestionably, that same admission was what Langston, through his own character, moral life, and ability, always exerted himself to win from his neighbors. Unprecedented events in early spring 1855 indicated that at least in Brownhelm township, with the voting majority, he had succeeded.

Politically, the winter had seemed relatively quiet after the hurly-burly over the Kansas-Nebraska Act and the victories of Philemon Bliss and other candidates of the new coalition in the fall congressional elections. In Brownhelm where Whigs, as well as Democrats, still fielded tickets in local races, John Mercer had aligned himself with the Independent Democrats. Later in March 1855, the Independent Democrats held a township caucus to nominate candidates for local offices. That evening, according to Langston's telling, he set off on horseback for the schoolhouse where the meeting would be held. On the way he encountered a neighbor, Charles Fairchild, a member of the prestigious Grandison Fairchild family that had been among the original settlers of Brownhelm. Brother of two Oberlin professors, James H. Fairchild, later president of the college, and E. H. Fairchild, later president of Berea

College in Kentucky, Charles Fairchild had inherited both family homestead and strong antislavery beliefs. After the two men had ridden companionably for some distance, Fairchild turned to the Negro lawyer and announced his intention to nominate him for township clerk, a position that entailed a number of legal duties. Langston objected strenuously that his name would kill the ticket. Not to be dissuaded, Fairchild nominated him in a speech enumerating his obvious qualifications for the post. Never once, Langston would gratefully recall, did Fairchild mention his race. "Without the least opposition," Langston was nominated.[53]

The election was held on April 2, 1855. Not bothering to conceal his elation, John Mercer described the outcome to Frederick Douglass. "The Independent Democrats were wise for once in making and sticking to their own nomination. They put up a colored man and he was elected clerk of Brownhelm, by a handsome majority indeed. Since I am the only colored man who lives in this township, you can easily guess the name of the man who was so fortunate as to secure this election." No coattail candidate, the new township clerk had run sixty votes ahead of his ticket. John Mercer Langston had become the first Negro elected to public office by popular vote in the United States.[54]

Two factors, one external to Brownhelm and political, the other internal and psychological, doubtless contributed to this outcome. Just before the Brownhelm elections, on March 30, the first territorial elections were held in Kansas. When thousands of pro-slavery Missourians crossed the border into Kansas, took over the polls by force, and elected a pro-slavery territorial legislature, northern forebodings of the Slave Power's intent to subvert democratic institutions seemed to be substantiated. Lorain County abolitionists, many of whom had helped send parties of Free Soil settlers to Kansas, were outraged. Even northerners of lesser antislavery convictions suddenly felt, as Horace Greeley put it, that slavery issues had become "close and practical."[55] At the same time, in the person of their black neighbor, Brownhelm residents closely and practically confronted, or probably felt they were confronting, the issues of slavery and prejudice. Even as the antislavery cause was becoming increasingly internalized by Langston's neighbors, it seems probable, it was becoming increasingly personalized by the young colored lawyer and gentleman farmer. The Brownhelm voter who cast his ballot for Langston for township clerk may well have felt he personally was striking back at the usurping Slave Power.

As an undergraduate, John Mercer had dreamed of someday being a black man in public office, a "sagacious statesman" or "wise legislator in the halls of Congress."[56] His election, accomplished with deceptive ease, thus was a realization of what he had had every reason to think never could be more than a fantasy. Moreover, it seemed to epitomize, as it confirmed, his belief in self-reliance; his conviction of the primacy, among matters of concern to black Americans, of suffrage; and his persuasion that the black man could win an equal place in the American democracy.

Langston early had come to believe that self-reliance provided the philosophical underpinnings for his own and the black American struggle against hostile social, political, and economic forces. It had been Finney who had first impressed on John Mercer, then a struggling student, Ralph Waldo Emerson's admonitions to throw off the shackles of tradition, history, and custom, and to heed the inner voice. These ideas seemed to Langston particularly liberating for the black American. For by refusing to conform to the expectations of a society permeated by racism, or to permit attitude, institution, or custom to dictate behavior, the black American might shake off his or her subordinate role and free his or her energies to achieve individual ends. On a personal level, both as a young orator and black leader, John Mercer doubtless had profited from particular points in the Emersonian doctrine.

Emerson's bidding to speak without undue regard for authority, past or present, may have guided Langston's own conduct. It was self-reliance, he would declare, that had given black Cincinnatian John I. Gaines the courage to speak his own mind "in the midst of men who were greatly his superiors in age, experience, and wisdom, in the first colored men's convention held in Ohio." Emerson's famous dismissal of consistency—"the hobgoblin of little minds"—surely had reinforced the young intellectual's tendency to consider alternatives and, as with emigration, to feel free to reject a course he had once advocated. But most important for Langston was the overall injunction to believe in the almost infinite possibilities of what might be achieved by effort and use of natural faculties. "Every man comes from the plastic hand of his Creator bearing an appropriate individuality, and if true to the convictions of his own nature," Langston thought, "his life and conduct will furnish the world a record distinguished for its originality and freshness." More, adherence to this "individuality," this "peculiar genius," was "the true secret of greatness. A great man is always himself." Self-reliance led to "industry and perseverance, . . . keen insight into life and its responsibilities, . . . determination not to exist merely, but to live, and to act a manly part in life." Despite the restrictions of white supremacist society, the black individual, through hard work, intelligence, morality, and will, might still achieve. This belief

served Langston as a functional myth, encouraging a continuing struggle against unfair, sometimes overwhelming odds. "Self reliance, the
secret of success"—it would be engraved upon the frontispiece of
Langston's autobiography.[57] And he probably never felt it more
strongly than at the moment of his election to be clerk of Brownhelm
township.

As for black enfranchisement, Langston held, long before Reconstruction, that no gain, whether it be land, schools, or jobs, could be
protected unless blacks had political power. "What we so much need
just at this juncture and all along the future," he wrote Douglass in
announcing his election, "is political influence, the bridle by which we
can check and guide, to our own advantage, the selfishness of American demagogues. How important, then, it is, that we labor night and
day to enfranchise ourselves. We are doing too little in this direction. And I make this charge against white anti-slavery persons, as well
as colored ones. I hope that before a great while, we will amend our
ways in this particular."[58] Despite the repulses he had met with during
previous enfranchisement campaigns, it was obvious that the Ohio
leader was already gearing up for the renewed effort he would mount
in 1856.

Finally, the election—a telling contradiction to the argument of black
emigrationists that blacks stood no chance of ever holding public office
in the United States—bolstered Langston's faith in the likelihood that
blacks could win freedom and justice under the American Constitution
and Declaration of Independence. From his position only three years
earlier that "mutual repellency" between the white oppressors and the
black oppressed precluded the possibility of the races ever living together "on terms of equality," he had swung round the circumference.
His election victory, he felt in his jubilation, "argues the steady march
of the anti-slavery sentiment, and augurs the inevitable destruction and
annihilation of American prejudice against colored men."[59]

Reports of Langston's triumph[60] brought him a speaking opportunity that he always regarded as one of the most important of his life.
The American Anti-Slavery Society would observe its anniversary week
in New York City in early May. Although the society had been driven
from its meeting hall during its anniversary ceremonies in the city only
five years earlier, and for two years thereafter had been forced to meet
in other cities for lack of a New York proprietor willing to lease it an
auditorium, it was a sign of changing northern sentiment that the
society expected its 1855 celebration to be one of its most successful.
Participants, in addition to William Lloyd Garrison, were to include

such luminaries as Wendell Phillips and theologian Theodore Parker, co-defendants in the celebrated Anthony Burns rescue case. The Brownhelm township clerk was invited to speak on the morning of May 9, anniversary day.

It was by far the most prominent platform yet extended to the twenty-five-year-old orator. The previous winter, through a miscarriage of his reply, Langston had lost the proffered opportunity to lecture in New York City under the sponsorship of the Garrisonian state society. He was pleased by the national society's offer to pay his expenses and a $50 fee, the first such compensation he had ever received—Langston's reform work, Douglass had noted, was "at his own expense." But the chief thrill was the challenge of speaking before the preeminent antislavery orators of the day. His address was to last thirty minutes. In planning his draft, Langston decided to achieve novelty in "general features": a startling opening, tightly controlled argument with fresh examples, dramatic climax, rather than in subject matter. The time for new ideas in the abolitionist movement had passed, the major themes achieved maturity, before his coming of age. But he did not wish to settle either for the broadly appealing motif, favored by less radical antislavery politicians, of the Slave Power's threat to northern institutions. Rather, he decided to deal with the larger question of slavery's impingement on the freedom of every American. Excitedly, he set to work on preparation of his "strongest word."[61]

He brought to the task a style based on the persuasion that eloquence consisted "in the sentiment, the truth of one's utterance, and not in mere diction, gesticulation, movement, smile or frown, even where accompanied by finished and effective rhetoric." That was his mature judgment. Earlier, as a pupil of elocution, he had looked for models in the "lofty, finished, masterly periods" of Lord Chatham, Lord Brougham, and Burke, the "grace, eloquence, and power" of Webster, Clay, and Calhoun. But rhetorical standards, he believed, had been altered by abolitionist orators. Phillips and Sumner, Parker and Beecher, Douglass and Seward, Remond and Burleigh, among those he most admired, had demonstrated that excellence of technique could enhance but not substitute for sincerity and moral purpose. Abolitionist orators, he thought, "possess the noblest of all themes—a theme whose simple announcement touches the human heart, and . . . affords the most ample field for the display of the stoutest faculties of thought and reason, of imagination and fancy." His own rhetoric had a twofold aim: through "stubborn facts" to convince the judgment, and through "earnest and pathetic appeals in behalf of freedom" to charm and captivate the emotions.[62]

Unlike those antislavery rostrum rousers who overstated the case that they might be heard, Langston, then, put his trust in the eloquence of fact. William C. Nell, after accompanying Langston on a lecture tour in 1856, would call him "a walking and talking encyclopedia of the colored American's position, aspirations, and capacities." His ready wit and broad education provided "a fertility of resource." Deploying, with comparative economy, classical, literary, historical, and Biblical allusions, mingled with snippets of poetry, to illustrate and leaven the text, he drove home his theme through evidence, lucidity, and logic. Although William Howard Day's "gaiety of imagination" was not characteristic of Langston, it could have been said of him, as it was of Day, that he possessed a "quick, practical ability, that hits the nail on the head at once, and combines all reasons that may be developed by argument into a conclusion. . . ." His sentences, only occasionally notable for poetic effect, were balanced, direct, and well crafted. His organization was firm, sustaining his theme to a logical and emotional climax. "He is not fragmentary in his speeches"; noted William Wells Brown, fugitive slave, abolitionist lecturer, and author, "but, as a deep, majestic stream, he moves steadily onward, pouring forth his rich and harmonious sentences in strains of impassioned eloquence." Because Langston's approach was "adapted to sway the strongest minds," Brown judged that he represented "the highest idea of the orator."[63]

In attempting to touch his auditors' hearts, Langston adopted a dignified, earnest, and affirmative approach. Eschewing both the flamboyant and conservative extremes of abolitionist costume, John Mercer appeared to audiences a rather sparely constructed young man "of good figure," who, in a high-collared era, often wore black frock coat and doeskin pants, satin vest, and cravat. The moustache and most of the beard that he would affect during the following decade had not yet made their appearance, leaving unguarded except for sideburns the full-lipped, firm-jawed face. In the earliest written description of him, Brown in the early sixties singled out his "full, but not prominent" eyes, "high and well-formed forehead, . . . mild and amiable countenance," and "modest deportment." His posture was erect, his gestures were uncommonly graceful. Moreover, his enunciation was "very clear and distinct," his "strong, musical voice" was "striking in its range." He consciously tried to communicate the depth and intensity of his convictions. "Without formality of expression," he managed to give the impression of a man speaking under oath. Although Douglass's use of mimicry and Brown's skill at imitations (both devices of the "character" speaker) were effective means of engaging any audience, for the young Langston such techniques were unnatural. Rather, he relied on a style

that was "bold and energetic, full of spirit." Lacking neither the asper-
ity of youth nor the self-righteousness of the reformer, Langston could
throw the barbed phrase, and his cultivation of irony, even at this early
date, was capable of provoking hearty laughter. Still, he resorted infrequently to the leaden sarcasm and stinging wit that marked the
oratory of black co-workers like Douglass, Remond, and Peter Clark,
and indeed, many white abolitionists. Typically, his language was more
bold than bitter. In the tradition of his fellow westerners, John I.
Gaines, Andrew J. Gordon, and Joseph Henry Perkins, his characteristic tone was positive, intended to uplift and unify. By the mid-fifties,
this was especially apparent, when he like Day, began to sense more
acutely the "good time coming," or as he expressed it, "the sure coming
of the millennium of liberty." In sum, the manliness and authority of
his appearance, the earnestness of his voice and manner, and the
"stubborn facts" combined with "earnest and pathetic appeals" conveyed a sense of moral exigency. In 1856, Nell described Langston's
effect: "In most of his public efforts, often two hours in length, he
presents arguments, appeals, facts and statistics, in such a fearless,
eloquent, and irresistible manner as to leave the friend proudly satisfied, and our enemies evidently confused." During one such effort,
a white Buckeye farmer, unstrung, threw his hands heavenward like
a repentant sinner, and shouted, " 'My God! Can these things be
true?' "[64]

On the morning of May 9, 1855, although a cold rain saturated New
York City, three thousand persons filled the vast pit and tiers of galleries of the Metropolitan Theatre for the American Anti-Slavery Society
anniversary day. On the platform such prominent antislavery political
figures as Gerrit Smith, Henry B. Stanton, and Henry Wilson, well-
known ministers Theodore Parker and Henry Ward Beecher, and
women's rights advocates Lucy Stone and Antoinette Brown sat alongside the Garrisonian veterans: H. C. Wright, William Wells Brown, C.
C. Burleigh, Oliver Johnson, Charles Lenox Remond, Abby and
Stephen Foster, Samuel May Jr., James and Lucretia Mott, Robert Purvis, and Wendell Phillips. At the completion of his welcoming address,
William Lloyd Garrison without ado introduced John Mercer Langston
as an Oberlin graduate and colored lawyer recently elected clerk of
Brownhelm township in Ohio.[65]

"Some great man," Langston began simply, "has remarked that a
nation may lose its liberty in a day, and be a century in finding it out.
Does our own nation afford illustration of this statement? There is not,
within the length and breadth of this entire country, from Maine to
Georgia, from the Atlantic to the Pacific Oceans, a solitary man or

woman who is in possession of his or her full share of civil, religious and political liberty. . . . Why? Because slavery is the great lord of this country, and there is no power in this nation today strong enough to withstand it." He drew first applause with a poem about a caged eagle: like the eagle, "the colored man hates chains, loathes his enslavement and longs to shoulder the responsibilities of dignified life. He longs to stand in the Church, in the State, a man; he longs to stand up a man upon the great theater of existence, everywhere a man; for verily he is a man, and may well adopt the sentiment of the Roman Terence, when he said, 'Homo sum. . . .' 'I am a man.'"

In making good his "proposition," Langston discussed the unfreedom of the American slave, slaveholder, northern white, and northern black. The slave's condition was obvious, but the curbs on the slaveholder, if less apparent, were exacting: "Let but a sentiment tending toward abolition escape and what is the consequence?" In response, he cited the destruction of the Parkville, Missouri, *Luminary* by a mob. The restrictions on white northerners he illustrated with two favorite examples, which he had probably witnessed himself. Two conventions held in Cleveland, a political antislavery convention in 1850, and the National Women's Rights convention of 1852, both had discussed holding subsequent meetings in the slaveholding District of Columbia. But both had abandoned the idea for fear of violence. On the latter occasion, Langston recalled, Lucy Stone objected, "'I am opposed to going to the city of Washington. They buy and sell women there, and they might outrage us.'" At greatest length, Langston spoke, to appreciative laughter and applause, "of that class which I have the honor to represent—the free people of color." Calling prejudice "the fruit of Slavery," he declared that in Ohio whites refused to enfranchise blacks partly because Kentucky slaveholders objected that their "slaves will hear of it and become restless, and directly we shall have an insurrection and our throats will be cut." After touching on the effects of prejudice on the schools, he went on to a novel discussion of Ohio prison conditions. "If a colored man knocks a white man down, perhaps in defense of his rights—he is sent to the penitentiary; and when he gets there, there is not discrimination made between him and the worst criminal; but when he marches out to take his meal, he is made to march behind the white criminal, and you may see the prisoners marching—horse-thieves in front, colored people behind." In New York, he continued, the property qualification for black suffrage was insulting: "It is not his manhood but his money that is represented. But that is the Yankee idea—the dollar and the cent!" In Illinois, he further noted, a residency law provided for the sale of blacks who could not put up a $10 bond, proceeds to go toward court costs and maintenance of poor whites. Public sentiment "will soon, I hope, be the death of [Illinois Sen. Stephen A.] Douglas, and of that sort of legislation."

Although slavery had "pervaded every crevice and cranny" of society, he predicted "a great change is coming on." Slavery, no longer seen simply as affecting Negroes alone, increasingly was being perceived as "a National question, in which every man and woman is more or less interested. And when the people of the North shall rise and put on their strength, powerful though slavery is and well-nigh omnipotent, it shall die!" Building toward his conclusion with a series of rhetorical questions ("Shall our free institutions triumph and our country become the asylum of the oppressed of all climes?"), he soared: "May God help the right!"

"Amen!" intoned a voice from the parquet. The next speaker, his friend Antoinette Brown, complimented "our brother Langston" for touching each heart with his expression of longing "to be a man and to exercise the attributes of his humanity." The next day's New York newspapers printed the full text of his speech; antislavery journals and periodicals also spread it abroad. Although the Democratic New York *Herald* snorted mildly at his criticism of New York's voting restrictions, the commentary was overwhelmingly positive. Langston felt his speech "produced effects which were highly advantageous, personally . . . and as its friends claimed, of great service to the antislavery cause in the United States."[66]

Aside from the excitement of his own performance, the young westerner reacted most strongly to the speeches of Massachusetts's two radical antislavery senators. The just-elected Henry Wilson—"hot shot from abolition cannon," as Chase called him—spoke on the night of May 8, his elegant senior colleague, Charles Sumner, the following evening. It seemed to Langston that both men "spoke indeed as moved by the holy spirit of liberty itself." Langston, possibly the "one handsome doubloon colored man" on the platform for the Sumner lecture, would establish a close relationship with the civil rights champion in postwar Washington. From that vantage point, he would recall fondly this first impression of Sumner, when "numbers of great men and women were present, and he was the greatest of all." Sumner's oration, which has been deemed one of the most successful of his career, was so brilliant, Langston remembered, that Wendell Phillips, called upon to speak afterward, wisely forebore. The black student of oratory himself had felt stirred to his depths by Sumner's closing declaration " 'that the Slave Oligarchy shall die!' "[67]

John Mercer did not leave New York without renewing black connections. The badly splintered National Council, set up by the 1853 national convention at Rochester, was holding what would turn out to be its final meeting in Dr. J. W. C. Pennington's church during anniversary week. Langston entered the council meeting on the second day and was voted to an honorary seat. Earlier, Philip A. Bell of New York had told the council that Langston's election was a sign of black progress. On another front, he may have joined briefly with black New Yorkers in their fight for integrated seating on the Sixth Avenue railroad line, spearheaded by Dr. Pennington and his parishioners. Years later Langston would relate that he had ridden in a street car in New York City, after he and his companions had been turned out by conductors in eight other cars, by virtue of declaring that he would not go out alive.[68]

The AASS anniversary celebration, overall, provided John Mercer Langston with one of the peak experiences of his young manhood. Not only did it, in a sense, extend and put a seal on the jubilation of his election, but it also gave him the gratification of having participated in an event that he, with others, took to be a landmark in abolitionist agitation. Like the earlier Cincinnati abolitionist conventions that he had attended, but on a larger scale, the anniversary seemed to promise greater unity of the political and nonpolitical abolitionists—in Sumner's words, "a general union of the anti-slavery elements on a broad foundation." Moreover, on a personal level, this favorable exposure of his talents paid "largely in its far-reaching results" for the young reformer's career.[69]

On return home, Langston's attention was quickly drawn to the problems of coalition politics. Although the continuing Kansas crisis presented the fledgling Ohio Republican party with an opportunity for victory in the fall state elections, radicals, hoping to make the strongly antislavery Salmon Chase their nominee for governor, had somehow to pacify ex-Whigs and other conservative members, stave off the anti-foreigner, anti-black Know Nothing challenge, and prepare to deal with a Democratic opposition certain to focus on racial issues. Langston, who had seen Senator Chase on the platform for his fellow radical Sumner's oration, had every reason to support him. But Langston's hopes for black enfranchisement, his call for a greater commitment from "white anti-slavery persons, as well as colored ones," he had to recognize, were jeopardized by powerful forces for compromise of black rights.[70]

Langston encountered these forces quickly on home territory. On July 7, with the state convention in Columbus less than a week away, Lorain County Republicans staged a mass meeting in Oberlin. The Brownhelm clerk, appointed to the resolutions committee, helped draw up statements endorsing Chase and declaring the party's objective to be the restriction of slavery and the maintenance of freedom. Furthermore, flouting both Know Nothing nativists and conservatives, Langston's committee issued an invitation to membership to "all citizens, of whatever name, birthplace, color, or religion." With a short, pertinent speech from Langston, these resolutions were easily approved by the meeting. But Langston apparently had been unable to persuade fellow committee members to submit a resolution on black enfranchisement, despite traditional endorsement of black suffrage by local Independent Democrats and earlier antislavery political groups. Nonetheless, a separate resolution "that the colored people are entitled to have the elective franchise given them" was introduced from the floor and, doubtless with Langston's strong backing, approved.[71]

At the Republican state convention in Columbus, however, all mention of black rights was studiously avoided. Still, by compromising with the Know Nothings on nominations for lesser state offices, the radicals did win an antislavery platform and make Chase the gubernatorial candidate. Subsequently, the Democrats, moving quickly to compensate for the Republican omission of black rights, not only raked over Chase's abolitionist past, but also, in particular, publicized his 1845 declaration to Cincinnati blacks that "the exclusion of the colored people . . . from the elective franchise [is] incompatible with true democratic principles." Chase refused to repudiate the statement although, particularly in populous Cincinnati, it made "a potent electioneering argument against him."[72]

Langston and other Ohio black leaders, refusing to be cowed by what a black Cincinnatian called the "bitter and malignant" race-baiting of the Democratic press, took a keen interest in the Republican campaign. Besides stumping for Chase, Langston supported with particular enthusiasm James Monroe, Oberlin professor of rhetoric and belles lettres, and a long-time ally in abolitionism, who was the local Republican nominee for the Ohio Assembly. William Howard Day, too, joined in the campaign. After one of Day's speeches "in favor of 'Brudder Chase,' " the Tiffin *Advertiser* pronounced it "part of the [Republican] programme: negro stump-speakers! negro voters! negro jurors! negro office-holders!"[73] Both Langston and Peter Clark, who since June had been publishing the short-lived *Herald of Freedom*, addressed a large and spirited First of August ceremony in Cincinnati, at which Langston, at least, doubtless urged the Republican cause. Many "nearer white than black" mulattoes in Ohio, although entitled to the ballot by terms of the same 1842 Supreme Court decision under which Langston had been admitted to the bar, had never exercised the privilege. Justifiably, they feared humiliation at the hands of election judges, who arbitrarily could decide they were too black to vote, and maltreatment from rowdy white voters. But on election day in Cincinnati, many mulatto men, as one of them noted, "for the first time in their lives" believing an election worth the risk, lined up at the polls to vote for the Republican candidates.[74]

Langston and his Lorain County neighbors elected Monroe to the Assembly and contributed an 1,800-vote majority to the victory of Chase in the overall Republican triumph. The election, which some saw as a culmination of two decades of antislavery agitation, firmly established the Republican party in Ohio. At the same time, the Ohio victory measurably strengthened the party's position in the entire North. Henceforward, on the political level, the black struggle for liberation would be conducted within the boundaries of a major party. Langston and his black movement colleagues recognized not only the reform limitations of the new party, but also its possibilities. The resolutions that, as chairman of the business committee, Langston helped pen for the state black convention the following January insisted that the "real political party of freedom" would be one declaring "there can be no law for slavery." Still, Langston and black Ohioans rejoiced at "the death of the Whig party, once a strong ally of Despotism," as well as at "the waning influence of the Democratic party—the black-hearted apostle of American slavery." They welcomed the inauguration of the Republican party, "which, although it does not take so high anti-slavery ground as we could wish, demanding the immediate and unconditional abolition of slavery in the States as well as its eternal prohibition in the Territories. . . ., may do great service in the cause of Freedom."[75]

For John Mercer Langston, Esq., of Brownhelm, these were mainly happy, productive days. His optimism was reinforced by his establishment of a law practice, his marriage, his participation in the political and social life of his community, his unprecedented election to public office, his appearance at the American Anti-Slavery Society anniversary, and the transformation in state politics that he had helped bring about. The cumulative effect of these events, he felt, "exerted a potent directing influence" upon him at the beginning of his professional and political career. Afterward, he would not relinquish his faith that a self-reliant black American could overcome most obstacles and win "a well ordered and dignified life."[76]

In late summer 1855, his happy outlook was reinforced by the birth of his first child. On August 3, with John Mercer barely home from the Cincinnati celebration of the West Indies Emancipation, Carrie Langston gave birth to a son. Charles Langston was in his brother's home, brought north by his own speaking date in late July in Cleveland to

raise money to purchase an ex-slave's wife and four children. Carrie
conceded to Mercer and Charles the honor of naming the firstborn.
Together, the brothers settled on names that recognized the importance of both the personal and public black past: Arthur, for their
father's slave who had accompanied them to Ohio, a man of "constitutional want of energy" but thorough likability; and Dessalines, for the
great Haitian hero.[77]

During the next months, his health fully recovered, John Mercer
decided to move his young family. Probably the discomforts of caring
for an infant during a rural winter made Carrie, in particular, realize
the advantages of a less isolated setting. Economically, too, a move
seemed sensible. Confident now that a sufficient living could be obtained from his profession without need for proceeds from the farm,
the black lawyer reasoned that he needed a more central location from
which to build his practice. In the spring of 1856, his term as township
clerk expired, John Mercer Langston, with his wife and baby, left the
Brownhelm farm to take up life in Oberlin.[78]

NOTES

1. Record of Deeds, Lorain County, VI, p. 5, Lorain County Courthouse,
Elyria. The deed between Ebenezer Jones and Langston is dated March 23,
1854. Receipt for lots of hay and corn, sold to Langston for $200, signed by
Jones, Elyria, March 25, 1854; Lorain County tax receipt, Dec. 8, 1854, both
in John Mercer Langston Papers, Fisk University Library; James Harris Fair-
child, "Early Settlement and History of Brownhelm: Presented at the Jubilee
Celebration" (Oberlin, 1867), pp. 1–24, Oberlin College Library; John Mercer
Langston, *From the Virginia Plantation to the National Capitol; or, The First and Only
Negro Representative in Congress from the Old Dominion* (Hartford, 1894; repr. New
York: Johnson Reprint, 1968), pp. 126, 136–37; Population Census of 1860,
Roll 1002, Lorain County, Ohio, Brownhelm township, National Archives.

2. Langston, *Virginia Plantation*, p. 126; William J. Simmons, *Men of Mark:
Eminent, Progressive, and Rising* (Cleveland, 1887; repr. Chicago: Johnson Publishing, 1971), p. 513; *Frederick Douglass' Paper*, July 22, 1853.

3. St. Louis *Globe-Democrat*, Oct. 5, 1890, John Mercer Langston Scrap-
books, 4 vols., III, Moorland-Spingarn Research Center, Howard University;
Langston, *Virginia Plantation*, p. 130; Frederick Douglass to Harriet Beecher
Stowe, Mar. 8, 1853, *Proceedings of the Colored National Convention . . . Rochester,
July, 1853* (Rochester, 1853); James Oliver Horton and Lois E. Horton, *Black
Bostonians* (New York, 1979), pp. 56–57.

4. Contract with Thomas Slater, Jan. 18, 1854, Langston Papers; New York
Freeman, May 14, 1887, JML Scrapbook, II.

5. Augustus Wattles to Dear Brother Wright, Sept. 1, 1837, *Philanthropist*,
Oct. 13, 1837; Augustus Wattles to Dear Bro Wright, Dec. 15, 1837, Elizur

Wright Papers, Library of Congress; J. Mercer Langston to Francis Barry, Dec. 1, 1854, *Frederick Douglass' Paper*, Dec. 15, 1854.

6. St. Louis *Globe-Democrat*, Oct. 5, 1890, JML Scrapbook, III; Fairchild, "Early Settlement and History of Brownhelm," p. 3; Henry Howe, *Historical Collections of Ohio*, 2 vols. (Cincinnati, 1888), II, p. 135; William C. Cochran, *The Western Reserve and the Fugitive Slave Law* (Cleveland, 1920; repr. New York: DaCapo Press, 1972), p. 138.

7. St. Louis *Globe-Democrat*, Oct. 5, 1890, JML Scrapbook, III; Simmons, *Men of Mark*, pp. 346–47; Langston, *Virginia Plantation*, pp. 130–32. Samuel Curtis mentioned in Fairchild, "Early Settlement and History of Brownhelm," p. 3.

8. Cleveland *Leader*, Nov. 4, 9, 1854; Robert S. Fletcher, *A History of Oberlin College*, 2 vols. (Oberlin, 1943), I, pp. 339–40.

9. Langston, *Virginia Plantation*, pp. 133–34; *Official Proceedings of the Ohio State Convention of Colored Freemen . . . Columbus . . . Jan., 1853* (Cleveland, 1853); J. E. Rankin, introductory sketch, John Mercer Langston, *Freedom and Citizenship* (Washington, 1883; repr. Miami: Mnemosyne Reprint, 1969), p. 13; New York *Freemen*, May 14, 1887, JML Scrapbook, II.

10. Langston, *Virginia Plantation*, pp. 134–35.

11. Ibid., pp. 134, 140.

12. *Palladium of Liberty*, May 22, Apr. 3, 1844; Davis Day, "Instruction of Colored People," *Philanthropist*, Oct. 13, 1841. Alumni and former student files of Oberlin College contain material on many black women who had careers as teachers. See also Ellen N. Lawson and Marlene Merrill, "The Antebellum 'Talented Thousandth': Black College Students at Oberlin Before the Civil War," *Journal of Negro Education* 52 (1983):142–55; Ellen NicKenzie Lawson with Marlene D. Merrill, *The Three Sarahs: Documents of Antebellum Black College Women* (New York, 1984), passim.

13. *Palladium of Liberty*, Apr. 27, 1844.

14. Cincinnati *Enquirer*, June 2, 1841; *Philanthropist*, July 14, 1841; Cincinnati *Gazette*, July 23, 1844; *North Star*, June 9, Aug. 11, 1848; *Anti-Slavery Bugle*, Mar. 31, 1855, Dec. 13, 1856; Cleveland *True-Democrat*, Feb. 14, 1850; Lawson, *The Three Sarahs*, pp. 148–67; Sarah Early, "The Great Part Taken by the Women of the West in the Development of the African Methodist Episcopal Church," reprinted in Lawson, *The Three Sarahs*, pp. 171–76.

15. Cincinnati *Sun*, n.d., quoted in *Anti-Slavery Bugle*, Mar. 29, 1856; *Proceedings of the State Convention of Colored Men . . . Columbus, Ohio, . . . Jan., 1856* (Columbus, 1856); *North Star*, May 26, 1848.

16. *Report of the Second Anniversary of the Ohio Anti-Slavery Society . . . Mt. Pleasant . . . Apr., 1837* (Cincinnati, 1837), p. 64; Rev. B. W. Arnett, ed., *Proceedings of the Semi-Centenary Celebration of the African Methodist Church of Cincinnati Held in Allen Temple, Feb. 8th, 9th, and 10th, 1874* (Cincinnati, 1874), p. 120; *Frederick Douglass' Paper*, Oct. 1, 1852, Apr. 28, 1854; Cincinnati *Sun*, n.d., quoted in *Anti-Slavery Bugle*, Mar. 29, 1856; Cleveland *Leader*, July 5, 1858; *North Star*, July 13, 1849.

17. Arnett, ed., *Proceedings*, pp. 122–23, 129–32; Cleveland *Leader*, Feb. 4, 1856.

18. On boarders and extended kinship responsibilities, see Horton and Horton, *Black Bostonians*, pp. 16–19. Wilbur Henry Siebert, *The Mysteries of Ohio's Underground Railroads* (Columbus, 1951), p. 32 and passim.

19. "Cincinnatus" to Editor, July 3, 1848, *North Star*, Aug. 11, 1848.

20. *Minutes . . . of the State Convention of the Colored Citizens of Ohio . . . Columbus . . . Jan., 1849* (Oberlin, 1849); *Anti-Slavery Bugle*, Aug. 20, 1859.

21. *State Convention . . . 1849.*

22. Sara Stanley to George Whipple, Mar. 4, 1864, American Missionary Association Archives, Amistad Research Center, Tulane University (hereafter cited as AMA Papers); *State Convention . . . 1856*; Lawson, *The Three Sarahs*, pp. 47–147.

23. Wilmington *Herald of Freedom*, Oct. 29, 1852; Cincinnati *Atlas*, n.d., quoted in *Voice of the Fugitive*, Apr. 8, 1852; *Aliened American*, Apr. 9, 1853; "Ethiop" to Editor, *Frederick Douglass' Paper*, Mar. 17, 1854; *Herald of Freedom*, n.d., quoted in *National Anti-Slavery Standard*, Oct. 13, 1855.

24. *Proceedings of a Convention of the Colored Men of Ohio . . . Cincinnati . . . Nov. 1858* (Cincinnati, 1858); *Proceedings of the First Annual Meeting of the Ohio State Anti-Slavery Society . . . Xenia . . . Jan. 1860* (title page missing).

25. Langston, *Virginia Plantation*, p. 236.

26. Caroline M. Wall, Alumni Records, Oberlin College Archives; *Oberlin Alumni Magazine* ll (May 1915):342; J. G. DeRoulhac Hamilton, ed., *Papers of Thomas Ruffin* (Raleigh, N.C., 1918), I, p. 409; John Mercer Langston, "A Representative Woman—Mrs. Sara K. Fidler," *A.M.E. Church Review* (July 1887):463.

27. Stephen Wall's will, June 23, 1845, Richmond County Wills, 1779–1915, North Carolina State Archives. Grant of Power of Attorney for Sara K. Fidler estate, Feb. 23, 1888; J. R. Galbraith to O. S. B. Wall, Aug. 24, 1887; Napoleon B. Wall to Langston, Jan. 21, 1887; M.[ial] Wall to Caroline Wall, Mar. 16, 1853, all in Langston Papers; R. G. Galbraith to Izariah S. Root, Jan. 5, 1900, Sara K. Wall Alumni Records, Oberlin College Archives. Both John Wall, who was born July 11, 1852, and Albert Wall attended the Oberlin preparatory department before enlisting in the 54th Massachusetts Regiment of black soldiers. John Wall Alumni questionnaire, Apr. 17, 1908, Oberlin College Archives; Henry Cowles, "Oberlin College Catalogue and Records of Colored Students, 1835–1862" (hereafter cited as Cowles List) ms., Henry Cowles Papers, Oberlin College Library.

28. Langston, *Virginia Plantation*, pp. 141–42; Langston, "A Representative Woman," p. 464; Levi Coffin, *Reminiscences of Levi Coffin* (Cincinnati, 1898; repr. New York: Arno Press, 1968), p. 581; Douglass A. Gamble, "Garrisonian Abolitionists in the West: Some Suggestions for Study," *Civil War History* 23 (March 1977):61; Howe, *Historical Collections of Ohio*, II, p. 775; INTERESSARE to Editor, *Herald of Freedom*, Dec. 5, 1851.

29. *Minutes of the National Convention of Colored Citizens Held at Buffalo . . . Aug., 1843 . . .* (New York 1843), p. 34, reprinted in *Minutes of the Proceedings of the National Negro Conventions, 1830–1864*, ed. Howard H. Bell (New York, 1969); A. Brooks to Editor, Aug. 2, 1842, *Philanthropist*, Aug. 27, 1842; Warren County black meetings reported in *Herald of Freedom*, Dec. 12, 1851, Jan. 7,

1853; *Anti-Slavery Bugle*, Jan. 25, 1851; *Frederick Douglass' Paper*, Oct. 15, 1852; Mahoning *Free Democrat*, Aug. 18, 1853; *Minutes of the State Convention of the Colored Citizens of Ohio . . . Columbus . . . Jan., 1850* (Columbus, 1850); *Proceedings of the Convention of the Colored Freemen of Ohio . . . Cincinnati . . . Jan., 1852* (Cincinnati, 1852).

30. Langston, "A Representative Woman," p. 464; "Negroes of High Rank," untitled, n.d., JML Scrapbook, II; *Free South*, n.d., quoted in *National Anti-Slavery Standard*, Oct. 9, 1858; Langston, *Virginia Plantation*, pp. 141–42.

31. Langston, "A Representative Woman," pp. 463–64; M.[ial] Wall to Caroline Wall, Mar. 16, 1853, Langston Papers; codicil to Stephen Wall's will, Aug. 28, 1845, Richmond County Wills, 1779–1915, North Carolina State Archives.

32. Cowles List; Langston, "A Representative Woman," pp. 473–74.

33. Langston, *Virginia Plantation*, pp. 140–42; Record of the Proceedings of the Ladies Board, July 21, 1851, June 16, 1853, Robert S. Fletcher Papers, Oberlin College Archives; Fletcher, *Oberlin College*, II, p. 672.

34. *Herald of Freedom*, Dec. 12, 1851.

35. M.[ial] Wall to Caroline Wall, Mar. 16, 1853, Langston Papers.

36. O.S.B. Wall to Langston, Jan. 23, 1854, Langston Papers; *Herald of Freedom*, Jan. 7, 1853; Cleveland *True-Democrat*, June 13, 1853. An Oberlin black meeting chose Wall and Langston delegates to the 1853 national convention. Ibid.

37. Langston to Dear Sister, Oct. 23, 1853, Langston Papers.

38. Langston to Sister Carrie, Mar. 9, 1854, Langston Papers; Record of the Proceedings of the Ladies Board, June 16, 25, 1853, Fletcher Papers, Oberlin College Archives.

39. Young Ladies' Literary Society Constitution and Minutes, 1851–54, Fletcher Papers, Oberlin College Archives.

40. Langston, *Virginia Plantation*, pp. 140–42; "Negroes of High Rank," untitled, n.d., JML Scrapbook, II; Carrie to Mercer, Mar. 18, 1887 (?), Langston Papers.

41. Langston, *Virginia Plantation*, pp. 142–43; contract with Thomas Slater, Langston Papers; Marriage Record, Lorain County, 11, p. 267, Lorain County Courthouse; affidavit of C. M. and John M. Langston, Oct. 26, 1891; Amanda A. [Thomas] Wall Declaration for Widow's Pension, May 29, 1891, both in O. S. B. Wall, Military Service Records, (NNCC), National Archives; *General Catalogue of Oberlin College 1883–1908* (Oberlin, 1909), p. 968; Ellen Henle and Marlene Merrill, "Antebellum Black Coeds at Oberlin College," Oberlin *Alumni Magazine* 75 (Jan.-Feb. 1980):21.

42. Langston, *Virginia Plantation*, p. 160; Potsdam (N.Y) *Courier and Freeman*, n.d., 1889, Langston Scrapbook, II.

43. J. Mercer Langston to Francis Barry, *Frederick Douglass' Paper*, Dec. 15, 1854.

44. Langston, *Virginia Plantation*, pp. 126–27, 135; James Frisbie to Editor, Mar. 14, 1855, *Frederick Douglass' Paper*, Apr. 6, 1855; Fairchild, "History of Brownhelm," p. 3.

45. Montgomery (Ala.) *State Sentinel*, Feb. 3, 1868.

46. J. Mercer Langston to Julia Griffiths, Oct. 29, 1854, *Frederick Douglass' Paper*, Nov. 10, 1854; Antoinette L. Brown to Julia Griffiths, Nov. 8, 1854, *Frederick Douglass' Paper*, Nov. 25, 1854.

47. Antoinette L. Brown to Julia Griffiths, Nov. 8, 1854, *Frederick Douglass' Paper*, Nov. 25, 1854; J. M. Langston to Julia Griffiths, *Frederick Douglass' Paper*, Dec. 1, 1854; Samuel A. S. Lowery to Editor, Feb. 28, 1855, *Provincial Freeman*, Mar. 17, 1855; Francis Barry to Editor, *Liberator*, Oct. 6, 1854; Francis Barry to J. Mercer Langston, *Frederick Douglass' Paper*, Nov. 24, 1854, Jan. 4, 1855. On Lowery, see Loren Schweninger, "The Free-Slave Phenomenon: James P. Thomas and the Black Community in Ante-Bellum Nashville," *Civil War History* 22 (1976): 296–97, 302, fns. 22, 47; Simmons, *Men of Mark*, pp. 77–80.

48. J. Mercer Langston to Francis Barry, *Frederick Douglass' Paper*, Dec. 15, 1854, Jan. 26, 1855.

49. Letter to Editor, Mar. 14, 1855, *Frederick Douglass' Paper*, Apr. 6, 1855; J. A. Spencer to Editor, Jan. 8, 1855, *Anti-Slavery Bugle*, Jan. 13, 1855; Cleveland *Leader*, n.d., quoted in *Anti-Slavery Bugle*, Dec. 30, 1854.

50. Langston, *Virginia Plantation*, pp. 128–30; Fairchild, "History of Brownhelm," p. 3.

51. William C. Nell to William Lloyd Garrison, *Liberator*, Nov. 14, 1856.

52. Louisville *Courier-Journal*, July 16, 1869.

53. Langston, *Virginia Plantation*, pp. 143–45.

54. J. Mercer Langston to Editor, *Frederick Douglass' Paper*, n.d., quoted in *Anti-Slavery Bugle*, Apr. 28, 1855; Oberlin *News*, Aug. 12, 1875; Langston, *Virginia Plantation*, p.144.

55. New York *Tribune*, May 12, 1855.

56. J. Mercer Langston, "Speech Before the Union Society," May 23, 1848, ms., Langston Papers.

57. Lorain County *News*, Aug. 4, 1870; John M. Langston, "Eulogy on the Life and Character of John I. Gaines, Delivered at the First Annual Meeting of the Ohio State Anti-Slavery Society by John M. Langston, at Xenia, Ohio, January 3d, 1860," *Liberator*, Apr. 27, 1860; Langston, *Virginia Plantation*, frontispiece and dedication; Louisville *Courier-Journal*, July 16, 1869; Montgomery *State Sentinel*, Feb. 3, 1868.

58. J. Mercer Langston to Editor, *Frederick Douglass' Paper*, n.d., quoted in *Anti-Slavery Bugle*, Apr. 28, 1855.

59. John I. Gaines to Editor, Jan. 8, 1855, *Provincial Freeman*, Jan. 20, 1855; Peter H. Clark to Henry Bibb, Jan. 31, 1852, *Voice of the Fugitive*, Feb. 12, 1852; J. Mercer Langston to Editor, *Frederick Douglass' Paper*, n.d., quoted in *Anti-Slavery Bugle*, Apr. 28, 1855.

60. *National Anti-Slavery Standard*, Apr. 28, 1855; *National Era*, May 3, 1855.

61. *Frederick Douglass' Paper*, Jan. 16, 1854; *National Anti-Slavery Standard*, n.d., quoted in *Liberator*, Dec. 29, 1854; J. Mercer Langston to Editor, Jan. 1, 1855, *National Anti-Slavery Standard*, n.d., quoted in *Frederick Douglass' Paper*, Jan. 19, 1855; Langston, *Virginia Plantation*, pp. 145, 150.

62. Langston, *Virginia Plantation*, pp. 147–48; John Mercer Langston, "The World's Anti-Slavery Movement: Its Heroes and its Triumphs," a lecture

delivered at Xenia and Cleveland, Ohio, Aug. 2 and 3, 1858, Langston, *Freedom and Citizenship*, p. 62.

63. William C. Nell to William Lloyd Garrison, *Liberator*, Nov. 14, 1856; *National Anti-Slavery Standard*, Dec. 7, 1867; New York *Tribune*, n.d., quoted in *Frederick Douglass' Paper*, July 22, 1853; William Wells Brown, *The Rising Son; or, The Antecedents and Advancement of the Colored Race* (Boston, 1874; repr. Miami: Mnemosyne Reprint, 1969), p. 448.

64. Brown, *The Rising Son*, p. 448; Potsdam (N.Y.) *Courier and Freeman*, n.d., 1889, JML Scrapbook, II; Langston, "World's Anti-Slavery Movement," *Freedom and Citizenship*, p. 66; William C. Nell to William Lloyd Garrison, *Liberator*, Nov. 14, 1856.

65. New York *Times*, May 10, 1855; New York *Tribune*, May 10, 1855; *National Anti-Slavery Standard*, May 12, 19, 1855.

66. *National Anti-Slavery Standard*, May 19, 1855; *Annual Report Presented to the American Anti-Slavery Society* (New York, 1855), pp. 131–36; New York *Tribune*, May 10, 1855; New York *Times*, May 10, 1855; New York *Herald*, May 10, 1855; *Liberator*, May 18, 25, 1855; Langston, *Virginia Plantation*, p. 150.

67. Salmon P. Chase to E. S. Hamlin, Feb. 9, 1855, American Historical Association, *Diary and Correspondence of Salmon P. Chase* (Washington, 1903; repr. New York: DaCapo Press, 1971), p. 270; New York *Times*, May 10, 1855; David Donald, *Charles Sumner and the Coming of the Civil War* (New York, 1960), p. 271; Hartford *Courant*, Jan. 7, 1887, JML Scrapbook, II; Langston, *Virginia Plantation*, p. 149.

68. New York *Tribune*, May 10, 11, 1855; New York *Times*, May 11, 12, 1855; New York *Herald*, May 10, 1855; *Liberator*, June 8, 1855; Hartford *Courant*, Jan. 7, 1887, JML Scrapbook, II.

69. Donald, *Charles Sumner*, p. 271; Langston, *Virginia Plantation*, pp. 145, 150.

70. Salmon P. Chase to A.M.G., Feb. 15, 1855; Salmon P. Chase to L. D. Campbell, May 25, 1855, both in *Diary and Correspondence of Salmon P. Chase*, pp. 271–74; Richard H. Sewall, *Ballots for Freedom* (New York, 1976), pp. 273–74.

71. Cleveland *Leader*, July 12, 1855.

72. J.W. Schuckers, *Life and Public Services of Salmon Portland Chase* (New York, 1874; repr. Miami: Mnemosyne Reprint, 1969), pp. 79–80, 166–68, 172.

73. "Cincinnatus" to Editor, Oct. 19, 1855, *Frederick Douglass' Paper*, Oct. 25, 1855; Clayton S. Ellsworth, "Oberlin and the Anti-Slavery Movement Up to the Civil War," Ph.D. diss., Cornell University, 1930, pp. 118–23; Langston, *Virginia Plantation*, p. 255; Tiffin (Ohio) *Advertiser*, n.d., quoted in *Liberator*, Oct. 12, 1855.

74. *Frederick Douglass' Paper*, July 20, 1855; Cincinnati *Gazette*, Aug. 2, 1855; "Cincinnatus" to Editor, *Frederick Douglass' Paper*, Aug. 31, 1855; "Cincinnatus" to Editor, Oct. 19, 1855, *Frederick Douglass' Paper*, Oct. 25, 1855.

75. Cleveland *Leader*, Nov. 1, 1855; Sewall, *Ballots for Freedom*, pp. 273–74; Eugene Holloway Roseboom and Francis Phelps Weisenburger, *A History of*

Ohio (New York, 1934), pp. 247–48; *Proceedings of the State Convention of Colored Men . . . Columbus . . . Jan., 1856* (Columbus, 1856); *Liberator*, Feb. 15, 1856.

76. Langston, *Virginia Plantation*, p. 146; Preamble and Constitution of the National Equal Rights League, *Proceedings of the National Convention of Colored Men . . . Syracuse, N.Y. . . . Oct., 1864* (Boston, 1864).

77. Langston, *Virginia Plantation*, pp. 156–57; Cleveland *Leader*, July 23, 26, 1855.

78. Langston, *Virginia Plantation*, p. 157.

CHAPTER 9

Life and Labor in a Biracial Town

1856–65

O N a bright spring morning in 1856 the black lawyer, with his wife and infant son tucked warmly beside him in the wagon, touched his prized chestnut sorrel team off the Brownhelm road and onto the still-unpaved streets of Oberlin. Even though his wagon was heavy with meats and root vegetables from the farm, as well as some household goods, and the thaw-struck road had become clay sludge, John Mercer figured contentedly to have made the nine-mile trip in an easy two hours. The bright sunshine burnished his "buoyant and happy" mood. Twelve years had passed since he shyly awakened in the Oberlin hotel to the Sunday morning spectacle. Now, at the age of twenty-six, Langston confidently looked forward to establishing himself socially and professionally in what he called "the most noted Abolition town in America."[1]

In preparation for the move, Langston had swapped the Brownhelm farm to his brother-in-law, O. S. B. Wall, receiving in exchange two parcels of Oberlin land. One included a brand new two-story frame house and was situated in a choice location on East College Street in an expensive and all-white neighborhood. Here Mercer and Carrie intended to live, "the first of their class who had undertaken to purchase and locate a home in that particular section." But just as John Mercer turned his horses onto East College, a white resident hailed him down. Langston, already in the habit (shared with other northerners during that intensely political decade) of identifying men by political party, knew the white man as an "extremely doubtful" Republican and an "officious and meddlesome" personage. Ignoring Carrie, although black women were addressed as ladies in Oberlin, the man demanded brusquely: "Are you coming to live among us aristocrats? Do you think you can maintain yourself among us?" Langston interpreted the questions as a crude warning to himself and Carrie "that they would find the usual social barriers erected against their advancement even there." Rejecting the temptation of an "ungenteel, vulgar or blasphemous" response, Langston replied shortly, "We shall see," and urged his horses toward his new home.[2]

In the light of Langston's future career in Oberlin, it is no wonder that he would take a certain grim pleasure in recalling this insulting welcome. Or rather, half a welcome. For once he and Carrie reached their house, the more hospitable face of white Oberlin's attitudes toward blacks was revealed. The nearest of their new neighbors came out to greet them. On seeing boxes not yet unpacked, the child fretful, and the house unheated, these Oberliners cordially insisted that Carrie and Arthur should rest with them until Mercer could install some comfort. These neighborly gestures did much to revive the young family's spirits.[3]

During the subsequent fifteen years (until 1871) that Langston would live in Oberlin, he so nearly would exemplify the town's abolitionist-free labor ideology that some wag, paraphrasing Voltaire, might well have quipped that if Langston did not exist, Oberlin would have had to invent him. In a sense, it did. Although Langston believed that he, like every man, must make himself, he never hesitated to give full credit to Oberlin, both for his education and for the opportunity to live as an equal in a racially integrated society or, at any rate, in the closest approximation to one that existed at the time. In a host of ways, not the least of which was his election and repeated reelection to public office, Oberlin promoted his public and private careers. The law practice launched in Brownhelm, abetted by electoral recognition, became successful and lucrative. All the while, as will be discussed in later chapters, Langston deepened his involvements in antislavery politics and the black movement, assisted in both enterprises by Oberlin allies. In short, as family and professional man, town official, and political reformer, Langston seemed living proof that, as he himself would explain the Oberlin ideals to later audiences, the black man given an equal start in life with the white man, and equal opportunities along the way, would achieve equally. It was because of such equitable treatment, Langston would assert, that Oberlin black men stood " 'cheek by jowl' upon the same platform with white men."[4]

Yet, as the contradictory nature of Langston's own reception into Oberlin illustrated, the racial situation was far more complex than this declaration implied. Notorious as a haven for fugitive slaves and den of "amalgamationists," Oberlin was, to an extent, a community in conflict with its own image and high ideals. Beneath Oberlin's "agreeable pepper and salt aspect," as Professor John Morgan characterized it,[5] lay problems involving differences in cultural background, educational level, and social class, as well as persistent racial prejudice.

Langston's position was correspondingly difficult. As he attempted to broaden and extend Oberlin's commitment to racial equality, he would encounter white prejudice and black mistrust. On occasion, frustrated and insulted, John Mercer would give vent to his emotions. But most often, he would try to behave as a bridge between white and black communities, responsible to both. As he helped to lead white and black residents toward a fuller actualization of the vision of a racially equalitarian society, it could be said, not merely that Oberlin was inventing Langston, but that Langston, in important ways, was helping to invent Oberlin.

By the mid-fifties, Oberlin registered signs of growth and comfort. Its population, predominantly transplanted white New Englanders and New Yorkers and black southerners, had increased to more than two thousand. Stamped indelibly a western town by its tumble-down plank sidewalks and unpaved streets, haunts of wandering livestock and scratching chickens, it also boasted New England-style "neat white houses and tidy yards," and numerous handsome new residences built in mid-decade. Oberlin's economy continued to center on the college, which was thriving. But the town also was becoming a marketing center for the surrounding countryside. Fresh impetus to enterprise and business had come with the arrival of the railroad in October 1852—an occasion enthusiastically celebrated with an initiatory ride, supper, and speeches by theological student John Mercer Langston and leading townsmen. A lively Commercial Block included three dry goods stores, numerous small groceries, meat markets, shoe and book stores. Although many individuals were "afraid" to tell the census taker "anything near the precise value of their possessions," white wealth in Oberlin on the eve of Civil War appears to have been rather evenly distributed. There were few rich (only eight persons claimed $20,000 or more in property) and comparatively few poor (fifty persons claimed $100 or less in property). Well over one-third of the white heads of households had real and personal property holdings officially assessed at $1,000 to $5,000—"a fair share of this world's goods" in Oberlin's reckoning. Almost 75 percent of the white male heads of families (246 of 318) were employed in professional, entrepreneurial, artisanal, or proprietary occupations. In the spring of 1857 an Elyria editor would note "substantial prosperity" in Oberlin. But by that fall a financial panic would spread from Cincinnati across the West and North so that by the summer of 1858 Oberlin merchants and towns-people would lament, with Professor Henry Peck: "Money is very scarce hereabouts." Still, with recovery by decade's end, the editor of the newly instituted local newspaper would be calling Oberlin a "go-ahead Ohio village."[6]

If Oberlin's expanding economy offered certain advantages to an aspiring attorney, its peculiar racial make-up and practices held out particular promise to the young black lawyer. Oberlin, in a former student's apt phrase, represented the "phenomenon of the bi-racial town." For the nearly two decades from Oberlin's founding to the mid-fifties, the actual number of black residents had remained quite small. In 1850, only 136 blacks (71 female, 65 male) were recorded, although the proportion of blacks to whites was substantial—about 11.5 percent of the total village population of 1,133.[7] The Fugitive Slave Law apparently sparked a black exodus, for not more than twenty of those listed in the 1850 federal census would reappear in the official enumeration ten years later. Langston's 1854 memorial to the Ohio Assembly, using information compiled by Wall, listed only 135 Negro residents of Oberlin ("permanent colored persons," as Wall put it, obviously excluding fugitives in transit).[8] But in the second half of the pre-war decade, with increasing economic opportunities, especially for skilled craftsmen, the black population grew dramatically. Among the new black residents were newly emancipated slaves, brought or sent by their ex-masters. In one instance, Maxwell Chambers, a planter in Salisbury, North Carolina, in 1854 sent eighteen of his emancipated slaves to Oberlin; following his death the next year, forty-eight others arrived: Chambers's will provided funds to assist in the resettlement of all sixty-six. By 1860, four heads of household surnamed Chambers lived in Russia township where Oberlin was situated, and all were property owners.[9]

Fugitive slaves, too, apparently with renewed confidence in the village's ability to protect them, remained in Oberlin rather than going on to Canada. Some fugitives were long-term residents. John Ramsey, whom Langston would remember in his autobiography, was one of several Oberlin blacks who cautiously told the census taker in 1850 that his place of origin was "not known." But, a decade later, Ramsey admitted it to be Louisiana. Without job or property in 1850, by 1860 Ramsey had become an "engineer" (mechanic) and owned real estate worth $450. Mason James A. Stone, a Kentucky fugitive, maintained an Oberlin residence (valued at $1,400 in 1860) with his wife and five children for some thirteen years. Village leaders kept his race and fugitive status secret until, after volunteering and being accepted as a white soldier in the Union army, he was killed in battle in October 1862. By January 1, 1859, despite several attempts to recapture runaway slaves from Oberlin, John Watson, a prominent black resident, reported that some twenty-eight fugitives "with about 50 children born in freedom" resided in the village.[10] An additional factor in the black population growth was a substantial increase in the number of black students attending Oberlin Institute during the decade. In the period 1852–60, doubtless partly as the result of Langston's efforts to stimulate black Ohioans' interest in education, more than 160 Negro students attended Oberlin, almost 60 percent of the entire pre-war total. Thirty-five black students were counted in the 1860 census.[11] For the village of Oberlin overall, the 1860 census recorded 422 blacks (212 female, 210 male) in a total population of 2,115. The village was nearly 20 percent black, the highest black population proportionately of any predominantly white community in the state.[12]

During Oberlin's first three decades, the town founders' evolving efforts to promote racial equality were both concerted and broad, with opportunities in one area tending to reinforce and expand into another. Despite lingering problems, black men and women in Oberlin experienced unparalleled access to the educational, political, economic, religious, and social life of the community. In turn, black Oberliners, individually and overall, achieved measurable gains.

Educational opportunities were available not only through the preparatory and collegiate departments of Oberlin College. From the start, the village common school had been open to Negro children. Provision for unlettered Negro adolescents and adults initially was made through special classes at the college, but in 1844 these were moved to the Liberty School House. By the late fifties, the American Missionary Association would support a missionary teacher for black adults; during the sixties, Oberlin black student Fanny Jackson and two female assistants would conduct an evening school. Sunday schools, too, offered instruction. Langston would teach one of these classes in 1865, for "old gray haired colored men." (At the beginning, Langston would boast with teacherly zeal, some of his students "hardly knew A from the last letter of the alphabet," but after three months had learned to read "with ease and beauty in any of the fine passages of the New Testament.") Black children and adults appear to have taken full advantage of their chances for schooling. By 1860 more than one-fourth of all black Oberliners, exclusive of students enrolled at Oberlin College, were attending school. It seems equally telling that none of the thirty-three Negro illiterates (7.8 percent of the whole black population) recorded by the census taker was under eighteen years of age.[13]

When it came to politics, Oberlin males of more than "one-half Saxon descent" enjoyed the voting privileges supposedly guaranteed such persons by Ohio law but often denied in actuality. Whether Negroes with a lesser proportion of white ancestry also were permitted to vote is a matter of conjecture. Hostile report had it that the village's first act on receipt of the charter of incorporation in 1846 had been approval of a resolution entitling all Negro residents to vote. According to William Howard Day, fugitive slave William P. Newman had been the first Negro voter in Lorain County. From the mid-fifties on, each election brought bitter charges from the Democratic press that large numbers of legally disqualified blacks voted in Oberlin and Lorain County. In 1862 the Wayne County *Democrat* would even print sixty-seven names purporting to be those of blacks who had voted in the fall election, causing the Lorain County *News* to retort that half of the names were probably bogus and the others doubtless "whiter than the Oberlin Democrat who furnished the names for publication." But what seemed corroboration of the Democrats' darkest suspicions came ironically from John Mercer Langston. "Up in the upper part of the State, on the Lake Shore and Reserve," he would inform a safely out-of-state black audience in 1865, "we have gone so far as to say that anybody that will take the responsibility of swearing that he is more than half-white, shall vote. We do not care how black he is." In voting, as in other matters touching black freedom and citizenship, Oberlin apparently had determined that personal conscience should take precedence over law. How early this system might have been hit upon it is impossible to say. It is clear that Democrats sometimes foiled its execution. One, tavernkeeper Chauncey Wack, habitually mounted a pollside vigil to challenge "any man whose face seemed a shade too dark." Langston sarcastically recounted one such incident. He himself had accompanied a black ex-North Carolinian, once a voter in that state, to the polls, where "a man—somewhat in the shape of a man," successfully challenged his vote.[14]

Black access to Oberlin's economic life seems the most remarkable, although the least remarked upon, facet of the biracial town. While blacks in other northern communities often complained that abolitionist equalitarianism ended where economic interests began, in Oberlin, perhaps uniquely in the North, abolitionist ideals seemed practically wedded to the free labor ideology. The fact that so many white townsmen were themselves the beneficiaries of the notion that free men given an equal chance could achieve social mobility and economic independence reinforced Oberlin's official commitment to racial equality. Together with the other pertaining factors, economic self-sufficiency made it easier for white Oberlin citizens to understand that the half-free black man in the North might require a helping hand: initial assistance in finding work, training, compensation for past wrongs. Not all Oberlin employers were inherently just with their black workers, but in Oberlin blacks could appeal to a community sense of fair play. Kentucky fugitive Lewis Clarke, afterwards well-known on the abolitionist lecture circuit, while sheltering in Oberlin in the early forties, was overjoyed to work at digging a cellar until he learned that his white employer was notorious for "bad pay." Still, on completing the job, Clarke found an arbiter who persuaded the recalcitrant employer to pay him the promised wages. In Oberlin, white and black citizens regularly extended moral and material assistance to black immigrants.[15]

Such black men and women themselves often had demonstrated much energy and initiative in reaching Oberlin, qualities that proved useful in earning a living there. State Assemblyman James Monroe of Oberlin in 1857 made the point that black men "who emigrate with their families a thousand miles to send their children to school and hear the gospel preached, are not men whose presence you need to fear in your midst." Specifically, he mentioned Allen Jones, the burly blacksmith who boasted of earning huge sums for his North Carolina master before purchasing himself and family members at a cost totaling more than $5,000. Jones had transported his family in a wagon to Oberlin, where four of his seven children, including Langston's classmate James Monroe Jones, had become Oberlin College graduates.[16]

The result of white encouragement combined with black ambition was a black economic achievement almost certainly unmatched in any other northern community. "Businessmen are colored," the Oberlin correspondent of a Cleveland newspaper noted as early as 1852, "and for enterprise, as far as their capital allows, they are equal to their white competitors. . . . The usual prejudice against colored tradesmen exists here in a very slight degree, if at all. . . ." In like vein, Monroe assured the scoffing General Assembly: "In my own county, some of our most substantial citizens are colored men. They read the papers, they are shrewd businessmen, and they amass property." During the fifties, Oberlin black residents engaged in a variety of occupations. Many were self-employed. In unexampled ways, black employment in Oberlin reflected the free labor ideal described by Republican Congressman Philemon Bliss, Langston's legal mentor. In his part of Ohio, Bliss said, "the farmer works his own farm; the mechanic labors in his own shop, and the merchant sells his own goods. True, labor is there sold, but mainly as a temporary expedient to enable the laborer to acquire a small capital. . . ." By 1856 black abolitionist William C. Nell, visiting Langston in Oberlin, was able to report that there were "cabinet makers, house contractors and builders, carpenters, blacksmiths, stucco workers, masons, coach trimmers and harness makers, upholsterers, bootmakers, grocers, farmers"—all black.[17]

Overall, the economic gains were impressive. From 1850 to 1860, the number of blacks engaged in some form of skilled employment rose from eight to fifty-four. In 1860, more than 50 percent of the recorded black male heads of household were employed in skilled occupational categories. "Everywhere," exclaimed a visitor in 1867, "we saw white men and black men doing business together. They shook hands, conversed, discussed, and bartered precisely as though they had all been of one color. The Negroes were well dressed and exceedingly polite . . . manly and frank."[18]

From 1850 to 1860, moreover, advances in property holding, encouraged by the relatively high land availability in the village, matched the marked increases in the black population and in the number of blacks engaged in favored employment. In 1850, the total value of black property holdings was $9,850, with only five persons owning property worth $500 or more. In 1859, as part of the ongoing progress reports filed by Ohio blacks, provisioner John Watson announced that black residents owned fifty houses and other property to the value of $100,000. The federal census the following year showed the value to be $110,000—a sum more than 11 times as great as it had been a decade before, as compared to a population increase of only 3.1 times. Further, the number of persons with substantial property had increased greatly—thirty-seven blacks had wealth totaling $500 or more, nineteen were worth $1,000 or more. Given the effects of the panic of 1857 and the large number of fugitive slaves in the population, the improving economic health of Oberlin blacks was the more noteworthy.[19]

By the eve of Civil War, the twelve outstanding black political and social leaders in Oberlin were all exemplars of the free labor ideology. Besides Langston, they were the brothers Henry and Wilson Evans, cabinetmakers and upholsterers (Henry Evans was named town sexton in 1860); John H. Scott, saddler and harnessmaker, whose harnesses won first prizes in two county fairs in the fall of 1859; John E. Patterson and Henry T. Patterson, both master masons whose skills were employed in the erection of college buildings as well as private construction; John Campton, master carpenter; Solomon Grimes, blacksmith; David L. Watson and O. S. B. Wall, bootmakers (David Watson was also a farmer); John Watson; and Sabram Cox.[20]

Ex-slave John Watson was the leading Negro businessman. A "man of great energy," the short, stocky, light-skinned Virginian had been a drayman until his horse died and he could not raise the money to buy another. Subsequently, he had tried a hand at brick masonry before settling in as a grocer and confectioner. By 1852 he owned a grocery prominently situated in the middle of Commercial Block on Main Street. To its plainer comestibles, he gradually added such luxuries as oysters and homemade candy, and in 1857 opened an ice cream saloon with marble tables in the rear of his shop. On one occasion, Watson asked the county sheriff to convey a gift can of "splendid oysters" to George W. Washburn, editor of the Elyria *Independent-Democrat* and prominent Republican. Sheriff and editor enjoyed a midnight feast, the "bivalves soon went down," and Washburn pronounced Watson's Oyster and Cream Saloon "the best west of Nova Scotia."[21] Active in black protest, Watson often shared platforms in Oberlin and at state black conventions with Langston.[22] Although in 1850 at the age of thirty-two, Watson could neither read nor write, by 1860, apparently having taken advantage of Oberlin's adult instructional programs, he had attained literacy. And in 1871, upon Langston's resignation, he would be appointed to the Oberlin school board.[23]

Ex-slave Sabram Cox, a part of antislavery legend since boyhood, was a prosperous farmer. A Virginia-born mulatto, Cox had been only fifteen in 1837 when a mob attacked the press of his employer, abolitionist editor Elijah P. Lovejoy, in Alton, Illinois. "The only person who dared haul from the river in an express wagon the sunken printing press," the boy afterward had driven through the threatening crowds with a coffin in which to place Lovejoy's body. Sabram managed to save $600 and "attended to his family affairs" before setting off for Oberlin in 1839. He entered the preparatory department and studied until 1847, when he began farming.[24] Reputedly one of the village's most efficient underground railroad agents and an activist in the local and state black movement,[25] Cox lived with his wife, Elsie, and three children in the neighborhood of Oberlin's President Finney. In 1865, Sabram Cox would be elected to the Oberlin city council. In 1883, a writer assembling materials on escaping fugitives in early Oberlin would discover a prime source in Sabram Cox, who struck him as a person of "rare intelligence and noble qualities of mind."[26]

In several respects, the twelve black leaders reflected the predominant values of the black community. All were self-employed. Nine were officially worth $2,000 or more, five of them possessing real and personal property valued in excess of $3,000. All but one mulatto, they had a median age of thirty-eight. In a community where 75 percent of the black residents had southern roots (not counting children under twelve born in Ohio), all but one had origins in the slave states. In a community where 80 percent of the black families (54 of 67) were headed by males—the corresponding figure for whites was 77 percent (246 of 318)—all were married and had families, generally sizable ones. In fact, this leadership group, taken together with their extended families and boarders, accounted for nearly one-fourth of the town's black population. One or more apprentices resided in most of their homes and, with one or two exceptions, every child from five to nineteen years of age in their households was attending school. From among the children of seven of these leaders, ten became Oberlin College graduates, seven received some education in the college, and six received training in the preparatory department. Six of these men were to play prominent roles in the Oberlin-Wellington slave rescue case (chapter 10). While such matters cannot be documented conclusively, strong religious convictions and an active social conscience appear to have been governing influences on most, if not all, of their lives. By their own industry, integrity, and intelligence, these twelve leading citizens represented Oberlin's strongest argument in favor of free labor and biracialism as a workable and satisfying way of life.[27]

In Oberlin, social mobility and where one lived usually had more to do with capability than with color. Generally speaking, like his white counterpart, the wealthier the Oberlin black man, the more respectable the neighborhood in which he tended to live. A cluster of blacks lived in the southeast, the poorest part of town, and a smaller although somewhat better-off group lived in the northeast close by the Liberty School House (neither area was without whites of comparable economic status). At the other economic extreme was the otherwise all-white section where Langston lived. But with these three exceptions, housing patterns were fairly well mixed.[28]

The degree to which racial integration was sanctioned in Oberlin is perhaps best indicated by a protest lodged against a particular case of discrimination. During the summer of 1862 the village innkeeper began to refuse to serve Negro diners, although previously blacks had always been welcome at the table. A biracial committee condemned the new policy as "in direct violation of the principles held and averred by the founders, patrons, and present authorities of this College. . . .no man who persists in this policy deserves the hotel patronage of this community, and no such man shall ever have ours." Because the matter disappeared from the public prints, it may be assumed that the protest was effective. Significantly, in Oberlin it was the advocate or practitioner of segregation and discrimination who was on the defensive, rather than the reverse. Racial mixing in Oberlin extended into religion and even, to a lesser degree, into private social life. The nondenominational

Union church (later First church), the only one in the village until 1855, when mainly Democratic dissenters of its "politico-religious teaching" formed an Episcopal congregation, always surprised visitors by its non-discriminatory seating of blacks in choir and congregation. When it came to private parties and entertainments, whether hosted by whites or Negroes, personal preference determined the guest list. "Every man is emphatically master of his own house," a visiting journalist reported in 1867. "He invites in whom he wishes and keeps out whom he chooses." While it seems certain that most white and black socializing was done separately, it is equally certain that the Langstons and other prominent black families entertained, and were entertained by, whites of their own social level. By the same token, some white and Negro children played together. Langston himself would boast of "the community in which I live, . . . which, thank God, from the day it was built, . . . made no distinction on account of color in social life."[29]

In their attempt to extend the limits of racial equality, white and black Oberliners struggled against inevitable racial prejudice and differences of educational levels, cultural backgrounds, and reform values. Divisions existed not merely between races, but between classes, in the black as well as the white community. Ironically, it was in the church, Oberlin's most visible showcase of racial integration, that racial tensions surfaced. As early as 1853, an Oberlin critic observed that most blacks boycotted Sunday evening church services for their own gatherings in the Liberty School House, and further speculated that they would attend a separate black church, were one available. Blacks "usually" did prefer separate religious meetings, "especially those of the more social kind," the Oberlin *Evangelist* admitted regretfully. Finney's and Morgan's sermons, geared to a college audience, often proved too complex for men and women only months or years removed from slavery. Morgan agreed that "the preaching is necessarily for the most part above them—'the hay,' as one old colored playmate of mine . . . said of the New York preachings—'the hay is raising too high.' " Blacks may also have suspected that Finney, with his emphasis on soul saving, was not sufficiently sensitive to their reform needs. At the 1852 First of August observance in Oberlin, Finney argued that slavery was a "dispensation of providence" and that it would be better to train blacks in Christian forgiveness than "to stimulate their resentment" against their wrongs. Professor Timothy Hudson, one of the faculty's most active abolitionists, thought blacks had been "greatly tried" by Finney's remarks. They would be "more cool" toward him in future, he predicted. "They were too cool before."[30]

Alfred J. Anderson
(Ohio Historical Society)

Peter H. Clark
(Cincinnati Historical Society)

William Howard Day (From B. F.
Wheeler, *Cullings from Zion's Poets*
[1907])

John I. Gaines
(Cincinnati Historical Society)

David Jenkins
(Ohio Historical Society)

James P. Poindexter
(Ohio Historical Society)

Wallace Shelton
(Cincinnati Historical Society)

Frances E. W. Harper (Schomburg
Center for Research in Black Culture,
The New York Public Library, Astor,
Lenox and Tilden Foundations)

Unquestionably, many black men and women also shrank from encountering the real or imagined antipathy of white parishioners. The A.M.A. missionary to needy black residents in 1859–60, whose own first impulse had been to condemn Negroes who "stand aloof from all the means of grace that are in this place, *free to all,*" shortly changed her emphasis. "This place is by no means free from the spirit of prejudice which has kept free persons of color from rising to their proper place in society," she reported. Many whites, "if they had the power," would have barred blacks from common school and church. "Many of the colored feel this so strongly that they keep themselves away from both school instruction and the means of grace." At the other extreme, white benevolence discomfited black recipients. Poor blacks, "even some who had pressed me most to teach them," the A.M.A. worker found, were "too proud" to attend "a missionary school." Attendance picked up only after she began teaching in the privacy of her lodgings, and increased more when a black fugitive, whom she had earlier taught to read, began to conduct an evening school. Morgan advocated missionary work among blacks throughout the land, but conceded they might well resent it. "Conceit and self-sufficiency," he observed, "are great besetments of our colored friends."[31]

Black racial solidarity and cultural preferences contributed to separatist leanings. Like the separate black village meetings long held to protest, celebrate, or promote reform efforts (chapter 4), the separate black religious sessions often dealt with peculiarly black concerns. Even the most committed white Oberliners, the *Evangelist* pointed out, had difficulty entering "as fully as they do" into black sympathies, "deep and strong, as for example with their brethren in bonds." At the same time, the Union church seemed to many blacks, as Langston himself would put it, "the church of white persons of Oberlin." Many blacks preferred the forms of black worship. Besides, the *Evangelist* discerned some black prejudice against whites, attributing it to "common sympathy under abuse for their color" which "has fearful power both to harrow the sensibilities and to provoke towards jealousy and bitterness."[32]

By the spring of 1859, "a large number" of blacks regularly absented themselves from church services. Convinced that Oberlin's own resources were no longer adequate to deal with the needs of poor and uneducated blacks, many of them recent arrivals, Morgan requested and received A.M.A. funds to support a missionary to the Negro community. But the white missionary, Zeruiah Weed, the college's first female graduate, encountered immediate opposition from the "more prosperous" black citizens. She observed that "the power of caste is very strong here among the intelligent and wealthy colored people (of whom there are a few) and the poor and ignorant." The former opposed her work "because they say it is causing, or will cause, a separation between the colored and whites."[33] How much the mission actually contributed to the sequel is uncertain. Perhaps of greater importance was the black population increase, by then sufficient to support a separate institutional life. In early 1860, in a period of exacerbated racial tensions, the recently organized white Methodist Episcopal church held a revival. Its principal result was the formation of a small Wesleyan Methodist church with "an almost all colored" congregation. The "general judgment" of Oberlin opposed it as "uncalled for, unwise, and harmful," noted an Oberlin historian, but when blacks persevered in their demand, charitable whites offered generous assistance.[34]

Nonetheless, some black Oberliners did continue to attend Union church and, after the congregation divided for lack of space, Second church, where Negro cabinetmaker Wilson Evans served as a deacon. In December 1861, black worshippers at the predominantly white services "were not very numerous, to be sure, but they seemed to be at home and at ease, and they could not be distinguished from the whites in any respect except by their complexion." In dress and appearance, they were "genteel and respectable," in demeanor "unexceptionable."[35] While such patronizing assurances rang with irritating familiarity in the ears of some black Oberliners, it was an inconvenience that those of good social standing, in particular, were willing to tolerate.

To be sure, racial prejudice was a persistent and treacherous factor in the life of the Oberlin citizen. Oberlin was not "the pool of Bethesda for the sin of prejudice," Langston and his young friend, Fanny Jackson, volunteered in 1864. Still, they concluded, it came "nearer to it than any other place in the United States." Indeed, for all the misperceptions and myths, the patronizing and the miscues, the racial insults and incidents, Oberlin was the nation's biracial "city upon a hill." A perpetually reform-charged evangelical atmosphere; a self-reliant stimulation to realize oneself as broadly and as complexly as possible; the open access and the extended opportunities, importantly including a liberal education at all levels; the inspiring leadership emanating from the college and the fair-mindedness rigorously insisted upon by all branches of the local government; the stress on exercising the duties and responsibilities of citizenship; a town newspaper, which while keeping the focus on democratic and abolitionist values customarily reported on the activities of black citizens without designating their color and only rarely with insensitivity; the interracial commercial and housing configurations that tended to promote understanding rather than to perpetuate myth; a preponderance of educated, upwardly mobile, and self-denying white people and a goodly portion of alert, economically advancing, and self-sacrificing black people—these were the principal reasons that Oberlin seemed proof of the all but totally rejected American proposition that blacks and whites could live together, as Langston said, "cheek by jowl" in freedom and equality.[36]

Convinced that social equality depended primarily "on the ability to place oneself among those with whom one would associate," John Mercer set out to arrange his affairs in Oberlin so that even the most prejudiced white man would be forced to respect him. By his example, too, he hoped to inspire the black man toward self-respect and accomplishment. Late in life, Langston would confide that he and Carrie strove "to so order their conduct, wherever living, as to exert a good influence no more upon their own family than upon the general community and any members of colored society. . . ."[37]

His choice of a homesite in itself had extended the black claims in Oberlin into a neighborhood previously limited to the white elite. The house was imposing. It was a large harmoniously proportioned frame structure, with numerous bedrooms on the upper story, and, below, kitchen, laundry, dining and sitting rooms. Windows and doors of the parlor and hall opened out onto a long veranda. When Mercer and Carrie moved in, the newly constructed dwelling still needed various finishing touches: blinds to decorously mask the windows, painting and plastering, varnishing of banisters and bricking of chimneys, gate and fence for the front yard, wood storehouse, cistern, privy, and barn for the back. To do the fixing up, as well as laying in of supplies, Langston dealt with both black and white artisans and tradesmen, the former including John E. Patterson, the mason. (Later in the decade, when Langston wanted a house constructed on other Oberlin property he owned, he would contract with John Campton, the black master carpenter who, like John Patterson, had sizable holdings in real estate.) Doubtless, Langston intended that his home should, in a sense, announce his own character—dignified, substantial, in harmony with its surroundings, prepared to withstand severe weather. He was sensitive to a home's "moral effect," as he put it after visiting a black-owned house in Mississippi in 1869: "It was a beautiful place, white and clean; the curtains new and white. Everything wore an air of cleanliness, comfort and beauty. I said in my heart I liked this place. Why? Because of the moral effect. It not only suited my judgment, but it touched a nice place in my taste." When his own place was completed, he felt, "the general finish of the house, inside and out, was all that could be desired to make it attractive and inviting."[38]

Before long, the voices of children and young people filled the Langston home. In 1857, little Arthur was joined by a second son, Ralph Eugene, named for his paternal grandfather, Ralph Quarles. In 1858, Carrie and Mercer had their first daughter, Chinque, named after the *Amistad* hero, but she would die at the age of two and a half. On June 17, 1861, another baby girl, Nettie De Ella, was born. She helped to fill the emotional gulf left by the loss of "sweet little Chinque" and became her father's "pet." In March 1864, the third son and last child was born and named Frank Mercer, but nicknamed "Lamb" because—as his father would recall in later troubled years—of his normally sweet and docile temperament.[39]

Eschewing the more severe theories of child-rearing, the Quaker-trained Carrie never "severely scolded or punished, bodily, one of her children," but relied instead on affectionate attention to the individual needs of each. As they came of age, the children doubtless attended the popular Union Sabbath School and the Common School. Arthur showed himself a particularly apt scholar. Oberlin's musical atmosphere appealed most especially to Nettie, who early began lessons in piano and voice. The young Langstons enjoyed a privileged but far from idyllic childhood. Their father's frequent and, especially in the sixties, prolonged absences, as well as his prominence, put special strains on the household. When confronting their father's high attainments, the children, especially the boys, may well have felt the pressure of behaving exemplarily. Nor did being a Langston protect the boys from assault. In 1868, a drunken white youth, with two companions, attacked one of Langston's sons, whether Arthur or Ralph the newspaper did not report, while he was quietly standing on the sidewalk near his home. The next day the assailant was convicted of assault and battery and sentenced to county jail. Two years later "young Langston," holding 25 cent bets that several black companions had placed on a baseball game, found himself in trouble when a rainstorm broke up the game. "Young Burnett" demanded the stakes, young Langston refused, and Burnett gave him a black eye. The latter served a ten-day jail sentence.[40]

The Langston family circle also encompassed Miss Jane M. Percival, a sprightly young Englishwoman who came in the mid-sixties to help care for the children and became a permanent member of the household,[41] and several of Carrie's nearest kin. Her younger sister, Sara Kelley Wall, "sober-minded and earnest," was graduated from the Ladies' Course at Oberlin College in August 1856. (Four black women were among the twenty-one female graduates that year. The Cleveland *Plain Dealer*, commenting approvingly on the graceful picture presented by the young women in their white dresses with sky-blue scarves as they marched across the college green, could not resist a sneer at the "repulsive . . . sprinkling of faces in ebony.") Employed as a teacher, Sara made her home with the Langstons until her marriage to Abram Fidler, an enterprising stable owner in Chillicothe, during the sixties.[42] Mercer and Carrie continued their close friendship with O. S. B. Wall and his young wife Amanda. Along with their three children, whose ages nearly paralleled those of the small Langstons, the Walls lived in a racially mixed neighborhood and owned substantial real and personal property. The burly, good-natured cobbler, who would gain a reputation in Oberlin and beyond for a character as solid as his frame, worked side by side with Langston for the black cause during the fifties and sixties.[43] Two young half-brothers, Albert G. and John Wall, also lived with the Walls briefly during the early sixties while attending the preparatory department.[44]

Attentive to village mores and black needs, John Mercer and Carrie adapted readily to the rhythms of Oberlin life. Despite his non-church-member status, he paid $8 annually to rent a pew in First Church. The Langstons may well have been the "colored gentleman and his wife" that a visitor saw "enter one of the principal aisles and proceed to one of the best pews and take their seats, one at each end, with as much dignity and self-possession as any other persons, and evidently unconscious of any inferiority." By his own account, Langston and his family got along well with most of their white neighbors, who included bookseller James M. Fitch, the printer and publisher of the Oberlin *Evangelist* and superintendent of the Sabbath School, and directly across the street, Professor Henry E. Peck, the zealous abolitionist. But, Langston would observe in his autobiography, wherever he and Carrie lived, "members of colored society constitute[d] the great body of their friends and associates."[45]

Langston was particularly drawn to young black men and women studying at Oberlin. Even before his Oberlin residence, in 1854, he had helped David Watson, later Wall's partner in the shoe shop, by giving him a scholarship to finance his preparatory studies. Over the years at least thirty students (white as well as black), including three of his own children, took advantage of a number of scholarships provided by the grateful black alumnus. Fanny Jackson would remember that Langston's "comfortable home was always open with a warm welcome to colored students, or to any who cared to share his hospitality." In accord with Oberlin custom, John Mercer and Carrie took in student boarders, who included several young black women, three mulatto sons of a wealthy Louisiana planter, and an African boy. Numbers of other black students would remember gratefully, as Langston did the white benefactors of his own student days, their heartening relationships with him. The scholarly Richard Theodore Greener, who experienced the Langstons' "kind attentions" in 1862–63 before going on to become a Harvard College graduate in 1870, would call it a "fortunate acquaintance" and note that Langston inspired "many such blessed memories in the grateful hearts of colored students everywhere, whom he always encouraged and befriended." For a black woman student, the Langstons' "multiple acts of kindness" in Oberlin's "pure atmosphere" constituted a "green spot" in her memory. A third undergraduate found Langston's simple warm manner during their own first encounter unforgettable: he stopped the young couple, for the student was with his wife, "inquired whom we were—, bade us God's speed with a warm grasp of the hand. And his presence from that time on was an inspiration to us both."[46]

Many of the young persons that Langston aided would become locally or nationally prominent black leaders during Reconstruction and afterward. Fanny Jackson, later married to Levi J. Coppin, A.M.E. Church bishop, long served as principal of the prestigious Institute for Colored Youth in Philadelphia; Greener was an educator and attorney in South Carolina and Washington, D.C.; both were well-known orators.[47] Others included Blanche K. Bruce, U.S. senator from Mississippi and later registrar of the U.S. Treasury; George F. T. Cook, for thirty-two years superintendent of colored schools in Washington, D.C.; John H. Cook, Washington attorney and briefly law dean at Howard University; James M. Gregory, professor of mathematics and Latin at Howard University; John Mitchell, dean of the theological school at Wilberforce University; James C. Napier, Nashville businessman and registrar of the U.S. Treasury; James H. Piles, attorney and officeholder in Mississippi; Charles B. Purvis, surgeon-in-chief at the Freedmen's Hospital and dean of medicine at Howard University; Josiah T. Settle, attorney active in Republican politics in Mississippi and Tennessee; Thomas DeSaliere Tucker, African missionary convert who became a New Orleans newspaper editor, lawyer, and later president of a black college at Tallahassee; and J. Milton Turner, Missouri politician and consul general to Liberia.[48] Mifflin W. Gibbs, already a successful businessman and later an Arkansas politician, who lived briefly in Oberlin with his wife, Maria Ann Alexander, Carrie's college classmate, and probably took private law classes there, also dated his own friendship with Langston to this period.[49]

As Greener noted, Langston's cultivation of talented young men and women in Oberlin was only the beginning of a life-long practice. It extended, too, beyond personal hospitality to political encouragement. Langston shared and, indeed, often relinquished, black platforms to black students and townsmen. This generous encouragement of the young, who might by another man have been seen as potential rivals to be bested, became a hallmark of Langston's national leadership. Doubtless, it was a reaction to certain personal imperatives, as well as a response to his own conviction that the young represented the hope of the race. Perhaps crucially, the orphan thereby was enabled to act out the role of the father he never had, and, at the same time, "repay" the various surrogate fathers and role models, white and black, who had seen to his nurture. Like those Ohio black movement leaders who had encouraged him, John Mercer was fulfilling a black cultural obligation to forward black sons and daughters. At the same time, in his biracial world, he established his connection with the continuity of black life. Moreover, the relatively uncomplicated admiration of the young could offer emotional support to a man with a persisting need, in a culture determined to judge blacks worthless, to be deemed worthy, while their capacity for idealism could help him ward off despair. Langston's personal frustrations might find constructive release in the extending of his "good right hand" to black students; at the same time, consciously or not, he was building an important constituency for his rise to national prominence.[50]

Langston maintained an active relationship with his alma mater in other ways. He sometimes addressed collegiate debating societies, and contributed an essay on Louis Pacheco, slave rebel during the Florida wars, to the initial edition of the Oberlin *Students' Monthly* in 1858. For the alumni association, he served on various committees, was twice elected a vice-president, and performed as its principal speaker at the important 1866 commencement, which marked the retirement of Finney and inauguration of J. H. Fairchild as college president. At the 1870 alumni reunion he would propose endowing chairs in honor of Finney and Morgan, himself starting the fund with a contribution of $1,250. In 1870 also, Langston unsuccessfully nominated Lucy Stone for the next year's alumni speaker: she had distinguished herself as a "first class woman," "nobly worked" for the black man, and as for ability in speaking, she was "fully equal" to any of the gentlemen "in every respect." In 1876–78, after he had left Oberlin, Langston and Jacob Dolson Cox, ex-general and ex-Ohio governor, would be the alumni representatives to the Board of Trustees.[51]

On April 6, 1857, within the year of his having established his Oberlin residence, the voters of Russia township, which encompassed Oberlin, elected Langston township clerk. Never before had abolitionist Oberlin elected a Negro to public office. Given Langston's personal qualifications, his energetic advocacy of political rights for Negroes, and the controversy over Justice Taney's pronouncement on black citizenship in the Dred Scott case, the choice of Langston for the political post must have appeared singularly appropriate. Langston's election allowed Oberliners to express their own unusual views of black citizenship. At the same time, it enabled them to relieve themselves of the incumbent clerk, Anson P. Dayton, a young white lawyer of questionable professional qualifications and political loyalties. The full price that Dayton would try to exact for his retirement would not, however, become apparent until later.[52]

As clerk, a post to which he would be reelected in 1858, Langston was charged with handling the township's legal affairs and seeing to the collection of road and poor funds. Further, as the man who dispensed public money allocated for the care of fugitive slaves, Langston would be at the center of Oberlin's lively underground railroad operations. He also served on the town council and, on April 20, 1857, was named by the board of education to be acting manager of schools.[53]

In the latter post, which he held again in 1858, Langston began a fourteen-year involvement in directing the course of public education in Oberlin. During his two years as school manager, he oversaw the instructional program, administered finances, visited teachers and students, and ordered repairs for schoolhouses. He found the system underfinanced and in some disarray. Teachers earned only $20 monthly and, shortly after he took office, the public funds failed. School closed, and all the teachers were thrown out of work. A more fundamental problem was the lack of provision for public schooling beyond the elementary level. In the spring of 1859, having concluded his second term as school manager, Langston and several other concerned citizens conducted a successful campaign for reorganization under the Ohio school law of 1853 and for establishment of a high school. Oberliners elected Langston as one of six members on the first board of education, a position in which he would serve continuously for the next eleven years. From 1860 to 1866, the period of the board's major innovations, Langston was its secretary. He and fellow board member J. H. Fairchild worked with the newly appointed superintendent to develop a more thorough classification of pupils and programs according to grade levels. Besides sometimes loaning his law office for board meetings,

Langston repeatedly served on the committee on finances. His long service to Oberlin education both reinforced and reflected his belief that the racially integrated public school—the "incomparable district school"—was a major instrument of democracy. Having contended with governmental and public hostility in trying to establish black schools, he put full value on Oberlin's integrated system. In 1859, at Alliance in Stark County, he noted that some Ohio schools did accept colored children along with white, "but it is not by virtue of the law, but because the people are better than the law. I hope it is so in Alliance—it is so in Oberlin." When in 1871 Langston would be forced to resign from the school board, his fellow members would commend his large contributions. His dedication to raising expectations of pupil achievement rated special mention. His "long and honorable career" had helped create "a grade of school second to none in thoroughness and efficiency, in management and good results." If "my services have been at all advantageous to the community—," Langston would reply, "if I have been able in any sense to assist, in the least degree, in furnishing to the children of Oberlin good Schools—I am very thankful."[54]

Both the lecture tours for equal suffrage and settling in chores delayed for several months the opening of Langston's Oberlin law office. It was well into the fall of 1856 before a small wooden sign appeared outside a door on North Main Street, one door east of the Palmer House, the village hotel, bearing the legend: "John M. Langston, Attorney and Counsellor at Law, Solicitor in Chancery and Notary Public." The Elyria newspaper began to carry a similarly worded advertisement. Shelves inside the freshly painted chamber solidly lodged a new volume on contracts, a new law dictionary, and the just-purchased *Ohio Law Reports*.[55] The attorney, as much as the homeowner, was concerned about appurtenances.

His practice quickly grew brisk. Reputation and some clients had followed from Brownhelm. And, as Langston acknowledged, the "popular endorsement and advertisement" gained through his election as clerk, as well as his subsequent offices, worked to his advantage. Horse thieves and bootleggers might be a young lawyer's only clients at first, Langston would reminisce. But success in their defense, if combined with an unwavering professional integrity, would win more respectable patrons. "When one goes upon the market with an article for sale at reasonable rates which is in demand, it matters very little as a rule whether the vendor be Jew or Gentile, white or black," he would expatiate, in purest tones of optimistic nineteenth-century mercantilism and black protective psychology. "Have you what is in demand and is it of first quality? Is it a trifle better than any other of the sort offered? Here is the secret of success!"[56]

To the bootleggers and livestock thieves, Langston steadily added clients in civil matters: real property and mortgage, contracts, divorce, debt, personal property—bread and butter law in a rural and semirural framework. An extra line in his newspaper advertisement—"Real Estate Agent, Special Attention Given to All Collections"—would announce his expanding interests. As a realtor Langston handled some valuable local property and managed to accumulate considerable holdings himself in locations as far away as Winona County, Minnesota territory. As a bill collector, he worked for such prominent white Oberlin businessmen as livery stable owner Richard Whitney and innkeeper W. U. Plumb to obtain payment of "all costs, claims, rent" due them.[57]

But the courtroom most absorbed him. There, whether in civil or criminal law, it was skillful cross-examination and devastating argumentation that made his name. Black abolitionist William Wells Brown, who viewed an Oberlin trial in which Langston was the defense lawyer in a civil suit, reported that the black attorney so outshown his two white opponents that, on the second day, they were joined by a third white lawyer. To the gleeful Brown, this seemed "a exhibition of weakness, and proved the power of the 'black lawyer,' who stood single-handed and alone." After Langston capped his case with a powerful argument, the jury decided for his client. Students, Brown noted, taking Langston's oratory as "a model"—much as John Mercer had studied Finney's techniques—turned out in numbers for his trials.[58] Black student John Hartwell Cook, himself later a successful attorney, witnessed a trial in the Democratic stronghold of Medina County. "A *true* Democrat was arraigned for murder," Cook would recall, and "strangely enough," retained Langston, "imploring thereby a Negro's assistance in saving him from the penitentiary." Although the opposing counsel opened the case by expressing "jealousy and manifest lack of courtesy," the black lawyer soon gained the upper hand through a "praiseworthy display of legal ability in the examination of witnesses." After "an eloquent and convincing argument to the jury," Langston's client was acquitted. The trial ended with Langston and client both "triumphantly borne away from the court-room . . . on the shoulders of his Democratic confreres."[59]

The black lawyer regularly provided fireworks. The fact that he generally appeared "single-handed and alone"—for whether from design or necessity he worked infrequently with other attorneys—underscored the drama. Langston jousted with opponents with a verbal facility at the least spirited, and sometimes ferocious. The Oberlin newspaper in 1864, calling attention to the simultaneous absences from town of both Langston and fellow attorney Omar Bailey, jokingly supposed that "a suspension of hostilities has been agreed upon in court during their absence." An 1863 civil suit in the Elyria court, in which Langston represented the plaintiff against Cyrus R. Baldwin, another Oberlin attorney who was defending himself, "called out a fierce collision. . . . It was terrifically personal and of course amusing to the crowd." Although Baldwin "made a sharp speech, . . . his allusions were unfortunate for a man who was to be followed, and Langston improved them." The verdict went to Langston's client.[60]

Much of this courtroom sparring, like the "manifest lack of courtesy" that young Cook observed, had a cutting racial edge. Langston's long-cultivated attitude of well-bred self-restraint constituted his first line of defense, but he had also to develop a delicate sensitivity to emotion and circumstance. A measure of protection lay in the fact that, as in Brown-helm, most of his clients continued to come "from the Democratic element of society." Thus, political comradeship tended to blunt the potentially most violent opposition. Langston generally pretended to ignore lesser insults as the safest course for his client and himself. One of his cases, however, involving an unpopular client in unfamiliar territory developed into the sort of volatile situation that he judged called for more than disciplined silence. At stake was the recovery of fatted steers, an emotion-packed issue in the rural backwater of Florence Corners in Huron County, where the trial was to be held before a justice of the peace. Both the lawyer and the white drover he represented had been warned not to appear. As Langston and his client made their way to the court, against a background chorus of muttered insults and threats, one rustic announced: "The community has reached a pitiable condition when a *nigger* lawyer goes in pompous manner about this town." Inside the courtroom, during a lull in the hearing, the opposing lawyer took up the theme, playing to the "rabble" by needling Langston in "offensive, vulgar language." Langston abruptly unleashed a torrent of words and blows on his tormentor. The novel spectacle of the intended victim's besting his rival not only with words but also with the physical prowess so highly touted by the frontiersman apparently turned the popular mood. Langston won "the sympathy and applause of the bystanders, and finally the case which he was there to try," by his account. "If blows were used, it was because they were necessary."[61]

In Oberlin, too, the black lawyer sometimes encountered racial invective. During a recess in a breach of contract case between two

Oberlin residents, in which Langston appeared for the defense, he thought the plaintiff had addressed him and, failing to catch the words, asked politely what had been said. The agitated plaintiff moved threateningly toward Langston and spat out that he was talking to a *white* man. In a quick flush of anger, Langston struck him with his fist, knocking him to the floor. The courtroom was aghast. Explaining what had passed between them, Langston announced himself willing to accept whatever punishment the court decided upon, but added that any man who referred to his color "to insult and degrade him" could expect him to "resent it, with any and every means and method at his command." The judge refused to hold him in contempt.[62]

If Langston's large Democratic clientele seemed an irony, it was matched, during the first six years of his practice and his first four years in Oberlin, by the more painful paradox that the black attorney had no black clients. (This contrasted to the complaints of many black lawyers later in the century that only blacks would employ them.) Black Oberliners seemed unprepared to add the probable liability of a black lawyer to the proscriptions and prejudices they already faced. Finally, in December 1860, builder John Campton and his wife Mary engaged Langston, in association with the well known Elyria firm of Burke and Poppleton, to represent them in a boundary dispute. That case apparently passed off without incident. However, the first black client Langston alone represented would involve him in yet another violent encounter. In the war-worried early summer of 1861 a timidly determined Negro man asked Langston's help in recovering custody of his daughter from his estranged wife. After first warning the man of his possible mistake—I am the colored lawyer, but not the colored man's lawyer—John Mercer took the case eagerly. Later, Baldwin, the white attorney who had been getting the bulk of the black business, and the same opponent with whom Langston waged his later verbal clash in the Elyria court, accosted Langston's client. Had he really hired the "*nigger* lawyer"? "If you have," Baldwin warned, "he will sell you out." On hearing the incident, a furious Langston sought out his white rival, slapped him, and kicked him as he fled. Baldwin—charging that Langston "with great Violence did seize, strike and push and other wrongs" to him—had the black lawyer arrested. At his hearing, which followed immediately, Langston unapologetically pled guilty; the sympathetic Oberlin mayor prescribed a token $5 fine. Aggrieved, Baldwin took his case to the grand jury, and was again rebuffed. The jury foreman privately advised Langston that if he ever failed to deal with such an affront in an equally decisive manner, he would be indicted.[63]

During almost fifty years of public life, years in which Langston constantly performed at the edge of violence, he generally exerted masterful control over his inner stresses. Then why, on these occasions, did his anger erupt? In part, certainly, Langston's violent actions reflected the violent national mood. In the immediate pre-war period, Oberlin black men demonstrated an increasing willingness to resort to fists and guns. For them and Langston, antislavery geography provided opportunity. At rural Florence Corners, Langston's outburst seemed almost less passionate than tactical, a demonstration—in the comparative safety of the courtroom—timed to avert an ugly situation with the warning that this colored man was neither cowed nor compliant. But in Oberlin he acted under the virtual certainty of immunity from serious reprisal. Like all black Americans, and in excruciating ways reserved for the sensitive, educated black man, he suffered grievous insult, but not gladly. Most of the time, he kept his indignation subject to his discretion. His anger was selective. His retaliatory means of preference were his wit and skill; but he believed force was justified to protect one's self, and one's personal, and, as a lawyer, professional honor—and one's honor as a black man. Because he could not always act fully on that belief, the explosion when it came in Oberlin where he could was all the more violent. The cuffs and kicks he dealt Baldwin doubtless had many targets.

Subconsciously, at least, Langston also may have felt the need to prove himself to other blacks through force. Although he might accept the logic behind their refusal to employ him, the rejection hurt. His very success, privately and professionally, in a racially integrated context made him liable to the jealousy and mistrust of those less favored, and whispers of being a white man's Negro. The class consciousness that tended to divide the intelligent and wealthy Oberlin black residents from the poor and ignorant[64] made it the more difficult to establish his credentials with all segments of society. Some blacks felt betrayed on seeing Negro students or townsmen in easy intercourse with their white peers; some were suspicious of the better educated. And some seem to have accepted, to some degree, the prevalent white attitude of black inferiority. The blacksmith Allen Jones, himself an ex-slave but a staunch Democrat, reportedly believed Negroes were "not fit to be free."[65] To Oberlin blacks of conservative bent, who counseled others of their race to find their place and stay in it, who had advised young Langston not to attempt a white man's profession because he would surely fail, his mode of living itself, to say nothing of his ideas, could seem radical and dangerous.

Langston's attacks on white detractors, then, could be exhibitions for blacks who accepted their inferiority to whites, to those who were fearful, to those who suspected any black so apparently close to whites would "sell them out," that he was not compromised. Significantly, after his drubbing of Baldwin and successful management of the black client's case, he found himself, if not "the colored man's lawyer," then sharing at least evenly in the black legal business. The records that exist bear out Langston's own observation that he won "as many suits for them in proportion to the number tried as for any other class."[66]

Defense of a black client, Mary Edmonia Lewis, would prove Langston's most sensational case. Daughter of a black manservant and a Chippewa woman, Mary claimed to have lived from the age of four, after they died, with aunts among the Chippewa in Canada. When Wildflower, as she was then called, was thirteen, her brother, who was in business in California, had her sent off to school, first to McGrawville and in 1859, to Oberlin. During her first three years of study, she established a reputation for "exemplary" conduct. Her social relations with white students were "easy and rather unusual." She was seventeen and living in the eminently respectable boarding house of the venerable John Keep, the Oberlin trustee whose vote had determined the black admissions policy, when her difficulties began.[67]

On the frozen morning of January 27, 1862, Maria Miles and Christina Ennes, two of Mary's white fellow boarders, were dressing for a sleighride with two young men. Their plans, confided to Mary the night before, were to go to Christina's home in Birmingham, some nine miles distant. Mary invited her friends to fortify themselves against the weather with a warm draught. They accepted, and accompanied her to her room, where she heated spiced wine. On barely tasting it, Mary declared the drink bland and set it aside, but the two white girls drained their glasses before hurrying off on their sleighing party. But on the way, both girls developed violent stomach cramps. While their alarmed suitors whipped the horses on, the afflicted girls recalled previous hard words with Mary Lewis and, on reaching Christina's home, sobbed out that she had poisoned them.[68]

Against a rising clamor for Mary's arrest, Langston was asked to assume her defense. Alienated by Mary's close associations with whites, the majority of black Oberliners, Langston observed, joined in early condemnation of the girl. An "aged lady," acting as black spokesperson, urged the black attorney not to become entangled with her. As for the "deeply stirred" white community, as the case progressed, Langston saw it becoming "about equally divided" on the question of Mary's guilt.

"Many were prejudiced against the accused," he asserted, "on account of her color." Langston took the case.[69]

About a week after the alleged poisoning, while Maria and Christina still lay critically ill, the attorney and a white doctor traveled to Birmingham in search of evidence. Although the doctor succeeded in questioning the patients and their medical advisers, Langston had a narrow escape. As he and the doctor walked toward their hotel, Christina's outraged father, standing in the doorway of his grocery store, fired his rifle at the black lawyer. Luckily, a bystander deflected the gun barrel upward, and the shot lodged in the doorjamb. Langston was so absorbed in conversation that he was unaware of the attempt on his life until someone told him, at which point he and his friend departed by "sprightly team."[70]

Nor was the violence at an end. A few nights later, tolling bells, Oberlin's distress signal, summoned townspeople. Shortly after dark Mary Lewis had stepped into the backyard of her boarding house and had not returned. Eventually lantern-carrying searchers found the girl on the frozen ground of an adjacent field, alive but brutally beaten, clothing and jewelry torn off and scattered. Soon after, Mary was arrested, but her injuries were so serious that Langston secured a postponement of her hearing. On February 19, the Lorain County *News*, newly passed into the editorship of Professor Peck, belatedly reported the story for the first time. "Many friends" of the two white girls had charged that "the people of Oberlin are not willing to have the case brought to a trial," but, Peck asserted, from the first the accused and her friends had invited an examination. He reminded his readers that the young lady, "whose color subjects her to prejudice," was guaranteed "the common rights of law."[71]

On February 26, the hearing was held in the town business hall to accommodate the curious throng. Two attorneys, one from Birmingham and the other a prominent Elyria Republican, conducted the prosecution. Langston sat with the battered defendant, accompanied only by his medical friend and his clerk. Testifying for the prosecution, the two doctors who had first examined and treated the now fully recovered Maria and Christina agreed the young women had been the victims of poisoning by cantharides. Notorious as "Spanish fly," this concoction made from dried beetles was popularly known as an aphrodisiac, but it could have toxic effects. As for motivation, the two girls were said to have subjected Mary Lewis to rough teasing. In revenge, the hypothesis was, she had spiced their wine with "Spanish fly"—a cathardic—either in a naughty attempt to add fire to their winter romances, or in a try at murder. To these speculations, Mary would never give direct reply. Langston pounced early on a prosecutor's unwary question to open his main line of defense, the impossibility of proving the poisonings. Repeatedly, he brought out the evidence gained from his harrowing trip to Birmingham, that the doctors had neither examined nor preserved for examination any of the contents of the afflicted girls' stomachs and bowels. When the state rested, Langston dramatically declined to call witnesses and abruptly moved for dismissal of the case, contending no corpus delicti had been proved. Ensuing debate between the prosecutors and Langston was long, heated, and, according to the press, of high quality. Into Langston's extended summation, he poured all the medical and legal understanding, and passion, at his command. At the conclusion of the two-day hearing, the court freed Mary Lewis on the grounds of insufficient evidence. Excited student friends and well-wishers carried her in their arms from the courtroom.[72]

Nonetheless, Mary Lewis's career in Oberlin was to end on a less than happy note. In his autobiography, Langston would write that the girl, whom he never identified despite the lapse of thirty years, was "fully vindicated in her character and name." Although true legally, among skeptical classmates and others, Mary's notoriety with the complications of youth and race made for difficult relationships. When her name came up, student wits facilely quipped, "Look out for Spanish Flies!" For her part, the high-spirited adolescent apparently had no inclination to placate critics by shows of submissiveness. When a new student skating club omitted her from membership, one young man gossiped that she put up such a "tantrum" that an adult intermediary persuaded one of the officers "to invite the wench, but I'm blamed if I would have done it in his place." But almost a year to the day after her examination for attempted murder, Mary again appeared before one of the same justices of the peace, this time charged with stealing artist's materials. Again for insufficient evidence, the case was dismissed. Less than three months later, however, having been indicted by the grand jury for "aiding and abetting" in a burglary, Mary Lewis skipped town.[73]

Subsequently, her life took an upward turn. Arrived in Boston and assisted by William Lloyd Garrison, she studied under the noted sculptor Edward A. Brackett. Now known as Edmonia Lewis, the past behind her, the young artist embarked on a career that would win her prizes and important commissions in Europe and America. Except for brief visits to the United States, she would spend most of her life in Rome. So long, in fact, that Frederick Douglass, encountering her one day in 1887 on the Pincian Hill, observed that her English was much impaired. Studying the work of the woman who was the first recognized American black sculptor, modern scholars have praised its quality, noted her artistic courage in departures from the overweening neoclassicism of the day, and discovered a concern with black and native American themes in her most significant productions.[74]

With lawyerly reticence, in describing this courtroom "effort of his life" Langston came not much closer to disclosing what he knew of his client's actual behavior and motivations than to term the accusation as "perhaps without reason." Whatever that old truth, another "rule stood good—let the world be shaken, but the lawyer shall never neglect nor forsake the performance of that duty which he owes to a client!" In the 1890s Edmonia Lewis's "works of art as displayed in marble" seemed telling evidence of the wisdom of her attorney's labors "to vindicate justice and innocence."[75]

The black lawyer could have felt, without much exaggeration, that he had represented a second client in the case. If the biracial town and college were always on trial, this was never truer than during the war years. As the result of heightened interest in the black man and his destiny, two opposing attitudes both focused on and operated within Oberlin: rising prejudice against blacks and rising hopes for national and racial redemption. A few began to hold up Oberlin as a model for the remolding of black-white relationships. The convicted black student murderess would have seemed to validate the prejudice and invalidate the model. As it was, the Cleveland *Plain Dealer*, Oberlin's shrillest Democratic critic, muttered about "a dark affair" and punned that most of the trial participants had been black. But, as editor Peck rejoined, "That is very mild for the aged P.D." Sympathetic visitors to Oberlin, like one soon after, could still find the effects of "this association of sexes and colors" in the college not disastrous. "The reverse is true." For the outside world, Oberlin's image remained intact. Within the town, the most sober observers could only have been shaken by the prejudice that had swept the community and the vigilante violence done Mary Lewis (apparently the perpetrators were never apprehended). The racial tolerance and love of justice that Oberlin's leaders had worked long to instill had broken down. For them, it was this better face that the black advocate had represented. Professor John Clark, a native white southerner who served with Langston on the school board, visibly moved throughout the black lawyer's closing address, habitually greeted him thereafter with the words he had called out at trial's end: "My orator! My orator!" As for black Oberlin, the majority who had been quick to condemn the black girl with white friends, to disown her before her misbehavior imperiled their own hard-won security, perhaps their change of heart was best summed up in the action of the matriarch who had earlier demanded that Langston shun Mary Lewis's defense. This "excellent aged colored woman" made him the guest of honor at a dinner in her home, "distinguished as well for the number and character of her guests as the richness and abundance of her repast."[76]

Practicing law was congenial to Langston's nature. A child of his century, he wanted to be useful, but in his case to blacks and whites alike. He wanted to have his wits and his oratorical skills, his preparation and his discipline count for something. He wanted to demonstrate that black people were capable of discharging society's obligations with efficiency and with profit to the community. This man who conceived of himself as a bridge between the races wanted to be able to view reality from differing perspectives, to master all the arguments for as well as all the arguments against. He wanted to be self-sufficient, in control, the supporter of his family in style. His law practice ministered to all these personal directives.

Lawyers, Langston joked, showed little interest in intellectual discussion on topics like politics, theology, or medicine. "They would rather ask the question, 'Did he steal the sheep?' " Anyone who could cite Kent, Blackstone, Archibald or the Supreme Court, "having never read the books," could "aspire to the position of a lawyer." A believer in "long, arduous, and unremitting labor," John Mercer read the books. To his Howard University law graduates in 1874 he would urge "confidence, courage, and self-reliance." The lessons of physical courage that, as he said, he had been taught by experience—and that he hoped "no other young lawyer, even of the colored class" would have to apply—went hand in hand with the courage that "must always come of one's confidence in his own powers and the legal sufficiency of the ground-work of his cause."[77]

By most yardsticks, lawyer Langston enjoyed success. In the Lorain County courts alone—and his practice encompassed country towns in a fifty-mile radius, with occasional work as far away as Columbus—he argued cases at nearly every term from February 1857 through June 1867.[78] Although his fees were often modest, like the $6 he charged a client in 1858, by Oberlin standards he did well financially. In 1860, the federal census showed a valuation of $12,000 on his real property, $5,000 on his personal holdings. In 1865—a year when he was more attentive to the black man's business than his own—under the war revenue act, he reported his personal income at $1,100, a total well over that of some of his former professors. The next year it increased to $1,215. The Lorain County *News* listed him among the town's most prosperous citizens. In the fall of 1866, the pressures of public and private activities dictated taking in a partner, A. E. Isham, with whom he "fitted up a neat office" in the Commercial Block. The change was announced with the promise to give "faithful and keen-eyed attention" to business.[79] Contemporary observers, white and black, considered Langston a highly respected attorney. In the mid-sixties, a visiting journalist reported that the "colored lawyer" was "perhaps oftener consulted by whites than any other lawyer." Young Cook in 1870 proudly cited the consideration "long since" accorded Langston by the Lorain bar, and the "generous patronage" he had won.[80]

In his profession, in public office, and in his domestic life, Langston confronted townspeople, white and black, with his own vision of black manhood. He functioned as the racial groundbreaker, the eminently qualified black man who freed white Oberliners to recognize the potential of other blacks as well as his own, and encouraged black Oberliners to develop that potential. The first of Oberlin's black office-holders, strikingly, he had not been the last. Surely, watching Langston perform, knowing him intimately, helped to embolden such Oberlin leaders as editor Peck who in September 1863, to an Episcopalian journal's dirge over receiving "the colored race into a domestic and social equality with ourselves," would reply, almost flippantly, "Why not?"[81]

John Mercer, who had once wistfully written "esquire" after his name, could only be gratified by public references to "our townsman, J. M. Langston, Esq., whom everybody knows to be a man of standing, of talent, of education, and of great executive ability." A measure of sardonic satisfaction was to be found even in such grudging tribute as that rendered by a white student, new to Oberlin ways, in the spring of 1861. Oberlin had two major omnipresent faults—mud and Negroes, the boy complained. Everywhere he saw "Darkeys, one on every street corner and the dummest Set I ever Saw. I only seen one Smart Nigger in town and that is Langston." Langston, he allowed, "is [a] pretty Smart fellow."[82]

NOTES

1. John Mercer Langston, *From the Virginia Plantation to the National Capitol; or, The First and Only Negro Representative in Congress from the Old Dominion* (Hartford, 1894; repr. New York: Johnson Reprint, 1968), pp. 157–58.

2. Record of Deeds, Lorain County, vol. 8, pp. 550, 601, 602, Lorain County Courthouse. On March 18, 1856, Langston sold Wall the fifty-acre

property in Brownhelm for $2,500, and Wall sold Langston a half-acre lot in the center of College Street for $1,500 and part of another lot bounded on the south by College Street for $1,000. Langston, *Virginia Plantation*, pp. 158–59; Cincinnati *Gazette*, June 10, 1867.

3. Langston, *Virginia Plantation*, p. 159.
4. Louisville *Courier-Journal*, July 16, 1869.
5. John Morgan to Simeon S. Jocelyn, Apr. 18, 1859, American Missionary Association Archives, Amistad Research Center, Tulane University (hereafter cited as AMA Papers).
6. Robert S. Fletcher, *A History of Oberlin College*, 2 vols. (Oberlin, 1943), II, pp. 550–52, 555–56; New York *Independent*, Dec. 3, 1863; Oberlin *Evangelist*, Nov. 21, 1855, Oct. 13, 1852; Cleveland *Herald*, n.d., quoted in Oberlin *Evangelist*, Sept. 26, 1855; Cleveland *True-Democrat*, Nov. 8, Dec. 23, 1851, Oct. 21, 1852; Elyria *Independent-Democrat*, Oct. 20, 1852, June 30, 1857; Population Census of 1850, Ohio, Roll 705, Lorain County, Russia Township, National Archives; Population Census of 1860, Ohio, Roll 1002, Lorain County, Russia Township, NA; J. M. Fitch to George Whipple, July 5, 1858; Henry E. Peck to Lewis Tappan, July 28, 1858, both in AMA Papers; Lorain County *News*, June 30, 1870, Mar. 28, 1860.
7. Denton J. Snider, *A Writer of Books* (St. Louis, 1910), p. 99; Population Census of 1850, Ohio, Roll 705, Lorain County, Russia Township, NA. The census taker did not separate Oberlin from Russia township, but it is not difficult to determine from the recorded data where the village begins. Forty-five other blacks were recorded in the township, whose total population was 2,061 (8 percent black).
8. Population Census of 1860, Ohio, Roll 1002, Lorain County, Russia Township, NA; *Frederick Douglass' Paper*, June 16, 1854; O. S. B. Wall to J. M. Langston, Jan. 25, 1854, John Mercer Langston Papers, Fisk University Library.
9. William E. Bigglestone, *They Stopped in Oberlin: Black Residents and Visitors of the Nineteenth Century* (Scottsdale, Arizona, 1981), pp. 35–38; Population Census of 1860, Ohio, Roll 1002, Lorain County, Russia Township, NA.
10. Langston, *Virginia Plantation*, p. 183; Population Census of 1850, Ohio, Roll 705, Lorain County, Russia Township, NA; Population Census of 1860, Ohio, Lorain County, Russia Township, NA; Bigglestone, *They Stopped in Oberlin*, Roll 1002, pp. 171–74, 195–96; Lorain County *News*, Nov. 19, 1862; Oberlin *Students' Monthly* 1 (Feb. 1859):160.
11. Henry Cowles, "Oberlin College Catalogue and Records of Colored Students, 1835–1862," ms., Henry Cowles Papers, Oberlin College Library (hereafter cited as Cowles List); Population Census of 1860, Ohio, Roll 1002, Lorain County, Russia Township, NA.
12. Population Census of 1860, Ohio, Roll 1002, Lorain County, Russia Township, NA. The 1860 census total for Oberlin usually cited is 2,915, rather than 2,115, apparently a misreading of the scarcely legible figures. Actual count shows in Oberlin a total 1,693 whites, 304 mulattoes, and 118 blacks. In the remainder of Russia township the total is 1,182 whites, 60 mulattoes,

11 blacks. Fletcher, *Oberlin College*, II, p. 553, estimates that blacks made up 25 percent of the village population in 1860, but the actual count does not support this figure. In 1860, Ohio's black population was 36,673, only 1.6 percent of the whole population.

13. Oberlin *Evangelist*, July 17, 1844, Feb. 12, 1845; Morgan to S. S. Jocelyn, Apr. 18, 1859; John Morgan, George V. Allen, George Thompson to AMA, Apr. (n.d.), 1859; Zeruiah Porter Weed to S. S. Jocelyn, July 5, 1859, all in AMA Papers; Lorain County *News*, Feb. 4, 1863, Mar. 2, 1864; St. Louis *Democrat*, Nov. 29, 1865, John Mercer Langston Scrapbook, Fisk University Library; Population Census of 1860, Ohio, Roll 1002, Lorain County, Russia Township, NA.

14. A Democrat of Lorain to Editor, Cleveland *Plain Dealer*, May 25, 1856; *Aliened American*, Apr. 9, 1853; Lorain County *Eagle*, Oct. 13, 1857; Cincinnati *Enquirer*, n.d., quoted in *National Anti-Slavery Standard*, Nov. 7, 1857; Lorain County *News*, Dec. 24, 1862, Oct. 13, 1869; St. Louis *Democrat*, Nov. 29, 1865, JML Scrapbook (Fisk).

15. Oberlin *Evangelist*, Aug. 13, 1851; Lewis Clarke, "Questions and Answers," *Interesting Memoirs and Documents Relating to American Slavery* (London, 1846), p. 93; Mildred Fairchild, "The Negro in Oberlin," master's thesis, Oberlin College, 1925, pp. 11–12.

16. *Anti-Slavery Bugle*, Feb. 21, 1857; Cleveland *Herald*, n.d., quoted in *National Anti-Slavery Standard*, Oct. 11, 1856; *Report of the Proceedings of the Colored National Convention . . . Cleveland . . . Sept. 1848* (Rochester, Sept. 1848). A vice-president of the 1848 black national convention, Jones also had been a delegate to the Ohio black convention in 1843; see *Philanthropist*, Oct. 4, 1843.

17. KAPPA to Cleveland *True-Democrat*, n.d., quoted in *Frederick Douglass' Paper*, June 3, 1852; *Anti-Slavery Bugle*, Feb. 21, 1857; Eric Foner, *Free Soil, Free Labor, Free Men: The Ideology of the Republican Party Before the Civil War* (New York, 1970), p. 30; *Liberator*, Oct. 10, 1856.

18. Population Census of 1850, Ohio, Roll 705, Lorain County, Russia Township, NA; Population Census of 1860, Ohio, Roll 1002, Lorain County, Russia Township, NA; Cincinnati *Gazette*, June 10, 1867. The 1850 occupational breakdown was: 6 laborers, 6 sailors, 3 farmers, 3 students, 1 agency, 2 brick masons, 2 joiners, 1 carpenter, 1 ditcher, 7 not given, 7 none. In 1860, of 83 adult males for whom occupations were listed, the breakdown was: 5 professional (1 lawyer, 1 teacher, 3 clergymen); 4 farmers; 3 in business (1 merchant, 2 clerks); 35 in skilled labor (2 harnessmakers, 4 carpenters, 4 shoemakers, 2 cabinetmakers, 1 wagonmaker, 1 table-maker, 8 masons, 2 painters, 3 blacksmiths, 3 barbers, 3 engineers, 1 cook, 1 broommaker); 7 in semiskilled labor (1 sailor, 4 apprentices to artisans, 2 clerks [listed under business above]); and 31 unskilled (8 farm laborers, 3 teamsters, 1 table waiter, 2 ditchers, 17 laborers). Only 1 declared no occupation. Although employed women were not routinely listed by federal census takers, those included were: 1 teacher, 4 dressmakers or seamstresses, 1 milliner, 1 stewardess, 1 cook, 1 weaver, 10 domestics, and 4 washerwomen. Ten of the 17 black female heads of households gave no occupation.

19. Population Census of 1850, Ohio, Roll 705, Lorain County, Russia Township, NA; Oberlin *Students' Monthly* 1 (Feb. 1859):160; Population Census of 1860, Ohio, Roll 1002, Lorain County, Russia Township, NA.

20. Lorain County *News*, Oct. 3, 1860, Sept. 4, 1861; Elyria *Independent-Democrat*, Oct. 13, 1859; Delevan L. Leonard, *The Story of Oberlin: The Institution, the Community, the Idea, the Movement* (Boston, 1898), pp. 420–21. These men were selected on the basis of the frequency and prominence of their appearances in local and Cleveland newspapers, as well as in town records and those of black meetings.

21. Portage County *Democrat*, n.d., quoted in Cleveland *Leader*, May 14, 1859; Jacob R. Shipherd, compiler, *History of the Oberlin-Wellington Rescue* (Boston, 1859; repr. New York: Da Capo Press, 1972), p. 18; Fletcher, *Oberlin College*, II, p. 567; KAPPA to Cleveland *True-Democrat*, Oct. 21, 1852; Elyria *Independent-Democrat*, June 30, 1857, Apr. 14, 1858.

22. Both Watson and Sabram Cox were prominent in establishment of the Colored American League of Oberlin in 1849. *North Star*, Jan. 12, 1849; Cleveland *True-Democrat*, Sept. 24, 1849. Watson attended Ohio state black conventions in 1849, 1850, 1853, 1857, 1858, 1860. *State Convention . . . 1849, 1850, 1853, 1857, 1858, 1860*. Cleveland *Leader*, Aug. 5, 1857; Elyria *Independent-Democrat*, Aug. 11, 1857.

23. Population Census of 1850, Ohio, Roll 705, Lorain County, Russia Township, NA; Population Census of 1860, Ohio, Roll 1002, Lorain County, Russia Township, NA; Lorain County *News*, Oct. 5, 1871. In 1850 Watson, thirty-two, mulatto, and illiterate, is listed as a brick mason with $450 in real property; in 1860 he is listed as literate and a merchant, with $2,300 in real and $2,000 in personal property. His wife, Margaret, forty-three, owned $3,000 in personal property. See also Bigglestone, *They Stopped in Oberlin*, p. 222.

24. A.L. Shumway, *Oberliniana, 1833–1883* (Cleveland, 1883), p. 22; J. B. Meachum to T. Levi Burnell, May 29, 1839, Oberlin College Archives; Cowles List.

25. *Liberator*, July 10, 1846; *Anti-Slavery Bugle*, July 24, 1846; Cleveland *True-Democrat*, Sept. 11, 1848; *North Star*, Jan. 12, 1849. Cox was president of the September 1852 Ohio black convention; see Cleveland *True-Democrat*, Sept. 9, 1852.

26. Population Census of 1860, Ohio, Roll 1002, Lorain County, Russia Township, NA. Cox, thirty-eight, a farmer, held $1,800 in real and $350 in personal property; see Lorain County *News*, Apr. 5, 1865; Shumway, *Oberliniana*, p. 22; Bigglestone, *They Stopped in Oberlin*, pp. 59–61.

27. Population Census of 1860, Ohio, Roll 1002, Lorain County, Russia Township, NA; Shipherd, *History of the Oberlin-Wellington Rescue*, passim; Bigglestone, *They Stopped in Oberlin*, pp. 32, 70–71, 164–65, 183–84; Langston, *Virginia Plantation*, pp. 524–28.

28. John Geil, map of Lorain County, 1857, Oberlin College Archives; Population Census of 1860, Ohio, Roll 1002, Lorain County, Russia Township, NA; Leonard, *Story of Oberlin*, pp. 381, 385.

29. Lorain County *News*, Aug. 20, 1862; Fletcher, *Oberlin College*, II, pp. 583–84, fn. p. 584; Snider, *A Writer of Books*, p. 99; Cincinnati *Gazette*, June 10, 1867; Leonard, *Story of Oberlin*, p. 385; Louisville *Courier-Journal*, July 16, 1869.

30. "X" to Editor, Delaware (Ohio) *Democratic Standard*, n.d., quoted in Oberlin *Evangelist*, Sept. 14, 1853; Morgan to Jocelyn, Apr. 18, 1859, T. B. Hudson to George Whipple, Aug. 3, 1852, both in AMA Papers; Oberlin *Evangelist*, Aug. 18, 1852.

31. Zeruiah Porter Weed to S. S. Jocelyn, July 5, Dec. 21, 1859, Mar. 16, 1860; Morgan to Jocelyn, Apr. 18, 1859, all in AMA papers.

32. Oberlin *Evangelist*, Sept. 14, 1853; John Mercer Langston, "A Representative Woman—Mrs. Sara K. Fidler," *A.M.E. Church Review* 4 (July 1887):464.

33. Morgan to Jocelyn, Apr. 18, 1859; Morgan, Allen, Thompson to AMA, Apr. n.d., 1859; Weed to Jocelyn, July 5, 1859, all in AMA Papers.

34. Zeruiah Porter Weed to S. S. Jocelyn, Mar. 16, 1860, AMA Papers; Leonard, *Story of Oberlin*, pp. 384–85. See also Marcus Dale to George Whipple, Apr. 2, 1861, AMA Papers.

35. E. H. Fairchild to George Whipple, Sept. 23, 1865, AMA Papers; New York *Independent*, Dec. 12, 1861.

36. New York *Independent*, Dec. 12, 1861; *National Anti-Slavery Standard*, July 9, 1864; Lorain County *News*, Mar. 14, Nov. 21, 1860, Jan. 23, Mar. 27, July 7, Sept. 4, Sept. 23, 1861, Jan. 7, Mar. 25, Sept. 23, 1863, and passim; Louisville *Courier-Journal*, July 16, 1869.

37. Louisville *Courier-Journal*, July 16, 1869; Langston, *Virginia Plantation*, p. 532.

38. Receipts, Apr. 1, Apr. 13, May 12, May 19, July 3, Dec. 10, 1856, contract, June 21, 1859, all in Langston Papers; Louisville *Courier-Journal*, July 16, 1869; Langston, *Virginia Plantation*, p. 159. The house, at 207 E. College Street, still stands. Oberlin *News-Tribune*, Mar. 22, 1973.

39. Langston, *Virginia Plantation*, pp. 524–29; Population Census of 1860, Ohio, Roll 1002, Lorain County, Russia Township, NA; Arthur Desaline Langston and Nettie De Ella Langston, Alumni Records, Oberlin College Archives.

40. Langston, *Virginia Plantation*, p. 531; Lorain County *News*, Mar. 25, 1868, Aug. 4, 1870.

41. Langston, *Virginia Plantation*, pp. 533, 531; Washington *National Republican*, June 2, 1884.

42. Langston, "A Representative Woman," pp. 462–65; *Liberator*, Oct. 10, 1856; Cleveland *Plain Dealer*, n.d., quoted in *Liberator*, Oct. 10, 1856. Population Census of 1860, Ohio, Roll 1002, Lorain County, Russia Township, NA; W. E. M. (William Matthews) to Editor, *Christian Recorder*, Nov. 3, 1866.

43. Lorain County *News*, Mar. 8, 1865, May 9, 1866; Population Census of 1860, Ohio, Roll 1002, Lorain County, Russia Township, NA. In 1860 Wall, thirty-four, owned $1,600 in real property and $1,200 in personal property. With him lived his wife Amanda, twenty-three, his children Edward, four,

Stephen, three, and Clara, two; two students, Albert Wall, seventeen, and Ella Alexander, fourteen, of Kentucky, all listed as mulattoes; Thomas Weaver, twenty-one, of North Carolina, a black painter, and Charles Jones, twenty-one, of Africa, a black shoemaker's apprentice.

44. Fletcher, *Oberlin College*, II, p. 871 fn.; John Wall, Alumni Records, Oberlin College Archives; Cowles List.

45. First Congregational church, Treasurer's Records and Misc., 1860–65, Oberlin College Archives; New York *Independent*, Dec. 12, 1861; John Geil, map of Lorain County, 1857, Oberlin College Archives; Langston, *Virginia Plantation*, pp. 159–60.

46. J. M. Langston to D. L. Watson, Mar. 11, 1854, Langston Papers; Cowles List; Oberlin College Scholarships, 1864–69, 1870–75, 1876–1893, Treasurer's Vault, Oberlin College Archives; Fanny Jackson Coppin, *Reminiscences of School Life* (Philadelphia, 1913), p. 12; Langston, *Virginia Plantation*, p. 181; Richard T. Greener to Caroline Langston, Nov. 16, 1897, Ada H. Hinton to Caroline Langston, Nov. 17, 1897, J. E. Moorland to Caroline Langston, Nov. 16, 1897, all in Langston Papers. See also Mr. and Mrs. C. A. Dorsey to Caroline Langston, Nov. 16, 1897. In 1860 Louisa Williams, eighteen, and Susan Elizabeth Reid, twenty-one, both students and the latter a graduate of the Oberlin Ladies Course in August 1860, lived with the Langstons; see Population Census of 1860, Ohio, Roll 1002, Lorain County, Russia Township, NA.

47. John W. Cromwell, *The Negro in American History* (Washington, 1914; repr. New York: Johnson Reprint, 1968), pp. 213–18; William J. Simmons, *Men of Mark, Eminent, Progressive, and Rising* (Cleveland, 1887; repr. Chicago: Johnson Publishing, 1970), pp. 211–16.

48. Cowles List; Simmons, *Men of Mark*, pp. 365–68, 435, 483–87; Cromwell, *Negro in American History*, pp. 231–33; Lorain County *News*, Mar. 3, 1870; Rayford W. Logan, *Howard University: The First Hundred Years, 1867–1967* (New York, 1969), pp. 49, 50, 159–60, 212; Cleveland *Leader*, Aug. 5, 1857; biography of James Carroll Napier, J. C. Napier Papers, Fisk University Library; Necrology: printed in the Annual Reports for 1903–04, 1918–19, Oberlin College Archives; J. T. Settle to Caroline Langston, Nov. 18, 1897, Langston Papers; Thomas DeSaliere Tucker to J. A. Williams, Sept. 29, 1858, Tucker to George Whipple, Nov. 4, 1862, Feb. 22, 1864, all in AMA Papers; Louisville *Courier-Journal*, July 16, 1869; J. Milton Turner et al. to John M. Langston, Jan. 27, 1866, in *A Speech on "Equality Before the Law"* . . . *by J. Mercer Langston, in the Hall of Representatives, in the Capitol of Missouri* . . . *1866* (St. Louis, 1866); Irving Dilliard, "James Milton Turner, A Little Known Benefactor of His People," *Journal of Negro History* 19, (1934):372–411.

49. Simmons, *Men of Mark*, pp. 407–11; Juanita Fletcher, "Against the Consensus: Oberlin College and the Education of American Negroes, 1835–1865," Ph.D. diss., The American University, 1974, pp. 273–77; M. W. Gibbs to Caroline Langston, Nov. 19, 1897, Langston Papers.

50. New York *Globe*, Oct. 15, 1882; Boston *Courant*, Aug. 16, 1890, both in John Mercer Langston Scrapbooks, 4 vols., II, Moorland-Spingarn Research Center, Howard University.

51. Journal of the Phi Kappa Pi Society, 1856–65, Nov. 16, 1858, Oberlin College Archives; Oberlin *Students' Monthly*, 1 (Nov. 1858):33–35; Oberlin College Alumni Association Minutes, Aug. 25, 1857, Aug. 23, 1859, Aug. 26, 1862, Aug. 25, 1863, Aug. 22, 1865, Aug, 21, 1866, Aug. 1, 1876, Oberlin College Archives; Lorain County *News*, Aug. 5, 1863, Aug. 8, 22, 1866, Aug. 4, 11, 1870, Sept. 21, 1871; Cleveland *Leader*, Aug. 2, 1866; Cincinnati *Gazette*, Aug. 29, 1866.

52. Russia Township—Township Records, 1855–69, Oberlin College Archives.

53. Ibid.; Langston, *Virginia Plantation*, p. 168; Russia Township—Board of Education Records, 1842–71, Oberlin College Archives.

54. Fletcher, *Oberlin College*, II, pp. 589–90; Zeruiah Porter Weed to George Whipple, June 27, 1857, AMA Papers; "History of Oberlin Public Schools," *Historical Sketches of Public Schools in Ohio* (Columbus, 1876); Langston's final entry as school manager, June 11, 1859, in minutes of old board; his handwritten annual board reports, 1861–66, Annual Reports, Board of Education, 1861–72, both in Russia Township—Board of Education Records, 1842–71, Oberlin College Archives; Lorain County *News*, Mar. 7, 1860, Nov. 27, 1861, Mar. 3, 1869, Oct. 5, 1871; John Mercer Langston, *Freedom and Citizenship* (Washington, 1883; repr. Miami: Mnemosyne Reprint, 1969), pp. 63, 154–55; *Anti-Slavery Bugle*, Sept. 24, 1859; Langston, *Virginia Plantation*, pp. 168–69; J. M. Langston to Dr. Homer Johnson, Oct. 24, 1871, Russia Township—Board of Education Records, Oberlin College Archives.

55. Langston, *Virginia Plantation*, p. 162; Elyria *Independent-Democrat*, Dec. 10, 1856; Misc. Receipts, Nov. 6, Dec. 29, 1856, Langston Papers.

56. Langston, *Virginia Plantation*, p. 161.

57. Langston's local law practice may be traced through Lorain County Court Docket, Appearance Docket and Execution Docket, all in Lorain County Courthouse, Elyria; Russia Township Justice's Docket, 1860–62, Lorain County Courthouse; legal notices in Elyria *Independent-Democrat*, Aug. 18, Sept. 1, 1857, Jan. 9, 1861; Powers of Attorney and Receipts, Langston Papers. Real estate notices, Lorain County *News*, Mar. 7, 1866, Mar. 30, Apr. 10, 1867; entries in Record of Deeds, 8, 10–12, 14–17, 19–20, 24–25, 27, 31–32, 34, Lorain County Courthouse, Elyria; Columbus Record Duplicate, 1860, 1861; Franklin County Deed Book 50, 68, both at Franklin County Courthouse, Columbus; General Index of Deeds, Ross County Courthouse, Chillicothe; Powers of Attorney and Misc. Receipts, Langston Papers.

58. William Wells Brown, *The Black Man: His Antecedents, His Genius, and His Achievements* (New York, 1863; repr. New York: Johnson Reprint, 1968), pp. 236–37.

59. Washington *National Republican*, Feb. 11, 1870; Lorain County *News*, Mar. 3, 1870.

60. Langston, *Virginia Plantation*, p. 178; Brown, *The Black Man*, p. 236; Lorain County *News*, July 27, 1864, Feb. 4, 1863.

61. Langston, *Virginia Plantation*, pp. 164–65.

62. Ibid., pp. 165–66.

63. Elyria *Independent-Democrat*, Dec. 19, 1860; Langston, *Virginia Planta-*

tion, pp. 166–67; Mayor's Court of Oberlin, June 24, 1861, pp. 27–28,Oberlin College Archives; J. E. Rankin, introductory sketch, Langston, *Freedom and Citizenship*, p. 13.

64. Weed to Jocelyn, July 5, 1859, AMA Papers.

65. Langston, *Virginia Plantation*, p. 177; Snider, *A Writer of Books*, pp. 99–100. Jones was the Democratic candidate for justice of the peace in Russia township; see Lorain County *News*, Jan. 13, 1869.

66. Langston, *Virginia Plantation*, p. 163; Lorain County Appearance Docket, 1, pp. 431, 609, Lorain County Courthouse, Elyria.

67. *Daily Graphic*, n.d., quoted in San Francisco *Elevator*, Aug. 30, 1873; *The Athenaeum* (London), Mar. 3, 1866, p. 302; William Wells Brown, *The Rising Son; or, The Antecedents and Advancement of the Colored Race* (Boston, 1874; repr. Miami: Mnemosyne Reprint, 1969), pp. 465–68; Lorain County *News*, Feb. 19, 1862; Langston, *Virginia Plantation*, p. 177; Geoffrey Blodgett, "John Mercer Langston and the Case of Edmonia Lewis: Oberlin, 1862," *Journal of Negro History* 53 (1968):201–2.

68. Lorain County *News*, Feb. 19, 1862; Cleveland *Plain Dealer*, Feb. 11, 1862; Langston, *Virginia Plantation*, pp.171–75.

69. Langston, *Virginia Plantation*, p. 177.

70. Ibid., pp. 175–76.

71. Ibid., pp. 176–77; Lorain County *News*, Feb. 19, 1862.

72. Cleveland *Leader*, Mar. 3, 1862; Elyria *Independent-Democrat*, Mar. 5, 1862; Blodgett, "John Mercer Langston and the Case of Edmonia Lewis," 211–13; Langston, *Virginia Plantation*, pp. 178–79.

73. Langston, *Virginia Plantation*, p. 179; Fred Allen to A. A. Wright, Jan. 30, 1863, Feb. 18, 1863, both in Oberlin College Archives; no signature to "Dear Folks at Home," Feb. 26, 1863, Reed-Thayer Letters, R. S. Fletcher Papers, Oberlin College Archives; Lorain County *News*, Feb. 25, May 6, 1863.

74. *Liberator*, Feb. 19, 1864; *National Anti-Slavery Standard*, Dec. 3, 1864, Jan. 14, May 6, 1865; Benjamin Quarles, *Frederick Douglass* (Washington, D.C., 1948; repr. Boston: Atheneum, 1968), p. 310; James A. Porter, *Modern Negro Art* (New York, 1943), pp. 57–63; James A. Porter, *Ten Afro-American Artists of the Nineteenth Century* (Washington, D.C., 1967); David C. Driskell, *Two Centuries of Black American Art* (New York, 1976), pp. 48–49, 131.

75. Langston, *Virginia Plantation*, pp. 178–80.

76. Cleveland *Plain Dealer*, Mar. 3, 1862; Lorain County *News*, Mar. 5, 12, 1862; New York *Independent*, Dec. 3, 1863; Langston, *Virginia Plantation*, pp. 179–80.

77. Louisville *Courier-Journal*, July 16, 1869; "Address to Law Graduates," ms., Langston Papers; Washington *National Republican*, Feb.27, 1874; Langston, *Virginia Plantation*, pp. 161–62.

78. Brown, *The Black Man*, p. 237; Columbus Appearance Docket M (1856), pp. 335, 587, Clerk's Office, Franklin County Courthouse.

79. Power of Attorney, Feb. 28, 1858, Langston Papers; Population Census

of 1860, Ohio, Roll 1002, Lorain County, Russia Township, NA; Lorain County *News*, Sept. 13, 1865, July 25, Nov. 14, 1866.

80. Brown, *The Black Man*, p. 237; *Congregationalist*, n.d., quoted in New York *Independent*, Nov. 16, 1865; Washington *National Republican*, Feb. 11, 1870; Cincinnati *Gazette*, June 10, 1867.

81. Lorain County *News*, Sept. 23, 1863.

82. Lorain County *News*, Aug. 6, 1862; John Carey Leith to "Dear Father," May 6, 1861, Former Student File, Oberlin College Archives.

CHAPTER 10

Blacks and the Oberlin-Wellington Rescue

1856–59

OBERLIN'S township clerk left home early on the morning of September 13, 1858, bent on official business in a neighboring county. Around him Langston could see fields of turnips and potatoes ready to be dug. Harvest time had come to northern Ohio, but without a corresponding sense of well-being. No fugitive slave had ever been taken from Oberlin, and no attempt made for the past ten years. But Langston, who was involved in the town's extensive network to protect fugitives both by conviction and profession, for the clerk's duties included their care and boarding, had reason to worry that the "citadel of human freedom," as he thought of it, might be breached.[1]

His concern centered on Anson P. Dayton, the man he had superseded as clerk the previous year. Dayton, a hard-up mason when he first arrived in Oberlin, had read law and set up a practice, although with such ill success that town fathers had considered it a charity to his young family to put him in the "quite lucrative" clerkship. After his ouster, Dayton had switched allegiance from the Republican to the Democratic party, acting as clerk of the state legislature during the 1857–58 session. Subsequently, Matthew Johnson of Cleveland, federal marshal for Ohio's northern district, who was rumored to be interested in enforcing the Fugitive Slave Law on the Western Reserve, had appointed Dayton a deputy U.S. marshal.[2]

Langston and other Oberlin leaders had soon realized that Marshal Dayton, doubtless resentful over his loss to a black competitor, hopeful of further political preferment, and mindful of the financial gain that could result from the return of fugitive slaves, might use his post for that purpose. By the late summer their fears were realized. Dayton made several attempts at seizing blacks in Oberlin, only to be thwarted by the threatened parties themselves or by a vigilant citizenry. In one incident, James Smith, a black stonecutter, had confronted Dayton on the street, accused the marshal of having offered to deliver him to his owner in North Carolina, and cudgeled the lawman with a hickory stick until he ran away. At the town hearing held immediately thereafter, Langston had appeared to defend Smith, who was fined a token $5 which was quickly chipped in by bystanders. When Dayton sought Smith the next day, he was informed that the stonecutter had left town.[3]

Despite warnings to desist, Dayton next had teamed up with a slave-hunting Kentuckian, Anderson P. Jennings. After a fruitless tour of various ports of fugitive embarkation for Canada, including Painesville where a well-armed crowd gave them less than twenty minutes to get out of town, the two again focused their attention on Oberlin. With promised payments of as much as $100, Jennings brought in three experienced confederates: a deputy marshal and a deputy sheriff, both from Columbus, and another Kentucky slavecatcher. By late night of September 8 the four were assembled at a tavern run by Chauncey Wack, long-time Oberlin resident and prominent Democrat. As they matured their plot, one of Wack's regulars chimed in to advise them against trying to act in the town, particularly not at night when they "might get shot and never know who done it." He suggested the services of Shakespeare Boynton, who, as Langston would describe him, was "a fast young lad, about fourteen years of age," the son of a large landholder.[4]

Early on September 13, about the time Langston rode out from Oberlin, Shakespeare was going in search of a young black man named John Price. Ill and unable to provide for himself, Price, designated as a "pauper" in the township records (which customarily used this term, along with "transient" and "poor stranger," for fugitive slaves), had been cared for at public expense since the previous spring. As clerk, Langston had recorded payments for Price's accommodations beginning in late March and continuing through September 10, during most of the period to James Armstrong, a black laborer who often boarded fugitives at his place on the outskirts of town where Price was currently living.[5]

Under the pretext of needing help to locate another black man to work in the harvest on the Boynton farm, Shakespeare persuaded John Price to go with him. As the two rode in a buggy on a lonely country road, three of the conspirators, armed with Bowie knives and revolvers, intercepted them, dragged Price into their carriage, and sped toward

Wellington. Earlier that day, Dayton had helped arrange housing and travel accommodations. Jennings, after paying Shakespeare $20 for his services, left Oberlin to join his associates at the Wadsworth House in Wellington, there to await the afternoon southbound train.[6]

Back in Oberlin merchants were just reopening their shops after the noon dinner hour. Suddenly—"like a flash of lightening," as Charles Langston would put it—came word that an Oberlin black had been seized. Black and white townsmen and students, using any means of locomotion available, set off on the nine-mile road to Wellington. Charles, who had been enjoying a prolonged visit with Mercer and Carrie, strapped a revolver on his hip and rode out on horseback. O. S. B. Wall, Carrie's brother, rode in one of the fastest rigs in the county, at the side of Simeon Bushnell, a white clerk in his brother-in-law J. M. Fitch's bookstore. But John Watson, the light-skinned confectioner, was the first to reach Wellington. Carrying a gun and with an armed black companion in his buggy, Watson whirled into Wellington shortly after two o'clock, waving his hat and shouting, "Kidnappers!"[7]

Alarmed at Watson's appearance, the Kentuckians retreated to the attic of the hotel where they holed up with John Price in a small cock-loft. Below, the Columbus lawmen posted a quickly garnered posse, weapons at the ready, to guard the doors. The crowd swelled. A number of men attracted to Wellington earlier in the day by a now-extinguished fire remained to watch this new excitement, their numbers augmenting those arriving from Oberlin. From his high perch, the beleaguered Jennings thought that at least a thousand men, with "a good many" guns, jammed the square. Other observers put the number at less than half that, and declared that some thirty to forty black men and a few white students wielded most of the guns. Witnesses agreed that blacks "seemed the most warlike."[8]

Blacks also were the most purposeful. Throughout the long, hectic afternoon, Charles Langston, Watson, and Wall made concerted attempts to persuade the village constable to arrest John Price's captors for kidnapping and, failing that, to secure a habeas corpus. Langston calmed rowdies with the admonition that "it was best to take legal measures if any, and not to do anything by force." But force came to seem increasingly likely. As the five o'clock train rumbled through Wellington without its intended passengers aboard, he met in an attic room adjoining the cockloft with one of Price's captors. Deputy marshal Jacob Lowe of Columbus, who had known the black schoolteacher there for several years and considered him "a reasonable man," had sought him out in hopes that he might persuade the crowd to disperse. To

Lowe's chagrin, after a second conference twenty minutes later, Langston advised him the people were "bent upon a rescue at all hazards" and strongly urged him to convince Jennings, for their own safety, "to give the boy up." Lowe refused. Langston got up from the bed where the two had been sitting and, Lowe would testify, "just as he was about to go downstairs he said, 'we will have him anyhow.' "⁹

A group of armed Oberlin men, five or six blacks and several white students, waited near the back door of the inn for the results of Charles Langston's negotiations. On his return they moved swiftly. Three black men, the powerfully built Wilson Evans, tall young John Copeland, Jr., and a mulatto teamster named Jerry Fox, led a rush on the deputized guards at the door. Evans seized the outside sentinel and flung him away; "for about three minutes," one of the students would recall, the scene was one of "heavy breathing, struggles, guns hurled here and there, men on the floor"; then the rescue party made its way up the dark attic stairs. Although Jennings had a tight grip on the door latch of his refuge, someone managed to reach through a stovepipe hole and stun him with a punch to the head, causing him to loosen his hold. In the confusion of the struggle, a small English theological student named Richard Winsor led John Price rapidly to the outside, where he was nearly hurled into a buggy. Men threw their hats in the air and let out a great cheer.¹⁰

At sunset John Mercer returned home to find an all but deserted village. Apprised of events, he rode hard toward Wellington—only to be met by a fast-moving buckboard driven by an exultant Simeon Bushnell and carrying John Price, normally ebony but now "ashen-faced," by his side. The attorney pressed on until he saw his brother and brother-in-law among "the returning hosts, shouting, singing, rejoicing in the glad results." Back in Oberlin, John Mercer helped the rescuers raise the "holy hurrah," contributing a fiery denunciation of the Fugitive Slave Law and the Slave Oligarchy to the evening's celebration. Meanwhile, John Price was secreted first in Fitch's home and then in the attic of future Oberlin president James H. Fairchild, and later escorted to Canada. There was no public word on his future. But John Langston, in terms that reflected the community's view of the rescue, a Christian republican action as sanctified as a crusade, evoked the fugitive's image: "Today John Price walks abroad in his freedom, or reposes under his own vine and fig tree with no one to molest him or make him afraid."¹¹

The Oberlin-Wellington Rescue marked, in Langston's reckoning, "at once the darkest and the brightest day in the Calendar of Oberlin."

He was confident at the time that posterity would deem it "worthy of the most sacred remembrance." Frankly envious that he had missed the dramatic moment, he took solace in "a fact worthy of particular mention, that in this rescue the colored men played an important and conspicuous part." Not as evenhanded as Langston in extending "our hearty thanks and lasting gratitude" to white and black rescuers alike, history has all but obliterated the black protagonists. Yet the black participation was vital, not only in effecting the rescue, but also in creating what Langston called its "profound impression."[12]

The rescue of John Price was to have far-ranging consequences. It would inject new emotional fervor into the antislavery movement, reinvigorate the Ohio black movement, and critically affect the Republican party's evolution and standing in Ohio—and, by extension, in the North. Charles Langston would emerge an antislavery hero; John Langston would achieve new recognition as black leader and black Republican. Its net result would be to accelerate the process of national polarization. To begin to understand those consequences, it is necessary to trace the course of both the black and the antislavery causes in Ohio politics from the election of Salmon P. Chase as Ohio's first Republican governor in the fall of 1855 to the rescue itself in the fall of 1858.

During this period Langston, having helped organize the Republican coalition around opposition to slavery in the territories, faced the problem of how to move it to support black enfranchisement and the abolition of slavery. His major argument was that black and white Americans must unite against the common menace of the Slave Power. But his efforts in this regard posed considerable risks for his radical Republican allies, who had to contend with the conservative, anti-black Republican element for control of the party. A further obstacle was the Democratic party, which already charged its opponents with being "Black Republicans" and proponents of black political and social equality. Nonetheless, Langston hoped to use the countervailing moral influence of the black movement to win Republicans to a forthright endorsement of abolitionist principles. "If the Republican party is not Anti-Slavery enough," he urged Ohio blacks, "take hold of it and make it so."[13]

At the bidding of Langston and other Ohio black strategists, a black state convention met in Columbus in January 1856, just as the first Republican legislature convened. In a message prepared by a committee that included Peter Clark and the Langston brothers, the black delegates gave notice of their intention to seek repeal of the remaining

Black Laws. If Ohio insisted on continued sowing of injustice, on continued denial of equal rights, they warned, the state would "reap her harvest of sorrow and crime." A "discontented population— dissatisfied, estranged," black Ohioans would be "ready to welcome any revolution or invasion as a relief, for they can lose nothing and gain much." At the same time the convention launched the most extensive drive for black enfranchisement since 1850.[14]

As agent of the black movement's Central Committee, Langston threw himself into the organized enfranchisement effort at the beginning of the summer. By then, black spokesmen like David Jenkins had done considerable groundwork, circulating petitions for black suffrage and raising black political awareness to such a level that the touring Frederick Douglass judged Ohio blacks ready to put forth the requisite energy and commitment. "The open sesame for the colored man," Douglass exhorted, "is action! action! action!" Langston hit on the bold tactic of merging the roles of black protest agitator and radical party propagandist, campaigning simultaneously for black enfranchisement and the Republican presidential nominee, John C. Frémont. By insisting that "Frémont and Freedom" encompassed black freedom as well as white, Langston hoped to further the radicalization of the Republicans and win the party new adherents, notably among previously nonvoting abolitionists, and focus more attention on the black suffrage issue than it could otherwise command.[15]

Beginning in the populous southwestern counties, moving into central Ohio, and then working on the Western Reserve, Langston took the dual campaign to every part of the state. For several weeks in August, he was accompanied by William C. Nell, black abolitionist fresh from leading the successful black school boycott and integrated school petition drive in Boston. Everywhere Langston employed the saturation technique of the evangelist, often, like Finney, speaking for two hours or more. He wielded "arguments, appeals, facts and statistics" in a "fearless, eloquent, and irresistible manner" that, Nell observed, left "the friend proudly satisfied, and our enemies evidently confused." The reception was heartening, from the grizzled white farmer in central Ohio who threw up his arms and shouted: "My God! Can these things be true?" to the Elyria editor who judged the black lecturers' arguments "unanswerable in favor of 'the right.'"

Most notable was the First of August celebration of the British West Indies emancipation held at Urbana, northwest of Columbus. Although Nell identified the area as normally pro-slavery, a crowd of five thousand, including two thousand whites, was on hand for the largest such observance in Ohio history. Speaking in the forenoon for an hour and forty-five minutes, and again for nearly that long in the afternoon, Langston addressed such Republican themes as slavery's effect on free white labor in the South and its restraint on American liberties. "If such men as Chase, as Sumner, or Frémont" were to go South "and speak their sentiments," he declared (lifting wholesale from his 1855 American Anti-Slavery Society address), "the Southern slaveholders would hang them and then cut them into quarters." On the black condition, Langston rang the charges, as Nell put it, with "telling effect." He predicted that Ohio's black children, like those in Massachusetts, soon would take their "rightful position" in integrated public schools. Friends of the black cause must rally to the support of Frémont, "the Moses of the 19th century who would restore the colored man to his liberty and to his equality." A Democratic journalist deemed Langston's political appeal inappropriate; Nell, on the other hand, noted that his companion's "most radical sayings were enthusiastically applauded." At day's end, the throng waved the black abolitionists off at the depot with lusty cheers "for Langston and for Frémont and Freedom."[16]

On November 4, 1856, John Mercer was one of those Oberlin activists who, the Cleveland *Plain Dealer* complained, "got up in the morning savage and hungry, worked the wagons, sweat the negroes, and swept the county." That much urging was not needed for Negroes like Anthony Burns, the principal in a celebrated fugitive slave case in Boston in 1854 and now an Oberlin student, who had stepped out proudly in an Oberlin Frémont parade. The final count in Russia township showed 444 votes for Frémont, 77 for the Democratic candidate James Buchanan. Elsewhere in Ohio, despite frequent Democratic challenges and, in Cincinnati, a skirmish between Irish supporters of Buchanan and black advocates of Frémont, mulatto voters added their ballots to the Republican columns. To Langston's satisfaction, although Frémont narrowly lost to Buchanan nationwide, the Republican ticket scored a four-percentage-point triumph over the Democratic in Ohio.[17]

One little noted consequence of the 1856 elections was that a number of Negroes who claimed an ancestry more than half white but who had been denied the ballot by election judges immediately filed suit. Although similar cases brought in the aftermath of the 1855 elections had affected only the individual claimants, one of the 1856 challenges—brought by black movement leader Alfred J. Anderson, a barber in Hamilton—would make its way to the Ohio supreme court. The decision, reached in late 1859 and publicized in early 1860, would be hailed as the definitive establishment of voting rights for mulattoes.

Lewis Sheridan Leary
(Oberlin College Archives)

John A. Copeland, Jr.
(Library of Congress)

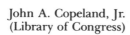

Urged by Langston and John Brown, Jr., these two young men, both residents of Oberlin, joined John Brown in his fatal raid on Harper's Ferry.

Oberlin-Wellington Rescuers, April 1859

In the meantime, such cases served to demonstrate black Ohioans' determination to use and maintain existing legal privileges.[18]

Frémont's Ohio victory—the third straight year of Republican electoral majorities in the state—gave Langston reason to indulge in guarded optimism for the success of his other, more fundamental cause. Now back in Boston, Nell predicted that the Ohio Central Committee's "zeal and efficiency bid fair to be rewarded with an early favorable response" unless politicians should decide "to play their old game and defer justice till a more convenient season." In any case, Nell asserted, the "present prominence and prospective triumph" of the equal suffrage drive was owing largely to the efforts of John M. Langston.[19]

With state elections coming up in the fall of 1857, however, Langston found few Republicans ready to commit themselves publicly for black enfranchisement. Governor Chase, himself facing a reelection campaign while trying to contain Know Nothings as well as former Whigs and Democrats within his coalition, judged the party "in no position to hold . . . advanced ground." Langston did garner the support of former legislator Norton Townshend, as well as two Reserve congressmen, his legal mentor Philemon Bliss and the veteran Joshua Giddings. As two prominent Republican newspapers voiced cautious approval of black suffrage, Oberlin's Representative James Monroe determined to introduce the required legislation.[20]

Langston and Monroe coordinated their efforts to gain maximum publicity for the black suffrage argument. On January 21, 1857, black delegates gathered in Columbus and elected Langston convention president for the second time in the decade. In an address to the state legislature, Langston based the black "demand" for enfranchisement and equal treatment both on the "inherent rights" of manhood and on American citizenship. He quoted Congressman Bliss's contention that neither American documents, principles, nor traditions justified denial of the franchise on account of color. Rather, black disenfranchisement had begun only with the ascent to power of pro-slavery forces that had "changed the whole policy of the Government from an enfranchising to an enslavery, from a propagandism of free labor to a propagandism of slavery." In an attempt to dispose of the colonization panacea that conservative Republicans were beginning to push in hopes of refuting slaveholder charges that their party's position on slavery would lead to black equality, Langston warned that black Ohioans would never emigrate en masse. "Your history and your destiny shall be ours. And while cruel and despotic statutes disgrace our State legislation, we will express, in every possible manner, our dissatisfaction and disapproval of them." The next day, with black petitions already in legislators' hands, Monroe delivered an eloquent speech and submitted a bill to amend the Ohio constitution to permit black suffrage. Oberlin's state senator also took positive action, reporting Langston's address to the judiciary committee. With at least half the Republicans in the assembly indicating they would side with Democrats in opposition to the bill, however, Monroe and radical allies decided against calling it up for a vote.[21]

Langston's disappointment fed his anger over the next national turn of events—Chief Justice Roger B. Taney's Dred Scott decision, denying that Negroes had citizenship rights. "So gross, so monstrous, so unparalleled a judicial outrage . . . overtaxes our patience, well-nigh extinguishes our hopes—almost goads us into madness," protested Charles Langston and other Columbus blacks in a letter to Governor Chase. Because "nearly four millions of disfranchised . . . colored men and women" were "too feeble" to administer the deserved retaliation, the black Columbians looked to those "aiding the anti-slavery cause" for "a rebuke and restraint of the Slave Power." In turn, Ohio's Republican lawmakers denounced Taney's decision and, despite their rejection of black suffrage, now expressly defended black citizenship. Moreover, they enacted three "personal liberty laws" designed to protect black Ohioans against kidnapping, including one submitted by Monroe providing habeas corpus rights to alleged fugitives. This radical thrust carried over into the state Republican convention, which renominated Chase for governor.[22]

But in the late summer and fall of 1857, Langston and his radical allies were dismayed as the northern electorate, soured by a financial panic and the onset of hard times, seemed swept by a conservative backlash. Republican candidates, embarrassed by an embezzlement scandal within the administration of Governor Chase, confronted Democratic charges of their dedication to a "Congo Creed." As evidence, Democrats cited the radical involvement in the black enfranchisement drive and some of Langston's own declarations for black equality. Langston and Monroe appeared jointly at the Oberlin First of August celebration, but this was the only time the black Republican was even reported during the campaign. On election day, Ohio mulattoes insisted on voting—in such numbers that Democrats claimed Chase's narrow reelection margin was due to two thousand black votes, many cast illegally in Oberlin and other abolitionist redoubts. Although Republicans retained the governor's office, Democrats won control of both houses of the Ohio legislature.[23]

The new year brought further setbacks to the black cause. The entire political climate seemed to be turning virulently anti-black. As a result of the national Democratic party split between followers of Stephen A. Douglas's doctrine of popular sovereignty and supporters of the Buchanan administration's attempt to force the pro-slavery Lecompton Constitution on Kansas, Ohio Democrats turned even more to racism as their most reliable appeal. Democrats in the assembly not only merely abrogated two of the three personal liberty laws, but also imposed a "gag rule" on Monroe when he tried to defend them. With Democrats threatening harsh new restrictive legislation, Frederick Douglass saw "the spirit of the bottomless pit" being loosed on the colored citizens of Ohio.

Meanwhile, conservatives in the Ohio Republican party mounted a strong drive to wrest control from the radicals. Declaring the entire "Negro question" settled for at least a generation, and asserting it was time to tend to white men's interests, southern Ohio's congressional candidate Thomas Corwin led the conservative Republicans in pressing for a coalition with the Douglas Democrats and an overall recasting of Republican doctrine to appeal to southern moderates. The evident strength of the conservatives was such that Chase privately worried that it might be necessary to resurrect the Free Soil party. While Langston and his fellow Oberlin Republicans staunchly reaffirmed their obligation to "press right on, until slavery is met at every assailable point and vanquished," they could not ignore the extent to which the radical-black strategy had backfired. Langston sadly received the returns from Republican caucuses to nominate congressional candidates at three traditionally radical strongholds on the Reserve. Three Republican stalwarts for black rights—O. P. Brown of Portage, Giddings, and, most disturbing of all to Langston, Philemon Bliss—all were defeated by conservative candidates.[24]

Langston may well have felt forced to a sober reassessment of his reform tactics and commitments. Could he continue to have faith that, as he and David Jenkins agreed, the rise of the Republican party and the disarray of the Democrats were "omens of hope for the colored people"? On this point, Peter Clark, for one, was skeptical that his rights would be safer, or slavery less secure, with the Republicans than with the Democrats. Could black ends be reached through the political antislavery movement? Were the best means to black ends moral or, perhaps, as a number of northern leaders were arguing since *Dred Scott*, violent?[25]

Langston's response to these questions came in a speech he delivered at Cleveland and at Xenia in early August 1858, at anniversary celebrations of the British West Indies emancipation. The Cleveland ceremonies, an elaborate day-long affair concluded with a ball, evoked the

praise of even the hostile *Plain Dealer*, while a Republican journalist
called Langston's speech "very stirring and excellent." In contrast,
threats of violence clouded the festivities in Xenia. Beforehand, local
whites and the Democratic press, reacting to the growing number of
black residents attracted to the area since establishment of Wilberforce
University for Negroes two years earlier, had clamored for removal of
the school and expulsion of "insolent blacks," and warned that the black
celebration would be "offensive." In consequence, a far smaller crowd
than usual gathered on the appointed day. Langston, too, had been
privately told by whites to stay away. Disregarding the threat, he took
the stand as a local black man named John C. Galley positioned himself
at his side, his hand resting conspicuously on his revolver. (Galley, a
delegate to the 1858 Ohio black convention, would become postwar
Xenia's town marshal.) Order prevailed, except for a small band of
inebriated white youths whom blacks quickly dispersed, and Langston
delivered his address.[26]

The speech, entitled "The World's Anti-Slavery Movement: Its Heroes and Its Triumphs," wrought on a theme suggested at the black
state convention six years earlier, was the only pre-war address that
Langston would include in his 1883 published collection of speeches. It
was a scholarly and ardent exposition of the struggles for freedom
throughout history. Comprehensive in his definition of the American
antislavery movement as encompassing all whose goals were the abolition of slavery and black enfranchisement, Langston excluded neither
moral, violent, nor political means toward these ends. "Whenever, wherever liberty has made a stand against oppression, whether with the
arms of 'truth and love,' or with the sword and bayonet, she has always
won the most brilliant, splendid triumphs." The West Indies emancipation had been a "great moral triumph," the Haitian insurrection a
"bloody contest," black-instigated and black-directed, in "one last,
mighty effort to throw off their yoke and gain their manhood, and
assert and maintain their rights." As for politics, the vote was "a source
of very great power," that would "stab the demon of slavery. . . . No
Democratic politician; no hollow-hearted politician of any party whatever; no man who is not a devoted, laborious anti-slavery man can ever
secure our vote."

In a perceptive analysis of the ongoing process of national polarization over the slavery question, Langston asserted that, "like the air we
breathe," it was "all-pervasive." The great national institutions, ecclesiastical and political, had broken apart over slavery; antislavery agitation, no longer merely "sectional," had become a "national" movement.
Because the "slave oligarchy" had transgressed on the rights of white as

well as black Americans, and thus had forged an "identification of the interests of the white and colored people of this country," white Americans would unite with blacks in the antislavery struggle to preserve their own freedom, their government, and "American liberty itself." Urging his listeners to retain "hearts full of hope, and a determination to battle for the right against the wrong," he pleaded: "Let us then, disenfranchised Americans, take new courage; for our cause and the cause of the slave shall triumph gloriously."[27]

The Oberlin-Wellington Rescue occurred less than six weeks later. Langston, typically sensitive to political opportunity, moved quickly to capitalize on this chance to mobilize his people and to agitate for the black and antislavery cause. Alongside Charles Langston and other black activists, he issued a call, widely advertised in the Republican and abolitionist press, for a black state convention to be held in late November in Cincinnati. Although Charles presided over the convention, both Langstons were the major proponents for the establishment of a new statewide black organization, the Ohio State Anti-Slavery Society. In opposition to the plan was Clark, who pointed out that numerous earlier organizational efforts during the decade had all ended in failure. The majority of delegates, however, concurred with Cincinnatian Josephus Fowler: "We must do or die!" and approved the new society. Together with the veterans Malvin of Cleveland and John Booker of Columbus, John Langston drew up a businesslike constitution. The society's aims were declared to be the abolition of slavery and the attainment of black rights; the phrase, to "secure [these objects] by political and moral means, so far as may be," deliberately left open the resort to force. Black women were accorded full membership privileges. In actuality, black orator and poet Frances Ellen Watkins participated prominently in the convention and, later, helped in fund-raising efforts for the society. Membership also was open to whites. (Oberlin whites, at least, did participate in the local chapter of the society.) Charles Langston agreed to serve the society as executive secretary, working out of a central office in Cleveland—an innovation designed to add organizational stability and facilitate quick response to crises. John Mercer served as president and chief traveling agent. With local auxiliaries shortly established around the state, the Ohio State Anti-Slavery Society would function until the outbreak of war.[28]

The Cincinnati convention provided John Langston an ideal platform from which to challenge the Buchanan administration. There may have been a grain of truth in a Democratic editor's later contention that federal officials and the other interested parties might well have ignored the Lorain County violators of the Fugitive Slave Law, but "were only driven to this prosecution by the belligerent demonstrations" of the rescuers and their allies.[29] Langston was plainly provocative. Counting on his race to make his already inflammatory declarations even more obnoxious to his political enemies, he devoted a full speech on the opening night to a biting attack on the Democratic party. Repeatedly characterizing the Democrats as pro-slavery, he as often jeeringly predicted the party's demise. His own motto, he said, referring to Cato's "Carthago delenda est," was "the Democratic party must be destroyed." In scornfully depicting the policies of the national and state Democrats, Langston employed a measured vocabulary of violence—"hate," "steal," "damn," "kill"—that reflected at once his genuine anger and his desire to prod both friends and opponents to action. He selected for special praise New York Governor William H. Seward's recent pronouncement of "irrepressible conflict" between northern and southern societies, and urged the further radicalization of the Republican party. The Democrats "can't stand in this State much longer, for the people are opposed to slavery and willing to trample under foot the Fugitive Slave Law as they did lately in Wellington." The Democratic administration, he taunted, was "afraid to prosecute the matter."

On two subsequent evenings, each, like the first, with large audiences and invited reporters on hand, Langston drove home the black determination to resist. Three militant resolutions he personally offered at one session demanded the repeal of all laws based on complexional discrimination, as well as the institution of full equality before the law; condemned the Dred Scott decision and the Fugitive Slave Law; and both lauded the Oberlin-Wellington rescuers and pledged to "imitate their worthy example." He was blunt about how far blacks might go in imitation. Joined on the final night by two prominent out-of-town guests, eastern protest leader William J. Watkins and William Howard Day, the former Ohioan who now lived in St. Catherine's, Ontario, Langston "reviewed with severity the action of the American people in regard to the colored race, and advocated the right and duty of resistance by force of arms, when it was feasible."[30]

Langston and the black leadership had thrown down the gauntlet. Meanwhile, his intensely political white townsmen had been scarcely less goading. In dispatches to newspapers ranging from Western Reserve weeklies to the New York *Tribune*, Oberlin citizens crowed: "The Fugitive Slave Law 'can't be did' in this part of the Reserve at least."[31]

A federal grand jury, empaneled in Cleveland, began hearing witnesses in the Oberlin-Wellington case in early November. The federal prosecutors were openly partisan. Only Democrats were selected as jurors, including Lewis D. Boynton, father of the boy who had betrayed John Price. According to the later admission of Anson Dayton, Oberlin Democrats supplied a list of suspects, as well as witnesses for the prosecution. (Although two Democrats were indicted, the charges against them were quickly dropped.) In his charge to the jurors, Democratic Judge Hiram V. Willson, who also would officiate at the trials, denigrated Higher Law—as Langston noted indignantly—as characterized "by intolerance and bigotry," and compared Oberlin leaders to "the subtle prelates of the dark ages . . . trained in certain schools in New England to manage words . . . [and] hearts" to the end of disrupting the federal union.[32]

Thirty-seven Oberlin and Wellington residents were indicted for the rescue of John Price. Most prominent among the whites were professor Henry E. Peck, attorney Ralph Plumb, and bookseller Fitch, who were charged with "aiding and abetting." The three men had not actually been on the scene in Wellington, although all were conspicuous in Oberlin's underground railroad operations and in the Republican party. Twelve blacks were indicted. They included Charles H. Langston, O. S. B. Wall, John Watson, David Watson, Wilson and Henry Evans, and John H. Scott. John Copeland, Jr., also was indicted but, like several other blacks, evaded arrest. The prosecutor's "most desperate efforts" to indict John Langston were thwarted by his proof of having been out of the county on the day of the rescue. All the indicted remained free on their own recognizance prior to trial.[33]

In early January 1859, Oberlin signalled its unrepentant attitude by holding a "Felon's Feast." Hosts for the dinner were the Oberlin rescuers, including six black men and their wives; guests were the indicted from Wellington and other localities, as well as several Republican newspapermen. John Mercer Langston offered a prophetic toast. In speaking to "Personal Sacrifices—The seed of today which brings the harvest of tomorrow," he forecast that reinstating the Declaration of Independence and the Constitution would require men to go to prison or to march in battle "to meet the Slave Oligarchy." Black Americans, he assured them, were only too ready to "fight against the enemies of their country, for it is their country now. We demand that we be permitted to exercise the rights of citizens." Langston yearned to take the field himself, "as a common soldier or in a more exalted rank," and "strike" for his country. The day would come, he ventured, when he would march to Camp Cleveland (the nearest military post) and be hailed by a former pro-slavery man: " 'I am glad you are going to fight with us; I was always in favor of it.' " The two then would march on side by side, agreeing to " 'let bygones be bygones.' " Without the aid of the Negro, Langston argued—his first statement of a major future theme—the "Slave Oligarchy" could not be overthrown. But when it should be vanquished, the black man "will stand free by your side."[34]

The trials began on April 5, 1859. By then the lines were drawn. Oberlin's defenders argued that individual and state rights were at stake; supporters of the administration upheld property and national rights. Langston characterized the rescue in more extreme terms, as pitting Christian republican values—"Justice and Christianity, the Declaration and the Constitution, Law and Order"—against those of the Slave Power—"Injustice and Atheism, Despotism and Slavery, Mob Violence and Misrule." Democrats reversed the coin. Federal prosecutors would fulminate against the "saints of Oberlin" whose Higher Law doctrine "would make a Hell upon earth" replete with "free love and infidelity." It was a "spirit which would tear down and annihilate the Government of these United States." The defense attorneys were four noted Republican attorneys from Cleveland: Rufus P. Spalding, A. G. Riddle, F. T. Backus, and S. O. Griswold, all of whom volunteered their services without charge. The prosecution team was composed of U.S. attorney George Belden and George Bliss, a private attorney who had been specially engaged. The jurors, hand-picked by Marshal Johnson, were all Democrats and included one deputy U.S. marshal. "The Court, the Prosecutor, the Jurors, and the witnesses, with one or two exceptions," Langston observed, "are Proslavery and Democratic in their connections and associations. It is well known, then, what we may expect. And, so far, we have not been disappointed." First tried, and duly convicted, was Simeon Bushnell, who had driven John Price back to Oberlin.[35]

The prosecution next called up the case of Charles H. Langston. Charles, like his brother, for whom he was often mistaken in the press, earlier had all but dared authorities to act, reportedly advising federal officers "to make their peace with God before they lay hands on him." In trying Langston, the prosecution may have calculated that it could hammer home the dangers of "nigger social equality" as practiced in Oberlin and promoted by "Black Republicans." Further, accustomed to routine convictions of blacks on the flimsiest of evidence, Belden doubtless hoped for a quick win. He was persuaded that with Langston's conviction and perhaps that of one more rescuer, "the Defendants will cease fighting, and that the remaining ones will plead guilty."[36]

But the case against Langston was far from clear-cut, and the trial proved long and expensive. A string of witnesses was required to make the case that all the while Langston overtly had engaged in legal methods to try to win Price's release, he surreptitiously had acted in concert with his violent black brothers. He had tried to bribe a servant to obtain a door key to the inn; he had given the signal for the rescue to commence. In sum, Belden argued, Langston's conduct in Wellington was "very cunning and very hypocritical, very shrewd, but very deceiving." In rebuttal, defense attorneys pled, "Lay aside all political bias or prejudice, forget his race and color, and try his case as though he were one of your equals; as though he were, as he is, a man, and had rights." After half an hour's deliberation, jurors declared Charles Langston guilty.[37]

On the morning of May 12, Judge Willson ordered Charles Langston to stand for sentencing and extended the usual invitation for a mitigating plea. This was the moment the Langstons had waited for. Having discarded the strategy of having John Mercer conduct Charles's defense, they had decided instead that Charles himself should deliver a carefully prepared and rehearsed address. In a full, melodic voice charged with deep feeling, the delicately built, thin-visaged forty-two-year-old "representative of the Negro Race"—as John Mercer aptly put it—responded with a richly wrought legal, ethical, and emotional challenge to the racially biased American system of justice. Despite constitutional guarantees of an impartial trial, "I was tried by a jury who were prejudiced; before a Court that was prejudiced; prosecuted by an officer who was prejudiced, and defended, though ably, by counsel that was prejudiced." He had gone to Wellington with full knowledge that, in the words of the Dred Scott decision, " 'BLACK MEN HAVE NO RIGHTS WHICH WHITE MEN ARE BOUND TO RESPECT.' " Had he himself been in John Price's position, claimed as a slave, "and my brother, being a lawyer, should seek to get out a writ of *habeas corpus* to expose the falsity of the claim, he would be thrust into prison under one provision of the Fugitive Slave Law, for interfering with the man claiming to be in pursuit of a fugitive, and I, by the perjury of a solitary wretch, would by another of its provisions be helplessly doomed to life-long bondage."

In impassioned climax, Charles Langston pledged himself to do again what he had done for John Price. Unprotected by the law, "I must take upon myself the responsibility of self-protection; when I come to be claimed by some perjured wretch as his slave, I shall never be taken into slavery. And as in that trying hour I would have others do to me, as I would call upon my friends to help me, as I would call upon you, your Honor, to help me, as I would call upon you [the prosecuting and defense attorneys] to help me, and upon you and upon you, *so help me God*! I stand here to say that I will do all I can for any man thus seized and held! . . . We have all a common humanity, and you all would do that; your manhood would require it, and no matter what the laws might be, you would honor yourself for doing it, while your friends and your children to all generations would honor you for doing it, and every good and honest man would say you had done *right!*"[38]

The courtroom applause was "great and prolonged," despite the marshal's attempts to quell it. Once order was restored, the judge, struggling to contain his own emotions, told Charles that he had done the court "injustice . . . in thinking that nothing you say could effect a mitigation of your sentence." Willson sentenced Charles Langston to twenty days in jail and a fine of $100 and costs, in contrast to the "exemplary" penalty meted out to Bushnell, a sixty-day sentence and $600 fine. "How the United States officials will collect the fines imposed upon these men," John Mercer reflected caustically, "it is impossible to tell. It is reported that they are very poor. Then blessed be nothing!"[39]

Charles Langston's speech evoked sympathy across the North. "The Children of the Free," the Cleveland *Leader* foretold, "will read it in their school books, and will execrate the memory of the Court and the Jury who consigned such a man to fine and imprisonment, for a crime so God-like!" An all-black meeting in Boston awarded the speech "high prominence in the annals of this the second revolution for liberty in the United States." To John Mercer's mind, as he would write in 1892 at Charles's death, it was "perhaps the most remarkable speech that has been delivered before a court by a prisoner since Paul pleaded his own cause before Agrippa." He was proud of its exposition of "genuine loyalty to the Negro race," its "fearless and eloquent expression in favor of the Negro and his rights."[40]

By this time, several developments had combined to build interest in the trials. At the commencement of Langston's hearing, the court had declared its plans to try him and the remaining defendants with the same jury that had convicted Bushnell, but defense attorneys refused to cooperate. The judge then ordered that the defendants' recognizances be canceled and that they be taken into custody. After court adjourned for the day, the marshal offered to release them, but the rescuers refused. Although the court later allowed a new jury for Langston's trial, the rescuers took up residence in the Cleveland jail. Under an indulgent antislavery sheriff, the prisoners exacted full propaganda value from their predicament. Besides countless newspaper interviews and articles, including a cover picture of the jailed rescuers on *Frank Leslie's Weekly*, they kept up a steady correspondence with the antislavery community, supplied sermon material to pastors across the North, printed a newspaper from the jail and issued pamphlets, sold writing paper imprinted with an image of the "stone castle," as the jail was called, and entertained a steady stream of visitors. For its part, the prosecution tried to isolate the Oberlin rescuers by freeing their counterparts from other localities on payment of token fines, while the Democratic press ridiculed their martyrdom as self-imposed. But the Oberlin men refused to submit. Despite the effects of confinement on "our business, our health, our families," they resolved, in the words of Sunday school superintendent Fitch, to "bear it patiently because we clearly see, as we think, that the time has come again when the truth must be sustained through suffering." Besides Bushnell and Langston, twelve Oberlin men, seven white and five black, remained in jail.[41]

Concurrently, the defense attorneys had undertaken to challenge the constitutionality of the Fugitive Slave Law in the Ohio supreme court. It was an effort encouraged by that body's all-Republican makeup. Although the state court in late April refused a writ of habeas corpus for release of the accused on the ground the cases were still pending, the defense attorneys later filed a second writ, this time only for the release of Bushnell and Langston. With the Ohio attorney general joining their suit, the defense looked with confidence toward the hearing. For their part, administration representatives in Cleveland appealed to Washington for support in the event of conflict with state authorities. Buchanan's attorney general Jeremiah Black responded with an order to stand firm: "the moral as well as the physical power will be on your side." In a show of force, President Buchanan ordered the U.S. war steamer *Michigan* to the port of Cleveland.[42]

All the while, Langston and other radical spokesmen employed the full range of agitational devices—speeches, demonstrations, articles, letters to the editor—to keep the rescuers' cause before the public. Langston underscored the black dimension of the rescue through an article he contributed to the *Anglo-African Magazine*, as well as through a campaign for an anti-kidnapping bill and for black suffrage that he spearheaded as president of the Ohio State Anti-Slavery Society. (Together with other society speakers, he delivered more than "three hundred lectures" in 1859 to "people of all classes," who, according to the annual report, manifested the "greatest anxiety to hear and receive the truth.") He spoke throughout the spring in villages and hamlets on and off the Western Reserve. After he portrayed the "abominable character" of the Fugitive Slave Law to an Erie County meeting in late May, a crowd resolved: "All enactments, State and National, that are founded in injustice and inhumanity, we despise and condemn as utterly null and void." The Lorain County Republican convention at Elyria, doubtless with Langston's presence felt, resolved: "It is absurd to contend, that the State Government is just as Sovereign within its sphere as the Federal Government is within its sphere, and yet make the latter the sole judge of the extent of the powers of both." Declarations coming out of other Republican county conventions, meeting to elect delegates to the state convention in early June, also indicated a heightened interest in disunion and nullification.[43]

Violent rhetoric was common coin. In late April before an excited crowd in the Oberlin chapel, Langston scornfully portrayed federal "idolatry" of the Fugitive Slave Law and set off cheers with the belligerent declaration: "As for me, if they come clothed with its authority, I will tear their documents in tatters and trample them under my feet." "We wait the action of the courts," he concluded amid "immense enthusiasm, . . . but let the Court remember what sympathies, what *action*, such men may call forth." Giddings, who took a jailhouse meal with the prisoners, led the formation of a chapter of the revolutionary Sons of Liberty at Ashtabula, where nearly a hundred citizens enrolled on the spot. Oberlin formed its own chapter and displayed posters emblazoned "Resistance to Tyrants, Obedience to God!" A former missionary who lived in Oberlin confided, "If deliverance fails, probably the *Populace* will rise, and I hope they will." Senator Ben Wade urged that if the supreme court should fail to grant the habeas corpus to the rescuers, "the People of the Western Reserve must grant it—*sword at hand if need be*." An Ashtabula County man spoke for the ordinary person: "We can't think of anything else, neither do we want to."[44]

On May 24, the day before the Ohio supreme court opened its hearing, Republicans held a mass meeting on the Cleveland public square. Such prominent politicians as Wade, Giddings, and Congressman James Ashley were among the five hundred signatories of the call. More than ten thousand aroused Ohioans poured into Cleveland for what was billed as the largest meeting ever held on the Reserve. Oberlin sent a 1,300-strong delegation; blacks came from as far south as Columbus. A crowd gathered at the Cleveland jail and called on Charles Langston for a speech. Then twelve days into his sentence, Charles mounted the wooden fence to explore the paradox of the peculiar country and age that celebrated freedom, yet imprisoned men who worked to let the "downtrodden and the oppressed go free." When he finished, the crowd seemed so wrought up that the incarcerated Peck, Plumb, and Fitch, successively called out, each deemed it prudent to caution against violence. When the formal program began on the city square, Giddings, as president, elicited roars of approval by suggesting the use of force should legal means prove inadequate to free the prisoners. But Governor Chase, who had made a last-minute decision to attend, soothingly stressed reliance on the state courts and the need to vote out of office the pro-slavery dominance in the federal government. In the event the Ohio supreme court ruled favorably on the habeas corpus proceedings, Chase promised to see the edict enforced—if necessary, by calling out the state militia.[45]

John Mercer Langston was the ninth of twelve speakers, the only Oberliner and only Negro on the program. More than anything else at this Republican-abolitionist indignation meeting, more even than the rebellious sentiments voiced by speakers and contained in a series of resolutions, the appearance of the black orator in the midst of the state's most illustrious Republican politicians signaled how far the Rescue cases had propelled the party down the radical road. Once again, John Mercer declared his "deep unalterable hatred" of the Democratic party. He "trampled the Fugitive Slave Law under his feet, for it incarcerated his own brother and his friends and neighbors for disobeying its bloody commands. If you but hate slavery because it oppresses the black man in the Southern States, for God's sake, hate it for its enslavement of white men. Don't say it is confined to the South, here it is on our neighbors and citizens." Invoking the spirit of radical Christian patriotism, he concluded: "As we love our friends, as we love our God-given rights, as we love our homes, as we love ourselves, as we love our God, let us this afternoon swear eternal enmity to this law. Exhaust the law first for these men, but if this fails, for God's sake, fall back upon our own natural rights, and say to the prison walls 'come down' and set these men at liberty."[46]

Six days later the Ohio supreme court handed down its decision. Relying on the U.S. Supreme Court's ruling in the Sherman Booth case (involving a Wisconsin fugitive rescue) only two months before, the Ohio justices, on a split decision, refused to intervene. Chief Justice Joseph R. Swan, a distinguished legal scholar, cast his lot with two jurists from southern Ohio, and against two from northern districts, to avert a constitutional crisis and probable confrontation between state and federal troops.[47]

"The Supreme Court of the State failing to sustain" them, Langston commented, "it was left for the Common Pleas Court of Lorain County to come to the rescue of its citizens." Although the heavily Democratic state legislature had repealed two of the three statutes to prevent kidnapping enacted in April 1857 by its Republican predecessor, one of these personal liberty laws remained. Under its terms, a Lorain County grand jury in February 1859 had indicted Anderson Jennings and his three companions on a charge of kidnapping John Price. The trial was now at hand. On instructions from Washington, District Attorney Belden intended to pursue the prosecution of the rescuers and to defend the slave catchers. But the latter, facing further loss of time and certain conviction in the county court, backed out. Lorain authorities dropped the case against the "kidnappers," in return for dismissal of the remaining indictments against the rescuers. "So the Government has been beaten at last," the Cleveland *Plain Dealer* commented sourly, "with law, Justice, and facts all on its side, and Oberlin, with its rebellious Higher Law creed, is triumphant." Slaveholders doubtless could only concur.[48]

Late in the afternoon of July 6, 1859, after eighty-five days' imprisonment, the Oberlin rescuers returned to jubilee. Only five days later, exultant townsmen celebrated the release of Simeon Bushnell. (Charles Langston earlier had completed his own sentence.) With four brass bands setting the cadence, the uniformed Oberlin fire brigade standing at attention, and six hundred white-gowned women waving banners, a huge crowd walked through the hot, dusty mid-day to the big church. Inside, the choir offered a spine-tingling rendition of the "Marseillaise." Monroe presided over speech-making galore. Prominent among the out of town speakers was Giddings, whom Langston later would credit as the single person outside Oberlin most responsible for having "compelled the government of the state of Ohio . . . to take an attitude in favor of American liberty." But "the most eloquent speaker of the occasion"—in the for once unanimous opinion of the *Plain Dealer* and its radical archenemy, the *Leader*—was the "colored man," John Langston. Called up by the crowd, he responded with the fluency and forcefulness that, along with his kinship to Charles Langston, had won him increased admiration in the last months. "In his characteristic bold eloquence," Langston damned the Fugitive Law, paid "a high and proud tribute" to his brother, and thanked "his noble friends who had gone up to Cuyahoga County jail—thanked them in his character as a negro—as a white man—as one in whom the blood of both races joined—as a man—and as an American citizen."[49]

While each of the celebrated slave rescue cases of the fifties contributed to the heightening of sectional tensions, none had more significant effects than the Oberlin-Wellington Rescue. In part it was a matter of timing, in part a mode of behavior. Previous cases, the most noted being that of Anthony Burns in Boston, transpired much earlier in the decade—before the Slave Power's perceived threat to liberty, equality, and self-government had taken firm lodging in the northern conscious-ness. But by the fall of 1858, outrage had been piled upon outrage, crisis upon crisis. The Kansas-Nebraska Act and the subsequent bitter and violent wrangling over slavery in the territories; the Dred Scott decision, interpreted by many as giving national legitimacy to slavery and white supremacy; the Buchanan administration's commitment to the fraudulent pro-slavery Lecompton Constitution and the consequent split within the Democratic party; the slaveowners' efforts to reopen the slave trade and to acquire new slave territory in Mexico, Cuba, and Central America; the southern demand for a slave code to protect slavery in the territories; the extreme pro-slavery arguments of south-erners like Virginia's George Fitzhugh, South Carolina's George McDuffie, and Alabama's William L. Yancey—each had lent substance to the abolitionist and Republican arguments that southerners were bent on controlling the country in the interests of slavery. In such a context, the protracted Oberlin-Wellington rescue case dramatically presented the northern public with a practical illustration of the Slave Power's alleged plot to destroy the Christian republican values it so long had taken for granted.

The conduct of the rescuers and the skill with which they and their friends exploited the crisis atmosphere effectively drove home the point. Their willingness to defend what Langston called the principles of "Liberty and Right" by risking themselves to free a fugitive slave and then cheerfully accepting the consequences by going to jail was not lost on that sizable segment of the northern population predisposed to be anti-southern and anti-Democratic. The longer the rescuers remained under confinement, the more they seemed, especially under the bar-rage of propaganda churned out by "the prisoners" and their allies, men of "indomitable purpose" whose actions were marked by "benev-olence and charity," as Langston portrayed them. More matter-of-factly, the respected Springfield (Massachusetts) *Republican* noted: "The per-secution of Christian men for showing kindness to runaway negroes is a losing operation socially and politically."[50]

As Langston felt confident would happen, the "conduct" of the res-cuers did forward "the interests of the Anti-Slavery cause." The wife of one of the rescuers would consider the heavy emotional and financial costs justified because "they were making anti-slavery sentiment very fast just then." A Michigan man visited Peck in jail to inform him of the "perfect *revival* of anti-slavery zeal in that state in consequence of our troubles," furthered by "a systematic effort to rouse the people by lec-tures and tracts." William Lloyd Garrison judged "this very persecution will give a fresh impetus to our noble cause"—an impetus evidenced in part by increased donations to antislavery organizations like the A.M.A. and Oberlin College. As one donor wrote, it was "high time for Antislavery men everywhere to show their faith by their works."[51] In the late summer and fall of 1859, Peck and E. H. Fairchild were instrumental in revitalizing the western evangelical antislavery movement through two well-attended Christian Anti-Slavery Conventions in Columbus and Chicago. Sending out speakers and petitions, the movement, recognizing the abolitionist clergy's considerable influence in previous Republican victories, forthrightly criticized the Republicans' *"prevalent tendency to overlook the claims of the oppressed themselves,"* and worked, as Peck put it, to infuse new principle into the party.[52]

Unquestionably, the biracial nature of the Rescue—the decisive actions of black men in securing John Price's freedom, the dignified martyrdom of black prisoners alongside white, the eloquent protests of Charles Langston in the courtroom and John Mercer Langston at black and white meetings around the state—heightened and extended its effect. Paradoxically freed by their race, as they were qualified by their attainments, both Langstons had been able to voice in the most radical terms the demand for recognition of black manhood—not just as a victim of oppression like Price, but, as Charles had put it, as an Ohio "citizen," as a United States "outlaw," as a human being set upon "employment of those means of liberation which belong to us all." Subsequent to the Rescue and the formation of the Ohio State Anti-Slavery Society under the leadership of the Langston brothers, the *Anti-Slavery Bugle* of Salem, Ohio, commented on the "utmost importance" of the black dimension in abolitionist protest: "their moral power on this question is not exceeded by any other class. Indeed, it may almost be said they carry in their hands the key of our American Bastille."[53]

While black participation in the Rescue strengthened the determination of white and black abolitionists, it unquestionably increased the pride and hope of ordinary black men and women as well. In the aftermath of the trials, Oberlin blacks showed no disposition to "meekly *lie still* under the heel of the oppressor." In early 1860 when Deputy Marshal Dayton was so imprudent as to show up in Oberlin, the black response was swift. After a citizens' committee ordered Dayton out of the village within the hour, five "active" black men, including rescuer Scott, followed Dayton's tracks in the snow, caught up with him, and forced a confession of his role in the kidnapping of Price and the names of his Oberlin accomplices, as well as a promise to resign. Some months later, a committee of Oberlin blacks, irritated by a local jeweler's display of an "image-clock"—evidently a Sambo caricature—explained to the proprietor that they found the clock "personally offensive" and requested its removal, "or they would assist him to it." A few nights later a gunshot shattered the window and the clock. Some white villagers worried that black vigilantism was getting out of hand. Oberlin blacks bore themselves as though they were "not afraid of the white man," black abolitionist William J. Watkins commented. "There is a sort of you-touch-me-if-you-dare about them."[54]

One measure of the impact of the Rescue was the hold it exerted on the black memory. It was in 1870 at a black Republican ward meeting in postwar Washington that one man would interject his own recollections of the Rescue—"the starting point of events that gave the colored men their freedom." It was in 1889, three decades after John Mercer Langston addressed the Republican mass gathering in the Cleveland square, that John P. Green of Cleveland, notable black Republican legislator, disclosed how that event had stimulated his own ambition. Barely fourteen years old at the time, the boy had "listened [to Langston] with my mouth and my ears, and I wished that the day might come that I might stand by his side."[55]

In addition to its beneficial effects on the antislavery and black causes, the Rescue bolstered the antislavery wing of Ohio's Republican party. On June 3, 1859, Giddings and Monroe, both fresh from the Republican state convention in Columbus, along with Langston, addressed some 1,200 Lorain County Republicans assembled in Oberlin to consider the radical gains evidenced in the party nominations and platform for the upcoming state elections. Over the heated objections of Corwin and other conservative leaders, the radicals had succeeded in denying renomination to Chief Justice Swan—consigning him, as Fitch gloated from his cell, "to the place of 'dead Swans.'" Although compromises had been necessary, and the party still fell short of the Oberlin standard, the Lorain County radicals professed themselves pleased with the emphasis of the state Republican platform on repeal of the Fugitive Slave Law. "Thus far we have not suffered in vain," Fitch believed. "The weak back of our Republican Party in Ohio has been strengthened." He did not mistake the temper of the electorate.[56]

In the largest voter turnout for state legislative offices in Ohio's history—an estimated 74.5 percent—the Republicans scored a solid victory in October 1859. Although Democratic sawing out of white supremacist tunes had been more strident than ever, it was apparent that the white and black Oberlin Rescuers, although they could not break the strings of the racist fiddle, for the moment had drowned it out with a music of their own. Although Democratic gubernatorial candidate Rufus P. Ranney of Cleveland, earlier identified with antislavery views, managed to run ahead of his ticket, Republican William

O. Dennison of Columbus, ex-Whig banker and railroad president, more closely aligned to the radical than conservative wing of his party, won the governor's chair by nearly twenty-four thousand votes more than Chase had mustered two years earlier. Republicans took all state offices on the ballot and regained control of both houses of the assembly by majorities of twelve to fourteen thousand. In danger of being subordinated to the conservative wing only a year before, radical Republicans reaped an impressive Rescue harvest. The Western Reserve sent to the state senate five radical representatives—veterans James Monroe; John F. Morse of Painesville, Townshend's coadjutor in the 1849 repeal of the Black Laws; and Francis D. Parish of Sandusky, Oberlin trustee and hero of an 1845 fugitive rescue; as well as noteworthy novices Jacob D. Cox of Warren, 1851 Oberlin graduate, future general and future Ohio governor, and the future president James A. Garfield of Hiram. The cap on the radical triumph would come in early 1860, when the assembly selected outgoing governor Chase to be U.S. senator, succeeding Democrat George E. Pugh as the associate of Ben Wade. If it were true, as the Cincinnati *Gazette* had contended in August 1858 on the eve of the rescue, that the radicals "constitute but a very small minority of the Republican party," the debt that the antislavery leadership owed to Oberlin was all the greater.[57]

John Mercer Langston's creative participation in the Rescue manifested his maturing skill and confidence as a black orator. In part this resulted from a heightened sense of belonging. As was likely in the Cincinnati riot of 1841, clearly with Oberlin-Wellington, he experienced the excitement of communality and self-sacrifice, a rejuvenating sense of bonding to a brotherhood that, under exacting pressures, had held to its interracial principles. In the ten months between the taking of John Price and the release of the rescuers, Langston, by his words and deeds, became even more attached to the Oberlin community than before. It was a symbiotic relationship for, if his conduct and that of the black rescuers strengthened the community's faith in biracialism as the proper American way of life, so its enthusiastic sponsorship of its best known black resident contributed to the bolder, more outspoken positions he was presently articulating.

Oberlin and the Rescue also gave Langston a broader white constituency. For what may well have been the first time in the history of a major political party, a black man not only had appeared on the same platform with white politicians prominent in that party—most of whom had shied away from his efforts to link the Republicans to black enfranchisement—but also had made incendiary remarks that had been soundly applauded by a predominantly white, although by no means exclusively abolitionist, audience. If a representative portion of the Western Reserve now appeared, at least in degree, to have accepted this militant black man as one of its own, he seems to have reciprocated. Writing about the impact of the Rescue on the Reserve, Langston spoke not of "their" but rather of "our deep love of liberty, our intelligent veneration for the precepts of Christianity . . . ." which could never be destroyed.[58]

An increased sense of belonging fostered a more complex identity. In 1849, in his senior year in college, it had been his contention that white prejudice subverted black manhood, robbed black people of a nationality which was necessary "before we can become anybody." By 1852 he was speaking as a black man, championing nationalist-emigration, arguing that the "mutual repellency of the races" foreclosed any possibility of the Negro's attainment of "Liberty and Equality" in his American birthplace. Although he would continue to call attention to "malignant Negro-hatred" and the "deep proslavery sentiment" against free Negroes that "pervades the whole country," the black-white cooperation in the Rescue, and the praise he and other blacks received for their significant part in it, caused Langston to reassess more positively both his American birthright and his white ancestry. In his speech at the Felon's Feast in January 1859, Langston was moved to declare that blacks were ready "to fight against the enemies of their country, for it is their country now. We demand that we be permitted to exercise the rights of citizens." At the jubilee celebration in July he represented himself as a man, an American citizen, a Negro, and a white man—"as one in whom the blood of both races joined." It was a theme he would pursue to the end of his days. Speaking to the annual meeting of the Garrisonian Western Anti-Slavery Society in Alliance, Ohio, in September 1859, Langston thanked God for "the two bloods that are coursing through my veins today. I stand before you as the representative of two classes of persons who are affected and seriously affected by American slavery in this country. . . . I demand a release from slavery for the white people of the North and South and shall never cease to demand it till I cease to breathe." Just as he functioned as a bridge between the blacks and whites in Oberlin, answerable to both, he was beginning to view himself as a connecting and responsible link between blacks and whites in the rest of the country.[59]

The heightened feeling of belonging and of his American and biracial identities helped to enlarge his perception of freedom. Through the Rescue, Langston received direct confirmation of one of the lessons of freedom he himself had earlier enunciated, namely, that ordinary men, embodying a "just and holy" cause and comporting themselves with "resolution" could empower themselves and effect change. For this abolitionist-politician, black freedom became more than ever the passion, the necessity. And the key to black liberation, Oberlin-Wellington seemed to verify, was through forceful, even violent, biracial confrontation with the Slave Power.

Glimpsing now the possibility of freedom in the foreseeable future, Langston articulated a vision that set him apart from his black contemporaries. Whereas a number of eastern black leaders in recent months had come to define the conflict in racial terms, predicting slave insurrection as inevitable, the black Ohioan, while giving his own endorsement to such insurrections, ventured the prediction that black men and white men fighting together in defense of Christian republican values would overthrow the Slave Power and, in the process, bring deliverance to slave and free, black and white alike.[60]

NOTES

1. John Mercer Langston, *From the Virginia Plantation to the National Capitol; or, The First and Only Negro Representative in Congress from the Old Dominion* (Hartford, 1894; repr. New York: Johnson Reprint, 1968), pp. 183–84; Cleveland *Leader*, Sept. 10, 1858; Russia Township—Township Records, 1855–69, Oberlin College Archives. The major source on the Oberlin-Wellington Rescue is Jacob R. Shipherd, compiler, *History of the Oberlin-Wellington Rescue* (Boston, 1859; repr: New York: Da Capo Press, 1972), a largely undigested compilation of newspaper articles and other documents, including much of the trial testimony. See also, William C. Cochran, *The Western Reserve and the Fugitive Slave Law* (Cleveland, 1920; repr. New York: Da Capo Press, 1972), pp. 118–211; Richard Winsor, "How John Price Was Rescued," in *The Oberlin Jubilee 1833–1883*, ed. W. G. Ballantine (Oberlin, 1883), pp. 251–52; William E. Lincoln, "The Oberlin-Wellington Rescue," ms., Palmer Papers, Western Reserve Historical Society; John Mercer Langston, "The Oberlin-Wellington Rescue," *The Anglo-African Magazine* 1 (July 1859):209–16, reprinted in *Anglo-African*, July 23, 1859.

2. Shipherd, comp., *Oberlin-Wellington Rescue*, p. 241; Lorain County *Eagle*, Sept. 15, 1857; Lorain County *News*, March 14, 1860; Cleveland *Leader*, Sept. 10, 1858.

3. Elyria *Independent-Democrat*, Sept. 15, Dec. 29, 1858; Cleveland *Leader*, Sept. 10, 1858; Cochran, *Western Reserve and the Fugitive Slave Law*, pp. 121–22; *Anti-Slavery Bugle*, Oct. 2, 1858.

4. Cleveland *Leader*, Sept. 10, 1858; Shipherd, comp., *Oberlin-Wellington Rescue*, pp. 77, 99–102, 35; Cochran, *Western Reserve and the Fugitive Slave Law*, p. 120; New York *Tribune*, Apr. 14, 1859; H. E. Peck to Anderson Jennings, Elyria *Independent-Democrat*, Dec. 29, 1858; Langston, "The Oberlin-Wellington Rescue."

5. Russia Township—Township Records, 1855–69.

6. Shipherd, comp., *Oberlin-Wellington Rescue*, pp. 35, 30.

7. Charles H. Langston, *Should Colored Men Be Subject to the Pains and Penalties of the Fugitive Slave Law?* . . . (Cleveland, 1859); Shipherd, comp., *Oberlin-Wellington Rescue*, pp. 104–5, 22, 26–27, 31, 106–7, 118.

8. Shipherd, comp., *Oberlin-Wellington Rescue*, pp. 25–27, 100, 37–39, 105, 114–16.

9. Ibid., pp. 26–27, 31, 34, 37, 40, 101, 107, 108–9, 114–24.

10. Ibid., pp. 104, 126, 33; Lincoln, "Oberlin-Wellington Rescue"; Winsor, "How John Price Was Rescued," pp. 251–52.

11. Langston, *Virginia Plantation*, pp. 184–86; New York *Tribune*, n.d., quoted in Cleveland *Leader*, Sept. 21, 1858; Shipherd, comp., *Oberlin-Wellington Rescue*, pp. 106–7, 109; Langston, "Oberlin-Wellington Rescue"; New York *Sun*, n.d., quoted in Cleveland *Leader*, Apr. 14, 1895; Lida Rose McCabe, "The Oberlin-Wellington Rescue, an Anti-Slavery Crisis . . . ," *Godey's Magazine* (Oct. 1896):361–76.

12. Langston, "Oberlin-Wellington Rescue." The aggressive role played by blacks is corroborated by trial testimony in Shipherd, comp., *Oberlin-Wellington Rescue*, passim. Accounts that omit or fail to treat black participation include James Ford Rhodes, *History of the United States from the Compromise of 1850 to the End of the Roosevelt Administration* (new ed.), vol. 2 (New York, 1928), pp. 317–23; Robert S. Fletcher, *A History of Oberlin College*, 2 vols. (Oberlin, 1943), I, pp. 402–14; Larry Gara, *The Liberty Line: The Legend of the Underground Railroad* (Lexington, Ky., 1967), pp. 138–40; Stanley W. Campbell, *The Slave Catchers: Enforcement of the Fugitive Slave Law, 1850–1860* (New York, 1972), pp. 164–67.

13. John Mercer Langston, "The World's Anti-Slavery Movement," in *Freedom and Citizenship* (Washington, 1883; repr. Miami: Mnemosyne Reprint, 1969), pp. 41–67; Eric Foner, *Free Soil, Free Labor, Free Men: The Ideology of the Republican Party Before the Civil War* (New York, 1971), pp. 133–34, 262–65; *Proceedings of a Convention of the Colored Men of Ohio . . . Cincinnati . . . Nov. 1858* (Cincinnati, 1858).

14. *Ohio Columbian* (Columbus), n.d., quoted in *Anti-Slavery Bugle*, Jan. 19, 1856; *Proceedings of the State Convention of Colored Men . . . Columbus . . . Jan. 1856* (Cleveland, 1856).

15. *Anti-Slavery Bugle*, Aug. 2, 9, 23, 1856, Jan. 10, 1857; *Frederick Douglass' Paper*, n.d., quoted in *Anti-Slavery Bugle*, Aug. 30, 1856; *Frederick Douglass' Paper*, Sept. 12, 1856; *Ohio State Democrat* (Urbana), July 3, 31, Aug. 7, 1856; Victor B. Howard, "The Election of 1856 in Ohio: Moral Issues in Politics," *Ohio History* 80 (Winter 1971):24–44.

16. *Anti-Slavery Bugle*, Aug. 2, 23, Sept. 27, 1856; Benjamin Quarles, *Black Abolitionists* (New York, 1969), pp. 111–12; William C. Nell to William Lloyd Garrison, *Liberator*, Aug. 15, Nov. 14, 1856; Elyria *Independent-Democrat*, Aug. 13, 1856; *Ohio State Democrat* (Urbana), Aug. 7, 1856.

17. Cleveland *Plain Dealer*, n.d., quoted in Elyria *Independent-Democrat*, Nov. 9, 1856; *Anti-Slavery Bugle*, Dec. 13, Nov. 1, 1856; Clayton S. Ellsworth, "Oberlin and the Anti-Slavery Movement Up to the Civil War," Ph.D. diss.,

Cornell University, 1930, pp. 132–33; Richard A. Folk, "Black Man's Burden in Ohio, 1849–1863," Ph.D. diss., University of Toledo, 1972, p. 81; Stephen E. Maizlish, "The Triumph of Sectionalism: The Transformation of Politics in the Antebellum North, Ohio, 1844–1860," Ph.D. diss., University of California, Berkeley, 1978, p. 445.

18. *National Anti-Slavery Standard*, Aug. 18, 1855; *Herald of Freedom*, n.d. quoted in *Anti-Slavery Bugle*, July 28, 1855; "Alfred J. Anderson to Judges of Elections," *Anti-Slavery Bugle*, Dec. 27, 1856; Cleveland *Leader*, June 25, 26, 1858, Dec. 15, 1856; *Alfred J. Anderson v. Thomas Milliken et al.*, 9 *Ohio State Reports* 568, 579–80 (Dec. 1859); Cleveland *Leader*, Feb. 16, 1860. In his deposition, Anderson claimed to have been born Feb. 24, 1824, in Wheeling, Va., the son of a woman who was three-quarters white, one-quarter Negro and Indian, and of a white man, lawyer James Shannon. (Anderson's uncle was Wilson Shannon, pro-slavery governor of Kansas territory in 1855 and 1856.) A frequent contributor to black and abolitionist newspapers during the 1840s, whose articles included a noteworthy series on the Black Laws and the black condition in Ohio [*North Star*, May 5, June 2, 1848, Feb. 16, Mar. 23, July 13, 1849], Anderson was active in local and state black protest until well into the postwar period. See Table 1, chapter 5.

19. Nell to Garrison, *Liberator*, Nov. 14, 1856.

20. James Brewer Stewart, *Joshua R. Giddings and the Tactics of Radical Politics* (Cleveland, 1970), pp. 250–51; *Anti-Slavery Bugle*, Jan. 10, 1857; Nell to Garrison, *Liberator*, Nov. 14, 1856; John Mercer Langston, "Address to the Legislature of Ohio," *Proceedings of the State Convention . . . Columbus . . . Jan. 1857* (Columbus, 1857); J. R. Giddings to D. Jenkins et al., Dec. 26, 1855, *State Convention . . . 1856*, Cleveland *Leader*, Nov. 4, 1856; *Ohio State Journal*, Jan. 13, 23, 1857.

21. *State Convention . . . 1857*; *Ohio State Journal*, Jan. 10, 23, 29, 30, 31, Feb. 2, Mar. 14, 1857; *Anti-Slavery Bugle*, Feb. 14, 21, 1857; *National Anti-Slavery Standard*, May 30, 1857; James Monroe, "Oberlin Thursday Lectures," pp. 111–12, quoted in Ellsworth, "Oberlin and the Anti-Slavery Movement," p. 126.

22. C.H. Langston et al. to Salmon P. Chase, Apr. 13, 1857, Salmon P. Chase Papers, Library of Congress; Don E. Fehrenbacher, *The Dred Scott Case: Its Significance in American Law and Politics* (New York, 1978), pp. 433–35; Cochran, *Western Reserve and the Fugitive Slave Law*, pp. 115–18.

23. Eugene H. Roseboom, *The Civil War Era, 1850–1873*, in *The History of the State of Ohio*, ed. Carl Wittke, 6 vols. (Columbus, 1944), IV, pp. 325–29; *Anti-Slavery Bugle*, Oct. 10, 1857; Lorain County *Eagle*, Oct. 13, 20, 1857; Toledo *Blade*, n.d., quoted in Elyria *Independent-Democrat*, Sept. 29, 1857; *Ohio State Democrat* (Urbana), Oct. 8, 1857; "A.P." to Editor, Aug. 3, 1857, Cleveland *Leader*, Aug. 5, 1857; Cleveland *Plain Dealer*, Sept. 12, Oct. 1, 1859; Cincinnati *Enquirer*, n.d., quoted in *National Anti-Slavery Standard*, Nov. 7, 1857.

24. Thomas D. Morris, *Free Men All: The Personal Liberty Laws of the North, 1780–1861* (Baltimore, 1974), p. 182; Elyria *Independent-Democrat*, Apr. 7, 21, July 7, Sept. 15, 1858; Cincinnati *Gazette*, Feb. 5, 1858; *Frederick Douglass'*

Paper, n.d. quoted in Cleveland *Leader*, Mar. 1, 1858; Richard H. Sewell, *Ballots for Freedom: Antislavery Politics in the United States 1837–1860* (New York, 1976), pp. 304–6; Daryl Pendergraft, "Thomas Corwin and the Conservative Republican Reaction, 1858–1861," *Ohio Archaeological and Historical Quarterly* 57 (Jan. 1948):123; Foner, *Free Soil, Free Labor, Free Men*, p. 131; *Anti-Slavery Bugle*, Sept. 18, 1858; Lorain County *Eagle*, Sept. 15, 1858.

25. *State Convention . . . 1858*; Jane H. Pease and William H. Pease, *They Who Would Be Free: Blacks' Search for Freedom, 1830–1861* (New York, 1974), pp. 240–46.

26. Cleveland *Leader*, Aug. 3, 4, 1858; Cleveland *Plain Dealer*, Aug. 2, 3, 4, 1858; *Ohio State Journal*, July 24, 1858; Xenia *Torchlight*, July 21, 28, Aug. 4, 1858; *Anti-Slavery Bugle*, Aug. 21, 28, Sept. 18, 1858; Xenia *Gazette*, Oct. 21, 1889, John Mercer Langston Scrapbooks, 4 vols., II, Moorland-Spingarn Research Center, Howard University.

27. *Proceedings of the Convention of Colored Freemen of Ohio . . . Columbus . . . 1852* (Cincinnati, 1852); Langston, "The World's Anti-Slavery Movement," pp. 41–67.

28. "To the Colored Citizens of the State of Ohio," Sept. 30, 1858, Cleveland *Leader*, Oct. 25, Dec. 7, 1858; Cincinnati *Gazette*, n.d. quoted in *Ohio State Journal*, Oct. 7, 1858; *Anti-Slavery Bugle*, Oct. 9, 1858; *Liberator*, Oct. 15, 1858; *State Convention . . . 1858*; Oberlin *Evangelist*, Jan. 19, 1859; Elyria *Independent-Democrat*, Jan. 19, 1859; Oberlin *Students' Monthly* 1 (Feb. 1859):160–61; *Proceedings of the First Annual Meeting of the Ohio State Anti-Slavery Society . . . Xenia . . . January 1860* (title page missing). Josephus Fowler was secretary and a member of the 1854–55 black school board in Cincinnati. *First Annual Report of the Board of Trustees for the Colored Public Schools of Cincinnati, June 30, 1855* (Cincinnati, 1855), p. 34.

29. Lorain County *Eagle*, Apr. 20, 1859.

30. *State Convention . . . 1858*; *Anti-Slavery Bugle*, Dec. 4, 1858; Cincinnati *Gazette*, Nov. 24, 1858. Quotations altered to present tense.

31. New York *Tribune*, n.d., and Sandusky *Register*, n.d., both quoted in Cleveland *Leader*, Sept. 21, 1858; Cochran, *Western Reserve and the Fugitive Slave Law*, pp. 132–33.

32. Cochran, *Western Reserve and the Fugitive Slave Law*, pp. 134–35, 139–40; Cleveland *Plain Dealer*, Feb. 24, 1860; Lorain County *News*, Mar. 14, 1860; Langston, "The Oberlin-Wellington Rescue"; Shipherd, comp., *Oberlin-Wellington Rescue*, pp. 3–4.

33. Shipherd, comp., *Oberlin-Wellington Rescue*, pp. 4–5; Elyria *Independent-Democrat*, Dec. 15, 1858; Cleveland *Plain Dealer*, Dec. 7, 1858; Langston, "The Oberlin-Wellington Rescue"; Langston, *Virginia Plantation*, p. 186.

34. Cleveland *Leader*, Jan. 13, 17, 1859; Elyria *Independent-Democrat*, Jan. 19, 1859.

35. Langston, "The Oberlin-Wellington Rescue"; Shipherd, comp., *Oberlin-Wellington Rescue*, pp. 82–83, 14; George W. Belden to Attorney General J. S. Black, Feb. 26, 1859, Attorney General's Papers, Department of Justice Records, Ohio 1824–64, National Archives.

36. Cleveland, *Plain Dealer*, Apr. 7, 12, 1859, Dec. 16, 18, 1858; Lorain County *Eagle*, Apr. 20, 1859; Belden to Black, May 2, 1859, Attorney General's Papers.

37. Shepherd, comp., *Oberlin-Wellington Rescue*, pp. 94–107, 114–69; *National Anti-Slavery Standard*, June 18, 1859.

38. Langston, *Virginia Plantation*, pp. 187–88; Langston, "The Oberlin-Wellington Rescue"; Charles H. Langston, *Should Colored Men Be Subject . . .?*

39. Elyria *Independent-Democrat*, May 18, 1859; Shepherd, comp., *Oberlin-Wellington Rescue*, pp. 178, 170; Langston, "The Oberlin-Wellington Rescue."

40. Cleveland *Leader*, May 13, 1859; *Liberator*, June 10, 1859; Charles H. Langston, *Should Colored Men Be Subject . . .?*, appendix; John Mercer Langston to Editor, Cleveland *Gazette*, Dec. 24, 1892.

41. Shepherd, comp., *Oberlin-Wellington Rescue*, pp. 88–94; "Statement of Oberlin Prisoners Now in Jail," May 13, 1859, Elyria *Independent-Democrat*, May 25, 1859; *Frank Leslie's Illustrated Weekly*, May 7, 1859; *The Rescuer*, July 4, 1859; William Fuller, Philemon Bliss, Reuben Hitchcock, "Why Do These Fathers and Husbands Stay in Jail," June 16, 1859, circular, American Missionary Association Archives, Amistad Research Center, Tulane University, (hereafter cited as "AMA Papers"); stationary sold by J. Goodrich, Oberlin, used by J. P. Bardwell to George Whipple, Aug. 19, 1859; J. M. Fitch to George Whipple, June 18, 1859, both in AMA Papers. See also Ralph Plumb to James Monroe, Apr. 30, 1859; H. E. Peck to James Monroe, Apr. 1859; J. M. Fitch to James Monroe, Apr. 22, 23, 24, 1859, all in James Monroe Papers, Oberlin College Archives.

42. Application for writ of habeas corpus to supreme court of Ohio, Apr. 21, 1859, copy in Attorney General's Papers, Department of Justice Records, Ohio 1824–64; Belden to Black, Apr. 28, 1859, Ibid.; J. M. Fitch to James Monroe, Apr. 24, 1859, Monroe Papers; H. V. Willson to President James Buchanan, Apr. 25, 1859, Attorney General's Papers; Black to Matthew Johnson, Apr. 26, 1859, Letter Book A, May 25, 1857–May 12, 1859, Attorney General's Office, Department of Justice Records; *Ohio State Journal*, Apr. 21, 26, 27, 1859.

43. Langston, "The Oberlin-Wellington Rescue"; Cleveland *Leader*, Feb. 9, 10, 15, May 25, 1859; Elyria *Independent-Democrat*, Jan 26, June 1, 1859; *State Convention . . . 1860*; Cochran, *Western Reserve and the Fugitive Slave Law*, pp. 171–80.

44. Cleveland *Leader*, Apr. 26, May 10, June 20, 1859; Cleveland *Herald*, n.d., cited in *Ohio State Journal*, Apr. 21, May 12, 1859; Ashtabula *Sentinel*, May 12, 1859; Ashtabula *Telegraph*, May 14, 1859; Portage County *Democrat*, May 11, 25, 1859, all in Cochran, *Western Reserve and the Fugitive Slave Law*, p. 178; Lorain County *Eagle*, May 25, 1859; George Thompson to Lewis Tappan, Apr. 26, 1859, William Handay to Lewis Tappan, May 29, 1859, both in AMA Papers.

45. *Ohio State Journal*, May 25, 26, 1859; Cleveland *Leader*, May 25, 1859; Elyria *Independent-Democrat*, June 1, 1859; *Anti-Slavery Bugle*, May 28, 1859; Shepherd, comp., *Oberlin-Wellington Rescue*, pp. 247–59; Cochran, *Western Reserve and the Fugitive Slave Law*, pp. 180–84.

46. Cleveland *Leader*, May 25, 1859.

47. *Ex Parte Simeon Bushnell and Charles Langston*, 9 *Ohio State Reports* (1859), pp. 77–325.

48. Langston, *Virginia Plantation*, p. 189; Lorain County *Eagle*, Feb. 23, May 11, 18, 25, 1859; Elyria *Independent-Democrat*, Apr. 27, May 18, 25, 1859; Cochran, *Western Reserve and the Fugitive Slave Law*, pp. 115, 118, 197–200; Shipherd, comp., *Oberlin-Wellington Rescue*, pp. 231–35, 264–65; Cleveland *Plain Dealer*, July 6, 1859.

49. Shipherd, comp., *Oberlin-Wellington Rescue*, pp. 264–79; Cleveland *Plain Dealer*, Oct. 26, 1889, JML Scrapbooks, II; Cleveland *National Democrat*, July 12, 1859; Cleveland *Plain Dealer*, July 12, 1859; Cleveland *Leader*, July 12, 1859.

50. Langston, "The Oberlin-Wellington Rescue"; Springfield *Republican*, July 7, 1859.

51. Langston, "The Oberlin-Wellington Rescue"; interview with Mrs. James M. Fitch, Cleveland *Leader*, Apr. 14, 1895; Henry Peck to S. S. Jocelyn, June 20, 1859, AMA Papers; William Lloyd Garrison to James Monroe, Apr. 22, 1859, Monroe Papers; Fletcher, *Oberlin College*, I, pp. 413–14; A. Fuller to Lewis Tappan, June 20, 1859, AMA Papers.

52. Peck to Jocelyn, June 20, 1859; E. H. Fairchild to Whipple, July 28, 1859, both in AMA Papers; *Ohio State Journal*, Aug. 9, 11, 12, 13, 19, Nov. 11, Dec. 19, 1859; Cleveland *Leader*, Aug. 15, 1859; Merton L. Dillon, *The Abolitionists: The Growth of a Dissenting Minority* (DeKalb, Ill., 1974), pp. 236–41; Howard, "The 1856 Election in Ohio," passim.

53. Charles H. Langston, *Should Colored Men Be Subject . . .?*; *Anti-Slavery Bugle*, Dec. 4, 1858.

54. *Anti-Slavery Bugle*, Dec. 4, 1858, Feb. 25, 1860; Cleveland *Leader*, Feb. 21, 1860; Cleveland *Plain Dealer*, Feb. 24, 1860; Lorain County *News*, Mar. 14, Sept. 25, 1860; Elyria *Independent-Democrat*, Sept. 26, 1860; *Pine and Palm*, Oct. 19, 1861.

55. Washington *National Republican*, Mar. 18, 1870; Cleveland *Plain Dealer*, Oct. 26, 1889, JML Scrapbook, II; Russell H. Davis, *Black Americans in Cleveland* (Washington, 1972), pp. 90–92.

56. C.W. [Chauncey Wack] to J. W. Gray, June 4, 1859, Cleveland *Plain Dealer*, June 7, 1859; Elyria *Independent-Democrat*, June 15, 1859; Foner, *Free Soil, Free Labor, Free Men*, pp. 136–37; Cochran, *Western Reserve and the Fugitive Slave Law*, pp. 191–95; Salmon P. Chase to Charles Sumner, June 20, 1859, American Historical Association, *Diary and Correspondence of Salmon P. Chase* (Washington, 1903; repr. New York: Da Capo Press, 1971), pp. 280–81; James Fitch to S. S. Jocelyn, June 18, 1859, AMA Papers.

57. Stephen E. Maizlish and John J. Kushma, eds., *Essays on American Antebellum Politics* (Arlington, Texas, 1982), p. 19; Elyria *Independent-Democrat*, Oct. 13, 19, 1859; Cochran, *Western Reserve and the Fugitive Slave Law*, pp. 205–11; Foner, *Free Soil, Free Labor, Free Men*, p. 144.

58. Langston, "The Oberlin-Wellington Rescue."

59. *Minutes . . . of the State Convention of the Colored Citizens of Ohio . . . Columbus . . . Jan., 1849* (Oberlin, 1849); *State Convention . . . 1852*; J. M. Langston,

"Louis Pacheco," Oberlin *Students' Monthly* 1 (Nov. 1858):35; Cleveland *Leader*, Jan. 13, 1859; *Anti-Slavery Bugle*, Sept. 24, 1859.

60. Langston, "The World's Anti-Slavery Movement," pp. 45–49, 52–57; Langston, "Oberlin-Wellington Rescue"; Pease and Pease, *They Who Would Be Free*, pp. 245, 242–43; Langston, "Louis Pacheco," pp. 34–35; Cleveland *Leader*, Jan. 13, 1859.

CHAPTER 11

Provoking the Conflict

1859–61

As the nation moved toward war, northern Democrats cried that the "irrepressible conflict" was, in actuality, a case of the "irrepressible nigger." The attempt to impose black political and social equality upon white men was at the root of the sectional troubles. John Brown's raid was a black invasion of the South; Republicans were "Black Republicans"; Abraham Lincoln's election to the presidency was a black victory. The Cleveland *Plain Dealer* even taxed John Mercer Langston personally with being a "leveler, determined to elevate the black or bring down the white to the same social condition. He wars with everything that stands in the way of this great object, becomes a rebel to the institutions of the country, and delights in revolution."[1]

Langston would have retorted that the "Slave Power," that "oligarchy of despotism" bent upon the destruction of "republican principles and doctrines," was driving the splintering wedge between North and South.[2] Yet he could, in a sense, agree with his enemies. He, and other blacks at his urging, did help John Brown, did push Ohio Republicans to uphold black rights, did work for Lincoln's election, did try to block compromise with the South. These activities reflected not only the aggressiveness of the black movement in Ohio that Langston had helped to build, but also his own comprehensive assessment of the black role. As black organizer and agitator, Langston saw self-help, protest, politics, and, when necessary and feasible, even violence as complementary rather than contradictory means to promote black rights and secure black liberation. The Negro must indeed be irrepressible in provoking the conflict that could bring freedom.

Long before Langston implicated himself in John Brown's conspiracy, he had made his peace with physical violence as a means of liberation. In an article he wrote in the fall of 1858, just after the Oberlin-Wellington Rescue, he justified the use of violence on several grounds. His subject was Louis Pacheco, a trusted slave who, acting as a U.S. army guide in December 1835 during the Florida wars, had betrayed an entire company of soldiers into massacre by Seminole Indians and fugitive slaves known as the Exiles. "Love of liberty," hatred of slavery, appreciation of his own manhood, "solicitude for the success" of the Exiles in their struggle for freedom, and longing to see the wrongs of his people avenged: these had prompted Pacheco's treachery. Langston vindicated his conduct—and, by inference, that of other slave insurrectionists—as "natural and praiseworthy."[3]

It was precisely because of his strong words in defense of violent means and his active participation in the underground railroad that Langston, early on, had been apprised of John Brown's intention to strike a direct blow against slavery. Richard J. Hinton, Brown's biographer and friend, would assert that Langston, along with other "prominent men of color . . . *knew* John Brown"—obviously meaning the scheme and possibly the man—by the spring of 1858. In May 1858, the white Kansas guerrilla captain, himself a man with northern Ohio roots and Oberlin connections, held a clandestine meeting of free blacks at Chatham, Canada.[4] Although Langston did not attend, among the thirty-four black (and twelve white) men who did were at least three with whom, at one time or another, he had been closely associated: James Monroe Jones; James H. Harris, a one-time Oberlin resident who had been a delegate to the 1856 Ohio black convention; and George J. Reynolds of Sandusky, who with Langston had championed black nationalist-emigration at the 1852 state black convention. At Chatham, Brown unfolded plans centered on his belief that slave insurrection would be the instrument of emancipation and that he and his followers could spark the revolt. On a public platform soon afterward, Langston appeared to be reinforcing Brown's argument as well as his penchant for historical prototypes when he recalled a slave revolt on the Greek island of Chios: fugitive slaves had taken refuge "in the mountain fastnesses," and then, inspired by their "noble" leader Drimacos, a man "determined . . . to make his life a holy sacrifice to liberty," had confronted the Chians and "vanquished them with great slaughter."[5]

Brown's machination hardly struck Langston as unique. He himself had been instrumental in establishing at least one all-black statewide network avowedly dedicated to underground railroad activities;

although the public record on conspiratorial organizations is necessarily scanty, it is likely that this group did not restrict its endeavors to merely helping whatever fugitives came its way. At the militant 1852 Ohio state convention, it will be remembered, the profoundly alienated Langston brothers, along with such irate young activists as Peter Clark and H. Ford Douglass, variously had espoused black military training, forcible resistance, slave uprisings, rebellion, and a willingness to "die for freedom." The explosive language had elicited a bold response from convention delegates. To the shocked disgust of a Cincinnati *Gazette* reporter, who railed against what was obviously "an extensive system of negro stealing," the black Ohioans openly discussed their fugitive assistance network and took measures to strengthen it. To "promote union and render our action beneficial," they authorized creation of central committees on a county level. Langston, as convention president, handpicked committee members. For Lorain County he named himself, future Rescuer John Watson, and carpenter and joiner John Copeland, Sr.[6]

This "negro-stealing" organization may well have evolved into, or in other ways been related to, a secret black military organization that by 1858 was known as the Liberators. Langston, if not a participant, certainly was cognizant of its operations. The Liberators stockpiled arms, drilled, and reportedly helped to maintain an escape route of legendary efficiency stretching from Syracuse to Detroit and reaching deep into the South, where black Ohioans prepared slaves for flight and rebellion. The society was particularly active on the Western Reserve, with branches in Oberlin, Cleveland, and Sandusky. Not long after returning from the Chatham convention, George Reynolds, a coppersmith in Sandusky who had been Langston's choice in 1852 to head Erie County's central committee, revealed the existence of the Liberators to George B. Gill, one of Brown's young white followers. Explaining that membership was exclusively black, Reynolds showed Gill the room where Liberators met and maintained their arsenal, "a fine collection of arms." Despite the pledge of secrecy he and the other Chatham conventioneers had taken, Reynolds had confided Brown's plans to other Liberators, and "they were only waiting for Brown, or someone else, to make a successful initiative move when their forces would be put in motion." Not surprisingly, John Brown, Jr., who would be charged with rounding up recruits for his father's Virginia expedition, would designate Reynolds as "one of those men who must be obtained if possible." (However, like all of the other convention participants except Osborne Anderson, who did go to Harper's Ferry, Reynolds would prove to be unavailable when the plot finally unfolded, eighteen months after Chatham.)[7]

With the Oberlin-Wellington Rescue on September 13, 1858, the tenuous cords connecting John Brown to black militants on the Reserve began to tighten. The black aggressiveness demonstrated throughout the Rescue and the intense emotions generated by it—when violence came to seem a necessary alternative to obeying the dictates of a southern-dominated federal government and when the idea of black violence, in particular, captivated the imagination of such antislavery radicals as Joshua Giddings, whose sole regret about the Rescue was that blacks had not hanged the slave catchers—[8] would prove fuel and catalyst for Harper's Ferry.

In Oberlin, alongside John Watson and other black and white townsmen, Langston had established a chapter of the Ohio State Anti-Slavery Society, the statewide organization the Langston brothers had helped to initiate on the heels of the rescue. Overtly committed to work for equal rights, the Oberlin Anti-Slavery Society, hinted the Oberlin *Evangelist*, also had "a practical purpose which would, perhaps, be illustrated if another attempt to arrest fugitives should be made hereabouts." In all likelihood, the Oberlin Anti-Slavery Society shared the aims and membership of the Oberlin Liberators. Despite an Oberlin white leader's later insistence that the village did not sanction operating "upon slave territory, for the release of slaves," the Oberlin Anti-Slavery Society counted on its rolls a young black man noted for doing just that—Lewis Sheridan Leary. Leary's militant kinsman, John Anthony Copeland, Jr., likewise was an enthusiastic member.[9]

John Brown arrived in Cleveland in March 1859 on the eve of the Oberlin-Wellington Rescue trials. He brought horses and mules that he and his band had "liberated," along with eleven slaves, in a bloody raid in Missouri. In spite of hefty federal rewards offered for Brown's capture, Marshal Matthew Johnson, warily gauging the rising radical sentiment, chose to ignore him. During Brown's nearly two-week stay, he strolled daily past the marshal's office, paid a call on Charles Langston, and auctioned off his captured livestock. In a public lecture, Brown declared it the duty of every man to liberate slaves whenever he could do so successfully. At 25 cents a ticket, his hearers were few, but they included Sheridan Leary. The marshal's failure to attempt an arrest instilled in Brown and some of his men a feeling of invulnerability; the combativeness of such black men as Charles Langston and Leary probably renewed his confidence that slaves would flock to his insurrectionary force.[10] It is also conceivable that the rescuers' subsequent success in arousing indignation across the North may have caused the old man to ponder the strategic power of martyrdom.

During the frenetic weeks of Rescue protest, John Mercer Langston became well acquainted with two of Brown's men, John Henry Kagi and C. F. Tidd. Publicly, the highly literate Kagi reported the Rescue trials for the New York *Tribune* and the Cleveland *Leader*; privately, he worked at converting black and radical enthusiasm to his leader's cause. At the request of the rescuers, Kagi traveled to Columbus so that he might give them a first-hand account of the state supreme court's deliberation on the habeas corpus. To Langston's knowledge, he also offered to free the jailed Oberliners by force—a proposition they rejected. Both Kagi and Tidd, under the alias of J. M. Greene, would be acknowledged in print for contributions to J. R. Shipherd's hastily compiled volume chronicling the Rescue.[11] It is likely that John and Charles Langston reciprocated Kagi's favors by furnishing names and introductions to local black men who might be interested in Brown's ideas. By the time Kagi departed for the East, he and Brown felt confident that their secret solicitations had secured four Negroes on the Reserve for their forces.[12]

Now that Brown's able lieutenant was gone, however, how to maintain enthusiasm for such a dangerous and vague enterprise, with not even a target date set, became cause for concern. For the time being, the task fell to J. Dennis Harris, a black plasterer in Cleveland, emigration advocate, and member of the executive committee and lecturer for the Langstons' antislavery society. On August 22, 1859, after visiting the four potential recruits and making a futile stab at fund-raising, Harris wrote Kagi in utter frustration: "All make such excuses until I am disgusted with myself and the whole *negro set*—God Dam 'em!" Charlie Langston, he suggested hopefully, if he wished to, would carry more weight with the wavering. The Rescue hero "says, 'it is too bad,' but what he will do, if anything, I don't know." But, noted a postscript, "Charlie goes to see Leary to-day."[13]

John Mercer Langston, having taken the field for the Ohio State Anti-Slavery Society, was not immediately available. But by the end of August he was back in Oberlin and in his law office when a stranger, who introduced himself as John Thomas, asked to see him. Busy with a client, Langston recommended a noon meeting. The stranger, a middle-aged white man of impressive height, joined the attorney as he walked home for his mid-day meal. At Langston's gate, his visitor confided that he was John Brown, Jr. "My father is John Brown of Ossawatomie," Langston remembered that he volunteered, who planned soon "to strike . . . a blow which shall shake and destroy American slavery itself."[14]

Langston knew something of this man through fellow attorney Ralph Plumb, who had been young Brown's neighbor during his residence in Ashtabula County. Indeed, at the Felon's Feast for the rescuers, Plumb had read a letter from his friend, an excerpt of which was subsequently published. "Friend Plumb, would you say, 'Oh! but that would be *Treason*.' Well, thank God! . . . Step by step the Slave Power is driving us on to take one or the other horn of the dilemma, either to be *false* to *Humanity* or *traitors* to the *Government*. If we 'would ordain and establish Justice,' and maintain our Constitution . . ., strange to say we are *forced* into the *attitude* of *resistance* to the Government."[15] Now, eight months later, the author of those words in support of treason stood at Langston's doorstep.

In the parlor after dinner, Langston's guest explained the purpose of his visit. Brown had come at the recommendation of Kagi and Tidd, who judged that Langston "would be likely to know" of any Ohioan, white or black, who might be persuaded "to strike and die for the American bondman." The emissary presented Langston with "a full statement of the purposes of his father with regard to the Harper's Ferry movement." Brown, Jr., himself was not aware that his father's destination was Harper's Ferry or his objective to seize the federal arsenal located there, or even of the date he planned to make his move.[16] Thus, the major information that Langston was likely to have received was simply confirmation from this authoritative source that the plot he already knew of, namely, a large-scale slave-liberating expedition in the Virginia mountains ultimately aimed at insurrection, was actually in the works. With confirmation came a direct plea for help, which in turn demanded that Langston define his own position.

If Langston's version many years later can be trusted, his valuation of Brown's insurrectionary scheme, or "any other such enterprise against any portion of the South, with a view to the abolition of slavery," was essentially pragmatic. "In every interview and conference" with enthusiasts of such plots, surely including the Liberators, he maintained that most slaves, far from being attracted to their would-be deliverers, would be frightened away by their "audacity." Therefore, "the ostensible and real object . . . in view"—a slave uprising in some form—was bound to be defeated. On the other hand, "the movements would at least tend to precipitate a condition of public feeling in the country which would sooner or later create disturbance and finally struggle, which would prove the greatest blessing to the slave and the country."[17]

Was this position one of hindsight or foresight? Although Langston, particularly since the Rescue, had made frequent public statements designed to instill a rebellious spirit in his black compatriots and to exacerbate the divisions between North and South, there is no record of his opinion of the likelihood of slaves to join with outside forces in rebellion. Only the preceding November at the black state convention, he had included the enslaved in his advocacy of "the right and duty of resistance by force of arms, when it was feasible." Then it had been John Gaines who had "deprecated such advice" on the grounds that armed resistance by slaves had no hope of success. But Langston clearly accepted violence as the means of last resort, and where "feasible," in the black struggle. He understood the uses of martyrdom, which he had portrayed, in reference to the failure of the first Haitian insurrection, as "the rallying-cry of the after-struggle." And, with the example of the Rescue still fresh, he naturally approved of black and white co-participation in forcible moves against the Slave Oligarchy. Notwithstanding his basic disagreement as to the practicality of Brown's plan, then (if indeed he did disagree), Langston unquestionably was predisposed to believe that its foreseeable psychological and political consequences were such that it warranted his support. But what kind of support? Should he himself, as old John Brown demanded of black leaders ranging from Harriet Tubman to Frederick Douglass, join Brown's band? Even though young Brown, less zealous than his father, probably did not pose the question to Langston, voiced or unvoiced, it existed. Like other prominent blacks, Langston's response was negative, conditioned, one suspects, more by his certainty of leadership priorities than by an intellectual's presumed inherent aversion to violence.[18] He could not have supposed that sacrifice of his energies and, perhaps, life to Brown's endeavor would be more efficacious in the black struggle than the work he was already pursuing. But he could use his influence to bolster Brown's movement.

Sometime during Langston's prolonged conference with Brown, Jr., the host invited to his parlor both Sheridan Leary and John Copeland, Jr. A handsome light-eyed man who wore his wide-brimmed hat at a rakish tilt, Leary, twenty-four, had been born free in Fayetteville, North Carolina, son of Guadeloupian Julie Memriel and Matthew Leary, a saddler and harnessmaker and plantation owner. In a day when the Revolutionary heritage counted, Sheridan Leary knew himself singularly endowed, for, on his father's side, both his Irish grandfather and free black great-grandfather had fought against the British.[19] In 1856, Leary had come to Oberlin, where one sister, Henrietta, was married to cabinetmaker and rescuer Henry Evans, and another, Delilah, to carpenter John Copeland, Sr. Leary's younger brother, John, who remained in Fayetteville to be schooled by both white and black teachers and to follow the family trade, after the war would study law under Langston at Howard University before becoming prominent in North Carolina politics. In Oberlin, Sheridan Leary had found employment as a harnessmaker with rescuer John Scott, who himself had learned the trade from Leary's father. About a year before he met John Brown in Cleveland, Leary married Mary S. Patterson, adopted in infancy by the industrious mason John E. Patterson and his dressmaker wife Mary, and at the time a student in the preparatory department. The young couple had an infant daughter named Lois.[20] "A Christian man," Leary impressed some of his neighbors as "a desperate fellow"; he seemed to Langston a man of great physical courage. Addressing the newly instituted Oberlin Anti-Slavery Society in early 1859, Leary exhorted: "Men must suffer for a good cause." The words were especially meaningful to those who knew Leary had been "driven forth amid a shower of rifle balls" for his efforts in an attempted slave escape and still pursued this "godlike calling."[21]

John Copeland, Jr., Leary's nephew, himself reputedly skilled with a gun, shared Leary's commitment and, quite probably, his clandestine work in slave liberation. Copeland, twenty-five, had lived with his family in Oberlin since childhood. The Copelands, before and certainly after John's involvement with Brown, appeared dedicated to the struggle for freedom. On the day of John's death, his mother Delilah, a domestic worker, announced to a group kneeling around the family altar, "If I could be the means of destroying Slavery, I would willingly give up all my menfolks." In 1862, his father, John Sr., then fifty-two, would sign on as a cook for J. G. W. Cowles of Oberlin, chaplain of the 55th Ohio Volunteers. Moreover, in January 1863, before black northern recruitment was officially sanctioned, his younger brother Henry would be serving as a lieutenant with the black First Kansas Volunteers.[22] In 1854–55, John Copeland, Jr., had been a student in the Oberlin preparatory department; afterward, he had worked with his father as a carpenter and joiner. Mustached and serious, a man of "few words," he had often attracted Langston's attention during the Liberty School night meetings where fugitives told their stories. He had appeared engrossed by the recitals, "signifying often by the deep scowl of his countenance, the moist condition of his eyes and the quivering of his lips, how deeply he was moved."[23] Conspicuous among the armed Oberlin men bent on rescuing John Price, the tall, muscular young man had been in the small group that had overpowered the guards below and then, above, had been the second one through the door to wrest Price from the cockloft. According to one story, he also had accompanied Price to Canada. After his grand jury indictment for his role in the Rescue, Copeland had refused to surrender, becoming, as Marshal Johnson would point out, "a fugitive from justice in Ohio." His fugitive status had not, however, prevented his involvement in the

Oberlin Anti-Slavery Society with Leary and Langston and others, whom he regarded as "friends and brothers." Two unlikely witnesses— the judge and the special prosecutor in the Harper's Ferry trials— would vouch for Copeland's intelligence, dignity, and manliness. As the latter would put it, Copeland was "the cleverest of all the prisoners . . . and behaved better than any of them. If I had the power and could have concluded to pardon any man among them he was the man I would have picked out."[24]

Langston was certain that personal history and Oberlin's influence, the familial and societal environments crucial to the shaping of his own radicalism, had brought both of these young men to a deeply held devotion to "freedom and free principles"—a devotion so deep that they would willingly risk their lives. By the late summer of 1859 the political environment, with extremism growing North and South and violence increasingly the method by which men demonstrated their adherence to principle, promoted such an interpretation. Nowhere was this truer than in Oberlin, where the Rescue rhetoric of honored black and white citizens still resounded: to suffer for humanity's sake is "a pleasure and not a pain" (Henry Evans); oppression must be shown "no quarter" (John Watson); no fear of consequences should "ever persuade any of us to draw back from any consecration which a good cause may require" (Henry Peck). And it was Langston himself who had written of Lewis Pacheco, "a man naturally brave, as he was, when fired by the sentiment of liberty, was ready to meet any danger, to make any sac- rifice, to achieve his own freedom, and that of his associates." Now, after talking to John Brown, Jr., and after hearing Langston explain his views, Leary and Copeland employed similar phrases in announc- ing their decisions. Leary thought the plans put forth by young Brown "satisfactory." The harnessmaker's sole reservation was that his wife and tiny daughter should "never know want," and Langston, it may be inferred from subsequent events, gave him that assurance. Both Leary and Copeland declared their readiness "to die, if need be," with John Brown as their leader.[25]

John Brown, Jr., returned to his West Andover farm heartened by the results of his Oberlin visit. "Friend L———y at Ob———will be on hand soon," he wrote Kagi on September 2. "Mr. C. H. L———n will do all he can here, but his health is bad . . . John L———n, brother of C. H. L., at O———, sympathizes strongly, and will work hard." On September 8 Leary, resorting to the conspirators' code, confirmed his commitment and informed Kagi: "I have a handy man who is willing and in every way competent to dig coal, but, like myself, has no tools. . . . His address is John Copeland, Jr., Oberlin, Ohio."[26]

Other than encouraging Leary and Copeland, John Langston himself would not claim to have participated in the conspiracy. But Hinton would assert that Langston, along with Ralph Plumb, "aided John Brown in money and counsel," as well as being aware "how and by whom" Leary and Copeland were sent to John Brown. On later questioning by a congressional investigating committee, Plumb would admit only to having passed the hat to collect $17.50 for Leary and Copeland's traveling funds for what Plumb assumed to be an attempt to extricate a young woman from slavery. But there is little reason to doubt Hinton's claim.

For his part, Charles Langston, convinced that "the hands" were "too few," would become "discouraged about the mining business," as Brown, Jr., informed Kagi on October 5. "Physical weakness is his fault," Brown added, perhaps an accusation of cowardice but more probably a reference to the bad health mentioned earlier. In any event, as the plot neared fruition, Charles would be in a Columbus courtroom for trial in a $20,000 suit for false imprisonment brought against the rescuers by U.S. Deputy Marshal Jacob Lowe.[27]

Taking leave of their families under the pretext of searching elsewhere for more lucrative employment, Leary and Copeland left Oberlin on Thursday, October 6. In Cleveland, where two or three other recruits were expected momentarily but did not arrive, Brown, Jr., gave them an additional $15. On Saturday, October 15, Leary and Copeland reached the ramshackle Kennedy farmhouse near Harper's Ferry. With a young white abolitionist who appeared nearly simultaneously, they brought Brown's total force to twenty-two men, five of them black.[28] Brown took the fresh recruits as good omens and decided to launch his mission the next night. In the resultant disaster, Sheridan Leary, while trying to swim the rapids of the Shenandoah, was shot and died ten hours later. In the same futile attempt at flight, Copeland was captured and jailed, barely escaping lynching.

An anxious Langston could only watch from Oberlin as one week later Copeland, with Brown and three other survivors, was indicted for treason, murder, and inciting slaves to insurrection. Although the first charge against him and Shields Green, the other surviving black raider, later was dropped on the grounds that blacks, noncitizens according to the Dred Scott decision, could not be traitors, Copeland, like his companions, was judged guilty and sentenced to death. In sensitive letters to family and friends in Oberlin written from prison, Copeland defended the enterprise, asserted that he blamed no one for his fate, and confidently informed his close friend Elias Green that even though the raid had not succeeded in freeing the slaves, it was "the prelude to that great event." On December 16, fourteen days after the execution of John Brown, John Copeland, Jr., alike mounted the scaffold and was hanged.[29]

Although Langston personally was not accused of conspiracy, all of Oberlin was suspect. In the midst of unrestrained insistence that Black Republicans bore responsibility for the Harper's Ferry attack, one Democratic editor called it a "second edition" of the Oberlin-Wellington Rescue. Democratic Congressman Clement L. Vallandigham of Dayton questioned the bloodied Brown only seven hours after capture, probing for connections with the Oberlin rescuers and "the insurrectionary movement at that time made in the Western Reserve to organize forcible resistance to the Fugitive Slave Act." Marshal Johnson of Cleveland likewise visited Copeland and extracted what newspapers called a "confession." Actually fabricated from the correspondence of Kagi, John Brown, Jr., Leary, and Ralph Plumb, found in the Kennedy farmhouse, the "confession" implicated both Plumb and Charles Langston.[30] Democratic newspapers in northern Ohio placed blame for the raid on Oberlin and the "fanatical views of such men as Giddings, Peck or Langston." "The blood of the poor ignorant blacks, Leary and Copeland, will forever stain the character of the whites of Oberlin and other places in Ohio!" jabbed Cleveland's *National Democrat*. "Too cowardly themselves to run the risk," the Oberliners "put forward comparatively innocent blacks." Nor were such judgments restricted to the Reserve. A nationally disseminated editorial charged: "Oberlin is the nursery of just such men as John Brown and his followers. . . . Here is where the younger Browns obtain their conscientiousness in ultraisms, taught from their cradle up, so that while they rob slaveholders of their property, or commit murder for the cause of freedom, they imagine that they are doing God service."[31]

Langston did not deny the accusation. Speaking for the Ohio State Anti-Slavery Society, he declared that "we most cheerfully approve the manly, the heroic, the patriotic, and the Christian course pursued by the noble and Christ-like John Brown and his compatriots." They had been courageous at Harper's Ferry, patient and Christian during incarceration, "firm and God-like" on the gallows. But in the raid's immediate aftermath, most Republicans disclaimed sympathy with Brown; Plumb and Giddings, like others among Brown's prominent contributors or co-conspirators, were emphatic in their disavowals. Not until after the November 1859 state elections across the North, when Republicans in every free state except Illinois and California won as handily as they had in Ohio in October, did the party's spokesmen adopt a more sympathetic tone.[32] Langston may well have shared his brother Charles's irritation at the Republican temporizing and found emotional release in the latter's public outburst. In a sardonic "card" to the press, Charles Langston reproved those who denied their connections with Brown. Were they afrighted at the prospect of "bloody gallows" or "a political grave?" As for himself, "I have no political prospects and therefore no political fears: for my black face and curly hair doom me in this land of equality to political damnation. . . . But I have a neck as dear to me as [Gerrit] Smith's, [John P.] Hale's, or Giddings', and therefore I must like them publish a card of denial. So here it is. But what shall I deny? I cannot deny that I feel the very deepest sympathy with the Immortal John Brown in his heroic and daring efforts to free the slaves.—To do this would be in my opinion more criminal than to urge the slaves to open rebellion." Charles, like his brother, justified Brown's movement on the basis of the "pure and righteous principles" expressed by the Bible, the Revolutionary fathers, and "all good" abolitionists.[33]

Both Langstons could be gratified at the militant black reaction to Harper's Ferry. As the day of Brown's hanging neared, Peter Clark and other black Cincinnatians expressed approval of Brown and his men, and the expectation that "the irrepressible conflict was now at hand, and the bloody days of Domitian would characterize the future of the Union, until the shackles should fall from the slave." They resolved that "the execution of John Brown and his associates will mark a new era in anti-slavery agitation"—the final phrase nearly identical to one Brown himself had spoken in support of insurrection. A black meeting in Cleveland resolved that "freemen of the North" had the "duty" to go to Charleston and "liberate John Brown."[34]

On December 2, the day of execution, Ohio black leaders, often in concert with whites, conducted ceremonies around the state. Exercises were held in Oberlin, certainly with a somber John Langston in attendance; Cincinnati, where the German community participated; and Columbus, where James Poindexter and David Jenkins led activities that began at 10 o'clock in the morning and continued well into the night. Charles H. Langston was the featured speaker at the Cleveland commemoration. In a black-draped hall with a gilt-framed picture of Brown at center stage, and flanked by two of the defense attorneys in the Rescue (the third had defended Brown at his trial), Charles Langston addressed some two thousand black and white mourners, on hand despite the blinding sleet and snow. He was in no mood for platitudes. If in Virginia he had expected no consideration, in Ohio he had found no rights. "A true man," Brown had assured Charles the previous spring that he found "black men to be equal to white," and Brown had believed this "practically and truthfully." Brown had been "murdered by the American people, murdered in consequence of your union with slavery. . . . But the 'irrepressible conflict' will go on. It cannot be stayed, and if the dissolution of the Union should take place, there would be a change by which here in Ohio the black man might be a free man." Until that occurred, white men too would be enslaved. Bitterly, Charles added: "All men speak of the matter from their own standpoint. I look at it from a colored man's standpoint—, one who hates your government as I hate the very devil."[35]

John Mercer, in cooperation with black and white townsmen, took steps to insure that the black raiders should not be forgotten. As John Copeland and Shields Green were mounting the gallows in Virginia, Langston, along with Professor James Monroe, John Watson, and black student James H. Muse, addressed a gathering in Oberlin to express sympathy for Copeland's family "and indignation against the cruel oppression that is so fast driving good men mad." Monroe subsequently traveled to Virginia in an attempt to recover Copeland's body, only to lose it to medical students who claimed the remains of both black raiders for use as cadavers. Oberlin spent Christmas day at a funeral service for the two men, with three thousand in attendance. Langston, appreciative of Copeland's manly bearing throughout, could only agree with Professor Henry Peck, who in his eulogy praised the Supreme Being for giving the black race a "not less firm, heroic and Christlike champion" at Harper's Ferry than the whites had in "the immortal John Brown." Langston served on a committee to initiate plans for a monument in the Oberlin cemetery honoring Leary and Copeland, "our martyred fellow-citizens," and Green as well. A fund-raising circular issued by the committee deemed the black raiders "representative men, of whom every colored person in the land has reason to be proud." Installed in 1865, the cenotaph, eight feet high and weighing half a ton, was inscribed: "These colored citizens of Oberlin, the heroic associates of the immortal John Brown, gave their lives for the slave."[36]

Through the memorial committee, Langston was able to begin to make good his assurance to Leary that his wife and baby would be cared for. The group early granted the twenty-three-year-old widow $50, a sum subsequently more than doubled. Charles Langston, with several others, published a commemorative booklet to be sold on behalf of the Brown and Leary families. The recipient of contributions from as far away as Haiti, Mary Leary, who had returned to the Patterson household, was able by February 1861 to consider buying the house she and Leary had shared, and supporting herself and her child by her work as a milliner. During the mid-sixties she went back to school, attending the preparatory department for two years. In January 1869, the Lorain County *News* directed readers to a special item: "a notice of the marriage of Charles H. Langston, Esq., brother of John M. Langston, and Mrs. Mary S. Leary, widow of Lewis Leary, one of the John Brown's 'raiders' who was shot while upon the rocks in the river near Harper's Ferry."[37]

"All that was done and suffered in such behalf was wisely and well done," John Mercer Langston would conclude some thirty-five years later, reflecting in one breath on Oberlin-Wellington and the John Brown affair. Yet, although the decision was their own and he almost certainly had not misled them as to the danger involved, two young men had gone to deaths he had, in all likelihood, felt were certain, partly at his urging. If Langston ever experienced that ambivalence felt by many whose lives were touched by John Brown, between having done too much or not enough, he never admitted it. In light of what he believed to be the "indirect but necessary effect of the Harper's Ferry Movement"—the War of the Rebellion resulting in the "overthrow of slavery followed by the enfranchisement of the emancipated classes," he appeared proud and not a little boastful of his contribution. In his final published word on the matter, Langston would write: "The sacrifices made must ever be considered large moral investments, profitable as well to the people generally, as to those who thus gained their freedom."[38]

At the time he could only agree with black Cincinnatians that the episode would "mark an era in anti-slavery agitation." It was as an agitator that he acted. Presiding over the Ohio State Anti-Slavery Society's first annual meeting in early January 1860 in Xenia, Langston chaired a special committee to draft a resolution on Harper's Ferry. Langston's resolution, then adopted, recommended that Virginia Governor Henry A. Wise, because of his conduct toward Brown and his "fellow Revolutionaries," be consigned to "a comfortable place in a Lunatic Asylum." As for "John Brown and his compatriots," they were "Heralds and Prophets of that new lesson, the lesson of Insurrection."[39]

Even while helping John Brown mass his fateful attack on slavery in the South, Langston had been mobilizing black Ohioans for an assault on prejudice in Ohio. As the boldness of the black reaction to John Brown indicated, the black temper was conducive to his efforts. Despite the firmly entrenched legal and social proscriptions upon black Ohioans as the 1850s drew to a close, Langston and his black protest co-workers found the self-help movement in a state of comparative health and heightened confidence. Although scholars generally have concluded that northern blacks in the 1850s faced a deteriorating economic situation and experienced growing demoralization, the situation in Ohio, at least, was different.[40] Although statistical evidence is lacking, other factors indicate that black Ohioans were, and perceived themselves as being, better off, better educated, and more morally and socially concerned than when Langston had entered the work in 1849.

On an economic level, Langston himself estimated in late summer of 1859 that some thirty thousand black Ohioans owned more than $7 million in property, on which they paid $65,000 in taxes, at least double the black estimate of 1851, when black residents of nineteen counties reported property holdings of something over $3 million. (Ohio's actual black population in 1850 was 25,279, in 1860, 36,673, both figures being well under 2 percent of the total population.) This relative economic achievement had come despite the competition of Irish immigrant workers and the severe depression of the late fifties, reflecting at least in part the state's generally robust economy for much of the decade, its improved antislavery climate, and black Ohio's propensity for exploiting opportunity while avoiding white competition. Although prospering Cincinnati had the largest black community (3,731 in 1860), more than 70 percent of black Ohioans lived in rural areas, many in all-black farming communities. In a number of these districts, Langston noted, blacks owned "large farms, well stocked and cultivated according to the most approved methods of modern agriculture."[41] That black Ohioans had made at least moderate economic gains may be inferred from statements made by emigration enthusiasts of the period, some from these selfsame rural communities. Prejudice, not poverty, was the motivation cited for their removal. Blacks in Mercer County, for example, took pride in having made Ohio's rough frontier "bloom and blossom like the rose," even as they contemplated emigration to Haiti, where they expected both economic opportunity and political rights.[42]

In no small part due to his own labors, Langston could also point to the improved state of black education in Ohio. Nearly half of the eligible young blacks were enrolled in public schools by the eve of war. Higher education was available not only at Oberlin, but also at Wilberforce University, founded near Xenia in 1856. Four years later it had some hundred males and females enrolled and a five-person teaching staff (including Sarah Jane Woodson, a black Oberlin graduate). Moreover, black adults and adolescents in urban and rural communities frequently took part in literary societies that maintained small libraries and sponsored debates, readings, and guest speakers. In Cleveland, where integrated schools had long been the norm, the black community demonstrated its own literary and artistic abilities in the spring of 1860 with a well-received serious drama, featuring music and dance, written by a black resident and employing an all-black cast.[43]

Langston also saw evidence of intensified moral awareness and endeavor. By 1860, a Baptist and a Methodist church occupied a central place in most black communities, along with associated Sunday schools and moral uplift and temperance organizations. In the larger urban areas, fraternal lodges, whose officers included such state leaders as Charles Langston, David Jenkins, and Alfred J. Anderson, and mutual aid societies offered their members sick and burial benefits, as well as fellowship and recreation. Women's groups and sororal affiliates of the lodges assisted the poor, the homeless, the orphaned. A fugitive aid society operated openly in Cleveland. By 1860, two black militia companies existed, Cincinnati's long-established Attucks Blues and a newly formed unit in Springfield. The annual First of August celebration of emancipation in the British West Indies, held in various localities, with well-ordered parades, picnics, and balls, exemplified the vitality of black-created institutions, while the eloquent antislavery oratory on such occasions testified to the moral values that sparked them. The 1860 celebration in Cincinnati was a case in point. Black Cincinnatians joined in a striking tribute to the late John I. Gaines, foremost in the local school effort as well as black protest, eulogized on a separate occasion by Langston as an exemplar of the "manly virtues" blacks should emulate. The Attucks Blues led a procession of some three thousand, mainly Negroes, to the black-owned cemetery, where a marble monument purchased by black contributions was dedicated at Gaines's grave. The ceremony may have seemed especially symbolic to those who remembered when Cincinnati's public cemetery, or potters' field, had buried blacks north to south and whites east to west, in an attempt to impose white supremacy even after death.[44]

After touring the state in the middle fifties, several of black abolitionism's most perceptive observers were ready to concur with Langston's estimate of the relatively advanced condition of black Ohio. William Wells Brown was especially impressed by Cleveland's black citizenry, comparing them "most favorably with an equal number of whites in any portion of Ohio." Boston's William C. Nell, while remarking on the "enterprise and prosperity" of black Cincinnatians in particular, contended that for "mechanical ingenuity, artistic skill, business attainments, moral development, and mental refinement" black Ohio was not to be "surpassed by any State in the Union . . ." And Frederick Douglass, having long been charmed by the black Ohioans, pronounced himself "much pleased with the general aspect of things" in most of the communities he had visited. Along the way he discovered a "large number of wealthy farmers" (300–500 acres) and "very little of the cringing Uncle Tom." Education, wealth, "elevating aspirations, indomitable energy, and perseverance, faith and hope must constitute the basis of black elevation here. They understand this."[45]

Langston likewise saw reason for at least guarded optimism in black Ohioans' advancing political understanding and involvement. Like other abolitionists, black and white, he viewed the economic, educational, social, and moral achievements of black Ohioans, individually and as a group, as contributions to the black struggle for equality. Like other blacks, he was able to measure black progress toward freedom on a continuum, rather than in absolutes, and in terms of generations and even lifetimes, not years. From this perspective, it was apparent that by 1860 a sizable number of black Ohioans were exercising some control over their destiny and manifesting a heightened degree of forcefulness. Nearly three decades of local and state black protest had produced a small but tenacious leadership group, an organizational framework, and a better informed constituency. Langston considered the leaders' educational role especially significant. By communicating their "very correct and thorough understanding of our national history, the genius of our institutions, and the philosophy of our politics," they had instilled in black Ohioans a deepened comprehension of the "very great power" of the "privileges and benefits" of citizenship and greater courage in urging their claim to it.[46]

Langston found substantiation in several areas. By 1860 lighter-skinned Negroes around the state were more forceful in claiming their privileges as voters. In such antislavery areas as Deer Creek in northeastern Ohio even darker-skinned Negroes voted for school and road officers in district elections where sympathetic authorities determined that the constitutional ban on black suffrage did not apply. In April 1860, Irvin Scott, a Negro, would be elected supervisor of a road district in Logan County, while later that year the Cleveland *Leader* reported that a local black man was serving subpoenas in his capacity as a deputy constable. Moreover, blacks had demonstrated repeatedly their willingness to go to court to secure their rights. Earlier in the year Sarah Walker Fossett mounted a protest against exclusion from the street cars in Cincinnati. In January, Fossett, an accomplished hairdresser with a large white clientele and manager of the Colored Orphan Asylum for more than twenty-five years, had been pushed off the car by the conductor. Aided by a number of well-to-do white women, she successfully sued the company and won black women the right to ride the cars.[47] From such modest achievements, fashioned against formidable odds, Langston and fellow blacks would derive inspiration and hope for the difficult years of Civil War and Reconstruction ahead.

For all their movement toward self-liberation, Langston did not let himself underestimate the weight of the disabilities still pressing on black Ohioans. In an "Appeal to the Public" in January 1860, Langston and his black colleagues noted that black residents were "exposed to all the outrages" of the Fugitive Slave Law and the Dred Scott decision, taxation without representation, exclusion from office, constitutional debarment from the militia, exclusion from benevolent institutions, denial of impartial trial by jury. "In short, this state of our nativity or adoption affords us no protection for our personal liberty, and denies us almost every civil and political right." At the same time, Langston believed it particularly important that blacks intensify, not moderate, their protest in these critical months. Seeking to exploit to the maximum an antislavery atmosphere that had Republicans in control of the Ohio statehouse and legislature, and simultaneously to build support for the Ohio State Anti-Slavery Society, Langston, as president, initiated a petition campaign aimed at black enfranchisement and passage of legislation to render the 1850 Fugitive Slave Law inoperative in Ohio.[48]

In laying the foundation for the proposed new laws, Langston and his co-workers extended the political process to the limit possible for blacks. Together with other agents, Langston delivered lectures throughout Ohio. In mid-August 1859, both John and Charles Langston addressed a mainly black young people's convention at Alliance that strongly condemned black disfranchisement and called on Ohio Republicans to grant black suffrage. As for the anti-Fugitive Slave Law campaign, Charles Langston, working as the society's executive secretary from its Cleveland office, helped to publicize a series of kidnappings of black Ohioans that occurred in the fall of 1859, keeping the issue "fresh in the minds of all." He saw to the circulation in more than fifty counties of the seven hundred petitions demanding repeal of the fugitive slave law, abrogation of the Black Laws, institution of black suffrage, and enactment of new personal liberty laws. In Cleveland the elder Langston personally secured the arrest of a white omnibus driver for kidnapping a black man; when a grand jury failed to indict, the "justly incensed colored people," as the Leader put it, abandoned the usual civility of black protest, and nearly lynched the suspect. Feeling also ran high in other kidnap localities. Through ad hoc indignation meetings, black Ohioans variously appointed investigating committees, subscribed funds to pay legal counsel, and assumed supervision of the petitions.[49]

Black leaders in Cincinnati, anxious to communicate their resentment, invited white reporters to a meeting called to promote the petition drive. Although several black Cincinnatians, recollecting the riot of 1841, counseled moderation, sentiment was decidedly with Peter Clark who denounced as scoundrels the men who "infest the Government offices of the city." "Who is afraid to call them scoundrels?" he demanded. "I will not lick the boot that kicks me. I hate them; and what I hate I would destroy." Josephus Fowler, Jr., a sometime state convention delegate, was even more emphatic: "Let each man prepare himself with a knife—a good stiletto, and when you are seized by one of these scoundrels, give him the knife to the hilt." The *Ohio State Journal*, the Republican party's official organ, picked up the story, quoting Fowler and adding: "In view of the actualities, who shall say he was a violent or sanguinary man?"[50]

To climax the petition campaign, Langston called the first annual meeting of the Ohio State Anti-Slavery Society for January 3–5, 1860, in Xenia. It was also the occasion for Langston to present a balance sheet on his organizational endeavors since the launching of the society in November 1858. Financing had been the major difficulty. Fund-raising attempts led by both Langstons, Clark, David Jenkins, and the antislavery lecturer and poet Frances Ellen Watkins had proved only partially effective. Not only were Ohioans still feeling the effects of the 1857–58 depression but, significantly, the Oberlin-Wellington Rescue, at the same time that it provided vital impetus to the black organization, diverted abolitionist funds and energies for much of 1859. (The same paradox, to a lesser degree, applied to John Brown's movement.) The first executive board meeting in February 1859 confronted a treasury of only $168, far short of the $500 goal. Consequently, agents and lecturers received no salaries and had to resort to taking up collections. Nonetheless, solid accomplishments had been registered. Rent had been paid on the Cleveland office, operating expenses met, and a modest salary allotted to Charles Langston. His Rescue address had been published and distributed, the petitions printed, and other antislavery tracts sold.[51] Most important, more than three hundred lectures had been delivered, with the Langston brothers doing much of the speaking themselves. The "truth," the Langstons reported, had been carried to "the ears and hearts of the people."

In short, against a record of failed organizational attempts during the decade, John Langston and his colleagues had constructed a viable statewide society. In welcoming the delegates to the Xenia conclave, Langston, as presiding officer (the third time he had served as president of an Ohio state black convention), could well regard the gathering as the culmination, not merely of the past year, but of a decade of organizational efforts. Those in attendance, agreeing with Langston that "this laudable, but arduous work" must be continued, reelected him president and Charles secretary. The extent of the society's constituency may be estimated by the appointment of one hundred thirty-four men and women to lead auxiliaries in thirty-one counties. The annual meeting itself was notable for the presence of women, not only as delegates, but also on committees.[52]

In his presidential address—as in the "Appeal" issued by the Xenia meeting—Langston called for removal of black legal disabilities. He especially underscored the "want of an efficient personal liberty law, for the protection of our wives, children, and ourselves, against the manstealer and the kidnapper. . . ." In response, delegates took the noteworthy step of designating him as lobbyist for black interests in the state capitol, the first time in Ohio that blacks had elected a representative to assume such a responsibility over a sustained period.[53]

In Columbus, "special agent" Langston caucused with Senator James Monroe and other supportive antislavery legislators, while the black Columbians, James Poindexter and John Booker, routed the petitions, "many" of which were "fully signed," to them.[54] To Langston's obvious satisfaction, his radical allies, with Senator Monroe in the forefront, proved anxious to channel momentum from the Rescue and Raid into pro-black, anti-southern legislation.

As a hardly surprised Langston was able to observe at close hand, the radical-conservative split among Republicans figured prominently in the 1860 assembly session. With the backing of outgoing Governor Chase and several influential Republican newspapers, James Monroe's bill to prevent slaveholding and kidnapping passed by a healthy margin in the senate, but failed in the house, where conservative Republicans, representatives of southern counties in the main and upholding the constitutionality of the Fugitive Slave Law, joined with Democrats to table it.[55] Another Monroe bill to repeal the so-called "visible admixture" law, an enactment of the preceding Democratic assembly that barred light-skinned Negroes like Langston from voting, likewise got through the senate only to have conservatives and Democrats combine to stall a similar measure in the house. The radicals decided against further action when word came in mid-February that the State supreme court, acting shortly before on the Alfred J. Anderson case (see chapter 10), had upheld earlier court decisions that persons of more white than black ancestry were entitled to electoral privileges. Although Monroe and others were interested in taking the "preliminary steps necessary" to alter the constitution so that black males, whatever their degree of color, might be eligible to vote, and were supported by many petitions, including those circulated by the Langstons, the strength of the opposition in both house and senate judiciary committees assured inaction.[56] On the other hand, a Democratic-initiated bill to bar black immigration, although clearly benefiting from a fear of racial inundation set off by the harsh treatment of free blacks in the post-Harper's Ferry South and backed by numerous petitions from the southern counties, was blocked by Republicans and moderates.[57]

Langston had reason to be encouraged by the radical legislators' success, over conservative opposition, in electing Chase to the U.S. Senate in 1860. At the same time, to the black man who wanted his American citizenship validated, the lip service paid to colonization by some of Ohio's staunchest antislavery men was deeply disturbing. Granted that such endorsement offered some defense against the Democratic bullyragging of the Republicans on race, still it could only make black Republicans, even such a stalwart as Langston, who denounced colonization on two noted occasions while the assembly was in session, uneasy about the party's future course. Indeed, the Republican legislature, "from which some expected so much in behalf of freedom," had been marked by timidity and division.[58] Langston may well have come away from Columbus even more convinced than before that violent conflict and social revolution were necessary if his people were ever to be fully free.

Langston committed himself wholeheartedly to Republican success in 1860. Whatever the Republican shortcomings on race, and they were many, the party's potential for forwarding the crusade against slavery and the "Southern Oligarchy" had never seemed greater. "It was well," Langston wrote in after years, that at the time of the Oberlin-Wellington Rescue and the John Brown Raid, a political party based on "Free Principles" was "thoroughly organized and established for state and national duty."[59] Gearing up for Ohio's off-year elections in October, to be followed in November by what most felt would be the most momentous presidential election in the nation's history, Langston felt confident that Republican victory would intensify southern alienation.

Through a Republican group that he had helped to initiate in Oberlin, Langston was involved in all phases of local party organizational work: planning strategy, canvassing the township, enlisting volunteers, organizing mass meetings, hanging posters and banners, lining up entertainment. Langston chaired the caucus that revived the Wide Awake Club, that emotion-stirring campaign innovation of 1856. Well-drilled young men in glazed varicolored capes and smart military caps, who bore torches and bright transparencies aloft while marching to

cadenced cheers and brass bands, the Wide Awakes added much to the
enthusiasm of the 1860 northern canvass. In particular, this was true
in Oberlin, where black Republicans stepped out side by side with
white.[60]

In late March, Langston joined with the local Republican faithful in
insisting that the party would be "the great party of freedom." As the
national convention in Chicago approached, the Republican Club of
Oberlin, buttressed by "inspirational music" from the Citizen's Brass
Band, met in the chapel to hear State Senator Monroe's account of his
somewhat frustrating labors in Columbus and to spell out the Oberlin
position. The resolutions offered by Ralph Plumb and unanimously
adopted affirmed "confidence in the earnestness and integrity of the
men who compose the great party of freedom, the Republicans of the
United States; and we believe that they are prepared to meet the crisis
which our country is fast approaching, in the decision of the conflict
between Freedom and Slavery." The meeting urged, without specific
mention of black rights, that the national platform adhere to the "principles of just government, as we find them expressed in the Bible, the
Declaration of Independence, and the Constitution of the United
States." Summoned by the crowd, Langston, who long had insisted
these documents contained ample moral and legal justification for
emancipation and black enfranchisement, offered a few well-chosen
words of support.[61]

Langston clearly would have preferred Chase, "the champion of
American liberty," or Seward, his brother's particular favorite, as the
Republican presidential nominee. He was one of those Oberlin Republicans who deemed Abraham Lincoln's "ground on the score of humanity toward the oppressed . . . too low. It did him no honor." Still, on
receipt of news that the Illinois man was to be the candidate, the
Oberlin Wide Awakes piled barrels and boxes twenty feet high and lit
a bonfire that illuminated the entire town. Later, reassured by direct
reports from Giddings and other allies as to Lincoln's soundness on
the slavery question, Langston and his townsmen declared themselves
for Lincoln and vice-presidential candidate Hannibal Hamlin, but "for
them only as they represent the principles of the Republican party, and
sustain those rights which we hold to be from the Creator of the
Universe." As an Oberlin representative, Langston took an active role at
the Republican county convention in Elyria on September 1 to nominate candidates for local office, where delegates "heartily endorsed"
the Chicago platform, but extended it to embrace condemnation of the
Fugitive Slave Law.[62]

Less in demand than Monroe who, while continuing to teach classes, delivered some thirty speeches in the congressional district, Langston nonetheless performed his share of stump speaking. In contrast to his widespread efforts during the Frémont campaign in 1856, he appeared mainly in the most rampantly radical nearby townships and, momentarily quiet on black suffrage, held to the radical party line. In a contest of intense, perhaps unparalleled, popular interest, nowhere more thrilling than among the Rescue and Raid-inspired inhabitants of the Western Reserve, the electorate turned out to hear "J. M. Langston Esq." of Oberlin deliver his latest word on "the great question of the day—Freedom and Slavery." His role in the campaign was not so much to win over the doubtful or bring back the vacillating as to fire up the white faithful and get out the black voter. To those ends, Langston—like Monroe, Peck, Ralph Plumb, James Fitch, and other Oberlin canvassers—naturally identified the Republican party with the mighty stream of righteousness, the source of Christian, republican, and antislavery justice.[63]

If his First of August oration on "the soul crushing system of slavery" is any indication, Langston rallied audiences with appeals to moral courage. The celebration, held at the Dayton fairgrounds, attracted a large crowd, black and white, from "almost every part of the State" and from neighboring Indiana as well. Acknowledging that slavery and prejudice remained strong, Langston, reminding his hearers of "the power in your own hands to rule the land for good or bad," implored them to "never desist" and "not despair. . . . It is a great cause, and success will ere long be ours. . . . Let our motto be upward, onward, right on, though fire-eaters of the South and dough-faces of the North oppose [us]."[64]

Langston, like other party regulars, regarded Ohio's elections for congressional and state offices as a harbinger for the presidential contest. On October 9, election day, the normal tranquility of Oberlin life gave way to an all-day mass meeting to bring out the vote. The "country people," some of their rail-pen wagons festooned with banners inscribed "Lincoln and Hamlin," began arriving as early as nine in the morning. While Langston and other Republican volunteers took turns distributing election tickets, poll watching, and escorting voters to the polls, rural folk and townsmen alike cast ballots, stood around talking crops and politics, and generally got caught up in the spectacle. A little after eleven, the parade embarked: a collection of carriages and floats representing the town's two fire engine companies and the wares of various black and white artisans; a student's room in miniature with three freshmen poring over their texts at a dilapidated desk; "three busloads of beauty and merriment" from Ladies' Hall; and, bringing up the rear, a host of "wide-awake Republicans" bearing fence rails on their shoulders. After the noonday dinner, the oratory rang out from the platform erected in front of Tappan Hall, with A. G. Riddle of Cleveland, one of the defense lawyers in the Rescue who was running for Congress, speaking for nearly two hours. Periodically throughout the festivities, the Lincoln Glee Club, "a quartet of gentlemen," and the Citizen's Brass Band performed partisan and religious airs. That evening, in the "warm and smoky atmosphere" of Indian summer, the Wellington Wide Awakes arrived by train and treated the crowd to a "rail-fence march." More speaking followed, and Lincoln and Hamlin were given a final salute with a dazzling torchlight procession by the "hale, hearty and good looking" Wide Awakes.[65] Had a stranger chanced upon Oberlin that day, he would have been struck forcibly by two aspects of the festivities—the absence of alcohol, and the full participation by black residents in every aspect of the political and social events that commonly transpired on an election day in nineteenth-century America.

The results gave Langston every reason for optimism. Having campaigned adroitly on the slavery issue in northern Ohio and on free labor and a protective tariff in the southern regions, the Republicans won handily in the state and congressional elections. Lorain County Republicans contributed a majority of 2,073 votes for the state ticket. Especially cheering to Langston was the reelection of State Supreme Court Justice Jacob Brinkerhoff despite the opposition of conservative Republicans as well as Democrats. In addition to his opinion in the Rescue hearing that the Fugitive Slave Law was unconstitutional, Brinkerhoff had participated in late 1859 in two controversial cases, siding first with the court minority in favoring the right of "nearer white than black" children to be admitted to white common schools, and then with the majority in the Anderson case in reestablishing the right of "nearer white than black" men to voting privileges. Only days before, the *Plain Dealer* had carped that under the Anderson decision "fourteen thousand negroes will vote the Black Republican ticket in Ohio." Negroes did, indeed, vote, reportedly even in heavily Democratic counties.[66]

A month later Lincoln carried Ohio, with an estimated voter turnout of 90 percent, by more than twenty thousand votes over the combined opposition. The great majorities piled up on the Western Reserve—an average of 67 percent for twelve counties, an 80 percent margin in Oberlin's township—were duplicated in other demonstrably antislavery areas in the northeast and midwest. With a local editor, Langston rejoiced: "Never in the history of American politics has so great a victory been achieved . . . never an election conducted on so important an issue."[67]

Langston's elation over the election soon dissolved into anxiety. In the tension-ridden period preceding the inauguration, as one after another of the Deep South states seceded and northerners waited to see what course the new president would adopt, there seemed reason to fear that the forces advocating compromise with the South once again might triumph. Langston confronted this possibility in an intensely personal way through the plight of Sara Lucy Bagby, a fugitive slave.[68] A pretty dark-haired woman who was pregnant with her first child, Lucy Bagby's ordeal began in mid-January 1861 when two wealthy Virginians, John Goshorn and his son William, bent on reclaiming her before the Republicans took charge in Washington, arrived in Cleveland. At the Goshorns' request, Marshal Johnson quickly apprehended her and placed her in the city jail. Congressman-elect Riddle, for whom Bagby had sometimes worked as a maid, and his partner Rufus P. Spalding, the prominent Republicans and Rescue attorneys, volunteered for her defense, but soon concluded there was no legal impediment to her return. Concerned that any attempt at prevention would fuel the "disunion flame" by furnishing southern extremists with proof that, despite avowals to the contrary, Republicans did not intend to abide by the laws regarding slavery, the city's Republican leaders, radical and conservative alike, repeatedly cautioned against a rescue.[69]

An incensed black citizenry disputed the Republican consensus. From the moment of Lucy Bagby's arrest, leaders like the Langstons, working through their Ohio State Anti-Slavery Society network, sought the means to extricate her. Crowds of black men and women, the latter especially aggressive, maintained a vigil near her jail cell. When the marshal attempted to move Bagby to a holding room near the federal court where the hearing was to be held, a throng including some sixty men from Oberlin—who had traveled to Cleveland for that purpose—surged forward and tried to wrest her free. A beefed-up squad of deputies clubbed them back. During the melee, John Wall, Carrie Langston's young half-brother who was carrying a pocketknife, and three other Negroes from Oberlin were arrested, jailed, and later fined.[70]

On January 23, the court remanded Lucy Bagby to her owners. The next day the Goshorns took the southbound train, riding in a special car and with the woman under heavy guard. Still, she was not without hope. Shortly after the court's decision, one of the Langstons had visited her with the news of another plan to free her. Working furiously, they had set about assembling a rescue party from across the Reserve. Armed with muskets, pistols, clubs, and "divers other weapons," more than a hundred men, most of whom were black, gathered near the train station in the small town of Lima. Meanwhile, further up the track at Ravenna, two men boarded the train. Muffled under a bulky coat, W. A. Tyler, a young white man from Oberlin, concealed two loaded pistols; in his arms, William J. Whipper, a strongly built young black man from the Youngstown area who was an Anti-Slavery Society agent, carried a formidable iron bar about a yard long.[71] The plan was straightforward. When the train made its scheduled stop at Lima, Tyler was to burst into the special car to hold the guards at bay while Whipper knocked loose the coupling pin to maroon the car, upon which the party of armed men would make good Lucy's escape. Unfortunately for the conspirators, the conductor and engineer, alerted to a possible rescue attempt and becoming suspicious when they spotted the crowd, took the train through at full throttle. Tyler and Whipper were later disarmed and put off the cars. Prominent among the armed men, John Mercer Langston could only watch in frustration as the train gathered steam for the journey south.[72]

It was a bitter moment, sharp with regret for the young woman and the baby that would be born into slavery, acrid, too, with the taste of political betrayal by Cleveland's white leaders of the party into whose building Langston had put such effort and tempered hope, and whose promise he continued to expound, not without cost, even when his brother and such close friends as Clark expressed their own skepticism and disillusionment over the Republican agenda. Although Cleveland, despite its relatively tolerant racial climate, had never been such a radical abolitionist redoubt as Oberlin, the spectacle of its antislavery politicians proclaiming willingness to abide by the Fugitive Slave Law if only the proper forms were observed—to say nothing of the praise, later softened, in the antislavery press for the thwarting of the rescue attempt—[73] was new and discomfiting. Langston's effort to free Lucy Bagby, despite the paucity of rational hope for success, was expressive, on the one hand, of his bold willingness to act decisively in a desperate situation and, on the other, of his restless need to involve himself in virtually every activity in sight that might combat slavery. The anguish and ambiguities, the triumphs and defeats of these frenzied last months, the unavoidably lost opportunity of helping to rescue John Price, the indirectness, secretiveness, and fatal consequences of his contribution to Harper's Ferry, the tension of the strange days of waiting, doubtless had added new dimensions to this need. The very audacity of

the try—the band of armed men ready to spring like train robbers—
lent its subsequent collapse something of the humiliating aspect of
farce, only adding to the pain.

At some point in these months, Langston's little daughter Chinque,
just two and a half, fell sick and, with the pounding inevitability of
many childhood illnesses of the day, died and was buried in the village
cemetery. Her death could only add to the sense of mounting catastrophe, her loss to his sensitivity to the fate of Lucy Bagby and her unborn
child, of all the children blighted by slavery. A glimpse forward in time
might have partially assuaged the pain. Despite reports that Lucy
Bagby had committed suicide in captivity, in actuality, she would survive to be liberated by the Union army and, through the instrumental-
ity of Cleveland black leader W. E. Ambush, brought back to the scene
of her rendition. On May 6, 1863, Langston would lead the speaking
at a Grand Jubilee in the city over her return.[74]

At the present, it afforded the radical black man some comfort that
the town that had done so much to shape his behavior and attitudes
remained, through the "cruel, deadly storm" he felt approaching, res-
olutely defiant. On February 4, as letters from two "shrewd" congressmen circulated in Oberlin warning that men "usually regarded as
'radical men' " were "deeply engaged in the business" of appeasement,
Langston participated in a mass local protest meeting. Following
prayerful consideration of the "crisis which the slave power has brought
upon our common country," the biracial audience approved an
"Oberlin manifesto." It protested to the just-convened compromise
convention in Washington "against any concession to slavery or to the
demands made by its abettors, in anything whatever, and especially
against making such concessions, at the behest of traitors in arms
against the Union."[75] Days later, in a poem, "To the Cleveland Union-
Savers," Frances Ellen Watkins Harper, Langston's fellow lecturer for
the Ohio State Anti-Slavery Society, expressed it another way:

> Ye may bind your trembling victims
> Like the heathen priests of old;
> And may barter manly honor
> For the Union and the gold.
>
> But ye cannot stay the whirlwind,
> When the storm begins to break;
> And our God doth rise in judgment,
> For the poor and needy's sake.
>
> And your guilty, sin-cursed Union
> Shall be shaken to its base,
> Till ye learn that simple justice
> Is the right of every race.[76]

Twelve of his thirty-one years invested in seeding the whirlwind, when the storm broke, Langston could only be glad. It was a significant thing to him that Ohio blacks had made a proportional contribution in bringing on the war—and that he himself, toward that end, had discharged his "responsibility and duty" as a man, a Negro, and an American.[77]

NOTES

1. Cleveland *Plain Dealer*, Oct. 18, Nov. 19, 1859, Dec. 13, 1860, Jan. 28, 1861.

2. John Mercer Langston, *From the Virginia Plantation to the National Capitol; or, The First and Only Negro Representative in Congress from the Old Dominion* (Hartford, 1894; repr. New York: Johnson Reprint Corp., 1968), p. 198.

3. John Mercer Langston, "Louis Pacheco," Oberlin *Students' Monthly* 1 (Nov. 1858):33–35.

4. Richard J. Hinton, *John Brown and His Men* (New York, 1894; repr. New York: Arno Press, 1968), p. 178; Robert S. Fletcher, "John Brown and Oberlin," Oberlin *Alumni Magazine* 28 (Feb. 1932):135–41; Mary Land, "John Brown's Ohio Environment," *Ohio State Archeological and Historical Quarterly* 57 (Jan. 1948):24–47.

5. Benjamin Quarles, *Allies for Freedom: Blacks and John Brown* (New York, 1974), pp. 43–51; Stephen A. Oates, *To Purge This Land with Blood* (New York, 1970), pp. 64, 244; John Mercer Langston, "The World's Anti-Slavery Movement," in John Mercer Langston, *Freedom and Citizenship* (Washington, 1883; repr. Miami: Mnemosyne Reprint, 1969), p. 46.

6. *Proceedings of the Convention of the Colored Freemen of Ohio . . . Cincinnati . . . Jan., 1852* (Cincinnati, 1852); *Voice of the Fugitive*, Feb. 12, 1852; Cincinnati *Gazette*, Jan. 19, 1852.

7. Hinton, *John Brown and His Men*, pp. 174, 262, 732–33; Wilbur H. Siebert, *The Underground Railroad from Slavery to Freedom* (New York, 1898), p. 180; Quarles, *Allies for Freedom*, pp. 73–74. George J. Reynolds was a delegate at the black emigrationist convention in Cleveland in 1854; see *Proceedings of the National Emigration Convention of Colored People . . . Cleveland . . . Aug., 1854* (Pittsburgh, 1854).

8. J.R. Giddings to Ralph Plumb, May 6, 1859, quoted in Cleveland *Plain Dealer*, June 2, 1859.

9. Oberlin *Evangelist*, Jan. 19, 1859; James H. Fairchild, *Oberlin: The Colony and the College, 1833–1883* (Oberlin, 1883), p. 156; Oberlin *Students' Monthly* 1 (Feb. 1859):160–61; *Liberator*, Jan. 13, 1860; John Copeland to "Dear Friends and Brothers of the Oberlin Anti Slavery Society," Dec. 11, 1859, John Brown manuscript materials used by Oswald Garrison Villard in preparing the life of John Brown, Columbia University Libraries (hereafter cited as "Villard ms.").

10. Oswald Garrison Villard, *John Brown: A Biography Fifty Years Later* (New York, 1910; repr. Gloucester, Mass.: Peter Smith, 1965), pp. 391–94; Charles

Langston quoted in Cleveland *Leader*, Dec. 3, 1859; Thomas Drew, *The John Brown Invasion: An Authentic History of the Harper's Ferry Tragedy* (Boston, 1860), p. 21; Cleveland *Leader*, Mar. 18, 22, 1859; Cleveland *Plain Dealer*, Mar. 22, Oct. 26, 1859; Katherine Mayo interview with Henrietta Evans, Mar. 5, 1908, Villard ms.; Oates, *To Purge This Land with Blood*, pp. 266–67, 221; confession of John Cook, quoted in Cleveland *Leader*, Nov. 28, 1859; Land, "John Brown's Ohio Environment," p. 40.

11. Langston, *Virginia Plantation*, p. 192; Hinton, *John Brown and His Men*, pp. 236–37; Ralph Plumb's testimony, "Select Committee of the Senate Appointed to inquire into . . . Harper's Ferry," 36 Cong., 1st sess., Senate Report 278 (Washington, 1860), p. 184; Cleveland *Plain Dealer*, Oct. 20, 1859; Jacob R. Shipherd, comp., *History of the Oberlin-Wellington Rescue* (Boston, 1859; repr. New York: DaCapo Press, 1972), viii.

12. J. D. H. [Joseph Dennis Harris] to J. Henrie [John Henry Kagi], Aug. 22, 1859, quoted in Cleveland *Plain Dealer*, Nov. 1, 1859. Harris identified the four only by last names: Leary, Smith, Davis, and Mitchell.

13. Ibid. Brown scholars have incorrectly assumed that J. D. H. was James H. Harris, a delegate to the Chatham convention. Villard, *John Brown*, p. 413; Quarles, *Allies for Freedom*, p. 80. The *Plain Dealer*, Nov. 1, 1859, identified the letter writer as Joseph D[ennis] Harris, No. 162, Ohio St., Cleveland. See *Proceedings of a Convention of the Colored Men of Ohio . . . Cincinnati . . . Nov. 1858* (Cincinnati, 1858); Cleveland *Leader*, Feb. 15, 1859; Floyd J. Miller, *The Search for a Black Nationality: Black Colonization and Emigration 1787–1863* (Urbana, 1975), pp. 237–38.

14. "Charlie" [Charles Langston] to Editor, *Anglo-African*, Aug. 20, 1859; Langston, *Virginia Plantation*, pp. 190–91. Langston's recollection that the visit occurred only three days before the attack on Harper's Ferry is faulty. The probable date was Aug. 29 or 30, 1859. John Smith [John Brown, Jr.] to Friend Henrie [John Henry Kagi], Aug. 27, 1859, *Calendar of State Papers*, Virginia (Virginia Historical Society); John Brown, Jr., to J. H. Kagi, Sept. 2, 1859; L. S. Leary to J. Henrie, Sept. 8, 1859, both quoted in Cleveland *Plain Dealer*, Nov. 1, 1859.

15. Plumb's testimony, Senate Report 278, p. 184; Cleveland *Leader*, Jan. 13, 1859.

16. Langston, *Virginia Plantation*, pp. 191–92; Oates, *To Purge This Land with Blood*, p. 268; John Brown, Jr., to John Cochrane, Feb. 28, 1878, quoted in New York *Tribune*, Mar. 23, 1878; J. S. [John Brown, Jr.] to Friend Henrie [John Henry Kagi], Sept. 27, 1859, quoted in New York *Herald*, Oct. 25, 1859.

17. Langston, *Virginia Plantation*, p. 196.

18. *State Convention . . . 1858*; Langston, *Freedom and Citizenship*, p. 54; Cleveland *Leader*, Jan. 13, 1859; compare Willie Lee Rose, *Slavery and Freedom* (New York, 1982), p. 133.

19. Photograph of Lewis Sheridan Leary in Oberlin College Library (see Robert S. Fletcher, *A History of Oberlin College*, 2 vols. [Oberlin, 1943], I, facing p. 414); interview with Henrietta Evans, Mar. 5, 1908, Villard ms.

20. William C. Nell, "Lewis S. Leary," *Pine and Palm*, July 27, 1861; interview with Henrietta Evans, Mar. 5, 1908; interview with James [John] Henry Scott, Dec. 7, 1908, both in Villard ms.; Quarles, *Allies for Freedom*, p. 87; Lida Rose McCabe, "The Oberlin-Wellington Rescue, an Anti-Slavery Crisis," *Godey's Magazine* (Oct. 1896):376; Langston, *Virginia Plantation*, p. 194; biographical sketch of John S. Leary in William J. Simmons, *Men of Mark: Eminent, Progressive, and Rising* (Baltimore, 1887; repr. Chicago: Johnson Publishing, 1970), pp. 285–86.

21. Elyria *Independent-Democrat*, Nov. 2, 1859; Langston, *Virginia Plantation*, p. 193; Oberlin *Students' Monthly* 1 (Feb. 1859):160; Nell, "Lewis S. Leary"; J. M. Fitch et al., Dec. 29, 1859, "Oberlin Monument Circular," quoted in *Liberator*, Jan. 13, 1860.

22. William E. Lincoln, "The Oberlin-Wellington Rescue," ms., Palmer Papers, Western Reserve Historical Society; biographical sketch in Villard, *John Brown*, p. 684; William C. Nell, "John A. Copeland," *Pine and Palm*, July 20, 1861; "W" to Editor, Dec. 16, 1859, quoted in New York *Tribune*, Jan. 6, 1860; Lorain County *News*, Mar. 26, 1862, Jan. 14, 1863.

23. Henry Cowles, "Oberlin College Catalogue and Records of Colored Students, 1835–1862," ms., Henry Cowles Papers, Oberlin College Library (hereafter cited as "Cowles List"); Fitch et al., "Oberlin Monument Circular"; Langston, *Virginia Plantation*, p. 195. The Population Census of 1860, Ohio, Roll 1002, Lorain County, Russia Township, National Archives, lists John Copeland, fifty, mulatto, and his wife Delilah, forty-nine, as having three sons and two daughters, four of them attending school. Copeland had $1,500 in real property and $100 in personal. There were seven children in all.

24. Shipherd, comp., *Oberlin-Wellington Rescue*, pp. 104–5, 126; Elyria *Independent-Democrat*, Nov. 2, 1859; Lincoln, "Oberlin-Wellington Rescue"; Copeland to "Dear Friends . . .," Dec. 1, 1859, Villard ms.; Villard, *John Brown*, p. 684.

25. Langston, *Virginia Plantation*, pp. 193–95; Shipherd, comp., *Oberlin-Wellington Rescue*, pp. 273, 270, 268; Langston, "Louis Pacheco," p. 35; Leary to J. Henrie [John Henry Kagi], Sept. 2, 1859; Leary to J. Henrie, Sept. 8, 1859, both quoted in Cleveland *Plain Dealer*, Nov. 1, 1859.

26. John Brown, Jr., to J. H. Kagi, Sept. 2, 1859; Leary to J. Henrie, Sept. 8, 1859, both quoted in Cleveland *Plain Dealer*, Nov. 1, 1859.

27. Interview with Richard J. Hinton, St. Louis *Globe-Democrat*, May 7, 1893, John Mercer Langston Scrapbooks, 4 vols., IV, Moorland-Spingarn Research Center, Howard University; Plumb's testimony, Senate Report 278, pp. 183, 180; John Smith [John Brown, Jr.] to Friend Henrie, Oct. 5, 1859, quoted in New York *Herald*, Oct. 25, 1859; Elyria *Independent-Democrat*, Aug. 17, 1859.

28. Interviews with Scott and Henrietta Evans, both in Villard ms.; John Smith [John Brown, Jr.] to Friend J. Henrie [John Henry Kagi], Oct. 6, 1859; Smith [Brown] to Henrie, Oct. 5, 1859, both quoted in New York *Herald*, Oct. 25, 1859; Oates, *To Purge This Land with Blood*, pp. 287–88, 296.

29. Quarles, *Allies for Freedom*, p. 110; Fletcher, "John Brown and Oberlin," pp. 137–39; Copeland to "Dear Friend . . .," Villard ms.; John A. Copeland to Friend [Addison] Halbert, Dec. 10, 1859; John Copeland to Dear Elias

[Green], Dec. 10, 1859, both in John Brown's Raid, Executive Papers, 1859, Box 477, Virginia State Library.

30. Lorain County *Eagle*, Oct. 26, 1859; Cleveland *Plain Dealer*, Oct. 18, 29, 26, 1859; New York *Herald*, Oct. 21, 1859; Clement Vallandigham to Editor, Cincinnati *Enquirer*, Oct. 22, 1859; Land, "John Brown's Ohio Environment," pp. 42–45; Elyria *Independent-Democrat*, Nov. 2, 1859; John Copeland's "Confession," Cleveland *Leader*, Nov. 1, 1859. Compare "Confession" and correspondence of Kagi, Brown, Jr., Leary, and Ralph Plumb, printed in Cleveland *Plain Dealer*, Nov. 1, 1859, and New York *Herald*, Oct. 25, 1859.

31. Cleveland *Plain Dealer*, Oct. 18, 20, 26, Nov. 1, 21, Dec. 15, 1859; Lorain County *Eagle*, Oct. 26, Nov. 16, 23, 30, Dec. 21, 1859; Cleveland *National Democrat*, n.d., quoted in Lorain County *Eagle*, Nov. 30, 1859; Philadelphia *Pennsylvanian*, n.d., quoted in Oberlin *Evangelist*, Dec. 7, 1859.

32. *Proceedings of the First Annual Meeting of the Ohio State Anti-Slavery Society . . . Xenia . . . Jan., 1860* (title page missing) (hereafter *State Convention . . . 1860*); Cleveland *Plain Dealer*, Nov. 21, 1859; James B. Stewart, *Joshua R. Giddings and the Tactics of Radical Politics* (Cleveland, 1970), pp. 269–71; Elyria *Independent-Democrat*, Nov. 30, 1859; Richard H. Sewall, *Ballots for Freedom: Antislavery Politics in the United States, 1837–1860* (New York, 1976), pp. 354–58.

33. Charles H. Langston, "Card," Cleveland *Plain Dealer*, Nov. 18, 1859; *State Convention . . . 1860*.

34. Cincinnati *Enquirer*, Nov. 16, 1859; Cincinnati *Gazette*, Nov. 15, 1859; *Liberator*, Feb. 4, 1859; Cleveland *Plain Dealer*, Nov. 18, 1859.

35. *Ohio State Journal*, Dec. 8, 1859; *Anglo-African*, Dec. 3, 1859; Cleveland *Leader*, Dec. 3, 1859; Cleveland *Plain Dealer*, Dec. 3, 1859; "Charlie" [Charles Langston] to Editor, *Anglo African*, Dec. 17, 1859; *Tribute of Respect, Commemorative of the Worth and Sacrifice of John Brown of Ossawatomie* (Cleveland, 1859). For black "Martyr Day" commemorations, see Quarles, *Allies for Freedom*, pp. 125–31.

36. Oberlin *Students' Monthly* 2 (Jan. 1860):93; Cleveland *Leader*, Dec. 28, 1859, Jan. 7, 1860; Elyria *Independent-Democrat*, Jan. 4, 1860; Fitch et al., "Oberlin Monument Circular," *Liberator*, Jan. 13, 1860; Lorain County *News*, July 5, 1865; Quarles, *Allies for Freedom*, pp. 140–42, 149–50, 192–93.

37. Oberlin *Evangelist*, Feb. 1, 1860; Lorain County *News*, July 5, 1865; Quarles, *Allies for Freedom*, pp. 147–50; Population Census of 1860, Ohio, Roll 1002, Lorain County, Russia Township, NA; W. E. Bigglestone, Oberlin College Archivist, to Authors, May 12, 1975; Lorain County *News*, Jan. 20, 1869.

38. Langston, *Virginia Plantation*, p. 196.

39. Cincinnati *Enquirer*, Nov. 16, 1859; *State Convention . . . 1860*.

40. Jane H. Pease and William S. Pease, *They Who Would Be Free: Blacks' Search for Freedom, 1830–1861* (New York, 1974), pp. 298–99; Leon F. Litwack, *North of Slavery: The Negro in the Free States, 1790–1860* (Chicago, 1961), p. 247; compare David A. Gerber, *Black Ohio and the Color Line 1860–1915* (Urbana, 1976), pp. 23–24.

41. *Anti-Slavery Bugle*, Sept. 24, 1859; William H. Day, Charles H. Langston, Charles A. Yancey, "Address to the Constitutional Convention of the State of Ohio, Now Assembled," *Minutes of the State Convention of the Colored Citizens of*

Ohio . . . Columbus . . . Jan. 15–18, 1851 (Columbus, 1851); U.S. Bureau of the Census, *Negro Population, 1790–1915* (Washington, 1918), p. 45; Gerber, *Black Ohio and the Color Line*, pp. 14–15; John Mercer Langston, "Address to the Legislature of Ohio," *Proceedings of the State Convention of the Colored Men . . . Ohio . . .Columbus, Jan. 21–23, 1857* (Columbus, 1857).

42. Medina *Gazette*, June 14, 1860; Cincinnati *Commercial*, Dec. 4, 1861; Cincinnati *Gazette*, Apr. 22, 1861; *Pine and Palm*, Aug. 14, 1862.

43. Leonard E. Erickson, "The Color Line in Ohio Public Schools, 1829–1890," Ph.D. diss., Ohio State University, 1959, p. 216; Cleveland *Leader*, May 31, 1860; Sarah Jane Woodson [Mrs. Jordan W. Early], Alumni File, Oberlin College; Ellen Lawson, "Sarah Woodson Early: Nineteenth Century Black Nationalist Sister," *Umoja* 5 (Summer 1981): 15–26; *Ohio State Journal*, Mar. 24, 1860; Gerber, *Black Ohio and the Color Line*, p. 13; Cleveland *Leader*, June 25, 1860; Cleveland *Plain Dealer*, June 26, 1860. The Ohio supreme court ruling in late 1859 that children of more white than black ancestry were not entitled to attend school with white children more firmly segregated the public school system. Gerber, *Black Ohio and the Color Line*, p. 8.

44. Ibid., pp. 20–21; "Charlie" [Charles Langston] to Editor, *Anglo-African*, July 14, 1860; Cleveland *Leader*, May 5, July 17, 25, Aug. 4, 1860; *Ohio State Journal*, Jan. 3, 1859; John B. Shotwell, *A History of the Schools of Cincinnati* (Cincinnati, 1902), p. 458; John M. Langston, "Eulogy . . . of John I. Gaines . . .," Xenia, Jan. 3, 1860, *Liberator*, Apr. 27, 1860; Litwack, *North of Slavery*, p. 279.

45. W. W. Brown on "Colored People of Cleveland," *Anti-Slavery Bugle*, Dec. 5, 1857; W. C. N., "A Recent Tour of Ohio," *Anti-Slavery Bugle*, Dec. 13, 1856; *Anti-Slavery Bugle*, Aug. 30, 1856.

46. Langston, "Citizenship and the Ballot," Oct. 25, 1865, in *Freedom and Citizenship*, p. 106; Langston, "World's Anti-Slavery Movement," Ibid., p. 63.

47. Cleveland *Plain Dealer*, Oct. 22, 1860; Cleveland *Leader*, Oct. 17, 1859, Sept. 29, 1860; *Anti-Slavery Bugle*, Apr. 17, 1858, Apr. 21, 1860; Cincinnati *Gazette*, Jan. 20, 1860; Wendell P. Dabney, *Cincinnati's Colored Citizens* (Cincinnati, 1926; repr. New York: Johnson Reprint, 1970), p.145.

48. *State Convention . . . 1860.*

49. Ibid.; *Anti-Slavery Bugle*, July 23, Aug. 20, 1859; Cleveland *Plain Dealer*, Oct. 1, 1859; "Charles" [Langston] to Editor, *Anglo-African*, Aug. 20, Nov. 26, 1859; Cleveland *National Democrat*, quoted in Lorain County *Eagle*, Nov. 16, 1859; Cleveland *Leader*, Nov. 12, 14, 1859; Xenia *News*, n.d., quoted in *Ohio State Journal*, Nov. 5, 1859; *Ohio State Journal*, Nov. 17, Oct. 29, Nov. 11, 1859.

50. Cincinnati *Gazette*, Nov. 15, 1859; Cincinnati *Enquirer*, Nov. 16, 1859; *Ohio State Journal*, Dec. 19, 1859.

51. *State Convention . . . 1860*; Charles H. Langston, A. M. Sumner, John Malvin to the Public, Portage County *Democrat*, Dec. 15, 1858; *Douglass' Monthly*, Jan. 1859; Elyria *Independent-Democrat*, Dec. 1, 1858, Jan. 19, 26, 1859; Cleveland *Leader*, Dec. 7, 1858, Feb. 9, 19, 15, July 9, Aug. 9, 1859; Charles H. Langston, "Should Colored Men Be Subject to the Pains and Penalties of the Fugitive Slave Law? . . ." (Cleveland, 1859).

52. *State Convention . . . 1860*; Pease and Pease, *They Who Would Be Free*, pp. 287, fn. 299; Gerber, *Black Ohio and the Color Line*, pp. 23–24.

53. *State Convention . . . 1860*.

54. Ibid.

55. Porter, *Ohio Politics*, pp. 28, 30–33; *Ohio State Journal*, Nov. 5, 1859; J. W. Schuckers, *The Life and Public Services of Salmon Portland Chase* (New York, 1874; repr. Miami: Mnemosyne Publishing, 1969), p. 193; Elyria *Independent-Democrat*, Feb. 29, 1860; Lorain County *Eagle*, Mar. 15, 1860; *Laws of Ohio*, 57, pp. 108–9; Cleveland *Leader*, Jan. 22, 1861.

56. Elyria *Independent-Democrat*, Feb. 22, 1860; Lorain County *News*, Apr. 18, 1860; Porter, *Ohio Politics*, p. 210; Lorain County *Eagle*, Mar. 15, 1860.

57. Porter, *Ohio Politics*, p. 34; *Frederick Douglass' Paper*, Feb. 6, 1860; Elyria *Independent-Democrat*, Feb. 22, 1860.

58. Porter, *Ohio Politics*, pp. 30, 35; Cleveland *Leader*, May 2, 1860; *Ohio State Journal*, Mar. 7, 1860; Sewall, *Ballots for Freedom*, pp. 321–36; Eric Foner, *Free Soil, Free Labor, Free Men: The Ideology of the Republican Party Before the Civil War* (New York, 1970), pp. 267–80; John M. Langston, "Eulogy of . . . John I. Gaines . . . Jan. 3rd, 1860," *Liberator*, Apr. 27, 1860; Cleveland *Plain Dealer*, Feb. 16, 1860; Ashtabula *Sentinel*, n.d., reprinted in *National Anti-Slavery Standard*, Apr. 7, 1860.

59. Langston, *Virginia Plantation*, p. 196.

60. Lorain County *News*, Jan. 13, Apr. 4, June 13, 20, Oct. 10, 1860.

61. Ibid., Apr. 4, 1860.

62. "Remarks of J. M. Langston of Oberlin," *Anti-Slavery Bugle*, Sept. 24, 1859; "Charlie" [Charles Langston] to Editor, *Anglo-African*, June 20, 1860; Oberlin *Evangelist*, May 23, 1860; Elyria *Independent-Democrat*, May 23, Sept. 5, 1860; "Beta" to Editor, May 22, 1860, Cleveland *Leader*, May 24, 1860.

63. Lorain County *News*, Nov. 21, Sept. 19, 1860; Langston, *Virginia Plantation*, p. 196.

64. *Anti-Slavery Bugle*, Aug. 18, 1860. Although the correspondent credited the address to "Dr. Charles H. Langston of Oberlin," Charles was the orator at a mass convention at Harrisville, Medina County, on Aug. 1, 1860, the day of the Dayton celebration. Both Langstons delivered First of August speeches. Cleveland *Leader*, July 9, 1860; *Douglass' Monthly*, Sept., 1860.

65. Lorain County *News*, Oct. 10, July 4, Nov. 7, 1860; St. Louis *Democrat*, Nov. 29, 1865, John Mercer Langston Scrapbook, Fisk University Library.

66. Eugene Holloway Roseboom and Francis Phelps Weisenburger, *A History of Ohio* (New York, 1934), pp. 261–64; Elyria *Independent-Democrat*, Oct. 10, 1860; 9 *Ohio State Reports* 407 (Nov. 1859); 9 *Ohio State Reports* 596 (Dec. 1859); Cleveland *Plain Dealer*, Oct. 1, 1860; Georgetown (Brown County) *Argus*, n.d., quoted in Cleveland *Plain Dealer*, Oct. 22, 1860.

67. Stephen E. Maizlish and John J. Kushma, eds., *Essays on American Antebellum Politics, 1840–1860* (Arlington, Tex., 1982), p. 19; Joseph P. Smith, *History of the Republican Party in Ohio*, 2 vols. (Chicago, 1898), I, p. 704; Elyria *Independent-Democrat*, Nov. 14, 1860.

68. See John E. Vacha, "The Case of Sara Lucy Bagby, a Late Gesture," *Ohio History* 76 (Autumn 1967):223–31. The case was extensively covered in *Anti-Slavery Bugle*, Feb. 2, 9, 16, 23, 1861, later issued as a pamphlet entitled, "The Cleveland Sacrifice."

69. Vacha, "The Case of Sara Lucy Bagby," pp. 224–28; Cleveland *Leader*, Jan. 21, 1861; Cleveland *Herald*, Jan. 21, 1861.

70. Cleveland *Plain Dealer*, Jan. 21, 22, 1861; Cleveland *Leader*, Jan. 21, 22, 1861; letter of W. R. Laine, Jan. 29, 1861, in "Some Civil War Memories," Oberlin *Alumni Magazine* 15 (Oct. 1918):11–12; Oberlin *Evangelist*, Feb. 16, 1861.

71. "N.A." to Editor, Cleveland *Plain Dealer*, Jan. 26, 1861; Cleveland *Plain Dealer*, Jan. 25, 1861; Cleveland *Leader*, Feb. 15, 1859; *Anti-Slavery Bugle*, Aug. 20, 1859. Whipper may have been the son of William Whipper, early black abolitionist and affluent lumberyard owner from near Philadelphia. Pease and Pease, *They Who Would Be Free*, p. 289.

72. Cleveland *Leader*, Jan. 25, 1860; William Hick to Editor, *Anti-Slavery Bugle*, Feb. 2, 1861; Cleveland *Plain Dealer*, Jan. 25, 1861.

73. Elyria *Independent-Democrat*, Feb. 6, 1861; Lorain County *News*, Jan. 30, 1861; *Anti-Slavery Bugle*, Feb. 16, 23, 1861; Cleveland *Leader*, Feb. 1, 1861.

74. Cleveland *Plain Dealer*, May 25, 1861, May 4, 1863.

75. Langston, *Virginia Plantation*, p. 198; Lorain County *News*, Jan. 30, Feb. 6, Mar. 6, 1861; M. W. Fairchild to Editor, Feb. 4, 1861, Cleveland *Leader*, Feb. 6, 1861; Cleveland *Plain Dealer*, Feb. 8, 1861.

76. Frances Ellen Watkins Harper, "To the Cleveland Union-Savers," *Anti-Slavery Bugle*, Feb. 23, 1861. (Frances Ellen Watkins had been married to Fenton Harper on Nov. 22, 1860 at Cincinnati. *Anti-Slavery Bugle*, Dec. 22, 1860.)

77. Langston, *Virginia Plantation*, p. 182.

CHAPTER 12

The Struggle to Fight for Human Liberty

1861–63

THE North could "not succeed in conquering the slave oligarchy unless it accepted the services of the Negro," Langston had predicted more than two years before the war's beginning. "When the North did conquer it, the Negro would stand free by the northern side." But his humanist vision of militant black manhood contending for the liberation of slave and freeman, for the freedom of both white and black Americans from the constrictions imposed by slavery,[1] was not widely shared. Instead, the North was virtually unanimous in insisting that the purpose of the war was simply to restore the Union. The realization of Langston's vision would put to severe test the strengths inculcated in black Ohioans by decades of pre-war black organizing and challenge the full range of his own leadership abilities.

As the call to arms vibrated across the North, blacks responded hopefully. "We understood the grand issue," Langston reflected proudly, "and said we wanted to fight." Within days of Lincoln's declaration of a state of insurrection, blacks in Oberlin, Cleveland, Cincinnati, Columbus, Xenia, and elsewhere—through such established spokesmen as Rescuers John Scott and Charles Langston, John Malvin, Peter Clark, and Captain Julius Hawkins of Cincinnati's Attucks Blues—attempted to enlist for the Union. White officials rejected all offers. While the rejections varied in tone, including on occasion a crumb of praise for black patriotism, a white policeman in Cincinnati, where the American flag was torn from an improvised black recruiting station, voiced the prevailing sentiment. Blacks "had nothing to do with the fight," he informed them, "it was a *white man's fight, with which niggers had nothing to do*." Nonetheless, black Ohioans persisted in trying to involve themselves in the struggle. Charles Langston and the sixty-six-year-old Malvin led a black Union meeting on the Cleveland public square in October to declare it the "sacred duty of those in authority to proclaim liberty throughout the land." Black Ohioans, who enjoyed the "blessings of personal, though not political freedom," recognized that a Confederate victory might mean their own enslavement. Should the government adopt an emancipation policy, "we will hold ourselves in joyful readiness to bare our bosums in battle in defense of the Union."[2]

Two days after the outbreak of hostilities, John Langston addressed a great Union rally of some two thousand citizens, white and black, at the old church in Oberlin. He served as an officer alongside two prominent Democrats, a signal of radical acceptance of the necessity of conciliating the opposition so as to present a united front to the Slave Power. Wary of further exciting their eager young listeners, Langston and the white orators, Henry Peck, James H. Fairchild, James Fitch, and Ralph Plumb, were "moderate" in tone; a local journalist thought the audience "prepared to endorse a little more enthusiasm in the speakers than they manifested." Although the meeting took no immediate steps toward enlistment, it did appoint a biracial vigilance committee, which included O. S. B. Wall. Within days, as the populace cheered from the depot, a hundred young white men, Latin and Greek grammars tucked in their gear, took the cars for Cleveland and induction into the Union forces, where they soon garnered the name of "the prayin' company."[3]

Just as Langston had helped initiate the Republican party, he participated in formation of the Union party, a coalition of Republicans and War Democrats, in Lorain County. He joined in the call for the first county Union party convention, and, when it was held in Elyria in early September, made a short patriotic speech. Resolving to cease discussing party issues and to help crush out the rebellion, the convention ratified the gubernatorial nomination of David Tod, a wealthy pre-war Democrat. Subsequently, Tod emerged the victor by an impressive margin and James Monroe won reelection to the state senate.

Although for the time being party unity demanded silence on issues concerning black rights, Langston and his townsmen did insist that emancipation was at the heart of the Union cause.[4] In late summer of 1861, when General John C. Frémont made his short-lived proclamation of freedom to the slaves of rebellious masters in border state Missouri, Langston and Monroe took to the platform of an outdoor meeting to express approval. Linking abolition with the will of God and the salvation of both American and world civilization, Langston called on the Lincoln administration to adopt an emancipationist policy "promptly and without hesitation." More than at any period in American history "our nation is a city upon a hill, . . . the eyes of the whole world are upon us." The rebellion could not be suppressed until slavery, its "sole cause," was eliminated. Once abolition was identified as the "purpose and aim of this struggle," the Union would not only have the "sympathy and approval" of God and all civilized nations, but also a moral purpose that would inspire its soldiers. "Let us not take counsel of our fears. Compromise is a very Devil. . . . God and Right are our mighty allies." As Oberlin pressed for emancipation with increasing vehemence in the spring and summer of 1862, Langston stood with Professors Henry Cowles and E. H. Fairchild in asserting that the war was "a Divine rebuke for the national sin of oppressing the slave, and that we cannot rationally expect peace until this sin is forsaken."[5]

Meanwhile, racial prejudice grew in Ohio and other parts of the Midwest. As a black Cincinnatian lamented in late 1861, "Even now when the final struggle of that hell-born hydra—slavery—is visible, that hatred to the Negro is intensifying." The white animosity fed on a growing black immigration from the South that would contribute to an unprecedented 72 percent increase (from 36,673 to 63,213) in Ohio's black population during the decade, even though blacks still would account for less than 3 percent of Ohio's people. At every turn, Democrats aggravated the attendant white anxieties of sexual violation and economic competition. In the spring of 1861, the Democratic minority and conservative Republicans in the Ohio assembly enacted the state's first law barring interracial marriage and sexual relations. Petitions calling for exclusion of black immigrants and, in some cases, for removal of black residents, flooded the 1862 and 1863 sessions of the assembly. As northern disaffection with the war grew, the Negro became an ever more convenient scapegoat. By late 1862, bemoaning the "good deal of prejudice," an Oberlin-educated black minister in Dayton observed, "Many are so consistently mean and ignorant as to seriously charge the negroes with being the cause of all the troubles now distracting and afflicting our country."[6]

In these difficult straits, Langston, feeling it strategically wise to alter his pre-war agitational stance, adopted a posture of watchful waiting. He advised beleaguered blacks who sought his counsel to "stand and suffer patiently the wrongs heaped upon them by a cruel and bitter prejudice. And when the time comes, as come it will, of the white man's sore need, by your deeds show that you can fight, dig or die for American liberty." Doubtless reasoning little positive could be extracted from state politicians, Langston and his black cohort held no state convention during the first two years of the war, relying instead on local meetings and frequent open letters to rally and inform their people. In the spring of 1862, blacks in Oberlin and in Cincinnati met to hail the emancipation of slaves in the District of Columbia. Still, racial tensions continued to build. In July 1862, violence exploded in the port cities of Toledo and Cincinnati when white steamboat workers, angered by wage disputes and the threat of black competition, launched attacks on Negroes. As the mob assaults spread from Cincinnati's docks into black neighborhoods, Peter Clark and fellow citizens described their plight in words nearly applicable to the overall condition of black Ohio: "If we remain quiet under the outrages, the mob attributes it to cowardice, and redoubles its violence; if we resist, we are said to be violent and disorderly, and the abuse we receive is said to be merited."[7]

Despite these difficulties, Langston thought he spied an opening for black military involvement. Staggering under a series of battlefield reverses, the North desperately needed more soldiers. Moreover, the second Confiscation Act and the Militia Act of July 1862 authorized both limited emancipation and military employment of persons of African descent, although in deliberately vague terms. With and without authorization, Union officers already had armed black men in a few areas, and several Ohio Republican editors had begun to urge some kind of utilization of black soldiers. Still, both proponents and opponents of black enlistment seemed mired in racism: conservative Union officers like General Lew Wallace in Cincinnati argued for "taking the nigger" in cases of military necessity; relatively enlightened journals like the Cincinnati *Commercial* postulated that Negroes would not fight for a prejudiced North; countless others contended that blacks were too ignorant, incompetent, and cowardly for military service.[8] To Langston, it seemed imperative that black Ohioans counter such speculation by their own forceful statement of their position. He decided to make an offer so generous that it might cut through official obduracy on the use of black soldiers.

The groundwork for his enlistment bid was characteristicly thorough. In mid-July 1862 at an Oberlin "war meeting" to raise bounty money for new recruits, Langston—liberal with his own funds for the Union cause throughout—first helped whip up enthusiasm with a speech and a pledge of $50. He then called for the reorganization and "perfect drill" of an Oberlin black military company, disbanded after its services had been rejected the preceding fall, declaring it should now form the nucleus for "a regiment, or, if possible, a brigade of colored men of Ohio." Black soldiers should be organized and "in readiness to offer their services to the President or to the Governor of Ohio, as soon as the way is opened."[9] Two weeks later, the Guards, led by William A.

Jones, the 1857 black graduate of Oberlin College and schoolteacher who had mustered the earlier company, met for recruitment and drill.[10]

Langston again promoted the issue at a large meeting—the climax of weeks of agitation for emancipation on the part of Oberlin leaders—in the chapel on July 29. Alongside such speakers as Finney, up from a sickbed for the occasion, he criticized Lincoln's inaction on emancipation, protested the administration's kowtowing to prejudice, and urged "acknowledging the humanity of the slaves, using the latent strength of the colored people north and south." Langston helped draft resolutions for forwarding to the eastern press and to the president. Then, responding to loud calls, he "stirred the blood of all present" with his declaration that blacks would fight for freedom. "The cause of the Union is the cause of God and humanity; the cause of liberty both to the slave and the freeman; to the white and to the black man."[11]

Langston drummed up further enthusiasm on the First of August when, in contrast to the quiet observances the year before, black Ohioans staged morale-boosting celebrations around the state. He was the principal speaker in Xenia, where some 3,500 celebrants gathered from throughout the southern region and "the greatest enthusiasm prevailed." Buoyed by this evidence of organization and resiliency, he soared "to one of his best flights" of oratory.[12]

From Xenia he went to Columbus. Supplied with letters of introduction from such influential Republicans as Monroe, now president pro tempore of the state senate, he secured an interview with Governor Tod. Langston asked permission to lead the recruitment of a black Ohio regiment numbering 1,001 men, without cost to the state government. The sole condition he wished to exact was equal treatment—that Ohio Negroes "be received, duly officered and employed as regular soldiers in the national service." Because the major recruiter of a regiment usually received a command post, the desire that Langston had voiced in 1859 of "taking to the field himself" was implicit in his plan. A few days later, the Lorain County *News* commented that he "would make about as good a colonel or brigadier, as could be found."[13]

The governor rejected the proposal. "Had the people elected a Colored Lieutenant Governor to serve with me," Tod candidly explained, "I would not have taken my seat, and I cannot ask the noble men from Ohio who are in the field, to do what I would not do myself." If the white soldiers should prove unsuccessful, "then we will see what should be done." Langston bowed his leave, outwardly calm but inwardly fuming, "Lord, how long!"[14]

Even after the failure of this initiative, neither Langston nor his comrades desisted. Only a day or so later, Cleveland's William E. Ambush offered to supply black guards for rebel prisoners at nearby camps. Although two white regiments would thereby have been relieved for field duty, Tod likewise declined that offer. But a strong indication that military necessity might yet overcome prejudice came from Cincinnati. When a Rebel invasion threatened the Queen City, a "black brigade" of some seven hundred Negroes, at first through brutal military impressment but later, under the sympathetic Judge William M. Dickson's command, as a matter of black community pride and patriotism, labored for three weeks at building fortifications. (The "black brigade" was the first utilization of northern Negroes in the war, apart from General James Lane's unauthorized recruitment of blacks in Kansas the month before.)[15]

All the more convinced that the trend was toward black enlistment, Langston chaired an Oberlin meeting on September 12. Despite the existence of the all-black Guards, the meeting formed a racially integrated drill company—quite possibly the only one in the North—whose object was to train each participant in infantry tactics as preparation for army service "whenever and wherever, in his individual judgment, duty may call him." E. R. Stiles, one of Oberlin's first white recruits who had recently returned from a Confederate prison, served as the captain. Elected a second lieutenant, Langston spent a part of each weekday in drill on Tappan Square.[16]

In late September came news of the preliminary emancipation proclamation. On January 1, 1863, President Lincoln proposed to emancipate the slaves in states whose people "shall then be in rebellion against the United States," justifying the action as a war measure. Despite the document's shortcomings—chief among them that it physically freed no bondsmen—Langston applauded its definition of the war as being against slavery. Five days later, as a member of the resolutions committee at the Lorain County Union party convention, he drafted a statement of approval and support. But in October, there was a political backlash. In Ohio, besides winning some state offices by sizable majorities, Democrats took fourteen of the state's nineteen congressional districts, including Langston's own. With Democratic victories in Pennsylvania and Indiana as well, rumors circulated that the president would draw back from his intended Emancipation Proclamation.[17]

From mid-morning to late evening of New Year's day, 1863, together with a "multitude" of friends and neighbors, Langston waited in Oberlin's First Church for news of the proclamation. He heard Finney's

morning sermon and applauded Professor Henry Cowles's set of resolutions during the afternoon "jubilee proper." The assembly agreed to
the formation of the Oberlin Freedman's Relief Association, which
would work with the American Missionary Association and similar
organizations in supplying teachers for the freed people in the Union-
occupied South, and elected five men—two black, Langston and Sabram Cox, and three white, Cowles, Samuel Plumb, and James Fitch—
to its executive committee. On through the hours, Fitch, John Keep,
E. H. Fairchild, Negro blacksmith Solomon Grimes, and Captain Ralph
Plumb, the latter just back from the field with tales of encounters with
slaves and their rebel masters, kept the waiting crowd entertained. The
dominant note was the historic importance of the moment, "second . . .
to none that had preceded it," both for the nation and the colored
people of the land.[18]

In the opinion of Fitch, who served as secretary, Langston made "the
great speech of the day, . . . sound in argument, burning with eloquence, sparkling with wit, and withering in invective," and the best
speech of Langston's he had ever heard. Beyond simple emancipation,
Langston asserted, freedom must entail full citizenship for black men
and women. Attorney General Edward Bates had recently ruled that
Negroes were entitled to national citizenship by reason of nativity;
certainly, they were also entitled by patriotism. Blacks were *"universally*
loyal, and that was more than could be said of any other race in this
land. All wanted to fight for liberty. . . . No white man would go lower
in the dirt or higher in the air for his country than the colored citizen.
But do what we may we can't whip the rebels without the help of the
negro. God has ordained it, and you must call the negro to your aid
or perish."[19]

But the day ended in anxious anticlimax. Although "all felt the great
moment was at hand," the proclamation did not arrive. Langston and
his townsmen were not reassured until evening of the next day when
the train brought newspapers. Then, spontaneously, the crowd on
the streets surged to the chapel. Eighty-two-year-old John Keep, the
trustee whose deciding vote had initiated Oberlin's own racial revolution, assumed the chair. At Keep's request, Langston read aloud the
entire proclamation. Everyone stood, and in "ringing tones" he read it
again. Only prayer, offered by Professor Cowles in trembling voice,
remained to complete the meeting. Once out into the night, the community delighted in fireworks, a great bonfire, and the roaring of the
"old six-pounder" cannon on Tappan Square. In the early dawn, black
Oberliners marched in procession to Langston's home. Touched by this

tribute, exultant in the historic moment, conscious of the "moral investments" of his black and white co-agents in abolitionism over the decades, Langston spoke only a few words "pertinent to the hour." The *News* concluded: "Never did we see an *extempore* demonstration on the part of a people so pleasant and appropriate. . . . We doubt if Oberlin ever felt more genuinely happy."[20]

With the announcement in the Emancipation Proclamation that the former slaves would be welcomed into the armed forces, Langston eagerly anticipated the commencement of black northern recruitment. Cleveland blacks organized a grand jubilee to celebrate the proclamation on the evening of January 16, 1863, and invited Langston to speak. Despite falling snow and bitter cold, the large National Hall was packed. Admission was 10 cents, supper, 40 cents. For Langston, it was an evening to evoke memories. The featured speaker was Frederick Douglass, whom an eighteen-year-old John Mercer first had met in Cleveland in 1848 at his own first black National Convention. One-time Lane Rebel James A. Thome, Langston's professor of rhetoric at Oberlin, was in attendance, a reminder not merely of boyish speeches. It was Thome who had called Harper's Ferry a "signal fire . . . to forewarn the South of the coming outburst that shall pour red hot lava into every master's dwelling." The program also included Oberlin's John Watson, retelling his role in the Rescue. Then there were David Jenkins and Peter Clark—fellow veterans of January's freezing convention halls and August's scorching picnic grounds as they had grappled with the intractable problems of a half-freedom shackled to slavery. In his speech, Langston, comparing the Declaration of Independence with the proclamation, declared that the latter marked the divorcement of the Republic from the slave oligarchy, rendering a "more perfect definition" of the Declaration with its promise of freedom and equality. Ardently, Langston advocated the right and duty of black men to fight alongside whites. Noting that his college friend Jacob Dolson Cox was now a general, he offered to fight as a common soldier under Cox's command. "Sooner or later" black Ohioans would fight for freedom and citizenship.[21]

Soon afterward, blacks across the North, as Langston proclaimed, got "just the opportunity they needed." In January 1863, Massachusetts's abolitionist Governor John A. Andrew, earlier advised to "Drop the nigger" when he proposed black recruitment, finally gained authorization for a black volunteer regiment. Because Massachusetts's small black population held an enlistment potential of only four hundred men, Andrew, who envisioned a select regiment that would be a model for the North, secured permission from other loyal governors to recruit in their states. With "neither means nor men," as Langston noted, supplied by the federal government, Andrew persuaded George L. Stearns, the affluent and socially prominent Boston merchant, to organize fund-raising and recruitment. One of John Brown's financial backers and a long-time abolitionist who boasted of having cultivated affiliations with black northern leaders "for years, and they now come in play," Stearns established white support committees across the North and sought out prominent black men as his chief recruiters.²²

For Langston, as for other black leaders, the major consideration was equity. Would black soldiers receive the same pay, treatment, and protection against southern reprisals as white soldiers? Governor Andrew, referring to his interviews with Secretary of War Edwin M. Stanton, repeatedly offered assurances. Because the commissioning of black officers was forbidden, Andrew intended to appoint young white men of abolitionist sympathies. But in every other respect—pay, bounty, equipment, protection—free black men would be "soldiers of the Union—nothing less and nothing different."²³

At Stearns's invitation, Langston conferred with him, first in Buffalo, where Stearns was setting up headquarters for the Organization for Recruiting Colored Men in the Free States, and, subsequently, at a large meeting in Philadelphia. Stearns was impressed. Besides Langston's capability as an orator and ties with black leaders, he boasted a broad popular following among the black citizenry—no small asset since Ohio, according to census projections, contained a black enlistment potential of some seven thousand, by far the largest of any northern state after New York and Pennsylvania, each with more than ten thousand. After the Philadelphia meeting, Stearns offered Langston appointment as the chief recruiting agent for the West, responsible for consulting on the recruitment effort and for addressing "great popular assemblies . . . in the great cities and important rural districts." Langston consented, satisfied that Andrew and Stearns "appreciated most fully" the black expectations surrounding this crucial enterprise.²⁴

Langston faced serious difficulties in helping raise the Massachusetts regiment. In Ohio, Illinois, and Indiana, all notorious for their Black Laws, the repeated rejection of black attempts to fight combined with the recent manifestations of racism to discourage many Negroes. Only too familiar with coarse jests from white northerners and threats from the South about the fate of "nigger soldiers," these men were justifiably skeptical of the terms of military service and its effectiveness in securing citizenship rights. General William Tecumseh Sherman of Ohio expressed the opinion of many whites, in and out of the army, when he hoped Negro soldiers would "be used for some side purposes and not be brigaded with our white men. . . . The Companies prefer now to be rid of Negroes—they desert the moment danger threatens. . . . I won't trust niggers to fight yet." A Republican editor in Cincinnati made the argument that, with northern white opinion inexorably opposed to granting the Negro either political rights or an economic foothold, the black man, "if he is a rational being, . . . must certainly see he has nothing to gain by becoming a partisan to the war." Nor could blacks find much motivation for enlistment in the cynical case advanced by white proponents that black soldiers would spare white lives. At the same time, blacks had to weigh their somewhat improved economic condition brought on by the war against a more realistic understanding of the brutality, boredom, and bloodshed that soldiering entailed. "The fact is," asserted William H. Parham, a black Cincinnati teacher, as recruitment got underway, "our men—or we, I should more properly say—are like the whites." In 1861, "every man you met with wanted to go to war; but now when they know that hard fighting is to be done, hardships to be suffered, and privations endured, it is rather difficult, in fact, impossible, to get their courage screwed to the fighting pitch." But Parham would prove a poor diagnostician of the state of the black soul.[25]

Langston recruited troops from late March until well into June, first for the 54th Massachusetts Regiment and subsequently for the 55th. In speeches delivered in major cities and important rural districts throughout the West, he attempted to overcome black suspicions by "cautious, truthful statements" about the terms of black enlistment, and to inspire black courage by appeals to the highest aspirations of black manhood. Reminding his listeners of the "great changes" in both public sentiment and law propelling blacks nearer to freedom and citizenship, Langston declared that "God was favoring the downtrodden and oppressed." The North "was pledged to the cause of Freedom" by the Emancipation Proclamation; the South was "simply fighting for slavery" in insane pursuit of its own destruction. Black southerners in the Union forces already were proving their mettle; black northerners "should not stand aloof from this contest and say they had not a country. They had a country, and it was their duty to fight for it. . . . They should be willing to pass through a baptism of blood, if need be, that the nation might at last come out purified." "The Government cannot crush out this wicked rebellion without the help of the Negro. It can't be did."[26]

Such speeches were a key element in an evolving recruitment pattern that made use of Langston's contacts with local black leaders and drew on a sense, dating from his boyhood in Cincinnati, that successful political drives as much as celebration should involve, as nearly as possible, all members of the black community. Young white army officers delegated by Stearns opened recruiting offices in the larger cities, frequently putting black recruiters in charge, and assembled a black committee to organize one or more "war meetings" that Langston addressed. A soldiers' aid society, including women, usually was formed, while Langston stimulated the creation of groups to raise funds to buy flags for the regiment. As a black Cincinnatian noted, the work proceeded "very privately" at the start. But Stearns's initial fear of exciting opposition soon faded, as he found that Republicans wanted Negroes in the war, and everyone else wanted them out of sight. Metropolitan dailies soon conferred respectable notice on Langston's appearances, such as: "Negro Recruiting," "Black Regiment," "What the Colored Men Think of the War."[27]

Langston's own family became deeply involved. Charles Langston, back from a stint as teacher among the contrabands in Kansas, became an agent, working sometimes with his brother and sometimes alone throughout the midwestern states. O. S. B. Wall left his cobbler's bench to serve as "state [Ohio] Agt to organize the colored settlements for the purpose of facilitating colored enlistments." By May, Wall would be manning an office in Columbus with several sub-agents. Carrie Langston, working with her friend Fanny Jackson, the Oberlin student who composed a long poem in honor of the 54th, started fund-raising for a regimental banner that ultimately would go to the 55th.[28]

Langston's efforts proved successful from the start. His earliest recruits for the 54th came from Cleveland and Oberlin. In Cleveland, where volunteers had been drilling on their own since mid-February, Langston addressed a mass meeting on March 30. Two days later some thirty men, led by barber J. C. Greene, left for Massachusetts, while another company, organized by Charles Langston, readied itself for departure.[29]

In the first days of April some of Oberlin's "most industrious and respected colored townsmen," including several fugitive slaves, left for Massachusetts, each man bearing a hurriedly collected purse of $4 and a Bible. Some twenty black Oberliners, including Carrie's two half-brothers, John and Albert Wall, were accepted into the 54th. At least five of the Oberlin men became noncommissioned officers: John Wall, regimental color bearer; Henry L. Patterson, orderly sergeant; Augustus Ward, first sergeant; John L. Barker, sergeant; and Henry J. Peal, corporal of the color guard. A wartime fugitive who had attended a school for contrabands in Oberlin, Peal wrote his former teacher: "It makes me proud that two of the Oberlin boys [John Wall and himself] carry the first flags that ever the Colored man could call his country's flag." In the 54th's famous charge on Fort Wagner, South Carolina, Color Sergeant Wall, severely wounded, fell in the outer trench, only to have the colors caught up and carried to the top of the parapet by Sergeant William H. Carney. Peal and Carney both were honored with the Gillmore medal for their gallantry in the assault. John Wall recovered to become town constable in postwar Oberlin; Peal, severely wounded at Olustee, Florida, in February, 1864, died of acute dysentery the following July 24 and was buried in the military cemetery at Beaufort, South Carolina.[30]

Accompanied by his brother Charles, Langston was in Chicago by April 13 to launch his western tour. Boasting a black population of about a thousand in 1860, the city was a favorable point of departure. Coincidentally, Charles Lenox Remond also arrived to recruit for the 54th, while Martin R. Delany likewise was on hand to solicit funds for his church in Chatham, Ontario. John Langston smoothly shaped this embarrassment of black talent into a "large and enthusiastic" mass meeting chaired by Chicago's most important black civic leader, the prosperous merchant-tailor John Jones.

As the major speaker, Langston elicited "storms of applause," after which he read a letter from Delany's son Toussaint asking his father's consent for his enlistment in the 54th. On this cue Delany, who was being wooed from emigrationist visions by new American realities, explained the terms of enlistment. Himself destined to be one of the scarcely one hundred black commissioned officers (the vast majority either in the Louisiana Native Guard or chaplains and surgeons) appointed during the war, Delany noted his own concurrence in the current bar on black field officers because he believed none yet "eligible or capable," but emphasized that otherwise equal treatment would apply. Within two days of the meeting, forty-five black Chicagoans volunteered.

While Charles Langston remained to manage a recruiting station, John Langston moved on to Galesburg, location of antislavery Knox College, where thirteen "stout able-bodied fellows" immediately joined the lists. When the Galesburg recruits passed through Chicago a few days later, the black citizenry there already was so well organized that black women "abundantly" supplied refreshments, and supporters cheered as the recruits marched to the depot. Jotting a quick note home that the work "was going on finely," Langston traveled on through the black settlements of Illinois and Indiana. At Richmond, Indiana, a large audience, both white and black, heard "that eloquent champion of freedom," and a number of black men responded to his call.[31]

In May, as the 54th filled and recruitment for the 55th began, Langston tirelessly concentrated his energies on the large black population in central and southern Ohio. He spoke in ten different towns and cities during one eleven-day period alone. At Xenia, where seventeen volunteers stepped forward after his first address to "an immense audience," Langston would recall that seventy-five men eventually were recruited for the 54th. In Cincinnati, besides a full company earlier enrolled, from May 13 to June 13 some two hundred men signed on at the office managed by a Negro agent; when spotted in Cleveland, some fifty of them were marching to the depot "singing the John Brown song." By the last days of May, when the 54th received its orders to move South, the rate of recruitment of black Ohio volunteers for the 55th was so brisk that 250 men reportedly passed through Cleveland during a single three-day period.[32]

Langston took justifiable pride in the numbers, competence, and performance of the men recruited under his charge for the pioneering Massachusetts regiments. Regimental rolls indicate an impressive contribution. The 54th listed 214 recruits from Ohio, Indiana, and Illinois. Of the 158 Ohioans, their ages ranging from 17 to 45, the great majority—more than two-thirds—had worked at skilled or semi-skilled occupations.[33]

Langston's contribution to the 55th was even greater. On June 10, with the regiment all but filled, he told hometown friends of having spoken through the West, from Buffalo to Chicago, and all over Ohio "with the most flattering success." Everywhere he had found "colored men enthusiastic for the Union, and ready and anxious to prove their loyalty by their deeds." The 55th's rolls show well over a third—375 recruits—from Ohio, Indiana, and Illinois. Ohioans alone numbered 222, a total nearly twice as large as Pennsylvania and far greater than any other northern state.[34]

In recognition of the 55th's origins, Langston, using the money earlier collected plus a healthy sum from his own pocket, $225 in total, ordered colors for the regiment in the name of the "Colored Ladies of Ohio." The heavy silk regimental banner in rich orange and blue featured an embroidered American eagle under a cloud pierced by the sun's rays and the inscription, "Liberty or Death." Three American flags, one large and two small, accompanied the banner. Displaying the colors at meetings that he arranged across the state, Langston exulted that the Stars and Stripes were "no longer typical to the slave of 'Fugitive Slave Laws,' but of Liberty itself."[35]

With Langston's success, Ohio Governor Tod's attitude toward black recruitment was changing. All that spring, as the 55th's commanding officer would recollect, white Ohioans had considered it "a good joke to get the 'darkies on to Massachusetts'—a joke that was bitterly repented when Ohio . . . tried in vain to get those same 'darkies' credited to her quota [of men to be supplied, by draft if the number of volunteers was insufficient, for the Union army]." Tod had maintained his opposition to an Ohio black regiment and ignored the Massachusetts effort until mid-May, when Langston secured a meeting with him. Aware that Tod's silence rankled black Ohioans, Langston informed him of the progress of black enlistment and tactfully requested his assistance in building morale through a statement of support and a request to Governor Andrew that black Ohioans be organized into separate companies. Tod complied. In a letter to Langston for use with the public, he gave assurances of the government's commitment to black recruitment and advised black Ohioans "disposed to enter the service" to join the Massachusetts regiments. Subsequently, Tod attempted without success not only to have the black recruits counted toward Ohio's draft quota, but also to secure the appointment of white Ohioans to command posts in the 55th. Tod's attempts reflected a growing sentiment, extending from Ohio's adjutant general to the irate Toledo Democrat who, on seeing fifty blacks from his city volunteer for Massachusetts, complained bitterly to Republican Congressman James M. Ashley. " 'Why,' said Ashley, 'I thought you wanted to get rid of them.' 'But,' said the Democrat, 'I want the city to have the benefit of them when the draft comes.' " Although Tod continued to deny any intention of forming a black regiment, on May 27 he requested authorization to do just that. Secretary Stanton refused the request, advising that the 55th be completed first. "If it proves a success there will be enough left to give a regiment or more in Ohio."[36]

When Langston arrived in Columbus in mid-June to show the 55th's banners, he received an urgent message from the Ohio chief executive. Tod explained that the war department had just granted permission to raise an Ohio Negro regiment and asked Langston to direct the effort. O. S. B. Wall, appointed on June 17 as general recruiting agent, already had persuaded fifty-eight volunteers who were in Columbus and no longer needed for the 55th to be the Ohio regiment's first enlistees. Not without pangs, for Langston had been looking forward to presenting the colors to the 55th in Massachusetts himself, he accepted the offer of a newly solicitous Tod to forward them at his own expense, and, although insistent on first receiving clearance from Governor Andrew, undertook organization of the Ohio recruitment.[37]

He anticipated two major obstacles in raising the regiment. Unlike Massachusetts, Ohio appropriated no state funds for bounties or for the welfare of black soldiers' dependents. The lack of provision for families, a black Cincinnatian believed, had led many black Ohioans to volunteer for the 54th and 55th rather than risk being drafted by their home state. Planning the recruitment in consultation with the governor's private secretary, Langston decided to try a private subscription drive headed by former governor Dennison to fund bounties "equal to that paid in Massachusetts." The second problem concerned what one Republican editor termed "a lingering suspicion on the part of the colored men" that Ohio would not accord its black volunteers the same impartial treatment as Massachusetts.

In the first days of recruitment, in person and through official statements, Tod promised that black volunteers would be "placed on the same footing, as to pay, bounty, equipments, rations, etc., as the White troops." While the flags destined for the 55th Massachusetts fluttered from the steps of the capitol's east front and Langston looked on, Tod adopted a radical tone in a speech to a group of black recruits. He advised black Ohioans that the only way to "get rid" of prejudice and enjoy the "rights and privileges" accorded white citizens was "to fight for them." Although the Ohio state bounty might not, he conceded, be as large as that of Massachusetts, in all other respects the black volunteer would "be treated like the white soldier."[38]

Within little more than a week, a buoyant Langston could report that nearly three hundred men had enlisted. "My Colored Reg't is progressing handsomely," Tod wired Stanton in late June. "They are expecting the usual pay & bounty allowed white Soldiers. Will they get it?" Stanton's reply was a bombshell. Army pay for whites ranged from $13 per month for privates and corporals, plus $3.50 in clothing allowances, to around $20 at the sergeant level. Federal bounty varied, but currently ran about $40 and, with other payments, could amount to as much as $400 over a five-year period. Coincident with creation of the Bureau for Colored Troops in May, Stanton, despite his earlier approval of equal compensation for Negro soldiers, had requested an opinion on the matter from department solicitor William Whiting. The solicitor's interpretation, based on the 1862 Militia Act, restricted payment of black soldiers to the specified amount for reimbursement of persons of African descent for incidental services to the military. Although Whiting's ruling had been promulgated in an order to all army commanders on June 4, Stanton had made no other announcement of the switch in policy. On June 27, he wired the news to Tod: no bounty—and $10 a month for all black soldiers. Three dollars for clothing also was to be deducted, dropping the monthly stipend to a mere $7.[39]

Langston was angry at this betrayal. Firing off urgent notes to Governor Andrew, Secretary of State William Seward, and other prominent white Republicans, he protested that black men were "asked to take an inferior position as soldiers." That same day, June 28, the governor's office made public the exchange of wires with Stanton, adding lamely that the already initiated subscription fund for state bounty payments also would make up the salary differential.[40] With the deception exposed to black Ohioans, Langston pondered his next step.

The irony of his position was that he could not publicly declare his conviction that the discriminatory payment policy rested on a faulty interpretation of the law without further hindering the Ohio recruitment effort. Still, working behind the scenes, he did his utmost to change it. His major instrument was Governor Andrew's response to his protest. Not yet aware that the ruling also affected the Massachusetts 54th and 55th regiments—both of which would engage in an extended pay boycott until their compensation was equalized—Andrew disputed Whiting's ruling. In a long letter to Langston, he contended that authorization for raising the Massachusetts black regiments lay not in the Militia Act of 1862, but rather in the July 1861 law governing regular volunteer recruitment, and encouraged Langston to seek the same authorization for the Ohio regiment. Delighted with this "clear and manly" interpretation, Langston quickly shared it with white Ohio officials. Dennison concurred that Andrew "states the law; his logic is irresistible"; U.S. Supreme Court Justice Noah H. Swayne of Columbus privately agreed. (Indeed, Andrew's argument essentially anticipated the later overturn of Whiting's ruling by Attorney General Bates, the basis for the congressional settlement finally arrived at in June 1864 that Negro troops from the North were entitled to equal pay from the date of enlistment.) In urgent pleas wired twice within a five-day period in mid-July, Governor Tod sought the desired authorization from Stanton, but without success.[41]

Langston may well have suspected that political, far more than legal, considerations underlay the decision to shortchange black soldiers.[42] Long before Lincoln's admission to Frederick Douglass that the discriminatory payment policy seemed "a necessary concession" to popular prejudice, it must have seemed evident that the administration was casting about for ways to diffuse the racial equality issue in the fall state election campaigns. In the event, Ohio Democrats would indeed charge that black enlistment was a poorly disguised instrument for achieving racial equality, and that the Negro was "a barbarian" who made war "by the destruction and rapine of women and children."[43]

Seeking to contain the damage, Langston appealed to his people. In a public letter issued July 3, less than a week after receipt of Stanton's telegram, Langston admitted that the unequal pay decision contradicted manifold prior assurances by "men high in authority, and men occupying exalted positions socially," offered "in private conversations, public addresses and carefully-written documents." Notwithstanding, military service offered blacks the chance to display "our genius and power; our skill and heroism as soldiers, and by our brave and manly deeds . . . challenge the respect and admiration of the world." Further—here Langston surely had in mind a heightening of group solidarity and political consciousness like that manifested by the 54th and 55th's subsequent pay boycott—military service offered "thorough organization . . . the great need of the colored American." Most importantly, it was the opportunity through which "we may achieve for ourselves and our race freedom and enfranchisement. . . . In our estimation, money is trash. But liberty is a living substance, and like God, its author, is immortal. . . . Let us not hesitate. Let our conduct be characterized by promptness and determination. Shall this regiment be promptly filled? To the Colored Men of Ohio the appeal is made. Let us not be disgraced, but let honor distinguish our conduct. . . . Pay or no pay, let us volunteer."[44]

The three companies already assembled at Camp Delaware, the training grounds north of Columbus, would furnish the first major test of the black resolve. These "fine looking and well-behaved colored soldiers," the nucleus of the regiment, as Langston put it, had volunteered before announcement of the discriminatory payment policy. Half had joined as the result of his personal effort. Soon after the Ohio recruitment began, Captain Asel P. Dunlap, one of Langston's young white assistants in the Massachusetts effort, had wired him that a large group of black irregulars, training at the Athens County fairgrounds, had refused to allow him to enter their camp. Langston immediately took the train to Athens and sought out the town banker, who provided him with a note of introduction and a saddle horse. Spirits lifting with the beauty of the late afternoon, the recruiter rode out to the fairgrounds. After formally presenting his credentials to a black sentinel, Langston was granted an interview—still outside the gate—with the "captain." This officer, who had raised his irregulars himself with the intention of joining a Massachusetts regiment, turned out to be "a mere boy," eighteen-year-old Milton M. Holland. Son of a one-time governor of Texas, educated at the Albany Colored School in Athens, and employed as a shoemaker, Holland struck Langston as a natural leader of "remarkable native intelligence." Holland interviewed the older man thoroughly before deciding to permit him to speak to his troops. Inside the camp, with mingled admiration and amusement, Langston heard the sounds of fife and drum and noted the rough military precision with which these rural recruits formed their hollow square. Before sundown, 149 men, on hearing Langston's appeal, signed his rolls. Overnight the friendly banker procured a silk flag from Cincinnati, and the next morning it was presented to the company in the town itself "with no little éclat," to Langston's eyes. The volunteers set off for Camp Delaware in high spirits.[45]

But Holland and his Athens County men, along with the other black recruits, who included a large Washington County contingent led by forty-four-year-old Thomas Solomon Grimes, soon had ample reason for disillusionment. White area farmers, smarting from the loss of chickens and pigs to white thieves from two regiments previously stationed in the camp, greeted the black recruits with fear and outrage. Far more serious, because it seemed to epitomize the government's attitude toward them, was the lack of proper medical care, weapons, and even clothing. As late as the last week of September, no surgeon would be attached to the regiment, no hospital stores could be drawn, and sixty men, many "very sick," lay in "narrow and inadequate" quarters with "no conveniences." For at least the first three months, moreover, drill was conducted with "inferior, condemned arms," although "first-class" weapons were promised before entrance into the field. Until mid-July, when Tod belatedly ordered clothing issued, the men lacked even the uniforms to identify them as soldiers.[46]

Thus, the announcement of the discriminatory pay came as the final straw. With the government having broken its contract with them on almost every count, many of the men prepared to quit the camp. Informed of their disaffection, Tod on July 17 wired Captain Lewis McCoy, the regiment's commander, to persuade the men to remain until he and a black recruiter, who turned out to be Langston, could arrive. "They will disgrace themselves and their Race forever by abandoning the Camp at this time." [47]

Once there, the governor and Langston candidly explained the situation and offered to release the men and pay their travel expenses home. Although the arrival of the uniforms and, probably, the payment of small bounties—$3 each—helped to mollify the soldiers, in Langston's estimation, the crucial factor was the conduct of Milton Holland. Both Grimes and Holland "held their respective companies completely under their influence and control, and either, when the explanations alluded to were given, might have directed his men to leave the camp and they would have gone." Nonetheless, Holland and his men "were decided and manly at once in their course, thus greatly influencing Mr. Grimes and his men to remain, and so not a single man of the three hundred left the camp." Holland, who impressed more than one observer as "Cromwellian" in his zeal, shared Langston's ardor for the black cause. "Though we shall fall struggling in our blood for right and justice, for freedom of our brothers in bondage, . . ." the young soldier would declare, "our home and fireside will be protected" by God, by Lincoln, the black man's "Moses," and by "our old friend, Governor Tod." The Negro soldier "must cast aside all mercenary compensation, spring forth to the call, and show to the world that you are men. . . . Give me liberty or give me death!" Langston left Camp Delaware with the patriotic vows of "the leaders and every man" ringing in his ears, a hopeful echo of his own faith sounding through the pall cast by the pay decision.[48]

But the discriminatory pay and bounty policy continued to fester. As David Jenkins informed Secretary of the Treasury Salmon Chase, "our men want the same pay." Possibly the politest expression of the sentiment Langston would hear came from a black man in southeastern Ohio, who stated simply: "Now men only want, when they do the work of men, to be assured they will be treated as men." The policy entailed a continuing psychological conflict for the black soldiers between the pride of their own patriotic sacrifice and the shame of accepting shoddy treatment for themselves and their families. By late September, as Oberlin's Professor Peck learned when he visited Camp Delaware, the financial pinch on some families had already become severe. Lt. Col. Giles W. Shurtleff, a thirty-two-year-old graduate of Oberlin College and seminary and one-time Latin tutor, told Peck that his men often asked for furloughs, showing him letters from home as justification. Their wives wrote "that they and their children are actually starving that their neighbors will not help them and that the County Commissioners say that the relief fund is 'not for niggers,' and that their husbands must come and bring help. 'We have to refuse them all,' the Col. added, 'but it is heartrending to do so.' "[49]

In spring of the following year, when the regiment had seen action and Congress still had taken no steps to equalize the pay, the strain would tell even on Orderly Sergeant Holland. During his several visits to the regiment, Peck, like Langston, had been impressed by the "clear, open intelligent countenance," soldierly figure, "modest and handsome" manners, self-respect and superior bearing of the youthful sergeant, singled out to him initially as "one of the best men in the regiment." Later, he was surprised to find Holland stripped of his chevrons and "slouching and sullen" in the ranks. Holland explained that his men had "kept coming to me until I was worried out," complaining of their families' deprivations. He had "gotten them into the scrape," and they wanted him to tell them " 'how we are to get out.' " Besides, he "was doing a commissioned officer's work in keeping company accounts, but my pay was only seven dollars a month, and when white sergeants asked me what I got, I was ashamed to tell them and almost ashamed to own that I was a sergeant." When the depressed and irritable Holland had snapped back at an officer's sharp words, he had lost his rank. Peck could only beg his young friend "not to throw himself away; there was a better day near at hand, and then all would be righted."[50]

In the meantime, although relieved and moved by the altruism of Holland and the other black recruits, Langston faced a Sisyphean task. The pool of black Ohioans able and willing to enlist had been shrunken by recruitment for Massachusetts, a Pennsylvania regiment, and the navy (which followed an equal payment policy)—a total estimated by one observer at a thousand men. Moreover, many other black Ohioans had found employment at better wages in the transportation service, or as army servants, teamsters, and cooks. To further complicate matters, a general economic improvement meant that by fall, even black civilian laborers were enjoying higher wages. For a state that had long abused them, for a government that, in Andrew's words, had "cruelly misled" them, for an insulting $7 a month, how could Langston convince black men in Ohio to risk their families and their own lives? Tod himself deemed the inferior pay an "insurmountable objection."[51]

At the same time, even Langston's organization of the recruitment was severely restricted by lack of funds. Despite his initial cheerfulness about the subscription fund's prospects, the fund-raising committee progressed at snail's pace. Reminders of white self-interest—"Every colored man who enlists, saves one white man from the conscription"—proved ineffectual. Scarcely $3,000, or about one-fourth of the initial goal, was raised between the end of June and early November. In addition to paying part of the transportation and subsistence costs of the black recruits, the fund paid meager bounties—about $3—and the standard $2 to recruiting agents for each man enlisted. By mid-September, the financial situation would be so bleak that Wall, by all accounts one of the most effective recruiters, had to be dropped from the roster. As Wall noted, Tod "told me that my services were very necessary, [but] that he had not a dollar to pay me with and that he could not ask me to work for nothing." [52]

In August, Langston would add fund-raising to his duties. Although Oberlin and Elyria neighbors would respond, most white Ohioans remained indifferent. In late September a Columbus correspondent would report: "Langston is now in the southern part of the State getting recruits, and excuses for not contributing to the expenses of raising this regiment." At a time when Rhode Island was advertising in Ohio a $275 bounty offer for each Negro who would join its own regiment, "How can our gallant John M. Langston, and other recruiting officers, with not a dollar to offer, compete with these distant States, save these recruits to the credit of Ohio, and lessen our numbers to be drafted?" In a last-ditch appeal, Judge Dickson of Cincinnati, formerly commander of the "black brigade," would remind his townsmen that, although large numbers of its black residents had volunteered, the city had "done little or nothing for this regiment." Committee chairman Dennison would add a final entreaty in early November. "No regiment in Ohio," he pointed out, "has been raised with so small an expenditure of money."[53]

The venomous racial climate surrounding the upcoming state election also exerted a discouraging effect on the potential black volunteer, and even made recruiting itself a hazardous undertaking. Some "Copperheads" and "Butternuts," as opponents called pro-South Democrats, reportedly had gone "nigger mad." Attempting to recruit in southeastern Ohio in early summer, Langston was prevented from even entering the town of Lancaster. "When we want niggers to go to war," a prominent citizen announced, "we will get them up ourselves." Racial tension in nearby Circleville was so taut that Langston, rather than risk arranging a meeting, saw potential recruits in private. "Your services in the rebellion in sending regiments of troops to the front," one of Langston's young admirers later would remark, was "accomplished frequently at risk of life."[54]

Nevertheless, Langston continued to throw himself into the Ohio recruitment, criss-crossing the state and speaking almost daily. On more than one occasion he arrived for his engagement seemingly exhausted in strength only to hold the "uninterrupted attention" of his audience for the better part of two hours. Again and again he appealed to black manhood and patriotism, reinforcing these appeals with reports of black heroism in battle, now involving black Ohioans. The Massachusetts 54th's assault on Fort Wagner in mid-July had dramatically vindicated the hope of Corporal Peal of Oberlin that he and his comrades would "prove themselves men."[55]

In his enlistment appeals, Langston also offered the inducement of sympathetic and well-qualified officers—men, as he promised, of "thorough anti-slavery character." Tod appointed an officer corps notable for its liberal education and abolitionist convictions, including former students of Western Reserve, Denison, and Ohio Wesleyan. Oberlin was prominently represented. Lieutenant Colonel Shurtleff, highest ranking of the Oberlin alumni, had been captain of Oberlin's first volunteer company and had spent time in Richmond's Libby Prison before his return in the fall of 1862. In September 1864, Shurtleff, promoted to colonel, would assume command of the regiment and later would become a brigadier general.[56]

Seeking to counter early reports of inferior accommodations at Camp Delaware, Langston solicited a statement from one of the Oberlin officers, J. B. T. Marsh, an 1862 college graduate and local editor of the Lorain County News before his appointment as quartermaster. Second Lieutenant Marsh supplied a glowing report on camp conditions: the food, good and plentiful; the clothing, "best quality"; the men, making "fine progress in drill and all soldierly accomplishments." A thin trail of Republican journalists also issued helpful reports. "A more cleanly camp or set of men I have never seen," noted humorist Alfred Burnett. Burnett recounted the regiments' reaction to an experimental test of bravery by the camp commander. In a manner "to excite fears," Captain McCoy told the men of Confederate John Morgan's raid into Ohio and called for volunteers. To his surprise, "every soldier save a dozen" stepped forward.[57]

Langston called upon black leaders and institutions to boost morale. The Ladies' Soldiers Aid Society of Cleveland donated clothing and stationery. The Colored Soldiers Aid Society of Columbus, organized by the Reverend James Poindexter and his wife, celebrated the First of August with a community picnic at Camp Delaware, where a special train of six cars, plus "several more loads" from regular trains, brought visitors carrying baskets heavily laden with "good things." The First of August celebration in Zanesville, with Langston speaking both in the afternoon and evening, yielded ten recruits and, as one of the organizers proudly disclosed, a citizens' contribution of more than $100, which "we gave to Mr. Langston for the regiment."[58]

Striving to build momentum, Langston's long-time colleagues of the State Central Committee called a state convention, the first since 1860. Twenty-four official delegates from nine counties attended the three-day meeting at Xenia. On August 4, opening day, a crowd gathered for festivities at the county fairgrounds and then marched to the depot to greet Langston, but the train arrived without him. The next afternoon, however, having recovered from a brief illness, Langston delivered his oration, "The Hour and Duty of Colored Men to the Government."

Politically, he "thanked the Government for what it had done, and hoped it would do more"; patriotically, he extolled the "noble and daring" exploits of black soldiers. As a recruiter, he urged the "imperative duty" of black men to "come forward to defend their country and win their freedom." Praising Lincoln's recent pronouncement of retaliatory action for southern mistreatment of black prisoners, the convention strongly resolved: "That it is the duty of the colored people of Ohio to fill up at once, by volunteering, the noble colored regiment now being formed at Camp Delaware." The convention furnished Langston $30 for the bounty fund, as well as several recruits.[59]

Despite momentary optimism that, as Stearns's Columbus agent reported, the recruitment had "begun to rise above the difficulties that meet us at every turn," the total inched upward with demoralizing slowness. By August 7 some 520 men had enlisted; more than 200 more were needed. With funds all but depleted, Langston, after another Cincinnati speech, headed back to Lorain County. At Elyria and Oberlin, on the latter occasion joined by Shurtleff and Charles Langston, he succeeded in raising several hundred dollars. He would continue to plead for contributions at each recruitment stop. Even so, barely scraping by and without Wall, he would be forced to rely more and more on the voluntary efforts of state and local black leaders.[60]

Although scheduled to deliver the alumni address at the Oberlin commencement, Langston waived the honor to begin another tour. He began in Cleveland, where Charles Langston, Malvin, Ambush, and others held a follow-up meeting a few days later, then came Dayton, Cedarville in central Ohio, and back to the southeast. On September 10, at Berlin in Jackson County, where Langston's father's freed slaves had put down stakes twenty-nine years before, Charles A. Yancy and James Woodson led a day-long "grand basket war meeting," complete with picnic, martial music, and resolutions. For more than two hours Langston held the crowd "spellbound . . ., forcibly setting forth the necessity of sustaining the Government till it shall triumph over rebellion, and justice be enforced all over the land."[61]

By now with the Union victories at Gettysburg and Vicksburg, white Ohioans had come to believe that the government might triumph over rebellion. Furthermore, the conspicuous black valor in military engagements (not to mention black freedmen's contributions on southern plantations and as military laborers) had furnished Republicans with a telling rebuttal to Democratic racism. In a letter to a Union meeting at Springfield, Illinois, an emboldened Lincoln contrasted "some black men . . . with silent tongue, and clenched teeth, and steady eye, and well-poised bayonet," who were helping mankind on to peace, with "some white ones, . . . with malignant heart, and deceitful speech," who were striving to hinder it. Despite the added advantage of an improving economy, Republican anxieties were acute as the Ohio election day dawned in early October. The Peace Democrats turned out an even larger vote for their gubernatorial candidate Clement C. Vallandigham than in their 1862 congressional victories. But the Unionists compiled a majority of more than one hundred thousand for John Brough, a one-time Democratic state auditor. "Glory to God in the highest," Lincoln telegraphed, "Ohio has saved the Union."[62]

Ohio—and black soldiers earning $7 a day, as Langston, indulging a private sardonic moment, might have reflected. But the election results gladdened the black Republican, all the more because they were widely interpreted as ratification both of the Emancipation Proclamation and the use of black soldiers. While a white friend and college classmate, J. A. R. Rogers, a former missionary in Kentucky who would teach at postwar Berea College, organized communities in southern Ohio for Langston's appearances, the black recruiter made one last swing across the state. "The work goes steadily on," noted the Lorain County *News* as late as November 4. "Langston is untiring in his efforts." And only a few days later, after more than four and a half months, the Ohio black regiment was declared complete.[63]

The 5th U.S. Colored Troops, as the unit was designated, was organized into nine companies comprising nearly eight hundred men (two hundred more than the six hundred originally planned). A relatively youthful unit, three-fifths of the soldiers were between the ages of eighteen and twenty-five, and most of this group were under twenty-one. Obviously, it was the very young, their idealism and daring bolstered by relative freedom from family responsibilities, who had felt most able to disregard the pay restriction. Although nearly every community in the state was represented, some 80 percent came from the populous southern section, the two counties most heavily represented being Hamilton and Milton Holland's Athens.[64]

Ohio's first black regiment had been slighted for political gain by the government it was sworn to defend and gotten up on the cheap to save white Ohioans from the draft. These distasteful realities were embedded in its history. But the mostly painfully young black men who, with their idealistic, young white officers, composed the regiment held these realities subordinate to ideas and emotions involving manhood and morality. To these soldiers, even more than most, Langston understood, the state's symbolic recognition of their status as men mattered deeply.

Acting on his determination "that no regiment going into the service of the government should do so under richer or more beautiful colors,"

Langston took money contributed by black Ohioans, together with his own, and ordered flags and banners from the same Cincinnati firm that had created the standards for the 55th. "All splendid silk pieces," as one witness noted, they were inscribed, "Victory or Death!" Langston, equally resolved to mount impressive presentation ceremonies, prevailed upon outgoing governor Tod to bring along a full complement of white officialdom, civilian and military, and himself invited black families and friends to Camp Delaware on November 9. As part of the ceremony, Langston had hoped to be able to present small purses to each volunteer from a fund of his own collection. When the fund broke down to a mere $2.50 per man—enough to do little more than remind the soldier of governmental and public parsimony— Langston decided on a gesture of almost reckless generosity. He took the entire amount and bought a golden ring for the regiment's commander, Captain McCoy, and a gold watch and chain for Mrs. McCoy, which he planned to present in the name of the regiment.[65]

On the appointed day, the train bearing Langston and the official party, along with large numbers of black Ohioans and the Chillicothe brass band, arrived at the depot near Camp Delaware simultaneously with the first blizzard of the season—typical of the hardship that had dogged the organization of the regiment. It was Tod's turn for gallantry. Peering through the driving snow at the company of black soldiers sent to welcome them, striving to hold themselves at strict attention, the governor ordered conveyances dispensed with. Some grumbling, others joking, the state officials, the congressmen, the generals, the entire retinue trudged through the storm from the depot to the camp. While the wind blew "a furious gale," everyone ate standing up. Then, with the 5th U. S. Colored Regiment assembled, Langston, in the name of the colored men of Ohio, presented the banners: to be "borne into the thickest of the fight, but returned in due time, tattered and torn, . . . but untarnished by the taint of dishonor, or of cowardice."

Langston's second speech, presenting the regiment's gifts to the McCoys, brought tears to the surprised officer's eyes and cheers from the men. But it was not so much Langston's words as the speeches of Tod, Dennison, and other white officials—"boldly" endorsing abolition and the elimination of "all distinctions as to natural rights"—that seemed most meaningful to several radical observers. Beginning by asking the soldiers for the privilege of calling them "his boys," which they granted with a roar, the governor addressed them with "fatherly counsel." Beyond paternalism, however, Tod promised his best efforts toward winning equal treatment and pay for them and equal compensation for their families. "Who, three years ago," marveled a journalist, "could

have fancied our worthy Governor following a colored man like Langston, in a speech from the same stand, enunciating the same
sentiments—to an audience of blacks. The world moves, verily."[66]

Langston and most black Ohioans doubtless would have agreed. At
least for the moment, the soldiers of the Fifth, as they moved to a camp
near Norfolk, Virginia, could believe the goals they had enlisted to
achieve had been brought nearer by their own actions. Within days, a
detachment of the Fifth, sent out on a scouting mission, would return
to camp with several hundred liberated slaves riding in carts and wagons and astride horses, including some seventy men who joined their
own ranks, as well as a few guerrilla prisoners.[67]

The 5th U.S.C.T. would dig, fight, and die along with, sometimes
literally alongside, the Massachusetts 54th and 55th. Particularly
through frequent letters home from the Fifth's Oberlin-educated
officers,[68] Langston followed its progress, taking special interest in the
career of Milton Holland. Restored to the rank of orderly sergeant and
his old task of compiling the payrolls after a white officer proved incompetent, Holland felt relieved and exonerated by the congressional
action in June 1864 to equalize the black soldiers' pay. Promoted in
September 1864 to sergeant-major by Colonel Shurtleff (who himself
had been elevated to the command of the regiment), Holland shortly
thereafter participated conspicuously in the fighting around New Market Heights, Virginia. In charges on two separate Confederate strongholds on the same day, Lt. E. F. Grabill wrote Oberlin friends, the Fifth,
which had begun the morning with 540 men, suffered 340 killed,
wounded, or missing. Of fourteen officers, only five emerged unin-
jured. When the captain of Holland's own Company C, composed
mainly of Athens County men, was wounded early in the day, Sergeant
Holland took over the command and later led the second charge. Of
the twenty-one Congressional Medals of Honor awarded to black soldiers and sailors during the war, four went to men of the 5th U.S.C.T.,
including Milton M. Holland. (As a prominent figure in postwar
Washington, D.C., the younger man would become an intimate of the
Langston family.)[69]

While young men like Holland compiled their admirable records,
Langston himself chafed under the war department's refusal to commission black men as field officers. Linking personal ambition with
racial goals, he wanted to be appointed a colonel, "with authority to
recruit his own regiment and to officer it with colored men taken from
regiments already in the service and who had given evidence of high
soldierly qualities on the field of battle." Throughout the war, as he had
proposed the black regiment to Governor Tod, drilled as a second

lieutenant with his little company on the Oberlin village square, contributed money and energy to entice white Ohioans into the army even while blacks were excluded, and mounted his recruitment effort, he was achingly aware of the opportunity being denied him because of his race. Like several other prominent black northerners, including Frederick Douglass who had given up his newspaper in the belief, illusory as it turned out, that he was about to be commissioned as a recruiting officer, Langston aspired to a share of the military glory that so many of his white peers were reaping. At the same time, convinced that black troops would never receive full credit for their exploits nor be free to perform at their highest capacity under all-white officers, he was equally certain, then and until the end of his life, that under black officers their performance would be so exemplary that it would provide the needed leverage for the winning of black equality—"the complete redemption of the colored American from every proscription, legal and social."[70]

Finally, in early 1865—heeding the mounting insistence of congressional radicals, which echoed the demands of northern blacks, as well as the acute manpower needs of the invading Union forces—the War Department cautiously began to change its all-white officer policy. In late February, O. S. B. Wall, who had taken a leading role in recruiting a second Ohio black regiment, the 27th U.S.C.T., besides his work on the two Massachusetts regiments and the Fifth, applied for a commission. Recommended by Professor Peck, himself about to be appointed minister to Haiti, Wall proferred his services through William O. Dennison, the new postmaster general, with whom he was acquainted through their mutual involvement in the Ohio recruitment. When the subject of commissioning Negroes was broached at a cabinet meeting, Dennison suggested Wall; in turn, Secretary of War Stanton insisted that Colonel J. W. Foster, the chief recruiting officer of Negro troops, who was hostile to the idea of black officers, put through the commission. Having written a formal application on March 3, Wall underwent a personal examination by Foster, after which he was appointed the Union's first regularly commissioned black captain.[71]

Two weeks later Langston returned home from a speaking tour in the East barely in time to see his brother-in-law off to war. Before a large, hastily assembled crowd in the Oberlin College chapel, Peck, Wall's fellow prisoner during the Oberlin-Wellington Rescue, presented him with an elegant sword. By thus honoring him, Wall declared, his friends were acknowledging the government's "recognition of the great principle of the equality of all men . . . in deed as well as word." Langston added a few timely remarks. Both Wall and Martin

Delany, the first regularly commissioned black major in the Union forces, were assigned to the 104th Regiment, U.S.C.T., in South Carolina, initially to serve as recruiters.[72]

Langston wrote to Stanton on March 20. "I think if I had a respectable rank, in the service, I could make myself of special use in the Recruitment and Organization of colored Troops. I therefore ask to be commissioned as a Colonel." After a brief unembellished description of his qualifications, he requested an early reply. Rather than mail the letter, he took it to Representative James A. Garfield, his friend and fellow Radical who had just returned home to Hiram at the close of the congressional session. On March 28, enclosing Langston's letter, Garfield wrote Stanton, with whom he was well acquainted through his service on the House Military Affairs Committee. Complimenting him for breaking the ice in the appointment of black officers, Garfield emphasized how important it was "that those who are commissioned should not fail—and I know of no colored man in the U.S. and but few if any men—who could succeed so well as [Langston] would in command of a regiment." Langston had "probably done much more" in black recruitment "than any other Colored man in the U.S."[73]

Shortly thereafter, both men traveled to Washington where Garfield conducted Langston first to see Stanton and then, at the latter's direction, Foster. Upon Stanton's agreement to approve the commission should Foster find it feasible, and with Foster seemingly receptive, the two Ohioans parted in the belief that Langston's appointment and the black-officered regiment were assured. But, as Langston lingered anxiously in Washington, the quickening pace of war threatened to overtake his hopes. On April 3, five thousand Negro troops marched into Richmond. In Washington as people blocked the streets, mounting spontaneous processions with flags and bunting, surrounding the war office to clamor for news, cheering, waving hats, singing "Rally Round the Flag," embracing, a smiling black man kept exclaiming, "I say, sar, d'ye hear, de niggahs took Richmond." Even then, one of the first actions by Union forces in the fallen Confederate capital was black recruitment. Langston's services still might be needed. But on April 10, booming guns shook him from his hotel bed at dawn. Happy pandemonium erupted once more. Lee had surrendered to Grant at Appomattox Court House the previous day. Through the shock of joy Langston painfully realized that his dream was a victim of victory.[74]

At a memorial service for the black war dead in 1874, Langston would allude to "the troubles which beset him in raising the Ohio regiment." His success with the Fifth, as well as with the Massachusetts regiments, attested to the fiber of his practical and moral leadership. Of the non-slaveholding Union states, only Pennsylvania, with a black population much in excess of that in Ohio, would contribute more black troops. Langston credited the black conduct in the military and at home under the bitter duress of the war years to the strengths of black Ohioans themselves—strengths instilled over some three decades by black and abolitionist-assisted institutions. For example, he had only to look to Circleville in southeastern Ohio where white enmity had forced him to conduct recruitment in private. For years, doubtless since Oberlin student-teacher George B. Vashon, his old mentor, had inspired it in the early forties, the village's comparatively small black population had maintained the Vashon Literary Society. Through its weekly meetings featuring declamations, debates and essays, a black villager reported, "Many of our young men made commendable progress and, in proportion as their abilities were developed, they, of course, were convinced of their manhood and, consequently, inspired with a deeper love of liberty." It was thus inevitable that "when Ohio called for colored troops, the able bodied members of our Society, with but few exceptions, immediately joined the Army of Freedom."[75]

Langston would recollect at war's end that Governor Tod, at their first meeting, had admonished, " 'Sir, I want you to understand that I am not going to call the negroes till I have exhausted every resource of the white population.' But God thundered from a moral Sinai, 'slavery is to die, the negro is to fight, the negro is to be emancipated.' And Mr. Lincoln called us into the fight, and when we went, we went with more terror to the slaveholders than ever Spartan caused in the breast of his enemy, and we fought like men, brave and true, and put your finger on the time when and the place where the negro disgraced his arms or his uniform. You can't do it."[76]

NOTES

1. Cleveland *Leader*, Jan. 17, 1859; Lorain County *News*, Aug. 6, 1862.

2. St. Louis *Democrat*, Nov. 29, 1865, John Mercer Langston Scrapbook, Fisk University Library; John H. Scott et al. to William O. Dennison, Apr., 1861, Governor's Official Papers, 1861, Ohio Historical Society; J. B. Carrington to C. H. Langston et al., Apr. 21, 1861, quoted in *Anti-Slavery Bugle*, Apr. 27, 1861; Wendell P. Dabney, *Cincinnati's Colored Citizens* (Cincinnati, 1926; repr. New York: Johnson Reprint, 1970), p. 200; Cleveland *Plain Dealer*, Apr. 20, 1861; Charles H. Wesley, *Ohio Negroes in the Civil War* (Columbus, 1962), p. 15; William H. Parham to Jacob C. White, Oct. 12, 1861, Jacob C. White Papers,

Moorland-Spingarn Research Center, Howard University (compare Peter H. Clark, *The Black Brigade of Cincinnati.* . . . [Cincinnati, 1864; repr. New York: Arno Press, 1969], pp. 4–5); Cleveland *Leader*, Oct. 16, 1861.

3. Lorain County *News*, Apr. 24, 1861; Henry Peck to Editor, Ibid.; Beta to Editor, Apr. 22, 1861, Cleveland *Leader*, Apr. 23, 1861; Robert S. Fletcher, *A History of Oberlin College*, 2 vols. (New York, 1943), II, pp. 843–48, 881.

4. Elyria *Independent-Democrat*, Aug. 14, Sept. 4, Oct. 2, 1861; Lorain County *News*, Aug. 21, Sept. 4, July 24, 31, 1861.

5. "John M. Langston on the War," *Anglo-African*, Sept. 21, 1861; Lorain County *News*, Aug. 7, 1861, Mar. 5, Aug. 6, 1862.

6. Parham to White, Oct. 12, 1861, White Papers; David A. Gerber, *Black Ohio and the Color Line, 1860–1915* (Urbana, 1976), pp. 26–29; W. R. J. Clemens to A.M.A., Nov. 20, 1862, American Missionary Association Archives, Amistad Research Center, Tulane University (hereafter cited as AMA Papers).

7. Lorain County *News*, Aug. 6, 1862; Oberlin *Evangelist*, May 7, 1862; Cincinnati *Gazette*, Apr. 21, 1862; Leonard Harding, "The Cincinnati Riots of 1862," *Bulletin of the Cincinnati Historical Society* 25 (Oct. 1967):229–39; Peter H. Clark et al., "To the Respectable Citizens of Cincinnati," July 16, 1862, Cincinnati *Commercial*, July 17, 1862.

8. V. Jacque Voegeli, *Free but Not Equal: The Midwest and the Negro During the Civil War* (Chicago, 1967), p. 100; Lorain County *News*, July 9, 1862; Cincinnati *Commercial*, Aug. 1, July 23, 1862.

9. Lorain County *News*, July 9, 23, Aug. 6, 1862; Oberlin *Evangelist*, July 16, 1862.

10. William A. Jones to Simon Cameron, Nov. 27, 1861, quoted in *The Negro in the Military Service of the United States: A Compilation of Official Records, State Papers, Historical Abstracts etc., Relating to His Military Status and Service from the Date of His Introduction into the British North American Colonies* (Washington D.C., 1888), p. 483 (hereafter cited as *Negro in Military Service*); Lorain County *News*, July 24, Aug. 7, Oct. 2, 1861.

11. Lorain County *News*, Aug. 6, 1862.

12. Lorain County *News*, July 18, Aug. 6, 20, 1862; Oberlin *Evangelist*, July 30, Aug. 13, 1862.

13. Lorain County *News*, Aug. 6, 1862; John Mercer Langston, *From the Virginia Plantation to the National Capitol; or, The First and Only Negro Representative in Congress from the Old Dominion* (Hartford, 1894; repr. New York: Johnson Reprint, 1968), pp. 205–6.

14. Lorain County *News*, Aug. 6, 1862.

15. Cleveland *Leader*, Aug. 13, 1862; Clark, *Black Brigade*, passim; "Aleph" to Editor, Sept. 11, 1862, *Christian Recorder*, Sept. 20, 1862; Edgar A. Toppin, "Humbly They Served: The Black Brigade in the Defense of Cincinnati," *Journal of Negro History* 48 (April 1963):75–97.

16. Lorain County *News*, Sept. 10, 17, 24, 1862.

17. Lorain County *News*, Sept. 24, Oct. 15, 22, Nov. 12, 1862; Elyria *Independent-Democrat*, Oct. 3, 22, 1862.

18. Lorain County *News*, Dec. 21, 1862, Jan. 7, 1863.

19. Lorain County *News*, Jan. 7, 1863.

20. Ibid.; Langston, *Virginia Plantation*, p. 196.

21. Cleveland *Leader*, Jan. 14, 17, 1863; Cleveland *Plain Dealer*, Jan. 7, 17, 1863.

22. Chicago *Tribune*, Apr. 15, 1863; James M. McPherson, *The Negro's Civil War* (New York, 1965), p. 22; Langston, *Virginia Plantation*, pp. 199–201; Jos. C. G. Kennedy to J. P. Usher, Feb. 11, 1863, quoted in *Freedom, a Documentary History of Emancipation, 1861–1867*, series II, *The Black Military Experience*, ed. Ira Berlin et al. (New York, 1982), p. 88; George L. Stearns to William Whiting, Apr. 27, 1863, quoted in ibid., pp. 91–92.

23. John A. Andrew to George T. Downing, Mar. 23, 1863, quoted in *Negro in Military Service*, p. 1133.

24. Langston, *Virginia Plantation*, pp. 201–2; Luis F. Emilio, *History of the Fifty-Fourth Regiment of Massachusetts Volunteer Infantry* (Boston, 1894; repr. New York: Johnson Reprint, 1968), p. 14; Table 1: "Black Soldiers . . . by State," in *Black Military Experience*, ed. Berlin et al., p. 12.

25. Voegeli, *Free but Not Equal*, pp. 98–103; W. T. Sherman to John Sherman, Apr. 26, 1863, quoted in Ibid., p. 101; Cincinnati *Commercial*, July 23, 1862; William H. Parham to Jacob C. White, Jr., Mar. 28, 1863, White Papers.

26. Chicago *Tribune*, Apr. 15, 1863; M. F. Thomas to Editor, May 20, 1863, *National Anti-Slavery Standard*, May 30, 1863; Lorain County *News*, Apr. 22, 1863; Xenia *Torch-Light*, May 6, 13, Sept. 2, 1863.

27. *Ohio State Journal*, May 22, 1863; M. F. Thomas to Editor, May 20, 1863, *National Anti-Slavery Standard*, May 30, 1863; G. H. Graham to Editor, *Christian Recorder*, May 9, 1863; Xenia *Torch-Light*, May 13, 1863; Joseph C. Bustill to Jacob C. White, Mar. 20, 1863, Carter G. Woodson Papers, Library of Congress; George L. Stearns to John A. Andrew, Apr. 3, 1863, *Negro in Military Service*, p. 1163.

28. Chicago *Tribune*, Apr. 15, 22, 1863; "Occasional," *Christian Recorder*, May 9, 1863; O. S. B. Wall to Col. C. W. Foster, Mar. 3, 1865, in *Black Military Experience*, ed. Berlin et al., p. 93; Capitol City (Columbus) *Fact*, n.d., quoted in Lorain County *News*, May 27, 1863; *Ohio State Journal*, May 22, 1863; Lorain County *News*, Mar. 26, May 21, 1862, May 13, 1863; *Anglo-African*, n.d., quoted in Ibid., June 10, 1863.

29. Cleveland *Leader*, Feb. 7, 9, 16, Apr. 1, 1863; Lorain County *News*, Feb. 18, 1863; Cleveland *Herald*, Feb. 19, 1863.

30. Lorain County *News*, Apr. 15, May 6, Aug. 5, 12, Sept. 2, 1863, Apr. 13, 1864; Henry T. Peal to "Kind Lady," May 22, 1863, Ibid., June 24, 1863; George Washington Williams, *A History of the Negro Troops in the War of the Rebellion 1861–65* (New York, 1888; repr. New York: Bergman Publishers, 1968), pp. 199–200, 339; John Wall, Alumni Records, Oberlin College Archives. The other Oberlin recruits included: Joseph Asberry, J. W. Bradley, James E. Brown, Fielding C. Brown, Leander L. Howard, Howard Howe, William Mitchell, Harrison Nichols, Oliver B. Ridgeway, William Rutledge, Samuel Smith, John Walker, Edward Williams, Isaiah Wilson. Ages ranged from twenty to thirty-six, with the average twenty-four; 14 were single; 14 were

either skilled (4 farmers, shoemaker, mason, tailor, engineer, barber, harness maker, carpenter) or semiskilled (teamster, wagoner, student). Compiled from Lorain County *News*, Aug. 5, 12, 1863; Emilio, *History of the Fifty-Fourth*, pp. 339–88 (Peal's death mentioned on page 168).

31. "Occasional," *Christian Recorder*, May 9, 1863; Chicago *Tribune*, Apr. 15, 22, 1863; Berlin et al., eds., *Black Military Experience*, p. 310; Lorain County *News*, Apr. 15, 22, 1863; M. F. Thomas to Editor, May 20, 1863, *National Anti-Slavery Standard*, May 30, 1863.

32. A.P. Dunlap to Editor, *Ohio State Journal*, May 18, 1863; Lorain County *News*, May 13, 27, 1863; Xenia *Torch-Light*, May 6, 13, 20, 1863; Langston, *Virginia Plantation*, p. 201; Elyria *Independent-Democrat*, June 10, 1863; Belmont *Chronicle*, June 11, 1863; Cincinnati *Commercial*, May 13, 1863; Cincinnati *Gazette*, May 12, 29, June 13, 1863; Cleveland *Herald*, June 11, 1863.

33. Langston, *Virginia Plantation*, pp. 202–5; compiled from Emilio, *History of the Fifty-Fourth*, pp. 339–88.

34. Lorain County *News*, June 17, 1863; Norwood P. Hallowell, *The Negro as a Soldier in the War of the Rebellion* (Boston, 1897), pp. 7–8, 23–25.

35. Cleveland *Leader*, June 8, 1863; Cincinnati *Gazette*, June 9, 1863; *Liberator*, June 12, 1863; *Douglass' Monthly*, Aug. 1863; *National Anti-Slavery Standard*, Aug. 1, 1863; Lorain County *News*, June 10, 17, 1863.

36. Hallowell, *Negro as a Soldier*, p. 7; G. H. Graham to Editor, *Christian Recorder*, May 30, 1863; David Tod to John M. Langston, May 16, 1863; David Tod to John A. Andrew, May 16, 1863; Gen. David Hunter to Tod, May 4, 1863, all in Lorain County *News*, May 20, 1863; Cincinnati *Gazette*, May 20, 1863; *Ohio State Journal*, May 22, 1863; Whitelaw Reid, *Ohio in the War: Her Statesmen, Generals, and Soldiers*, 2 vols. (Columbus, 1893), I, pp. 176–77; David Tod to Edwin M. Stanton, May 27, 1863; Stanton to Tod, May 27, 1863, both in *Negro in Military Service*, pp. 1270, 1268.

37. Tod to Stanton, June 16, 1863; Stanton to Tod, June 16, 1863, both in *Negro in Military Service*, p. 1329; Cleveland *Leader*, June 25, 1863; David Tod to Press of Cincinnati, June 17, 1863, Cincinnati *Gazette*, June 18, 1863; Elyria *Independent-Democrat*, June 24, 1863; Cincinnati *Commercial*, June 27, 1863; O. S. B. Wall to George L. Stearns, Oct. 29, 1863, O. S. B. Wall, Military Service Records, National Archives; Index to Letters Sent, Administration of John A. Andrew, Apr. 15, 1861 to Jan. 6, 1866, pp. 353–54, no. 32460, Massachusetts Historical Society.

38. Joseph C. Bustill to Jacob C. White, June 11, 1863, Woodson Papers; Cincinnati *Gazette*, June 27, 1863; Elyria *Independent-Democrat*, July 1, 8, 1863; Cleveland *Leader*, June 25, 1863; Medina *Gazette*, June 27, 1863.

39. David Tod to E. M. Stanton, June 26, 1863, Edwin M. Stanton to Governor Tod, June 27, 1863, both in *Black Military Experience*, ed. Berlin et al., pp. 370, 362–64; Dudley Taylor Cornish, *The Sable Arm: Negro Troops in the Union Army, 1861–1865* (New York, 1956), pp. 184–87, 192; Elyria *Independent-Democrat*, July 8, 1863.

40. William H. Seward to J. M. Langston, July 1, 1863; Judge W. M. Dickson to J. M. Langston, June 30, 1863, both in Lorain County *News*, July 22, 1863; *Douglass' Monthly*, Aug. 1863; John A. Andrew to John M. Langston, July 4,

1863, *National Anti-Slavery Standard*, May 28, 1864; Cincinnati *Gazette*, June 27, 1863; Elyria *Independent-Democrat*, July 1, 8, 1863; State of Ohio, Executive Department, June 27, 1863, in Cincinnati *Commercial*, July 1, 1863.

41. John A. Andrew to John M. Langston, July 4, 1863; John M. Langston to Oliver Johnson, n.d., both in *National Anti-Slavery Standard*, May 28, 1864; David Tod to E. M. Stanton, July 14, July 18, 1863, both *Black Military Experience*, ed. Berlin et al., pp. 370–71.

42. Compare Herman Belz, "Law, Politics, and Race in the Struggle for Equal Pay During the Civil War," *Civil War History* 22 (Sept. 1976):197–213.

43. Frederick Douglass, *Life and Times of Frederick Douglass* (Hartford, rev. 1892; repr. New York: Collier Books, 1962), pp. 347–49; Voegeli, *Free but Not Equal*, pp. 125–31; Cincinnati *Enquirer*, July 8, 1863; Eugene Holloway Roseboom and Francis Phelps Weisenburger, *A History of Ohio* (New York, 1934), p. 283.

44. John M. Langston to the Colored Men of Ohio, July 3, 1863, Cincinnati *Gazette*, July 9, 1863.

45. Ibid.; Langston, *Virginia Plantation*, pp. 213–16; *Ohio State Journal*, May 18, 1863; G. H. Graham to Editor, *Christian Recorder*, May 30, 1863; Milton M. Holland, Co. C, 5th U.S. Colored Infantry, WC 710107, Military Service Records; H. W. Peck, "Sketches . . .," No. 5, Lorain County *News*, Dec. 7, 1864; *Official Roster of the Soldiers of the State of Ohio in the War of the Rebellion, 1861–1866* (Cincinnati, 1886), pp. 600–3.

46. Langston, *Virginia Plantation*, pp. 207–10; Lorain County *News*, Sept. 30, 1863; State of Ohio, *Executive Documents 1863* (Columbus, 1864), pt. 1, pp. 276, 275; Reid, ed., *Ohio in the War*, II, p. 916; Frank R. Levstik, "The Fifth Regiment, United States Colored Troops, 1863–1865," *Northwest Ohio Quarterly* 42 (Fall, 1970):87–88.

47. David Tod to Capt. Lewis McCoy, July 17, 1863, Adjutant General's Papers, Ohio Archives, Ohio Historical Society.

48. Langston, *Virginia Plantation*, pp. 207–8; William O. Dennison to People of Cincinnati, Cincinnati *Commercial*, Nov. 9, 1863; M. M. Holland to Editor, Athens *Messenger*, Feb. 4, 1864; Peck, "Sketches."

49. David Jenkins to Salmon P. Chase, July 24, 1863, Chase Papers, Library of Congress; D[avid] Cooper to editor, *Christian Recorder*, July 4, 1863; Lorain County *News*, Sept. 30, 1863.

50. Peck, "Sketches."

51. "Aleph" to Editor, Sept. 26, 1863, *Christian Recorder*, Oct. 3, 1863; Cincinnati *Commercial*, July 30, 1863; John A. Andrew to John Wilder, May 23, 1863, *Negro in Military Service*, pp. 1264–65; William H. Parham to Jacob C. White, Jr., Aug. 7, 1863, White Papers; David Tod to E. M. Stanton, July 18, 1863, in *Black Military Experience*, ed. Berlin et al, p. 371.

52. Cincinnati *Gazette*, July 2, 1863; Cincinnati *Commercial*, July 2, 30, 1863; Cincinnati *Enquirer*, July 8, 1863; Elyria *Independent-Democrat*, July 8, 1863; *Ohio State Journal*, July 1, 11, Nov. 5, 1863; William O. Dennison to People of Cincinnati, Cincinnati *Commercial*, Nov. 9, 1863; O. S. B. Wall to George L. Stearns, Oct. 29, 1863, O. S. B. Wall, Military Service Records.

53. Lorain County *News*, Aug. 19, 1863; Elyria *Independent-Democrat*, Aug.

19, 1863; Cincinnati *Gazette*, Sept. 26, 1863; W. M. Dickson to the People of Cincinnati, Nov. 9, 1863, Cincinnati *Commercial*, Nov. 9, 1863; *Ohio State Journal*, Nov. 5, 1863.

54. Sandusky *Register*, n.d., quoted in Elyria *Independent-Democrat*, June 10, 1863; D[avid] Cooper to Editor, *Christian Recorder*, July 4, 1863; Washington *National Republican*, Feb. 11, 1870.

55. *Anglo-African*, June 13, Aug. 22, 1863; Henry T. Peal to "Kind Lady," May 22, 1863, Lorain County *News*, June 24, 1863.

56. John M. Langston to the Colored Men of Ohio, July 3, 1863, Cincinnati *Gazette*, July 9, 1863; Ulysses L. Marvin, "Giles Waldo Shurtleff," Oberlin *Alumni Magazine* 7 (June 1911): 312–13; Cincinnati *Gazette*, Sept. 26, 1863; David Tod to Waldo G. Shurtleff, July 20, 1863, *Executive Documents, 1863*, p. 275.

57. Lorain County *News*, July 29, 1863; J. B. T. Marsh to J. M. Langston, July 28, 1863, Elyria *Independent-Democrat*, Aug. 19, 1863; Cincinnati *Commercial*, Aug. 4, 1863; Delaware *Gazette*, Aug. 7, 1863.

58. Geo. Vosburg to Editor, Nov. 15, 1863, *Anglo-African*, Nov. 28, 1863; *Ohio State Journal*, June 25, Aug. 4, 1863; *Anglo-African*, Aug. 22, 1863.

59. Lorain County *News*, July 29, 1863; *Ohio State Journal*, Aug. 4, 1863; *Liberator*, Sept. 4, 1863; Cincinnati *Gazette*, Aug. 13, 1863; "Convention of Colored Men in Xenia, Aug. 4–6, 1863," in Xenia *Torch-Light*, Aug. 12, 1863.

60. George L. Stearns to Edwin Stanton, Aug. 10, 1863, *Negro in the Military Service*, p. 1471; Cincinnati *Gazette*, Aug. 6, Sept. 8, 1863; Lorain County *News*, Aug. 19, 1863; Elyria *Independent-Democrat*, Aug. 12, 19, 1863.

61. Cleveland *Leader*, Aug. 21, 25, 1863; "O.K." to Editor, Aug. 22, 1863, Xenia *Torch-Light*, Sept. 2, 1863; Jackson *Standard*, Sept. 24, 1863.

62. Voegeli, *Free but Not Equal*, pp. 120–26, 129; Roseboom and Weisenburger, *History of Ohio*, pp. 283–84.

63. Voegeli, *Free but Not Equal*, pp. 123–24, 131–32; Lorain County *News*, Oct. 21, Nov. 4, 11, 1863.

64. Cincinnati *Commercial*, Nov. 10, 27, 1863; Cincinnati *Gazette*, June 27, 1863; *Official Roster*, pp. 593–624; compilation by Levstik, "The Fifth Regiment," p. 88.

65. Langston, *Virginia Plantation*, p. 210; Lorain County *News*, Nov. 18, 1863; Cincinnati *Gazette*, Nov. 12, 1863.

66. Delaware *Gazette*, Nov. 13, 1863; *Ohio State Journal*, Nov. 5, 1863; Elyria *Independent-Democrat*, Nov. 18, 1863; Lorain County *News*, Nov. 18, 1863; A. M. Taylor to Editor, Nov. 16, 1863, *Christian Recorder*, Nov. 28, 1863; Cleveland *Leader*, Nov. 12, 1863.

67. E. F. Grabill to Editor, Lorain County *News*, Dec. 9, 1863.

68. Levstik, "The Fifth Regiment," pp. 86–98, passim; Emilio, *History of the Fifty-Fourth*, passim; Hallowell, *Negro as a Soldier*, passim; Lorain County *News*, Dec. 9, 30, 1863, Jan. 20, Feb. 3, May 25, July 6, 20, Aug. 17, Sept. 14, Oct. 19, 1864.

69. Peck, "Sketches"; E. F. Grabill to Editor, Oct. 2, 1864, Lorain County *News*, Oct. 19, 1864; Cornish, *The Sable Arm*, pp. 278–80; Milton M. Holland,

Military Service Records; McPherson, *Negro's Civil War*, p. 237; Cincinnati *Colored Citizen*, Dec., 1863, quoted in New Orleans *Tribune*, Jan. 7, 1864; Langston, *Virginia Plantation*, pp. 216–17.

70. Langston, *Virginia Plantation*, pp. 219–23.

71. Berlin et al., eds., *Black Military Experience*, pp. 303–12; O. S. B. Wall to Col. C. W. Foster, Mar. 3, 1865, W-172 1865, Letters Received, ser. 360, Colored Troops Division, RG 94; C. W. Foster to Brevet Maj. Genl. R. Saxton, Mar. 3, 1865; C. W. Foster to Capt. Henry Keteltas, Mar. 3, 1865, all in *Black Military Experience*, ed. Berlin et al., pp. 93, 394.

72. Lorain County *News*, Mar. 15, 22, 1865; G. G. Collins to Editor, *Anglo-African*, Apr. 8, 1865; Special Orders, No. 106, War Department, Adjutant General's Office, Washington, Mar. 3, 1865, and Office Muster-in, Co. K, 104th U. S. C. T., both in O. S. B. Wall, Military Service Records. Assigned to the Quartermaster Corps of the 104th, Captain Wall would serve with the regiment until Feb. 5, 1866, when it was mustered out at Beaufort. For another three months he would work as civilian agent of the Freedmen's Bureau. O. S. B. Wall to Editor, Lorain County *News*, July 19, 1865, May 9, 1866; Company Musterout Roll, Co. K, 104th U. S. C. T., in O. S. B. Wall, Military Service Records.

73. J.A. Garfield to E. M. Stanton, Mar. 28, 1865, enclosing John M. Langston to E. M. Stanton, Mar. 20, 1865, both filed with W-276 1865, Letters Received, ser. 360, Colored Troops Division, RG 94, in *Black Military Experience*, ed. Berlin et al., pp. 346–47.

74. Langston, *Virginia Plantation*, pp. 219–23; Cincinnati *Gazette*, Apr. 4, 5, 7, 1865; Philadelphia *Press*, Apr. 7, 1865; A. A. Genl. C. W. Foster to John M. Langston, May 17, 1865, W-276 1865, Letters Received, ser. 360, Colored Troops Division, RG 94, in *Black Military Experience*, ed. Berlin et al., p. 347.

75. Baltimore *Sun*, June 2, 1874; Table 1, in *Black Military Experience*, ed. Berlin et al; p. 12; *Christian Recorder*, July 30, 1864.

76. St. Louis *Democrat*, Nov. 29, 1865, John Mercer Langston Scrapbook, Fisk University Library.

CHAPTER 13

The Emergence of a National Leader

1863–65

No sooner had Langston completed his recruitment labors than he began to put forward in earnest his program for reconstruction. Developed and refined during the remaining months of war, his ideas were representative, in the main, of the northern black leadership, as well as of many white radicals. He called for an "entire national regeneration" based on the "total abolition of slavery and the enfranchisement of the Negro race."[1] The program encompassed black self-help and solidarity, interracial cooperation, and a measure of governmental assistance, but its nucleus was legal and political recognition of the Negro, North and South.

The obstacles were formidable. Langston deceived himself neither about the obduracy of white prejudice in the North and the virulence of white enmity in the South, nor about the fundamental damage wrought by slavery: it would take years to erase its cursed effects on blacks and whites.[2] Nonetheless, schooled as he was in Oberlin perfectionism, democratic-republican ideals, antislavery politics, and the northern black civil rights movement, Langston held that people were educable.

Although the "white man was the white man" the world over, as Langston was wont to say, simple self-interest must lead to the recognition that in tolerating slavery for blacks, whites "manufacture[d] shackles for themselves."[3] No advanced civilization could remain callous to the Negro's demands for liberty and justice. The black man could count as allies a goodly number of Christian philanthropic reformers, while the practical lessons that Union soldiers had absorbed in the

Confederacy had changed the honest and candid among them into sincere opponents of slavery.

Yet it was not so much northern commitment as southern intransigence that would effect the eradication of slavery, just as southern excesses had brought on the war. The South was mad and, he might hope, would remain so until the Slave Power was destroyed, and Jefferson Davis and his kind dispatched to the "bottomless pit where they belonged."[4] As military necessity had led to the Emancipation Proclamation and the use of black soldiers, so the political necessity of subduing the traitors all over the South at war's end would force the government to grant black suffrage. "You will need the black man with the ballot box as you have with the bayonet, and when you want him you know he is ready to cry, 'Here I am.' "[5]

Insofar as blacks themselves could bring about change, Langston was confident of their fundamental capacity to make their way, gradually but surely, in freedom. Both on a personal level and in the creation of community institutions, "the energy, the enterprise, the purpose and the genius of the colored American" had been demonstrated. What was true of black Ohioans, with their southern origins—to speak only of those with whom he was most closely associated—might prove equally true of the newly freed men and women. Many of the North's "most sober, industrious and thrifty men," including seven-eighths of the black artisans, came from the South, produced not by, but in spite of, the institutions of slavery. Holding up their example, Langston felt that the freed people should primarily rely on the traditional means of self-help. They should be hardworking, frugal, and temperate in the effort to accumulate property and acquire education, "grow strong in knowledge, secure character and influence, and use them as moral levers to elevate yourselves to the dignity of manhood and womanhood."[6]

Although a firm adherent of the free labor ideology, Langston understood that government and northern reformers must step in to assist the former slaves. Jointly with other Oberlin leaders, he urged as early as January 1, 1863 that the government employ large numbers of the freedmen for military or other purposes, paying them fairly, supervising them kindly, and protecting their rights. Protection, in particular, as he continued to stress, was essential.[7] Agreeing with Oberlin's longtime advocates of land confiscation and redistribution to the former slaves, Langston joined his townsmen (again on Emancipation Day) in requesting the government to provide for the settlement of the freedmen on lands adequate for their support. Nonetheless, after both Lincoln and a host of influential Republicans rejected as unconstitutional the attempts of congressional radicals to secure permanent confiscation of Rebel properties, Langston did not publicly renew the plea. As a lawyer and a real estate agent, he appreciated the deep-seated republican aversion to governmental interference with the sanctity of private property; as a student of American racial prejudice, he was reluctant to cast the black man too starkly in the role of supplicant. Thus, making land for the landless a conspicuous plank in any early black reconstruction program could only seem folly. Instead, Langston urged blacks to avail themselves of access to the public lands, wherever feasible.[8]

Northern sympathizers, coalescing in missionary and freedman's aid societies, should act as the freed people's natural allies, helping to impart a "useful education, and instruction in a pure Christianity." Langston himself not only loaned his voice to raise funds for such endeavors, but also assisted in organizing the Freedman's Relief Association of Oberlin, which worked with the American Missionary Association to supply male and female teachers of both races to the South.[9] Furthermore, building on his long-standing argument that white people, particularly the "poor, ignorant, and degraded non-slaveholders" of the South, had also been the victims of slavery, he espied in the elevation of the latter group through "a *free* school, a *free* church, and all incentives to industry" the potential for a fruitful interracial alliance. "Indeed, the poor white man of the South and the slave ought to be linked in friendship stronger than iron chains, for a common enemy preys upon their freedom."[10]

Recognition of the civil and political equality of all men, North and South, was key to the nation's peace and welfare, as to the fulfillment of its democratic destiny. Without full rights, emancipation would be a mockery.[11] The Negro wanted no favors, but simply "a fair, open field." He wanted to be subjected to the same burdens, and to be endowed with the same privileges, that white Americans enjoyed, no more, no less. Subjected to taxation, the Negro claimed the correlative rights of citizenship: trial by a jury of his peers, equal access to public education and to other public institutions, and the vote. Black attainment of the ballot was "the next step to be taken to perfect American democracy."[12] Langston asserted that Attorney General Edward Bates's opinion repudiating the infamous strictures on blacks contained in the Dred Scott decision had, in effect, cleared the title of black Americans to national citizenship. Thus, because suffrage was a natural and political right of the American citizen, Langston "would make his argument and rest his cause" on the Declaration of Independence and the

Constitution. Exactly like the white American, the black American expected the right to vote on the basis of his manhood. The Negro's valiant military service made it impossible for even his bitterest enemies any longer to advance the objection "that the black man is not a man."[13]

Despite the strength of their claims, black Americans must beware. Lulled neither by recent gains nor by expectations of national magnanimity, they must unite to demand equality without delay. Black patriots in earlier wars alike had hoped for justice, "but we know too well by our bitter experience of wrong and degradation, how they were treated after those wars. Wisdom, then, dictates that we should profit by this lesson. . . . When this, our present war, shall have ended, it will be our duty to see to it that we have indeed a standing place under American law."[14]

Langston advised Negroes to "demand their rights," even as "white men, in self-defense, should give Negroes their rights." The latter should file antidiscrimination suits in the courts where, before long, it would be "decided that a man's rights in this country were not to be measured by the color of his skin."[15] Rejecting the contention of some abolitionists that the demand for enfranchisement should be deferred until blacks were better educated and morally prepared, Langston told his people: "Until you are in possession of the rights and powers of full citizenship, the partial rights and privileges you now enjoy will be entirely at the disposal of those whose prejudice or supposed interest may be against you. See to it, . . . that you are the custodians of your own liberties. . . . Justice . . . demands that you should move in the great matter of reconstructing our nation, upon the basis of liberty to all."[16]

Langston brought his arguments for emancipation and enfranchisement to Washington in early December 1863. Although worn from his marathon recruitment labors and barely recovered from an illness that had prevented his participation in the landmark thirtieth anniversary celebration of the American Anti-Slavery Society in Philadelphia, he grasped this chance to visit the national capital for the first time. Buoyantly aware that black Ohioans in the Fifth Regiment, posted just to the south in Virginia, already were adding to the dramatic proofs of black manhood and patriotism, he was eager to test both antislavery sentiment and his own powers of persuasion. His arrival coincided with the opening of the Thirty-eighth Congress, which was expected to consider a constitutional amendment to abolish slavery as well as other measures vital to black interests. Optimism, generated by the recent Union party victories over the Peace Democrats in Ohio and elsewhere, as well as the preceding northern military advances at Gettysburg and Vicksburg, was surging, with a number of leading Republicans and abolitionists confident that both the war and slavery were almost at an end. Even should that be the case—and events soon exposed the falsity of this unseasonal antislavery spring—Langston and other black leaders felt only an increased urgency to press for black rights.[17]

Langston attended a speech by Frederick Douglass on the evening of December 7. The program, sponsored by the black Contraband Relief Association, whose president was the socially prominent Elizabeth Keckley, was held in the Fifteenth Street Presbyterian Church, the black religious showplace known for its carpeted floors, chandeliers, and splendid organ and choir. Langston was scheduled to appear a week later under the same auspices in the same place. Then at the meridian of his fame, Douglass drew a huge, diverse crowd, everyone from "statesmen down to clodhoppers," who pushed and shoved to be among the thousand admitted. When "every bench was crammed full, white and colored, all squeezed in snug," the choir struck up the "Star Spangled Banner" and the newly elected chaplain of the House of Representatives, abolitionist William Henry Channing, introduced the speaker. In his address and in an elaboration before another full-house audience the following night, Douglass called for equal rights: "the black man must have his vote given him, the right to the ballot box, without which he is weak, and is of no use to the country and its glories." After a thunderous ovation for Douglass, Langston was called to the podium. Complimenting Douglass and crediting him, in apparent reference to the 1848 national black convention in Cleveland, with having been the first person to encourage Langston to make a public speech, he asserted that now "Mr. Douglass was pleading the President of the United States' cause, as well as the bondsman's." Langston, too, won loud applause. A correspondent informed Oberlin newspaper readers: "Report says his speech 'took.' "[18]

Langston's own address on the evening of December 15 was one part recruitment, one part justification for black suffrage. Predicting that black men in the District of Columbia would have the vote within six months of the war's conclusion, he refuted the standard objection of black ignorance, contending that ignorance existed in about equal proportions among white and black populations, excluding the slaves. Only the faulty perspective fostered by segregation and discrimination, the distortion produced because "we are a great way from white people," made whites "look large when they are very small." Although his audience was sparse, the Ohioan won appreciative notice in both the black and white radical press.[19]

Like the New England abolitionists George T. Downing and Charles Lenox Remond and other distinguished black visitors—currently mounting, as a black Washingtonian noted, "one grand congress of motion and interest"—Langston availed himself of the recently won access to federal institutions, helping to create a new black visibility at the seat of government that Remond interpreted as symbolic of the increasing official recognition of the Negro's enhanced role. The symbol was flawed, with seating in the congressional galleries segregated and the visiting dignitaries as liable as any black man to the requirement of showing a government pass to enter or leave the city.[20] Still, as he walked down Pennsylvania Avenue, admired the bronze statue of Freedom that had just been hoisted to the apex of the newly finished huge iron dome of the Capitol, and actually stood inside the Capitol building, Langston, who in his college days had dreamed of becoming a congressman, felt a special pride. Exploiting his Radical connections, he doubtless lobbied for the black cause at every open office door; his old ally Salmon P. Chase, now secretary of the treasury, prudently recorded the black Republican's address for possible use. At the same time, Langston made "a host of friends" among Washington's black elite. Aware of the need and opportunity for dismantling social barriers between the races in the capital, as he had observed in his speech, he may well have encouraged several black men of stature who were planning an assault on one important white bastion. On New Year's Day, after he had left the city, four Negroes—including Remond, the Reverend Henry Johnson of Ithaca, New York, once sold as a slave in Washington, and Alexander Ferguson, a former Cincinnatian now living in San Francisco whom Chase would shortly appoint a special treasury agent to convey government gold to California—attended a public reception at the White House and received cordial greetings from the president.[21]

Langston lectured on emancipation and enfranchisement whenever he could during the next nine months. He scarcely participated with his family in the Christmas season before he was off in the worst of weather to attend the Michigan black state convention on New Year's day 1864. Held in Adrian, reputed to be the most antislavery town in the state, the conclave drew only a modest representation, in part because of the intense cold. Langston delivered the keynote address and, when a great snow storm prevented the arrival of H. Ford Douglass from Chicago, spoke again in his stead at the evening session. Out of the convention came a petition to the legislature asking removal of all legal distinctions based on color, and expressly calling for the elective franchise.[22] Blacks in Adrian were so impressed that they asked

Langston back in more seasonable weather. In early June—despite competition from a circus and two other "exhibitions," and even though only about thirty black families lived in the area—he attracted a good crowd, enabling his sponsors, the Union Literary Association, to pay expenses ($32) and realize a profit of $15, which was promptly turned over to the local branch of the Freedman's Association of Chicago. The reporter for the local conservative journal commented that the audience reacted with great delight to Langston's resolute defense of the equal rights doctrine and to his obvious pride in his black identity. The response was equally enthusiastic to Langston's First of August address that year in Marietta, Ohio, where he spoke for two and a half hours before a large number of blacks and whites.[23]

With 1864 a presidential election year, Langston favored Abraham Lincoln. Like black northerners generally, Langston genuinely feared that the Democratic party aimed to restore slavery and to return the national government to southern domination; unlike the many black spokesmen who manifested ambivalent attitudes toward Lincoln and his party, Langston continued strongly to sustain them. Despite the Republicans' timidity, temporizing, and prejudice, he considered the "good done, however forced" an outgrowth of their actions; he "intended to vote with and for them." He deemed Lincoln "cautious and for that reason he was the man of the hour. His head and his heart were right." In a speech in Toledo in the last days of May, Langston announced his gratitude to the Heavenly Father that the nation had such a president and predicted Lincoln's renomination and reelection. Wary of splinter movements, Langston timed his endorsement shrewdly. Within days a convention called by some of Lincoln's Radical critics, Frederick Douglass among them, was to meet in Cleveland, where the candidacy of John C. Frémont was launched on an equal rights platform.[24]

Langston remained steadfast in support of the Republicans throughout a turbulent political season. The congressional session proved a disappointment. The Thirteenth Amendment failed to materialize; a bill to equalize black soldiers' pay with that of white soldiers passed belatedly, but not all were to benefit uniformly from it. No reconstruction plan to emerge, whether originated by Lincoln or the Congress, was predicated on equal rights; nor had the freedmen won guarantees of land or fair compensation for their labor. Despite the ease of Lincoln's renomination and the forthrightness of the Union party pledge to secure constitutional abolition of slavery, both Radical dissatisfaction with the administration and racism among the electorate surged during the summer of 1864, as Union armies floundered. By late summer as Democrats prepared to nominate General George B. McClellan on a platform calling for peace and the preservation of slavery, even Lincoln privately conceded defeat. Only with the fall of Atlanta in early September and a subsequent tightening of the Republican coalition did the pessimism begin to dispel. Even so, the shaken administration, confronting a Democratic campaign of unbridled racial demagoguery, showed signs that it might negotiate a peace with slavery intact. When Langston led a meeting of Oberlin blacks in voicing support of the administration in mid-September, he specified that it was contingent upon continuation of the emancipation policy and "vigorous prosecution of the war."[25]

To underscore the demand for emancipation and enfranchisement, some one hundred fifty black leaders met at a national convention in Syracuse, New York, on October 4, 1864. The delegates represented seventeen states, South and North, and the District of Columbia, constituting the most truly national black convention that had been held since the movement's beginning in 1830.[26] Nine years had elapsed since the last, lacklustre gathering in 1855. The major reason for the hiatus was the polarization within the black northern leadership over the question of black nationalist emigration, an issue that continued to stir discord, although recently submerged by the pressing concerns of war. Nonetheless, the black men (and women, although not as official delegates) were gathered in an attempt to set a course and forge a national union at a critical juncture in the Afro-American experience.

As temporary chairman, Langston presided over the opening session of the convention. The choice of the young Ohioan with the distinguished recruitment record as presiding officer extended recognition to the West and to the rising generation of black leaders—men who, quipped Douglass, had "come up in this time of whirlwind and storm, and would very naturally give them thunder." In a juxtaposition suggestive of the hope for unity animating the gathering and of the obstacles in the path, Langston shared the platform with Henry Highland Garnet, the eminent black protest veteran who had originated the call for the convention. As Langston, the thirty-four-year-old light-skinned lawyer, wielded the gavel with tact and efficiency, and Garnet, the forty-nine-year-old dark-skinned eastern preacher noted for his emotive powers, convened the delegates, read the call, led the singing of "Blow Ye, the Trumpet Blow" (John Brown's favorite hymn), and held forth in fervent prayer and address, the obvious contrasts in their age, regional background, and personal style underlined the more important philosophical differences between them. In the ideological cleavage over black nationalism, the two had embraced opposing views: Langston as a political-integrationist committed to waging the black struggle in an American context, Garnet as a leading spokesman for a nationalist-emigration movement.[27]

Langston's prominence on the platform was not without irony, for he had been slow to support the convention proposal, his reluctance in sharp variance with the black northern mood. The idea of a national conclave, informally broached as early as January 1864, had elicited favorable comment from blacks across the North during the winter and spring, mirroring the interest in equal rights manifested in suffrage drives as far afield as Louisiana, the District of Columbia, and Kansas.[28] (In Kansas, Charles H. Langston, who had gone to the Leavenworth area in 1862 to teach and work among the former slaves, had helped inaugurate a sustained enfranchisement campaign, beginning with a state convention on January 1, 1863.)[29]

Garnet's call for a national convention, issued in early July, thus had quickly garnered support.[30] Yet the assent in some instances was less than wholehearted. The influential intellectual John S. Rock of Boston—the dark-skinned dentist and physician who had been admitted to the Massachusetts bar and appointed a justice of the peace in 1861, and who in February 1865 would become the first black lawyer admitted to practice before the Supreme Court—had been privately skeptical when a group of his townsmen proposed to initiate their own convention call in early April. An anti-emigrationist, Rock had confided to such ideological allies as George Downing, Charles Remond, and Frederick Douglass that he questioned the wisdom of holding a convention, "knowing as I do the materials of which it must be composed." Once Garnet's preemptive summons appeared, however, Rock, having maneuvered himself into the position of spokesman for the Boston committee, publicly compromised with him in making key decisions on convention arrangements.[31] As for Langston, he and other Ohioans had maintained a studied silence until September, when they tardily called meetings and elected delegates.[32] Like other blacks with a western outlook, Langston doubtless resented Garnet's failure to consult more than a handful of his peers, virtually all from New York and the District of Columbia, before issuing his call—an omission the more striking given the history of East–West rivalry in the national convention movement. The subsequent haphazardness of the planning, with the site undecided until less than a month before the convention was to occur, did little to inspire confidence.[33] But for Langston, as for some other leaders, the most questionable factor may well have been Garnet's involvement.

Famous for his 1843 advocacy of slave insurrection, Garnet had engaged in diverse forms of protest and abolitionism, including political activism, over a long notable career. In 1858, he had become president of the African Civilization Society, an organization that, while professing to endorse only limited African emigration, shared working quarters, officers, and funding with the American Colonization Society's New York branch. Garnet promoted Afro-American settlement among the Yoruba as well as emigration to Haiti under a plan sponsored by the Haitian government during the early sixties. Although these and other colonizationist schemes of the early war years attracted considerable black interest, their subsequent collapse, with the attendant suffering of the emigrants, only served to further embitter such confirmed opponents as George Downing, the noted civil rights leader and businessman in Rhode Island and New York.[34]

In early 1864, when the magnetic Garnet exchanged his old pulpit at the Shiloh Presbyterian in New York City for the Fifteenth Street Presbyterian in Washington and the African Civilization Society publicly switched its focus to schooling the freedmen in the capital, new suspicions arose. Had the organization actually changed direction, or was it merely promoting black nationalism and colonization in a new guise, moving into the area of freedmen's relief to repair its image and attract new converts from among the land-hungry former slaves who—in their uprooted, insecure, and poverty-stricken condition—might prove susceptible to its message. Not only did Downing and other political-integrationists think the latter was the case but, they charged, programs sponsored by the society fostered segregation. They were further incensed by the encouragement the black nationalist-emigrationists offered to the conservative and moderate Republican predilection to view colonization as the simple solution to the complex problems posed by black freedom. Indeed, Garnet and his followers—who had recently applied to the administration for a large grant to advance the society's aims—often offered public assurances of the Negro's willingness, once freed, to emigrate to foreign lands or to withdraw to some unsettled portion of the United States.[35]

Whether for these reasons or others, opposition to Garnet in Washington proved so strong that the black citizenry refused to elect him as a delegate to the 1864 National Convention of Colored Men, thus forcing him, at the eleventh hour, to go as a representative of the Civilization Society in New York City. Unexpectedly, however, the civilizationist ranks themselves harbored a mutineer, the volatile young clergyman J. Sella Martin of Brooklyn. Recently returned from a well-publicized tour of the British Isles, Martin—who was born a slave in

North Carolina in 1832 but escaped his master in 1856 before becoming a Baptist preacher, first in Boston and then in Brooklyn—had been Garnet's top lieutenant in the African Civilization Society for several years. Martin would later claim to have been Garnet's chief convention foe. Although a generational rivalry for leadership of the society may have been the major cause for Martin's behavior, his own explanation was that Garnet was unduly ambitious and had proved himself undeserving of high position.[36]

Whatever Langston's pre-convention thoughts, the scene that greeted him in Syracuse on the morning of October 4 was calculated to harden doubts about Garnet's qualities as a leader and to fire his own determination to wield a controlling hand. Even though the convention was not supposed to begin until that night, Langston found other early arrivals excitedly gathered in an upper room of the Wesleyan Methodist church. The previous evening, a mishap had befallen Garnet. As he stood outside his hotel chatting with the white proprietor and several black men, four white toughs had assailed them, prostrating the one-legged Garnet. They ran off with his cane, along with papers that detailed his plans for convention business and that had fallen out of his hat. Now, alarmed that the incident portended a mob attack, Garnet, noting that a few delegates already had left, proposed an immediate transfer of the whole proceedings to some other city. Langston opposed a retreat. In concert with Douglass and Downing, he argued that it would be unbecoming to the dignity and courage of black men and their cause. The meeting decided to stand firm, but only after Jermain W. Loguen of Syracuse, the long-time abolitionist who was in charge of local arrangements, secured a promise of protection from the mayor. Thereupon, the delegates moved downstairs where Garnet called the convention to order, Langston, on motion, was named temporary chairman, and committees were appointed. But all this turned out to be mere dress rehearsal when a delegation from Pennsylvania arrived and, pointing out that the announced starting time was 7 p.m., indignantly forced adherence to the original schedule.[37]

Langston and Garnet resumed their places on the platform that night as the convention finally got underway. For all the controversy, it was an impressive assembly. In the caliber of their leadership, the delegates—who included most of the seasoned northern spokesmen, a sizable contingent of well-educated younger men, emigrationists returned from abroad, northern-trained teachers working in the South, free men from liberated areas, and even soldiers like Captain James H. Ingraham of New Orleans who created a stir by exhibiting the flag used by black troops in the assault on Port Hudson—outstripped any previous national convention, with the possible exception of the Rochester gathering of 1853. Two women, the well-known Frances Ellen Watkins Harper, who had been so active in black protest in Ohio, and a twenty-year-old teacher of the freedmen, Edmonia Highgate of Syracuse, delivered speeches during the proceedings. Although both the Democratic and Republican press largely ignored the gathering because coverage could serve the campaign interests of neither party, public attention would prove so intense that more than two thousand spectators, most of whom were white, crowded the evening sessions devoted to public address.[38]

Langston early disposed of the potentially nettlesome issue of deciding on the credentials of the delegates by appointment of a prestigious committee composed of Douglass, Peter Clark, and Massachusetts abolitionist William Wells Brown. But sharp debate erupted over conflicting proposals for choosing officers, either in open convention—a plan backed by some of the fifty strong New York delegation, in which Garnet's supporters were prominent—or by nominating committee—favored by Pennsylvania, next largest with thirty-six delegates. The latter plan was ultimately adopted. The committee's choice of Douglass as president brought rounds of applause and quick approval.

The following morning, Douglass wielded his appointive powers to construct a twenty-five-member business committee, representative of each state. Garnet headed a list that included Langston, Peter Clark, George Downing, Sella Martin, and John Rock. Once inside the committee room, Garnet, frankly disappointed that he had not been chosen as president of the convention, attempted to claim the chairmanship of the committee by virtue of the order of his appointment. After Martin and Downing mounted a lively opposition, the group instead elected two attorneys, Langston as chairman and Rock as secretary. Irate, Garnet resigned from the committee.[39]

Although Langston also delivered a well-received address on the second night of the convention, his most vital contribution was coordination of the group that originated all of its business. He directed the production of several documents reflective of his own views that, taken together, constituted a Negro blueprint for Reconstruction. The committee gave final shaping to a trenchant "Declaration of Wrongs and Rights," prepared in its initial form by Dr. P. B. Randolph of New York City, and approved a remarkable "Address to the People of the United States," written by Frederick Douglass. It originated a series of resolutions on the major issues confronting black Americans, many of which were written by Ebenezer D. Bassett of Philadelphia, principal of the Quaker-operated Institute for Colored Youth and later U. S. minister to Haiti. Infused with the American ethos of revolution, democracy, and religious faith, and marked by a sense of historic moment, these documents demanded the "immediate and unconditional" abolition of slavery. To the freedmen, Langston and his colleagues recommended the course of elevation long considered essential in the North: industry, thrift, the acquisition of property, education, morality, and religion. Forced colonization at home or abroad was unacceptable. Blacks were entitled to a "fair share" of public lands, whether acquired by confiscation, conquest, or other means, and should, so far as possible, settle on them. Calling for full enfranchisement North and South, Langston and his colleagues, even as they recognized the "powerful reactionary forces arrayed against us," expressed the hope "that the generosity and sense of honor inherent in the great heart of this nation will ultimately concede us our just claims, accord us our rights, and grant us our full measure of citizenship, under the broad shield of the Constitution."[40]

So adroit was Langston's management of the committee that—aside from Garnet, who grumbled that he had been unable to get any of his business presented—only one delegate lodged a complaint. The Reverend Singleton T. Jones of New York, later a bishop of the A.M.E. Zion church, charged Langston with having pocketed a proposed resolution commending the contemplated union of the A.M.E. Zion and A.M.E. churches. Langston, who had been publicly critical of black religionists as far back as 1850, replied derisively that he was unaware a resolution was included in the bundle of papers that Jones had handed him, and which he had withheld from the business committee because he "did not wish to bring sectarian matters into the convention." With what surely struck his more sophisticated hearers as false modesty and dubious sincerity, he apologized for his "youth and inexperience." The majority of delegates, not of Langston's mind, approved the resolution.[41]

The convention created a new national black organization, the National Equal Rights League. Langston brought the constitution for the league, drafted in the main by Peter Clark, to the floor on the third day of the convention. In contrast to the defunct National Council of 1853, the league was to be unencumbered of any specific project. Instead, it was to devote itself to two broadly stated goals: to encourage black self-improvement and to obtain the full rights of citizens "by appeals to the minds and consciences of the American people, or by legal process where possible." Authority in the National League was to reside in the executive officers and eight-man executive board, with a permanent office to handle routine affairs and an annual convention to set policy. State and local adjuncts, which were to be open without distinction of color or sex, would initiate their own programs while cooperating with the National League and supporting it financially.[42]

Although Langston could be pleased at the convention's handy approval of the league in concept, disputes over key questions of implementation—involving such traditionally disruptive issues as class, sectionalism, and ideology, as well as personal rivalries, each of which took on an added dimension with the participation, for the first time, of representatives from the South—exposed the fragility of the hope for national black unity. On the question of representation at the National League's annual meeting, the first of which was scheduled nearly a year thence, Garnet was vehement in opposition to the proposal that each state auxiliary pay $100 for every delegate, arguing that the business committee intended to discriminate against the common people and those less wealthy than themselves. After his attempt to substitute a $10 fee was narrowly voted down, 55–45, an amendment offered by D. D. Turner of Philadelphia was accepted that lowered the cost to $50 for the first and $30 for each additional delegate.[43]

The traditional East–West rivalry fired the debate over the location of the league headquarters, with support divided between Philadelphia, Cleveland, and, to a lesser extent, Cincinnati. Langston endorsed Cleveland on the grounds of centrality and biracial sympathies; it was a measure of his influence when it was selected. That evening, however, a startling reversal occurred. Elisha M. Weaver of Philadelphia, editor of the *A.M.E. Christian Recorder*, moved for reconsideration, the vote was retaken, and Philadelphia was chosen.

Thereupon Army Sergeant Alfred M. Green of Philadelphia rose to nominate Langston for the league presidency. "This seemed to take several members by surprise," observed emigrationist William Howard Day, Langston's erstwhile Ohio ally who reported convention proceedings for the nationalist journal, the New York *Anglo-African*. Day added that some votes for the headquarters site had been cast with the tacit understanding that either Douglass or Garnet would be president. That boosters of the rival cities had privately come to terms was apparent: Langston himself—it was later charged—had engineered the deal. But this sectional compromise only unleashed ideological acrimony. Robert Hamilton, editor of the *Anglo-African*, immediately nominated Garnet for the presidency. "Spirited discussion" ensued. On the verge of a vote, Clark suggested that nominations be referred to a committee to be appointed by Douglass, who apparently had declined to have his own name considered.[44] Douglass, whose disagreements with Garnet extended back some two decades, and who may have tangled with him on this occasion—a black journalist later would recall the "disgraceful and disastrous partisanship manifested in the Douglass and Garnet *imbroglio* which occurred at the Syracuse convention"[45] —turned the podium over to the militant nationalist. Garnet said he had been "asked that night to define his position," a request that "at this late day in his career, was exceedingly humiliating." Because of his ties to the African Civilization Society, "there had been a strong disposition to throw him on the shelf," but he had acted in accordance with his belief in a "Negro nationality." Going on to delineate the depredations of the mob during the New York City draft riot of the previous summer and to extol the deeds of the black soldiers, he displayed the emotional power that had long swayed public assemblies. But here it neither answered his critics, nor proved effective against their joined forces. The nominating committee appointed by Douglass consisted of P. N. Judah of Philadelphia, the anti-emigrationist William J. Wilson of Washington, and Langston. (The group evidently later merged with the business committee.)[46]

But Langston's nomination was not to be achieved without final skirmishing. As the last session unfolded the following morning with a number of delegates already having left, Richard Harvey Cain of Brooklyn—an A.M.E. minister educated at Wilberforce who was later an important Reconstruction leader and congressman from South Carolina—moved to insert the name of the African Civilization Society, of which he was a member, in a resolution thanking several organizations for their work among the freedmen. William P. Newman, the former Oberlin College student just returned after spending more than a decade in Canada and the Caribbean to his old Baptist pastorate in Cincinnati, seconded the motion. This brought George Downing to his feet. In an angry review of the society's history, the New England civil rights leader attacked it as "the child of prejudice; and its originators assert that the colored man cannot be elevated in the United States; that the black men must be 'massed to themselves,' and have a grand fight for a 'Negro nationality,' before they can be respected!" Besides barring abolitionists from its platforms, its leaders had maintained "that we are out of our place here, and that 'it would be well if every colored man was out of the country'!" As for working with the freedmen, "the exertions of this Society have been where friends have been numerous and springing up daily; where the Society was needed, it did not go." Downing pointed sternly to the African Society's affiliation with "our old enemy, the Colonization Society," and warned that the resolution might be construed as an endorsement of colonizationist aims. "We must be careful not to be made tools of."[47]

Garnet again defended himself. Claiming to be poor because of his lifelong refusal to be "the tool" of the white man, he attempted to equate the society's financing with the contributions that white spectators had made to the collection plates passed at the convention. "If Mr. Downing has intended to cripple my influence in this convention," Garnet concluded bitterly, "to keep me out of office and off of committees, he has successfully accomplished that purpose." Langston's old friend, George B. Vashon of Pittsburgh, tried to calm the combatants with a resolution commending the society's work with the freedmen although opposing colonization, but Garnet rejected it. Cain's motion finally won acceptance, but it seemed less victory than conciliatory gesture.[48]

Minutes later, Rock, speaking for the business committee, nominated Langston for president. Even then, Garnet's supporters persisted, this time from within Langston's own Ohio delegation. Newman and Henry Lee—the latter like the former a clergyman with Oberlin schooling, both men runaway slaves from Virginia and both noted for their litigious and independent behavior[49]—sought to discredit the nominee. Disappointed in his own advocacy of Cincinnati as host city for the league, Newman urged that Langston should be barred from the presidency because he had engineered a "corrupt bargain and sale": the agreement to make Philadelphia, rather than Cleveland, the league headquarters in exchange for the Philadelphians' support of Langston for the presidency.

Lee, a twenty-eight-year-old freshman who was just beginning to assert his own claims for black leadership in Oberlin, claimed to have witnessed the negotiations. Ignoring Newman and the issue at hand, Langston, bursting onstage from the committee room, launched a fierce counterattack on Lee, contending that he lacked the requisite credentials to act in the convention, that even so Langston had "taken him up and treated him courteously," but that Lee, while professing friendship, "had attempted thus to stab him." In the heat of the moment, Langston boasted that he represented white Oberliners as well as black, and the former had helped pay his way to Syracuse. After Douglass ruled Lee out of order, the delegates, disregarding the allegations against Langston, overwhelmingly approved his nomination. Shortly thereafter, Langston presided over the first hurried meeting of the league, into which the convention had reconstituted itself, at which the departing delegates enthusiastically pledged financial support.[50]

In victory Langston had taken a prize of uncertain value. Just as partisanship, lack of interest, and, as Clark put it, "the captiousness of our leading men" had helped to scuttle earlier vessels of black unity, the convention disputes augured ill for the league. Indeed, within days Garnet, reacting to public criticism of him by Martin, branded the league undemocratic and an instrument of the "milk and water colored codfish aristocracy," and, as Downing and Clark joined the fray, even threatened to call a new convention, a "people's convention," to set up a rival organization.[51] Although Garnet did not specifically attack Langston, Newman did, in an article in the Cincinnati *Colored Citizen* that Langston's Cleveland allies termed slanderous. Even three years later, Day, disappointed in his own desire for political preferment, would charge in his newspaper that Langston had resorted to "difficult and political chicanery" to obtain the league presidency.[52]

Although, despite the charges of his critics, Langston's backstage manuevers appear to have been neither unusual nor unethical, it is true that his convention conduct, particularly his pursuit of the presidency, suggests aspects of his personality with important implications for his national leadership. His driving dedication to the black cause, animating him since adolescence and nearly frenzied in the months since the Emancipation Proclamation, carried its own expectation of reward. His activism was intertwined with emotional tensions rooted in the deep hurt of his double orphaning and his residual hunger for approval. The obverse of the nightmare of helplessness and loneliness is the dream of power and recognition. It was intertwined, too, with cultural tensions, reflective of the ambiguity of his racial inheritance and half-privileged and half-oppressed social status, and of an almost inevitable ambivalence toward a white culture whose dominant mores he respected even as he despised its failure to practice its own professed ideals, and toward his own people, whose struggle he so deeply espoused and from whose lives he was, in so many ways, set apart. Although he tried to resolve these oppositions philosophically through embracing a broad humanism, and emotionally through personal achievement and public service, such resolutions could only be partial and required a rigorous self-discipline that, in turn, exacted an emotional toll. He put a just estimate on his capabilities and harbored commensurate ambitions. Thus, it was hardly surprising that, exercising his considerable political skills, he should have seized the opening presented to win the league presidency.

What is surprising is his clumsiness in self-defense. When accused of having underhandedly contrived the trade of the league headquarters from Cleveland to Philadelphia in exchange for the presidential nomination, he might better have called on delegates from the former city who, after all, had the most to lose, but who seemed fully supportive of his position. He might even have left the field to the Pennsylvanians who, in fact, did vigorously protest the charges. Instead, his attack on Lee, mounted with an able lawyer's tactical agility but without his better judgment, only proved effective in killing debate while leaving the issue alive. Although obviously intended to bolster his position, his reference to his white supporters in Oberlin simply served to betray his insecurity and to underline how much his social status differed from that of most of those he would lead. Langston's reaction was a reflection of his extreme sensitivity to criticism, particularly criticism of his integrity, that derived from his personal conflicts and seemed to reflect a rather naive belief that his black peers would estimate his conduct nearly as highly as he did himself. In expending his verbal artillery on Lee, who could scarcely be considered an equal opponent, Langston was assuaging his own pique at what he deemed to be the man's ingratitude, but he was also—in departing from his deliberate practice of publicly ignoring critics—making himself vulnerable to their future charges, including the notion that he was part of a black parvenu aristocracy.

Still, the 1864 National Convention of Colored Men installed Langston as a truly national leader. Prominent as he had been in northern black and abolitionist circles for virtually his entire adult life, indisputable as was his leadership in Ohio, he had hitherto been regarded primarily as a westerner. But with his election to head the National League, many Afro-Americans were ready to agree with the black Chicagoan who characterized Langston and Douglass as "the Aurora Borealis of our people." In a letter to a New Orleans friend, "Natchitoches" predicted: "The time will come when one or both of these men will occupy places in the hearts of the people of our country seldom reached by man. I need say nothing of Mr. Douglass, the world already knows him; and as an orator and thinker John Mercer Langston has no superior upon this continent." Yet in this contraposition with outstanding black easterners, who generally had tolerated rivals grudgingly, there were risks, particularly at a moment when black spokesmen were attaining increased power and influence, however limited and tenuous. By dint of geography as well as disposition, Langston previously had avoided this sort of antagonism. An aged Clark would remember, however, that rivalry between Douglass and Langston adversely affected the league.[53]

More than simply a personal victory, Langston's election marked the choice of an ideology. In contrast to Garnet, Langston stood as an unequivocal advocate of freedom and citizenship. Professionally, socially, politically, and personally, he exemplified an American nationalism that embodied both pride in race and faith in the ideals of the Declaration of Independence. In abandoning his own enthusiasm for black nationalist-emigration a decade before, he had embraced the ideas that found expression in the 1864 convention resolve: "That, as natives of American soil, we claim the right to remain upon it: and that any attempt to deport, remove, expatriate, or colonize us to any other land, or to mass us here against our will, is unjust, and here we hope to remain in the full enjoyment of enfranchised manhood, and its dignities." In the great numbers of the enslaved could they be freed and enfranchised by a government somehow persuaded to live up to its democratic standards, and in a black people aroused, instructed, and organized, North and South, there was the promise that Negroes might cease to be a despised minority and become a citizenry commanding respect. This image guided convention actions, nowhere more than in the choice of Langston to lead the National Equal Rights League. Putting black nationalism on the shelf where it would rest until darker days came again, the national convention of 1864 had decided to risk the grand attempt for American citizenship.[54]

Before trying to forward the league, Langston awaited the outcome of the fall elections. Returning home just before the Ohio balloting for congressional candidates, the black Republican, who had been one of Oberlin's delegates at the county convention of the Union party earlier that fall, doubtless pressed through the pelting rain to First church on October 8 to hear his ally Congressman James Garfield at a final exciting rally. The following Tuesday, the Union party in Ohio reversed its 1862 losses, electing seventeen candidates to Congress, as opposed to only two Democrats.[55]

By November, Lincoln's victory seemed so secure that Langston devoted election eve to rousing spirits for a new round of army recruitment in Oberlin rather than electioneering proper. Late the next day Colonel Giles W. Shurtleff of the Fifth U.S. Colored Regiment, limping from a thigh wound he had sustained in the devastating battle of Chapin's Farm in Virginia, appeared at the polls and, to shouts and applause, tendered his vote for "Lincoln and the Union." As the officers and men of Shurtleff's command cast their own ballots at improvised polls in a field far to the south in Virginia, a dark-skinned Negro orderly sergeant stepped up, only to be challenged under Ohio's "more white than black" suffrage restriction. In response, the sergeant pointed to an ugly scar on his throat that, he said, had earned him "the right to vote anywhere." In full agreement, Langston set about trying to capitalize on the possibilities for the black cause offered by Lincoln's reelection.[56]

The immediate response to the National Equal Rights League was encouraging. To the accompaniment of an approving tattoo from the black press, Negroes in a number of localities, on hearing reports from their representatives to the Syracuse convention, had commended its work, expressed support for the league, and formed local auxiliaries.[57] In North Carolina, where sub-leagues named for John Brown, Lincoln, and Garnet were set up, the first state league was born three days after Lincoln's reelection. One of Langston's admirers, James H. Harris—a former North Carolina slave who had migrated to Ohio in 1850, received some schooling in Oberlin, attended Brown's Chatham convention, and traveled "40,000 miles in search of a better country" before returning to recruit black soldiers—was from the start its driving force. Harris was to become an important black leader in North Carolina Reconstruction. Meanwhile, in Tennessee on Thanksgiving day a group of blacks, led by livery stable owner Peter Lowery and Ransom Harris, both men ministers who had represented Nashville at the national convention and the latter a member of the National League's executive board, also adopted a constitution for a state Equal Rights League.[58] On the state and local level, enthusiasm for the league would continue to grow during the next months, with at least seven more states—Louisiana, Michigan, Pennsylvania, Massachusetts, Ohio, Missouri, and New York—forming state leagues by the end of the war.[59]

On the level of the national board, however, as the result of personal rivalry or misunderstandings between black leaders, or the difficulty of long-distance travel and the press of personal business, or some combination of these and other factors, organization proved more difficult. Langston, reasoning that the holiday would encourage attendance and perhaps unaware that Harris, at least, would have to be absent, called the first meeting of the executive board for Philadelphia on November 24, Thanksgiving day.[60]

For their part, black Philadelphians, renowned for their hospitality, lived up to their reputation in their welcome to the league president, honoring him with a reception, several invitations to speak, and a $52 contribution to the league. But most memorable for Langston was his introduction to the famous black war hero Captain Robert Smalls. In May 1862, Smalls, a slave pilot who was destined to become an important politician in Reconstruction and post-Reconstruction South Carolina, had commandeered the *Planter*, a Confederate steamer, in Charleston harbor and delivered it to the Union blockading fleet. When Langston and several black Philadelphians took the Camden ferry to the Brooklyn navy yard to tour the *Planter*, Smalls himself welcomed them aboard and gave them a guided tour. "In behalf of the Colored of the United States," Langston formally congratulated the captain for his services to the cause of freedom. Two days later at Smalls's invitation Langston headed a party of thirteen that sat down to Sunday dinner at the captain's table.[61]

Despite the festivities, the board meeting was little short of a fiasco. With only himself and the two league secretaries, St. George R. Taylor of Altoona and Davis D. Turner of Philadelphia, of the eight-member board in attendance—Langston found himself unable to declare a quorum. The board thus was blocked not just from moving ahead but even from resolving a critical piece of unfinished business. Only a limited number of the minutes of the Syracuse convention with Douglass's address thus far had reached the public. John Rock, charged with publication, later would explain that, because the funds on hand were insufficient for a larger printing, he had written to Langston in early November requesting that an order for the additional sum be sent to the treasurer, William Rich of Troy, New York, who afterward informed him that Langston had never responded. Although Langston refrained from public comment, he did attempt without success to summon Rock and Rich, both board members, to the meeting by telegram.[62]

The situation at the second meeting of the board in Philadelphia on March 14 was only marginally improved. Although the presence of a fourth member, Ransom Harris of Nashville, enabled Langston to declare a quorum, meaningful action—such as the employment of agents, which he was eager to undertake—was precluded. Wherever culpability lay for the failure to publish the minutes, Rich still had made no accounting of funds, and Rock's committee on publications still had made no report. It was not until the middle of April that the proceedings would finally be published for general distribution.[63]

On both occasions, Langston chose to eschew controversy. Without criticism of other board members for their inability or unwillingness to attend, indeed, without public hint at their absence, he and the secretaries in November and again in March broadcast ardent pleas for cooperation. "While the devotion, the gallantry, and the heroism" displayed by black soldiers were still fresh in the public consciousness, went the former, "let us . . . not fail to make every effort in our power to secure for ourselves and our children all those rights, natural and political, which belong to us as men and as native-born citizens of America." The time was ideal to "enter upon . . . a well defined, energetic and manly course of action."[64]

Carpetbag in hand, Langston shortly began to carry out this resolve. Aside from presiding over the regular meetings of the league and of the executive committee, his charge as president was broadly defined: to see that its decrees were "duly executed" and to perform any other duties imposed by the league. Holding with his black cohort in Columbus that the "watch-word" must be "agitate, agitate, agitate,"[65] he interpreted that charge in characteristically activist terms. Although the organization lacked the means to hire the agent or agents prescribed in its constitution, Langston's popularity as an orator, enhanced by his new office, provided him with the opportunity to function informally in that role. In response to invitations from local black committees and organizations in the South, West, and Northeast, Langston would spend the last winter of the rebellion on his appointed rounds. He would stand on platforms, exploring freedom and citizenship in their manifold aspects, and he would meet black people in private, concerning himself with their hopes and fears and lending the political expertise that he had accumulated as a black organizer and radical politician in Ohio.

Alongside some of his longtime co-workers, he helped to form the Ohio Equal Rights League. In Ohio, enthusiasm for the league, which soon had auxiliaries in Cincinnati, Columbus, Cleveland, and elsewhere, had grown rapidly. Instrumental in setting up the Oberlin League, where black students expressed pride in his position at the head of the national organization, Langston, on his way to Philadelphia in November, also had attended the organizational meeting in Cleveland. With the veteran John Malvin as presiding officer, a large assembly had not only set up a league but had collected and entrusted to Langston the $25 its representatives in Syracuse had pledged to the National League. The secretary of the meeting was a future civil rights activist and Latin professor at Howard University, fifteen-year-old James M. Gregory, born in Virginia to free parents, who would enter the Oberlin preparatory department in 1865 and participate in the Oberlin League—which he would consider a shaping influence in his life.[66]

On January 10, Langston was among the fifty-nine black Ohioans representing twenty-four counties who gathered in Xenia for a three-day state convention. With James Poindexter of Columbus as president, the delegates included such leaders as John Booker and J. T. Ward of Columbus, Alfred J. Anderson of Hamilton, plaintiff in the Ohio Supreme Court's important 1859 decision protecting the voting privileges of those more white than black, "Rescuer" John Scott of Oberlin, shortly to volunteer for the Fifth Ohio Cavalry Regiment,[67] A. J. Gordon of Yellow Springs, the Cincinnati orator of Langston's boyhood, Henry Hurd of Carthagena, pioneer of the Mercer County black farming community, Dr. Joshua McCarter Simpson of Zanesville, composer of black folk music,[68] Charles A. Yancy of Berlin Cross Roads, and Daniel A. Payne of Wilberforce University, the future A. M. E. bishop.

In forming the Ohio Equal Rights League, the delegates chose Peter Clark as president and Cincinnati as headquarters, while pledging "a constant and manly endeavor" to obtain complete freedom and enfranchisement. With a petition for black suffrage already in circulation, the convention appointed David Jenkins as the league lobbyist in Columbus and praised him for his persuasive efforts with the preceding legislature. A petition drive led by Jenkins had resulted in several changes in the school law, whose effect was to allow the establishment of more schools for black children. At his urging—as well as that of outgoing Governor Tod in fulfillment of his promise to the Fifth Regiment—the legislators also had provided for the support of the families of black soldiers. Further signs of the change in the racial climate brought about by black contributions to the war came in the current assembly session, which repealed the infamous 1859 act barring light-skinned Negroes from the polls (which had remained on the books despite the negating effect of the Anderson decision) and abrogated an 1863 enactment barring black immigrants from obtaining a residence in Ohio.[69]

In addition to explaining the workings of the league to the convention, Langston delivered a public address at a special evening session designed to raise money to mail three black newspapers—the *Colored Citizen*, *Anglo-African*, and *Christian Recorder*—to black soldiers and sailors. The editors of two of these papers, John P. Sampson of the *Colored Citizen* and Robert Hamilton of the *Anglo-African*, were on hand. Despite his support of Garnet at the Syracuse convention, Hamilton, who was touring the West to publicize his journal and had just stopped over in Oberlin where he had met Langston's wife, now showed every sign of willingness to cooperate with the league president—a willingness that Langston obviously reciprocated. With word having just arrived that slavery had been abolished in Missouri—for which, at Langston's suggestion, delegates had joined in a "prayer of thanksgiving to Almighty God"—the general mood was jubilant. His speech, at 25 cents a ticket, drew a full house.[70]

During February and March, Langston spoke extensively in the Northeast. Under black sponsorship, he appeared in Boston with his friends William C. Nell and Frances Ellen Watkins Harper for a commemoration of Crispus Attucks, the Negro who was the first man killed in the American Revolution, and in Philadelphia, Brooklyn, and New York. Although his audiences were not always large, he received respectful notices in the white radical and black press. "President Langston" had "created a furore among our people to hear more of him, for he is not only able but versatile and can keep on lecturing with increased interest for a dozen evenings at least," the *Anglo-African* declared. He "had a flow of words and an intonation that were pleasing in the extreme, and was both earnest and eloquent in the whole of his speech. In the latter part particularly, his enthusiasm was not to be mistaken, and we, the reporter, can only say that we will drink his health and that of the gay 5th from the south of Ohio in the very first glass of wine we can muster, and beg for success to both him and them."[71]

Of all of Langston's efforts during these months, the most remarkable was his first foray among the newly freed people. During the final week of 1864 he set out for Nashville where he was to be the speaker at the celebration of the second anniversary of the Emancipation Proclamation. He admittedly felt apprehensive about the reception to be extended him by a South in the death rattle of impending defeat. Only days before his departure, Confederate forces under John Bell Hood had clashed with Union defenders under George Thomas in two days of murderous battle outside Nashville and, although the latter had been victorious, guerrilla attacks continued in the Tennessee countryside. In Kentucky as well, through which he had to pass, marauders still operated at will.[72]

On Langton's arrival in Louisville, however, a group of black women asked him to speak; then and on five subsequent occasions he succeeded in addressing several thousand black men and women. "Now is the time," he advised an audience at Quinn A.M.E. Chapel, "for you to assert your manhood and to convince the world that you are worthy of a place among free men." In the city, filled with black soldiers—"many splendid men, entirely dark, in fine uniforms and with guns," as he characterized them—he suffered nothing more onerous than the requirement for a pass which, he later joked, the officer was reluctant to issue until given assurances by a black Kentuckian that the light-skinned man from Ohio actually was a Negro. Unable to dissuade Langston from his plans to continue on to Nashville despite their warnings that few recent southbound trains had safely made it through bushwhacker territory, his friends convinced him to accept the services of William Howard of Louisville. While the latter, watching over the traveler's carpetbag and papers and ready to rush to his defense, rode in the smoker, Langston, seated in the regular car, thoughtfully observed a landscape cluttered with wrecked locomotives and the burned-out husks of once fine manor houses on what turned out to be an uneventful trip to the Tennessee capital.[73]

In Nashville, Langston found black leaders who were determined and innovative in their push for emancipation and political rights. Even before the war, free and "freeslave" Negroes—men and women who with the acquiescence of their owners had attained a high degree of self-sufficiency—had composed a small enterprising black community within a restricted society. Taking advantage of a private school that had functioned intermittently since the 1830s, many of these individuals, a number of whom would be prominent during Reconstruction, possessed at least the rudiments of an education.[74] The thousands of former bondsmen who took refuge in the capital following the Confederate evacuation in 1862 contributed their own needs and energies to the developing black political consciousness. After a black mass meeting to support enlistment in the Union army in October 1863 was held despite the legal bars on black convocations, an emerging black leadership, whose identifiable members were largely free and "freeslave" businessmen, artisans, and clergymen but which probably also included runaway slaves, had mounted frequent demonstrations for their rights. In addition to marches and meetings, they had set up a mock polling place during the presidential election at which all but one of nearly 3,500 ballots cast favored the Union ticket. Three men from Nashville and two from Memphis (including Horatio N. Rankin, an Oberlin student working as an A.M.A. teacher) had attended the national convention at Syracuse. Langston had been invited to speak in Nashville the previous summer but had been unable to keep his engagement. Now, on the eve of a state convention to draw up a new constitution for Tennessee, and with a black petition for the granting of full civil and political rights in circulation,[75] his appearance could not have been more timely.

Langston was pleased to discover that an elaborate celebration of the anniversary of the Emancipation Proclamation had been planned without white assistance. His hosts, a black soldiers' aid society, the Nashville Sons of Relief, had secured the permission of Andrew Johnson, military governor of Tennessee and the vice-president-elect, to hold an evening meeting in the hall of the state house of representatives. During the day Langston received the public at a hotel for Negroes. Its owner was Henry Harding, a member of the host committee, who, although still a slave, had amassed sufficient earnings as a wheelwright to buy the three-story hotel on Cherry Street and to begin to accumulate considerable property. Besides Harding, the committee included Wade Hickman, an attendant of Governor Johnson at the capitol and a restaurateur; William Sumner, a livery stable operator, grocer, and liquor dealer with extensive property holdings; James Sumner, a hack driver; Abraham Smith, a vice-president of the National Equal Rights League, who worked as a porter at the capitol and would later become a jailor and Harding's real estate partner; and William C. Napier, a hack driver and deliveryman who had established close associations with upper-class whites. Not only Harding, but also Hickman and Smith were still classed as slaves; the others were freeborn.[76]

On the evening of January 2, 1865, Langston was at the center of an unprecedented scene. Making their way through miserably muddy streets congested with army vehicles and soldiers, well-dressed black men and women began arriving early at the Tennessee statehouse, an imposing, still unfinished structure of native limestone in classical style situated on a hill that afforded a view of the city around it, the Cumberland River, and the distant rim of mountains. Soon a crowd of some three thousand, mainly civil and orderly Negroes, as a local newspaper noted, filled the floor and galleries of the hall, an august chamber divided by sixteen massive fluted stone columns. About five hundred whites, Union officers in full military attire making colorful clusters among them, were seated at random in the throng. As Governor Johnson took his place on the platform alongside such dignitaries as the commanding general of the Nashville Military District, Langston accepted a chair—the very one occupied in 1861 by the president of the convention that had voted Tennessee out of the Union. Imbued with Oberlin's abolitionist legends, Langston knew that just outside the hall almost thirty years before, a student, Amos Dresser, had suffered a public flogging for having antislavery pamphlets in his possession. On introduction, Langston rose to round after round of applause.[77]

Although plagued by a severe cold and hoarseness, he spoke for an hour and a half on his enduring theme—newly reworked into a speech titled "The War, Our National Emancipator"—that the war-induced end of slavery would signal the beginning of freedom for both whites and blacks to fulfill America's democratic destiny. On northern platforms during this period Langston called for enfranchisement for the emancipated Negro in the South as well as for the free Negro of the North, bluntly stating that there had never been "a more fitting time to discuss Negro equality." Here, although his basic message was the same, his tone was tactful, designed at once to reassure white southern Unionists and to inspire the freed men and women. Calling attention to his mixed racial inheritance, he staked his familiar claim to an identity of interest with white as well as black Americans and his belief in "a full freedom for all men of whatever race or complexion." The privileges of citizenship belonged not to "white men only," but "apply as well to him who has knotty hair, chalky eyes, long heels and flat nose, as to him who has flaxen hair and blue eyes. The federal Constitution says not one word about color. . . . I would say then, to the colored

Americans around me tonight, the Government owes you protection, and you owe it allegiance." While extending gratitude to the "noble white men" assisting the black cause, the freed men and women must learn the precepts of self-reliance. As for the Emancipation Proclamation whose issuance they were celebrating, it "should be hung on the walls of your dwellings; let your children learn to read it. The nation has said to us, 'Come forth,' and we have come forth, it may be with our old grave clothes bound about us, but resolved on progress."[78]

The speech—praised by the local Union newspaper that printed large portions of it and commented that it had been listened to with "profound and unbroken attention"—caused Andrew Johnson to invite Langston to call on him. In recent months Johnson himself had been exploring the idea that the war had "freed more whites than blacks," and, with his promise to be the black man's Moses—to which Langston had flatteringly alluded—had held out prospects of freedom and possibly equal rights, declaring that control of Tennessee's future should be in the hands of "loyal men, whether white or black." The following morning Langston, accompanied by the host committee, went to the governor's office. During a long interview, it became clear that Langston's stress on black self-reliance had particularly appealed to Johnson, speaking to the concerns of southern whites about the freed man as a worker and, more specifically, to his own experience and philosophy as a self-made man.[79] (Langston could have reminded him that the Patterson family of North Carolina, the black family who had helped Johnson when he was a poverty-stricken youth, were now his own neighbors in Oberlin.)[80] Thanking Langston for his advice to the colored people, the governor asked him to urge the freed men and women to be up and doing for themselves. Langston's arguments for equal rights, however, were less successful. At the constitutional convention that opened within the week, Johnson would successfully insist upon deletion of a proposed amendment to extend suffrage to black soldiers, although the convention did agree to leave the setting of suffrage qualifications in the hands of the first legislature after the constitutional referendum. The convention would propose, and loyal white voters subsequently approve, the emancipation of the slaves. Grateful for Johnson's hospitable treatment and aware that Nashville black leaders found him cooperative in a number of respects, Langston received a favorable impression of the man who was shortly to become vice-president.[81]

Johnson asked a favor. During the recent Battle of Nashville, eight regiments of black troops, some only just plucked from plantations, had borne the brunt of the fighting and suffered extremely heavy losses. Their valor had inspired the wounded white soldiers to refuse to be moved from the battlefield before or without the black casualties—a "nobility of soul" that, Langston told audiences in the North, should be held up as an example to all white people. With every appearance of sincerity, he would recollect nine years later, Johnson declared, "When I forget these men [the black soldiers], may my God forget me." Explaining that emotion might overcome him should he try to address the survivors himself, he requested that Langston "tell them for me that I think them the bravest men under the sun." The Negro accepted the honor; the white man was relieved of a burden.[82]

Colonel J. A. Dewey, a white Oberlin alumnus who was commanding officer of the 111th U.S. Colored Infantry, took Langston out to the camp in an ambulance cart. Light snow covered the ground. While five thousand black soldiers—"covered equally with blackness and with glory," as he put it—stood drawn up in a hollow square, Langston, using an army wagon as a platform, tried to convey his appreciation of their deeds. As he was lowered on the wagon tongue to the ground after his remarks, an already emotion-filled experience was intensified when he met the aged black corporal Robert J.—the Louisa County fugitive whose aggressive entry into Ralph Quarles's Great House had terrified Langston as a child. "You were never a slave!" Langston blurted to the erect old man. "Always a slave, John, always a slave; but always a fugitive slave." Afterward, Colonel Dewey identified the corporal as a natural leader who exercised an unrivalled influence over his troops.[83]

After leaving Tennessee, Langston took advantage of a further opportunity to witness the condition of black men and women as they stood on the verge of freedom. When the state constitutional convention abolished slavery in Missouri, he was summoned to St. Louis to take part in the celebration. Traveling there directly from the Ohio state black convention, he appeared before a large audience at a festival in Veranda Hall and delivered a speech that a hostile journalist termed brilliant. A businessman involved in organizing free schools for blacks in the city, Preston G. Wells—or "Father Wells," as Langston had called him at the Syracuse convention where, as Missouri's sole representative, he had been named a vice-president of the National Equal Rights League—had helped to arrange for his appearance. Young Oberlin-educated J. Milton Turner, the future minister to Liberia, also took part in the festivities. "At St. Louis I wanted no pass—colored men now look up at the stars and walk erect without fear and the freest city in the

Union is now St. Louis," Langston exulted a few weeks later. That black Missourians intended to work to make this vision an actuality became clear soon afterward with the formation of the Missouri Equal Rights League.[84]

What Langston would term his "first general trip of observation of the colored people of the South" deeply touched him. The "great bodies of [newly freed men and women], now in early movement, searching for a spot upon which to place their feet for life and its achievements," impressed him at once with their resourcefulness, courage, hope, and religious faith and their vast need. Although the army, especially the black soldiers, agents of the Freedmen's Bureau, and workers from charitable and religious groups in the North offered some help, nonetheless, in the border states it was the free black families—exemplified by his host committee in Nashville—that Langston saw assuming the most vital role. By the example of their own lives, the modest homes, churches, and sometimes schools they had managed to establish despite their restrictive environment, and their wartime efforts toward improving the political and social condition of their people, they exercised the most potent influence on the freed people. Black women, with their "business understanding and tact," were particularly energetic and effective in projects for black betterment.[85]

Sobering as the situation was, Langston was exhilarated to witness and be part of the transformation from slavery to freedom. "It is no longer—'Susan, you must do so and so or you'll be whipped.' But its 'Susan, do so and so,' and Susan says 'no—I am going to dress up and go to the Soldiers' Aid Fair.'" He himself "had the impudence to walk all about" and "no man molested him." As he told black and white friends in Oberlin, who gave him a near hero's welcome at the completion of his southern travels, and elsewhere, wherever he went he had managed to speak "always with perfect freedom, withholding no truth he wished to utter."[86]

On the strength of his observations South and North, he judged—as he noted in his plea for cooperation with the National Equal Rights League issued in March—"that colored Americans in all localities of the Republic in which circumstances have lent the least assistance have been untiring in their efforts to elevate themselves from the depths of debasement to which pro-slavery policy had consigned us all." At the same time, "there is scarcely a community in the United States in which some outrage and conspiracy against colored men's rights is not in daily practice. . . . Justice to the tens of thousands of our brothers, relatives, and friends, who have stubbornly opposed the public enemy upon many bloody fields, giving us still greater claims to all which belongs to the loyal citizen, demands that you should move in the great matter of reconstructing our nation, upon the basis of liberty to all."[87]

For a few fragile moments of rejoicing over the defeat of the South, Langston took hope that Reconstruction might be based on universal liberty. Having gone to Washington in pursuit of his commission as an army colonel, he stood among the immense throng in front of a White House ablaze with lights two evenings after the surrender, staring up at the gaunt face of Abraham Lincoln. Although the president justified his plan for reconstructing Louisiana and appealed for forgiveness of the Confederates, he also declared his preference that the elective franchise "were now conferred on very intelligent colored men, and on those who serve our cause as soldiers." Less than Langston desired, it was enough to make his heart leap. Three nights later Lincoln was murdered.[88]

"The foul assassination of Abraham Lincoln . . . this day makes us indeed a nation of mourners," Langston said. A year later he would recall that Negroes in the capital had "felt as though they had lost their best friend." Nonetheless, even in mourning, they were thrilled on the "sweet, lovely" day of the funeral procession when—through an organizational snarl that he ascribed to providence—the 22nd U.S. Colored Troops led the line of march down Pennsylvania Avenue. Standing near the southwest corner of the Capitol, he himself was filled with gratitude at the sight of the black soldiers. Not everyone was pleased. Lost somewhere in the crowd of fifty thousand, a white man remarked to no one in particular, "What a shame." When questioned, he explained: "Oh, it seems too bad to put a *negro* regiment in the advance."[89]

At this historic juncture, cognizant of the symbolic as well as the potential practical significance of such a meeting, Langston was anxious to present the black brief for equality to the new president, Andrew Johnson. Despite the scandal Johnson had created by his intemperate performance at his inauguration as vice-president, radicals tended toward cautious optimism about his future conduct toward the South. Langston's friend Henry E. Peck—the Oberlin professor newly appointed minister to Haiti, where he would die of yellow fever in 1867—also visiting Washington, was inspired "with hope and encouragement of the highest kind," convinced that Lincoln's successor would "do all his duty and justify the public expectations of him." During these eventful days, Langston had renewed his acquaintance with Wade Hickman, one of his hosts in Nashville, who had accompanied Johnson to Washington as his private servant, and quite probably with his help—in keeping with the hoary protocol of seeking access to high places through the back stairs—secured an audience with the president.[90]

On the morning of April 18, 1865, Langston, at the head of a delegation somehow gathered from among prominent black men then in Washington, faced Andrew Johnson. Because, just three days after the assassination, the president was not yet installed in the White House, the interview took place in an office in the Treasury Building. Speaking as president of the National Equal Rights League—"an association whose membership may be numbered by thousands—an association having its branches in well nigh all the loyal States of the Union—an association representing in a truly national sense the patriotism and loyalty of the colored American"—Langston offered congratulations, sympathy, and assurances of black support. "Your past history, as connected with the rebellion, gives us full assurance that in your hands our cause shall receive no detriment, and that our liberty and rights will be fully protected and sustained. We are not ignorant of the many noble utterances of freedom which you have made to the colored people of your own State, Tennessee, nor are we ignorant of the high estimate in which they hold you as their friend and benefactor."[91]

"The colored American asks but two things," the president of the National Equal Rights League told the president of the United States. "He asks, after proving his devotion to his country by responding to her call in the hour of her sorest trial, and after demonstrating, upon many hotly-contested battle-fields, his manhood and valor, that he have, first, complete emancipation, and secondly, full equality before American law."[92]

NOTES

1. "Oscar" to Editor, *National Anti-Slavery Standard*, Mar. 18, 1865; Lorain County *News*, July 6, 1864; August Meier, *Negro Thought in America, 1880–1915* (Ann Arbor, 1963), pp. 3– 6; James M. McPherson, *Ordeal by Fire: The Civil War and Reconstruction* (New York, 1982), pp. 391–408.

2. *Proceedings of the National Convention of Colored Men, . . . Syracuse, N.Y., Oct. 4, 5, 6 and 7, 1864 . . .* (Boston, 1864) (hereafter cited as *National Convention . . . 1864*); *Anglo-African*, Mar. 11, 1865.

3. *Proceedings of the First Annual Meeting of the National Equal Rights League . . . Cleveland, Ohio . . . Sept. 19, 20, and 21, 1865* (Philadelphia, 1865) (hereafter cited as *First Annual Meeting . . . 1865*); Philadelphia *Press*, Mar. 11, 1865.

4. "Oscar" to Editor, *National Anti-Slavery Standard*, Mar. 18, 1865; Chicago *Tribune*, Apr. 15, 1863.

5. *Anglo-African*, Mar. 11, 1865.

6. John Mercer Langston, "Citizenship and the Ballot," in John Mercer Langston, *Freedom and Citizenship* (Washington, 1883; repr. Miami: Mnemosyne Reprint, 1969), pp. 106–7; "Oscar to Editor, *National Anti-Slavery Standard*, Mar. 18, 1865.

7. Lorain County *News*, Jan. 7, 1863; speech of J. M. Langston, Nashville *Times*, Jan. 4, 1865.

8. Oberlin *Evangelist*, Aug. 13, 1851; Lorain County *News*, Jan. 7, 1863; *National Convention . . . 1864*.

9. Lorain County *News*, Dec. 17, 1862, Jan. 7, Mar. 11, 1863; Oberlin *Evangelist*, Dec. 3, 1862. For Langston's activities with various freedmen's aid groups, see Washington *Chronicle*, Dec. 16, 1863; *Anglo-African*, Mar. 12, 1864, Feb. 11, 1865. On Oberlin A. M. A. teachers in the Civil War South, see, for example, Lorain County *News*, Feb. 25, May 27, Sept. 23, 1863; E. H. Fairchild to George Whipple, Aug. 8, 1863; Horatio N. Rankin to George Whipple, Sept. 7, 1863; Thomas De. Tucker to George Whipple, Feb. 22, 1864; Sara Stanley to George Whipple, Mar. 4, 1864; Lucie S. Day to George Whipple, Apr. 26, 1864, all in American Missionary Association Archives, Amistad Research Center, Tulane University (hereafter cited as AMA Papers).

10. *Anti-Slavery Bugle*, Sept. 24, 1859; John Mercer Langston, "The World's Anti-Slavery Movement," Langston, *Freedom and Citizenship*, p. 60.

11. *Anglo-African*, Mar. 11, 1865.

12. "An Observer" to Editor, June 3, 1864, *Anglo-African*, June 11, 1864; "Oscar" to Editor, *National Anti-Slavery Standard*, Mar. 18, 1865.

13. Washington *Chronicle*, Dec. 16, 1863; *National Convention . . . 1864*; Nashville *Times*, Jan. 4, 1865; *Christian Recorder*, Mar. 18, 1865.

14. John M. Langston et al., "Executive Board of National Equal Rights League, Nov. 24, 1864, to the Colored People of the United States," reprinted in *Christian Recorder*, Jan. 7, 1865.

15. Philadelphia *Press*, Mar. 11, 1865.

16. John Mercer Langston et al., "An Appeal, National Equal Rights Bureau, Mar. 14, 1865," reprinted in *Christian Recorder*, Apr. 15, 1865.

17. Thomas H. C. Hinton to Editor, Dec. 12, 1863, *Christian Recorder*, Dec. 26, 1863; John M. Langston to William Lloyd Garrison, Dec. 3, 1863, William Lloyd Garrison Papers, Boston Public Library; James M. McPherson, *The Struggle for Equality: Abolitionists and the Negro in the Civil War* (Princeton, 1964), p. 240; McPherson, *Ordeal by Fire*, pp. 391–92.

18. Washington *Chronicle*, Dec. 8, 1863; Constance McLaughlin Green, *The Secret City* (Princeton, 1967), pp. 51–52; Thomas H. C. Hinton to Editor, Dec. 12, 1863, *Christian Recorder*, Dec. 26, 1863; "Mc." to Editor, Dec. 9, 1863, Lorain County *News*, Dec. 16, 1863.

19. Washington *Chronicle*, Dec. 16, 1863; "Our Washington Correspondence," Dec. 27, 1863, *Anglo-African*, Jan. 9, 1864.

20. Thomas H. C. Hinton to Editor, Dec. 12, 1863, *Christian Recorder*, Dec. 26, 1863; Thomas H. C. Hinton to Editor, Jan. 23, 1864, Ibid., Jan. 30, 1864; Washington *Chronicle*, Jan. 6, 1864; Boston *Commonwealth*, n.d., quoted in San

Francisco *Pacific Appeal*, Mar. 5, 1864. After black protests the "pass" system was abrogated by the House of Representatives in March of 1865; Boston *Commonwealth*, Mar. 18, 1865.

21. Speech of J. M. Langston, Nashville *Times*, Jan. 4, 1865; Salmon P. Chase Memoranda, 1864, "Addresses," Salmon P. Chase Papers, Historical Society of Pennsylvania; "Our Washington Correspondence," Dec. 27, 1863, *Anglo-African*, Jan. 9, 1864; Washington *Chronicle*, Dec. 16, 1863; *Anglo-African*, Jan. 23, 1864; San Francisco *Pacific Appeal*, Mar. 12, 1864.

22. *Anglo-African*, Dec. 19, 1863, Dec. 10, Jan. 23, 1864.

23. Adrian *Expositor*, quoted in *Anglo-African*, June 11, 1864; *Anglo-African*, Aug. 20, 1864.

24. *National Convention . . . 1864*; Chicago *Tribune*, Apr. 15, 1863; Toledo *Blade*, May 28, 1864; McPherson, *The Struggle for Equality*, pp. 269–70.

25. McPherson, *Ordeal by Fire*, pp. 391–408, 440–42, 447–49; Lorain County *News*, Oct. 5, 1864.

26. *National Convention . . . 1864*; Howard H. Bell, "Negro Emancipation in Historical Retrospect: The Nation—The Condition and Prospects of the Negro as Reflected in the National Convention of 1864," *Journal of Human Relations* 11 (Winter 1963):221–31; Meier, *Negro Thought in America*, pp. 4–8.

27. *National Convention . . . 1864*; *Anglo-African*, Oct. 15, 1864.

28. "ANIMUS," "A Call for Unity," *Christian Recorder*, Jan. 16, 1864; San Francisco *Pacific Appeal*, Mar. 5, 1864; Washington *Chronicle*, Mar. 22, 1864; "An Appeal in Behalf of the Elective Franchise to Colored People of the U.S.A.," *Christian Recorder*, Jan. 23, 1864; Sattie Douglass to Editor, July 5, 1864, *Anglo-African*, July 30, 1864. See also Larry E. Nelson, "Black Leaders and the Presidential Election of 1864," *Journal of Negro History* 63 (Jan. 1978):42–55.

29. C.H. Langston to Editor, Lorain County *News*, Mar. 26, May 21, 1862; C. H. Langston, William D. Matthews, John Turner to Governor Charles Robinson, Dec. 17, 1863, Charles Robinson Collection, Kansas State Historical Society; Sattie Douglass to Editor, July 4, July 5, 1864, *Anglo-African*, July 23, July 30, 1864. See also Eugene H. Berwanger, "Hardin and Langston: Western Black Spokesmen of the Reconstruction Era," *Journal of Negro History* 64 (Spring 1979):105–7.

30. *Anglo-African*, July 2, 16, 23, 30, Aug. 6, 13, 20, 27, Sept. 3, 1864; New Orleans *Tribune*, Sept. 20, 1864; *Christian Recorder*, July 23, 1864.

31. John S. Rock to C. L. Remond, Geo. L. Downing, John J. Smith, Wilson et al., Apr. 19, 1864; John S. Rock to H. H. Garnet, Robt. Hamilton, S. G. Brown and others, July 15, 1864; John S. Rock to Rev. H. Highland Garnet, July 23, 1864, all in George L. Ruffin Papers, Moorland-Spingarn Research Center, Howard University; J. B. Smith to Editor, Aug. 6, 1864, *Anglo-African*, Aug. 20, 1864; John S. Rock to Messrs. Garnet, Hamilton, and others, Sept. 5, 1864, *Anglo-African*, Sept. 10, 1864.

32. Geo. B. Collins to Editor, Sept. 22, 1864, *Anglo-African*, Oct. 8. 1864; J. E. Sampson to Editor, Sept. 2, 1864, *Anglo-African*, Sept. 17, 1864; "L'Occident" to Editor, Sept. 19, 1864, Ohio Soldier to Editor, Sept. 13, 1864, both in *Anglo-African*, Oct. 1, 1864.

33. "A Call," *Anglo-African*, July 2, 1864; R. H. Cain to Editor, *Christian Recorder*, July 16, 1864; Henry Highland Garnet to Editor, July 20, 1864, *Christian Recorder*, July 30, 1864; *Anglo-African*, Aug. 13, 20, 1864; Robert Wilson to Messrs. Henry Highland Garnet et al., Aug. 1, 1864, *Anglo-African*, Aug. 20, 1864; W. E. W. to Editor, Aug. 5, 1864, *Anglo-African*, Aug. 20, 1864; P[eter] H. C[lark] to Editor, Nov. 8, 1864, *Anglo-African*, Nov. 26, 1864.

34. Joel Schor, *Henry Highland Garnet: A Voice of Black Radicalism in the Nineteenth Century* (Westport, Conn., 1977), pp. 150–215; Sterling Stuckey, "A Last Stern Struggle: Henry Highland Garnet and Liberation Theory," in *Black Leaders of the Nineteenth Century*, ed. Leon Litwack and August Meier (Urbana, 1988), pp. 129–47; Richard K. McMaster, "Henry Highland Garnet and the African Civilization Society," *Journal of Presbyterian History* 48 (Summer 1970):95–112; Jane H. Pease and William H. Pease, *Bound with Them in Chains: A Biographical History of the Antislavery Movement* (Westport, Conn., 1972), pp. 162–90; James M. McPherson, *The Negro's Civil War: How American Negroes Felt and Acted During the War for the Union* (New York, 1965), pp. 261–64; *Liberator*, June 12, 1863; Floyd J. Miller, *The Search for a Black Nationality: Black Colonization and Emigration, 1787–1863* (Urbana, 1975), pp. 183–93, 197, 228–31, 258–63.

35. *Christian Recorder*, Feb. 13, 1864; Geo. T. Downing to Editor, Nov. 1, 1864, *Anglo-African*, Nov. 19, 1864; Miller, *The Search for a Black Nationality*, pp. 262–263. For the view that the African Civilization Society no longer had emigrationist aims in 1864, see Schor, *Henry Highland Garnet*, pp. 201–2.

36. "Reply of Rev. Henry Highland Garnet to Rev. J. Sella Martin, Oct. 14, 1864," *Anglo-African*, Oct. 29, 1864; William Wells Brown, *The Rising Son; or, The Antecedents and Advancement of the Colored Race* (Boston, 1874; repr. New York: Johnson Reprint Corp., 1970), pp. 535–36; Miller, *The Search for a Black Nationality*, p. 228; Jane H. Pease and William H. Pease, *They Who Would Be Free: Blacks' Search for Freedom, 1830–1861* (New York, 1974), pp. 270–72; "Rev. J. Sella Martin on the National Convention," *Anglo-African*, Oct. 22, 1864. On Martin, see R. J. M. Blackett, *Beating Against the Barriers: Biographical Essays in Nineteenth-Century Afro-American History* (Baton Rouge, 1986), pp. 185–285.

37. "Howard" [William Howard Day] to Editor, *Anglo-African*, Oct. 8, Oct. 29, 1864; "TYPES" to Editor, *Anglo-African*, Oct. 22, 1864.

38. *National Convention . . . 1864*; *Syracuse Journal*, Oct. 7, 1864, reprinted in *National Anti-Slavery Standard*, Oct. 15, 1864; *Christian Recorder*, Oct. 15, 1864.

39. *National Convention . . . 1864*; "Howard" to Editor, *Anglo-African*, Oct. 15, 1864; "Rev. J. Sella Martin on the National Convention," *Anglo-African*, Oct. 22, 1864; "Reply of Rev. Henry Highland Garnet," Oct. 14, 1864, *Anglo-African*, Oct. 29, 1864.

40. "Howard" to Editor, *Anglo-African*, Oct. 15, Oct. 22, 1864; *National Convention . . . 1864*.

41. "Howard" to Editor, *Anglo-African*, Oct. 22, 1864; *Minutes of the State Convention of the Colored Citizens of Ohio . . . Columbus . . . Jan., 1850* (Columbus, 1850); *Anglo-African*, Nov. 26, 1864.

42. William J. Simmons. *Men of Mark: Eminent, Progressive and Rising* (Baltimore, 1887, repr. Chicago: Johnson Publishing, 1970), p. 246; *National Convention . . . 1864.*

43. "Howard" to Editor, *Anglo-African*, Oct. 15, 1864; "Reply of Rev. Henry Highland Garnet . . .," Oct. 14, 1864, *Anglo-African*, Oct. 29, 1864; *National Convention . . . 1864.*

44. "Howard" to Editor, *Anglo-African*, Oct. 15, Oct. 22, 1864; *National Convention . . . 1864.*

45. "Editor's Budget," *Christian Recorder*, Dec. 8, 1866.

46. "Howard" to Editor, *Anglo-African*, Oct. 22, 1864; *National Convention . . . 1864.*

47. Ibid.

48. Ibid.

49. On Newman, see chapter 4, note 10. On Henry Lee, see William E. Bigglestone, *They Stopped in Oberlin: Black Residents and Visitors of the Nineteenth Century* (Scottsdale, Ariz., 1981), pp. 127–35; Rev. Henry Lee to Rev. Geo. Whipple, Mar. 28, 1864, A.M.A. Papers; Henry Lee to Editor, Jan. 19, 1865, Lorain County *News*, Feb. 8, 1865.

50. "Howard" to Editor, *Anglo-African*, Oct. 22, 1864; *National Convention . . . 1864.*

51. P. H. C. to Editor, Nov. 8, 1864, *Anglo-African*, Nov. 26, 1864; "Reply of Rev. Henry Highland Garnet," *Anglo-African*, Oct. 29, 1864; Geo. T. Downing to Editor, Nov. 1, 1864, *Anglo-African*, Nov. 19, 1864; P. H. C. to Editor, Nov. 1, 1864, *Anglo-African*, Nov. 12, 1864; Henry Highland Garnet to P. H. Clark, Dec. 3, 1864, *Anglo-African*, Dec. 10, 1864.

52. James M. Gregory to Editor, Nov. 22, 1864, *Christian Recorder*, Dec. 7, 1864; *Zion's Standard and Weekly Review*, Sept. 4, 1867, enclosed in John Mercer Langston to Oliver O. Howard, Sept. 13, 1867, in Letters Received, vol. 10, 1867, Bureau of Refugees, Freedmen, and Abandoned Lands, Office of the Adjutant General, National Archives; Editorial, *Christian Recorder*, June 22, 1867.

53. "Natchitoches" to Editor, Feb. 19, 1865, New Orleans *Tribune*, Mar. 8, 1865; Peter Clark to John W. Cromwell, n.d., in John W. Cromwell, *The Negro in American History* (Washington, 1914; repr. New York: Johnson Reprint, 1967), pp. 37–38.

54. *National Convention . . . 1864.*

55. Lorain County *News*, Aug. 10, Oct. 5, 12, 1864; Elyria *Independent-Democrat*, Oct. 5, 12, 1864.

56. Lorain County *News*, Nov. 9, 16, 23, 1864; "p" [Henry E. Peck] to Editor, Nov. 24, 1864, Lorain County *News*, Dec. 7, 1864.

57. *Christian Recorder*, Oct. 15, Dec. 3, 1864; R. H. [Robert Hamilton], Oct. 13, 1864, *Anglo-African*, Oct. 22, 1864; *Anglo-African*, Dec. 17, 1864; New Orleans *Tribune*, Dec. 29, 1864; James M. Gregory to Editor, Nov. 22, 1864, *Christian Recorder*, Dec. 7, 1864.

58. *Anglo-African*, Dec. 17, 1864; S. L. [Samuel Lowery] to Editor, Nov. 24, 1864, *Anglo-African*, Dec. 31, 1864. On James H. Harris, see Leon F. Litwack,

Been in the Storm so Long: The Aftermath of Slavery (New York, 1979), pp. 504, 506–7, 549–50; Benjamin Quarles, *Allies for Freedom: Blacks and John Brown* (New York, 1974), pp. 80, 131; *Proceedings of the State Convention of Colored Men . . . Columbus . . . Jan., 1856* (Columbus, 1856); *First Annual Meeting . . . 1865*. On Peter Lowery, see Loren Schweninger, *From Tennessee Slave to St. Louis Entrepreneur: The Autobiography of James Thomas* (Columbia, 1984), pp. 6–7.

59. *Christian Recorder*, Mar. 18, Feb. 18, Apr. 15, 1865. By September, when the National League held its first annual meeting, leagues also would be underway in Virginia, Alabama, Illinois, New Jersey, and Connecticut, bringing the total number of state leagues to at least fourteen. In Pennsylvania by then, twenty-one subleagues would have been formed. *First Annual Meeting . . . 1865.*

60. *Anglo-African*, Nov. 26, 1864.

61. *Christian Recorder*, Dec. 3, 1864; "Spectator" to Editor, *Anglo-African*, Feb. 11, 1864.

62. *First Annual Meeting . . . 1865*; *Anglo-African*, Nov. 26, 1864; John S. Rock to Editor, Dec. 24, 1864, *Anglo-African*, Jan. 14, 1865.

63. John M. Langston to Editor, *Christian Recorder*, Feb. 18, 1865; "L'Ouverture" to Editor, Mar. 20, 1865, *Anglo-African*, Mar. 25, 1865; John Mercer Langston et al., "An Appeal, National Equal Rights Bureau," Mar. 14, 1865, reprinted in *Christian Recorder*, Apr. 15, 1865; *First Annual Meeting . . . 1865*; *Christian Recorder*, Apr. 15, 1865.

64. John M. Langston et al., "To the Colored People of the United States," reprinted in *Anglo-African*, Dec. 17, 1864.

65. *National Convention . . . 1864*; J. H. Roney to Editor, Dec. 22, 1864, *Ohio State Journal*, Dec. 28, 1864.

66. *Proceedings of a Convention of the Colored Men of Ohio . . . Xenia, . . . Jan., 1865* (Cincinnati, 1865) (hereafter cited as *State Convention . . . 1865*); J. H. Roney to Editor, Dec. 22, 1864, *Ohio State Journal*, Dec. 28, 1864; "Oberlin correspondent" to Editor, *Anglo-African*, Dec. 10, 1864; James M. Gregory to Editor, Nov. 22, 1864, *Christian Recorder*, Dec. 7, 1864; Simmons, *Men of Mark*, pp. 433, 435.

67. *Lorain County News*, Apr. 5, 1865.

68. On Simpson, an Oberlin student in 1846 and 1847, and his music, see Henry Cowles, "Oberlin College Catalogue and Records of Colored Students, 1835–1862," ms., Henry Cowles Papers, Oberlin College Archives; Concord (Ohio) *Free Press*, n.d., reprinted in *North Star*, Dec. 7, 1849; Charles Thomas Hickok, *The Negro in Ohio, 1802–1870* (Cleveland, 1896; repr. New York, AMS Press, 1975), p. 47.

69. *State Convention . . . 1865*; Cincinnati *Gazette*, Mar. 8, 24, Apr. 11, 1865.

70. R.H. [Robert Hamilton] to Editor, *Anglo-African*, Jan. 28, Feb. 4, 1865; *State Convention . . . 1865*.

71. Boston *Transcript*, Mar. 6, 8, 1865; Philadelphia *Press*, Mar. 11, 1865; "Oscar" to Editor, *National Anti-Slavery Standard*, Mar. 18, 1865; New York *Post*, reprinted in *National Anti-Slavery Standard*, Mar. 11, 1865; New York *Tribune*, Mar. 13, 1865; Boston *Commonwealth*, Feb. 25, Mar. 18, 1865; *Anglo-African*, Feb. 11, Mar. 11, 25, 1865.

72. Louisville *Journal*, Dec. 20, 1864, Jan. 5, 1865.

73. Louisville *Union*, n.d., reprinted in New Orleans *Tribune*, Jan. 20, 1865; "J. Mercer Langston at Cooper Institute," *Anglo-African*, Mar. 11, 1865; John Mercer Langston, *From the Virginia Plantation to the National Capitol; or, The First and Only Negro Representative in Congress from the Old Dominion* (Hartford, Conn., 1894; repr. New York: Johnson Reprint, 1968), pp. 224–25, 232–33.

74. Loren Schweninger, "The Free-Slave Phenomenon: James P. Thomas and the Black Community in Ante-Bellum Nashville," *Civil War History* 22 (1976):294, 296–98, 302–6.

75. John Cimprich, "The Beginning of the Black Suffrage Movement in Tennessee, 1864–1865," *Journal of Negro History* 65 (Summer 1980):185–95; *Anglo-African*, Dec. 19, 1863; Sept. 10, 1864; Lorain County *News*, July 6, 1864; Nashville *Dispatch*, Aug. 16, 1864; *National Convention . . . 1864*.

76. Langston, *Virginia Plantation*, pp. 224–26; Nashville *Times*, Jan. 2, 1865; Cimprich, "The Beginning of the Black Suffrage Movement," pp. 187–88; Nashville *Press and Times*, reprinted in San Francisco *Elevator*, June 19, 1868; Boston *Commonwealth*, Mar. 4, 1865; San Francisco *Elevator*, Mar. 8, 1873. William C. Napier's son, James C. Napier, who would marry Langston's daughter Nettie, would become a leading businessman and politician in Nashville and in 1911 would be appointed registrar of the Treasury. "A Biographical Sketch of James Carroll Napier," James Carroll Napier Papers, Fisk University Library.

77. Nashville *Times*, Jan. 4, 1865; "Occasional" to Editor, Jan. 4, 1865, Lorain County *News*, Feb. 1, 1865; Amos Dresser, *Narrative of the Arrest, Lynch Law Trial, and Scourging of Amos Dresser, at Nashville, Tennessee, Aug., 1835* (Oberlin, 1849).

78. "Speech of J. M. Langston," Nashville *Times*, Jan. 4, 1865; "J. Mercer Langston at Cooper Institute," *Anglo-African*, Mar. 11,1865; "J. Mercer Langston, the War Our Emancipator," Philadelphia *Press*, Mar. 11, 1865.

79. Nashville *Times*, Jan. 3, 4, 1865; "Occasional" to Editor, Jan. 4, 1865, Lorain County *New*, Feb. 1, 1865; Nashville *Times and True Union*, Nov. 14, 1864.

80. Lorain County *News*, Dec. 13, 1865; John E. Patterson to Andrew Johnson, July 2, 1861, in *The Papers of Andrew Johnson, 1860–1861*, ed. Leroy P. Graf and Ralph W. Haskins, vol. 4 (Knoxville, Tenn., 1976), pp. 537–38; Bigglestone, *They Stopped in Oberlin*, p. 163.

81. "Occasional" to Editor, Jan. 4, 1865, Lorain County *News*, Feb. 1, 1865; Cimprich, "The Beginning of the Black Suffrage Movement in Tennessee," p. 190; Boston *Commonwealth*, Mar. 4, 1865; R. H. [Robert Hamilton] to Editor, *Anglo-African*, Feb. 4, 1865.

82. Langston, *Virginia Plantation*, pp. 226–27; "J. Mercer Langston at Cooper Institute," *Anglo-African*, Mar. 11, 1865; Baltimore *Sun*, June 2, 1874, in John Mercer Langston Scrapbooks, 4 vols., I, Moorland-Spingarn Research Center, Howard University.

83. "Occasional" to Editor, Jan. 4, 1865, Lorain County *News*, Feb. 1, 1865; "J. Mercer Langston at Cooper Institute," *Anglo-African*, Mar. 11, 1865; San Francisco *Post*, Apr. 5, 1877, in John Mercer Langston Scrapbooks, 4 vols., I,

Moorland-Spingarn Research Center, Howard University; Langston, *Virginia Plantation*, pp. 224– 29.

84. Missouri [St. Louis] *Democrat*, Jan. 20, 19, 1865; "Howard" to Editor, *Anglo-African*, Oct. 22, 1864; Langston, *Virginia Plantation*, p. 242; "J. Mercer Langston at Cooper Institute," *Anglo-African*, Mar. 11, 1865; John Mercer Langston et al., "An Appeal, National Equal Rights Bureau," Mar. 14, 1865, reprinted in *Christian Recorder*, Apr. 15, 1865.

85. Langston, *Virginia Plantation*, pp. 233–37.

86. "J. Mercer Langston at Cooper Institute," *Anglo-African*, Mar. 11, 1865; R. H. to Editor, *Anglo-African*, Jan. 28, 1865; Lorain County *News*, Feb. 1, 1865; *National Anti-Slavery Standard*, Mar. 18, 1865.

87. John Mercer Langston et al., "An Appeal, National Equal Rights Bureau."

88. Langston, *Virginia Plantation*, p. 223; *National Anti-Slavery Standard*, Mar. 18, 1865.

89. Philadelphia *Press*, Apr. 21, 1865; Cincinnati *Gazette*, Mar. 26, 1866; Langston, *Virginia Plantation*, pp. 229–30; New York *Independent*, Apr. 27, 1865.

90. Lorain County *News*, Apr. 26, 1865; Langston, *Virginia Plantation*, pp. 230–31.

91. Philadelphia *Press*, Apr. 21, 1865.

92. Ibid.

Afterword

LANGSTON's meeting with President Johnson was an indication, not only of the position of genuine national leadership he had attained by the close of the Civil War, but also of how he would evince that leadership. In the years ahead, following his work in the South as educational inspector for the Freedmen's Bureau and organizer for the Republican party, he became professor of law, first law dean, and then acting president of Howard University. As a member of the first Board of Health of the District of Columbia, he helped to devise a model sanitation code for the capital. From 1877 to 1885 he was the U.S. minister to Haiti as well as for some time the U.S. consul to Santo Domingo. Afterward, he returned to Virginia to head the state college for Negroes at Petersburg. When Democratic control of the state made the post untenable, Langston resigned and in 1888 ran for Congress in the district encompassing Petersburg. Finding not just Democrats but also the state Republican party pitted against him, he campaigned as an independent, lost, contested the election results, and eventually won his seat—so late, however, that a scant three months remained of his term. Nonetheless, until his death in 1897, he continued to engage in protest, politics, education, and the law.

In the transformation from regional leader to national statesman, Langston faced complex questions. Although his urging of self-reliance had always reflected his aloneness as well as his convictions, his emphasis of this theme during the war years took on an added dimension. It seemed a recognition of the distance that his increasing prominence was forcing between him and the individuals, black and white, whose support had been crucial to his development, and of the probability that he would be even more isolated in the future. At the same time, his constituency was growing to include the former slaves whose condition he had never shared, but to whom, as well as to northern blacks, he hoped to translate his ideal of human dignity—a black American manhood and womanhood based on self-reliance, self-respect, and self-assertion.

Although black unity could prove vital in forwarding that ideal and gaining political rights, the difficulty of forging it was already apparent. Cognizant of the special significance of symbols to an oppressed people and adept at fashioning them, Langston nonetheless confronted the danger that the abstract might be confused with the actual. The National Equal Rights League might never become a real vehicle of unity, the recognition of black patriotism might never go beyond the symbolic. As a national representative of black Americans and also as a black politician, he himself might be subject to manipulation, and thus be simply another means of misleading his people. Although it was true, as he had triumphantly pointed out, that the American flag no longer stood for the Fugitive Slave Law, could it now be made to stand for freedom? Still, in his interview with Andrew Johnson, himself representative both of promise and peril for black Americans, Langston had found it useful to wield these symbols as he asked for complete emancipation and full equality before American law.

With the ratification of the Thirteenth Amendment completed by the end of the year, emancipation would become a reality for some four million slaves. Langston could count as significant his own part in that achievement. Absorbed since adolescence in what he considered the transcendent issue of human freedom, he had brought to the fight zeal, energy, uncommon intelligence, education, and training, an aristocratic style and a democratic temperament, a rare combination of abilities as organizer and executive, agitator and negotiator, and a compelling talent for oratory.

Drawing on many and various models, he had attempted to mold himself and his leadership on broad humanistic lines. As the 19-year-old Langston had insisted, quoting the Roman slave Terence: " 'I am a man, and there is nothing of humanity, as I think, estranged to me.'. . . The spirit of our people must be aroused. They must feel and act as men." His redefinition of manhood on his own exceptional terms had helped to shape his strategy for forwarding his vision of freedom and equality. Availing himself of access to the abolitionist biracial community of Oberlin and to white radical politicians, he had engaged in antislavery politics. At the same time, he had involved himself in black communities in Ohio and the North. By centering a political movement for freedom and civil rights within the Afro-American culture, he and other black leaders had made a significant impress on the hot wax of critical events that had sealed the fate of slavery.

Although their very struggle had taken these men and women nearer to freedom, an abyss of folly and barbarism still lay between black Americans and the complete emancipation and full equality before American law that John Mercer Langston sought. Still, in the coming ordeal of black citizenship, he could hold to a hope: that black and white Americans would join hands to overcome racism and discrimination and, side by side, work out their common destiny and glory. It was a hope that had taken form from his early years, that had been contradicted a thousand times, and yet was reaffirmed by a practical man brave in his commitment to possibility.

Index

Abolitionism/antislavery, 18, 71, 87, 88–89, 107, 213, 221, 226: in Virginia, 16; in Chillicothe, 30, 31, 33, 37–38, 39, 40–42; and formation of American Anti-Slavery Society, 33; blacks in, 33, 49, 55, 46, 47, 71, 72, 85–89, 90, 95, 96, 103–5, 109–11, 135, 137, 145–46, 147, 148–50, 151–52, 153–54, 156–57, 158, 159, 169, 170, 171, 172–73, 179, 181–82, 183, 187–88, 191, 193–94, 206–7, 209, 211, 213–18, 220, 222, 224–25, 226–27, 230–31, 248, 249, 252, 253, 255, 257, 258, 265–67, 286, 318–20, 321–22, 325–27, 328, 329, 331–32, 333–34, 335, 338–39, 350, 351–54, 355–59, 362, 366, 368, 372–75, 384–85, 418; and Ohio Anti-Slavery Society, 40; and black education and uplift, 41–42, 53–54, 59, 180, 181–82, 183; in Cincinnati, 49–50, 53–54, 55, 56, 57, 59–60, 61, 65, 71, 72, 187, 206–7; and underground railroad, 49, 57, 59–61, 150, 187, 206, 248, 281–82, 316, 317, 329, 350–51; and Lane Rebels, 53, 54, 59; women's involvement in, 54, n.119 10, 157, 183, 206, 215, 249, 289–90; and Liberty party, 65; and repudiation of American Colonization Society, 66,

172–73, 191, 220, 226–27, 253; and *Amistad* case, 71; and Oberlin, 85–89, 90, 91, 92, 93, 94, 99–103, 104–5, 106, 109–11, 118, 171, 182–82, 183–84, 185, 207, 209, 230, 231, 279, 281–82, 283–85, 287–88, 289–90, 290–91, 317, 328, 329, 336, 352, 353–54, 355–59, 361–62, 373, 385; and support of black emigration, 174, 175, 188–89; and Western Anti-Slavery Society, 175, 177, 197, 233, 250, 341; conventions of, 206–7, 215–18, 262–63, 265–67, 421; salience of black rights in, 213–14, 215–16, 228; and Kansas-Nebraska protest, 229–31, 234; in Brownhelm township, 243, 257–58, 259–60; involvement of Quakers in, 250; Oberlin-Wellington Rescue and, 318–20, 332–33, 334–35, 337–38, 339; and Ohio and John Brown, 350, 351–62

Adams, John Quincy, 71, 72

Adrian (Michigan): black community in, 423–24

Africa, 150, 173, 195: cultural associations with, 33, 61, 63, 70–71; Oberlin and, 86, 91; "Ohio in Africa" and, 173, 210; movements for emigration to, 189, 427

students, 293–95; provides
scholarships, 293; as alumnus, 295;
profession and personal life: attempts to
study law, 130–33; law schools reject,
132–33, 227; owns property, 179–80,
278, 291, 292; apprentices with Bliss,
226–27; admitted to bar, 233–35; as
farmer in Brownhelm, 243, 245,
255–56; health of, 243–44; white
tenants of, 244–45; on reformer, 245,
255; tries first case, 245–46; practices
law in Brownhelm, 246–47; weds
Caroline Wall, 247, 251–54, 254–56,
258; on Wall family, 250–51;
prejudiced neighbor and, 258–59;
influence of self-reliance on, 261–62;
children of, 270–71, 292, 375; moves
to Oberlin, 271, 278–79; lives in white
neighborhood, 278, 291; on racial
equalitarianism in Oberlin, 279, 288,
290, 291; speaks to welcome railroad,
280; teaches adult Sunday school, 282;
family and community life of, 291–97,
318; on school board, 296–97;
practices law in Oberlin, 297- 307,
317; as realtor and bill collector, 298;
as target of prejudice as lawyer, 298,
299–301; uses violence in self-
defense, 299–302; defends Edmonia
Lewis, 302–6; on lawyers, 306;
succeeds as lawyer, 306–7;
black leadership: on black-white sexual
relationships, 16–17, 103–4, 115–16,
209; addresses black troops, 21, 445;
and Nell, 66, 222, 258–59, 264, 265,
285, 321–22, 440; attends national
conventions, 112–13, 218–20, 425; and
Douglass, 113, 154–55, 157–60,
196–97, 206, 207, 220, 221, 260, 263,
390, 422, 425, 428, 429, 431–32, 435;
as state leader, 113–16, 135–36, 151,
152–55, 187, 190–91, 211, 215, 222,
323, 350–51, 362, 366, 367–68,
439–40; as black nationalist-
emigrationist, 113–16, 170–71,
173–76, 185–97, 231–32; on
prejudice, 114, 116, 191, 229, 256,
257, 262, 266–67, 341, 385, 446; on
black manhood, 114, 116, 117, 118;
criticizes racial discrimination at

Oberlin, 116; criticizes black
religionists, 144, 154, 430; on John I.
Gaines, 146, 151, 261, 364; on
socioeconomic status of black Ohioans,
147, 219, 363; collects black statistics,
153, 228, 281, 363; urges black
newspaper, 154–55, 176, 215; urges
enfranchisement, 155–61, 176–77,
228–29, 281, 320–22, 323–24, 333,
366–69; makes first tour, 155–60; on
enfranchisement, 156–57, 161–62,
262, 326, 328; mobbed, 158;
description of, at 20, 159; seeks advice
of Chase, 161, 162, 170, 173; protests
Fugitive Slave Law, 169, 170–72, 319,
328, 333, 333–36, 366; opposes
colonization, 172–73, 191, 195, 207,
213, 226–27, 323–24, 369; aids black
public schools, 180–85, 282; on
education, 182, 185; as president of
state conventions, 187, 190–91, 323,
362, 366–68; and underground
railroad, 187, 296, 316, 317, 350–52;
and unity of oppressed, 194; opposes
attempt to revive Black Laws, 213; as
temperance advocate, 214, 246, 257;
defends black productivity, 219; wins
regard of black abolitionists, 221–22;
speaks in East, 221–22, 229; as First
of August orator, 222, 231, 269,
321–22, 324, 325–27, 371, 387, 404,
424; defends Clark, 224; protests
assembly's refusal to grant hearing,
228–29; on agitation, 229;
emigrationists criticize, 232–33; on role
of women, 249; discriminated against,
256–58; aids attempt to integrate
street cars, 268; on integrated schools,
297, 322; on Slave Oligarchy (Slave
Power), 319, 326–27, 329–30, 349,
355, 419; denies chance of mass
emigration, 323–24; threatened, 326,
403; pragmatic about means, 326, 349;
activates Ohio State Anti-Slavery
Society, 327, 333, 352, 353, 359, 362,
366–68; on Dred Scott decision, 328,
366; favors violent resistance, 328,
349–51, 355, 359, 362; urges
anti-kidnapping bill, 333, 366–68; aids
John Brown, 349–50, 353–58, 362;

About the Authors

William Cheek is professor of history at San Diego State University. He has also taught at Hollins College, the University of Virginia, the University of Arkansas, and as a visiting professor in Montreal, Aix-en-Provence, and Paris, the last under a Fulbright grant. He is the author of *Black Resistance Before the Civil War*.

Aimee Lee Cheek is a writer and community activist in San Diego.

BOOKS IN THE SERIES
BLACKS IN THE NEW WORLD

Black Leaders of the Nineteenth Century
Edited by Leon Litwack and August Meier

Charles Richard Drew: The Man and the Myth
Charles E. Wynes

John Mercer Langston and the Fight for Black Freedom, 1829-65
William and Aimee Lee Cheek

Reprint Editions

King: A Biography
David Levering Lewis
SECOND EDITION

The Death and Life of Malcolm X
Peter Goldman
SECOND EDITION

Race Relations in the Urban South, 1865-1890
Howard N. Rabinowitz,
with a Foreword by C. Vann Woodward

Race Riot at East St. Louis, July 2, 1917
Elliott Rudwick

W. E. B. Du Bois: Voice of the Black Protest Movement
Elliott Rudwick

The Negro's Civil War: How American Negroes Felt and Acted
during the War for the Union
James M. McPherson

Lincoln and Black Freedom: A Study in Presidential Leadership
LaWanda Cox

Slavery and Freedom in the Age of the American Revolution
Edited by Ira Berlin and Ronald Hoffman